中國思想下的全球化管轄規則

陳隆修◆著

以「王道」觀世界
——讀陳隆修老師
《中國思想下的全球化管轄規則》有感

劉仁山*

初識陳隆修老師是2008年在西安召開的海峽兩岸國際私法研討會上。此前十多年裡，我一直是在書本上聞其名悅其文而已。

1990年代初，我在跟隨大陸原中南政法學院[1]的張仲伯教授[2]念碩士研究生的期間，根據張老師的讀書清單，讀過陳

* 法學博士，中南財經政法大學教授、法學院院長；大陸「中國國際私法學會」副會長；加拿大約克大學奧斯古德法學院訪問學者，德國馬克斯普朗克比較法與國際私法研究所訪問學者，美國國務院「國家訪問學者領導專案」訪問學者；大陸地區人力資源與社會保障部、教育部等七部門「新世紀百千萬人才工程國家級人選」，教育部「霍英東基金會第九屆高校優秀青年教師獎（科研資助類）」獲得者。

1 大陸原中南政法學院是直屬於大陸司法部的五所政法院校之一（其他四所政法院校分別為中國政法大學即原北京政法學院、西南政法學院即今西南政法大學、華東政法學院即今華東政法大學、西北政法學院即今西北政法大學），其源於1948年在河南寶豐縣設立的中原大學（該校創建之初，就有一些法學專業課程的設置，如有的課程涉及民法）。1952年9月，中原大學成立了政法學院，其中包含法律教研室和政治教研室。1953年4月，以中原大學政法學院為基礎，合併中山大學、湖南大學、廣西大學的政法系科，成立中南政法學院（其中，原中山大學法學院是整體併入原中南政法學院的）。1958年10月，中南政法學院與中南財經學院、中南政法幹校、武漢大學法律系合併成立湖北大學，上述政法類院校組成湖北大學法律系，之後演變為湖北財經學院法律系。1977年大陸地區結束「文革」，恢復高考制度，原湖北財經學院法律系與北京大學法律系、吉林大學法律系同批于當年招收恢復高考制度後的首批法律專業本科生，並于1979年開始招收法學碩士研究生（大陸地區招收法學研究生的首批單位之一）。1984年12月，以湖北財經學院法律系為基礎，正式恢復中南政法學院。2000年5月，中南財經大學、中南政法學院合併組建成中南財經政法大學（大陸地區教育部直屬的「211工程」和「985工程」優勢學科創新平臺項目重點建設高校之一），並以原中南政法學院的主體和中南財經大學法律系組成法學院。

2 2011年陳隆修老師來中南財經政法大學法學院傳道期間，張仲伯教授曾專程與陳老師會晤交流。張仲伯教授是大陸地區國際私法衝突法學派的重要代表者。

老師撰寫的《國際私法管轄權評論》和《美國國際私法新理論》。由於《國際私法管轄權評論》是我學生時期看過的第一本用中文編寫、系統介紹英美國際管轄權判例的著作，所以印

1957年初，張老師第一次為中南政法學院法律系本科生授課。他編寫的《國際私法綱要》認為：國際私法是以解決法律衝突為目的，以間接調整為方法，由衝突規範、規定外國人的民事地位規範和涉外民事訴訟程序規範所組成的國內部門法。該《綱要》的體系為：國際私法概論（主要包括國際私法的概念、淵源、與鄰近法律部門的關係、名稱、體系）；衝突規範及其制度（主要包括衝突規範的概念、結構、種類，准據法的確定，識別，反致，公共秩序保留，法律規避，外國法的查明）；國際私法主體（外國人及其待遇，外國自然人，外國法人）；幾種涉外民事關係的法律衝突和法律適用（主要包括所有權、合同、侵權行為、婚姻家庭、財產繼承等方面）；涉外民事訴訟程序（主要包括涉外民事訴訟的概念，外國人的民事訴訟地位，涉外民事案件管轄權，司法協助，外國法院民事判決的承認與執行）。由於1957年的《國際私法綱要》在「文革」期間丟失，在上世紀80年代初期，張老師又編寫了《國際私法教學大綱》。該《大綱》認為：國際私法是調整涉外民事關係的法律規範的總稱，是與國內民法相平行的獨立的法律部門。該《大綱》的體系為：各國國際私法立法中規定的各項法則，就是指那些解決國籍、住所衝突在內的外國人（含無國籍人）的民事法律地位（含外國人在內國民事主體資格的確定）；涉外身份能力、物權、債權、婚姻家庭、財產繼承等民事關係的法律適用；還包括如何確定涉外民事案件的管轄權、司法協助，即包括法院等機構的文書的國外送達、涉外調查取證、被適用外國法內容的查明、以及外國法院判決及仲裁裁決的承認與執行等諸多問題。張老師認為國際私法的物件是特殊的涉外民法關係。即不完全是泛指的涉外民法關係，而是專指間接調整這一特殊方法即選擇適用法律的方法所調整涉外民法關係。他認為，這樣界定國際私法物件的好處在於：首先，可以排除統一實體規範和調整涉外民法關係的國內實體規範大量湧入，致使國際私法的範圍膨脹起來；其次，應當維護國際私法作為「間接法」具有的本質特徵；張老師認為國際私法的主要任務是：當某一涉外民商事案件觸及不同國家的法律內容和體系，在適用於具體案件而引起法律衝突時，怎樣按照國內法或公約中的衝突規則，並援用涉外民事程序法規定的要求，正確而妥善地處理有關的涉外民事案件；張老師認為國際私法主要是衝突規範，同時，還應包括外國人民事地位規範和涉外民事訴訟程序規範。但不應該將統一實體規範納入國際私法範圍之中。張老師認為，如果使那些本屬於其他法律部門組成範圍的一攬子實體規範一齊進入國際私法領域，把「實體法」和「衝突法」湊合成一個拼盤，其結果不僅將導致肢解始自「法則區別說」以來形成的國際私法這一傳統的結構體系；同時，這也會損害國際私法相臨近的其他法律部門，如國際經濟法、涉外經濟法及其各分支學科的研究和發展。參見張仲伯：《關於國際私法的物件、範圍和體系問題》，載《中南政法學院學報》1988年第1期；劉仁山：《國際私法與國際民商事交流規制之衝突法論——張仲伯教授學術思想概覽》，載《私法研究》（第8卷），法律出版社2010年8月版，第387-394頁。

象頗深。1994年——1997年，我在武漢大學韓德培[3]先生門下念國際私法博士研究生期間，無論是閒暇，還是做論文時，仍會繼續研讀和引注陳老師的著作。事實上，在那個年代，很多同我年紀相仿、在大陸修讀國際私法的學生，都應該讀過陳老師寫的書。儘管這些書當時尚未在大陸正式出版，大家能夠找到的也只是複印版（上世界80年代中期到90年代初，人們似乎還沒有盜版概念），但這並不影響年輕學子閱讀和求知的熱情。陳老師的這些以英美判例法為專題內容的著作，無疑是給那個年代身處成文法環境下的大陸學子打開了一扇瞭望之窗，這也使得我對於海峽彼岸的這位國際私法前輩油然而生好奇與敬慕。然而，當時除了手中的書之外，我幾乎查閱不到任何有關陳老師個人的資訊或介紹。1990年代後期，我曾向有關同行探詢陳老師的相關情況，想與他取得聯繫，但遺憾未果。

輾轉到2008年11月，在西北政法大學召開的海峽兩岸國際私法研討會上，我才第一次見到陳隆修老師。見面的那一刻，我還一時無法將自己學生時代仰慕的學術前輩同眼前這位清雅

---

3 武漢大學法學院教授韓德培先生是大陸地區國際法學界的一代宗師，國際私法學泰斗。韓德培先生生前曾提出「一機兩翼論」觀點。韓先生認為：「國際私法就如同一架飛機一樣，其內涵是飛機的機身，其外延是飛機的兩翼。具體在國際私法上，這內涵包括衝突法，也包括統一實體法，甚至還包括國家直接適用於涉外民事法律關係的法律。而兩翼之一則是國籍及外國人法律地位問題，這是處理涉外民事法律關係的前提；另一翼則是在發生糾紛時，解決糾紛的國際民事訴訟及仲裁程序，這包括管轄權、司法協助、外國判決和仲裁裁決的承認與執行。」1996年6月初，應時任上海財經大學余先予教授之邀，韓德培先生赴上海參加余先予教授主持的課題成果鑒定會。其間，韓德培先生應復旦大學法學院張乃根教授和時任上海外貿學院法學院教授的周漢民及朱照敏兩位的邀請，先後在復旦大學和上海外貿學院作了兩場學術報告。在兩場報告中，韓先生先後從不同角度系統闡述了關於國際私法範圍的「一機兩翼論」。本人當時作為韓先生的弟子，有幸陪同韓先生前往上海，聆聽並見證了韓先生的精彩報告及其「一機兩翼論」。參見劉仁山主編：《國際私法》，中國法制出版社2010年版，第9頁。

溫和的紳士聯繫起來。與我多次想像中的陳老師相比，陳老師本人似乎要年輕許多。記得當我提到很多大陸學者在學生時期就讀過他的書時，他很是驚訝，還謙遜地回應說自己沒有想到會在大陸國際私法學界有這樣的影響。

那年與陳老師的初識，成為我那次西安之行的最大收穫。之後，我們之間的接觸和交流就漸漸多了起來。2010年4月，趁我去臺灣中央研究院參會之餘，陳老師邀我赴東海大學法學院與學生交流；同年6月，第五屆海峽兩岸國際私法研討會在我們法學院召開，陳老師應邀隨臺灣地區的各位前輩和同行參會。客觀地講，陳老師的第二次大陸之行讓我們中南國際法學科受益良多。在會議間隙，陳老師開啟了在中南傳道的序幕。在該次會議期間的一個晚上，陳老師為法學院兩百多名學子作了以「從歐盟經驗論中國式國際私法」為題的報告。[4]陳老師在報告中關於他的「中國式國際私法」思想的闡述，引得青年學子群起激昂。2010年歲末，蒙陳老師厚愛，我也應邀赴東海大學參加「國際私法高峰論壇」，並因此能榮幸地與中正大學、政治大學、逢甲大學、亞洲大學的各位先進和同道認識或敘舊。在陳老師的促成下，東海大學法學院和我們中南的法學院簽訂了合作協定，陳老師還屈尊欣然接受我和我同事們的請求，成為中南國際私法的客座教授；2011年10月下旬，陳老師再次受邀來中南傳道，他不辭辛勞，為法學院本科生和國際法專業的碩士和博士研究生先後作了三場報告。我印象很深的是我親自主持的那場報告會，主題是「美國的選法規則——最低限度關連點」。陳老師在報告中講解了「最低限度關連點」這一選法規則的確立過程，揭示了該規則的實質，並對該規則

4 http://fxy.znufe.edu.cn/contents/157/734.html.

可能的後果作了鞭辟入裡的剖析；[5]陳老師無疑是我們法學院最為勤勉辛勞的客座教授。2011年以來，他已經出版了三本冠以「中南財經政法大學法學院國際私法叢書」之名的系列國際私法新作。[6]我們法學院有三十多位從事國際法教學的同行，在「中國法學創新網」關於科學研究實力的排名中，我們也一直居於前列。[7]但我的這些同事每每看到學院圖書館所排列的陳老師的這些新作時，無不心悅誠服。

陳老師是位正直的仗義執言的知識份子，但他身上也洋溢著中華文化薰陶下特有的謙遜和誠懇。陳老師是位健談的哲人，多年來對英美普通法的潛心研究，使得他對兩岸國際私法中諸多問題的看法，總是會讓人生出撥雲見天醍醐灌頂之感慨。

這本《中國思想下的全球化管轄規則》，是陳老師撰寫的「中南財經政法大學法學院國際私法叢書」收關之作。即將付梓之際，陳老師囑余為序。身為晚輩，我對於這一囑託既感且愧！謹此，我只有惶恐地在前言部分輔添數語，將我讀書後的幾點心得拙見藉機呈現，以求教讀者諸君。

「中國式法學」這一議題，很早就為大陸地區包括國際私法學者在內的所有法學學者所關注。大陸地區近三十年來在國際私法領域的雖然成績卓著，[8]但大陸地區國際私法學的研

---

5 http://fxy.znufe.edu.cn/contents/157/4090.html.

6 參見陳隆修、宋連斌、林恩偉著：《國際私法——新世紀兩岸國際私法》，五南圖書出版公司2011年版；陳隆修、劉仁山、許兆慶著：《國際私法——程序正義與實體正義》，五南圖書出版公司2011年版；陳隆修著：《中國思想下的全球化選法規則》，五南圖書出版公司2012年版。

7 http://www.lawinnovation.com/html/fxpd/7716.shtml.

8 這些成績可以歸納為：第一，培養了一大批國際私法專業法律人才。大陸地區「文革」結束初期，全國健在的從事國際私法教學研究的人員不足20人，但從中國社科院法學研究所國際法研究室1978年率先恢復招收國際私法專業的碩士

究，無論是過去還是現在，主要還是處於引進階段。許多學者所構建的國際私法體系（如果可以稱之為構建的話），似乎是前蘇聯體架構下的英美國際私法；儘管早在唐《永徽律》中，就有關於適用外國法的規定，[9]但在國際私法學的若干基本理論問題上，我們至今尚無自己的理論。譬如，對於中國法院審理相關涉外民商事案件適用外國法的理論依據問題，雖然早在上世紀80年代，大陸有學者提出法律適用應堅持「平等互利說」，但該觀點一方面深受前蘇聯學者的「對外政策需要說」的影響，另一方面，平等互利說到底是法律適用中應堅持的原則、還是依據？還有待進一步闡述。[10]因此，在2009年海峽兩岸國際私法會議上，黃進教授和趙相林教授等再次提出兩岸應

研究生和1982年武漢大學和北京大學招收國際私法專業博士研究生開始，到現在已經有16所高校和科研機構擁有國際法專業博士授權點，可以招收國際私法專業博士研究生。到目前，大陸地區的「中國國際私法學會」不僅已經有了20多年的歷史，而且，註冊會員已經達到300餘人；第二，國際私法的教學科研成果豐碩，並惠濟立法及司法實踐，充分顯現了國際私法在我國對外開放中的作用。在韓德培先生等的帶領下，探索並形成了較為成熟的國際私法教學體系。截至2010年底，全國有各類國際私法教材達100餘部。自上世紀80年代初韓德培先生和李雙元老師在《武漢大學學報》上發表的較有影響的國際私法論文《應當重視對衝突法的研究》開始，到2011年9月底，僅在全國核心期刊上發表的國際私法論文已達1700餘篇。中國國際私法學會還創辦有《中國國際私法與比較法年刊》，目前已經出版到第14卷，並在法學界享有盛譽。「中國國際私法學會」2000年正式出版的《中華人民共和國國際私法示範法》，以及1990年韓德培先生和黃進教授起草的《大陸地區與臺灣、香港、澳門地區民事法律適用示範條例》，對大陸地區的相關立法及實踐均產生了重要影響。參見劉仁山：《中國國際私法學養成意識之培育問題》，載《武漢法學》2012年第1期。

9 在唐《永徽律》頒佈後的永徽四年即西元653年，司典大臣長孫無忌等19人奉詔撰寫《唐律疏議》，對《永徽律》逐條進行注釋。就《名例律》中的「化外人相犯條」注釋到：「化外人謂蠻史之國別立君長者，各有風俗，制法不同。其有同類自相犯者，須問本國之制，依其俗法斷之。異類相犯者，若高麗之與北濟相犯之類，皆以國家律典論定刑名。」這就是說，外國人所屬國的風俗習慣和法律都有所不同，如同一國籍的外國人之間發生的糾紛，須適用本國法；不同國籍的外國人之間發生糾紛，則以唐朝法律論處。唐律關於化外人的規定，是中國歷史上最早的，在同時期的世界範圍內也絕無僅有的。

10 參見劉仁山：《中國國際私法學養成意識之培育》，載《法學研究》2011年第6期。

發展具有中華文化特色的國際私法。三年來，陳隆修老師一直沿循此研究路徑，致力於從中華文化的精髓中去探尋國際私法相關問題的解決之道。本書也正是基於上述路徑，探討全球化管轄規則同中國傳統文化中「王道」思想的碰撞與交融。

本書以「全球化法學的共同核心」為主線，用「王道」思想來審視兩大法系管轄權規則之間的對立與默契，展現全球化管轄規則的應然與實然格局。在王道「思想」的映照之下，作者對於西方管轄權理論和實踐的修正，集中體現在以下幾方面：

第一，在協議管轄問題上，管轄條款（以及仲裁條款）受法院地和合同履行地強行法的制約，已成為國際法上的一種常態，這無疑是國際私法為順應全球化潮流的一種表現。但是，賦予管轄條款及仲裁條款獨立性的做法，有時可能會違反契約法基本原則。因為解決跨國民商事案件的實踐表明，一味強調管轄條款及仲裁條款之獨立性，往往會導致強勢一方將法律的可預測性置於弱者要求正義的利益之上。對於一個因涉及欺詐或脅迫而無效的契約而言，如果仍要求受害一方去遵守契約中的管轄權條款，不僅嚴重違背法律上公正之精神和原則，同時也有違背人類生活之常理，因此，應予以摒棄。

第二，在外國禁訴令的承認問題上，大陸法上的誠信原則與英美法上要求的「合理性」遙相呼應。如果當事人于外國所提的程序是「困擾性」或「壓迫性」的行為、濫用程序、或違反誠信原則，對禁訴令的許可，當然是符合正義利益之要求的，其他法院亦應承認該禁訴令的效力。但由於契約的成立、效力以及履行等均應受到全球化契約法共同核心強行法的制約，特別是有關契約強行法中當事人平衡條款的規定、以及各種人權公約中強行規定的制約，所以，如果當事人所提起的訴訟，即使違反了契約中的協議管轄條款，但法院還應審查該行為是否符合契約法的基本原則及人權法的若干基本原則。只有對該既違反契約本身，也違背契約法的基本原則及人權法的若干基本原則的行為，法院才能被作出禁訴令，其他國家法院也只有在此前提下才能承認該禁訴令的效力。

第三，在管轄權與判決承認的關係上，基於美國和英國衝突法均將「既有權力」（present power）作為對人管轄基礎這一事實，「不方便法院」可以作為對相關管轄權行使的限制。而在外國法院的判決違反自然和實質正義之時，「不方便法院」還應成為拒絕承認該外國判決的理由。即英美法寬泛的管轄基礎與其靈活的法院裁量權（方便與不方便法院）構成同一制度下不可分割的兩面。這種制度設計將引導原告對被告的訴訟于「自然」（the most real and substantial connection，即最真實與實質性關聯）法院被提起，使之順其自然的符合「王道」思想對公平正義的要求。

第四，在管轄權邏輯一致性與個案實質正義的關係上，判例法對於邏輯一致性的政策要求，應當受限於實現個案正義的基本目標，而後者才是判例法的最高價值所在。排除過分技術性的法律論述，關注個案公平正義的達成，「天道無親，恒與善人」，如此才是21世紀全球化法學的自然道法。

通覽全書，本人還有如下感受需一吐為快——

記得有種哲學觀講，事物的發展軌跡，是螺旋式的。產生這種現象的原理為：每一事物都是多面而立體的，需要旋轉地——至少正反互換地觀察它，才能獲得逐漸完整的認識。本書的研究主旨，無疑充分體現了上述哲學思想。對於本書的「全球化法學的共同核心」這一主旨問題，陳老師首先用相當的筆墨來論證，全球化法學無論是實體法還是程序法，都已經具備了一個共同核心管轄基礎。比如，合同法上要求的誠實信用原則與平衡性原則，訴訟法上要求當事人立足點平等和避免因當事人貧富不均所產生的不公正，這些制度在許多國家的管轄規則中都有所體現。之後，本書進一步揭示，儘管全世界主要文明國家的管轄規則是相似的，但是不同國家背後的「心態」卻南轅北轍，即對跨國管轄的最基礎認知上並沒有形成共同核心。對於這一觀點，我深以為然。因為在21世紀全球化法學中，人類文明對於正義的要求更為嚴格，但是共同認知的缺失不僅掣肘了全球化法學的發展，還導致最初那個真正實現人類公平與正義的法治之夢漸行漸遠。這一點是任何法律技術與經驗的進化都無法彌補的。但是，本書對人類社會探尋爭議解決之道，給出的是自信而不是悲觀的結論：聯合國數次高峰會中針對「全球化的利益及代價並未平均分配」，而要求降低生活水準差距所形成的宣言，如《環境與發展宣言》、《可持續發展宣言》，已經為21世紀全球化法學提供了共同核心政策。這些共同核心政策，更是與中華民族千年傳承的「不患寡患不均」、「禮運大同」的「王道」思想相契合。我個人認為，這是一種跨越了意識形態、文化隔閡乃至歷史時空的默契。通過「以德示人」來獲得認同感的「王道」思想區別於西方「以力服人」的「霸道」處世哲學，是智慧的華夏祖先留給我們的寶貴財富，我們理應對這些經典的傳統文化心懷敬畏。中華民族的王道祖訓可以成為、且應當成為醫治當今全球化管轄規則中諸多弊病的良方。

當下正是一個經濟高速發展、思潮迭起的過渡時代。尤其當唯經濟論被提升到崇高地位，社會對物質利益的過分關注，我們可能會因此偏離祖宗留給我們的核心價值觀。在這樣一個快速奔跑的年代，我們似乎更需要時時提醒自己，最初啟程的意義究竟是什麼？這並非厚古薄今，盲目貶損當下的文明，而恰恰是因為，孕育中國現代文明的那些傳統文化和精神財富是如此的厚重深邃，想要隔斷這樣一個「文化臍帶」，似乎絕無可能。

因此，我們要建設一個法治社會，就必須從國情出發。這應當是我們確立依法治國方略時的重要依規。在作為「中國國情」的一個不可或缺的組成部分之傳統文化當中，諸多傳統的價值觀與道德觀，是值得我們堅守和傳承的。一個具有前瞻性的民族，一定是重視文化傳承、且懂得揚棄的民族。在我們這樣一個有著深厚傳統文化積澱的國度裡，對於法律文化的傳承也需要有更深層次的領悟：從傳統文化中汲取養分，從最樸素的道理中尋求破題之法；發掘傳統思想的魅力，讓中華民族的法學理論真正走向世界。在任重而道遠的法治建設旅途中，我們無疑應當以「王道精神」為基礎，實現法學意義中的「禮運大同」。

這些，似乎正是陳老師通過本書于讀者的希冀和啟迪。

此外，「文如其人」是我閱讀完陳老師大作後的深刻感受。本書對諸多原本嚴肅的話題，在以幽默犀利的語言深入淺出的同時，又貫穿著富有條理的論證和鞭辟入裡的批判，這是既是本書行文風格上的一大特色，也是陳老師長久以來所秉持良知與追求真理的鐵骨風範。書中看似率性灑脫的筆調，卻是經過了陳老師反復的凝思與揣摩；看似信手拈來的旁徵博引，卻始終因循陳老師嚴密的行文邏輯。在陳老師筆下，資本主義國家「高雅精緻的法學傳統」，被解剖為中國人俗稱的「人嘴兩片皮」，可幽默謔之為「兩片皮法學」；而美國憑藉其經濟實力推行霸權主義、罔顧司法正義的做法，卻被陳老師戲稱為「神話法學」。陳老師堅定的表達了自己對於歐美發達國家管轄權現時制度的態度和立場，並堅定地認為：中國式法學，應當以「王道」文化為基礎，而避免以「利益」作為法學之目的；多次將自己稱為「法律的學生」之陳老師，對美國和英國法院管轄權判例中的「實質正義」，提出了讓其無以遮羞的質疑。尤其對它們某些損害第三世界國家利益、顯失公平的做法，甚至發出強烈拷問，並籍此表達出自己對於未來世界利益格局的擔憂。陳老師由此認為，21世紀全球化法學的心與靈魂，在於個案正義是否能被達成。在法學的這一基本核心政策之下，21世紀全球化管轄規則的心與靈魂應當是：於某地訴訟是否最能實現個案當事人的真正利益。

還應該提及的是，本書並不僅僅是一部限於研究國際私法領域相關問題的著作。全書的諸多論述，不僅反映出作者深厚的知識底蘊和開闊的治學視野，更是折射出其他相關國際私法著作所缺乏的人本主義思想的鋒芒。全書的靈魂，始終在於對管轄權個案中的實質正義、以及當事人個體權益尤其是弱勢一方權益的關注。但陳老師在書中對很多問題的探討，其實已經超越了跨國訴訟管轄權本身，甚至超越了法學的範疇。陳老師關於意識形態、國家政策、文化傳統、以及國際經濟與政治關係等問題的認識，以及對於其相互之間千絲萬縷的關聯深刻剖析，仿佛大地春綠上點綴的朵朵鮮花。

三十年來的實踐表明，我們的法律制度目前正經受著國際化與本土化激烈博弈之考驗。在學習和借鑒世界範圍內的優秀法治成果時，對於他國的制度經驗，我們無疑應要有客觀清醒之認識。社會體制、現實國情、文化傳統之差異，或許會讓我們尋尋覓覓一圈，還是難以找到值得追隨之標杆，更是無法從中獲得具有普世價值的啟示。因此，撥開那些繁雜的法律技術和利益紛爭，我們可能會恍然：解決問題的答案竟是如此返璞歸真。

正如陳老師所言：「如果一幅畫勝過千句言語，那麼一顆正義的心勝過一千個人權公約。」

掩卷沉思，私下揣測：這大概是陳老師給讀者最為深刻的留白吧。

中國思想下的全球化管轄規則

Globalization of Jurisdictional Rules Based on Chinese Philosophy

於2009年在台北舉辦的第5屆兩岸國際私法研討會中，趙相林教授及黃進教授倡議兩岸應發展具有中華文化特色的國際私法。後2010年黃進教授與個人於台中共同認為我們民族綿延兩千多年的「王道」精神（the way of heavenly beneficence）或許應為中國式法學之核心基礎思想。而於2012年個人就此問題在長沙受教於李雙元教授，其亦欣然同意以此中國固有的「人本思想」做為中國式法學之基礎。

聖經路加福音第18章：「不可姦淫、不可殺人、不可偷盜、不可作假見證、當孝敬父母。那人說，這一切我從小都遵守了。耶穌聽見了，就說，你還缺少一件，要變賣你一切所有的，分給窮人，就必有財寶在天上，你還要來跟從我。他聽見這話，就甚憂愁，因為他很富足。耶穌看見他就說，有錢財的人進上帝的國，是何等的難哪。駱駝穿過鍼的眼，比財主進上帝的國，還容易呢。」個人真誠的以為這是與我們傳統文化上盛行的「禮運大同」、「不患寡患不均」的基本社會政策，於大方向上是一致的。而中國傳統上兩千多年來的「王道」哲學、「禮運大同」思想、及「不患寡患不均」的至高政策，又是與現代聯合國1948人權宣言、1992 Rio宣言、及2002 Johannesburg宣言之理想是一致的，故而21世紀的全球化法學自然應順理成章的以中國「王道」思想及聯合國上述宣言為共同核心之基礎——而這或許亦是黃進教授所主張的「中國法學革命」（Chinese legal revolution）應有之特色。

於國際民事訴訟上無論是在大陸法的國家或英美法的國家，平行訴訟（parallel proceedings）或複數訴訟（multiple proceedings），通常是不受歡迎的。歐盟法院是被有些英國同僚號稱為「大陸法思想的堡壘」（a bastion of civil law thinking），其於解決會員國間之「平行訴訟」或「複數訴訟」，是依布魯塞爾公約（Brussels Convention）21、22條或布魯塞爾規則（Brussels Regulation）27、28條之先繫屬優先原則（lis pendens）。而英美法系統於解決國際訴訟上所可能發生之「平行訴訟」或「複數訴訟」上之問題，通常是以「不方便法院」（forum non conveniens）來停止法院地之訴訟，或作成「禁止訴訟命令」（anti-suit injunctions）禁止當事人於外國法院提起訴訟。

大陸法的先繫屬優先或其台灣的突變版〈民訴182之2〉，會造成鼓勵當事人先起訴以選購法院的不良後果。這種鼓勵訴訟的拙劣法學是與中國二千多年來的「訟，終凶」的文化思想不合的。而相對的自1821起英國法院已行使管轄權去限制當事人於外國法院之程序或停止國內之訴訟。見Leach V.-C., Bushby v. Munday (1821), 5 Madd. 297, 56 E.R. 908, at p. 307 and p. 913, “Where parties Defendants are resident in England, and brought by subpoena here, this Court has full authority to act upon them personally with respect to the subject of the suit, as the ends of justice require; and with that view, to order them to take, or omit to take, any steps and proceedings in any other Court of Justice, whether in this country, or in a foreign country.” 故無論是停止國內之訴訟（不方便法院）或限制當事人於外國之程序（禁訴令），其起源皆是在於「正義的目的之需求下」。

於英國禁訴令之作成是不能僅以「更為合適」為理由，於

Airbus Industrie GIE v. Patel中，Lord Goff認為通常欲作成禁訴令時，國際禮誼要求英國法院對該問題必須有足夠之利益或關連，以便有正當之理由去間接的干擾外國法院。但個人真誠的認為國家的利益或關連點是與個案的正義無直接關係的，所牽連的全球化實體政策才是衡量個案正義的標準。

於可謂是本書的上冊「全球化選法規則」之序中，個人認為「誠信原則與合理性之標準既然是數千年來人類文明及法律科學的最核心主流價值，自然是21世紀人類國內法及國際私法黑死病——公序良俗、強行法及合法性——的最佳救贖。」因此對於英美法院機械式的經常依當事人之管轄或仲裁條款而作成禁訴令之死硬判例法，個人是無法認同。統一商法1-304條的註釋1與歐盟契約法原則1：201條的註釋A，皆認為誠信原則是「基本原則貫穿了整個統一商法」或「貫穿整個契約的原則中之基本原則」。故而契約法上議價能力的平衡性與附隨而來於訴訟程序上立足點之平等，以及ALI/UNIDROIT Principles of Transnational Civil Procedure的3.2條所規定對第三世界人民參加外國訴訟之困難必須加以考慮，這些很明顯的應屬於歐盟契約法原則15：101條「契約違反歐盟會員國（事實上應為全世界）間所承認之法律基本原則之範圍內是無效的。」主張管轄條款、仲裁條款、及附隨而來之禁訴令、以及2005年海牙選擇法院公約所代表之契約條款之效力應超越一切全世界目前所公認的既有契約法共同核心基本原則及訴訟法立足點平等〈武器對等〉之要求的人，請問他們憑什麼可以超越這些全球化法學的共同核心強行法、基本政策、及超越性考量？

ALI/UNIDROIT Principles 3.2條之解釋要求避免「嚴格、過分、不合理」條款的適用，管轄及仲裁條款超越性的適用，對第三世界弱勢之商人、社會所可能造成之毀滅性傷害，第一

世界可能必須摸著良心重新再唸一次：「因為那字句是叫人死，聖靈是叫人活」。〈新約哥林多後書第3章〉

英美法——特別是英國法長久之傳統——經常會制止當事人之濫用程序，但大陸法並非沒有這概念。於ALI/UNIDROIT Principles of Transnational Civil Procedure之第2.5條之comment P-2F中，有趣的將停止或駁回訴訟之方法，比喻為英美法之不方便法院法學及大陸法的防止濫選法院之法學。而且更有趣的是註釋中闡明本2.5條應與第3條的當事人程序上公平條款一起被解釋，特別是應去防止可能發生3.2條基於國籍、居所、及外地人參加訴訟之困難而來的歧視之情形。尤其是其第11條更是明文當事人有著誠信、道德上之責任，去避免濫用程序。故而在全球化法學的概念下，禁訴令隨著全球化經濟市場的擴展，亦可視為全球化法學日益拓展之一個環節。若外國法院所作成禁訴令之基礎為當事人於程序上的濫用程序違反自然正義，或其之行為違反誠信原則的自然法概念，則為了達成當事人間之公平正義，在符合法院地法濫用程序或誠信原則之既有標準下，自然可以執行外國法院之禁訴令。但是外國禁訴令之作成基礎若不符合法院地既有的濫用程序自然正義之標準，亦不符合法院地既有的實體上誠信原則之自然法概念，自然可以不承認外國法院所作成之禁訴令。因為美國聯邦各州間、歐盟會員國內、及英國法院於傳統上皆沒有承認外國法院所作成之禁訴令之義務，故中國法院若不承認外國（通常是英美法）法院所做之禁訴令，自然不會違反國際禮誼及既有的國際慣例。

在Erie Railroad v. Tompkins, 304 U. S. 64 (1938)中，美國最高法院禁止聯邦法院於依憲法應以州法為依據之範圍內，去適用或創造聯邦判例法。但其仍舊於管轄規則及選法規則上先後創造及適用一個於各州管轄規則及選法規則上最低限度之標準。先前美國最高法院因為沒有正視英國母法對送達境外視為「過度、例外」之法理，故而對所引發之情形，個人認為minimum contacts於管轄規則上在美國已造成「最大程度之混亂」（minimum contacts cause maximum chaos）；於選法規則上因為忽視所牽連的實體政策，故構成「最大程度之欺騙」（minimum contacts constitute maximum deception）。

一百多年前美國最高法院在Pennoyer v. Neff中，公開的接受英國判例法的「所在權力」（presence power）一般管轄權基礎，但是後於International Shoe Co. v. Washington及Shaffer v. Heitner中又分別建立「最低限度關連點」或以其對「所在權力」試圖加以修正，但較近於Burnham v. Superior Court又回到原點而接受「所在權力」。美國最高法院在一連串令人目眩神搖驚心動魄的管轄權革命後，卻又極度低調的回歸原點，故個人稱之為「鬼打牆法學」（a ghost hitting the wall legal doctrine）

就管轄權之規則而言，無論是於大陸法所通常分類的一般管轄或特別管轄上（英國無此分類，美國則接受），全球化管轄規則的共同核心是存在的。但是這種將國內管轄的概念詭異的套在國際訴訟上，其阿奇里斯腳踝即為其不符合現實生活經驗的完全忽視了「外國當事人參加訴訟的困難」（ALI/UNIDROIT Principles of Transnational Civil Procedure 3.2），對第三世界的人民而言有時甚至可能近乎違反了人權公約上人道的基本超越性考量。

個人於此再次引用先前著作之論述：「或許是無論於英國方便法院原則之公開確認，或美國於Burnham對短暫過境管轄之確認，至今皆不滿二十年，個人甚為訝異的發現國際私法界有一個驚天動地的新潮流又鋪天蓋地的席捲而來，而全世界仍然白目的視而不見——英國與美國皆不約而同的對送達至境外加以重新規範，英國以『方便法院』原則而美國以『最低限度關連點』原則為裁量權行使之規範。雖然學理與名稱不同，但基本精神乃是將送達至境外的過度管轄權加以適度合理的規範，如前述歐盟與海牙會議數十年來忙著對過度管轄消極的加以撻伐及限制，然而最近不到二十年來英國及美國卻不約而同的以不同的手段積極的對送達至境外加以制度化及合理化。或許歐陸國家應擺脫消極禁止的態度，而積極的去制度化境外送達。個人不知是否有其他衝突法的同僚注意到英、美此處異曲同工之創見，如若是沒有，那麼如同個人近三十年前於實體法方法論一般，於此處管轄權理論驚濤駭浪般澎湃洶湧的新趨勢中，本文很榮幸的於此為衝突法管轄權歷史作一個大時代潮流的新見證。」（陳隆修、許兆慶、林恩瑋、李瑞生四人合著，《國際私法-管轄與選法理論之交錯》，204、205頁。）

因此個人務實的根據英國判例法經歷近兩百年時空淬鍊順天應人所形成的判例法之自然寫實（Cheshire and North's Private International Law, 13th ed, 313; 14th ed., 426, 427,），而建議全球化之管轄規則應如下：「於民商管轄規則上，歐盟Council Regulation No.44/2001之第2及第5條、1999海牙草約、美國各州送達境外被告之長手法規及英國法院允許送達境外被告之R.S.C. Order 11, rule 1 (1)（即現今之1998 C.P.R. s. 6. 20），與大陸法各國之國內管轄規則相去並不遠，故個人建議於行使民商管轄權時：各國仍得以既有的國內或國際管轄規則為基礎（英美則仍為所在權力理論及送達境外之規則）。但訴訟之通知若於境內已適當的送達給被告，或被告承認法院之管轄權時，若有其它更適合之法院時法院得以『不方便法院』法則為拒絕或停止訴訟裁量之依據（例如訴因與法院地沒有合理之牽連時）；而若法院欲允許送達至境外時，首先必須認知此為一種例外之過度管轄，其判決有可能不為外國法院所承認，應以『方便法院』法則來確認法院是否為合適、自然之管轄法院以作為允許送達境外之適用基礎（例如為了公平正義之目的或訴因與法院地有強烈之牽連時）。」但是有鑑於美國法院的利用「不方便法院」法則去剝奪第三世界弱勢人民人權法上保障的訴訟權及財產權，個人於此必須不厭其煩的再次重申英國判例法中之核心超越性考量——"conveniens"並不是指「方便」之意，而是合適去達成正義之目的之意。

美國所行使的「不方便法院」法學是被1999年海牙草約22(3)條及UNIDROIT Principles 3.2條所公開禁止其基於國籍或居所而對外國當事人加以歧視之行為。其所行使的「公共利益」考量，是為英國最高法院於Lubbe v. Cape PLC中明確的表示與當事人的私利益及正義的目的無關（"public interest considerations not related to the private interests of the parties and the ends of justice have no bearing on the decision which the court has to make."），又採用蘇格蘭判例法認為「司法的自尊與政治上之利益或責任與此無關」（"questions of judicial amour propre and political interest or responsibility have no part to play."）。

美國最高法院於Piper Aircraft Co. v. Reyno中說：「當家園地之法院被選定時，去假設這個選擇是便利的是為合理的。但是當原告是外國人時，這個假設就是非常的沒有那麼合理。因為任何不方便法院的諮詢之中心目的就是去確保審判是便利的，一個外國原告的選擇是較不值得順服的。」（Because the central purpose of any forum non conveniens inquiry is to ensure that the trial is convenient, a foreign plaintiff's choice deserves less deference.）相對的英國最高法院於Lubbe v. Cape PLC中則氣勢萬千的宣示，如果在「更合適的」南非法院進行訴訟會等同於「正義的拒絕」（if these proceedings were stayed in favour of the more appropriate forum in South Africa the probability is that the plaintiffs would have no means of obtaining the professional representation and expert evidence which would be essential if these claims were to be justly decided. This would amount to a denial of justice.）。

Dicey and Morris解釋如下：「不方便法院法學，亦即所謂其他法院是更『合適』指的就是為了正義的目的是更適合」。故而所謂「合適」的自然法院指的就是為了正義的目的更適合之意思。彷彿這樣還不夠明確，其又於註解中引用判例法而更白紙黑字的明確宣示：「conveniens不是指『便利』」。於確立「方便與不方便法院」法學之領頭案例Spiliada中，Lord Goff宣示所謂「合適法院」就是能更妥善的處理所有當事人之利益及正義之目的之法院。因此個人於此請求美國同僚注意，你們判例法的母法鏗鏘有力的宣布「conveniens不是『便利』，因此「不方便法院的諮詢中心的重點是便利性」是與母法之判例法不合的。」（“Conveniens does not mean ‘convenient’: see The Atlantic Star [1974] A.C. 436, 475; GAF Corp v Amchem Products Inc [1975] 1 Lloyd’s Rep. 601, 607; Spiliada Maritime Corp v Cansulex Ltd [1987] A.C. 460, 474-475.”）個人認為任何「方便與不方便法院」法學之重點若不是以正義為目的，就不是「道法自然」之行為。自然原告應對自然被告於自然法院提起自然訴訟。

事實上受到這個資本主義及自由貿易主義所創造的「神話法學」所荼毒的亦不限於極低度開發國家。1998年美國跨國企業本著「金融自由流通」的概念於東南亞攫取暴利而造成亞洲金融風暴，而2009年更變本加厲的造成全世界金融海嘯。所有全世界的受害者皆無能力到美國求償，所有的美國跨國企業皆受到這個「神話法學」的保護。美國法院的「神話法學」不但違反「以原就被」及一般管轄的訴訟法共同核心，亦違反產品責任及保護投資消費者於實體法上之共同核心。這個「神話法學」不但違反實體法及程序法上之全球化共同核心，亦違反了幾乎所有文明國家憲法及人權公約中所保障的訴訟權、財產權、生命權、平等權、及適當程序權，更應特別指出的是它違反了聯合國1966年兩個人權公約第1條2項中之生存權。第2項規定：「在他們自己的目的下，所有的人得自由的處分他們的自然財富及資源，但不得違反基於國際法與互利原則而來的國際經濟合作所產生的任何義務。無論於何種情形下，沒有任何人得被剝奪其賴以生存之依據。」很明顯的，在1998年及2009年美國跨國企業以金融自由之名所引起的金融風暴，已違反了「自然財富之處分不得違反互利原則下國際經濟合作所產生之義務」，對第三世界人民而言這更是「剝奪其賴以生存之依據」。美國法院違反實體法與程序法在全球化法學的共同核心，允許跨國企業「逆向選購法院」以躲避其產品責任，這是一種「逆向不方便法院」（reverse forum non conveniens）之行使。對這違反「傳統上公平與實質正義」的「逆向不方便法院」神話法學，個人再次重申——這是一個20世紀的唯一霸主赤裸裸的展現出逆天而行不可一世之暴力法學，中國文化自古稱之為霸道法學。

當Lord Denning豪情萬丈氣吞河嶽的宣示：「沒有人到這些法院來要求正義會徒勞無功……這個到這裡來的權力並不只侷限於英國人。它拓展至任何友好的外國人。如果他願意如此做，他可以要求我們法院的幫助。如果你願意你可以稱這是『選購法院』，但如果法院是在英國，同時在貨的品質及服務的速度上，它是一個選購的好地方。」（No one who comes to these courts asking for justice should come in vain.... This right to come here is not confined to Englishmen. It extends to any friendly foreigner. He can seek the aid of our courts if he desires to do so. You may call this 'forum shopping' if you please, but if the forum is England, it is a good place to shop in, both for the quality of the goods and the speed of service.）而Lord Goff亦高調的宣佈英國的「不方便法院」法學：「可被視為最文明的法學原則之一」。（can be regarded as one of the most civilised of legal principles.）請問「所有」的美國同僚——你們可以直視第三世界人民的眼睛而重覆這些話嗎？請問WTO與諾貝爾和平獎——你們可以直視第三世界人民的眼睛而重覆這些話嗎？

無論是於契約法上之要求平衡性原則，於訴訟法上要求立足點平等及避免當事人貧富不均所產生之不公正，及最重要的聯合國數次高峰會針對「全球化的利益及代價並未平均分配」，因而要求「降低生活水平之差距」，以上這些實體法、訴訟法、及聯合國高峰會宣言不但是21世紀全球化法學的共同核心基本政策，更是中華民族二千五百年來我們祖先的「不患寡患不均」「禮運大同」的「王道」思想。

很明顯的中國的「王道」哲學是與聯合國數次宣言之理想是一致的，故而21世紀的全球化法學自然應以中國「王道」思想及聯合國上述宣言為基礎及共同核心。「天道無親，恆與善人」，21世紀文明的進展使得全球化法學提昇至以個人之人權為中心，故個人認為21世紀全球化管轄規則之心與靈魂在於個案正義的真正利益在那裏最能被達成（whether the true interests of justice would be best served by trying the question here, or leaving it to the foreign tribunal.），而21世紀全球化法學之心與靈魂在於個案之正義是否能被達成。（「你們明顯是基督的信、藉著我們修成的。不是用墨寫的、乃是用永生上帝的靈寫的。不是寫在石版上，乃是寫在心版上。我們因基督所以在上帝面前纔有這樣的信心。並不是我們憑自己能承擔什麼事、我們所能承擔的、乃是出於上帝。他叫我們能承擔這新約的執事。不是憑著字句、乃是憑著精意。因為那字句是叫人死、精意是叫人活。」「精意或作聖靈」）

本書承蒙東海陳美蘭助教打字，研究生林郁甄小姐與陳奕彣先生的校稿及編排及中南財經政法大學劉仁山院長賜序，於此特別致上真誠的謝意。

近年來個人與許多大陸的同僚一起努力於「中國思想下的全球化法學」（legal globalization based on Chinese philosophy）之發展，於漫長的過程中經常回想起於LSE時大學、碩士、博士之指導教授Prof. Trevor C. Hartley不辭辛勞的輔導與耐心的授業，故謹以本書敬呈最尊敬的恩師Prof. Trevor C. Hartley——“you are not only a scholar, but also an English gentleman.”

目錄

第1章　禁訴令、不方便法院、先繫屬優先

一、跨國管轄與禁訴令—chickens talking to a duck; and if it is, it is pointless to say that one approach is right and the other is wrong.*

2008年第4屆兩岸國際私法會議於西安舉行時，杜新麗教授對於實務上法院面對英國法院所作成之禁止訴訟命令（anti-suit injunctions）的裁決（這包含中間裁定及最後決定）之困擾，鄭重的提出請求希望其他同僚給予意見。英美法的禁訴令的確經常讓大陸法的同僚「挑起對英美法懷疑的眉毛」。甚至Professor Adrian Briggs於評論大陸法與英美法同僚在禁訴令上之對話是如同：「雞同鴨講；並且如果是如此的話，去論述一種方式是對的而他種方式是錯，那就沒有意義。[1]」

儘管大陸法的同僚對禁訴令的普遍不滿，甚至以「禁訴令是個核子炸彈」來加以形容[2]，但有些年輕氣盛的英美法同僚仍舊堅持[3]：「但是在這

* Adrian Briggs, The Impact of Recent Judgments of the European Court on English Procedural Law and Practice, Zeitschrift fur Schweizerisches Recht 124 (2005) II 231, 234, 244.

1 Adrian Briggs, The Impact of Recent Judgments of the European Court on English Procedural Law and Practice, zeitschrift fur Schweizerisches Recht 124 (2005) II 231, 234, 244. "chickens talking to a duck; and if it is, it is pointless to say that one approach is right and the other is wrong."

2 "L'antisuit injonction est une bombe nucleaire." Renaud Carrier, L'antisuit injonction, Centre de Droit Maritime et des Transports 5 (2001), available at http://junon.u-3mrs.fr/ad210w00/memoires/2001/m01care.html

3 Daniel Tan, Enforcing International Arbitration Agreements in Federal Courts: Rethinking the Court's Remedial Powers, 47 Va. J. Int'l L. 545, 591, 592 (2007), "Suffice it to say that in this dialogue where civilian chickens talk to the common law ducks, it is the chickens who have managed to get through to the ducks. The mantra in modern antisuit cases is that because antisuit injunctions infringe judicial comity, they should only be issued in the most exceptional circumstances. Evidently, the civilian distaste for the injunction has permeated common law antisuit practice. This is not a good thing. The common law courts should not simply accept the ipse dixit of the foreign courts that these orders cause offense,

個大陸法的雞群與判例法的鴨群之對話中，是可以這樣說的，應是雞群已經穿過鴨群了。在現代禁止訴訟案例中之例行咒語是，因為禁訴令侵犯了司法禮誼，他們只能於最例外之情形下而被作成[4]。很明顯的，大陸法對禁訴令的不喜歡已經影響到判例法禁訴令的實施。這並不是一個好事。外國法院認為這些命令會造成侵犯是他們自己的說辭，判例法法院不應就如此的接受，而是應相反的去檢驗他們的敵意是否有良好的依據。它可能是沒有的。」

這些年輕的英美法同僚將戰鼓擂向大陸法，這種單向的敵意是否過於簡化？由於以歐盟法院[5]（European Court of Justice）為首的大陸法系，通常拒絕作成禁訴令或承認外國之禁訴令，故而事實上於英美法與大陸法間反而較為單純。反而於實施禁訴令之英美法國家間戰況較為詭譎。德國同僚即陳述：「因此在1980年代早期之Laker案件訴訟期間，美國與英國

---

but should instead examine whether their hostility is well founded. It may not be."

4 Daniel Tan, note 161
Quaak v. Klynveld Peat Marwick Goerdeler Bedrijfsrevisoren, 361 F. 3d 11, 18 (1st Cir, 2004), "Issuing an international antisuit injunction is a step that should 'be taken only with care and great restraint.'" (citing Canadian Filters (Harwich) Ltd. v. Lear-Siegler, Inc., 412 F.2d 577, 578 (1st Cir. 1969)); Laker Airways v. Sabena, Belgian World Airlines, 731 F. 2d 909, 927 (D.C. Cir. 1984), "Thus, only in the most compelling circumstances does a court have discretion to issue an anti-suit injunction."; China Trade & Dev. Corp. v. M.V. Choong Yong, 837 F. 2d 33, 36 (2d Cir. 1987), "An anti-foreign-suit injunction should be 'used sparingly', and should be granted 'only with care and great restraint.'"

5 於Turner v. Grovit, Case c-159/02, 2004 E.C.R.I-3536中，歐盟法院認定一會員國法院作成禁訴令以限制其他會員國法院之程序是違反布魯塞爾公約（Brussels Convention）。但稍早之前法國最高法院（Cour de cassation）卻維持下級法院禁止破產程序中之一請求人再於西班牙提起破產程序，Cass.1e civ., Nov. 19, 2002, Banque Worms v. Brachot, 92 REVUE CRITIQUE DE DROIT INTERNATIONAL PRIVÉ [REV. CRIT. DIP] 816 (2003).該案之討論見Horatia Muir Watt, Injunctive Relief in the French Courts: A Case of Legal Borrowing, 62 CAMBRIDGE L. 573 (2003).法國法院之可以作成禁訴令或許可能應是破產程序並非是布魯塞爾公約及規則適用範圍內之原因。但是鑑於歐盟法院對於英國在非會員國法院之管轄上行使不方便法院之裁量權，及不在公約及規則範圍內之仲裁上行使禁訴令之限制，法國法院卻得以在破產程序上行使禁訴令。個人以為或許法國法院之禁訴令是符合全球化法學之共同核心政策之故—亦即每個同梯次之債權人應得到相同比例之賠償。見UNCITRAL Model Law on Cross-Border Insolvency with Guide to Enactment
Articl 32. Rule of payment in concurrent proceedings
Without prejudice to secured claims or rights *in rem*, a creditor who has received part payment in respect of its claim in a proceeding pursuant to a law relating to insolvency in a foreign State may not receive a payment for the same claim in a proceeding under *[identify laws of the enacting State relating to insolvency]* regarding the same debtor, so long as the payment to the other creditors of the same class is proportionately less than the payment the creditor has already received.

法院間之禁止訴訟命令及反禁止訴訟命令於司法上升格為『禁止命令之戰爭』……這是不可能於德國與美國法院間被重覆。[6]」Laker Airways Ltd. 破產案及相關之其他案件為反托辣斯法及禁訴令上之經典案例，其於美國之相對案件為Laker Airways Ltd. v. Sabena, Belgian World Airlines[7]。於Laker案中英國法院作成禁止當事人於美國訴訟之命令，但之後美國聯邦地院即作成反禁訴令以禁止當事人去執行英國禁訴令。因為涉及鉅額之利益故引起其時雷根總統及柴契爾首相之洽商，及甚多同僚之討論[8]。於英美法法院間之司法上之「禁止命令戰爭」，不但會以「反禁止訴訟命令」（anti-anti-suit injunction）之方式而進行，甚至偶會有「反反禁止訴訟命令」（anti- anti-anti-suit injunction）之情形發生。亦即申請人要求法院作成禁止命令，以禁止被申請人去要求外國法院去作成命令，而該外國法院之命令是意圖限制申請人之申請對其加以禁止訴訟命令[9]。

美國的Anti-Injunction Act是美國最古老的條文之一[10]，其禁止聯邦法院去作成禁止命令以停止州法院之訴訟程序，「除非於國會有明示立法，或為了幫助其管轄權之必要情形，或為了保護或執行其判決」[11]之情形。但正如大部分國際私法上之範圍，美國國會尚未對國際上之禁止訴訟命令加以規範，因此有聯邦上訴法院認為這是「完全屬於地院之裁量權範

---

6 Moritz Bälz and Felix Blobel, Collective Litigation German Style, in conflict of Laws in a Globalized World, edited by Eckart Gottschalk, Ralf Michaels, Giesela Rühl, Jan von Hein, p. 146, note 86, "Therefore, a judicial escalation of antisuit-injunctions and antiantisuit-injunctions into a 'battle of injunctions,' as fought between English and U.S. courts in the course of the Laker litigation in the early 1980s (see British Airways Board v. Laker Airways, [1985] AC 58 [House of Lords, 1984]) has no prospect of being repeated between German and U.S. courts."

7 731 F.2d 909 (D.C. Cir. 1984).

8 雷根總統並下令法務部調查該事件。George A. Bermann, The Use of anti-suit Injunctions in International Litigation, 28 Colum. J. Transnat'l L. 589, 591-93, 608 n. 75 (1990).

9 Cf. Smith Kline French Laboratories Ltd v Bloch [1983] 1 W.L.R. 730 (CA). Shell UK Exploration and Production Ltd v Innes, 1995 S.L.T. 807; General Star International Indemnity Ltd v Stirling Cooke Browne Reinsurance Brokers Ltd [2003] EWHC 3 (Comm.), [2003] I.L.Pr. 314; national Australia Bank Ltd v Idoport [2002] NSWSC 623.見Dicey and Morris, the Conflict of Laws, 14th ed., p. 501, note 91.

10 於Atl. Coast Line R.R. Co. v. Bhd. Of Locomotive Eng're, 398 U.S. 281, 282 (1970)中，美國最高法院陳述國會於1793年即通過the Anti-Injunction Act.

11 28 U.S.C. §2283 (1948), "except as expressly authorized by Act of Congress, or where necessary in aid of its jurisdiction, or to protect or effectuate its judgments."

圍」[12]。這個美國早期的國內規定，於國際場合上卻有時會造成外交上的緊張關係。與其他英美法的國家偶而會升級成為「司法上之禁止命令戰爭」，而與大陸法國家間之對話是形同「雞同鴨講」之情形。美國法院於懲罰性賠償、反托辣斯法、及集體訴訟之運作上，經常被德國同僚視為「法律帝國主義」及「霸權法律制度」，於禁訴令之運作上亦被視為「司法霸權主義」之一環。Professor Ralf Michaels即如此的表達歐洲同僚的不滿：「因為美國法院會在忽視其他國家之情形下主張管轄權，歐洲人經常控訴美國法院的司法霸權主義。[13]」

Cheshire and North[14]說：「如果牽連相同當事人及相同爭點之訴訟，是同時於兩個不同國家間進行，這是被稱為lis alibi pendens之案件。於這種案件時英國法院所面對之問題並不只是去決定請求人應於那一個可替代的法院去提起訴訟。反而於另一方面而言，其選擇是在於英國之審判加上外國之審判（如果停止訴訟之請求是被拒絕），及於另一方面，於外國之審判（如果停止訴訟之請求是被允許）。於英國及外國同時有著訴訟是非常不好的：相較於若訴訟只是於一個國家舉行，這對當事人而言牽涉到更多的費用及不方便；這亦可能造成兩個相衝突的判決，導致當事人間會有著不良的競爭以企圖去首先取得判決及後續產生禁反言之問題[15]。通常

12 Seattle Totems Hockey Club, Inc. v. Nat'l Hockey League, 652 F. 2d 852, 855, "squarely within the discretion of the district courts."

13 "Europeans frequently accuse U.S. courts of judicial hegemonialism, because U.S courts assert jurisdiction without regard to other countries." Ralf Michaels, Two Paradigms of Jurisdiction, 27 Mich. J. Int'l L. 1003, 1058 (2006).

14 PM North, JJ Fawcett, Cheshire and North's Private International law, 13th ed., p. 347, "If litigation involving the same parties and the same issues is continuing simultaneously in two different countries, this is referred to as a case of lis alibi pendens. In such cases the issue facing the English court is not simply that of deciding to which of the alternative fora the claimant should have to go to bring his action. Instead, the choice is between, on the one hand, trial in England plus trial abroad (if a stay refused) and, on the other hand, trial abroad (if a stay is granted). It is very undesirable to have concurrent actions in England and abroad: this involves more expense and inconvenience to the parties than if trial were held in merely one country; it can also lead to two conflicting judgments, with an unseemly race by the parties to be the first to obtain a judgment and to subsequent problems of estoppel. The objection to concurrent proceedings is said to be even stronger if this involves in one of the two states proceedings for a negative declaration (a declaration that a person is not liable in an existing action)." 14th ed., pp.440, 441.

15 The Abidin Daver [1984] AC 398 at 412 (per Lord DIPlOCK), 423-424 (per Lord BRANDON); The

是認為如果兩個國家之一的訴訟是牽連到否認之訴（確認一方當事人對於一既存之訴訟並無責任），這種對同時訴訟的反對是更為強烈。[16]」無論是在大陸法的國家或英美法的國家，平行訴訟（parallel proceedings）或複數訴訟（multiple proceedings），通常是不受歡迎的[17]。

於Gubisch Maschinenfabrik KG v. Giulio Palumbo中歐盟最高法院（ECJ）解釋布魯塞爾公約第8段之21及22條之目的為：「在本聯盟適當的執行正義之利益下，本段條文是意圖被用來防止不同訂約國法院間之平行訴訟及去避免因此可能產生的判決間之衝突。這些規則因此是被設計來一開始就儘量排除27(3)條所提及情況發生之可能，亦即與在該判決被請求承認之國家，對於相同當事人間所發生的紛爭所作成的判決不一致之理由而不承認該判決之情況。[18]」歐盟法院是被有些英國同僚號稱為「大陸法思想的堡壘」[19]，其於解決會員國間之「平行訴訟」或「複數訴訟」，是以布魯塞爾公約（Brussels Convention）21、22條或布魯塞爾規則（Brussels Regulation）27、28條之先繫屬優先原則（lis pendens）。而英美法系統於解決國際訴訟上所可能發生之「平行訴訟」或「複數訴訟」上之問題，通常是以「不方便法院」（forum non conveniens）來停止法院地之訴訟，或作成「禁止訴訟命令」禁止當事人於外國法院提起訴訟。

Messiniaki Tolmi [1983] 1 Lloyd's Rep 666 at 672.

16 First National Bank of Boston v Union Bank of Switzerland [1990] 1 Lloyd's Rep 32 at 38-39. See also saipem Spa v Dredging V02 BV and Geosite Survrys Ltd, The Volvox Hollandia [1988] 2 Lloyd's Rep 361 at 371, CA; sohio supply Co v Gatoil (USA) Inc [1989] 1 Lloyd's Rep 588 at 593.有關否認之訴（即大陸法之確認之訴）與先繫屬優先，見陳隆修，《2005年海牙法院選擇公約評析》，台北，五南圖書公司，2009年1月，初版1刷，128、129頁。

17 陳隆修，《國際私法管轄權評論》，台北，五南圖書公司，民國75年11月，初版，84-101頁。

18 Case C-144/86, 1987 E.C.R. 4861, "Article 21, together with Article 22 on related action, is contained in Section 8 of Title II of the Convention; that section is intended, in the interests of the proper administration of justice within the Community, to prevent parallel proceedings before the courts of different Contracting States and to avoid conflicts between decisions which might result there-from. Those rules are therefore designed to preclude, in so far as is possible and from the outset, the possibility of a situation arising such as that referred to in Article 27(3), that is to say the non-recognition of a judgment on account of its irreconcilability with a judgment given in a dispute between the same parties in the State in which recognition is sought."

19 Tan, 47 Va. J. Int'l L. 545, 592, "Professor Briggs insightfully remarked that the European Court of Justice, a bastion of civil law thinking..."

或許是禁訴令的作成會間接的影響到外國法院管轄權之運作[20]，因而會牽涉到國際禮誼（comity）之問題，故而通常英美法院會於較謹慎的情況下才會作成，大陸法有些年輕同僚會將大陸法的先繫屬優先原則直接與不方便法院原則對比，而有時忘了將禁訴令相提並論[21]。事實上「禁訴令」亦是於國際訴訟上處理「平行訴訟」之重要（或有爭議）工具之一種。有美國年輕同僚將英美法之不方便法院與禁訴令區分如下：「當一個法院拒絕一個基於不方便法院而要求停止訴訟之請求時，其並未禁止一個於外國進行之訴訟，而只是保留自己之管轄（訴訟）而已。相對的，禁訴令主要是主張比起外國法院美國是更合適處理該案件，並且該外國訴訟因此應被禁止。基於不方便法院的駁回訴訟是順從外國法院；而禁訴令是試圖關閉外國法院的門。[22]」事實上於英國禁訴令之作成是不能僅以「更為合適」為理由，於Airbus Industrie GIE v. Patel中，Lord Goff認為通常欲作成禁訴令時，國際禮誼要求英國法院對該問題必須有足夠之利益或關連，以便有正當之理由去間接的干擾外國法院[23]。

20 禁訴令之運作被大陸法視為對本國管轄權具有敵意之干涉，見Andreas F. Lowenfeld, Forum Shopping, Antisuit Injunctions, Negative Declarations and Related Tools of International Litigation, 91 Am. J. Int'l L. 314 (1997).

21 Martine Stuckelberg, LIS PENDENS AND FORUM NON CONVENIENS AT THE HAGUE CONFERENCE, 26 Brooklyn J. Int'l L. 949, 950, 951 (2001), "Linked with the question of forum non conveniens is the question of lis pendens. This is a rule applied in many civil law countries, giving the court first seised of a case a priority for deciding that case. Its primary goal is to avoid parallel proceedings in different courts. As both forum non conveniens and lis pendens deal with declining jurisdiction in certain circumstances, they had to be negotiated together in The Hague."

22 Laural Eddleman Heim, District of Columbia v, Heller: Note: Protecting Their Own?: Pro-American Bias and the Issuance of Anti-Suit Injunctions, 69 Ohio St. L.J. 701, 737, "When a court denies a forum non conveniens dismissal it does not bar proceedings in a foreign court, it simply retains its own jurisdiction. In contrast, anti-suit injunctions essentially assert that the United States is in a better position than the foreign court to judge the action and that the foreign action should be barred as a result. Forum non conveniens dismissals defer to foreign courts; anti-suit injunctions attempt to shut the foreign courthouses' doors."

23 [1991] 1 AC 119 at 138, "As a general rule, before an anti-suit injunction can properly be granted by an English court to restrain a person from pursuing proceedings in a foreign jurisdiction in cases of the kind under consideration in the present case, comity requires that the English forum should have a sufficient interest in, or connection with, the matter in question to justify the indirect interference with foreign court which an anti-suit injunction entails."有關英國禁訴令，見陳隆修、許兆慶、林恩瑋、李瑞生四人合著，《國際私法-管轄與選法理論之交錯》，台北，五南圖書公司，2009年3月，初版1刷，244-247頁。

禁訴令或許充滿著爭議性，並且基於國際禮誼應被謹慎的（restrictive）的作成，但於國際貿易發達的今日它卻是個日益重要的議題。不同於大陸法之先繫屬優先或英美法之不方便法院皆侷限於不同國家間法院之平行訴訟或複數訴訟，禁訴令並不侷限於法院間之平行訴訟或複數訴訟，它亦可以基於契約之仲裁條款而被作成。無論是英國判例法[24]或美國判例法[25]皆充滿著法院作成禁訴令以限制違反仲裁協議之衡平救濟[26]。甚至事實上於國際仲裁上，已有仲裁協會在討論仲裁庭是否可能作成禁訴令[27]。有趣的是於Telenor Mobile Communication AS v. Storm LLC[28]中，聯邦地院認為根據紐約公約（the New York Arbitration Convention）其只是第二順位之管轄，故維持仲裁庭所作成禁訴令之效力，允許一挪威公司之請求，禁止一烏克蘭公司於烏克蘭提起訴訟。根據美國第2新編於判決上之第84條（Restat 2d of Judgments, s.84），一個有效及最後之仲裁判斷，通常是與法院的判決一般具有一事不再理的效力[29]。但亦有美國同僚認為

---

24 Aggeliki Charis Compania Maritima S.A. v. Pagnan S.p.A. (The Angelic Grace), [1995] 1 Lloyd's Rep. 87, 96 (Eng. C.A.); Welex A.G. v. Rosa Martime Ltd. (The Epsilon Rosa II), [2002] 2 Lloyd's Rep. 701, para. 23. (Eng. Q.B.), affd [2003] 2 Lloyd's Rep. 509(Eng. C.A.).見陳隆修、許兆慶、林恩瑋、李瑞生四人合著，《國際私法-管轄與選法理論之交錯》，台北，五南圖書公司，2009年3月，初版1刷，247頁。

25 Paramedics Electromedicina Comercial v. GE Med. Sys. Info. Techs., 369 F. 3d 645 (2d Cir. 2004); Affymax, Inc. v. Johnson & Johnson, 420 F. Supp. 2d 876 (N.D.Ill. 2006); Ibeto Petrochemicak Indus. v. M/T Beffen, 412 F. Supp. 2d 285 (S.D.N.Y. 2005); SG Avipro Fin. Ltd. v. Cameroon Airlines, No. 05 Civ. 655 (LTS)(DFE), 2005 U.S. Dist. LEXIS 11117 (S.D.N.Y. June 8, 2005).

26 禁訴令之作成是法院衡平管轄權之行使，E & J. Gallo Winery v. Andinal Licores S.A., 446 F. 3d 984, 989, 993 (9th Cir, 2006), "Courts derive the ability to enter an anti-suit injunction from their equitable powers…. involving equity jurisdiction.". 見Daniel Tan, Enforcing International Arbitration Agreements in Federal Courts: Rethinking the Court's Remedial Powers, 47 Va. J. Int'l L. 545, 612. 613 (2007), "In addition, as pointed out, the courts have used the equitable remedy of the antisuit injunction to restrain breaches of arbitration agreements. These cases further demonstrate how the courts liberally use extra-statutory equitable remedies to effectively enforce arbitration agreements. Moreover, as discussed, the federal courts have asserted an inherent power to stay court and arbitral proceedings in support of arbitration agreements. This power is wider than the statutory power to stay court proceedings in the FAA, and has been exercised in circumstances not explicitly envisioned by the FAA."

27 Int'l Arbitration Inst., Anti-suit Injunctions in International Arbitration 115, 126 (Fmmanuel Gaillard ed., 2005).

28 524 F. Supp. 2d 332, 359, 363, 364 (S.D.N.Y. 2007).

29 S. 84 Arbitration Award
(1) Except as stated in Subsections (2), (3), and (4), a valid and final award by arbitration has the same effects under the rules of res judicata, subject to the same exceptions and qualifications, as a judgment

紐約公約為美國所簽訂，故依紐約公約而作成之仲裁判斷自然應有排除效力（preclusive effect），但其他仲裁判斷則不見得會有排除效力。如果基於上述於禁反言（estoppel）之論述，對於非紐約公約之仲裁判斷於禁訴令上是否應如同禁反言上應有區別？

個人並不以為法院基於仲裁條款而作成禁訴令前，必須先認定該仲裁判斷是否為依紐約公約而被加以作成。如第2新編判決篇第84條註釋(a)所說：「仲裁是決定法律紛爭的一種方式，而方式是經由紛爭之當事人間以契約所授權的。[30]」正如當事人間所訂定之法院管轄條款，整個仲裁或仲裁條款皆是以當事人間所協議的契約內容為依據，故而英美之法院亦是依據此當事人間之契約協議而作成不方便法院（停止法院之訴訟）或禁訴令（禁止違約之一方至其他法院提起訴訟）之決定。因此於作成禁止令前法院所應確認的是仲裁條款協議之成立、存在、與效力，而非辨認該仲裁是否為紐約公約之仲裁。

二、不方便法院與先繫屬優先

許多大陸法的國家於國內之平行訴訟上，採先繫屬優先原則[31]，有趣的是這個國內法的作法亦為大陸法系適用至國際平行訴訟上。如大陸法同僚所述：「大部分大陸法的國家並沒有一個不方便法院理論，他們亦不行使禁訴令。為了限制平行訴訟，他們採用一種稱為先繫屬優先之原則。根據這個規則，如果對相同當事人間之紛爭兩個法院皆已繫屬，並且是牽連到相同之訴因，第二繫屬之法院必須停止或駁回該案件而以第一繫屬法院為優先，這就是『第一及時規則』，亦即只是允許第一繫屬法院去決定案

of a court.

30 Comment a. Scope. “Arbitration is a method of determining legal disputes that is authorized by contract between the parties to the dispute. There are forms of dispute-resolution procedure that are called ‘arbitration’ but which are made obligatory by law instead of being prescribed by contract, for example, some proceedings in ‘no fault’ insurance schemes. These procedures might perhaps better be regarded as adjudication before specialized tribunals.”

31 例如Societe A v. S., ATF 118 II 1888. Swiss Federal Supreme Court (1992) (in French).

件之實體。[32]」採用先繫屬優先原則最具代表性的自然就是歐盟布魯塞爾公約的21、22、23條，及布魯塞爾規則的27、28、29條。

歐盟與美國為當今全世界最具影響力之聯邦，而歐盟的布魯塞爾公約及規則更是被美國同僚稱為「歐洲版的充分互信條款」（European full faith and credit clause），但是這兩個巨大的聯邦間對聯盟內部之平行訴訟之處理法則並不相同。於美國聯邦法院間所發生的平行訴訟之情形，美國最高法院於Landis v. North American Co.中[33]，認為聯邦地院有著固有的權力去停止訴訟。美國最高法院要求地院於決定停止訴訟前必須先平衡停止訴訟的益處及困難之處，而該檢驗的標準是近似不方便法院之分析。但是於後來之Colorado River Water Conservation District v. United States[34]中，美國最高法院認為聯邦法院間之平行訴訟應與聯邦法院及州法院間之平行訴訟之情形不同。除非於有些例外之情形下，聯邦法院對於適當的被呈現於其前面之紛爭是有著去決定的責任，因此通常是不能將案件交給州法院而停止訴訟。至於有關因為在外國之平行訴訟因而停止訴訟之情形，最高法院尚未有著判例。因此有些下級法院遵守Landis規則於平行訴訟時對是否停止訴訟，則於衡量利益及困難之情形下行使裁量權。而其他法院則遵守Colorado River規則，要求必須有特殊情形下才會停止訴訟[35]。但無論其內部民事訴訟法學是如何區分，一般於國際私法學上是認

---

32 Martine Stuckelberg LIS PENDENS AND FORUM NON CONVENIENS AT THE HAGUE CONFERENCE 26 Brooklyn J. Int'l L. 949, 958 (2001), "Most civil law countries do not have a forum non conveniens doctrine, nor do they use antisuit injunctions. In order to limit parallel litigations, they apply a rule called lis pendens. According to this rule, if two courts are seised of a dispute between the same parties, involving the same cause of action, the court second seized must stay or dismiss the case in favor of the court first seised. It is a 'first in time' rule, allowing only the court first seised to decide the case on the merits."

33 299 U.S. 248 (1936).本案為兩個控股公司對the Holding Company Act是否合於憲法而對the Securities & Exchange Commission於聯邦地院提出訴訟，但由於其他公司與the Securities & Exchange Commission在其他聯邦地院之訴訟而被停止，以等待有關the Holding Company Act是否合乎憲法的決定。

34 424 U.S. 800 (1976).本案為有關the Colorado River的水權而由美國聯邦政府在聯邦地院提出告訴，但由於聯邦訴訟中被告之一在州法院提出平行訴訟而被駁回。該案中美國最高法院認為，因為聯邦有著清楚的政策去避免在有關河流之制度裡作成在水權上碎片式的決定，故已形成特殊之情形，因而聯邦訴訟的駁回是合乎道理的。

35 Martine Stuckelberg, 26 Brooklyn J. Int'l L. 949, 960, 961 (2001); Gary B. Born, International Civil

為於平行訴訟上，在國際案件美國法院是以「不方便法院」之法理加以處理[36]。

但是在有關聯邦法院間審判地之移轉（venue transfers），國會於1948年28 U.S.C. 1404（a）之立法使得不方便法院變得幾乎為不需要[37]，其規定：「為了當事人及證人之便利，正義之利益，一個地院得將任何民事訴訟移轉至任何其得被提起之其他任何地院或部門。[38]」故而依據成文法上之權力（statutory powers）聯邦地院是有權力將不方便之請求，移轉至其他州有管轄權之較合適法院。因為美國憲法之「充分互信條款」（full faith and credit clause）保障一個州之判決會為其他州所承認，故而於移轉管轄之情形下，原告之權利還是受到應有之保障。有趣的是與因不方便法院而停止法院地之訴訟不同的是，於因不同州籍案件（diversity cases）而移轉管轄之情形，美國最高法院於Van Dusen v. Barrack中規定為保護原告故不得改變應適用之法律[39]。法院認為於被告依Section 1404(a)而提出移轉之請求後，被移轉之法院應遵照原來移轉出法院

Litigation in United States Courts (3d ed. 1996), 459.

36 Gulf Oil Corp. v. Gilbert, 330 U.S. 501 (1947); Piper Aircraft Co. v. Reyno, 454 U.S. 235 (1981).另外Restatement (Second) of Conflict of Laws (1969), s. 84亦規定如果明顯而清楚的顯示法院並非是合適而方便的法院，則該法院不應行使管轄權。這亦是有著不方便法院之意涵。

37 Alexander Reus, A Comparative View of the Doctrine of Forum Non Conveniens in the United States, the United Kingdom, and Germany, 16 Loy. L.A. Int'l & Comp. L.J. 455, 464-466 (1994).

38 "For the convenience of parties and witnesses, in the interest of justice, a district court may transfer any civil action to any other district or division where it might have been brought." 28 U.S.C. 1404(a) (1948).另外由於法院沒有權力將案件轉至其他州之法院，因此如果法院認定自己為不方便法院，其應駁回訴訟，或附帶條件的駁回，或於等待原告於更方便法院提起訴訟時暫停訴訟。或於聯邦地院間若無法依不方便法院而駁回訴訟時，則得以s. 1404(a)而將訴訟移轉。見the American Law Institute的Restatement (Second) of Conflict of Laws § 84 (1971)的註釋(e): "e. Action taken when forum inappropriate. A court lacks power to transfer a case to the courts of another state. For this reason, a court which finds itself to be an inappropriate forum under the rule of this Section must dismiss the action outright, or do so conditionally (as by requiring that the defendant stipulate to accept service of process and not plead the statute of limitations in some second state that is deemed a more convenient forum), or else stay the action pending institution of suit and service of process upon the defendant in a more convenient forum. The federal district courts are authorized by statute (28 U.S.C. § 1404(a) 'for the convenience of parties and witnesses, in the interest of justice' to transfer 'any civil action to any other district or division where it might have been brought.' A transfer under § 1404(a) may be granted in situations which would not justify dismissal of the case under the doctrine of forum non conveniens. Norwood v. Kirkpatrick, 349 U.S. 29 (1955).

39 376 U.S. 612, 639 (1964).

之選法規則。後來於Ferens v. John Deere Co.中，最高法院又將Section 1404(a)對當事人之保護更加以推展[40]。法院認為無論是何人提出移轉管轄之請求，Van Dusen案之規則皆應被加以適用。Ferens案法院之決定是本於Section 1404(a)之政策及Van Dusen中所確認之國會對該法之立法意旨，其認為28 U.S.C. 1404(a)是聯邦法院處理案件之規則，故既不應剝奪當事人在設若沒有不同州籍訴訟時州法律應會給予之保護，亦不應給予當事人選購法院之機會。它所應可考量的是便利的因素，而非去造成準據法適用上之可能不利之改變。但亦因這個管轄移轉的內部規則，今日於美國不方便法院法則主要是適用於國際案件。

大部分大陸法的國家於平行訴訟上通常既不採不方便法則，又不作成禁止訴訟命令，他們通常採用先繫屬優先原則（lis pendens）。歐盟COUNCIL REGULATION (EC) No 44/2001 of 22 December 2000 on jurisdiction and the recognition and enforcement of judgments in civil and commercial matters（布魯塞爾規則）的27條規定：「1.直至第一繫屬法院之管轄權確立為止，當牽連到相同當事人及他們間相同訴因之訴訟於不同會員國間之法院被提起時，除了第一繫屬之法院外之任何其他法院皆應自動停止其訴訟程序。2.當第一繫屬法院之管轄權確立後，任何非第一繫屬之其他法院應順從第一繫屬法院之管轄，而拒絕該案之管轄。[41]」至於

---

40 494 U.S. 516, 525-527 (1900).

41 Article 27

1. Where proceedings involving the same cause of action and between the same parties are brought in the courts of different Member States, any court other than the court first seised shall of its own motion stay its proceedings until such time as the jurisdiction of the court first seised is established.
2. Where the jurisdiction of the court first seised is established, any court other than the court first seised shall decline jurisdiction in favour of that court.

而舊有的條文規定於CONVENTION of 27 September 1968 on jurisdiction and the enforcement of judgments in civil amd commercial matters的第21條。

Article 21

Where proceeding involving the same cause of action and between the same parties are brought in the courts of different Contracting States, any court other than the court first seised shall of its own motion stay its proceedings until such time as the jurisdiction of the court first seised is established.

Where the jurisdiction of the court first seised is established, any court other than the court first seised shall decline jurisdiction in favour of that court.

有關布魯塞爾1968公約之評析，見陳隆修，《國際私法管轄權評論》，台北，五南圖書公司，

相關訴訟（related actions）間之先繫屬優先則規定於28條：「1.當相關的訴訟是繫屬於不同的會員國間之法院時，除了第一繫屬之法院外，任何其他法院皆得停止其程序。2.當這些訴訟是繫屬於第一審時，如果第一繫屬法院對這些爭議中之訴訟是有著管轄權並且其法律是允許這些訴訟的集中處理，於當事人之一之請求下，任何其他非第一繫屬之法院並得拒絕管轄。3.為了本條文之目的，當案件是如此的密切關連，以致為了避免由於不同的程序所可能產生的不相容判決的風險，而他們是方便被一起處理及決定時，這些訴訟是被視為相關的。[42]」

傳統上英國判例法通常視訴訟繫屬日期之先後為偶然之因素，並不特別給予重視。但歐盟是採先繫屬優先法則，故對繫屬之次序是給予重要的法律意義。布魯塞爾規則30條對「繫屬」加以規定如下：「為了本條文之目的，於下列情形之一法院是被視為已被繫屬：1.如果原告對於它所被規定應對被告加以送達之行為，於後來並未被不履行，則於構成起訴之文件或類似之文件已被呈送至法院之時，或2.如果原告對於他所被規定應

民國75年11月，初版，7-26頁。

[42] Article 28

1. Where related actions are pending in the courts of different Member States, any court other than the court first seised may stay its proceedings.
2. Where these actions are pending at first instance, any court other than the court first seised may also, on the application of one of the parties, decline jurisdiction if the court first seised has jurisdiction over the actions in question and its law permits the consolidation thereof.
3. For the purposes of this Article, actions are deemed to be related where they are so closely connected that it is expedient to here and determine them together to avoid the risk of irreconcilable judgments resulting from separate proceedings.

而布魯塞爾公約則規定於第22條。

Article 22

Where related actions are brought in the courts of different Contracting States, any court other than the court first seised may, while the actions are pending at first instance, stay its proceedings.

A court other than the court first seised may also, on the application of one of the parties, decline jurisdiction if the law of that court permits the consolidation of related actions and the court first seised has jurisdiction over both actions.

For the purposes of this Article, actions are deemed to be related where they are so closely connected that it is expedient to hear and determine them together to avoid the risk of irreconcilable judgments resulting from separate proceedings.

規則的第一項並不似公約第一項要求訴訟必須繫屬於第一審；但規則第二項則不似公約第二項反而要求必須繫屬於第一審。這是因為規則第二項希望維護當事人保有上訴之權利。台灣的民訴182之2條對這點似乎亦有澄清之必要。

呈送於法院之文件，於後來並未不履行，又於文件被呈送至法院前已被送達，則於應負責送達文件之機構接收該文件之時。[43]」通常許多大陸法的國家是以訴訟通知之送達日為依據，而英國法則經常是以法院接受訴訟程序日為依據，故而布魯塞爾規則30條對此加以實質上之規範。

[43] Article 30

For the purposes of this Section, a court shall be deemed to be seised:

1. at the time when the document instituting the proceedings or an equivalent document is lodged with the court, provided that the plaintiff has not subsequently failed to take the steps he was required to take to have service effected on the defendant, or
2. if the document has to be served before being lodged with the court, at the time when it is received by the authority responsible for service, provided that the plaintiff has not subsequently failed to take the steps he was required to take to have the document lodged with the court.

但是如果僅就送達而言，或許Hague Convention on the Service Abroad of Judicial and Extrajudicial Documents in Civil or Commercial Matters 1965的第15條是較為實際的規定。其規定於送達至國外並且於被告未出席時，判決不應被作成，除非「(a)依當事人所在地法該文件是依該國於國內案件中所規定送達文件之方式而被加以送達，或(b)依本公約所規定之其他方式，該文件是於實際上被交付至被告本人或其之居所，並且於上述兩種情形之一，送達或交付必須給能予被告足夠的時間去幫助其抗辯該訴訟。[1]」而且該通知通常是應告知被告被起訴之理由，否則被告是無法有充分之準備時間。個人非常認同英國司法之慣例，送達境外基本上是一種過度（exorbitant）或例外（extraordinary）之管轄基礎[2]，經常冒著不被外國法院所承認的風險，因而必須於非常謹慎下方得行使此種裁量權以送達通知至境外[3]。故而於此種情形下，舉證責任在於原告，並且於請求之階段因不須通知他方，故必須完全而且公平的陳述[4]。個人認為

1 Article 15
Where a writ of summons or an equivalent document had to be transmitted abroad for the purpose of service, under the provisions of the present Convention, and the defendant has not appeared, judgment shall not be given until it is established that-
a) The document was served by a method prescribed by the internal law of the State addressed for the service of documents in domestic actions upon persons who are within its territory, or
b) the document was actually delivered to the defendant or to his residence by another method provided for by this Convention, and that in either of these cases the service or the delivery was effected in sufficient time to enable the defendant to defend.

2 Spiliada Maritime Corpn v. Consulex Ltd [1987] AC 460 at 481.

3 Cordova land Co. Ltd., v. Victor Bro Inc [1966] 1 WLR 793 at 796.

4 Kuwait Oil Co. (KSC) v. Idemitsu Tankers KK, The Hida Maru [1981] 2 Lloyd's Rep 510.但應注意的是於主張不方便法院而要求停止訴訟之情形，至少於第一階段的舉證責任是在於主張不方便法院的被告。見陳隆修、許兆慶、林恩瑋、李瑞生四人合著，《國際私法-管轄與選法理論之交錯》，台北，五南圖書公司，2009年3月，初版1刷，203、204頁。

為著避免濫訴，於國際訴訟之通知不但應具備理由，並且原告目前所掌握之證據亦通知國外被送達之被告，以使得送達境外之訴訟成為「最大誠意之訴訟」。

一、境外送達、所在權力與裁量權之行使

英國司法於傳統上對境外送達的戒慎恐懼表現在Civil Procedure Rules 1998之規定上，其s. 6.20(3)(a)規定：「3.一個請求是針對某一個人（被告）而請求的文件已經或將會送達給他，並且(a)於請求人與該某人間存在著真正的問題，而該問題合理的需要法院去審理」[5]。而與舊法不同的又增加了「合理勝訴的機會」，其s. 6.21(1)及(2)又規定：「依據規則6.20而申請（送達境外）法院之許可，必須有著書面之證據以支持其說明如下：(a)其申請所依據之理由及所據的6.20規則之項目；(b)申請人相信其申請有著合理的勝訴機會……(2)當所被提出之申請是有關規則6.20(3)所提及之請求時，書面證據必須亦說明證人相信請求人與請求文件已被送達，或將被送達，之人間有一個真正的問題合理的需要法院去審理之理由。（2A）除非滿意英格蘭及威爾斯是提起請求之合適之地方，法院不會給予許可。[6]」故而於境外送達上，英國法律不但要求當事人間

---

[5] 6.20 Service out of the jurisdiction where the permission of the court is required
In any proceedings to which rule 6.19 does not apply, a claim form any be served out of the jurisdiction with the permission of the court if-- ...
(3) a claim is made against someone on whom the claim form has been or will be served and –
(a) there is between the claimant and that person a real issue which it is reasonable for the court to try.

[6] 6.21 Application for permission to serve claim form out of jurisdiction
(1) An application for permission under rule 6.20 must be supported by written evidence stating –
(a) the grounds on which the application is made and the paragraph or paragraphs of rule 6.20 relied on;
(b) that the claimant believes that his claim has a reasonable prospect of success; and
(c) the defendant's address or, if not known, in what place or country the defendant is, or is likely, to be found.
(2) Where the application is made in respect of a claim referred to in rule 6.20(3), the written evidence must also state the grounds on which the witness believes that there is between the claimant and the person on whom the claim form has been, or will be served, a real issue which it is reasonable for the court to try.
(2A) The court will not give permission unless satisfied that England and Wales is the proper place in

必須「有一個真正的問題合理的需要法院去審判」，而且「必須有著書面的證據去相信其請求有著合理的勝訴之機會」，另外「法院必須為提出請求之合適法院」[7]。

隨著全世界於經濟、社會、科技、及文化上之全球化，二十一世紀人類各部門之法學（包含憲法、程序法、刑法、民法、親屬繼承、商法、及國際私法等）之全球化已成為必然之趨勢。於國際訴訟上對境外之被告加以送達仍舊應被視為「過度」或「例外」之管轄，仍應被所有的法院視為應被加以戒懼謹慎之司法行為。但於鋪天蓋地而來之全球化潮流下，全世界的法院皆不得不順應時勢的擴張其管轄範圍。在此種沛然莫之能禦的時勢下，英國Civil Procedure Rules 1998, 6.20及6.21規則中所代表的判例法對送達境外的限制，不但代表著尊重被告所在地國司法主權的國際

---

which to bring the claim.

7 對於Civil Procedure Rules 1998, s. 6.20送達境外之規定，英國之前規定於Rules of the Supreme Court, Order 11, rule 1,英國法院有裁量權（discretion）將訴訟之通知或命令（notice of a writ or a writ）送達於法院境外。對於英國是否為合適之方便法院，個人早期於陳隆修，《國際私法管轄權評論》，台北，五南圖書公司，民國75年11月，初版，46、47頁中如此評述：「英國有關法院行使裁量權的標準，於The Hagen中有規定如下：

1.使居住於國外之被告到法院地來為其權利辯護不是不正當（unjustifialb）。

2.當法院對於是否應適用法規而將訴訟之通知送達於國外，若有疑問時，對於外國被告之利益應給優先之考慮（benefit of doubt）。

3.由於被告居於國外，並且通常無代理人，故原告有義務將案件之事實完全告訴法院，並且說明法院將訴訟之通知送達於國外是符合法律上之規定。

除了以上規定外，英法院又於Cordova Land Co, Ltd. v Victor Brothers Inc.表示，如果其他外國法院為處理本訴訟之更方便法院，則英國法院不會接受該訴訟之管轄權。例如證人較易出席於於外國法院，證物之搜集於該外國較方便，該係爭法律行為皆於外國進行，或契約之準據法為該外國法等因素都可能促使英國法院行使裁量權而不接受該案之管轄權。英國法院行使裁量權時對被告之利益固然應加以保護，但對於原告之利益亦會加以考慮。對於原告若無法於法院地起訴時，是否有其他合適的法院可以請求救濟的考慮，美國於對『方便法院』（forum conveniens）下定義時有明示規定。英國雖因為沒有採『方便法院』之理論，對此似乎沒有美國那麼明顯，但於Oppenheimer v. Louis Rosenthal & Co,中，亦對原告是否可以到其他法院請求救濟的因素加以慎重考慮。於該案中一德國公司違背法律的規定而解除其倫敦之經理之職務，該經理為德國籍之猶太人。英國法院認為依通常情形德國法院應為方便法院，因為德國法為契約之準據法。而依該法解約前若無事先給予六個月之通知則該解約行為無效。因為倫敦有甚多熟悉德國法之法學者，故被告德國公司依德國法來保護其利益之權利並未被剝奪。反過來說，若原告到德國法院去請求救濟，則其無法找到律師替其辯護，並且極有可能被捉到集中營。故雖然雙方當事人皆為德國人，並且德國法又為準據法，法院仍判德國法院為『不方便法院』，而決定將訴訟之通知送達國外。」[1908] p. 189; [1966] 1 W.L.R. 793; [1937] 1 All E.R. 23.英國判例法於早期送達境外即採「方便法院」理論，現今於停止英國訴訟亦採蘇格蘭的「不方便法院」理論，見陳隆修、許兆慶、林恩瑋、李瑞生四人合著，《國際私法-管轄與選法理論之交錯》，台北，五南圖書公司，2009年3月，初版1刷，197-215頁。

禮誼（comity），對濫用訴訟程序的禁止，更是在保障被告的訴訟權、財產權、適當程序權及維護司法正義。**故而CPR 1998, ss. 6.20及6.21所要求的條件，「有一個真正的問題合理的需要法院去審判」，「有著書面的證據去相信其請求有著合理的勝訴之機會」，及「法院必須為提出請求之合適法院」，應成為21世紀中國際訴訟上對境外被告加以送達之前提要件—亦即前述之要件應成為21世紀境外送達之實質核心共同基本政策**。可悲的是如果採用大陸法的先繫屬優先原則，不但會硬性且機械性的拒絕給予法院裁量之機會，違反國際禮誼的不尊重被告所在地國之司法主權，無法有效的制止濫用訴訟程序之行為，更無法保障被告於憲法及人權法上之訴訟權、財產權、及適當程序權，亦無法達成司法的有效正義。

歐盟的布魯塞爾公約及規則的第3條，鄭重其事的宣布禁止會員國間的適用其各自的「過度管轄」之規則於會員國之住民上。規則第3條規定：「1.住所於會員國之人只能依據本章第2至7條所規定之法規而於其他會員國之法院而得被起訴。2.特別是附件I所列舉的各國管轄規則對他們不得加以適用。[8]」故而除了第2條以「住所」為一般管轄[9]及第5至7條特別管轄之規定外，大陸法有些國家傳統上以物之所在地或國籍等為管轄基礎之過度管轄[10]，於會員國間是被禁止的。但有趣的是歐盟卻公然的於第4條中給予其住民權利，去根據各國此種過度的管轄基礎對非歐盟住民提

---

8 Article 3
1. Persons domiciled in a Member State may be sued in the courts of another Member State only by virtue of the rules set out in Sections 2 to 7 of this Chapter.
2. In particular the rules of national jurisdiction set out in Annex I shall not be applicable as against them.

9 Article 2
1. Subject to this Regulation, persons domiciled in a Member State shall, whatever their nationality, be sued in the courts of that Member State.
2. Persons who are not nationals of the Member State in which they are domiciled shall be governed by rules of jurisdiction applicable to nationals of that State.

10 見陳隆修、許兆慶、林恩瑋、李瑞生四人合著，《國際私法—管轄與選法理論之交錯》，台北，五南圖書公司，2009年3月，初版1刷，176-180頁。

起訴訟[11]。這種雙重標準的「岳不群法則」自然會引起美國同僚之不滿[12]。恩師美國之歐盟國際私法權威Arthur von Mehren如此不平的論述著：「對於西方文化所展現出的正義的標準感到敏感的人，對於不能如同美國憲法之適當程序條款，無論國籍或住所將其之保護及於所有之人一般，將第3條之保護及於所有之被告，只能表示震驚。[13]」做為一個第三世界的國際私法學生，「對於西方文化所展現出的正義標準」，在歐盟規則第4條的規則上，自然同樣的「只能表示震驚」。但是美國法院於不方便法院上所顯示對第三世界人權之踐踏，這種「掠奪式新殖地主義法學」是更令第三世界的法律學生震驚的。無論是歐盟及美國間如何的指責對方為「法律霸權主義」[14]（hegemonic legal system）或「司法帝國主義」[15]（judicial imperialism），這些都僅限於他們自己的內部法則。但是於2005年海牙法院選擇公約中，歐美則聯手以優越的法學霸權主義雷霆萬鈞勢不可擋之姿，強迫弱勢的第三世界人民必須毫無條件的順服第一世界資方所指定之管轄法院條款。這種霹靂手段是剝奪第三世界人民聯合國1966年兩

---

11 Article 4

1. If the defendant is not domiciled in a Member State, the jurisdiction of the courts of each Member State shall, subject to Articles 22 and 23, be determined by the law of that Member State.
2. As against such a defendant, any person domiciled in a Member State may, whatever his nationality, avail himself in that State of the rules of jurisdiction there in force, and in particular those specified in Annex I, in the same way as the nationals of that State.

除了有管轄條款之約定及相關專屬管轄之情形外，對於非會員國住民之被告是依各會員國之法律。而任何會員國住民皆可根據各會員國之過度管轄之規則，對非會員國住民之被告提起訴訟。

12 陳隆修，《2005年海牙法院選擇公約評析》，台北，五南圖書公司，2009年1月，初版1刷，147-149頁。

13 “One sensitive to the standards of justice that have emerged in Western culture can only express shock at the failure to make the Article 3 protections available to all defendants just as due process protections under the Constitution of the United States extend to all persons, regardless of nationality or domicile”; Arthur T. von Mehren, *Recognition and Enforcement of Foreign Judgments – General Theory and the Role of Jurisdictional Requirements*, 167 REGUEIL DES COURS 9, 98 (1980-II).

14 “The *Campabell* decision has been hailed as a welcome contribution given European apprehension of a perceived excessive and hegemonic legal system in the United States at the hands of American plaintiff.” Oliver Furtak, Application of Foreign Law to Determine Puntive Damages, in Conflict of Laws in a Globalized World, edited by Eckart Gottschalk, p. 272.

15 Jens Adolphsen, *The Conflict of Laws in Cartel Matters in a Globalised World: Alternatives to the Effects Doctrine*, 1 J. PRIVATE INT’L L. 151, 157 (2005), “has clearly reduced the tendency towards judicial imperialism in U.S. cartel law.”

個人權公約中第1條2項的生存權，這是對第三世界人民侵門踏戶的法律帝國主義加上岳不群法學。個人幾年前以此公約違反人權法中之訴訟權、財產權、適當程序權，及違反國際私法傳統判例法規則，更亦是違反人類共通契約法共同核心政策而加以抗衡[16]。不信公義喚不回，不信青史盡成灰。**然而第一世界之所以如此顢頇野蠻，第三世界之所以如此任人宰割，皆是因為沒有公開確認送達境外是一種「過度」的「例外」管轄之基本共同核心政策之故。**

個人早期即如此寫著[17]：「英國法院對人訴訟的管轄基礎，由歷史上的原因都是本於程序上法院訴訟的通知是否可以送達給被告（a writ of notice of a writ can be served on the defendant）。於三種情況下法院可以送達給被告：(1)當被告親自於法院地時；(2)被告承認法院之管轄權時；(3)雖然被告於法院地外，但依照英國法規[18]允許法院將訴訟之通知送達於法院地外。」「除了有外交豁免權之人外，任何人無論其國籍為何，只要其身體於英國國境內都必須對英國有效忠之義務。此義務自亦包含遵從傳達女皇命令的法院訴訟之通知。故而只要被告接受送達時身體於英國，法院即對其有對人訴訟之管轄權。但是當被告是為了此目的而被詐欺致引入英國時，其可以不接受法院之送達，此外美國法規定被告被脅迫進入法院地，則法院亦不接受管轄權」。

對於這種「所在權力」（presence power）理論之適用於個人上，Dicey and Morris非常權威的加以論述如下：「任何所在於英國之個人是有責任於對人訴訟之程序中受到送達，無論其於英國所在之期間是如何的短暫皆是如此。因此一個美國人其由紐約飛至倫敦並且意圖同一天離開，是有責任接收訴訟程序之通知，而該訴訟是由於請求人要求該美國人給付其應於紐約支付之債務而被提起。無疑的於某些情形下這種管轄之行使是

16 陳隆修，《2005年海牙法院選擇公約評析》，台北，五南圖書公司，2009年1月，初版1刷，142-153頁。

17 陳隆修，《國際私法管轄權評論》，台北，五南圖書公司，民國75年11月，初版，36頁。英國管轄基礎見27-28頁。

18 先前rule 1, Order 11, Rules of the Supreme Court；現今規定於s.6.20, Civil Procedure Rules 1998.

可能會構成過度管轄，並且亦有主張認為這種程序不能被合適的送達給嚴格而言並非居住於英國之外國人。但以短暫性的所在（停留）做為管轄基礎是為上訴法院所強力的認同[19]，並且是為Lord Russell of Killowen於其有份量的判決中之附帶意見所支持[20]。英國程序法的歷史證明了這個觀點；英國法院審理案件之權力之依據，是源自依據被告於英國受到國王命令之送達而來，而同樣的這只是基本理論之一部分而以，而該理論是任何人當於英國時至少對國王負有短暫忠誠的義務。但是法院在如果可能會造成不正義之情形下，是有著裁量權去拒絕接受訴訟程序的，例如當該請求是被加以抗辯並且該案件與英國沒有關連時。[21]」而所謂依「所在權力」

---

19 *Colt Industries Inc v Sarlie* [1966] 1 W.L.R. 440 (CA); *Maharance of Baroda v Wildenstein* [1972] 2 Q.B. 283 (CA), *Adams v Cape Industries Plc* [1990] Ch. 433, 518 (CA).

20 *Carrick v Hancock* (1895) 12 T.L.R. 59m 60, *See also Forbes v Simmons* (1914) 20 D.L.R. 100 (Alta); *Laurie v Carroll* (1958) 98 C.L.R. 310, 323.但是當一個人依法被帶至加拿大的另一省，或澳洲的另一州時，該第二省或州是被認定為有權力對其加以送達。*Doyle v Doyle* (1974) 52 D.L.R. (3d)143 (Newf.); *John Sanderson Ltd v Giddings* [1976] V.R. 421; *Baldry v Jackson* [1976] 1 N.S.W.L.R. 10, *affirmed on different grounds* [1976] 2 N.S.W.L.R. 415.但是若一個外國人被以詐欺之方式而誘引至法院地，該送達得被撤銷。*Stein v Valkenhuysen* (1858) E.B.E. 65; *Watkins v North American Lands, etc. Co.* (1904) 20 T.L.R. 534 (HL); *Perrett v Robinson* [1985] 1 Qd.R. 83.
至於有關替代送達（substituted service）於*Porter v Freudenberg* [1915] 1 K.B. 857, 887-888 (CA)中，Lord Reading認為於下列3種情形下是得被允許的：(1) "The general rule is that an order for substituted service of writ of summons within the jurisdiction cannot be made in any case in which, at the time of the issue of the writ, there could not be at law a good personal service of the writ because the defendant is not within the jurisdiction." (2) "The general rule is not applied where the court is satisfied that the defendant went outside the jurisdiction before the issue of the writ in order to evade the service of the writ within it." (3) "If the defendant went out of the jurisdiction after the issue of the writ, although not for the purpose of evading service, substituted service may be allowed if the court is satisfied that the issue of the writ came to his knowledge before he went outside the jurisdiction and special circumstances show that such substituted service would be just."但澳洲高院對此第(2)個建議於Laurie v Carroll (1958) 98 C.L.R. 310, 332.中加以反對"open to the objection, first, that it departs altogether from the principles upon which the exercise of English jurisdiction in action *in personam* rests; secondly, that it cannot be reconciled with the doctrine, that where the writ may not be served personally, an order for substituted service may not be made; thirdly, that it ignores the implications of Order 11, r.1(1); fourthly, that it does not involve a matter of procedure but an extension of jurisdiction."後來上訴法院於Myerson v Martin, [1979] 1 W.L.R. 1390 (CA)中，對作成送達命令時被告不在法院地，拒絕允許替代送達，Lord Denning認為於此情形下不可能作成替代送達。Dicey and Morris, the Conflict of Laws, 14th ed, p. 348認同後兩者之論述如下："It is submitted that the view of the High Court of Australia and of Lord Denning M.R. is the preferable one, and that there is no jurisdiction to order service by an alternative method of process for service within the jurisdiction on a defendant who was outside the jurisdiction at the time of issue."

21 "Any individual who is present in England is liable to be served with process in proceedings *in personam*, however short may be the period for which he is present in England. Thus an American who has

而來的管轄，這顯然包括美國所謂的「過境管轄」（transient jurisdiction）在內，「法院在如果可能會造成不正義之情形下，是有著裁量權去拒絕接受訴訟程序的」，Dicey and Morris於註解中即指明此即為規則31之不方便法院之裁量權[22]。

於國際私法上，正如美國法律協會於許多方面之新編（或整編）一般，Dicey and Morris之規則經常為英國各級法院引為判決之依據。其規則31如此規定：「(1)當為著防止不正義的發生而有必要時，英國法院有管轄權去停止或駁回英國之程序[23]。(2)除了歐盟（EC）44/2001規則，及布魯塞爾與魯加諾於民商事項之管轄及執行公約之規定外（「判決規則」、「1968公約」及「魯加諾公約」之個別規則），在英國法院是個不合適法院之基礎上（不方便法院），於下列情形一個英國法院是有著權力去停止訴訟：(a)被告證明有著其他有管轄權之法院，對於審理該訴訟比起英國是清楚的或明顯的更為合適，並且(b)對於請求人被剝奪於英國之訴訟權是不會不正義的[24]。(3)於考慮是否接受規則27所規定的任何案件時（經過法院許可而送達境外時），法院[25]一般會要求請求人去證明在審理該請求上，英國為最合適之法院。[26]」

---

flown from New York to London and intends to leave on the same day is liable to be served with process in proceedings brought to recover a debt due to the claimant incurred by the American and payable in New York. No doubt in some cases the exercise of such a jurisdiction may be exorbitant, and it has been contended that process cannot rightly be served on a foreigner who is not strictly speaking resident in England. But temporary presence as a basic of jurisdiction was emphatically affirmed by the Court of Appeal and has the support of weighty dicta by Lord Russell of Killowen. The history of English procedure bears out this view; the right of an English court to entertain an action depended originally upon a defendant being served in England with the King's writ, and this again was only part of the general doctrine that any person whilst in England owed at least temporary allegiance to the King. But the court has a discretion to refuse to entertain proceedings if to do so might work injustice, where, for example, the claim is contested and the case has no connection with England." Dicey and Morris, the Conflict of Laws, 14th ed, p. 346.

22 同上。

23 *Spiliada Maritime Corp v Cansulex Ltd* [1987] A.C. 460; *Connelly v RTZ Corp Plc* [1998] A.C. 845; and *Lubbe v Cape Plc* [2000] 1 W.L.R. 1545 (HL).

24 *Spiliada Maritime corp v Cansulex Ltd* [1987] A.C. 460, 475-478; *Connelly v RTZ Corp Plc* [1998] A.C. 854, 871-873; *Lubbe v Cape Plc* [2000] 1 W.L.R. 1545, 1553-1555 (HL).

25 *Amin Rasheed Shipping Corp v Kuwait Insurance Co* [1984] A.C. 50, 72; *Spiliada Maritime Corp v Cansulex Ltd* [1987] A.C. 460, 478-482.

26 Rule 31 – (1) English courts have jurisdiction, whenever it is necessary to prevent injustice, to stay or

上述的「所在權力」理論自1891以後，對於在英國經商而合夥人在送達時不在英國之合夥亦可適用[27]。雖然表面上只是對合夥之訴訟，但Civil Procedure Rules規定，以合夥之名於英國經商之合夥，無論合夥人是否於英國，可被送達至合夥於英國之主要或最後已知之營業地[28]。但是對合夥起訴之訴訟只能對合夥於英國之財產加以執行。若欲對合夥人於英國之財產加以執行，必須其於英國受到送達，承認法院管轄，或經法院之許可於境外受到送達[29]（亦即CPR, r.6.20之情形）。

而於英國登記之公司，即使其營業地是在外國，皆得依Companies Act 1985而送達至其於英國之登記地[30]。另外根據Civil Procedure Rules，於英國登記之公司得被送達至其主事務所（principal office），或於境內與請求有真實關連之營業地[31]。於外國成立之有限公司若於英國有分行，則依Companies Act 1985, s.690A對於該分行之營業其必須指定於英國之接收送達之人。而任何「有關該分行之營業」（“in respect of the carrying on of the business of the branch”），依s.694A(2)得送達至該被登記之指定接收人。但若該被登記之指定接收人無法被加以送達或拒絕接收，

strike out proceedings in England.
(2) Subject to the provisions of Council Regulation (EC) 44/2001, and the Brussels and Lugano Conventions on jurisdiction and the enforcement of judgments in civil and commercial matters (“the Judgments Regulation”, “the 1968 Convention” and “the Lugano Convention” respectively), an English court has power to order a stay of proceedings on the basis that England is an inappropriate forum (forum non conveniens) if:
(a) the defendant shows there to be another court with competent jurisdiction which is clearly or distinctly more appropriate than England for the trial of the action, and
(b) it is not unjust that the claimant be deprived of the right to trial in England.
(3) In considering whether to assume jurisdiction in any of the cases mentioned in Rule 27 (service out of the jurisdiction with the permission of the court) the court will generally require the claimant to show England to be the most appropriate forum for the trial of the claim.
Dicey and Morris, the Conflict of Laws, 14th ed, pp. 461, 462.

27 “... any two or more persons claiming to be entitled, or alleged to be liable, as partners in respect of a cause of action and carrying on businesss [in England] may sue, or be sued, in the name of the firm (if any) of which they were partners at the time when the cause of action accrued.” Rules of the Supreme Court, Ord. 81, r.1 (in CPR, Sch.1).

28 CPR, rr.6.4(5), 6.5(6), and 6PD, para. 4.

29 RSC, Ord. 81 r.5 (in CPR, Sch. 1). *Lindsay v Crawford and Lindsays* (1911) 45 Ir. L.T. 52.

30 見s.725(1). *Addis Ltd v Berkeley Supplies Ltd* [1964] 1 W.L.R. 943.

31 CPR. rr.6.2(2)(a), 6.5(6).

依s.694A(3)得送達至該公司於英國之任何營業處。於外國成立之公司若於英國有營業處，依s.691亦必須指定於英國之送達接收人。依s.695(1)對該公司之送達可送達至該被登記之指定接收人，該接收人死亡、停止居住於英國、拒絕接受送達、或其他原因而不能被送達，則對該公司之送達依s.695(2)得送達至該公司於英國之任何營業處。有趣的是依s.694A該送達必須是為「與該分行之營業有關」之案件，而依s.695之送達則未規定請求與營業處（"the place of business"）須有任何關連。於Saab v Saudi American Bank[32]中，s.694A所規定的「有關該分行之營業」，被認定為與「由於該分行之行為所引起」（"arising out of the operations of the branch"）並不一樣，只要該訴訟程序可以被合理的認為部分是與該分行之營業有關即可滿足規定。但若訴訟程序與該分行之營業間之關係是甚為「少量」（de minimis）時，則不能符合規定。於該案中，上訴法院認為「分行」相較於「營業處」，是為較永久的機構（a more permanent establishment）[33]。Clarke L.J.認為ss.694A及695之效力之不同已造成異常的結果[34]，並認為這應是立法歷史的緣故。

雖然於the Companies Act 1985及the Civil Procedure Rules中對「營業處所」（place of business）並未加以定義，但其應包含股份之轉讓或股份登記處[35]，因此是具有寬廣的意義[36]。判例法顯示營業之「處所」

---

32 [1999] 1 W.L.R. 1861 (CA).

33 但是the Companies Act 2006之s. 1044對overseas company的定義為於外國組織成立之公司，這個定義是較the Companies Act 1985, s. 744所規定的於外國組織成立並於英國有營業處的定義為廣。對於可能通過的行政規則意圖將外國公司於英國之分行與營業處合而為一之作法，Cheshire and North, 14th ed., p.364，表示歡迎："The intention of the Steering Group is that two separate regimes under the 1985 Act, one for foreign companies that have a branch in Great Britain and the other for foreign companies that have established a place of business, which is not a branch, in Great Britain, will be replaced by a single regime. This is very much to be welcomed. First, it simplifies the law. Secondly, it avoids having to determine whether an established place of business in the United Kingdom is a branch or not."

34 *Saab v Saudi American Bank*, [1999] 1 W.L.R. 1861, 1868; Dicey and Morris, the Conflict of Laws, 14th ed, p. 352.但*Sea Assets Ltd v PT Garuda Indonesia* [2000] 4 All E.R. 371認為s. 694A並不是唯一送達之方式，見CPR, Pt 6.

35 s. 698: *The Madrid* [1937] P. 40; *cf. A/S Dampskib Hercules v Grand Trunk Pacific Ry of Canada* [1912] 1 K.B. 222 (CA); *and contrast Badcock v Cumberland Gap Co* [1893] 1 Ch. 362.

36 見Dicey and Morris, the Conflict of Laws, 14th ed., p.353.

（place）應是有一個固定而明確的地方[37]，其行為必須進行一段之時間以致可被認為是為經營商業。但判例法顯示於展覽會上之擺攤，9天就可被認為已構成充分之時間[38]。於South India Shipping Corp Ltd v Export-Import Bank of Korea[39]中，一個外國銀行與其他銀行進行外部之關係，並且對給予貸款或取得貸款進行前置作業，但尚未完成任何銀行交易行為，被認定為得於英國營業處被加以送達。故於英國之行為並不一定須構成外國公司主要目的之重大或附隨的部分。

當公司之營業是由代表人或代理人所作為，而其並非公司之員工或職員時，如果是有關公司之營業，仍得將通知送達給該代表或代理人。如果該代表或代理有權替公司訂定契約，並且其行為是以公司之名而為之，則自然滿足「公司營業處所」之要求[40]。於此方面著名之案例Adams v. Cape Industries plc[41]中，一家全球性開採及經銷石棉之公司透過其美國子公司而在美國經銷。後206位受傷之工人於德州聯邦地院對其起訴，其並未出席並且被判應予賠償。英國上訴法院認為子公司完全獨立營業，並有自己之債權與債務人，而且子公司雖為中間人但所作之行為並不能對其有契約上之拘束力，故不執行該缺席判決。但原告卻主張美國式理論[42]，認為被告與其子公司為同一經濟單位（a single economic unit）。如Cheshire and North所說：「這個激進的想法，是根據經濟情況的現實，並且於美國是受到認同的，但是卻為上訴法院所拒絕，其仍是強調母公司與子公司是獨立法律實體之傳統公司法之觀念。這即是認為英國公司得於外國以這

[37] *The Theodohos* [1977] 2 Lloyd's Rep. 428; *Saccharin Corporation Ltd v Chemische Fabrike AG* [1911] 2 K.B. 516 (CA); *Okura Co Ltd v Forsbacka Jernverks A/B* [1914] 1 K.B. 715 (CA).

[38] *Dunlop Pneumatic Tyre Co Ltd v AG Gudell Co* [1902] 1 K.B. 342 (CA).

[39] [1985] 1 W.L.R. 585 (CA).

[40] Saccharin Corporation Ltd v Chemische Fabrik AG [1911] 2 K.B. 516 (CA); contrast Okura Co Ltd v Forsbacka Jernverks A/B [1914] 1 K.B. 715 (CA). See also Rakusens Ltd v Baser Ambalaj Plastik Sanayi Ticaret AS [2001] EWCS Civ. 1820, [2002] 1 B.C.L.C. 104; Harrods Ltd v Dow Jones & Co Inc [2003] EWHC 1162 (QB).

[41] [1990] Ch. 433.

[42] Bulova Watch Co Inc v K Hattori and Co Ltd 508 F Supp 1322, 1342 (1981)

種方式營業而不會構成所在或居住於當地。[43]」於該案中上訴法院對於子公司是否為母公司之代理或代表（alter ego）採判例法[44]，而以當地代理人是否須事先得到母公司之同意才可訂定對其有拘束力之契約為依據[45]。Adams案中之原則亦為判例法適用於被告公司透過同一集團中有著股份之非子公司於外國經營商業之情形[46]。於Adams v Cape Industries Plc中，上訴法院對於為了執行外國判決之目的，一個公司是否於外國有著居所或著所在於外國，對於判例法加以詳細的檢驗[47]，例如代理人是否有固定營業處所、公司是否支付其費用或其他費用、代理人是否因交易行為而得到報酬、公司對代理人營業之控制程度、代理人是否利用其設施或員工進行公司之營業、代理人是否引用公司之名稱、代理人是否只是經營自己之業務、代理人是否以公司名義訂約或其行為對公司有拘束力、如果對公司有拘束力是否須事先得到公司之授權。雖然代表公司訂約之能力並非為唯一或必要之條件，但卻是重要及主要之標準[48]。

二、方便與不方便法院

故而英國歷史上對人訴訟之傳統管轄基礎，是本於程序上法院訴訟

43 PM North, JJ Fawcett, Cheshire and North's Private International Law, 13th ed. p.410, 14th ed., pp. 519, 520, "This radical idea, which is based on the economic reality of the situation and has found favour in the United States, was rejected by the Court of Appeal, who emphasised the traditional company law notion that parent and subsidiary are separate legal entities. This means that an English company can set up its business abroad in such a way that it is not present/resident there."事實上這種美式「同一經濟單位」之理論是較為符合現代工業全球化之經濟現實，亦較符合中國「不患寡而患不均」之「禮運大同」文化。英國上訴法院這種拘泥於傳統法律邏輯之作法，是種過時資本主義的法律邏輯，而可能擋不住21世紀全球化法學注重環保及個案正義的共同核心價值。於陳隆修，《2005年海牙法院選擇公約評析》，台北，五南圖書公司，2009年1月，初版1刷中，個人曾對此案加以論述，乃是在「以此案舉例說明2005年海牙公約第9條f款、g款所可能產生之相類似問題，不在是否應依申請地法或作成地法，而在子公司是否因獨立營業故而有獨立人格，或與母公司是個同一經濟單位之實體問題。」見141、142頁。

44 F & K Jobbour v Custodian of Israeli Absentee Property [1954] 1 W.L.R. 139, 146.

45 "Mere façade concealing the true facts". [1990] Ch. 433, 531, 539。其引用*Woolfson v Strathclyde Regional Council*, 1978 S.L.T. 159, 161 (HL)亦即刺穿法人之外衣（piercing the corporate veil），親子公司是否為母公司之分身而決定母公司是否應負起責任。

46 *Akande v Balfour Beatty Construction Ltd* [1998] IL Pr 110.

47 [1990] Ch. 433, 523-531 (CA).

48 [1990] Ch. 433, 531.

的通知是否可以送達給被告為依據。因此除了被告承認法院之管轄權外，通常是以被告於法院地受到送達為依據，而此種管轄基礎於美國適當程序條款上經常以「所在權力」加以稱呼。而對送達給境外之被告則傳統上視為「過度」或「例外」之管轄，英國法院通常是只有於法院是「合適之法院」下才有可能准許送達給境外之被告[49]。如Dicey and Morris對境內送達所下之評論：「無疑的於某些情形下這種管轄之行使是可能會構成過度管轄」。**因此長久以來英國司法的歷史就給予法院裁量權，以便「法院在如果可能造成不正義的情形下，是有著裁量權去拒絕接受訴訟程序的」。而如其規則31所述，這種法院為了防止不正義情形之發生而所有之裁量權，於境內送達（或於被告約定法院之管轄權[50]上亦類似）即為著**

[49] Civil Procedure Rules 1998之s, 6.20是有關判例法傳統上須得到法院允許才能送達境外之規定，而s.6.19則是為送達境外有關歐盟布魯塞爾公約及已有其他立法不須法院同意之情形。
6.19 Service out of the jurisdiction where the permission of the court is not required
(1) A claim form may be served on a defendant out of the jurisdiction where each claim included in the claim form made against the defendant to be served is a claim which the court has power to determine under the 1982 Act and –
(a) no proceedings between the parties concerning the same claim are pending in the courts of any other part of the United Kingdom or any other Convention territory; and
(b) (i) the defendant is domiciled in the United Kingdom or in any Convention territory;
(ii) Article 16 of Schedule 1, 3c or 4 to the 1982 Act refers to the proceedings; or
(iii) the defendant is a party to an agreement conferring jurisdiction to which Article 17 of Schedule 1, 3c or 4 to the 1982 Act refers.
(1A) A claim form may be served on a defendant out of the jurisdiction where each claim included in the claim form made against the defendant to be served is a claim which the court has power to determine under the Judgments Regulation and –
(a) no proceedings between the parties concerning the same claim are pending in the courts of any other part of the United Kingdom or any other Regulation State; and
(b) (i) the defendant is domiciled in the United Kingdom or in any Regulation State;
(ii) Article 22 of the Judgments Regulation refers to the proceedings; or
(iii) the defendant is a party to an agreement conferring jurisdiction to which Article 23 of the Judgments Regulation refers.
(2) A claim form may be served on a defendant out of the jurisdiction where each claim included in the claim form made against the defendant to be served is a claim which, under any other enactment, the court has power to determine, although –
(a) the person against whom the claim is made is not within the jurisdiction; or
(b) the facts giving rise to the claim did not occur within the jurisdiction.
(3) Where a claim form is to be served out of the jurisdiction under this rule, it must contain a statement of the grounds on which the claimant is entitled to serve it out of the jurisdiction.

[50] 見陳隆修、許兆慶、林恩瑋、李瑞生四人合著，《國際私法—管轄與選法理論之交錯》，台北，五南圖書公司，2009年3月，初版1刷，199、200頁，The Sennar (No.2) [1985] 1 WLR 490 at 500，又見陳隆修，《國際私法管轄權評論》，台北，五南圖書公司，民國75年11月，初版，43、44頁。

名的「不方便法院」原則之行使（即法院為不合適之法院“an inappropriate forum”）；而於送達境外之被告時，除了歐盟公約及其他既有法律之規定外，一般是將其視為「過度」或「例外」之管轄權行使，法院通常會行使裁量權要求請求人去證明在審理該請求上，英國為「最」合適之法院，即美國與大陸法所經常忽略的有關境外送達的「方便法院原則」（於該請求之審理上英國為「最」合適之法院“the most appropriate forum”）。

美國法院所引用之不方便法院原則，事實上是主要源自蘇格蘭法院，個人於學生時期英國法院並不使用「不方便法院原則」。早期個人如此論述[51]：「於現代國際社會，各國不得不擴大法院之管轄權，但相對地，隨著其權力之擴大，法院亦應有著適當之裁量權，於特殊案例中去拒絕行使該案件之管轄權。台灣與歐洲共同市場公約於此方面皆無規定，甚為可惜。英國於此方面之法規，或許可謂為全世界最週詳[52]。因為英國法院於訴訟會造成困擾（vexation）或壓迫（oppression）之情形下，為避免造成不正當（unjust）的後果，可以命令停止（stay）或駁回（dismiss）當事人於英國之訴訟，甚至可以禁止（injunction）當事人於國外起訴或繼續進行國外之訴訟，或強制執行國外之判決。此種管轄上之權力為英法院之自由裁量權（discretionary power），法院必須很謹慎地使用此種權力。法院必須於當事人之一方，若繼續進行其於法院地或法院外之訴訟，會很明顯地對他方當事人造成困擾或壓迫，或者濫用法院之訴訟程序時才可使用此種權力。另一要件為法院欲停止訴訟之進行時，必須不能對原告造成不公平（injustice）之現象。」

個人早期又如此論述[53]：「由以上最後三個判例可知[54]，即使訴訟只

51 陳隆修，《國際私法管轄權評論》，台北，五南圖書公司，民國75年11月，初版，84頁。

52 Supreme Court of Judicature (Consolidation)Act 1925, s. 41, proviso (a).見Ionian Bank Ltd v. Couvreur [1969] 1 W.L.R. 781及陳隆修，《國際私法管轄權評論》，台北，五南圖書公司，民國75年11月，初版，84-96頁中所討論之案件。

53 陳隆修，《國際私法管轄權評論》，台北，五南圖書公司，民國75年11月，初版，91頁。

54 Logan v. Bank of Scotland (No 2)中，住所於蘇格蘭之原告，由於一蘇格蘭公司之目錄不實而受損害，故於英國提起訴訟告蘇格蘭公司之董事，其董事並未出席法庭。由於蘇格蘭銀行亦於該

於英國提起，而不在他地提起，英法院亦有權力停止或駁回該訴訟。此種情況通常都是由於法院認為，該案在其他地方之法院審理較為方便（conveinient）。例如當訴因是於國外發生，並且被告若要於英國應訴時，可能會產生困難，而當事人又可於訴因發生之國家之法院提起訴訴訟之情形。」「但『方便法院』為蘇格蘭法院之技巧，英國法院不若美國法院，並無引用此技巧。於The Atlantic Star[55]中，一荷蘭船the Atlantic Star與另一荷蘭船及一比利時船相撞，後the Atlantic Star之船東於比利時被告。六個月後the Atlantic Star抵英國港口，原告又於英國提起對物訴訟，被告提出擔保以免除該船之被扣押。英國最高法院同意停止英國訴訟之進行，但其很明白地拒絕蘇格蘭技巧『不方便法院』（forum non conveniens），重申只要原告之訴若構成困擾性或壓迫性之訴訟，或濫用司法程序（abuse of the process of the court），則法院有權停止訴訟之進行。[56]」但事實上於英國尚未引用「不方便法院」主義前，個人早已建議「困擾性」及「壓迫性」主義應與「不方便法院」主義一起使用[57]。

早在18世紀時蘇格蘭法即以「法院沒有權力」（“forum non compe-

不實之目錄上，故原告亦將蘇格蘭銀行及其負責人任列為共同被告。該銀行之主事務所於蘇格蘭，並於倫敦有分行。由於該案之結果須依蘇格蘭法及蘇格蘭之證人，故英法院停止原告對蘇格蘭銀行及其董事之訴訟，[1906] 1 K.B. 141 (C.A.).

Re Nortions Settlement中，先生與太太之住所皆於英國。先生之居所（residence）為印度，而太太居住於法國。太太宣稱其欲永久居住於英國，而來到英國，並於英國告先生及其約定婚姻財產（marriage settlement）之信託人，要求給予其應有之金錢。先生及其他兩位信託人皆居住於印度，但當他們於英國做短暫之停留時，法院之訴訟通知已於英國交給他們。其約定婚姻財產之契約之準據法為印度法，財產亦於印度，全部之證人亦於印度。英法院認為原告非善意地提起該訴訟，其目的為壓迫先生（被告）與其和解，故停止該訴訟之進行。[1908] 1 Ch. 471 (C.A.).

Egbert v. Short中，先生為住所於印度之美國人，先生同意與太太分居，並給予贍養費。被告（律師）為贍養之被信託人（trustee）。當先生沒有付贍養費後，太太宣稱被告故意等先生離開印度後才起訴，故太太無法取得其應有之贍養費。當太太與被告皆於英國做短暫之停留時，太太於英國起訴，告被告違背其義務，及送達通知給被告。但於送達通知後，原告返回美國，而被告返回印度。英國法院依被告知請求，駁回（dismiss）原告之訴。法院認為原告於離開印度前已知其權利受損，而其並非善意地提起訴訟，其目的在於試圖強迫被告與其達成和解，因為被告若要應訴，則會造成甚大之不便及花費相當多之金錢。[1907] 2 Ch. 205.

55 [1973] 2 W.L.R. 795.

56 陳隆修，《國際私法管轄權評論》，台北，五南圖書公司，民國75年11月，初版，92、93頁。

57 陳隆修，《國際私法管轄權評論》，台北，五南圖書公司，民國75年11月，初版，93頁。

tens"）之名而駁回訴訟[58]（dismissal of actions）。雖然名稱是「沒有權力」，因而法院是沒有管轄權，但法院還是使用forum non competens之名稱去拒絕有管轄權之案件[59]。因此於19世紀末時這個法則的名稱被改稱為「不方便法院主義」（forum non conveniens doctrine）[60]。蘇格蘭法創造這種法則以便於扣押外國人財產而迫使外國人必須進入蘇格蘭法院答辯時（arrestment ad fundandam jurisdiction），若會產生不適當之情形時即可依此法則加以平衡[61]。於Sim v. Robinow[62]中，Lord Kinnear對不方便法院主義適用之論述不但為蘇格蘭法於此方面之基礎，亦為英國最高法院日後適用不方便法院及方便法院法則[63]之參考：「這種主張（基於不方便法院之理由而要求停止訴訟程序）是永遠不能被許可的，除非法院能確定還有著其他有充分管轄權的法院，且於該法院中該案件可以為了所有當事人之利益及正義之目的下而被更合適的加以審判。[64]」但是此種「最合適法院」（"most suitable forum"）法則之使用方式於Sim v. Robinow之前並不穩定，因為這種法則是與英國傳統的「困擾性」與「壓迫性」法則及「濫用訴訟程序」一起存在[65]，但是在Societe du Gaz de Paris v. SA de Navigation, "Les Armateurs Francais"[66]案中再次確認Lord Kinnear之

58 Alan Dashwood et al., A Guide to the Civil Jurisdiction and Judgments Convention (1987) 425 n. 76.

59 Robert Braucher, The Inconvenient Federal Forum, 60 Harv. L. Rev. 908 (1946-47).

60 Edward L. Barrett, The Doctrine of Forum Non Conveniens, 35 Cal. L. Rev. 380, 389 (1947);見Alexander Reus, A Comparative View of the Doctrine of Forum Non Conveniens in the United States, the United Kingdom, and Germany,16 Loy. L.A. Int'l & Comp. L.J. 455, 460 (1994).

61 A. Gibb, The International Law of Jurisdiction in England and Scotland (1926), 212, 213; 16 Loy. L.A. Int'l & Comp. L.J. 455, 460 (1994).

62 1892 Sess. Cas. 665 (Scot. 1st Div.).

63 Spiliada Maritime Corpn v. Consulex Ltd [1987] AC 460;見陳隆修、許兆慶、林恩瑋、李瑞生四人合著，《國際私法-管轄與選法理論之交錯》，台北，五南圖書公司，2009年3月，初版1刷，195-215頁。

64 1892 Sess. Cas. 665, 668 (Scot. 1st Div.), "The plea [for staying proceedings on the ground of forum non conveniens] can never be sustained unless the court is satisfied that there is some other tribunal, having competent jurisdiction, in which the case may be tried more suitably for the interests of all the parties and for the ends of justice."

65 有關「困擾性」及「壓迫性」法則，見陳隆修，《國際私法管轄權評論》，台北，五南圖書公司，民國75年11月，初版，84頁。

66 1926 Sess. Cas. 13 (Scot.).

論述後，「最合適法院」之法則就超越了「濫用程序」法則[67]。但是不方便法院原則之使用是有限制性的，因為一直到英國法院於MacShannon v. Rockware Glass Ltd.[68]時，「最合適法院」法則才被用來保護法院地之被告。

故而若對不方便法院則加以追本溯源，其較為原始的要件應為：1.有其他有管轄權之法院；2.該法院能合適的處理所有當事人之利益及達成正義的目的。如Dicey and Morris所說：「**不方便法院主義，亦即就是有著其他更『合適』之法院，而所謂更合適是指為了正義的目的更為適當之意思，這是蘇格蘭法院於十九世紀所發展出來[69]，並為美國[70]（有著一些改變）所採納。**[71]」又說：「於英國，方便法院與依現在民事程序規則第6篇法院給予許可去送達境外的裁量權之行使永遠是個有關的因素[72]」。因此或許可以如此加以論述：「不方便法院」與「方便法院」的中心重點是在為了達成正義的目的而去確認合適處理該案之法院。即使是美國縱使於國際上以不方便法院之名霸凌第三世界之人民，但於國內聯邦法院審判地

67 David W. Robertson, Forum Non Conveniens in American and England: A Rather Fantastic Fiction, 103 Law Q. Rev. 398, 412 (1987); 16 Loy. L.A. Int'l & Comp. L.J. 455, 460.

68 1978 App. Cas. 795 (appeal taken from Q.B.).

69 Société du Gaz de Paris v SA de Navigation "Les Armateurs Français," 1926 S.C. (HL) 13, (1925) 23 L1.L.R. 209.

70 Gulf Oil Corp v Gilbert, 330 U.S. 501 (1947); Piper Aircraft v Reyno, 454 U.S. 235 (1981)。美國並未完全遵循蘇格蘭法，自創了「公利益」的考量因素，近數十年來藉此考量因素操弄管轄規則，欺壓第三世界人民，見陳隆修、許兆慶、林恩瑋、李瑞生四人合著，《國際私法-管轄與選法理論之交錯》，台北，五南圖書公司，2009年3月，初版1刷，207頁；陳隆修，《2005年海牙法院選擇公約評析》，台北，五南圖書公司，2009年1月，初版1刷，304-306頁。

71 "The doctrine of *forum non conveniens*, i.e. that some other forum is more 'appropriate' in the sense of more suitable for the ends of justice, was developed by the Scottish courts in the nineteenth century, and was adopted (with some modifications) in the United States. The Scots rule is that the court may decline to exercise jurisdiction, after giving consideration to the interests of the parties and the requirements of justice, on the ground that the case cannot be suitably tried in the Scottish court nor full justice be done there, but only in another court." Dicey and Morris, the Conflict of Laws, 14th ed., pp. 465, 466.

72 "In England, *forum conveniens* was always a relevant factor in the exercise of the discretion to grant permission to serve out of the jurisdiction under what is now Pt 6 of the Civil Procedure Rules, i.e. Rule 27, but until 1984 the English courts refused to accept that the jurisdiction to stay actions commenced against defendants who were sued in England as of right could be based *forum non conveniens* grounds."同上，p. 466；因「方便法院」而送達境外，見陳隆修，《國際私法管轄權評論》，台北，五南圖書公司，民國75年11月，初版，45-48頁。

之移轉，其1948年28 U.S.C. 1404(a)亦規定「為了當事人及證人之便利，正義之利益」，而得將訴訟移轉至其他地院[73]。**為了避免對「不方便法院」或「方便法院」中「conveniens」一詞產生混淆，Dicey and Morris還特別說明：「conveniens並不是指『方便』[74]」**。故而於此"conveniens"所指的通常或許應是「appropriate」（合適）之意，這雖然包含證人、證據、及準據法的便利及當事人的利益，但最主要的還是指「更合適達成正義目的」（more suitable for the ends of justice）之法院。個人之所以不厭其煩的對此名詞一再重複贅述，乃是兩岸法學皆採「不方便法院」主義[75]，如果過分惑於「方便性」之表面語詞，可能會忽略法院追求個案正義之基本天職。

個人早期對於在平行訴訟時英國傳統上在判例法上所採之困擾性及

---

73 "For the convenience of parties and witness, in the interest of justice, a district court may transferr any civil action to any other district or division where it might have been brought." 28 U.S.C. 1404(a)(1948).

74 Dicey and Morris, the Conflict of Laws, 14th ed., p. 465, note 25, "*Conveniens* does not mean 'conveniens': see *The Atlantic Star* [1974] A.C. 436, 475; *GAF Corp v Amchem Products Inc* [1975] 1 Lloyd's Rep. 601, 607; *Spiliada Maritime Corp v Cansulex Ltd* [1987] A.C. 460, 474-475."

75 對於平行訴訟台灣民訴新增加於182之2條：「當事人就已繫屬於外國法院之事件更行起訴，如有相當理由足認該事件之外國法院判決在中華民國有承認其效力之可能，並於被告在外國應訴無重大不便者，法院得在外國法院判決確定前，以裁定停止訴訟程序。但兩造合意願由中華民國法院裁判者，不在此限。法院為前項裁定前，應使當事人有陳述意見之機會。」本條文看似採歐盟之先繫屬優先，但不似歐盟的硬性機械式規則，卻給予後繫屬之台灣法院裁量權去決定是否會停止訴訟。歐盟的先繫屬優先法則是嚴禁所有相關法院去私自加以裁量而背離該法則，一般認為裁量權之行使是英美法院之作法，故而182之2條是明顯的同時採納大陸法先繫屬優先及英美法不方便法院兩種近似衝突之作法，故而相當詭譎。在有關不方便法院之規定上182之2是如此規定：「被告在外國應訴無重大不便者……法院得……停止訴訟程序」。如主文中所強調"conveniens"並不是指「方便」，而是指「更合適去達成正義的目的」。如果過分迷惑於「方便性」之適用。則整個不方便法院法則之引用可能再次淪為「有禮無體」的台灣法學特徵。另外為182之2所忽略但卻為英美法院於實施不方便法院法則所經常附帶實施之作法為，法院於裁定停止訴訟前會要求被告承認其他所認定之方便法院之管轄權、該法院未來所可能作成之判決、於法院地審判前所作成之事實調查於該其他法院亦應被承認、放棄時效之利益（大陸法可能會有爭議，但歐盟契約法源則已接受此種合理的英美法作風）、對未來可能不利之判決之執行提出擔保。見Restatement (Second) of Conlict of Laws § 84 (1971), REPORTER'S NOTE, "Some courts will dismiss on the ground of forum non conveniens on condition that the defendant submit to jurisdiction in a more conveniens forum. Vargas v. A.H. Bull Steamship Co., 44 N.J. Super. 536, 131 A. 2d 39 (1957), cert. den., 355 U.S. 959 (1958); AEtna Insurance Company v. Creole Petroleum Corporation, 27 A.D.2d 518, 275 N.Y.S.2d 274 (1st Dep't 1966); Wendel v. Hoffmam, 259 App. Div. 732, 18 N.Y. S.2d 96 (2nd Dep't 1940)."另外又見comment (c), "The same will be true if the plaintiff's cause of action would elsewhere be barred by the statute of limitations, unless the court is willing to accept the defendant's stipulation that he will not raise this defense in the second state."

壓迫性主義如此陳述[76]：「此種情況最常發生的為，相同之當事人為著相同或類似之糾紛，於英國及其他國家發生訴訟。學理上，同一原告對同一被告於不同之國家提起相同之訴訟，並無任何不適之處（但於國內案件則自然不可）。蓋依英國觀點，原告有權利合法地引用任何國家對其之司法上之保護，例如其可能是為了儘速取得於任何一國之判決；或者為了取得更有效之救濟手段，例如於海商案件中對停留於法院地之船舶或貨物行使權利，故原則上除非被告能證明訴訟之進行，對其造成困擾或壓迫，否則英法院不會行使此種權力，而且舉證責任在於被告。[77]」「當相同之原告於英國及其他國家告相同之被告，且訴因（cause of action）亦為相同時，於管轄權上英國法院有三種裁量權：(1)讓原告選擇（election）其願意放棄那一國家之訴訟程序；(2)或依當事人一方之建議，停止英國之訴訟程序，而不予原告選擇權；(3)或命令當事人停止國外之訴訟程序[78]。以上之司法管轄權，英國法院欲使用時必須十分謹慎。於例外情況下，當各訴訟不是同時於數國法院被提起時，而是先後於數國被提起時，法院亦有此等裁量權。」「當同一原告於不同之國家對同一被告提起訴訟時，法院較容易依被告之聲請，而停止其中之一訴訟之進行。但當訴訟當事人雖皆相同時，若一訴訟中之原告於他訴訟變為被告，而另一當事人之地位於不同之訴訟亦有變更時，英法院較上述之情形更不願意停止任何訴訟之進行[79]」。

---

76 陳隆修，《國際私法管轄權評論》，台北，五南圖書公司，民國75年11月，初版，84-89頁。

77 Ionian Bank Ltd. v. Couvreur [1969] 1 W.L.R. 781;於Sealey v. Callan中，太太居住於英國，依英國法規定其於英國提起離婚之訴。其先生之住所於南非居所亦於南非，後來亦於南非提起離婚之訴，並要求英法院停止太太於英國之訴。英法院拒絕先生之請求。[1953] p. 135.

78 The Christiansborg (1886) 109. D. 141. (C.A.).

79 Cohen v, Rothfield [1919] 1 K.B. 410, (C.A.),於英國訴訟中之原告於英格蘭及蘇格蘭經營生意，被告為其經理，當原告被判犯罪入監受罰時，被告拿了原告所應有之金錢，故原告於英格蘭起訴，要求被告返還其金錢。數日後被告亦於蘇格蘭起訴，宣稱該些金錢為其所有。原告要求英格蘭法院禁止被告於蘇格蘭法院進行訴訟。英格蘭法院判被告於蘇格蘭之訴訟並非為困擾性或壓迫性之訴送，雖然無直接證據顯示於蘇格蘭之訴訟會給予被告任何益處，但法院認其不能假定無此利益存在，故拒絕原告之請求。另外又見陳隆修，《國際私法管轄權評論》，台北，五南圖書公司，民國75年11月，初版，86-92頁之案例，下面為幾個案例。於Peruvian Guano Co. v. Bockwoldt中，一英國公司於英國告一法國公司沒有履行交付船上之貨物之責任。當英國訴訟開始時，船還停留於英國領海，後該貨被移至法國，並由該法國公司所占有，故該英國公司後又

但自英國加入歐盟，上述傳統的英國法律邏輯自應受到布魯塞爾公約及布魯塞爾規則之先繫屬優先法則的拘束，故而於歐盟會員國間之案件，上述傳統英國法則並不能被加以適用。另外更有可能因近二十多年來採納不方便法院法則，原告之利益不若以往的被給予如此重大的份量[80]。個人較近如此敘述[81]：「對於英國於原告利益司法作風的改變，個人因為屬於old school故有些適應不良，並很驚訝的發現英國新版的教科書不約而同的證實個人之感受。個人認為除了因新近採納不方便主義外，另外可能因加入歐盟而感受到壓力。」而Cheshire and North更是對相關原告的利益如此直接的表白：「於以前一段時期這個因素（原告的利益）是被給予重大的份量，並且如果請求人可以由英國的審判取得重大的利益法院是不太可能允許去停止英國的訴訟。當於行使決定是否停止訴訟之裁量權時，最高法院於spiliada[82]案中試圖減少對請求人之利益所給予考量之份量。因此請求人僅在事實上於英國之訴訟程序有著合法的私人或司法上之利益之法則是不構成決定性之影響。[83]」故而或許英國資深同僚權威性之評述，間

於法國告該法國公司，要求交付貨物。該法國公司於英國申請要求原告選擇（election）法國訴訟或英國訴訟，英法院拒絕其聲請。(1883) 23 Ch. D. 225 (C.A.).於The Christianborg中，一德國船與一丹麥船於公海中發生碰撞，德國船東於荷蘭扣押該丹麥船隻，並對其提起對物之訴送。後該丹麥船隻之船東提起擔保，而解除扣押，該丹麥船隻並航行至英國。德國船東又於英國扣押該丹麥船，並對其提起對物訴訟。英國法院判英國之訴訟應被停止，因為該丹麥船東於荷蘭提出擔保後，該船已享有免除被扣押之權。(1886) 109. D. 141 (C.A.).於Orr-Lewis中，太太於英國法院提起離婚之訴，先生出庭法院之目的只為抗辯其住所於法國，故英法院無管轄權，但英法院仍判其住所為英國。同時先生亦於法國提起離婚之訴，太太於英國請求英法院禁止先生於法國提起訴訟。英法院拒絕發給禁止命令。[1949] p.347.於Sealey v. Callan中，先生與太太之住所皆於南非，但太太因居住於（resides）英國滿三年，故可於英法院提起離婚之訴，後來先生亦於南非提起離婚之訴。先生要求英法院停止英國之訴訟程序，因為其無法於英法院反訴，並且英法院之判決將無法被其夫妻住所地國南非所承認。但有證據上顯示除非雙方同意，否則南非法院無法給予贍養費之命令，故英法院拒絕停止英國之訴訟。[1953] p.135.

80 有關原告之利益，見陳隆修、許兆慶、林恩瑋、李瑞生四人合著，《國際私法-管轄與選法理論之交錯》，台北，五南圖書公司，2009年3月，初版1刷，211-215頁。

81 陳隆修、許兆慶、林恩瑋、李瑞生四人合著，《國際私法-管轄與選法理論之交錯》，台北，五南圖書公司，2009年3月，初版1刷，213頁。

82 [1987] AC 460.

83 Cheshire and North's, Private International Law, 13th ed. p. 345, "At one time great weight was attached to this factor, and if the claimant obtained a substantial advantage from trial in England the courts were unlikely to grant a stay of the English proceedings. The House of Lords in the Spiliada case sought to reduce the weight given to the advantage to the claimant when exercising the discretion to stay. Hence the principle that the mere fact that the claimant has a legitimate personal or juridical advantage in pro-

接的支持個人較近之論述：「如前述於最早採納困擾性及壓迫性主義時，個人覺得英國法院對於原告有利之點（advantage）較為尊重。迫於現代社會之流動性，英國法院不得不放寬管轄權基礎，故較近亦不得不採納較為寬鬆而具彈性之不方便法院主義，因而對原告之利益之解釋亦較為嚴格。[84]」

相較之下較早採納蘇格蘭不方便法則之美國似乎較為注重原告之利益[85]。美國法律學會（the American Law Institute）第2新編國際私法第84條Restatement (Second) of Conflict of Laws §84（1971）亦採納不方便法院法則[86]，其comment (c)中認為法院保留訴訟的兩個最重要因素為：若對原告而言沒有其他更合適的法院，該訴訟不會被駁回；及「因為應由原告去選擇訴訟之地方，除非有重大之理由其所選之法院不應受到干擾。[87]」另外於決定是否為合適之法院時，其comment (f)對原告住所之州

ceedings in England cannot be decisive."14th ed., p. 437.

84 陳隆修、許兆慶、林恩瑋、李瑞生四人合著，《國際私法-管轄與選法理論之交錯》，台北，五南圖書公司，2009年3月，初版1刷，211、212頁。又個人如此論述：「傳統上所認為的利益有個人的、司法上的及程序上的利益。有關個人的利益之情形，例如：原告居住於法院地。司法上的利益則通常為英國之實體法對當事人較為有利情形，例如：英國的選法規則會使得原告取得快速之判決。而對原告較為通常發生之利益則為程序上的情形，例如：原告可以取得其請求權之完全擔保，較快的訴訟程序，較高的損害賠償額，利息的給付，費用的賠償，或較長的消滅時效。相較於英國，美國還是甚為遵循傳統之政策，對於原告之意願理論上還是甚為尊重。雖然於空難事件美國法院對於尋求高額賠償金的外國原告，常以不方便法院而駁回，但原告若為法院地真正的居民時，訴訟甚少被駁回。有些州甚至認為居民原告所提之訴不能被駁回（但可停止）。此乃因為各州有利益去保護其居民，免除他們去外州訴訟的不方便及花費。個人認為對居民之保護擴及管轄權，或許多少有受到『利益說』所影響之故。」

85 早期對此點個人於陳隆修，《國際私法管轄權評論》，台北，五南圖書公司，民國75年11月，初版，170、171頁中如此評述：當原告為法院地之居民時，法院一般甚少以不方便法院之理由將訴訟駁回。很明顯地，此乃因法院欲保護其居民，免得其必須遭受於他處起訴之不便與花費。有些州法院，如加州，明白地規定對當地居民所提起之訴訟，不得以不方便法院為理由將其駁回，至多法院只能停止該訴訟之進行，而等待所被提議的更方便法院之判決。作者對此類判決不甚贊同，蓋保護被告之利益乃為訴訟法之大原則，今加州之做法似與此大原則之基本精神不甚相合。此或許是由於加州現今於實體法上沈迷於Currie教授的「保護州民利益說」之故。Archibald v. Cinerama Hotels, 15 Cal 3d 853 (1976).

86 § 84. Forum Non Conveniens
A state will not exercise jurisdiction if it is a seriously inconvenient forum for the trial of the action provided that a more appropriate forum is available to the plaintiff.

87 "c. Factors to be considered. The two most important factors look to the court's retention of the case. They are (1) that since it is for the plaintiff to choose the place of suit, his choice of a forum should not be disturbed except for weighty reasons, and (2) that the action will not be dismissed unless a suitable alternative forum is available to the plaintiff. Because of the second factor, the suit will be entertained,

又如此論述：「於這個州起訴可能牽涉及對被告所造成之困難，但除了於例外之情形外，對原告於當地起訴之明顯的方便性，及該州對原告福祉的明顯利益，會使得該州是個合適的法院。[88]」另外其報告人之註釋中又說：「除非在『平衡所有的情況下相當強烈的有利於』被告下，法院不應駁回該訴訟。[89]」故而美國不方便法院法則之實施仍舊遵守判例法之傳統，而相當的尊重原告之利益-但非常可惜的所謂「原告之利益」，指的僅是美國人原告，而非第三世界的原告[90]。

三、司法的自大與司法的禮誼

如Dicey and Morris所說：「但是一直到1984年為止，對於在英國被

---

no matter how inappropriate the forum may be, if the defendant cannot be subjected to jurisdiction in other states. The same will be true if the plaintiff's cause of action would elsewhere be barred by the statute of limitations, unless the court is willing to accept the defendant's stipulation that he will not raise this defense in the second state."

88 "First, as stated in Comment c, plaintiff's choice of a forum will not be disturbed except for weighty reasons, and, second, there will in the ordinary case be one or more forums available to the plaintiff which, in the great majority of situations, will be appropriate. One of these is the state where the occurrence took place, which qualifies because its local law will usually govern the rights and liabilities of the parties, and because in the normal case, at least, the majority of witnesses will reside there. A second forum is the state of the defendant's domicil or, in the case of a corporation, the state of its incorporation or principal place of business. These states will presumably be convenient places for the defendant to stand suit, and the defendant's relationship to them makes it appropriate for their courts to hear the case. A third forum is the state of the plaintiff's domicil. Suit in this state may involve hardship to the defendant, but the obvious convenience to the plaintiff in bringing suit there, together with the clear interest of this state in the plaintiff's welfare, will make this state an appropriate forum except in unusual circumstances."

89 REPORTER'S NOTE, A court should not dismiss the action unless the "balance is strongly in favor" of the defendant. Mobil Tankers Co v. Mene Grande Oil Co., 363 F.2d 611 (3d Cir. 1966); Byrd v. Southern Railway Co., 203 A. 2d 37 (D.C.App. 1964). See also Thomson v. Palmieri, 355 F F.2d 64 (2d Cir. 1966); Kolber v. Holyke Shares, Inc., 213 A.2d 445 (Del. 1965).

90 早期於陳隆修，《國際私法管轄權評論》，台北，五南圖書公司，民國75年11月，初版中個人如此論述：「一般對原告選擇法院地起訴之意願應加以相當之尊重，除非其他法院很明顯地為更方便之法院，否則法院不應不尊重其意願。但於Piper Aircraft Co. v. Reyno中，法院決定當原告為外國人，且訴因亦為外國訴因時，若法院地非為該外國損害發生地時，原告不可僅以法院地之法律對其比該外國法律較為有利為理由，去抗辯法院地為不方便法院之裁定。故法院地之法律對原告較為有利之因素，並不構成法院是否為方便法院之特別考慮因素，而只為考慮因素之一而已。」102 S. Ct. 252 (1981).另外美國近年來對第三世界原告之冷酷暴行，個人近年來屢次加以撻伐，見陳隆修，《2005年海牙法院選擇公約評析》，台北，五南圖書公司，2009年1月，初版1刷，304-306頁。

起訴的被告之訴訟英國法院拒絕承認其有權力去根據不方便法院之理由而去停止訴訟。[91]」或許於早期科技尚未如此發達，流動性較低，困擾性及壓迫性法則因較為嚴守傳統的法律邏輯，故較能維護當事人之訴訟權及適當程序權，因此可能甚為符合當時之社會。個人早期如此論述：「許多英國學者認為英國之技巧，較『不方便法院』之技巧更為開明（liberal），作者亦同意他們之看法。但嚴格而言，此二技巧實有甚多相似之處。[92]」故個人早期即建議「兩者皆引用」[93]。另外又如此又如此論述：「美國由於長手法規普遍地被各州所接受，及憲法法條要求只要有最低限度之關連點法院即有管轄權，一非居民被告很可能於遙遠的法院地被起訴。於此寬廣之管轄基礎上，法院必須有適當之裁量權，於特殊案例中去避免對被告造成不公平之現象。此與英格蘭所採的避免『困擾性或壓迫性訴訟』之技巧，有異曲同妙之功。無論是採美國及蘇格蘭之技巧，或英格蘭之技巧，只要法院之管轄基礎愈為寬廣，則其愈需要有裁量權去拒絕接受會造成不公正之訴訟。[94]」

時光飛逝驀然回首已經過四分之一世紀，個人早期孤鳥般的喃喃獨白，已成為今日全球化法學中理所當然的共同核心事實。英國最高法院早就於Spiliada Maritime Corpn v. Cansulex Ltd[95]中採納不方便法院法則，而曾引起熱烈討論的海牙民商事項管轄及判決草約（1999）（Preliminary Draft Convention on Jurisdiction and Foreign Judgments in Civil and Commercial Matters 1999）第21條7項[96]（先繫屬優先之例外）及第

91 Dicey and Morris, the Conflict of Laws, 14th ed., p. 466, "but until 1984 the English courts refused to accept that the jurisdiction to stay actions commenced against defendants who were sued in England as of right could be based on *forum non conveniens* grounds."

92 陳隆修，《國際私法管轄權評論》，台北，五南圖書公司，民國75年11月，初版，93頁。

93 同上。

94 陳隆修，《國際私法管轄權評論》，台北，五南圖書公司，民國75年11月，初版，172、173頁。

95 [1987] AC 460.

96 7. This Article shall not apply if the court first seised, on application by a party, determines that the court second seised is clearly more appropriate to resolve the dispute, under the conditions specified in Article 22.這個胎死腹中的草案之條款，可能是台灣民訴182之2最近似之條款。

22條[97]亦曾試圖引用不方便法院。但最為指標性標竿條款則或許為ALI/UNIDROIT Principles of Transnational Civil Procedure（2004）對人管轄條款之2.5條[98]，因為是被ALI/UNIDROIT兩個具權威性之機構所共同採納，故而該2.5條中所引用之「不方便法院」法則或許已從判例法制度國家的共同法則，於某些方面而言已被提昇至全球化實質政策上共同基本主流核心之位階。個人於年輕時基於理想而來之建言，又再一次歷經時空之檢驗而成為今日之現實。個人早期篳路藍縷一生懸命的擎舉著「主流價值」、「實體法方法論」的大纛，但於三十多年前卻被前輩同僚視為「瘋子，應被送回台灣」，個人認為時間已還實體法論一個公道。個人早期大逆不道的所堅持的「主流價值」，今日已為全世界所視為勢不可擋的「全

---

97 Article 22 Exceptional circumstances for declining jurisdiction

1. In exceptional circumstances, when the jurisdiction of the court seised is not founded on an exclusive choice of court agreement valid under Article 4 or on Article 7, 8 or 12, the court may on application by a party, suspend its proceedings if in that case it is clearly inappropriate for that court to exercise jurisdiction and if a court of another States has jurisdiction and is clearly more appropriate to resolve the dispute. Such application must be made no later than at the time of the first defence on the merits.
2. The court shall take into account, in particular—
   a) any inconvenience to the parties in view of their habitual residence;
   b) the nature and location of the evidence, including documents and witnesses, and the procedures for obtaining such evidence;
   c) applicable limitation or prescription periods;
   d) the possibility of obtaining recognition and enforcement of any decision on the merits.
3. In deciding whether to suspend the proceedings, a court shall not discriminate on the basis of the nationality or habitual residence of the parties.
4. If the court decides to suspend its proceedings under paragraph 1, it may order the defendant to provide security sufficient to satisfy any decision of the other court on the merits. However, it shall make such an order if the other court has jurisdiction only under Article 17, unless the defendant establishes that sufficient assets exist in the State of that other court or in another State where the court's decision could be enforced.
5. When the court has suspended its proceedings under paragraph 1,
   a) it shall decline to exercise jurisdiction if the court of the other State exercises jurisdiction, or if the plaintiff does not bring the proceedings in that State within the time specified by the court, or
   b) it shall proceed with the case if the court of the other State decides not to exercise jurisdiction.

98 2,5 Jurisdiction may be declined or the proceeding suspended when the court is manifestly inappropriate relative to another more appropriate court that could exercise jurisdiction. 見其comment P-2F, "The concept recognized in Principle 2.5 is comparable to the common-law rule of forum non conveniens. In some civil-law systems, the concept is that of preventing abuse of the forum. This principle can be given effect by suspending the forum proceeding in deference to another tribunal. The existence of a more convenient forum is necessary for application of this Principle. This Principle should be interpreted in connection with the Principle of Procedural equality of the Parties, which prohibits any kind of discrimination on the basis of nationality or residence. See Principle 3.2.

球化法學」之潮流。請問大陸的年輕同僚——在當今全球化法學之浪潮中，中國的法律學生不曾於浪潮之最前端留下鴻泥嗎？

在英國於St Pierre v South American Stores（Gath and Chaves）Ltd中Scott L.J.即重申英國法院停止訴訟之法則[99]為，若訴訟之進行會對被告形成「困擾性或壓迫性」（vexatious or oppressive）之情形下而造成不正義之後果，及若訴訟之停止不會對請求人造成不正義之情形，則停止訴訟之請求會被允許。故而如Dicey and Morris所說[100]：「一直到最高法院於The Atlantic Star[101]之判決前，要求停止英國訴訟之被告是要負起相當大的舉證責任。」如前述雖然於The Atlantic Star中，英國最高法院明白的拒絕蘇格蘭「不方便法院」法則，重申只要原告之訴若構成困擾性或壓迫性之訴訟，或濫用司法程序，則法院有權停止訴訟之進行，大部分法官亦認為原告於英國訴訟之權利不可輕易的被拒絕，但又認為於未來「困擾性及壓迫性」應被更開放的解釋，於考慮是否停止訴訟時，應考慮到原告之利益及被告之任何不利之處。故而如Dicey and Morris所說：「前述在The Atlantic Star之前所決定之許多案件，於今日會被給予不同的決定。[102]」

事實上於英國法院正式採納不方便法院之前，英國法院已存在著自然法院（natural forum）之概念。繼The Atlantic Star之後，隨即於Rockware Glass Ltd v. MacShannon[103]中，4個上訴案件被集中審理。原告皆為蘇格蘭人，於蘇格蘭受到工業傷害，所有之證人及醫療證據皆於蘇格蘭。被各皆為英國公司，故於英國被送達，因而英國法院有著管轄權。英國最

[99] [1936] 1 K.B. 382, 398 (CA).

[100] Dicey and Morris, the Conflict of Laws, 14th ed., p. 466, “Until the decision of the House of Lords in *The Atlantic Star* a defendant who sought a stay of English proceedings had a very heavy burden.”

[101] [1974] A.C. 436.

[102] Dicey and Morris, the Conflict of Laws, 14th ed., p. 466, note 28, “Many cases decided before The Atlantic Star, above, would be decided differently today. *The more important decisions are McHenry v Lewis* (1882) 22 Ch. D. 397 (CA); *Peruvian Guano Co v Bockwoldt* (1883) 23 Ch. D. 225; *The Christiansborg* (1885) 10 P.D. 141 (CA); *Logan v bank of Scotland* (No.2)[1906] 1 K.B. 141; *Jopson v James* (1908) 77 L.J. Ch. 824 (CA); *St Pierre v South American Stores Ltd* [1936] K.B. 382 (CA).”

[103] [1978] AC 795.

高法院允許被告之請求而停止訴訟，法院認為合適或自然的審判地應為蘇格蘭。所謂自然法院地指的就是與訴訟有著最真實與重大關連（the most real and substantial connection）之地。於該案中原告雖然在取得法律意見後，真誠的認為他們可於英國訴訟程序中取得利益，但在沒有客觀之證據下，英國法院認定他們無法於英國訴訟中取得利益[104]。在MacShannon中，除了Lord Keith外，英國最高法院（House of Lords）之其他成員甚至進一步的偏向停止「困擾性或壓迫性」（oppressive or vexatious）之名詞。Lord Diplock重新論述停止訴訟之基本原則為應滿足兩要件，一為正面一為負面：(a)被告必須說服法院有著其他對被告有管轄權法院之存在，而該其他法院可在更重大的減少不便利及費用下於當事人間達成正義，及(b)該停止之許可不會剝奪原告如果其於英國法院訴訟所會享有之合法私人或司法上之利益[105]。但是個人認為至少很清楚的是於禁止當事人在外國提起訴訟程序上（restrain foreign proceedings），法院仍引用傳統的「困擾性或壓迫性」的標準[106]。於有關禁止當事人在外國提起訴訟上，新採納的「不方便法院法則」（forum non conveniens principles）於在有關停止英國訴訟之行使上，對其之影響有一段時期並不清楚。但是於Castanho v Brown & Root (UK) Ltd[107]中Lord Scarman說，自從The Atlantic Star[108]及MacShannon v Rockware Glass Ltd.[109]後就沒有必要去考慮先前之判例法，這個說法為其他大法官所同意。該案認為禁止外國訴訟之命令得於停止英國程序之相同情形下而被作成，亦即是在前述當時MacShannon之兩個條件之情形下[110]。但是在Société Nationale Industrielle

---

104 [1978] AC 795 at 812, 820, 830.

105 [1978] A.C. 795, 812.

106 South Carolina Insurance Co v Assurantie Maatschappij "De Zeven Provincien" NV [1987] A.C. 24, 41; Société Nationale Industrielle Aérospatiale v. Lee Kui Jak [1987] AC 871, 893.見陳隆修、許兆慶、林恩瑋、李瑞生四人合著，《國際私法—管轄與選法理論之交錯》，台北，五南圖書公司，2009年3月，初版1刷，206、207頁。

107 [1981] A.C. 557.

108 [1974] A.C. 436.

109 [1978] A.C. 795.

110 [1981] A.C. 557, 575. *See also British Airways Board v Laker Airways Ltd* [1985] A.C. 58, 80; *South*

Aérospatiale v. Lee Kui Jak[111]中Lord Goff of Chieveley代表大英國協最高法院（the Privy Council）認為，於禁訴令上去適用Spiliada Maritime Corpn v. Cansulex Ltd[112]所發展出來的「不方便法院法則」（“the doctrine of forum non conveniens”）是不對的，通常應於訴訟會對被告造成「困擾性或壓迫性」才會限制原告於外國之訴訟[113]。

但是由另一方面而言自採用不方便法院法則後，如Dicey and Morris所說：「依在the Atlantic Star及MacShannon v Rockware Glass Ltd中所建立的原則而被決定的案件，現在已經重大的減少其相關連性。[114]」雖然於the Atlantic Star及MacShannon v Rockware Glass Ltd中英國最高法院仍拒絕接受不方便法院原則作為英國法之一部分。但在MacShannon之判決中，如同Dicey and Morris之評論：「但是後者之判決是被認為，其對英國法院於這些案件中所行使的法則的改編，與蘇格蘭不方便法院法則之行使相差並不遠[115]。」有趣的是自英國最高法院（House of Lords）從The Atlanic Star開始之一系列判例後，Lord Diplock於The Abidin Daver

Carolina case [1987] A.C. 24, 40.

111 [1987] AC 871.

112 [1987] A.C. 460.

113 Société Nationale Industrielle Aérospatiale v. Lee Kui Jak [1987] AC 871 at 896, Lord Goff “in a case such as the present where a remedy for a particular wrong is available both in the English … court and in a foreign court, the English… court will, generally speaking, only restrain the plaintiff from pursuing proceedings in the foreign court if such pursuit would be vexatious or oppressive.”見陳隆修、許兆慶、林恩瑋、李瑞生四人合著，《國際私法-管轄與選法理論之交錯》，台北，五南圖書公司，2009年3月，初版1刷，244、245頁。

114 Dicey and Morris, the Conflict of Laws, 14th ed., p. 466, note 32, “Cases decided under the principles established in *The Atlantic Star* and *MacShannon v Rockware Glass Ltd* are now of sharply reduced relevance.”又參考 *The Wladyslaw Lokietek* [1978] 2 Lloyd’s Rep. 520; *The Wellamo* [1980] 2 Lloyd’s Rep. 229; *Trendtex Trading Corp v Crédit Suisse* [1980] 3 All E.R. 721, *affirmed* [1982] A.C. 679; *European Asian bank v Punjab Bank* [1982] 2 Lloyd’s Rep. 356 (CA); The Messiniaki Tolmi [1984] 1 Lloyd’s Rep. 267 (CA); The Abidin Daver [1984] A.C. 398; *The Forum Craftsman* [1985] 1 Lloyd’s Rep. 291 (CA); *Muduroglu Ltd v TC Ziraat Bankasi* [1986] Q.B. 1225 (CA).

115 Dicey and Morris, the Conflict of Laws, 14th ed., p. 466, 467, “ In the latter decision, however, it was recognised that the reformulation in these decisions of the principles on which the English court acted was not far removed in practice from the Scottish doctrine of *forum non conveniens*.”又見其p. 467, note 33, “See [1978] A.C. 795, at pp. 812 (Lord Diplock), 822 (Lord Fraser) and *Hesperides Hotels Ltd v Aegean Turkish Holidays Ltd* [1979] A.C. 508 at pp. 537 (Lord Wilberforce) and 544 (Lord Fraser). For an earlier (if premature) recognition of the same point cf. *Logan v Bank of Scotland* (No.2) [1906] 1 K.B. 141.”

中語出驚人的如此說：「至少於一個程度上司法的自大已經被司法的禮誼取代，亦即我認為現在應是坦白的承認的時候，在有關這個上訴的法律之部門是與蘇格蘭的不方便法院法律原則無法區分的[116]。」最後於Spiliada Maritine Corp v Cansulex Ltd[117]中，英國最高法院（the House of Lords）決定Lord Diplock對於英國停止訴訟重新論述之兩個基本原則太過注重原告之「合法個人或司法利益[118]」（legitimate personal or juridical advantage），而公開的採用不「方便法院法則」，認為訴訟只能基於「不方便法院」之理由而被加以停止。

於英國在法院之許可下得送達境外之R.S.C. Order 11, r.l (1)(d)（iii）[119][前r.l(1)(f)（iii）]，現在是規定於Civil Procedure Rules 1998，s. 6. 20(5)(c)，其規定若是根據準據法為英國法之契約而來之請求，則該請求之文件得於法院許可下而被送達至境外[120]。於Spiliada Maritime Corpn v. Cansulex Ltd[121]中，原告船東是一家利比亞船公司，其宣稱被告貨主，一家英屬哥倫比亞公司，之硫磺損害其船，並要求契約上之損害賠

---

116 [1984] A.C. 398, 411, "judicial Chauvinism has been replaced by judicial comity to an extent which I think the time is now right to acknowledge frankly is, in the field of law with which this appeal is concerned, indistinguishable from the Scottish legal doctrine of *forum non conveniens*."

117 [1987] A.C. 460.

118 有關原告之「合法私人或司法利益」，見陳隆修、許兆慶、林恩瑋、李瑞生四人合著，《國際私法—管轄與選法理論之交錯》，台北，五南圖書公司，2009年3月，初版1刷，211-215頁。

119 見陳隆修，《國際私法管轄權評論》，台北，五南圖書公司，民國75年11月，初版，53-55頁。

120 6.20 Service out of the jurisdiction where the permission of the court is required
In any proceedings to which rule 6.19 does not apply, a claim form may be served out of the jurisdiction with the permission of the court if –
(5) a claim is made in respect of a contract where the contract –
(a) was made within the jurisdiction;
(b) was made by or through an agent trading or residing within the jurisdiction;
(c) is governed by English law; or
(d) contains a term to the effect that the court shall have jurisdiction to determine any claim in respect of the contract.
(6) a claim is made in respect of a breach of contract committed within the jurisdiction.
(7) a claim is made for a declaration that no contract exists where, if the contract was found to exist, it would comply with the conditions set out in paragraph (5).

121 [1987] AC 460.有關送達境外，見陳隆修，《國際私法管轄權評論》，台北，五南圖書公司，民國75年11月，初版，45-79頁；陳隆修、許兆慶、林恩瑋、李瑞生四人合著，《國際私法—管轄與選法理論之交錯》，台北，五南圖書公司，2009年3月，初版1刷，196-205頁。

償。之前已有不同之原告對同一被告於英國法院提起類似訴訟。雖然第一審法院已認定契約準據法為英國法，但上訴法院認為本案並不適宜去行使裁量權而將訴訟之通知送達國外。但英國最高法院卻根據Lord Goff的原則而允許將通知送達國外。主要考慮的因素之一即為契約準據法為英國法，另外證人的便利性及同時於不同國家提起同一訴訟的不適宜性也被提出討論。但最主要之點為先前已發生類似的訴訟，如若本案亦於英國審判，則上次訴訟的律師團及專家，尤其是保險公司，皆可為本案盡力，亦會較有效率、快速、及更經濟的達成正義的目的。法院因此也可於做成正義的判決中得到助益，並且如同上次之訴訟一般，可能促成當事人的和解。故於英國審判，不但不會於形成對被告不利的情形下，造成對原告經濟上的利益，並且會在客觀的利益下做成符合正義的判決。

四、送達境內與送達境外之區分

於經過多年的反覆思慮後，英國最高法院終於在Splilada Maritime Corpn v Cansulex Ltd中正式宣佈，英國法院得基於「不方便法院」而行使裁量權停止英國之訴訟。而又如個人早期所述[122]，基於RSC, Ord. 11, r.1（現今之1998 CPR, s. 6.20）之規定，英國法院得基於「方便法院」之標準而行使裁量權，允許將訴訟之通知送達境外[123]。如Cheshire and North所說：「現在所已經被見證的是允許將訴訟的文件送達至境外的裁量權是依據方便法院的基礎而被加以行使。另外亦有著裁量權於有些特定之情形下依不方便法院之基礎（亦即特別是當英國不是審理案件之合適法院時）去停止訴訟之進行。[124]」

---

122 陳隆修，《國際私法管轄權評論》，台北，五南圖書公司，民國75年11月，初版，45-48頁。

123 PM North, JJ Fawcett, Cheshire and North's Private International Law, 13th ed, p. 313. "The courts may, rather than must, allow service of a claim form out of the jurisdiction. Where the case falls within one of the heads of Order 11, rule 1(1) the exercise of assumed jurisdiction in any given case lies within the discretion of the court. The critertion for exercise of the Order 11 discretion is that of forum conveniens, ie service out of the jurisdiction will only be allowed where England is clearly the most appropriate forum in the interests of the parties and the ends of justice." 14th ed., p. 399.

124 PM North, JJ Fawcett, Cheshire and North's Private International Law, 13th ed, 334, "It has already

但是無論是「方便法院法則」或「不方便法院法則」之行使，「conveniens」並不是指「方便」（conveniens）之意，而是如Dicey and Morris所說「為了正義的目的更為合適」之意思。事實上於一百多年前面對國際訴訟上可能形成之複數訴訟之問題，在Lopez v Chavarri中英國判例法甚早就對此問題之核心加以論述如下：「是否於本地審理該問題，或將其交付外國法院，最能達成正義的目的。[125]」而如前述於更稍早前Lord Kinnear在Sim v. Robinow中確立蘇格蘭不方便法院主義之適用時，亦認為欲基於不方便法院之理由而停止法院之訴訟程序前，法院必須「能確定還有著其他有充分管轄權的法院，且於該法院中該案件可以為了所有當事人之利益及正義之目的下而被更合適的加以審判。[126]」

英國最高法院（the House of Lords）於領導案例Spiliada Maritime Corp v Cansulex Ltd[127]中，由Lord Goff說明以不方便法院法則為基礎而停止法院之訴訟程序之適用規則如下：「基本原則是法院之訴訟只能基於不方便法院而被停止，而其要件是法院能確認有其他有管轄權之法院存在，並且該法院是合適處理該訴訟之法院，亦即該訴訟可以為了正義的目的及所有當事人的利益，可以在該法院更合適的被加以審判。[128]」而對於以方便法院法則為基礎而行使裁量權，允許將訴訟的文件送達境外之適用規則，Lord Goff說明所謂方便法院即為：「去辨別出案件可以在所有當

been seen that the discretionary power to allow service of a claim form out of the jurisdiction exercised on the basis of forum conveniens. There is also a discretion to stay actions on the basis of forum non conveniens (ie where England is not the appropriate forum for trial) in certain specific situations." 14th ed., p. 426.

125 [1901] W.N. 115, 116, "whether the true interests of justice would be best served by trying the question here, or leaving it to the foreign tribunal".

126 1892 Sess. Cas. 665, 668 (Scot. 1st Div.), "The plea [for staying proceedings on the ground of forum non conveniens] can never be sustained unless the court is satisfied that there is some other tribunal, having competent jurisdiction, in which the case may be tried more suitably for the interests of all parties and for the ends of justice."

127 [1987] A.C. 460.

128 Spiliada Maritime Corpn v. Cansulex Ltd [1987] AC 460 at 476, "The basic principle is that a stay will only be granted on the ground of forum non conveniens where the court is satisfied that there is some available forum having jurisdiction, which is the appropriate forum for trial of the action, i.e. in which the case may be tried more suitably for the interests of all the parties and the ends of justice."

事人的利益及達到正義的目的下而被合適的審判法院」[129]。故自Spiliada Matitime Corp v Consulex Ltd[130]後，英國法院於允許送達境外裁量權之行使是以方便法院法則為基礎，而於特定情形停止英國法院訴訟進行之裁量權之行使則是以不方便法院法則為基礎。

早期英國法院於停止訴訟上較為尊重原告合法之「私人或司法之利益」之「困擾性或壓迫性」法則，現今於spiliada後已正式採用以「所有當事人之利益及達到正義的目的」為基礎之「不方便法院法則」。Lord Diplock相當英國紳士的於The Abidin Daver中自制而謙謙君子的表示這是「司法的自大已為司法的禮誼所取代」[131]。這個論述自然是相當的有氣度及有氣魄，這種令人折服的論述是法律科學中少有的，但個人以為真正的理由應是全球化不可擋之潮流所導致這種法學之趨勢。如Dicey and Morris於評論在複數國際訴訟時英國法院所採之方法時說[132]：「英國法院是事實上已有著固有的管轄權，而這種權力是被成文法所再加強的[133]，於

---

129 同上，at 480, "to identify the forum in which the case can be suitably tried for the interests of all parties and for the ends of justice".

130 [1987] A.C. 460.

131 [1984] A.C. 398, 411.

132 Dicey and Morris, the Conflict of Laws, 14th ed., pp. 464,465, English courts have an inherent jurisdiction, reinforced by statute, to stay or strike out proceedings, whenever it is necessary to prevent injustice. The court also has an inherent power to order a stay to await the outcome of proceedings in a foreign court or arbitration in the exercise of case management. The jurisdiction may be exercised in cases which have nothing to do with the conflict of laws, or with the fact that a cause of action or ground of defence arises in a foreign country. But the cases in which a party to proceedings applies to have them stayed under this jurisdiction are very often, in some way or another, connected with transactions taking place in a foreign country or with litigation being conducted abroad. In such cases, according to English notions of the conflict of laws, an English court and a court in some foreign country may both be recognized as having jurisdiction to entertain proceedings, and the English court has a discretion to determine in which forum the dispute will be resolved, by using its power to grant or refuse a stay of the proceedings by the claimant in the English court, or by exercising or refusing to exercise its power to authorise the claimant to serve process out of the jurisdiction, or by using its power to enjoin a party subject to its jurisdiction, but who is or is threatening to become a plaintiff in to foreign court, from commencing or continuing proceedings in that court.

133 Supreme Court Act 1981, s. 49(3); Civil Jurisdiction and Judgment Act 1982, s. 49; cf. CPR, r.3.1(2)(f). 這個停止訴訟之請求是一般根據CPR, Pt 11而來，並且基本上欲抗議法院之管轄權必須於收到通知後14天內為之，申請停止之請求原則上是依據這個基礎而來，但商事法院是28天（the Commercial Court 28 days (CPR, r. 58.7)）。如果訴訟停止之請求被許可，「額外之請求」（"an additional claim for contribution"）仍得對停止訴訟之原告提出（Lister & Co Ltd v EG Thomson (shipping) Ltd (No.2) [1987] 1 W.L.R. 1614），或仍得加入其他被告（Rofa sport Management AG

無論何時有必要之情形下為防止不正義之發生，而去停止或駁回訴訟程序。於行使處理案件之程序權上，法院亦有著固有的權力去命令訴訟之停止，以等待外國法院或仲裁程序之結果[134]。這種管轄權之行使可能適用在與衝突法無關之案件上，或是訴因或抗辯的理由是基於在外國發生的事實之案件上。但是訴訟當事人依此管轄權而請求停止程序之案件是經常，至少於某些方面上，與在外國發生的交易或於外國進行之訴訟有關。根據英國衝突法的概念，於此種案件英國法院及某些外國法院可能被承認皆會有著管轄權去處理訴訟程序，及英國法院經由使用其允許或拒絕請求者要求停止英國訴訟程序之權力[135]，或經由行使或拒絕行使其權力去允許請求者將訴訟之文件送達境外，或經由行使其權力去禁止一個受到其管轄之當事人，但該當事人於外國法院卻已成為或威脅著要去成為原告，去於該外國法院提起或繼續訴訟程序[136]，而使得其（英國法院）具有裁量權去決定該紛爭應於那一個法院而被決定。」故而面對日益複雜詭譎多變的複數國際訴訟，英國法院（及同樣的美國法院，但卻無方便法院之名稱）有著固有的裁量權（an inherent discretion）去依方便法院法則而允許送達境外，或依不方便法院法則而停止英國訴訟，或在對當事人有對人管轄權下作成禁止當事人於外國法院提起或繼續訴訟之禁訴令。相對於大陸法於複數訴訟時所引以為傲的「先繫屬優先原則」，英美法院固有裁量權之行使顯得

v DHL International (UK) Ltd [1989] 1 W.L.R. 902）.法院雖然亦有權利依不方便法院法則去駁回訴訟，而不僅是停止訴訟（Haji-loannou v Frangos [1999] 2 Lloyd's Rep. 337, 348 (CA)），但似乎尚未有法院如此決定。

134 Retchhold Norwat ASA v Goldman Sachs International [2000] 1 W.L.R. 173 (CA); Klöckner Holdings GmbH v Klöckner Beteiliguns GmbH [2005] EWHC 1453 (Comm.) (stay of part of proceedings); Mazur Media Ltd v Media GmbH [2004] EWHC 1566 (Ch.), [2004] 1 W.L.R. 2966.於防止禁訴令之進行，見Al-Bassam v Al-Bassam [2004] EWCA Civ. 857.

135 於特殊情形下案件是為防止時效之屆至而被提起，於申請人提出請求後訴訟得被停止，見Att-Gen v Arthur Andersen & Co [1989] E.C.C. 224 (CA); see also Ledra Fisheries Ltd v Turner [2003] EWHC 1049 (Ch.); Klockner Holdings GmbH v Klockner Beteiliguns GmbH [2005] EWHC 1453 (Comm.) at [21]; cf. The Sylt [1991] 1 Lloyd's Rep. 240; cf. Centro Internationale Handelsbank AG v Morgan Grenfell [1997] C.L.C. 870. Contrast Australian Commercial Research and Development Ltd v ANZ Mc Caughan Merchant Bank Ltd [1989] 3 All E.R. 65, affirmed February 23, 1990 (CA, unreported); Doe v Armour Pharmaceuitical Co Inc [1994] 3 L.R. 78 (Sup Ct.);Manufacturers Life Ins Co v Guarantee Co of North America (1987) 62 O.R. (2d) 147.

136 British Airways Board v Laker Airways Ltd [1985] A.C. 58, 80.

較具彈性而較能維持個案正義。「先繫屬優先原則」不但過於機械式的硬性以致可能有時無法顧及個案正義，並且造成鼓勵當事人於和解前先下手為強選擇對自己有利之法院先行起訴之可能會發生現象。這種違反自然原告至自然法院起訴自然被告之自然訴訟之法律原則，是明顯的違反人類文明的常識，踐踏司法追求正義的基本目的，亦是違反國際訴訟法的倫理道德，故完全是違背了「道法自然」的逆天行為。「先繫屬優先原則」的鼓勵訴訟是與中國文化易經「訟，終凶」[137]之教誨不合的，於21世紀法學實質政策全球化之潮流下，任何與中華民族二千五百年生活經驗背道而馳的法學原則必須被加以三思。

如個人所一再指責的，「先繫屬優先原則」最荒謬之處即為其違反了近二十多年來法學全球化之潮流。對於允許送達訴訟文件至境外被告的「過度」或「例外」的管轄基礎，英國判例法上一向就認為必須於非常謹慎下才可行使此種裁量權[138]。有趣的是英國法院不但於Spiliada Maritime Corpn v. Consulex Ltd中再次重申允許境外送達是一種過度或例外的管轄基礎[139]，其亦宣示「方便法院原則」與「不方便法院原則」的適用基礎，自此法院之境內管轄與境外管轄裁量權之適用行使基礎更是涇渭分明趨於較為單純化、統一制度化。美國雖然追隨英國母法以「所在權力」（Presence power）作為基本的管轄基礎（Pennoyer v. Neff[140]），但其自作聰明的脫離英國母法於International Shoe Co. v. Washington[141]中自

137 坎下乾上
訟
有孚，窒惕，中吉，終凶。利見大人，不利大川。
象曰：訟，上剛下險；險而健。訟。「訟，有孚，窒惕中吉」，剛來而得中也。「終凶」，訟不可成也。「利見大人」，尚中正也。「不利涉大川」，入于淵也。
象曰：天與水違行，訟；君子以作事謀始。
上九：或錫之鞶帶，終朝三褫之。
象曰：「以訟受服」，亦不足敬也。

138 陳隆修，《國際私法管轄權評論》，台北，五南圖書公司，民國75年11月，初版，45-48頁。Cordova land Co. Ltd., v. Victor Bro Inc [1966] 1 WLR 793 at 796.

139 [1987] AC 460 at 481.

140 95 U.S. 714 (1877).

141 326 U.S. 310 (1945).

創「最低限度關連點」（minimum contacts）原則。後於Shaffer v. Heitner中又確認這個「最低限度關連點」原則亦應適用於對物及準對物訴訟中[142]。亦即憲法適當程序條款（the Due Process Clause）要求被告、法院地、及訴訟間必須有著最低限度關連點，以使得法院於行使管轄權時，不會違反「傳統上公平原則及實質正義的概念」（traditional notions of fair play and substantial justice）。於Shaffer後甚多人懷疑所在權力之基礎是否被推翻，但較近之Burnham v. Superior Court則確定「最低限度關連點」只有適用於被告不在法院地而主張之管轄權，而與於法院地受到送達之被告之管轄權無關[143]。無論是以「方便法院法則」或「最低限度關連點原則」，英國及美國最高法院皆不約而同的對傳統上視為「過度」或「例外」的允許送達至境外被告的管轄基礎，於近二十多年來以判例法儘量加以制度化、單純化、規格化。這是個到目前為止不為世所矚目的寧靜革命，就個人有限的認知似乎甚少（或個人甚至不知有其他同僚對此加以注目）同僚注意到這個國際民事訴訟的革命。這個寧靜革命雖不似上世紀60、70年代的美國選法革命般的喧騰一時，但卻是同樣重要的實質政策全球化的人類文明大躍進。

這個訴訟法的寧靜革命是符合全人類的生活經驗與常識，更重要的是其亦符合一般人的正義感。這個寧靜革命符合了中國文化「道法自然」的演進程序，「道大、天大、地大、人亦大」——自然的道法是可能隨著人類的演化而與時俱進的。歐盟抱殘守缺的守著「先繫屬先原則」是忽視了

---

142 443 U.S. 186 (1977)，但海商案件因有特殊商業需求，例如船及船員可能離港甚久，故因而不適用。

143 495 U.S. 604 (1990)重申至少於外州被告有意的進入法院地時，短暫過境管轄權（transient jurisdiction）不受最低限度關連點的影響。在Shaffer之後，有一度個人如同許多美國學者一般，以為Pennoyer會被推翻，見陳隆修，《國際私法管轄權評論》，台北，五南圖書公司，民國75年11月，初版，108、109頁，及陳隆修、許兆慶、林恩瑋、李瑞生四人合著，《國際私法-管轄與選法理論之交錯》，台北，五南圖書公司，2009年3月，初版1刷，204、205頁。但或許美國最高法院少數持保留意見的四位法官是有欠思慮的。雖然對案件結果一致同意，但少數法官在此「容易案件」中保留被告必須「志願」進入法院地的條件是多慮的。如前述「所在權力」之基本、一般管轄基礎於被告被詐欺、脅迫進入法院地時是不存在的。Burnham v. Superior Court中之美國最高法院及所有的美國同僚（至少就個人有限的知識範圍內）這個「志願」或「有意」的保留條件顯然是徒增困擾之不必要邏輯。

撲天蓋地而來的全球化法學的潮流，其固執的於國際訴訟中不去區分被告是否於法院地的作法亦是與人類的生活經驗與常識不合的顢頇頑固-全世界的人都知道被告若不在法院地國際訴訟會有差別，就只有歐洲大陸法的同僚不知道。

對於前述個人早期所述[144]：「美國由於長手法規普遍地被各州所接受，及憲法法條要求只要有最低限度之關連點法院即有管轄權，一非居民被告很可能於遙遠的法院地被起訴。於此寬廣之管轄基礎上，法院必須有適當之裁量權，於特殊案例中去避免對被告造成不公平之現象。此與英格蘭所採的避免『困擾性或壓迫性訴訟』之技巧，有異曲同妙之功。無論是採美國及蘇格蘭之技巧，或英格蘭之技巧，只要法院之管轄基礎愈為寬廣，則其愈需要有裁量權去拒絕接受會造成不公正之訴訟。」現今於英國採用「不方便法院法則」後，或許同樣的道理亦為Dicey and Morris所認同，並且其更詳盡的如此解釋著：「由於許多因素的結果，包括旅行與通訊的較為容易；許多國家的法院傾向對於在他們管轄區域外之事情或人擴張其管轄權；及對於外國法與程序上的較為知悉，而這可能造成『選購法院』的現象，這個議題已經成為最重要的議題。[145]」而這個鏗鏘有力之論述亦為其他英美法院所認同及引述[146]。於國際複數訴訟中，無論是以什麼名義，承審法院於個案中為了主持正義而行使的裁量權（discretionary power），無論是停止法院地之訴訟、允許送達訴訟之通知至境外之被告、或對有著對人管轄權的當事人作成禁訴令，於市場全球化的今日世界裡已變為「最重要的議題」。

而令人深有感觸的是早期於尚未流行「全球化」名詞前，個人早已

---

144 陳隆修，《國際私法管轄權評論》，台北，五南圖書公司，民國75年11月，初版，172、173頁。

145 Dicey and Morris, the Conflict of Laws, 14th ed., p. 465, "This topic has become of the highest importance as a result of a variety of factors including the greater ease of communication and travel; the tendency of courts in many countries to extend their jurisdiction over events and persons outside their territory; and a greater awareness of foreign laws and procedures, which in turn may lead to 'forum-shopping'."

146 Amchem Products Inc v Worker's Compensation Board [1993] 1 S.C.R. 897, 904 (Sup Ct Can).

數次於不同場合中將管轄權之拓展、不方便法院、濫訴、及法院之裁量權等概念加以結合而論述[147]。無論是以「主流價值說」、「立法實體化」、「實體法論」、「共同核心基本政策」、或現今流行的「法學全球化」，只要是符合人類生活經驗、常識、與基本正義的目的之理論，歷經時光歲月的洗鍊，最後總會有其他同僚或法院於不同時空下提出相同的認知。

不方便法院法則的躍上司法的舞台，除了上述Dicey and Morris之理由外，個人認為我們同僚太過低估人類的進化本能。「道大、天大、地大、人亦大」，於21世紀高度科技發展的文明中，人類不但對物質的需求及生產皆大幅的提高，我們對個案正義的需求亦隨著物質文明的進步而提高，這亦就是「自然的道法」。21世紀法學全球化的共同核心政策乃在儘量確保個案正義的達成，為了達成這個目的，無論於國內或國際訴訟法上法院所被賦予的裁量權是不得不被提高，以應付日益複雜的社會。於這種全球化潮流的背景下，較為嚴謹且較為遵守傳統法律邏輯的「困擾性」或「壓迫性」法學自然要在更為寬鬆的「不方便法院」法學前退讓。於科技文明的推動下，全球化的潮流促使美國法院於允許境外送達時是以「最低限度關連點」為最基本的限制（另外美國又於理論上同時的於境外

---

147 見陳隆修，《國際私法管轄權評論》，台北，五南圖書公司，民國75年11月，初版，除了前述172、173頁外，對歐盟早期之布魯塞爾公約的死硬，亦屢表不認同。例如對第5(5)條代理或分行之管轄個人如此論述：「但應注意的是，公約並沒有給予法院裁量權去拒絕此類案件之管轄權，由於現代貿易發達，一家公司之貿易網可能觸及全世界，故作者以為我國若要立法，似乎應予法院拒絕管轄之裁量權，方能有效的避免原告濫訴以困擾被告之情形。」見15頁。對17條的管轄條款之約定：「歐盟共同市場則似乎不給予法院任何裁量權而缺少彈性。除非我國與日、韓等達成歐洲共同市場似的協定，否則實不必如此，而應給予我國法院適當裁量權。蓋於實務上，作者發現我國廠商不但外語能力及國外關係欠缺，議價能力亦甚低，故我國法院應彈性地保有此不輕易使用的裁量權去保護我國商人。」見22、23頁。另外對同一訴訟或相關連訴訟的21、22、23條，個人亦曾於24-26頁中主張應給予法院裁量權，例如對21條的先繫屬優先個人如此論述：「英國法院用來取代『不方便法院』的技巧，為以訴訟的進行是否會對被告造成『困擾』（vexations）或『壓迫』（oppressive）為行使裁量權之依據，來拒絕接受案件之管轄。無論美國之『不方便法院』或英國之技巧，於數個國家對同一案件發生管轄權之競合時，都相當具有彈性。相反地，公約於此方面則表示出成文法一貫機械性之作法，而不具有彈性，法院無裁量權去按照個案之需要而去停止（stay）或駁回（dismiss）該訴訟。公約二十一條規定當有甚多訴訟於不同訂約國之法院被提起，而訴的要求與當事人皆相同時，除了第一個接受案件的法院外，其他法院應自動宣布其無管轄權。我國於此方便有關國際案件沒有直接明文規定，將來若欲直接明文立法，則似應採英國技巧或美國技巧為宜。」

及境內管轄之限制上皆適用不方便法院法則[148]）；於英國則在允許境外管轄之文件送達上是遵照傳統的以「方便法院」法學為適用之基礎，而於停止英國訴訟之進行上是以「不方便法院」法則為適用之基礎。全球化市場經濟帶動了全球化法學之進展，再一次人類文明的進展又促成了法律邏輯的同步進展，而再一次引領法學全球化浪潮的又是英國及美國的最高法院。更有趣的是兩個法院皆約於二十多年前不約而同的先後（幾乎相差不久）作成於各自管轄區域內具歷史指標性的轟動驚人判決-如果如個人解讀一般，將兩國最高法院的判決合併在一起而給予世界性、歷史性、指標性的詮釋，那麼他們對全世界人類在追求正義的發展史上，其重要性可能就只有過去上世紀美國選法革命才足以相比擬。

面對全球化市場所帶來不可避免的複數訴訟之增加，歐盟除了機械式的回應以「先繫屬優先」外，就只能消極的限制各會員國之「過度」管轄[149]。歐盟於較近除了自吹自擂「歐洲法學革命」外，還是應該從雲端下降到人世間之泥土上，虛心的學習送達境外之管轄與境內管轄之區別，特別是於個案上裁量權適用基礎之區別。如此才能符合全球化社會中之生活常識，並才能於全球化之生活經驗中達成個案正義之目的。個人於此必須重述近年來一再論述之理念：「如同大自然之進化，經過長久歷史演進而來之判例法，經常亦屬於宇宙進化之一環，學術理論之創作最好不要逆天而行與判例法相抗衡。[150]」「違反聲名卓越的法院所累積出來的實務判

---

148 陳隆修，《國際私法管轄權評論》，台北，五南圖書公司，民國75年11月，初版，170-173頁。

149 Council Regulation (EC) No 44/2001
of 22 December 2000
on jurisdiction and the recognition and enforcement of judgments in civil and commercial matters
Article 3
1. Persons domiciled in a member State may be sued in the courts of another Member State only by virtue of the rules set out in Sections 2 to 7 of this Chapter.
2. In particular the rules of national jurisdiction set out in Annex I shall not be applicable as against them.
至於布魯塞爾公約第3條，見陳隆修，《國際私法管轄權評論》，台北，五南圖書公司，民國75年11月，初版，9頁。

150 陳隆修，《2005年海牙法院選擇公約評析》，台北，五南圖書公司，2009年1月，初版1刷，94頁。

例法，於國際私法學上就是近乎逆天而行違抗大自然不環保的浪費行為。歐盟法院一再顯示出其不借鏡人類祖先多年來判例法演進之結果，因為其不珍惜人類祖先歷史經驗之累積，是個不環保的法院。[151]」或許個人這種論述是更為精準的被美國最高法院於Sun Oil Co. v. Wortman中所陳述如下：「如果一件事於大眾同意下已被實行二百年，那麼需要很強的證據才能以十四修正案去影響它」[152]。故而個人真誠的認為近二十多年來英、美最高法院不約而同的對送達境外與送達境內之區別加以更明確、更制度化之規定，不但符合二十一世紀全球化市場的社會生活經驗，亦符合一般人之常識，更為司法達成個案正義之基本目的所必須。個人亦認為近年來送達境外與送達境內管轄之區別，不但為二十一世紀法學基本政策全球化之共同核心，更符合二千多年來中華文化「道大、天大、地大、人亦大」天地人合一之「自然道法」之演進過程。

我們經常認為歷史會重覆發生，但於法學全球化的過程中我們現在亦見證了歷史於同時重覆發生。前述歐盟無視於英美最高法院近乎同時的對境外與境內送達的更為制度化、一致化的加以區分。同樣的情形亦發生於集體訴訟上。集體訴訟是現代工業社會中第三世界平民大衛對抗跨國企業巨人哥來亞的彈弓[153]。為了維護這個現代「法律制度中一個重要而

151 陳隆修，《2005年海牙法院選擇公約評析》，台北，五南圖書公司，2009年1月，初版1刷，108頁。

152 本論述為針對肯塔基適用自己之消滅時效是否違反憲法適當程序條款之問題。486 U.S. 717, 730, "If a thing has been practiced for two hundred tears by common consent, it will need a strong case for the Fourteenth Amendment to affect it." Jackman v. Rosenbaum Co., 260 U.S. 22, 31, 67 L. Ed. 107, 43 S. Ct. 9 (1922).

486 U.S. 717, 730, "State's interest in regulating the workload of its courts and determining when a claim is too stale to be adjudicated certainly suffices to give it legislative jurisdiction to control the remedies available in its courts by imposing statutes of limitations. Moreover, petitioner could in no way have been unfairly surprised by the application to it of a rule that is as old as the Republic. There is, in short, nothing in Kansas action here that is 'arbitrary or unfair,' Shutts III, 472 U.S. at 821-822, and the due process challenge is entirely without substance."

486 U.S. 717, 726, J. Kent, Commentaries on American Law 462-463 (2d ed. 1832): "The period sufficient to constitute a bar to the litigation of sta[1]e demands, is a question of municipal policy and regulation, and one which belongs to the discretion of every government, consulting its own interest and convenience."

153 見陳隆修，《智財法院97重附民1號》，載於〈國際私法：程序正義與實體正義〉，陳隆修、劉仁山、許兆慶合著，五南圖書出版公司，頁180。

寶貴的部分[154]」，於Phillips Petroleum Co. v. Shutts[155]中，美國最高法院不得不宣布集體訴訟制度是美國法於對人訴訟管轄基礎（Pennoyer所代表之「所在權力」原則）在一事不再理（res judicata）原則前讓步之表徵[156]。有鑑於英美兩國之法院氣勢磅礡的於集體訴訟或代表人訴訟中，對「所在權力」（presence power，此為美式名詞）之傳統要求加以讓步，而反之歐盟昧於時代之進化，仍舊要求傳統管轄規則之法律邏輯應被嚴格的遵守，個人不由得感慨萬千的如此論述[157]：「這正是Cardozo J.所論述：『法學的概念甚少，如果曾經有的話，被推展至邏輯的極限，亦即其並非絕對的，而是受到自我設限的常識與公平概念的節制[158]』。同樣的對法律邏輯加以設限，恩師Prof. Graveson於評述附隨問題時亦睿智的如此論述：『這個解決方法的可接受性乃基於邏輯並非判例法的最高價值。英國國際私法實現正義的概括性目的給予邏輯一致性的政策必要的限制。因此於附隨問題上一個英國法院可能判定一個小孩為婚生子女，而於主要問題上卻認定其父母之婚姻為無效[159]，為了達成這個目的可能會使用不同制

---

[154] Class Action Fairness Act of 2005
SEC. 2. FINDINGS AND PURPOSES.
(a) FINDINGS. – Congress finds the following:
(1) Class action lawsuits are an import and valuable part of the legal system when they permit the fair and efficient resolution of legitimate claims of numerous parties by allowing the claims to be aggregated into a single action against a defendant that has allegedly caused harm.

[155] "The burdens by a State upon an absent class-action plaintiff are not of the same order or magnitude as those it places upon an absent defendant." 472 U.S. 797, 808.
"In Hansberry v. Lee, 311 U.S. 32, 40-41 (1940). Which explained that a class or representative suit was an exception to the rule that one could not be bound by judgment in personam unless one was made fully a party in the traditional sense. Ibid., citing Pennoyer v. Neff, 95 U.S. 714 (1878)." 472 U.S. 797, 808.

[156] 見陳隆修，《2005年海牙法院選擇公約評析》，台北，五南圖書公司，2009年1月，初版1刷，130, 261-264頁。

[157] 見陳隆修，《智財法院97重附民1號》，載於〈國際私法：程序正義與實體正義〉，陳隆修、劉仁山、許兆慶合著，五南圖書出版公司，頁126、127。

[158] Boris N. Sokoloff v. The National City Bank of New York, 239 N.Y. 158, 165, "Juridically, a government that is unrecognized may be viewed as no government at all, if the power withholding recognition chooses thus to view it. In practice, however, since juridical conceptions are seldom, if ever, carried to the limit of their logic, the equivalence is not absolute, but is subject to self-imposed limitations of common sense and fairness, as we learned in litigations following our Civil War.

[159] In Hashmi v. Hashmi [19720 Fam. 36.

度的國際私法。判例法的法官將規則視為工具，而非束縛，去提升，而非防止，他們功能的實現。[160]』於此方面有著相同的意義，但更為早遠，更為磅礴，二千多年前我們的祖先教導我們：『人法地，地法人，天法道，道法自然。[161]』於21世紀全球化的實質政策共同核心價值上，『自然』應就是本世紀中符合環保、人權概念而順天應人的為一般舉世所共同接受的全球化『常識』，亦即為擺脫過時的法律邏輯的桎梏而為共同核心『公平正義』之理念。法律邏輯本就是人類為適應環境所創，自然應與時俱進，於二十一世紀瞬息萬變之新環境裡理所當然的會有新法律邏輯產生之需要。」

當如果連ALI/UNIDROIT Principles of Transnational Civil Procedure的s. 2.5都採納英美法的不方便法院法則[162]時，大陸法對於美國及英國制度化的區分境內與境外送達，如果仍然無動於衷那就不符合常識與全球化的生活經驗。如恩師Arthur von Mehren生前所說：「沒有任何國際私法的制度可以逃脫與比較法學科有著一些牽連。[163]」於全球化的市場下，全球化法學的基礎是必然本著比較法為基礎，故而於現代社會「每一種法學」皆必須本著參考其他制度的法律而來。於甚早Justice Story即曾給予

---

160 R.H. Graveson, Conflict of Laws, p.79 (7th ed. 1974), "The acceptability of this solution rests in the fact that logic is not the highest value in the common law. The necessary limits on the policy of logical consistency are imposed by the general purpose of positive justice of English private international law. An English court may thus uphold the legitimacy of children as the subsidiary question and declare null and void the marriage of their parents as the principal question, using different systems of conflict of laws for the purpose. Common law judges regard rules as tools, not as fetters, to promote, not prevent, the fulfillment of their function."

161 老子，道德經，25章，「有物混成，先天地生。寂兮寥兮，獨立而不改，周行而不殆。可以為天下母。吾不知其名，字之曰道。強為之曰大。大曰逝，逝曰遠，遠曰反；故道大、天大、地大、人亦大。域中有四大，而王居其一焉！人法地，地法天，天法道，道法自然。」

162 2.5 Jurisdiction may be declined or the proceeding suspended when the court is manifestly inappropriate relative to another more appropriate court that could exercise jurisdiction.
2.6 The court should decline jurisdiction or suspend the proceeding, when the dispute is previously pending in another court competent to exercise jurisdiction, unless it appears that the dispute will not be fairly, effectively, and expeditiously resolved in that forum.這個條文卻亦有先繫屬優先之意涵。

163 The Role of Comparative Law in the Practice of International Law, in FESTSCHRIFT FÜR KARL H. NEUMAYER 473, 483 (Werner Barfuß et al. eds., 1985), "No system of private international law can escape some involvement with the discipline of comparative law."又見Arthur T. von Mehren, The Contribution of Comparative Law to the Theory and Practice of Private International Law, 26 Am. J. COMP. L. Supp. 31 (1977-1978)

如此之論述：「如果一個文明的國家對於其自己法院之判決欲尋求其他地方對其效力加以認可，則他們應該公正的考慮到其他文明國家之慣例及權利，及於行使正義時國家法律及公共之原則。[164]」因此「如果歐盟對自己法院之判決欲尋求其他地方對其效力加以認可，則應該公正的考慮到其他文明國家之慣例及權利（於此指的應就是英、美對送達境內及境外管轄之區分與限制），及於行使正義時國家法律及公共之原則（於此指的應是其布魯塞爾公約及規則第四條對其他國家人民所行使的不公義過度管轄）。」

隨著市場全球化的趨勢席捲而來，於國際訴訟上如Dicey and Morris所說的平行訴訟所產生的「選購法院」與各國法院的「傾向擴張域外的人或事情的管轄權」，已經成為「最重要的議題」[165]。歐盟布魯塞爾公約的先繫屬優先法則只會造成鼓勵訴訟及刺激當事人先下手選購對自己有利之法院之惡性後果；而其第四條更是公然的鼓吹對外人加以歧視的過度管轄。反之英、美兩國最高法院較近的區分境內與境外送達之作法，不但符合英國判例法一貫的發展歷史，又配合人類現代生活的經驗與常識，更能給予法院裁量的空間以便於個案有例外之情形下達成主持正義的基本司法目的及人權法上之政策。

於評論The Tatry[166]時，對於布魯塞爾規則先繫屬優先及相關訴訟的27、28條，Dicey and Morris有些絕望的如此低調哀吟：「法院認為現今的27及28條是應被適用於英國法院的程序上：這些條文是不論請求的性質或程序上的性質皆應被加以適用，並且即使訴訟程序是為了選購法院的目的而被提起是無關的，就算是被證明真的亦是如此。……結果是在最近幾年內，比起三十年前有更多的否認之訴的被允許提出。[167]」方便法院與

---

164 "If a civilized nation seeks to have the sentences of its own courts held of any validity elsewhere, they ought to have a just regard to the rights and usages of other civilized nations, and the principles of public and national law in the administration of justice" Bradstreet v. Neptune Ins. Co., 3 Sumner, 600, 608.

165 陳隆修，《2005年海牙法院選擇公約評析》，台北，五南圖書公司，2009年1月，初版1刷，147-149頁。

166 Case C-406/92 [1994] E.C.R. I-5439, [1999] Q.B. 515.

167 Dicey and Morris, the Conflict of Laws, 14th ed., p.487, "Likewise, in *The Tatry*, where proceedings

不方便法院的核心目的固然是在主持正義，但於確認「合適」去主持主義的「自然法院」的過程中，經常會排除不自然的選購法院行為及濫用否認之訴（確認之訴）之不適當的行為，而且更會對「例外」、「過度」管轄權的行使加以篩選。因此當於幾年前個人發現英、美法院殊途同歸的將送達境外與境內之管轄加以更為有效的制度化，個人如此喜悅的寫著：「或許是無論於英國方便法院原則之公開確認，或美國於Burnham案對短暫過境管轄之確認，至今皆不滿二十年，個人甚為訝異的發現國際私法界有一個驚天動地的新潮流又鋪天蓋地的席捲而來，而全世界仍然白目的視而不見——英國與美國皆不約而同的對送達至境外加以重新規範，英國以『方便法院』原則而美國以『最低限度關連點』原則為裁量權行使之規範。雖然學理與名稱不同，但基本精神乃是將送達至境外的過度管轄權加以適度合理的規範，如前述歐盟與海牙會議數十年來忙著對過度管轄消極的加以撻伐及限制，然而最近不到二十年來英國及美國卻不約而同的以不同的手段積極的對送達至境外加以制度化及合理化。或許歐陸國家應擺脫消極禁止的態度，而積極的制度化境外送達。個人不知是否有其他衝突法的同僚注意到英、美此處異曲同工之創見，如若是沒有，那麼如同個人近三十年前於實體法方法論一般，於此處管轄權理論驚濤駭浪般澎湃洶湧的新趨勢中，本文很榮幸的於此為衝突法管轄權歷史作一個大時代潮流的新見證。國際私法的江山如此的多嬌，難怪60、70年代的前輩美國選法革命論者

---

were brought in the Netherlands for a declaration that the carrier had no liability for alleged cargo damage, and subsequently an action was brought in England by the cargo owner in respect of damage to the cargo, it was held that what are now Arts 27 and 28 were capable of applying to the proceedings in the English court: the Articles apply without regard to the nature or procedural nature of the claim and it is irrelevant, even if true, that the proceedings were instituted for the purpose of forum shopping. Indeed, Tesauro A.-G. went so far as to characterize proceedings for a declaration of non-liability as being 'generally allowed under the various national procedural laws and [as] entirely legitimate in every respect'. The result is that, in recent years, more actions for negative declaratory relief have been brought and permitted to proceed than was the case thirty years ago. *Messier Dowty v Sabena SA* confirms the Court of Appeal's adoption of the new approach to such claims." [2000] 1 W.L.R. 2040 (CA).見陳隆修，《2005年海牙法院選擇公約評析》，台北，五南圖書公司，2009年1月，初版1刷，128、129頁，有關歐盟先繫屬優先、選購法院、及否認之訴。

直以生死相許。[168]」

對於英國最高法院的明示確認以「方便法院」法則作為允許送達境外的裁量權適用之基礎；而美國最高法院的明示確認即使是短暫過境（transient jurisdiction）亦是滿足憲法適當程序條款的要求[169]，因此依據適當程序條款而來的「最低限度關連點」之限制標準自然於邏輯上只能適用於境外被送達之被告。因此基於英國及美國近二十多年來其最高法院對允許送達境外的「例外」或「過度」管轄權行使適用之基礎或限制的加以制度化及合理化，個人即對國際訴訟管轄權行使之基礎或限制於前幾年嘗試著提出看似大膽之創新建議[170]。但事實上個人拒絕承認這個「建議」有任何創新之處。如前述Cheshire and North已陳述英國現今於裁量權之行使上是如下：「現在所已經被見證的是允許將訴訟的文件送達至境外的裁量權是依據方便法院的基礎而被加以行使。另外亦有著裁量權於有些特定之情形下依不方便法院之基礎（亦即特別是當英國不是審理案件之合適法院時）去停止訴訟之進行[171]。」個人所提之「建議」事實上是如Cheshire and North之論述一般，只是單純的對英國最高法院（及或許個人亦加上美國最高法院）較近之判例法所代表之法律事實加以整編而已。

---

168 陳隆修、許兆慶、林恩瑋、李瑞生四人合著，《國際私法—管轄與選法理論之交錯》，台北，五南圖書公司，2009年3月，初版1刷，204、205頁。

169 Burnham v. Superior Court, 495 U.S. 604, JUSTICE SCALIA, "The short of the matter is that jurisdiction based on physical presence alone constitutes due process because it is one of the continuing traditions of our legal system that define the due process standard of 'traditional notions of fair play and substantial justice.' That standard was developed by analogy to 'physical presence,' and it would be perverse to say it could now be turned against that touchstone of jurisdiction." JUSTICE BRENNAN, "For these reasons, as a rule the exercise of personal jurisdiction over a defendant based on his voluntary presence in the forum will satisfy the requirements of due process."如個人前述「自願」出現於法院地之要件是不具有重大的意義的，因為如果以詐欺或脅迫之手段誘導被告之出現於法院地是不具有法律上之效力的，見陳隆修，《國際私法管轄權評論》，台北，五南圖書公司，民國75年11月，初版，110頁。

170 陳隆修、許兆慶、林恩瑋、李瑞生四人合著，《國際私法—管轄與選法理論之交錯》，台北，五南圖書公司，2009年3月，初版1刷，248頁。

171 P M North, JJ Fawcett, Cheshire and North's Private International Law, 13th ed., 334, "It has already been seen that the discretionary power to allow service of a claim form out of the jurisdiction is exercised on the basis of form conveniens. There is also a discretion to stay action on the basis of forum non conveniens (ie where England is not the appropriate forum for trial) in certain specific situations. 14th ed., p. 426.

五、全球化之共同核心管轄基礎

國際私法早期之重心雖是在各國管轄權於對人及對物訴訟上之確認，但是不可否認的一般普遍的認為國際管轄是如愛麗絲於夢幻仙境（Alice-in-Wonderland）般的不可捉摸及確認。基於全球化之潮流下，本著較近的英、美最高法院之判例法，個人認為21世紀的國際管轄規則已存在著一個既有的（至少於英美）共同核心實體政策。因此幾年前本著這個既存的全球化管轄規則上的實體（或實質）共同核心基本政策，個人提出對這個既存的事實（至少於英美）應加以明確的追認之建議[172]：**「於民商管轄規則上，歐盟Council Regulation No.44/2001之第5條、1999海牙草約、美國各州送達境外被告之長手法規及英國法院允許送達境外被告之R.S.C. Order 11, rule 1 (1)（即現今之1998 C.R. s. 6. 20），與大陸法各國之國內管轄規則相去並不遠，故個人建議於行使民商管轄權時[173]：各國仍得以既有的國內或國際管轄規則為基礎（英美則仍為所在權力理論**

---

[172] 陳隆修、許兆慶、林恩瑋、李瑞生四人合著，《國際私法—管轄與選法理論之交錯》，台北，五南圖書公司，2009年3月，初版1刷，見「序言」及248頁。

[173] 有關婚姻案件管轄基礎之建議，見陳隆修、許兆慶、林恩瑋、李瑞生四人合著，《國際私法-管轄與選法理論之交錯》，台北，五南圖書公司，2009年3月，初版1刷，251、252頁。「全世界各國立法程序大部甚為曠日廢時工程浩大，我國如欲為國際婚姻事件訂立管轄規則之法律，可能緩不濟急。更重要的乃是國際私法近年變化甚大，瞬息萬變，於未來不可預測之情形下，不必冒著訂立死硬法規之風險，不如本著既有的國內民事訴訟規則，授權給法院『司法立法』。既然現今文明國家對離婚大都不採過失主義，而且相關之國際公約對離婚長久以來接秉持著尊重當事人意願之原則，個人建議民訴第568條『訴之原因事實發生地』，於國際案件上或許可以將之擴大解釋為『事實發生地即為當世人慣常生活所在地』，亦即原因事實發生地即為雙方當事人任何一方之慣居地。由現實生活而言，原因事實自然發生於當事人日常生活之慣居地。如此以雙方當事人任何一方之慣居地為離婚法院之管轄基礎，不但配合我國民訴第568條，而且更重要的乃是與歐洲國家之國際私法與歐盟No. 2201/2003規則第3條第1項(a)款配合。我國法院於國際離婚案件之判決既本著國際上所通行之管轄基礎而來，則該判決於國際社會自然會被加以認定。另由於我國民法仍規定夫妻需有同一住所，故民訴第568條所規定之『夫妻住所地』自然符合國際私法上一般所謂『婚姻住所地』（『matrimonial domicile』）之概念。所謂『matrimonial domicile』並非為一正式嚴肅之法律概念，故甚少有判例專門為其下定義，一般所指應是於婚姻生活持續中夫妻之住所皆在同一地之義。我國民訴第568條之夫妻住所地自然符合這個概念。婚姻住所地自然較慣居地為一更嚴格之離婚管轄基礎，不但英國、美國皆認可此一管轄基礎，亦可比擬配合歐盟No.2201/2003規則第3條第1項(b)款之類似規定，於國際上亦並非為一唐突之規則，故個人認為我國法院仍可適用此一規定於國際離婚案件上。
故在我國目前尚無立法之情形下，個人建議我國應本著民訴第568條之規定，而以婚姻住所地及夫妻任何一方之慣居地為國際離婚案件之管轄基礎。或者秉持我國傳統上保護婦女之基本政策，亦不妨將慣居地侷限於被告配偶之慣居地。」

及送達境外之規則）。但訴訟之通知若於境內已適當的送達給被告，或被告承認法院之管轄權時，法院得以『不方便法院』法則為拒絕或停止訴訟裁量之依據（例如訴因與法院地沒有合理之牽連時）；而若法院欲允許送達至境外時，首先必須認知此為一種例外之過度管轄，其判決有可能不為外國法院所承認，應以『方便法院』法則來確認法院是否為合適、自然之管轄法院以作為允許送達境外之適用基礎（例如為了公平正義之目的或訴因與法院地有強烈之牽連時）。」但是有鑑於美國法院的利用「不方便法院」法則去剝奪第三世界弱勢人民人權法上保障的訴訟權及財產法，個人於此必須不厭其煩的再次重申英國判例法中之核心超越性考量—「conveniens」並不是指「方便」之意[174]，而是合適去達成正義之目的之意。

英國司法制度自The Spiliada[175]後，停止英國法院訴訟程序之裁量權適用之基礎，由原先的「困擾性」或「壓迫性」法則變為「不方便法院」法則；而法院於允許送達境外之「過度」或「例外」管轄權之裁量權適用之基礎上，亦即於R.S.C. Order 11, rule 1(1)（現今1998 C.P.R. s. 6.20）之規定上正式的冠予「方便法院」之說詞。「方便法院」法則與「不方便法院」法則雖然大致上是本著「合適去達成正義之目的之審理案件之法院」之相同基礎，但仍是一體之兩面，目前仍是無法將兩種法則合而為一。個人曾如此加以論述[176]：「基於方便法院之原則而將通知送達至境外，與基於不方便法院之原則於通知送達至境內後方停止訴訟，兩個裁量權行使的裁量因素、內容、甚至判例基本上皆相似，故而個人前述稱之為一體之兩面，但仍有相異之處。首先送達至境外基本上就被認為是過度管轄[177]，而於不方便法院之情況基本上法院是已有管轄權之後才去裁量是否停止管轄。另外於方便法院之情況下，舉證責任在於原告，並且於請求之

174 Dicey and Morris, the Conflict of Laws, 14th ed., p. 465, "conveniens does not mean 'convenient': *see The Atlantic Star* [1974] A.C. 436, 475; *GAF Corp v Amchem Products Inc* [1975] 1 Lloyd's Rep. 601, 607; *Spiliada Maritime Corp v Cansulex Ltd* [1987] A.C. 460, 474-475."

175 [1987] AC 460.

176 陳隆修、許兆慶、林恩瑋、李瑞生四人合著，《國際私法—管轄與選法理論之交錯》，台北，五南圖書公司，2009年3月，初版1刷，203、204頁。

177 Spiliada Maritime Corpn v. Consulex Ltd [1987] AC 460 at 481.

階段因不須通知他方，故必須完全而且公平的陳述[178]；而於不方便法院的情況，至少於第一階段舉證在於不方便法院的被告。[179]」

於領導案例（the leading case）Spiliada Maritime Corp v Consulex Ltd[180]中，英國最高法院對這個判例法的規則加以定義，認定英國法院是較其他有管轄權的外國法院「清楚或明顯的合適」[181]，或認定其他法院為「表面上看起來是審理該訴訟為清楚的更合適之地。[182]」雖然這個標準所尋找的是較其他法院「清楚的更為合適」之法院，而非尋找「自然法院」（the natural forum）。但如Dicey and Morris所說：「但是必須承認的是『自然法院』之名詞已經成為不可抗拒，並且這個方便的簡稱已經被法院於比較一個法院與爭執間之關連的相關強度時所現今例常的使用著。[183]」於不方便法院法則被適用來決定是否停止英國之訴訟時，於The Spiliada中Lord Goff說：「……如果有著其他表面上是清楚的更合適去審理訴訟的法院是存在的，通常法院會允許訴訟的停止，除非有著基於正義的理由要求訴訟的停止是仍然不應該被允許的情形。[184]」故而於主張基於不方便法院而停止訴訟時，通常於第一階段被告須證明有著清楚的更合適的有管轄權的外國法院外；於第二階段法院必須考慮到是否為了正義的需求，停止訴訟之請求應被駁回，此時原告須證明其於英國提起訴訟之正當性，故而第二階段的舉證責任在於原告[185]。

---

178 Kuwait Oil Co. (KSC) v. Idemitsu Tankers KK, The Hida Maru [1981] 2 Lloyd's Rep 510.另外在對法律解釋有疑問時，應以對被告有利之方式解決。

179 The Spiliada, [1987] AC 460, at 474.

180 [1987] A.C. 460.

181 同上，p.477, "clearly or distinctly more appropriate".

182 同上，p.478, "which prima facie is clearly more appropriate for the trial of the action"

183 Dicey and Morris, the Conflict of Laws, 14th ed., p. 464, But it must be acknowledged that the terminology of 'the natural forum' has become irresistible, and that this convenient shorthand is now routinely used by the courts in comparing the relative strengths of connection between a court and a dispute.

184 The Spiliada [1987] AC 460 at 476, Lord Goff: "...if there is some other available forum which prima facie is clearly more appropriate for the trial of the action, it will ordinarily grant a stay unless there are circumstance by reason of which justice requires that a stay should nevertheless not be granted."

185 Connelly v. RTZ Corpn. Plc [1998] AC 854, HL.又「不方便法院」法則第一階段與第二階段之區別，見陳隆修、許兆慶、林恩瑋、李瑞生四人合著，《國際私法—管轄與選法理論之交錯》，台北，五南圖書公司，2009年3月，初版1刷，207-215頁。

而如前述送達境外之管轄基本上是被視為「過度」或「例外」之管轄，Civil Procedure Rules 1998 s. 6.20(3)(a)規定當事人間必須有一個真正的爭點合理的需要法院去審理[186]。而s. 6.21(1)(b)則規定原告須證明其請求有著合理的勝訴機會[187]。送達境外管轄裁量權之行使是以「方便法院」法則為適用之基礎，更為s. 6.21（2A）所明白的規定：「除非法院能被說服英格蘭與威爾斯是提出請求之合適的地方，法院是不會給予允許（送達境外）。[188]」對於現今送達境外的方便法院法則，Dicey and Morris綜合判例法而陳述：「請求人必須可以顯示出為何訴訟程序的通知應該被允許送達給一個外國被告，並且於考慮這個問題時法院應該考慮爭執的性質，所牽連的法律與實際上之問題，相關之問題例如當地情況之認知、證人及他們證據的可提供性、及費用。[189]」而Scott L.J.於判例法中早

---

[186] (3) a claim is made against someone on whom the claim form has been or will be served and—
(a) there is between the claimant and that person a real issue which it is reasonable for the court to try.
對於當事人間之「真正爭點」，個人以前於陳隆修、許兆慶、林恩瑋、李瑞生四人合著，《國際私法—管轄與選法理論之交錯》，台北，五南圖書公司，2009年3月，初版1刷，197頁中對英國判例法曾加以論述。「首先要決定英國法院是否為方便法院之前，原告必須先證明有著實體上嚴重的爭點（serious issue on the merits）應被審判，而該爭點是基於書面證據所顯現出來的重大法律、事實、或兩者都有的重大問題而原告真誠的希望被加以審判。」Seaconsar Far East Ltd v. Bank Markazi Jomhouri Islami Iran [1994] 1 AC 438.「此時於確認法院對這個案件之管轄權階段，為了證明於實體上有嚴重之爭點，選法規則之問題可能被提出討論。」於Metall and Rohstoff AG v. Donaldson Lufkin and Jenrette Inc, [1990] 1 QB 391，為了決定原告是否於實體上能建立爭點，英國上訴法院採用英國侵權法選法規則。「由此點可見法國人所謂『即刻適用法』不適用一般選法規則之論點似乎應略加修正；另外國內有人主張定性應本於原告之聲明而來，於邏輯上之次序可能亦有些問題。」因為全世界文明國家無論於國內或國際案件，通常必須於被告放棄抗辯或抗辯失敗後管轄權之爭議才能被加以確定，這點於國際管轄特別具有重要性。「另外歐盟Council Regulation (EC) No. 44/2001 Article 27及1999 Draft Hague Convention on Jurisdiction Article 21皆採相同訴因主義，故與國內此等獨特創見不合，但應注意的是英國採用的卻是更鬆的相同issue或dispute.」

[187] (b) that the claimant believes that his claim has a reasonable prospect of success.

[188] (2A) The court will not give permission unless satisfied that England and Wales is the proper place in which to bring the claim.

[189] Dicey and Morris, the Conflict of Laws, 14th ed., p.488, "The modern law on the role of *forum conveniens* in service out of the jurisdiction cases is to be found in the speeches of Lord Wilberforce in *Amin Rasheed Shipping Corp v Kuwait Insurance Co* and of Lord Goff of Chieveley in *Spiliada Maritime Corp v Cansulex Ltd*. The effect of the latter decision was to endorse Lord Wilberforce's statement of principle that in cases governed by Rule 27 the claimant must show good reason why service of process on a foreign defendant should be permitted, and in considering this question the court must take into account the nature of the dispute, the legal and practical issues involved, such questions as local knowledge, availability of witnesses and their evidence, and expense." [1984] A.C. 50, 72. [1987] A.C. 460, 478-482.

就表示方便法院與停止訴訟之裁量無關[190]，對於送達境外的Order 11規則之案件則如此論述：「如果訴因的真實事實是屬於某一外國，而非本國，並且尤其是當這是一個問題……於外國可能會被更好的加以審判時，（送達境外）許可是不應被允許的。[191]」

同樣的個人以前亦如此評述[192]：「欲主張方便法院時，原告必須證明英國為合適審判之法院（appropriate forum）[193]。此時法院會注意爭執的性質，及法律上和實際上的問題[194]，例如外國被告於英國訴訟之費用及便利之問題[195]，及當事人與訴因跟其他外國法院之關係[196]等。英國法如是準據法，則有利於英國法院被認定為方便法院[197]，但如會造成同樣當事人同樣的爭點（issue）於英國與其他國家同時進行訴訟，則構成英國法院拒絕將訴訟之通知送達境外之理由[198]。」

因為有關「方便法院」與「不方便法院」兩個法則的較為條理性與系統性的介紹，個人以前即有較為詳細的論述[199]，故於此不再贅述，但無疑的兩個法則的核心重點皆是於確認「自然」、「合適」去處理案件之法院。Cheshire and North如此論述[200]：「自從MacShannon後『自然法

[190] *St Pierre v South American Stores Ltd* [1936] 1 K.B. 382 (CA).

[191] *Kroch v Rossell et Cie* [1937] 1 All E.R. 725, 731 (CA), "if the reality of the cause of action is one which belongs to a foreign country, and not to this country, and above all, where it is a question which probably would be better tried …. in the foreign country, leave ought not to be granted."

[192] 陳隆修、許兆慶、林恩瑋、李瑞生四人合著，《國際私法—管轄與選法理論之交錯》，台北，五南圖書公司，2009年3月，初版1刷，198頁。

[193] ISC v. Guerin [1992] 2 Lloyd's Rep 430.

[194] Amin Rasheed Shipping Corpn v. Kuwait Insurance Co., [1984] AC 50.

[195] Société Général de Paris v. Dreyfus Bro. (1885) 29 Ch. D 239.

[196] Kroch v. Rossel et Cie [1937] 1 All ER 725.

[197] Cordoba Shipping Co Ltd v. National State Bank, Elizabeth, New Jersey, The Albaforth [1984] 2 Lloyd's Rep 91.

[198] The Hagen [1908] p.189.見陳隆修，《國際私法管轄權評論》，台北，五南圖書公司，民國75年11月，初版，46頁。

[199] 陳隆修、許兆慶、林恩瑋、李瑞生四人合著，《國際私法—管轄與選法理論之交錯》，台北，五南圖書公司，2009年3月，初版1刷，195-215頁。

[200] P M North, JJ Fawcett, Cheshire and North's Private International Law, 13th ed., pp.338,339, The term "natural forum" has frequently been employed since MacShannon. Lord Keith in that case said that it refereed to the country with which the action has the most real and substantial connection. Although in theory this raises the question of whether the issue of litigational convenience is given as much emphasis under the notion of the "natural forum" as it is given under the notion of appropriateness, it appears,

院』的名詞就已經經常被引用。Lord Keith在那個案件中說它是指與案件有著最真實與重大關連的國家[201]。雖然於理論上這引起一個問題，亦即於有關訴訟便利之問題，於『自然法院』之概念下是否如同於合適之概念下被給予同樣的重視，但於實際上看起來『自然法院』與『合適的法院』是相同意義的被使用著。[202]」而Lord Goff於Spiliada[203]中解釋法院於決定外國法院是否為清楚的更合適的法院，亦是以Lord Keith於自然法院（natural forum）之定義為基礎。於Spiliada[204]中Lord Templeman（而Lord Griffiths及Lord Mackay皆加以認同）說法院於決定一個法院是否較其他法院為合適之法院所應考慮之因素很多，而是否應於英國或外國法院審理該案是由第一審的法官先行決定。其希望法院只是參考Lord Goff所作成之論述而非根據其他事實而來之其他決定，並且其認知當事人之提議是應於數小時內而非數天內被決定。

雖然於Amin Rasheed Shipping Corp v Kuwait Insurance Co中英國最高法院認為法院不會「著手去比較相對於比起其他國家的法院，一個國家法院的程序、或方法、或名譽、或地位[205]」。故而相對於英國審判前之

---

in practice, that the terms "natural forum" and "appropriate forum" are used synonymously. Rockware Glass Ltd. v. MacShannon [1978] AC 795. 又見14th ed., p. 431. In ascertaining whether there is a clearly more appropriate forum abroad, the search is for the country which the action has the most real and substantrial connection. The court will look for connecting factors "and these will include not only factors affecting convenience or expense (such as availability of witnesses), but also other factors such as the law governing the relevant transaction ..., and the place where the parties respectively reside or carry on business". *Spiliada Maritime Corpn v Cansulex* Ltd [1987] AC 460 at 478.

201 [1978] AC 795 at 829. See also *The Abidin Daver* [1987] AC 398 at 415 (Lord Keith); *The Forum Craftsman* [1984] 2 Lloyd's Rep 102 at 108 (Sheen J); affd by the Court of Appeal [1985] 1 Lloyd's Rep 291.

202 See *Rockware Glass Ltd v MacShannon* [1978] AC 795 at 812 (per Lord Diplock); *see also Trendtex Trading Corpn v Crédit Suisse* [1980] 3 All ER 721 at 734; *European Asian Bank AG v Punjab and Sind Bank* [1982] 2 Lloyd's Rep 356 at 364.

203 [1987] AC 460 at 477-478.

204 [1987] A.C. at 465. *The Nile Rhapsody* [1994] 1 Lloyd's Rep. 383, 388 (CA); *Haji-Ioannou v Frangos* [1999] 2 Lloyd's Rep. 337, 356 (CA); *Askin v Absa Bank* [1999] I.L.Pr. 471, 473 (CA).

205 "to embark upon a comparison of the procedures, or methods, or reputation or standing of the courts of one country as compared with those of another". *Amin Rasheed Corpn v Kuwait Insurance Co* [1984] AC 50 at 72 (per Lord Wilberforce), at 67 (per Lord Diplock). *Jayaretnam v Mahmood* (1992) Times, May 21; *New Hampshire Insurance Co v Strabag Bau AG* [1992] 1 Lloyd's Rep 361 at 371; *Bank of Baroda v Vysya Bank Ltd* [1994] 2 Lloyd's Rep 87 at 98; *Trade Indemnity v Försäkrings AB Njord* [1995]

事實調查，美國是較為廣泛而大陸法是較為限縮，但於The Abidin Daver[206]中英國最高法院認為於行使裁量權時，通常不合適去比較於同一類似案件於英國法院與不同程序之制度中之國家的法院所能取得正義的品質。而於Spiliada[207]中Lord Goff認為如果一個當事人是於實際上被強迫去接受所被相當認可之制度之一的程序法，則不能說不正義的事情已被作成。於Connelly v. RTZ Corpn. Plc[208]中Lord Goff又對於Spiliada中之經典論述再加以闡述如下：「如果於外國有一個清楚的更為合適的法院已經被確認出來，通常而言即使是於某些方面對原告而言較其於英國法院為不利，其仍是應接受其所能找到有管轄權之法院。[209]」

但是判例法曾認定外國法院經過十年的拖延仍未進入審判程序的訴訟是不尋常的遲延，因此構成正義的拒絕[210]；同樣的外國法院所給予的低到可笑的限制賠償額亦是構成正義的拒絕[211]。如果原告依被認定之準據法可能會有一個請求權，而其卻被要求去於會簡單的拒絕其請求之外國法院起訴，這是被認為會對正義之達成沒有助益[212]。法院亦會考慮到例如因司法的不獨立而無法於外國達成正義之情形[213]，但是提出主張的當事人所呈現的證據若「只是如報紙或政治性之評論」[214]，則會受到強烈的質疑，故必須為有力之證據[215]。另外於英國訴訟程序中的原告若返回另一個有管轄權

1 All ER 796 at 809.

206 [1984] A.C. 398.

207 [1987] A.C. at 482,483,其引用Trendtex Trading Corp v Crédit Suisse [1982] A.C. 679，於該案件中瑞士法院雖然沒有如英國法院般的有著廣泛的審判前事實調查庭，英國法院仍停止訴訟程序。

208 [1998] AC 854, HL.

209 同上，872, “if a clearly more appropriate forum overseas has been identified, generally speaking the plaintiff will have to take that forum as he finds it, even if it is in certain respects less advantageous to him than the English forum”.

210 *The Vishva Ajay* [1989] 2 Lloyd’s Rep 558 at 560. 又見*Konamaneni v Rolls-Royce International Industrial Power (India) Ltd* [2002] 1 W.L.R. 1269; XN *Corp Ltd v Point of Sale Ltd* [2001] I.L.Pr. 525.

211 *BMG Trading Ltd v A S Mckay* [1998] IL Pr 691; *The Adhiguna Meranti* [1998] 1 Lloyd’s Rep 384 at 395-396, *Hong Kong Court of Appeal; The Falstria* [1988] 1 Lloyd’s Rep 495.

212 *Banco Atlantico SA v British Bank of the Middle East* [1990] 2 Lloyd’s Rep 504 at 509.

213 *The Abidin Daver* [1984] AC 398 at 411. *Muduroglu Ltd v TC Ziraat Bankasi* [1986] QB 1225, [1986] 3 All ER 682, CA. *Middle East Banking Co SA v Al-Haddad* (1990) 70 OR (2d) 97.

214 “no more than press or political comment”, *Dornoch Ltd v Mauritius Union Assurance Co Ltd* [2005] EWHC 1887 (Comm.).

215 即使雙方當事人皆為外國人，並且即使他們權利義務的準據法為外國法，由於原告可能基於政

的外國法院其可能會遭受囚禁時，停止英國訴訟程序是被認為不符合正義的[216]。

Dicey and Morris如此論述[217]：「於Spiliada中已見證了Lord Goff of Chieveley表示英國法院應去尋找與爭執有著最真實與重大關連之法院，並且他特別指出影響便利或費用（例如證人的可利用性）之因素，及包含相關行為之準據法等其他因素。[218]」「如果法律爭點是相當直接，或如果（管轄權）有競爭性的法院是有著重大相同的國內法[219]，去辨識出應適用的準據法是等於為幾乎沒有意義的因素[220]。但是如果法律問題是複雜，或

治或其他理由無法於外國接受公平的審判，法院於此情形下即可能允許送達境外。*Oppenheimer v Louis Rosenthal and Co AG* [1937] 1 All ER 23.但是這種證詞必須具有高度標準的說服力（a high standard of cogency），*International Marine Services Inc v National Bank of Fujairah* [1997] IL Pr 468 at 470, CA.基於同樣的理念，個人於陳隆修、許兆慶、林恩瑋、李瑞生四人合著，《國際私法-管轄與選法理論之交錯》，台北，五南圖書公司，2009年3月，初版1刷，232頁所論及之台中地院94年家訴字253號民事裁定，及陳隆修，《2005年海牙法院選擇公約評析》，台北，五南圖書公司，2009年1月，初版1刷，290、291頁中所述日本名古屋裁判所平成8（ワ）1433與平成7（ワ）4179號有關華航名古屋空難事件之判決，個人即是本著英國判例法傳統上主持正義之目的，而要求台灣法院重新接受案件之管轄去達成個案正義。

216 *Purcell v Khayat* (1987) Times, 23 November.

217 Dicey and Morris, the Conflict of Laws, 14th ed., p.478, "It has been seen that in *Spiliada* Lord Goff of Chieveley indicated that the English court should look for the forum with which the dispute had the most real and substantial connection, and he referred in particular to factors affecting convenience or expense (such as availability of witnesses) and other factors including the law governing the relevant transaction." "If the legal issues are straightforward, or if the competing fora have domestic laws which are substantially similar, the identity of the governing law will be a factor of rather littler significance. But if the legal issues are complex, or legal systems very different, the general principle that a court applies its own law more reliably than does a foreign court will help to point to the more appropriate forum, whether English or foreign."

218 [1987] A.C. at 478. See also The Elli 2 [1985] 1 Lloyd's Rep. 107; *MacSteel Commercial Holdings (Pty) Ltd v Thermasteel (Canada) Ltd* [1996] C.L.C. 1403 (CA).

219 *Marconi Communications International Ltd v PT Pan Indonesia Bank Ltd TBK* [2004] EWHC 129 (Comm.), [2004] 1 Lloyd's Rep. 594; affirmed [2005] EWCA Civ. 422, [2005] 2 All E.R. (Comm.) 325.

220 這個見解為判例法所引用，見*Navigators' Insurance Co v Atlantic Methanol Production Co LLC* [2003] EWHC 1706 (Comm.). at [48]. cf. *The Rothnie* [1996] 2 Lloyd's Rep. 206.故而如果在沒有重大不同之影響下，「去辨識出應適用的準據法是幾乎沒有意義的因素」。個人早期於陳隆修，《比較國際私法》，台北，五南圖書公司，78年10月，初版，33頁中曾對附帶問題加以論述。依一般英國看法可能分為三種要件：「其之所以被稱為附帶問題，乃因其雖可構成一獨立之問題，但於本案件中，乃附帶於主要問題而產生。又所以被稱為先決問題，乃因其必須先於主要問題而被解決。一案件中欲造成有先決問題之情形必須滿足三要件。第一、主要問題必須依法院地之國際私法，準據法為外國之法律。第二、附帶之問題牽連外國因素，且可為獨立之問題，並有其獨自之法律選擇法則（choice-of-law rule）。第三、亦為最重要之點，依法院地之國際私法該附帶問題之結果，必須與該主要問題準據法之國際私法對該附帶問題之結果，有著不同看法。第三點乃為自然之要件，蓋實際上自然亦必須上述兩種法律之國際私法對該附帶問題

法律制度是非常不同，那麼相較於一個外國法院，法院適用自己的法律是較為可信賴的基本原則，是對尋找更合適的法院是有助益的，無論該法院是英國或外國法院。[221]」如英國判例法所論述，適用自己法院地法是較為可信賴為「一種於常識上之事情」[222]。並且如果法律被引用錯誤時，於所適用之準據法之法院上訴是遠較為容易[223]。

當於外國法院會為了適用自己之公共政策或法律而無視於所被明示為準據法之英國法時，英國法院會視外國法院為無法給予公平之審判。於Coast Lines Ltd v Hudig & Veder Chartering NV中，英國上訴法院即認為外國法院會「被迫去適用一個違反商業人士一般的認知之法律」[224]，故

有著不同之看法，方會產生問題。」但亦有大陸法同僚認為應為四要件，可能德國同僚認為所適用之準據法不同亦甚為重要，但個人認為畫蛇添足。因為對當事人而言結果既然一致，法律邏輯則變得無關緊要。對大陸法而言外國法律雖被視為法律而加以適用，但大陸法並不如英美法一般給予判例之拘束性。依英美法外國法是以事實而被加以適用，故亦無拘束力。

221 Charm Maritime Inc v kyriakou [1987] 1 Lloyd's Rep. 433 (CA); Muduroglu Ltd v TC Ziraat Bankasi [1986] Q.B. 1225, 1246 (CA); El du Pont de Nemours & Co v Agnew [1987] 2 Lloyd's Rep. 585 (CA); Standard Steamship Owners' Protection and Indemnity Association (Bermuda) Ltd v Gann [1992] 2 Lloyd's Rep. 528. The Varna (No. 2) [1994] 2 Lloyd's Rep. 41.

222 *The Eleftheria* [1970] p. 94, 105 ("a matter of common sense").

223 既然這是「一種於常識上之事情」，除了有關上訴外，美國法律協會的Restatement (Second) of Conflict of Laws §85 (1971)的comment (a)及案例1及2亦與英國判例法相似的作出下列評論："If the plaintiff could conveniently bring suit against the defendant in the state of the applicable law, the court will usually dismiss the action if it believes that the relief which it could grant is substantially different from the relief which would be obtained in the latter state. So if the only relief which the forum could grant is a lump sum judgment, whereas in the state of the applicable law the defendant would be ordered to make payment in periodic installments whose amount would be dependent in part upon subsequent events, the forum would probably dismiss the action if jurisdiction could be obtained over the defendant in the state of the applicable law and if the plaintiff could bring suit there without undue inconvenience to himself (see Illustration 1). Similarly, the suit might be dismissed if the courts of the state of the applicable law are open to the plaintiff and if the relief sought is of a kind which is novel to the forum and which would depend in its amount largely upon the discretion of the court (see Illustration 2). In such a case, the court might feel that since any judgment it might grant would probably differ considerably in amount from one rendered in the state of the applicable law, justice would better be served by relegating the plaintiff to the courts of the latter state. On the other hand, the court would probably entertain the action in such a case, if, for some reason, it would either be impossible or unduly burdensome for the plaintiff to bring suit in the state of the applicable law. If the alternative forum readily accessible to the plaintiff is not in the state of the applicable law, the court might also dismiss the action if this other forum would be in a better position to render relief similar to that which would be granted in the state of the applicable law."故而於今日全球化的潮流下，如comment (a)所作之論述平行訴訟於全球化法學之核心政策乃在「更好的達成正義」，這是與上述英國判例法一致的。

224 "compelled to apply a law which is contrary to the general understanding of commercial men" [1972] 2 QB 34, 45.又見*Sawyer v Atari Interactive Inc* [2005] EWHC 2351 (Ch.), [2006] I.L.Pr. 129, at [59];

而不是公平的審判地。或者是於有關英國公共政策時，外國法院是否能合適之法院亦可能被懷疑。於El du Pont de Nemours & Co v Agnew中，是有關英國契約效力中公共政策之問題，任何外國法官皆被質疑「是否有信心的能真誠的達成正確的答案」[225]。另外應注意的是台灣與大陸於海商案件上所引用的國際公約經常不同，導致台灣可能甚至不承認大陸之判決。依英國判例法由於各國適用之國際公約不同，導致有些國家對於海商請求權的損害賠償之限制額度較英國為低，這種情形並不能構成外國審判不符合正義之情形[226]。既然仍有其他公約之存在，就表示英國所適用之公約因此並非一個國際所共同認可之公約，亦因此而無法有一個符合正義的客觀標準。另外有一個所謂的「Cambridgeshire factor」，亦即若有法院對一特定種類之複雜問題已有著解決問題之專業知識，則允許該法院去處理該案件是符合正義的利益，並且於特殊之情形下或許可能對自然法院之確認有影響[227]。但如前述英國最高法院已表示不會「著手去比較相對於比起其他國家的法院，一個國家法院的程序、或方法、或名譽、或地位」。故而Dicey and Morris陳述：「但是接受這種抗辯的案例是非常稀少的。[228]」可是英國上訴法院（court of Appeal）仍於決定方便法院時要求其他法院必須維持最低限度標準的正義[229]，並且警告：「法院於遵循其作法時不可太脫離俗世……世界上有其他的地區，在那裡事情是極度糟糕的。[230]」即

Cadre SA v Astra Asigurari SA [2005] EWHC 2504 (Comm.). See also The Magnum [1989] 1 Lloyd's Rep. 47. Contrast Nima SARL v Deves Public Insurance Co Ltd (The Prestrioka) [2002] EWCA Civ. 1132, [2003] 2 Lloyd's Rep. 327.

225 "could conscientiously resolve with any confidence that he was reaching a correct answer", [1987] 2 Lloyd's Rep. 585, 595; *cf. Mitsubishi Corp v Alafouzos* [1988] 1 Lloyd's Rep. 191. cf. *Britannia Steamship Insurance Association v Ausonia Assicurazioni SpA* [1984] 2 Lloyd's Rep. 98 (CA); *Midland Bank Plc v Laker Airways Ltd* [1986] Q.B. 689 (CA); *Banco Atlantico SA v British Bank of the Middle East* [1990] 2 Lloyd's Rep. 504. *Irish Shipping Ltd v Commercial Union Assurance Co Plc* [1991] 2 Q.B. 206, 229-230 (CA).

226 *Herceg Novi v Ming Galaxy* [1998] 4 All ER 238, CA.

227 Spiliada Maritime Corpn v. Cansulex Ltd [1987] AC 460, 484-486.

228 Dicey and Morris, the Conflict of Laws, 14th ed., p.480, note 34, "where it is referred to as the 'Cambridgeshire factor', after the ship which gave its name to the earlier litigation. But examples of cases in which this argument has been accepted are extremely rare."

229 Amin Rasheed Shipping Corpn v. Kuwait Insurance Co., [1984] AC 50 at 67.

230 Muduroglu Ltd v. TC Ziraat Bankasi [1986] QB 1225 at 1248, "the court must not be too unworldly in

使「事情是極度糟糕」的情況沒有發生，但是於現代化複雜的社會裡，對於海商、保險、金融等類型的案件，有些國家的法院是沒有「信心的能真誠的達成正確的答案」，這是「一種於常識上的事情」。故而於Islamic Arab Insurance Co v Sandi Egyptian American Reinsurance Co中，沙烏地阿拉伯於有關保險之事項上並沒專業法庭及律師，而英國卻有，故被認為若審判於該地舉行可能會產生不正義之後果[231]。

its approach ... there are other parts of the world where things are badly wrong."

[231] [1987] 1 Lloyd's Rep 315 at 319-320.

第3章 屏東地院92重訴字4號裁定——江春水向東流

台灣屏東地院92重訴字第4號裁定為因外國輪船於屏東墾丁外海失事而污染海岸之事件，由環保署於屏東地院提起訴訟之案件。原告主張：「民國90年1月14日於屏東縣墾丁外海地區，因船長即被告Evangelos Lazaridis、輪機長及被告Vasileios Sardis之過失致阿瑪斯號船舶發生擱淺及漏油事故，造成原告之損害，又船舶所有權人即被告Nissos Amorgos Shipping Corporation（下稱AMORGOS）應就船長與輪機長所造成之損害負連帶賠償責任，又被告Gard則因承保阿瑪斯號船東責任，亦得直接向被告Gard訴請賠償，爰依海洋污染防治法（下稱海污法）第33條向被告Amorgos等三人請求賠償，同法第34條向被告Gard訴請賠償，又原告請求係以〔侵權行為〕為請求權基礎，主張本件事故發生於本院所轄屏東縣墾丁外海，故依民事訴訟法第15條之規定，本院應有管轄權云云。」法院認定侵權行為之準據法為台灣法，而保險契約準據法為挪威法。

「就此一事件實質審理面以觀，如前述原告對責任保險人被告Gard請求之準據法應為挪威法，則就挪威法之適用，挪威法院應為審理本案最適當之法院，至對被告Amorgos等三人雖以我國法為本件準據法，然依原告主張依海污法第三十三條被告應就本件事故負賠償責任。然而我國海污法甫於89年11月1日公布施行，實務上尚未有關於適用海污法第33條之案例；再者海污法乃參酌1969 CLC公約立法例制定（見本院卷一第241頁，故若本案件於我國法院為審理時，應參酌1969 CLC公約及相關外國法院判例、國際慣例為解釋，我國並非該公約之簽約國，就公約之審理適用較為生疏，需花費較多的勞費審理此案，勢必壓縮其他案件審理的時間及勞費，不符合中華民國人民之公共利益，參以，所有與本件相關之證據（如前述「船東責任保險規則」）及專業評估報告均係以外文做成，則在本院進行審理本案為證據調查時（或就擱淺漏油之發生歸責原因，或就相關損害額進行調查時），尚須耗費時日就前揭報告加以譯文或詢問相關國外鑑定證人時，不能使被告等人之訴訟上（要求迅速經濟裁判）權益受到保護，且難謂無就其必要防禦之不利益情事發生，反觀挪威不但自始即為該公約之簽約國，且自1969年起之二十一年間，曾經多次適用該公約於其管轄之相類案件而有相當之經驗。從而考量訴訟之經濟、法庭之便利性、及裁判公平妥適，雖被告Amorgos等三人之請求以行為地法即我國法為準據法，本案仍應以挪威法院進行審理為宜。」故而法院之認定為：「綜上，本件挪威法院應為實質審理本案最適當之法院，本院乃『不便利之法庭』，即本案應由挪威法院管轄，基於國際實務上關於解決國際管轄衝突之『不便利法庭之原則』，則應認我國法院均無管轄權，從而原告向本院提起本件訴訟，本院並無管轄權且因管轄法院為外國法院，復不能為民事訴訟法第28條之移送裁定，應依民事訴訟法第249條第1項第2款之規定，以裁定駁回原告之訴及假執行之聲請。」個人或許應是台灣正式立書首先引進國際管轄及不方便法院[1]之法律學生，不方便法院法則應是如此的被引用嗎？這種作法符合個人對中國法院於新時代的期望嗎？

一、專屬管轄與直接訴訟

首先對1969年的石油污染公約個人早期是如此的加以論述[2]：「英國the Merchant Shipping（Oil Pollution）Act 1971引進the Brussels Convention on Civil Liability for Oil Pollution Damage（1969）。英國1971年海上石油污染法強制規定漏出石油之船之船東須負民事責任；及強迫船東對海上污染責任加以強制保險；並規定對其保險人有直接起訴（direct

1 見陳隆修，《國際私法管轄權評論》，台北，五南圖書公司，民國75年11月，初版，及170、171、172頁。

2 陳隆修，《國際私法管轄權評論》，台北，五南圖書公司，民國75年11月，初版，75、76頁。

action）之權。依照布魯塞爾公約[3]，只有損害發生地之訂約國法院方有管轄權。故如損害發生於英國，英法院仍有將訴訟之通知送達於國外之船東或保險人。

我國雖為一地處世界航運要衝之海洋國家，然而對於此方面之規定甚為不週到，未免令人深覺遺憾。我國民事訴訟法第15條規定侵權行為地之法院有管轄權，但若船之漏油處為公海，而造成損害之海飄向我國沿岸，則此第15條就較難適用。而最嚴重之缺點為，我國並未規定受害人得直接向保險人起訴請求，此對我國人民之權益保護甚為不週到，政府機關之有關部門對此似乎應詳加考慮。」如今受害人雖有著直接請求權，但法院對「專屬管轄」似乎視若無睹。

事實上這個石油污染事件專屬管轄之概念，於聯合國的the International Convention on Civil Liability for Oil Pollution Damage, 1992中是被延續的。其同樣的第9條[4]中第1項白紙黑字斬釘截鐵的宣示：「當於一

---

[3] Act. 9 (1).
International Convention on Civil Liability for Oil Pollution Damage (Brussels, 29 November 1969)
Article Ⅸ

1. Where an incident has caused pollution damage in the territory including the territorial sea of one or more Contracting States, or preventive measures have been taken to prevent or minimize pollution damage in such territory including the territorial sea, actions for compensation may only be brought in the Courts of any such Contracting State or States. Reasonable notice of any such action shall be given to the defendant.
2. Each Contracting State shall ensure that its Courts possess the necessary jurisdiction to entertain such actions for compensation.
3. After the fund has been constituted in accordance with Article Ⅴ the Courts of the State in which the fund is constituted shall be exclusively competent to determine all matters relating to the apportionment and distribution of the fund.

故除了第一項規定專屬管轄外，第二項規定各國必須確保有著處理損害賠償的管轄法院。第7（8）條則規定對保險人或其他保證人之直接請求訴訟權。

8. Any claim for compensation for pollution damage may be brought directly against the insurer or other person providing financial security for the owner's liability for pollution damage. In such case the defendant may, irrespective of the actual fault or privity of the owner, avail himself of the limits of liability prescribed in Article V, paragraph 1. He may further avail himself of the defences (other than the bankruptcy or winding up of the owner) which the owner himself would have been entitled to invoke. Furthermore, the defendant may avail himself of the defence that the pollution damage resulted from the wilful misconduct of the owner himself, but the defendant shall not avail himself of any other defence which he might have been entitled to invoke in proceedings brought by the owner against him. The defendant shall in any event have the right to require the owner to be joined in the proceedings.

[4] Article Ⅸ

個或更多訂約國的領土，包含其領海或第2條所提及之地區，發生造成污染傷害的事故，或預防性的措施被採取以防止或減少於該領土，包含領海或地區，之污染性之損害時，損害賠償之訴訟只得於任何該訂約國之法院而被提起。於任何這種訴訟中被告應被給予合理的通知。」第2項甚至規定「每一訂約國應確保其法院有著必要的管轄權去處理這種損害賠償的訴訟。」**故而個人感慨萬分的請教台灣法院—那一個地球上的國家會給予法官權力去認定「專屬管轄法院」為不方便法院？**聯合國規定每一個訂約的國家應確保有著處理石油污染的「必要管轄法院」，台灣的法院顯然位階高於聯合國之公約，台灣的法院再一次證明其適用「任我行」法學的決心—諸法皆空，自由自在。問台灣法院、學界能有幾多頑固顢頇之處，恰似一江春水向東流。

為了確保損害賠償的被執行，聯合國又訂了the International Convention on the Establishment of an International Fund for Compensation for Oil Pollution Damage, 1992，而第3條則為該基金之管轄範圍之規定。第7條8項則為被害者對保險人或對船舶所有人污染責任之其他保證人之直接訴訟請求權之規定，有趣的是該項最後又規定：「被告無論如何有權利要求所有人去被加入訴訟。[5]」

---

1. Where an incident has caused pollution damage in the territory including the territorial sea or an area referred to in Article II of one or more Contracting States, or preventive measures have been taken to prevent or minimize pollution damage in such territory including the territorial sea or area, actions for compensation may only be brought in the Courts of any such Contracting State or States. Reasonable notice of any such action shall be given to the defendant.
2. Each Contracting State shall ensure that its Courts possess the necessary jurisdiction to entertain such actions for compensation.
3. After the fund has been constituted in accordance with Article V the Courts of the State in which the fund is constituted shall be exclusively competent to determine all matters relating to the apportionment and distribution of the fund.

[5] 8. Any claim for compensation for pollution damage may be brought directly against the insurer or other person providing financial security for the owner's liability for pollution damage. In such case the defendant may, even if the owner is not entitled to limit his liability according to Article V, paragraph 2, avail himself of the limits of liability prescribed in Article V, paragraph 1. He may further avail himself of the defences (other than the bankruptcy or winding up of the owner) which the owner himself would have been entitled to invoke. Furthermore, the defendant may avail himself of the defence that the pollution damage resulted from the wilful misconduct of the owner himself, but the defendant shall not avail himself of any other defence which he might have been entitled to invoke in proceedings brought

更有趣的是較近聯合國的International Convention on Civil Liability for Bunker Oil Pollution Damage, 2001，除了照例於7條10項[6]規定對保險人或其他應負責之保證人之直接請求之訴訟權外，亦於第9條[7]中規定管轄規則。其9(2)、(3)條照例規定必須給予被告適度之通知及要求各國必須確保有著能處理損害賠償之法院，更有趣的是第1項規定：「當於一個或更多訂約國之領土，包含其領海或2(a)（ii）條中所提之地區，中發生造成污染損害之事故時，或於這些領土，包含其領海或這些地區中，為了防止或減少污染損害所採取的預防性措施，而對船東、保險人、或其他為船東之責任提供擔保之人，所提起之損害賠償之訴訟只能於任何這些訂約國之法院而被提起。」

故而聯合國於此方面之公約，自1969、1992到2001年之公約，其內容皆大致上本著類似之架構：亦即船東須負民事責任；強迫船東對海上污染責任加以強制保險；對保險人或擔保人有直接訴訟權；損害發生地國法院有著專屬管轄權。很明顯的這一系列之公約即為人類文明於此方面之共

---

by the owner against him. The defendant shall in any event have the right to require the owner to be joined in the proceedings.

6 10. Any claim for compensation for pollution damage may be brought directly against the insurer or other person providing financial security for the registered owner's liability for pollution damage. In such a case the defendant may invoke the defences (other than bankruptcy or winding up of the shipowner) which the shipowner would have been entitled to invoke, including limitation pursuant to article 6. Furthermore, even if the shipowner is not entitled to limitation of liability according to article 6, the defendant may limit liability to an amount equal to the amount of the insurance or other financial security required to be maintained in accordance with paragraph 1. Moreover, the defendant may invoke the defence that the pollution damage resulted from the willful misconduct of the shipowner, but the defendant shall not invoke any other defence which the defendant might have been entitled to invoke in proceedings brought by the shipowner against the defendant. The defendant shall in any event have the right to require the shipowner to be joined in the proceedings.

7 Article 9
Jurisdiction

1. Where an incident has caused pollution damage in the territory, including the territorial sea, or in an area referred to in article 2(a)(ii) of one or more States Parties, or preventive measures have been taken to prevent or minimise pollution damage in such territory, including the territorial sea, or in such area, actions for compensation against the shipowner, insurer or other person providing security for the shipowner's liability may be brought only in the courts of any such States Parties.
2. Reasonable notice of any action taken under paragraph 1 shall be given to each defendant.
3. Each State Party shall ensure that its courts have jurisdiction to entertain actions for compensation under this Convention.

同核心全球化實體政策。而或許隨著實務經驗的累積，於2001年公約第9條的專屬管轄範圍更明確的將被告明文列出為船東、保險人、及提供擔保之人。1969及1992之公約[8]之專屬管轄範圍只是規定為污染事故之損害賠償，而2001年公約除了規定專屬管轄範圍為污染事故[9]之損害賠償外，更進一步對被告加以明示。故而92重訴4號應該深切反省於判決前1969及1992年聯合國公約數十年來一貫的給予海洋油污染發生地專屬管轄權，並且明文要求全世界文明國家必須確保有著對污染損害賠償之管轄法院。污染事故地法院對當地之損害是最合適去評估損害的，挪威法院是不可能

---

8 1969公約及1992公約對「石油」的定義較類似，其分別規定於其公約第1(5)條中。
5. "Oil" means any persistent oil such as crude oil, fuel oil, heavy diesel oil, lubricating oil and whale oil, whether carried in board a ship as cargo or in the bunkers of such a ship.
5. "Oil" means any persistent hydrocarbon mineral oil such as crude oil, fuel oil, heavy diesel oil and lubricating oil, whether carried on board a ship as cargo or in the bunkers of such a ship.
雖然3個公約之架構、內容、精神、及目的皆一致，但2001年公約指的是船用油，見第1(5)條。
5. "Bunker oil " means any hydrocarbon mineral oil, including lubricating oil, used or intended to be used for the operation or propulsion of the ship, and any residues of such oil.

9 所謂「污染損害」及「事故」，1969公約規定於1(6)及(8)條。
6. "pollution damage" means loss or damage caused outside the ship carrying oil by contamination resulting from the escape or discharge of oil from the ship, wherever such escape of discharge may occur, and includes the costs of preventive measures and further loss or damage caused by preventive measures.
8. "Incident" means any occurrence, or series of occurrences having the same origin, which causes pollution damage.
1992公約規定於1(6)及(8)條。
6. "pollution damage" means:
(a) loss or damage caused outside the ship by contamination resulting from the escape or discharge of oil from the ship, wherever such escape or discharge may occur, provided that compensation for impairment of the environment other than loss of profit from such impairment shall be limited to costs of reasonable measures of reinstatement actually undertaken or to be undertaken;
(b) the costs of preventive measures and further loss or damage caused by preventive measures.
8. "Incident" means any occurrence, or series of occurrences having the same origin, which causes pollution damage or creates a grave and imminent threat of causing such damage.
2001公約規定於1(8)及(9)條。
8. "Incident" means any occurrence or series of occurrences having the same origin, which causes pollution damage or creates a grave and imminent threat of causing such damage.
9. "Pollution damage" means:
(a) loss or damage caused outside the ship by contamination resulting from the escape or discharge of bunker oil from the ship, wherever such escape or discharge may occur, provided that compensation for impairment of the environment other than loss of profit from such impairment shall be limited to costs of reasonable measures of reinstatement actually undertaken or to be undertaken; and
(b) the costs of preventive measures and further loss or damage caused by preventive measures.

「有信心真誠的」知道墾丁海洋在台灣人心中之地位的。一個國際上被課予應提供管轄法院義務的地區，並且該地區之法院又為舉世所公認之專屬管轄法院是不可能亦不應該被認為是不方便法院的。更何況於92重訴4號判決前3年，聯合國2001年公約又白紙黑字的公告船東、保險人、及擔保人皆為該專屬管轄範圍內之被告。

二、No Law No Heaven

於英國不方便法院領導案例Spiliada中Lord Goff說：「……如果有著其他表面上是清楚的更合適去審理訴訟的法院是存在的，通常法院會允許訴訟的停止，除非有著基於正義的理由要求訴訟的停止是不應該被允許的情形。[10]」所謂的「清楚的更合適」的法院自然是舉世公認的專屬法院，所謂「最真實與重大關連」法院自然是海岸被污染地之法院，離台灣墾丁半個地球的挪威法院一點也不「自然」。92重訴4號法院的停止（事實上是幾乎前所未有的駁回[11]）訴訟，不但是「不方便」，更是不正義的。92重訴4號所實施的不方便法院法則並非個人二十多年前所引進的法則，很難想像一個國際公認的專屬管轄會被認為是「不方便」，於文明世界中或許只有四月一日才可能產生這樣脫離俗世的判決。英國上訴法院於對不方便法院加以論述時警告：「法院於遵循其作法時不可太脫離俗世……世界上有其他的地區。在那裡事情是極糟糕的。[12]」台灣又一次於92重訴4號中證明英國上訴法院所警告的「其他地區」就是這裡。台灣的學界及法界又再一次的忽視了我們的祖訓：「爾俸爾祿，民脂民膏，下民易虐，上天

10 The Spiliada [1987] AC 460 at 476, Lord Goff: "...if there is some other available forum which prima facie is clearly more appropriate for the trial of the action, it will ordinarily grant a stay unless there are circumstance by reason of which justice requires that a stay should nevertheless not be granted."

11 通常依各國慣例，停止訴訟是有可能重新接受管轄，而駁回訴訟則通常不會再接受管轄。因此雖然於此方面美國法院較不注重，但英國法院於行使不方便法院法則時，通常皆只是停止訴訟，而幾乎不曾駁回訴訟。一個「專屬」的「自然法院」會以不方便法院之名而停止自然原告對自然被告之自然訴訟已是令人瞠目結舌，如果加以駁回則已是超乎人類想像力的極限。

12 Muduroglu Ltd v. TC Ziraat Bankasi [1986] QB 1225 at 1248, "the court must not be too unworldly in its approach ... there are other parts of the world where things are badly wrong."

難欺」。不僅外國人會火燒圓明園，中國人又再一次證明自己會火燒比圓明園更珍貴的自然遺產。於另一時空，另一角落，中國人又充分的證明其另一天賦——no law no heaven。

英國於尚未引用不方便法院法理時，所依賴之「對被告造成困擾性或壓迫性」理論之重點乃在保護原告之合法利益，即使於現在訴訟當事人雖相同，但於他國之訴訟中地位不同時，英國法院仍會對當事人依他國法律而來之可能利益而加以考量[13]。而於評述美國不方便法院法則時，個人早期所論述之第1及第2要件即為有關原告之利益[14]：「1.尊重原告之意願。一般對原告選擇法院地起訴之意願應加以相當之尊重，除非其他法院很明顯地為更方便之法院，否則法院不應不尊重其意願。……2.當原告為法院地之居民時，法院一般甚少以不方便法院之理由將訴訟駁回。很明顯地，此乃因法院欲保護其居民，免得其必須遭受於他處起訴之不便與花費。有些州法院，如加州，明白地規定對當地居民所提起之訴訟，不得不以方便法院為理由將其駁回，至多法院只能停止訴訟之進行，而等待所被提議的更方便法院之判決。[15]」

美國法律協會（the American Law Institute）第2新編國際私法第84條（Restatement （Second） of Conflict of Laws § 84 （1971））之comment (c)認為法院保留訴訟的兩個最重要原因之一為「應由原告去選擇訴訟之地方，除非有重大之理由其所選之法院不應受到干擾」[16]。而comment (f)於論述原告之州是否為合適之法院地時則如此下結論：「於這個州起訴可能牽涉及對被告所造成之困難，但除了於例外之情形下，對原告於當地起訴之明顯的方便性，及該州對原告福祉的明顯利益，會使得該州是個合適的法院。[17]」另外於其報告人之註釋中又說：「除非在『平

[13] 陳隆修，《國際私法管轄權評論》，台北，五南圖書公司，民國75年11月，初版，86、87頁。
[14] 同上，170、171頁。
[15] Archibald v. Cinerama Hotels, 15 Cal 3d 853 (1976).
[16] "The two most important factors look to the court's retention of the case. They are (1) that since it is for the plaintiff to choose the place of suit, his choice of a forum should not be disturbed except for weighty reasons".
[17] "Suit in this state may involve hardship to the defendant, but the obvious convenience to the plaintiff

衡所有的情況時相當強烈的有利於』被告下，法院不應駁回該訴訟。[18]」92重訴4號於不方便法院法則之行使上是明顯的違反判例法的經驗法則。

即使我們無視於憲法上之合法訴訟權，墾丁是侵權行為作成地兼主要損害發生地，國際法的歷史上似乎沒有不認為其為合適管轄地。92重訴4號的否定自然原告對於自然被告於自然法院起訴之自然訴訟是極度「不自然」。這個作法不但違背聯合國數十年來相關公約之一貫共識及規定，亦違反了Cardozo J.的「法律邏輯的推展應受到常識的限制」，及違反了Prof. Graveson的「法律邏輯一致性之要求應受到判例法達成正義基本目的限制」，更違反了我們祖先「道法自然」的數千年生活經驗。墾丁是台灣國家公園所在地，對於天堂被污染成地獄固然是人類自然資產的喪失，但面對92重訴4號這個直接在地獄所作成之裁定，個人對人性（humanity）之喪失只能無語問蒼天。

挪威法院的母國法歐盟法於REGULATION（EC）NO 864/2007 OF THE EUROPEAN PARLIAMENT AND THE COUNCIL of 11 July 2007 on the law applicable to non-contractual obligations（Rome II）中，在其序言要點之24[19]特別說明環境的損害就是對自然資產的傷害。羅馬II的要點之25[20]中又特別說環境的損害應根據「預防性原則而給予高度之保護」，「對於污染源加以矯正行為之優先原則及製造污染者應付費之原則，使得偏向對受害人有利原則之被適用是完全有正當性的」。因此羅馬

---

bringing suit there, together with the clear interest of this state in the plaintiff's welfare, will make this state an appropriate forum except in unusual circumstances."

18 Reporter's Note, A court should not dismiss the action unless the "balance is strongly in favor" of the defendant.

19 (24) 'Environmental damage' should be understood as meaning adverse change in a natural resource, such as water, land or air, impairment of a function performed by that resource for the benefit of another natural resource or the public, or impairment of the variability among living organisms

20 (25) Regarding environmental damage, Article 174 of the Treaty, which provides that there should be a high level of protection based on the precautionary principle and the principle that preventive action should be taken, the principle of priority for corrective action at source and the principle that the polluter pays, fully justifies the use of the principle of discriminating in favour of the person sustaining the damage. The question of when the person seeking compensation can make the choice of the law applicable should be determined in accordance with the law of the Member State in which the court is seised.

II在其侵權行為基本條款之準據法選擇上，雖然於第4條[21]通常是以損害發生地法為依據，但基於「偏向有利受害人之原則」，其第7條[22]有關環境保護之損害賠償確有特別規定。其第7條規定：「由於環境之損害所產生之非契約責任，或由於這種損害之結果導致對人或財產上之傷害，所應適用之法律應根據4(1)條而決定（即損害發生地法），除非要求損害賠償之當事人選擇去以引起損害發生的事故所在地國之法律（行為地法）為其請求之依據。」無論是依行為地法或損害發生地法，墾丁皆是環境損害之行為作成地[23]及損害發生地，於21世紀全球化法學的共同核心政策策上，環境汙染之被害人應受到較有利的對待是「完全有正當性。」92重訴4號之裁定不但違背聯合國數十年來一系列公約，亦違反了挪威母法及全世界21世紀法學的共同核心主流價值。92重訴4號證實了的英國上訴法院的警告：「法院於遵循其作法時不可太脫離俗世……世界上有其他的地區，在那裡事情是極度糟糕的。」

---

21 Article 4 General rule

1. Unless otherwise provided for in this Regulation, the law applicable to a non-contractual obligation arising out of a tort/delict shall be the law of the country in which the damage occurs irrespective of the country in which the event giving rise to the damage occurred and irrespective of the country or countries in which the indirect consequences of that event occur.
2. However, where the person claimed to be liable and the person sustaining damage both have their habitual residence in the same country at the time when the damage occurs, the law of that country shall apply.
3. Where it is clear from all the circumstances of the case that the tort/delict is manifestly more closely connected with a country other than that indicated in paragraphs 1 or 2, the law of that other country shall apply. A manifestly closer connection with another country might be based in particular on a pre-existing relationship between the parties, such as a contract, that is closely connected with the tort/delict in question.

22 Article 7 Environmental damage

The law applicable to a non-contractual obligation arising out of environmental damage or damage sustained by persons or property as a result of such damage shall be the law determined pursuant to Article 4(1), unless the person seeking compensation for damage chooses to base his or her claim on the law of the country in which the event giving rise to the damage occurred.

23 羅馬II對行為發生地的安全及行為標準規定於17條。

Article 17 Rule of safety and conduct

In assessing the conduct of the person claimed to be liable, account shall be taken, as a matter of fact and in so far as is appropriate, of rules of safety and conduct which were in force at the place and time of the event giving rise to the liability.

三、實體法論與道法自然

事實上不但是聯合國於石油汙染的1969、1992、及2001公約有規定強制保險及受害者向保險人直接請求之規定，保險法上許多規定已成為現代社會中許多國家之國內法及國際法上之強行法規。台灣保險法54條[24]規定除了有利被保險人外，強行規定不得變更之。而第94條第2項[25]亦規定被害人向保險人之直接訴訟權。羅馬II 16條[26]自然亦有法院地強行法之規定，而這個強行法指的不只是當事人所同意之準據法不得違背[27]，更包括了本應適用之準據法亦不得違背之最強行之法規（與公共政策同一位階之強行法規）。第18條[28]則規定於該行為之準據法或保險契約準據法之許可下，被害人對保險人有直接訴訟權。第18條這個規定德國1999年國際私法侵權行為之主要條文第40條即有規定，其規定於第4項[29]。

24 第54條：「本法之強制規定，不得以契約變更之。但有利於被保險人者，不在此限。保險契約之解釋，應探求契約當事人之真意，不得拘泥於所用之文字；如有疑義時，以作有利於被保險人之解釋為原則。」

25 第94條：「保險人於第三人由被保險人應負責任事故所致之損失，未受賠償以前，不得以賠償金額之全部或一部給付被保險人。被保險人對第三人應負損失賠償責任確定時，第三人得在保險金額範圍內，依其應得之比例，直接向保險人請求給付賠償金額。」

26 Article 16 Overriding mandatory provisions: Nothing in this Regulation shall restrict the application of the provisions of the law of the forum in a situation where they are mandatory irrespective of the law otherwise applicable of the non-contractual obligation.

27 羅馬II允許當事人於適當條件下選定準據法。
Article 14 Freedom of choice:
1.The parties may agree to submit non-contractual obligations to the law of their choice:
(a) by an agreement entered into after the event giving rise to the damage occurred;
or
(b) where all the parties are pursuing a commercial activity, also by an agreement freely negotiated before the event giving rise to the damage occurred.
The choice shall be expressed or demonstrated with reasonable certainty by the circumstances of the case and shall not prejudice the rights of third parties.

28 Article 18 Direct action against the insurer of the person liable
The person having suffered damage may bring his or her claim directly against the insurer of the person liable to provide compensation if the law applicable to the non-contractual obligation or the law applicable to the insurance contract so provides.

29 見陳隆修、許兆慶、林恩瑋，《台灣財產法暨經濟法研究叢書（十三）—國際私法：選法理論之回顧與展望》，台灣財產法暨經濟法研究協會發行，2007年1月，初版，178-180頁。
(4) The injured person may bring his or her claim directly against the insurer of the person liable to provide compensation if the law applicable to the tort or the law applicable to the insurance contract so provides.

於保險法的進化過程中，「保險是用來賠償責任而非製造責任」的傳統法律邏輯是個堅強的傳統法學的最後堡壘之一，但是這個法律邏輯最後亦不得不適度的讓步。如個人早期所述[30]：「事實上，現代工業社會中，保險制度的普遍已使得不利於被告的判決，不再只是將一個人的損失轉嫁給另一個人，而是使該損失由所有的保單持有人來分擔。被告成為訴訟中名義上的一造，只是損失分擔程序起點的管道[31]。」對於被害人於有關保險契約之直接訴訟權，早期於進化過程中對於其是屬於程序法或實體法，或於國際法上是屬於準據法之選法規則或管轄權之規定上，是經常混淆不清的。個人以前對相關的美國判例法如此評述[32]：「至於美國有關被害人之直接訴訟權之判例則甚為有趣，並且似乎互相矛盾。於Roberts v. Home Insurance Indemnity Co.[33]中，加州居民於路易斯安那受傷後，於加州提起訴訟直接告保險人。保險契約於路州所訂，路州法並允許直接訴訟。法院判直接訴訟為有關實體上之規定，路州法因而被引用。但於Watson v. Employers Liability Assurance Corp.中[34]，路州居民於路州法院對英國保險人提起直接訴訟。路州法允許直接訴訟，而保險契約準據法伊利諾伊法並不允許直接訴訟。路州法院認為有關直接訴訟之規定應屬程序性，故而引用路州法院地法之規定。兩個法院於定性學理上看似不一樣的作法，事實上只要符合實體法之發展趨勢而給予被害人迅速合理的賠償，則看似矛盾的判例事實上是一致的。故而作者一再主張實體法方法論，不但能保證個案結果之公平正義，並且能促成判決的一致性。個案正義（individual justice）與判決一致（consistency）的並不相容性是國際

30 陳隆修，《美國國際私法新理論》，台北，五南圖書公司，民國76年1月，初版，129-131頁。

31 Stig Jørgensen, "The Decline and Fall of the Law of Torts", 18 AM. J. Comp. Law 39 (1970), at 53; J. G. Fleming "The Collateral Source Rule and Loss Allocation in Tort Law," 54 Cal. L. Rev. 1478 (1966), at 1548; Lord Denning, *Post Office v. Norwich Union* [1967] 2 Q.B. 363, 375; J.G. Fleming, *Law of Torts*, 5th ed., p. 11.

32 陳隆修、許兆慶、林恩瑋，《台灣財產法暨經濟法研究叢書（十三）─國際私法：選法理論之回顧與展望》，台灣財產法暨經濟法研究協會發行，2007年1月，初版，188頁。

33 48 Cal. App. 3d 313 (1975).

34 348 U.S. 66 (1954).

私法界百年來的迷思，或許實體法方法論於此再度證明這個迷思可能是謬誤的，是應該被打破的。」

被害人對保險人的直接請求權，如果依傳統法學邏輯之定性，到底是屬於實體法（選法規則）或程序法（管轄規則），不但混淆不清且很有可能於個案造成不正義之判決。但經過時間的演進及三個聯合國的石油汙染公約，已證明它們都是一體之兩面－－既是實體法（選法規則）又是程序法（管轄規則）。這樣子的法學進化過程之歷史是一再重覆的，例如個人數十年來所再三強調的，契約通常不得違反履行地法之法則[35]，它已被證實既是國內法亦是國際法。故而個人近年來於遵照黃進教授及趙相林教授的指示，於自不量力的試圖建立王道之中國法學基礎時[36]，一再重申判例法的演進為大自然進化之一環，若無明顯的理由不應輕易違背其法則[37]。並且一再引述Cardozo J.的論述：法學的概念甚少被推展至邏輯的極限，應受到常識的節制[38]。及又同時一再引用恩師Prof Graveson一生懸念的經典結晶：「邏輯並非判例法的最高價值。英國國際私法實現正義的基本目的給予邏輯一致性的政策必要的限制。[39]」因此個人亦一再大聲重申我們祖先二千多年來氣勢磅礴的宣示：「道法自然」。

---

35 陳隆修，《2005年海牙法院選擇公約評析》，台北，五南圖書公司，2009年1月，初版1刷，92-95頁。

36 兩個月前個人與黃進教授於台中晤談，我們皆認同中國法學之基礎應本於王道之祖訓。

37 Sun Oil Co. v. Wortman, 486 U.S. 717, 730, "If a thing has been practiced for two hundred years by common consent, it will need a strong case for the Fourteenth Amendment to affect it." Jackman v. Rosenbaum Co., 260 U.S. 22, 31, 67 L. Ed. 107, 43 S. Ct. 9 (1922).「如果一件事於大眾同意下已被實行二百年，那麼需要很強的證據才能以十四修正案去影響它」。

38 Boris N. Sokoloff v. The national City Bank of New York, 239 N.Y. 158, 165, "Juridically, a government that is unrecognized may be viewed as no government at all, if the power withholding recognition chooses thus to view it. In practice, however, since juridical conceptions are seldom, if ever, carried to the limit of their logic, the equivalence is not absolute, but is subject to self-imposed limitations of common sense and fairness, as we learned in litigations following our Civil War."

39 R.H. Graveson, Conflict of Laws, p. 79 (7th ed. 1974), "The acceptability of this solution rests in the fact that logic is not the highest value in the common law. The necessary limits on the policy of logic consistency are imposed by the general purpose of positive justice of English private international law. An English court may thus uphold the legitimacy of children as the subsidiary question and declare null and void the marriage of their parents as the principal question, using different systems of conflict of laws for the purpose. Common law judges regard rules as tools, not as fetters, to promote, not prevent, the fulfillment of their function."

如個人以前所述：「個案正義與判決一致性的不相容性是國際私法界百年來的迷思，或許實體法方法論於此再度證明這個迷思可能是謬誤的，是應該被打破的。」無論基於什麼樣的名詞，主流價值、共同核心政策、實體法方法論或法學全球化，國內法及國際法的基本目的皆在達成個案正義，不正義的判決是不會被承認的，因而法學一致性的目的亦不可能達到。於二十一世紀全球化法學之概念下，隨著人類文明的提昇，個案正義的要求亦更被提昇，惟有對個案正義的概念達成一致性，判決一致性的目的才能水到渠成的被達成。如Story J.甚早以前就說：「如果一個文明的國家欲尋求其自己法院的判決於其它地方被認定為有效，他們應該公平的注意到其他文明國家的權利及慣例，及於行使正義時各國及國際共同的原則。[40]」故而早於全球化形成前，不符合自然慣例法及實證國內法及國際法之公平正義理念之判決是不會被承認的，一致性之目的自然是無法達成的。二十一世紀之中國國內法及國際法或許必須本著禮運大同之王道祖訓，以個案正義為最高目的。不符合我們祖先仁道文化的判決會由根本上去破壞中國法治的理想，於法學政策全球化之二十一世紀，沒有個案正義就沒有中國式法學之建立。

台灣的法界及學界人士應深深認知沒有人性就沒有法學正義，不具備常識性之人性的人是不能有資格號稱法律學生的。在台灣的法院中，有時（或經常）道不大、天不大、地不大、人更不大，有些判決是學界與法界直接在地獄作成之泯滅人性之魔性判決[41]。對這種不具常識性基本人性

---

40 "If a civilized nation seeks have the sentences of its own courts held of any validity elsewhere, they ought to have a just regard to the rights and usages of other civilized nations, and the principles of public and national law in the administration justice" Bradstreet v, Neptune Ins. Co., 3 Sumner, 600, 608.

41 TVBS記者洪彩綸，2010/11/25 20:07，於抬頭為「『兒讓我養』台荷搶童！母反悔出養 敗訴」之報導中，一出獄之媽媽因生活困難將6歲之兒童出養給一對荷蘭夫妻，經法院裁定收養。但事後兒童家人反悔向法院提出終止收養之訴，但為最高法院所裁定敗訴。家人向總統陳情，同時再提上訴。記者報導：「小兄妹的外婆拿出孫子的照片，6歲的小孫子笑的很開心，生日時抱著外婆許了一個大心願。林童外婆：『他說阿嬤求求你，救救我，不要去荷蘭，阿嬤我的生日心願就是不要跟阿嬤分開。』」（98家上字276；99台上字2059））
聯合國1989年Convention on the Rights of the Child開宗明義的規定任何有關兒童之行為應以兒童之最佳利益為第一考量："Article 3, 1. In all actions concerning children, whether undertaken by public or private social welfare institutions, courts of law, administrative authorities or legislative bodies,

the best interests of the child shall be a primary consideration."個人數十年來於所有的著作中皆不厭其煩的重申這個普世價值萬國公法（陳隆修、許兆慶、林恩瑋、李瑞生四人合著，《國際私法-管轄與選法理論之交錯》，台北，五南圖書公司，2009年3月，初版1刷，149-160頁）。海牙會議之Convention of 29 May 1993 on Protection of Children and Co-operation in Respect of Intercountry Adoption即是根據1989年聯合國公約而被通過，1993年公約特別對1989公約21條加以闡明。海牙公約之序言即承認只有於兒童之本國無法找到合適之家庭時，才會有跨國收養。"Recognising that intercountry adoption may ofter the advantage of a permanent family to a child for whom a suitable family cannot be found in his or her State of origin."但是更重要的是其再一次「提醒各個訂約國應優先採取合適之措施以使得兒童能繼續留在其原來家庭之照顧下」。"Recalling that each State should take, as a matter of priority, appropriate measures to enable the child to remain in the care of his or her family of origin"其序言亦照例再次重申以兒童最佳利益為行為之準則。"Convinced of the necessity to take measures to ensure that intercountry adoptions are made in the best interests of the child and with respect for his or her fundamental rights, and to prevent the abduction, the sale of , or traffic in children."而第1條(a)款即宣示："Article 1, The objects of the present Convention are- (a) to establish safeguards to ensure that intercountry adoptions take place in the best interests of the child and with respect for his or her fundamental rights as recognized in international law"
尤其更重要的是台灣法院及學界必須注意根據第4(c)(1)及(3)條，兒童原來之政府（台灣）不但必須確保兒童之監護人同意收養，更必須確認該同意並未被撤銷。"Article 4
An adoption within the scope of the Convention shall take place only if the competent authorities of the State of origin-
a) have established that the child is adoptable;
b) have determined, after possibilities for placement of the child within the State of origin have been given due consideration, that an intercountry adoption is in the child's best interests;
c) have ensured that
(1) the persons, institutions and authorities whose consent is necessary for adoption, have been counselled as may be necessary and duly informed of the effects of their consent, in particular whether or not an adoption will result in the termination of the legal relationship between the child and his or her family of origin,
(2) such persons, institutions and authorities have given their consent freely, in the required legal form, and expressed or evidenced in writing,
(3) the consents have not been induced by payment or compensation of any kind and have not been withdrawn."
個人於此公開的質疑台灣最高法院—兒童血親家庭已表明願意照顧小孩，並已撤銷同意，請問你們可以超越聯合國人權公約及海牙公約嗎？「世界上有其他地方在那裡事情是極度糟糕的」，台灣的法院再一次「諸法皆空自由自在」，no law no heaven。
另外第4(d)條亦規定小孩之願望應被加以考量。
"d) have ensured, having regard to the age and degree of maturity of the child, that
(1) he or her has been counseled and duly informed of the effects of the adoption and of his or her consent to the adoption, where such consent is required,
(2) consideration has been given to the child's wishes and opinions,
(3) the child's consent to the adoption, where such consent is required, has been given freely, in the required legal form, and expressed or evidenced in writing, and
(4) such consent has not been induced by payment or compensation of any kind."
但是很明顯的台灣的法院採納不聽、不說、不見三隻猴子哲學，或許應再加一隻猴子哲學——沒天良。事實上公約規定即使到了接收國後，為了兒童最佳利益可將其送回原來國家。"Article 21
(1) Where the adoption is to take place after the transfer of the child to the receiving State and it appears to the Central Authority of that State that the continued placement of the child with the prospective

adoptive parents is not in the child's best interests, such Central Authority shall take the measures necessary to protect the child, in particular –

…………….

(c) as a last resort, to arrange the return of the child, if his or her interests so require.

(2) Having regard in particular to the age and degree of maturity of the child, he or she shall be consulted and, where appropriate, his or her consent obtained in relation to measures to be taken under this Article."

另外台灣法院應深感慚愧的是，即使收養行為已成立，於小孩最佳利益下，訂約國可拒絕承認該收養。"Article 24 The recognition of an adoption may be refused in a Contracting State only if the adoption is manifestly contrary to its public policy, taking into account the best interests of the child."

兒童之血緣家庭最後要求台灣政府出面，這是常識之問題。依法律學理而言，個人一再強調基於parens patriae之地位，政府才是兒童之保護者。（陳隆修，《比較國際私法》，台北，五南圖書公司，78年10月，初版，296頁；陳隆修、許兆慶、林恩瑋、李瑞生四人合著，《國際私法-管轄與選法理論之交錯》，台北，五南圖書公司，2009年3月，初版1刷，218頁）有關收養個人早期如此論述：「收養本即為一甚謹慎之行為，對未成年之被收養者利益之考慮，為此類案件中惟一且最高之價值及政策。於英美法因收養皆須經法院之許可，故美國法院視收養為一程序法規，而無法律選擇法規（Choice-of-law rules）問題之存在，一向皆以法院地法為準據法，以求得未成年被收養者最大幸福之保障。有些英國國際私法之教科書，甚至不將收養列入其中。」（陳隆修，《比較國際私法》，台北，五南圖書公司，78年10月，初版，290、291頁）在60年前，大英國協最高法院於著名的Mckee v. Mckee [1951] AC 352 at 365中說："It is the law … that the welfare and happiness of the infant is the paramount consideration in questions of custody … To this paramount consideration all others yield. The order of a foreign court of competent jurisdiction is no exception. Such an order has not the force of a foreign judgment: comity demands not its enforcement, but its grave consideration. This distinction … rests on the peculiar character of the jurisdiction and on the fact that an order providing for the custody of an infant cannot in its nature be final."

於半世紀前國協最高法院即擲地有聲的宣示，在兒童最佳利益的「至高無上考量下所有其他考量應退讓」，即使「國際禮誼只能要求被慎重的考量，而非被執行」，「外國有管轄權的法院之命令亦不能構成例外」。數十年來個人一向聲嘶力竭的主張，要求台灣遵守文明世界的慣例，於台灣「這個世界上有其他地方在那裡事情是極度糟糕的」，個人還有多少年可以做這萬國公約普世價值的守護者？做為一個國際法的學生，個人於此再一次的向台灣當局、學界、及法界提出抗議。這是一個由學界及法界聯手在地獄作成之沒有人性的魔性判決，在判決中道不大、天不大、地不大、人更不大。

全世界的文明國家已經透過1989聯合國公約及1993海牙收養公約，來確保於收養中「兒童的最佳利益應是最高考量」，而「收養行為成立之法律邏輯的一致性應受到判例法達成公平正義基本目的之限制」。1989聯合國公約規定："Article 21

State Parties that recognize and/or permit the system of adoption shall ensure that the best interests of the child shall be the paramount consideration and they shall:

a) Ensure that the adoption of a child is authorized only by competent authorities who determine, in accordance with applicable law and procedures and on the basis of all pertinent and reliable information, that the adoption is permissible in view of the child's status concerning parents, relatives and legal guardians and that, if required, the persons concerned have given their informed consent to the adoption on the basis of such counselling as may be necessary;

b) Recognize that inter-country adoption may be considered as an alternative means of child's care, if the child cannot be placed in a foster or an adoptive family or cannot in any suitable manner be cared for in the child's country of origin;

c) Ensure that the child concerned by inter-country adoption enjoys safeguards and standards equivalent to those existing in the case of national adoption;

d) Take all appropriate measures to ensure that, in inter-country adoption, the placement does not result

之判決，相對於我們中國法制史將「情」字放進法典正文中，個人只能說這種判決no law no heaven。「爾俸爾祿，民脂民膏，下民易虐，上天難欺。」

四、歐盟規則與岳不群法學

事實上除了台灣保險法及於非契約責任歐盟之羅馬II有規定相關保險事故之強行法外，羅馬I（REGULATION （EC） NO 593/2008 OF THE EUROPEAN PARLIAMENT AND OF THE COUNCIL of 17 June 2008 on the law applicable to contractual obligations （Rome I））是有關契約責任，其對保險契約上亦有強行規定。除了例行的強行規定外[42]，其又

---

in improper financial gain for those involved in it;

e) Promote, where appropriate, the objectives of the present article by concluding bilateral or multilateral arrangements or agreements, and endeavour, within this framework, to ensure that the placement of the child in another country is carried out by competent authorities or organs.

而這個21條之規定又如前述被1993海牙公約再次更詳細的加以確認。如Story J.於Bradstreet v. Neptune Ins. Co., 3 Sumner, 600, 608中所說「如果一個文明國家的判決欲被認為有效，應注意到於行使正義時各國及國際共同的原則」。個人三十多年來魂縈夢繫一生懸命於主流共同核心基本價值的確認—亦即主流價值的確認就是通常能同時促進個案正義與法律（判決）一致性的自然達成。如此順天應人的透過主流價值的確認，以使得個案正義與法律一致性的相衝突變為和諧，這亦就是我們祖先所謂的「自然道法」。

個人一再主張人類文明的進化，使得21世紀全球化法學的共同核心基本政策便是在於確保個案正義的達成，沒有個案的正義就無法於世界各國被達成全球化的認可。黃進教授與個人皆認為21世紀的中國法學應以王道為基礎，個人期盼或許大陸年輕同僚應體認沒有個案正義就沒有禮運大同的王道境界。「鰥、寡、孤、獨、廢疾者皆有所養」，禮運大同指的不只是弱勢經濟人權之確保而已，更積極的指向弱勢者之所有人權及公平正義之確保。最高法院的這個裁定不但違反中國五倫中之親情，亦同時違反了聯合國人權公約及海牙公約。「情」字為有些西方先進同僚翻為"compassion"，而個人數十年來一貫認為是"human sentiments"，但無論如何本案至少證明中國文化中之「情哲學」是可能於個案上與現代人權法是相通的。如個人於第六屆兩岸國私會議中所主張「情」字是中國法的特色，中國法學欲領導全球化法學，「情法學」是個重要的因素。個人真誠的認為21世紀的全球化法學如果不加入「情文化」，則或許全球化法學的個案正義與人權上之進展會受到很大的傷害。（**本注釋為較近臺灣家事事件審理細則第110條所採納**）

42 Article 9 Overriding mandatory provisions

1. Overriding mandatory provisions are provisions the respect for which is regarded as crucial by a country for safeguarding its public interests, such as its political, social or economic organisation, to such an extent that they are applicable to any situation falling within their scope, irrespective of the law otherwise applicable to the contract under thus Regulation.
2. Nothing in this Regulation shall restrict the application of the overriding mandatory provisions of the law of the forum.
3. Effect may be given to the overriding mandatory provisions of the law of the country where the ob-

於有關保險契約的7(4)(b)條[43]對強行法加以規定。另外7(5)條[44]規定若契約涵蓋的危險跨及不同會員國，則該契約應被視為由數個保險契約所組成，而這些保險契約只是各自與一會員國相關而已[45]。保險法的共同核心基本價值在於保護保單持有人及被保人之利益，這種規定可能是在確保各個會員國於此方面之強行政策不會有衝突，並進而保障各會員國於此方面強行法之被加以執行。

對於保險人之直接訴訟權，及對保單持有人、被保人、受益人、及受害人之保護既然是全球化實體政策上之共同核心，自然會反映在各國之國內與國際法，及實體與程序法。歐盟的羅馬I及羅馬II既然於實體上之選法規則有相關之規定，布魯塞爾規則（COUNCIL REGULATION（EC）No 44/2001 of 22 December 2000 on jurisdiction and the recognition and enforcement of judgments in civil and commercial matters）於相關之程序上之管轄規則自然亦有著甚多配合性之規定。第5(3)條照例以侵權行為或準侵權行為地或可能發生地為特別管轄[46]，而這個行為地於解釋上是包含行為作成地及損害發生地。92重訴4號應注意的是歐盟建立這個規則的判例法，Handelskwekerij G. J. Bier B.V. v Mines de Potasse d'Alsace S.A.[47]，亦是為有關水污染之判例。而歐盟法院甚早就明白的宣示行為作

---

ligations arising out of the contract have to be or have been performed, in so far as those overriding mandatory provisions render the performance of the contract unlawful. In considering whether to give effect to those provisions, regard shall be had to their nature and purpose and to the consequences of their application or non-application.

43 (b) by way of derogation from paragraphs 2 and 3, a Member State may lay down that the insurance contract shall be government by the law of the Member State that imposes the obligation to take out insurance.

44 5. For the purposes of paragraph 3, third subparagraph, and paragraph 4, where the contract covers risks situated in more than one Member State, the contract shall be considered as constituting several contracts each relating to only one Member State.

45 The American Law Institute, Restatement of the Law, Second, s. 193, comment (f)，亦做同樣之論述，可見這是個全球化法學的共同核心。

46 3. In matters relating to tort, delict or quasi-delict, in the courts for the place where the harmful event occurred or may occur;

47 [1976] ECR 1736.見paras. 16, 17, 20, 21, 22.
"16 Liability in tort, delict or quasi-delict can only arise provided that a causal connexion can be established between the damage and the event in which that damage originates."
"17 Taking into account the close connexion between the component parts of every sort of liability, it

成地與損害發生地皆與侵權行為之發生有必要之關連，故而兩者中之任何一個連結因素皆應構成管轄基礎。同樣的於92重訴4號案中兩連結因素皆發生於台灣，而依許多歐盟國家之國際及國內法任何一個連結因素皆可構成管轄，台灣屏東地院卻認為「台灣不方便」，台灣屏東地院必須對「方便」的定義給予全世界一點白色的曙光。

另外對於保險布魯塞爾規則規定於第3段，而其亦充斥著保護保單持有人、被保險人、受益人、及被害人之全球化共同核心政策。其第9條[48]除了規定保險人得於其住所地被起訴外，保單持有人、被保險人、或受益人得於自己之住所地對保險人起訴。故而92重訴4號應知道保險人於原告之住所地被提起訴訟，非但不是不方便而且是二十一世紀中全球化經濟潮流中之生活寫實。保險人被為利害關係人之原告於原告住所地起訴，已是

---

does not appear appropriate to opt for one of the two connecting factors mentioned to the exclusion of the other, since each of them can, depending on the circumstances, be particularly helpful from the point of view of the evidence and of the conduct of the proceedings."

"20 This conclusion is supported by the consideration, first, that to decide in favour only of the place of the event giving rise to the damage would, in an appreciable number of cases, cause confusion between the heads of jurisdiction laid down by Article 2 and 5(3) of the Convention, so that the latter provision would, to that extent, lose its effectiveness."

"21 Secondly, a decision in favour only of the place where the damage occurred would, in cases where the place of the event giving rise to the damage does not coincide with the domicile of the person liable, have the effect of excluding a helpful connecting factor with the jurisdiction of a court particularly near to the cause of the damage."

"22 Moreover, it appears from a comparison of the national legislative provisions and national case-law on the distribution of jurisdiction – both as regards internal relationships, as between courts for different areas, and in international relationships – that, albeit by differing legal techniques, a place is found for both of the two connecting factors here considered and that in several States they are accepted concurrently."

故而於侵權行為上，行為作成地與損害發生地任何一個連結因素皆可於國內或國際管轄上構成充分而合理之管轄基礎，並且這亦是許多歐盟國家的國內及國際判例法及成文法。

48 Article 9

1. An insurer domiciled in a Member State may be sued:
   (a) in the courts of the Member State where he is domiciled, or
   (b) in another Member State, in the case of actions brought by the policyholder, the insured or a beneficiary, in the courts for the place where the plaintiff is domiciled,
   (c) if he is a co-insurer, in the courts of a Member State in which proceedings are brought against the leading insurer.
2. An insurer who is not domiciled in a Member State but has a branch, agency or other establishment in one of the Member States shall, in disputes arising out of the operations of the branch, agency or establishment, be deemed to the domiciled in that Member State.

二十一世紀之常識及生活經驗，並且這個生活經驗已成為二十一世紀之全球化法學之共同核心政策，92重訴4號之裁定是與二十一世紀之生活經驗、常識、及全球化法學之共同核心相違背的。

另外第10條[49]又規定責任保險或不動產之保險，保險人亦額外的得於損害發生地被起訴。對於墾丁這個損害發生地，92重訴4號卻認為「不方便」去起訴保險人，屏東地院充分證明，「世界上有其他地區，在那裡事情是極度糟糕的」。92重訴4號特殊的地方是其幾乎違背了相關聯合國之公約、保險法、民事訴訟法、國際私法、不方便法院法學、及侵權法每一相關部門最基本核心的概念，而且跟二十一世紀的生活經驗、常識、及全球化法學共同核心概念亦背道而馳。問台灣法界及學界有幾多野蠻無知之概念，恰似一江春水向東流。

另外挪威法院之母法歐盟布魯塞爾規則第11條[50]對被害人（台灣）之訴訟權更有明示規定。11(1)條規定：「有關責任保險，如果法院地法許可下，被害人於對被保險人之訴訟中，得將保險人加入訴訟程序。」而11(2)條亦規定：「於直接訴訟被允許下，被害人直接對保險人之訴訟得適用8、9、及10條。」因為台灣法允許直接訴訟，故除了保險人之住所地外，被害人得於其住所地（台灣）或損害發生地（台灣），直接向保險人起訴；或者被害人於向被保險人在台灣起訴時，得要求將保險人加入訴訟。於後者之情形，台灣民訴53條是有著共同訴訟之規定[51]，但無論國內

---

49 Article 10
In respect of liability insurance or insurance of immovable property, the insurer may in addition be sued in the courts for the place where the harmful event occurred. The same applies if movable and immovable property are covered by the same insurance policy and both are adversely affected by the same contingency.

50 Article 11
1. In respect of liability insurance, the insurer may also, if the law of the court permits it, be joined in proceedings which the injured party has brought against the insured.
2. Article 8, 9 and 10 shall apply to actions brought by the injured party directly against the insurer, where such direct actions are permitted.
3. If the law governing such direct actions provides that the policyholder or the insured may be joined as a party to the action, the same court shall have jurisdiction over them.

51 民事訴訟法第53條
二人以上於下列各款情形，得為共同訴訟人，一同起訴或一同被訴：

法是否有著規定，因應21世紀之時勢，應將其視為有著規定。根據11(1)及(2)條，92重訴4號再度侵犯了被害人之直接訴訟權，這個瘋狂的裁定不但踐踏了聯合國所給予的相關公約、全球化法學的共同核心，更直接的藐視挪威的母法。

更有趣的是12(1)[52]條規定：「於不影響11(3)條下，無論被告是保單持有人、被保險人、或受益人，保險人只得於被告住所地之會員國法院提起訴訟。」於案中被告保險人於2003年6月6日向挪威「管轄地方法院主張其無庸負責」，這個否認之訴（確認債權不存在之訴）自然是向保單持有人、被保人提起。這種否認之訴之被提起，已違反挪威法院母法布魯塞爾規則12條之規定，但或許因被害人為中國人而非歐盟人故挪威法院擺明著踐踏歐盟的法律尊嚴，以攫取跨國保險公司的利潤。這個現象是個人一再指控「岳不群法學」、「掠奪式殖地主義」是西方法學的潛在基礎之故。這亦是個人一再認為西方法院以「利益」為基礎之理由，個人認為中國式法學應以「己所不欲，勿施於人」之王道、仁道為基礎，以替我們子孫建立一個千秋萬世的恢宏制度。個人已一再指出殷鑑不遠，美國近幾十年來一再以「不方便法院」為莫須有之理由，拒絕受害之第三世界人民要美國跨國企業為其暴行負起責任，然美國國勢仍是繼續下跌。是故個人主張中國式法學應以王道為主，而拒絕短暫「利益」的誘惑。中國式王道法學不爭一世，而爭千秋。

如果保險人只能對相關被告於其住所地起訴，那麼很明顯的被害人於其住所地之屏東地院起訴是不可能構成不方便法院。但非常遺憾的是原告

---

(1) 為訴訟標的之權利或義務，為其所共同者。
(2) 為訴訟標的之權利或義務，本於同一之事實上及法律上原因者。
(3) 為訴訟標的之權利或義務，係同種類，而本於事實上及法律上同種類之原因者。但以被告之住所在同一法院管轄區域內或有第四條至第十九條所定之共同管轄法院者為限。」

52 Article 12

1. Without prejudice to Article 11(3), an insurer may bring proceedings only in the courts of the Member State in which the defendant is domiciled, irrespective of whether he is the policyholder, the insured or a beneficiary.
2. The provisions of this Section shall not affect the right to bring a counter-claim in the court in which, in accordance with this Section, the original claim is pending.

於2004年3月5日在挪威地院提起反訴—於國內及國際訴訟法上這即意味著原告放棄抗辯而承認挪威之管轄。這到底是怎麼回事？中國人沒有國際法的學生嗎？不必根據國內及國際訴訟法之常識，布魯塞爾規則13(1)[53]條即規定上述之強行法得於事故發生後經由當事人之同意而放棄（當事人於事後得以契約加以放棄，故是第二級強行法，非為第一級任何應適用之法律皆不可違背之強行法）。

五、否認之訴

事實上台灣法院應注意到被告保險人於挪威所提的為否認債權存在之訴（確認之訴）、「被告Gard於同年（2003）6月6日向管轄地法院起訴主張無庸負責」。這是典型的否認之訴（確認之訴）。海牙會議於1999年草約（Preliminary Draft Convention on Jurisdiction and Foreign Judgments in Civil and Commercial Matters）之21條雖然採先繫屬優先法則，但詭異的是除了採納這個大陸法的法則外，其又於21(7)條及22條採英美法的不方便法院法則。有趣的是不似布魯塞爾公約及規則的將先繫屬優先視為不可侵犯的聖牛，其21(6)[54]條規定：「如果於第1個接受訴訟的法院

53 Article 13
The Provisions of this Section may be departed from only by an agreement:
1. which is entered into after the dispute has arisen, or
2. which allows the policyholder, the insured or a beneficiary to bring proceedings in courts other than those indicated in this Section, or
3. which is concluded between a policyholder and an insurer, both of whom are at the time of conclusion of the contract domiciled or habitually resident in the same Member State, and which has the effect of conferring jurisdiction on the courts of that State even if the harmful event were to occur abroad, provided that such an agreement is not contrary to the law of that State, or
4. which is concluded with a policyholder who is not domiciled in a Member State, except in so far as the insurance is compulsory or relates to immovable property in a Member State, or
5. which relates to a contract of insurance in so far as it covers one or more of the risks set out in Article 14.

54 6. If in the action before the court first seised the plaintiff seeks a determination that it has no obligation to the defendant, and if an action seeking substantive relief is brought in the court second seised –
a) the provisions of paragraph 1 to 5 above shall not apply to the court second seised, and
b) the court first seised shall suspend the proceedings at the request of a party if the court second seised is expected to render a decisions capable of being recognised under the Convention.

中，原告要求確認其對被告並無義務，並且如果於第2繫屬的訴訟中是有關實質上之救濟-(a)本條文第1至5項之規定（即先繫屬優先）應不能適用至第2繫屬法院，及(b)如果第2繫屬法院是被認為會作成依公約會被承認之判決，在當事人之要求下，第1繫屬法院應停止其程序。」1999年草約雖然最後未能付之實施，但亦可於某些方面上充分的代表著全球化法學對否認之訴之疑慮。通常全球化法學是會包括國際法與國內法。事實上台灣民訴247條[55]亦對否認之訴（確認之訴）的提起多所限制，必須原告有法律上利益，及以原告不能提起他訴訟者為限。92重訴4號非常奇怪的是不但視國際法上之全球化法學之共同核心價值如蔽屣，亦視自己所宣誓效忠的台灣民事訴訟法如無物。台灣法界及學界（包含國內及國際法）所作成的見解，有時（或經常）已經達到任我行法學的境界。「諸法皆空，自由自在」，是二十一世紀現代版的no law no heaven。

對於國際案件上之否認之訴Cheshire and North[56]是如此的論述：「去

---

55 民事訴訟法第247條：
確認法律關係之訴，非原告有即受確認判決之法律上利益，不得提起之；確認證書真偽或為法律關係基礎事實存否之訴，亦同。
前項確認法律關係基礎事實存否之訴，以原告不能提起他訴訟者為限。
前項情形，如果利用同一訴訟程序提起他訴訟者，審判長應闡明之；原告因而為訴之變更或追加時，不受第二百五十五條第一項前段規定之限制。
又見Messier-Dowty v Sabena SA (No 2), [2000] 1 WLR 2040, 2050 CA, Lord Woolf MR: "The deployment of negative declarations should be scrutinised and their use rejected where it would serve no useful purpose. However, where a negative declaration would help to ensure that the aims of justice are achieved the courts should not be reluctant to grant such declarations. They can and do assist in achieving justice."

56 PM North, JJ Fawcett, Cheshire and North's Private International law, 13th ed., p. 318, "One important factor that is taken into account in deciding whether the case is a proper one for service out of the jurisdiction, not mentioned by Lord Goff in the Spiliada Case, is that the claimant seeks a negative declaration from the English courts. The jurisdiction to grant such a declaration is exercised with caution, and most of the cases where a negative declaration has been sought have been held not to be proper ones for service out of the jurisdiction. If the possibility exists that the claimant in the English proceedings will be sued by the defendant in an alternative forum abroad, the English court must be particularly careful to ensure that the negative declaration is sought for a valid and valuable purpose and not in an illegitimate attempt to pre-empt the jurisdiction in which the dispute between the parties is to be resolved. However, this factor is not an absolute bar to such service. 又見14th ed., p. 408: The modern approach towards the grant of negative declarations is set out in Messier-Dowty v Sabena SA (No 2), where Lord Eoolf MR said that:
The deployment of negative declarations should be scrutinized and their use rejected where it would serve no useful purpose. However, where a negative declaration would help to ensure that the aims of

允許這種宣示的管轄權是謹慎的被行使著，並且於否認之訴被提出時，在大部分案件中是被認定為不合適去送達境外[57]。如果於英國程序的原告會為被告在外國的另一法院起訴的機會是存在的，英國法院一定必須特別謹慎以確保該否認之訴是基於有效及有價值的目的而被提起，而不是非法的企圖先搶得解決當事人糾紛的管轄權[58]。但是這個因素並不是這種送達（境外）的絕對限制。[59]」於92重訴4號中自然原告已於自然法院（損害發生之專屬管轄法院）向自然被告（行為人及其保險人）提起自然之訴訟，被告在遙遠的法院（a remote forum）提起否認之訴（negative declaration），自然是有著選購法院（forum shopping）之目的，「非法的企圖先搶得解決當事人糾紛的管轄權」。這並非國際法高級的技術性問題，而是Cardozo J.所謂「常識」的問題，亦是恩師Prof. Graveson所強調的「正義的基本目的」的問題。而自然原告於自然法院告自然被告，更是我們祖先所說的「道法自然」。92重訴4號已明顯的違反美、英、及中國前輩同僚之法理，台灣的法院在這種全世界矚目的石油污染案中，有義務透露一些白色曙光來啟蒙全世界。

但是不同於布魯塞爾公約及規則拙笨的忽視了選購法院及否認之訴的負面效果，亦不同於海牙1999年草約的硬性停止否認之訴的進行。英美

justice are achieved the courts should not be reluctant to grant such declarations. They can and do assist in achieving justice.

No valid reason could be seen for taking an adverse view of negative declaratory relief. The crucial question therefore is whether such a declaration would serve a useful purpose. An example of whether it would do so is where the person against whom it is sought is "temporizing" (ie was not prepared to come forward and make his claim). Where the negative declaration would serve a useful purpose the normal forum conveniens principles (or forum non conveniens) will then apply. Where the negative declaration would serve no useful purpose, permission for service out of the jurisdiction should be refused or, in a case of forum non conveniens, a stay granted. Careful scrutiny must be exercised not just to test utility but also to ensure that inappropriate forum shopping is not allowed. [2000] 1 WLR 2040, 2049, CA.

57 *Insurance Corpn of Ireland v Strombus International Insurance Co* [1985] 2 Lloyd's Rep 138 at 144, CA; *The Volvox Hollandia* [1988] 2 Lloyd's Rep 361, CA; DR Insurance Co v Central National Insurance Co [1996] 1 Lloyd's Rep 74 at 83 et seq; *New Hampshire Insurance Co v Aerospace Finance Ltd* [1998] 2 Lloyd's Rep 539. See also *Akai Pty Ltd v People's Insurance Co Ltd* [1998] 1 Lloyd's Rep 90 at 106.

58 *New Hampshire Insurance Co v Phillips Electronics North American Corpn* [1998] 1 L Pr 256, CA.

59 *HIB v Guardian Insurance* [1997] 1 Lloyd's Rep 412.

法院視給予法院充分的裁量權去拒絕否認之訴的進行，但於正義之需求下亦得允許否認之訴的進行。Cheshire and North[60]又說：「請求人於英國法院提起否認之訴的事實，於實際上會造成有利於停止訴訟的因素。這是一種例外的救濟形式，並且只有在請求者有主張的好理由時才能被考慮[61]。當管轄權可能有衝突時應被加以慎重的警惕[62]。但是，在一個案件中雖然有著英國法院管轄條款，而否認之訴的被提起是被視為維持當事人所同意之準據法之方法[63]，訴訟仍得被停止。於正義的利益下否認之訴仍是得以被允許的，例如當其能確保有關連的類似行為會同時於一次審判之程序中被處理。[64]」

雖然德國法傳統上比起英、美及法國法傳統上較能接受確認之訴，德國民事訴訟法256條亦有本著當事人「法律上之利益」（legal interest）概念而來之「確認之訴」（declaratory action），而其「訴因」之觀念與歐盟法院不儘相似[65]。但無論如何自然被告所提之確認之訴當可被自然原

---

60 PM North, JJ Fawcett, Cheshire and North's Private International law, 13th ed., p. 339, "The fact that the claimant seeks a negative declaration from the English courts, in effect, operates as a factor in favour of granting a stay. This is an extraordinary form of relief and will only be considered if the applicant has good reason to seek it. Great caution is needed where there may be conflicts of jurisdiction. Nevertheless, a stay may be granted and was in one case where there was an English choice of jurisdiction clause and the negative declaration sought was seen as a way of upholding the agreed law governing the contract. A negative declaration will be granted if this is in the interests of justice, for example where it ensures that proceedings in relation to comparable transaction will all be tried at one and the same time." 14th ed., pp. 432, 433.

61 *Camilla Cotton Oil Co v Granadex SA* [1976] 2 Lloyd's Rep 10; *New Hampshire Insurance Co v Phillips Electronics North American Corpn* [1998] IL Pr 256, CA.

62 *The Volvox Hollandia* [1988] 2 Lloyd's Rep 361; *Sohio Supply Co v Gatoil (USA) Inc* [1989] 1 Lloyd's Rep 588.

63 *Akai Pty Ltd v People's Insurance Co Ltd* [1998] 1 Lloyd's Rep 90.

64 *Smyth v Behhehani* (1999) Times, 9 April, CA.

65 Zivilprozessordnung [ZPO][Code of Civil Procedure] Jan. 30, 1877, Reichsgesetzblatt [RGBl.] [Imperial Gazette] at 83, last amended by Gesetz, Apr. 19, 2006, Bundesgesetzblatt I [BGBl. I] [Federal Gazettee, Part I] at 866, art. 50, translated in: GERMAN COMMERCIAL CODE & CODE OF CIVIL PROCEDURE IN ENGLISH (Charles E. Stewart trans.) (2001) 191, at 277. ZPO §256(1) reads as follows: "An action may be brought for the declaration of the existence or nonexistence of a legal relationship (Rechtsverhältnis) [...], provided the plaintiff has a legal interest (rechtliches Interesse) in having promptly determined the legal relation [...]."以上引自Martin Gebauer, "Lis Pendens, Negative Declaratory-Judgment Actions and the First-in-Time Principle", in "Conflict of Laws in a Globalized World", edited by Eckart Gottschalk, Ralf Michaels, Giesela Rühl Jan Von Hein, p. 95.

告所提之要求救濟之訴訟可取代時，則較無決定性之效力[66]。至於什麼情形下能構成有關當事人「正當的利益」之問題，為否認之訴、選購法院、規避法律（亦即牽涉到三權分立之問題）、不方便法院、及濫訴之禁止等國內法及國際法問題之核心，於此不再贅述。

即使各國國內法通常對否認之訴、規避法律[67]、不方便法院（至少於未成年兒童之監護權上）、選購法院、及濫訴之禁止[68]皆有著不同程度上之規定，且歐盟為了達成統一判決的鐵血政策，布魯塞爾公約及規則先繫屬優先的鐵血規則超越了一切訴訟法上的常理與常識上的正義概念。英國於加入歐盟三十年後，Dicey and Morris[69]如此哀怨的評述著：「其結

---

66 "Under the traditional German approach, a natural plaintiff has the choice between litigating a declaratory action brought by a natural defendant or by initiating a coercive action himself. It is probably due to this solution that German law traditionally was more receptive to declaratory action than were Franch, English, or U.S. law: the declaratory action is less decisive when it may be displaced by a coercive action."同上，95頁。有趣的是布魯塞爾公約與規則英文版皆使用「訴因」，但歐盟法院卻認定德國與英國於此問題上必須有著相同的意義。"The doctrinal explanation for the traditional German approach lies in the concept of 'legal interest,' which is required for a declaratory action according to §256 of the Code of Civil Procedure, and in the concept of 'the cause of action' (Streitgegenstand), which differs somewhat from the Brussels concept as developed by the European Court of Justice (supra II.1). Under German law, the coercive action does not have the same cause as has the negative declaratory action, but it goes further. By initiating a coercive action, the plaintiff demands more than a clarification of an existing legal relationship. The purpose of coercive relief is to compel the defendant to actually do something for example, to pay a certain amount of money, which includes, however, answering the incidental question as to whether the defendant is obliged to do so. As a consequence, lis pendens (Rechtshängigkeit) does not apply if the negative declaratory action was a first-in-time action. It does rule, however, if the coercive action was a first-in-time action. In addition, the legal interest that is a precondition for a declaratory action disappears if a subsequent coercive action is brought before the same court or another court."德國這種過分重邏輯的分類，或許會增加判決不一致之可能，而且或許可能有時會導致違反一事不再理或禁反言之程序正義，故而這種「訴因」之定義不太可能為英美法所接受。如果德國訴訟法能引進訴因及爭點禁反言，或許就不會振振有詞的玩起庸人自擾的邏輯遊戲，於個案正義的追求上就會多放熱而少放光。

67 另外非常遺憾的是，個人之另一重要主張長期被忽略。個人早期已陳述過英國並無禁止「規避法律」（evasion of the law）之判例，此法國式作風英國並不認同。因為基於三權分立之原則，法院是執法單位，法律若有漏洞，應由立法機關補足。在這之前，人民之行為縱使其目的是在規避法律，只要不違法，法院無權干涉。見陳隆修，《國際私法契約評論》，台北，五南圖書公司，民國75年2月，初版，頁28。但如大陸法的誠信原則，英美法亦要求契約必須「合理」，所選的準據法必須是"bona fide and legal"。

68 見陳隆修，《國際私法管轄權評論》，台北，五南圖書公司，民國75年11月，初版，84、85、86、280、281頁。

69 Dicey and Morris, the Conflict of Laws, 14th ed., edited by Lawrence Collins, p. 487. "The result is that, in recent years, more actions for negative declaratory relief have been brought and permitted to proceed than was the case thirty years ago." See also Trevor C. Hartley, *How to abuse the law and*

果是，在近幾年，比起三十年前的情形有更多的否認之訴之請求被提起及被允許進行。」但是即使是依歐盟布魯塞爾規則的鐵血規定，92重訴4號仍是：(1)有著充分的管轄基礎；(2)符合先繫屬優先的荒唐機械式鐵血規定。

六、天道無親

對於歐盟為著市場利益而不惜犧牲司法個案正義，以求得法律之快速統一，個人主張這是有著二千五百年王道文化的中國式法律所應引為殷鑑的警惕[70]。先繫屬優先為西方法學以利益為核心基礎的代表性標竿鐵血野蠻規則，個人較近如此評述[71]：「於國際上有複數訴訟時，毫無選擇的以原告所偏好的第一個法院為唯一有管轄權的法院，自然對被告甚為不公，不但違背了以原告就被告（actor sequitur forum rei）這個訴訟法上的基本理念，並且自然會造成原告選購法院（forum shopping）的國際私法夢魘。」另外對歐盟為著統一會員國之判決，將先繫屬優先原則（lis pendens）的置於選購法院及否認之訴上，又如此的評述[72]：「原告若於英國提起否認債權存在之訴（negative declaration），因為被告將可能於外國對原告提起告訴，故而英國法院於此情形下會非常謹慎的去避免原告先取得管轄權之優勢，而通常不會送達通知至外國。但與1999年海牙民商管轄草約不同的是，如若原告之目的乃是為了有效及有意義的解決當事人間之紛爭時，則法院之通知可被送達至國外[73]。於現代之商業訴訟中，特別

(maybe) come out on top: bad-faith proceedings under the Brussels Jurisdiction and Judgments Convention, in Law and Justice in a Multistate World, Essays in Honor of Arthur T. von Mehren 73, James A. R. Nafziger & Symeon C. Symeonides eds.

70 陳隆修，《由歐盟經驗論中國式國際私法》，載於〈新世紀兩岸國際私法〉，五南圖書公司，2011年11月。

71 陳隆修，《2005年海牙法院選擇公約評析》，台北，五南圖書公司，2009年1月，初版1刷，36頁。

72 同上，36頁。

73 The Rama [1996] 2 Lloyd's Rep. 281,291; A Kai Pty Ltd v. People's Insurance Co Ltd [1998] 1 Lloyd's Rep.539, 543; Tryg Baltica International (U K) Ltd v Boston compania de Seguros SA [2004] EWHC 1186 (Comm.), [2005] Lloyd's Rep. L. R. 40.

是於保險業中，當事人可能有正當的需求去早點決定其是否負有責任。例如保險公司可能想知道是否應替其被保人之責任進行辯護[74]，或者廠商可能想知道其是否有義務繼續供給其經銷商[75]。歐盟1968 Brussels Convention, Lugano Convention，及2000年管轄規則於管轄基礎及lis pendens的適用上，對於negative declaration的案件並未特別規定；另外大陸法系特別憎惡之選購法院（forum shopping）亦未明文禁止。故而在歐盟較近牽涉到多重訴訟之案件中[76]，即使其中之一訴訟為否認債權之訴，歐盟法院仍堅持先繫屬優先原則。」如果略過歐盟利欲薰心的顢頇無知，依照傳統判例法，於92重訴4號中被告保險公司的確「有正當的需求去早點決定其是否負有責任」。但是這個理由於92重訴4號中是不存在的，台灣法院已經處理該爭點中。於92重訴4號中，自然原告（被害人）已經於自然法院（污染發生地之損害發生法院及專屬法院）向所有的自然被告（行為人及保險人）「一併」提起自然之訴，自然被告（保險人）於一個「遙遠的法院」再次提起平行訴訟，顯然是「困擾性」、「壓性」的「選購法院」之「濫用訴訟程序」之不符「誠信」之行為，其「壓迫性」、「困擾性」之濫訴，不但可能造成會有著不一致結果的複數訴訟，而且明顯的會拖延判決的程序之不自然訴訟。這是個人所一再指責的第一世界的跨國公司欺壓第三世界人民的「掠奪性新殖民主義」（predatory neocolonialism）、「掠奪性恐怖主義」（predatory terrorism）、及「岳不群法學」。做為第三世界的國際法學生，個人必須鄭重的指出小國寡民的挪威等西方第一世界，只要一有機會能夠聞到第三世界人民的血汗，馬上拋棄聯合國人權公約、諾貝爾和平獎的經咒，立即恢復第一世界嗜血食肉的掠食動物天性，而與黑暗帝國美國所實施的「不方便法院」並駕齊驅，在全球化的市場上揮舞著「自由市場」、「比較經濟利益」的刀劍，四處追逐第三世

[74] HIB Ltd v Guardian Insurance Co Inc [1997] 1 Lloyd's Rep. 412.

[75] Smyth v Behbehani [1991] I. L. Pr. 599(CA).

[76] Gubisch Maschinenfabrik KG v Palumbo 144/86[1987] E.C.R.4861; The Tastry [1994] E.C.R.I-5439; Overseas Union Insurance Ltd v New Hampshire Insurance Co [1991] E.C.R.I - 3317.

界人民的血肉。於WTO中第一世界所揮舞「自由市場」、「比較經濟利益」的偽善雖早已為第三世界所看見，但於國際法上第一世界所施放的各種「岳不群法學」煙幕並非法律科學落後的第三世界所能抗衡。「天道無親恆與善人」，再次崛起的中華民族唯有本著「王道」法學才能於二十一世紀的全球化法學中領袖全球，達成聯合國人權公約中1966年兩個人權公約第1條的生存權，及真正的平等權。

(一)不患寡患不均法學

於評述契約法時，個人主張中國式法學（國內及國際法）應以二千多年來「不患寡而患不均」之祖訓為核心，並且這個千年不易的祖訓應為二十一世紀全球化法學的共同核心最基本的主流價值。個人之所以如此強調再三乃是針對英美法的「促進商業」傳統。20世紀見證了資本主義所引發的對第三世界的掠奪、環境的污染、貧富的不均、司法正義的傾向資本持有者（無論是個人或國家）、及一再循環發生的世界性金融風暴，而歐盟與英美卻仍然迷信於自由資本的流竄得以掠奪第三世界以維持第一世界的繁榮。自Victoria時代英國法院即信奉著Jeremy Bentham的功利主義，或許於兩百年前工業革命時這種法學的確能促進社會之生產。但個人深信二十一世紀的全球化法學之核心是應本著「禮運大同」、「不患寡而患不均」的中國王道哲學而來——於二十一世紀人類文明的重心已進化到以個案正義為共同核心，沒有個案正義就沒有全球化法學的一致性。二十一世紀聯合國人權公約應是本著「己所不欲，勿施於人」之中國式「王道」、「仁道」法學為詮釋之基礎，而不是剝奪第三世界1966年兩個人權公約第一條生存權的WTO的「比較經濟利益」、「自由經濟」為假平等的詮釋基礎。所謂的「比較經濟利益」、「自由經濟」於實際上是享有資本、技術、行銷的一方之「比較利益」及「自由經濟」，這是違反1966年人權公約的真平等權，亦違反「不患寡而患不均」之中國哲學，故應不符合二十一世紀全球化法學之潮流。二十一世紀全球化之經濟學及法學，皆應以中國二千五百年之「中庸」哲學為共同核心主流價值。

於92重訴4號中保險人之「正當的需求去早點決定其是否有負責任」之傳統判例法如果被推至極限則可能會是個過時的產物。二十一世紀全球化法學所重視的不是「利潤的提高」，而是「個案正義的維護」。現今保險法的共同核心是在保護保單持有人、受益人、及被害人，這個全球化保險法的共同核心已由保險法、管轄規則、及選法規則中充分被證明。故而個人一再強調已有二千多年的中國文化應於二十一世紀中華民族再次崛起時，取代英美法本著十九世紀資本主義而來的過時法學。是故「天行健，君子以自強不息」，是故「道法自然」。

(二)共同訴訟與第三人訴訟

除了上述管轄基礎外，於共同訴訟上92重訴4號或許於國際管轄上得將台灣民訴53條(1)、(2)[77]款擴張適用於國際案件上。而歐盟布魯塞爾規則如前述對保險已有規定，故於第6條[78]共同訴訟上或許不需要適用於保險案件。其6(1)條規定於數個被告時，如果數個請求是密切關連，為著避免個別訴訟造成相衝突判決，並且方便一起審理之情形下，得於任何被告之會員國住所地對被告提起訴訟。相較之下92重訴4號之保險人被告之於挪威再提起訴訟，挪威法院及被告明顯的違反大陸法歐盟母法強調判決一致的鐵血政策，這是岳不群法學的另一次展現。而6(2)條為有關保證人或

---

77 民事訴訟法第53條（共同訴訟之要件）
二人以上於下列各款情形，得為共同訴訟人，一同起訴或一同被訴：
一為訴訟標的之權利或義務，為其所共同者。
二為訴訟標的之權利或義務，本於同一之事實上及法律上原因者。

78 Article 6
A person domiciled in a Member State may also be sued:
1. where he is one of a number of defendants, in the courts for the place where any one of them is domiciled, provided the claims are closely connected that it is expedient to hear and determine them together to avoid the risk of irreconcilable judgments resulting from separate proceedings;
2. as a third party in an action on a warranty or guarantee or in any other third party proceedings, in the courts seised of the original proceedings, unless these were instituted solely with the object of removing him from the jurisdiction of the court which would be competent in his case;
3. on a counter-claim arising from the same contract or facts on which the original claim was based, in the court in which the original claim is pending;
4. in matters relating to a contract, if the action may be combined with an action against the same defendant in matters relating to rights in rem in immovable property, in the court of the Member State in which the property is situated.

擔保人及其他第三人訴訟得於原來之訴訟被起訴之規定，故而92重訴4號是符合歐盟規則，並且不太可能是不方便法院。

而1999年海牙草約14條[79]的多數被告訴訟中，規定對於非慣居地被告為了避免判決不一致及重大關聯下亦得起訴。但更直接適用的應是英美法所慣稱的第三人訴訟。其16條[80]規定若訂約國法允許下，若被告主張第三人對其所被請求的義務有賠償之責任，而訴訟地（法院地國）與牽連該第三人之紛爭有著重大關聯，則該法院亦有管轄權處理被告對第三人之請求。但這個規定不能違反被告與第三人間之專屬管轄條款。故除非當事人間訂有專屬管轄條款，否則92重訴4號是沒有理由主張台灣為不方便之地。

英國的Civil Procedure Rules 1998, S. 6.20(3)[81]規定於法院允許下得將訴訟的文件送達境外（亦即法院因而有管轄權）：「(3)對於請求的文

---

79 Article 14 Multiple defendants

1. A plaintiff bringing an action against a defendant in a court of the State in which that defendant is habitually resident may also proceed in that court against other defendants not habitually resident in that State if –
   a) the claims against the defendant habitually resident in that State and the other defendants are so closely connected that they should be adjudicated together to avoid a serious risk of inconsistent judgments, and
   b) as to each defendant not habitually resident in that State, there is a substantial connection between that State and the dispute involving that defendant.
2. Paragraph 1 shall not apply to a codefendant invoking an exclusive choice of court clause agreed with the plaintiff and conforming with Article 4.

80 Article 16 Third party claims

1. A court which has jurisdiction to determine a claim under the provisions of the Convention shall also have jurisdiction to determine a claim by a defendant against a third party for indemnity or contribution in respect of the claim against that defendant to the extent that such an action is permitted by national law, provided that there is a substantial connection between that State and the dispute involving that third party.
2. Paragraph 1 shall not apply to a third party invoking an exclusive choice of court clause agreed with the defendant and conforming with Article 4.

81 6.20 Service out of the jurisdiction where the permission of the court is required

In any proceedings to which rule 6.19 does not apply, a claim form may be served out of the jurisdiction with the permission of the court if –

(3) a claim is made against someone on whom the claim form has been or will be served and –

(a) there is between the claimant and that person a real issue which it is reasonable for the court to try; and

(b) the claimant wishes to serve the claim form on another person who is a necessary or proper party to that claim.

件已經或將會送達之人提起請求並且－(a)請求人與被請求人間有一真正的紛爭合理的需要法院去審理；並且(b)對於該請求是一個必須或合適之當事人之其他人，請求人欲送達請求之文件。」故而如果第三人對該請求是必須或合適之當事人，亦可一併提起訴訟。但如個人前述送達境外基本上是屬於例外或過度之管轄，故除了必須有一個真正的紛爭合理的需要法院去審判外，s. 6.21(1)(b)還要求請求人「有著合理的勝訴機會」[82]，s.6.21（2A）又規定法院地須為「合適去提起請求之地」[83]。於92重訴4號中，台灣國家公園之沿岸被徹底的污染破壞，自然是「超過合理的勝訴機會」；而依據聯合國的油污染公約台灣是專屬法院地，故自然是「專屬、排他的合適提起請求地」。反觀於挪威之否認之訴，保險人是「超過合理的敗訴機會」；挪威法院是個違反聯合國公約專屬管轄的「不自然、選購法院、濫用訴訟」之後繫屬法院，其規避國際訴訟法的不誠信行為是昭然若揭，故不是個「合適提起請求之地」。

另外有趣的是92重訴4號法院認為：「雖被告Amorgos等三人之請求以行為地法即我國法為準據法，本案仍應以挪威法院進行審理為宜。」個人已一再重申準據法為法院地法時，無論於英、美都對法院於認定自己為

---

82 (b) that the claimant believes that his claim has a reasonable prospect of success.

83 (2A) The court will not give permission unless satisfied that England and Wales is the proper place in which to bring the claim.
見陳隆修，《國際私法管轄權評論》，台北，五南圖書公司，民國75年11月，初版，頁66、67。
「1.對原被告所提起之訴訟必須為『適當的』（proper）。所謂『適當的』提起訴訟即原被告必須為一『主要的』（principal）或『真正及重要的』（real and substantial）被告。亦即原被告被提起訴訟而做為被告之目的，不可只是為了使法院對於居住法院地外之共同被告有管轄權而已。此外，即使於英國之原被告對該訴訟之標的有著真實之利益，並且原告提起訴訟之目的並非只是針對法院地外之共同被告，假如於英國之原被告有著絕對的抗辯權，而原告之訴一定會失敗，則此訴訟之提起不能構成『適當的提起訴訟』之要件。如於The Brabo案中，由於英皇室友司法豁免權，故英國最高法院（the House of Lords）拒絕將訴訟之通知送達到法院地外之比利時共同被告。[1949] A.C. 326.」
「3.居於法院地外之共同被告必須於該訴訟中為一必要或適當之被告。一般英國法院判定法院地外之共同被告是否為該訴訟中之必要共同被告之標準（test）為：設若原被告與居住於法院地外之被告皆於法院地內時，它們是否皆為該訴訟之適當被告？若為肯訂之答案，則自然符合此款之要件。」

方便法院有甚大之影響[84]。如美國最高法院於Gulf Oil Corp. v. Gibert[85]中所說：「於不同州籍案件之審判，由對應處理案件之州法較為熟悉的法院來審判，是比起其他的法院去解決國際私法及其所陌生的法律所造成的問題，是亦較為合適。」主要案件之準據法為法院地法，而法院卻宣稱自己為「不方便法院」，這是違反常識、判例法實現正義的基本目的、及自然道法。個人至此已無語問蒼天。

七、管轄權之行使或限制

至於法院是否必須有著管轄權後才能宣布「不方便法院」以暫停訴訟之邏輯性問題，個人一向遵從恩師Prof. Graveson之指示，法律邏輯一致性的要求必須受限於判例法達成正義的基本目的。92重訴4號則似乎將「不方便法院」引為管轄權之基礎，而非行使之限制：「基於國際實務上關於解決國際管轄衝突之『不便利法庭之原則』，則應認我國法院均無管轄權，從而原告向本院提起本件訴訟，本院並無管轄權」。這個問題於Sinochem International Co., Ltd. v. Malaysia International Shipping Corporation[86]中，被美國最高法院認為是：「這是一個即刻的以不方便法院駁回的教科書案例。[87]」於該案中上訴法院對地院主體（實體、訴因）管轄權之問題於第一印象中認為是具備的，並且下級法院對這個問題是相當的加以考慮的。「但是有關對人管轄權的檢驗卻會使Sinochem（被告）於費用及遲延上產生負擔。而所有的這些努力是幾乎不會有任何目的：於地方法院仔細的評估不方便法院之下，其不可避免的會駁回該案而不會達

84 陳隆修、許兆慶、林恩瑋、李瑞生四人合著，《國際私法—管轄與選法理論之交錯》，台北，五南圖書公司，2009年3月，初版1刷，198、199、207頁。
Cordoba Shipping Co Ltd. V. National State Bank, Elizabeth, New Jersey, The Albaforth [1984] 2 Lloyd's Rep. 91.

85 330 U.S. 501 at 508,
"There is an appropriateness, too, in having the trial of a diversity case in a forum that is at home with the state law that must govern the case, rather than having a court in some other forum untangle problems in conflict of laws and in law foreign to itself."

86 127 S. Ct. 1184; 549 U.S. 422 (2007)。

87 127 S. Ct. 1184, 1194, "This is a textbook case for immediate *forum non conveniens* dismissal."

成實體上之認定。由於訴訟程序於中國已進行很久，在賓州東區繼續訴訟是無法達成司法經濟。[88]」而原告主要的爭辯是有關被告於中國海商法院之爭點是不實的，美國最高法院認為是應最好由中國法院決定。一般訴訟法是認為錯誤是沒有抗拒禁反言之空間，而美國許多洲是認為唯有外部詐欺才可加以抗辯[89]，英國國內法是認為唯有法院受到影響及當事人其時不能發現才可加以抗辯，英國同僚認為國際案件應比照國內案件[90]。美國最高法院於Sinochem中有關方便法院之認定不但符合訴訟法禁反言之程序自然正義，亦符合Prof. Graveson正義的基本目的之要求。

該案為一中國公司（Sinochem）與一美國公司訂約購買鋼捲，於鋼捲裝上船後美國公司即應受到信用狀之給付，美國公司又包租一馬來西亞公司之船以運送鋼捲。中國公司於中國海商法院以馬來西亞公司不實記載提單日期而對其起訴並加以扣船。中國上訴法院維持第一審拒絕馬來西亞公司於國際管轄權上之抗辯。隨後馬來西亞公司即於聯邦地院以中國公司於中國法院之報告不實而對其起訴要求損害賠償。中國被告主張美國法院為不方便法院。美國地院及高院皆認為美國法院有著對訴因的主體（實體）管轄權，但對是否有著對人管轄權則尚需進一步之探討。地院認為中國為決定訴訟更合適更方便之法院地，故以不方便法院駁回。高院則認為沒有確認其明確的有著對主體及對人管轄權之前，不得以不方便法院駁回訴訟。

---

88 同上,
"The District Court's subject-matter jurisdiction presented an issue of first impression in the Third Circuit, see 436 F.3d, at 355, and was considered at some length by the courts below. Discovery concerning personal jurisdiction would have burdened Sinochem with expense and delay. And all to scant purpose: The District Court inevitably would dismiss the case without reaching the merits, given its well-considered *forum non conveniens* appraisal. Judicial economy is disserved by continuing litigation in the Eastern District of Pennsylvania given the proceedings long launched in China. And the gravamen of Malaysia International's complaint—misrepresentations to the Guangzhou Admiralty Court in the course of securing arrest of the vessel in China—is an issue best left for determination by the Chinese courts."

89 陳隆修，《國際私法管轄權評論》，台北，五南圖書公司，民國75年11月，初版，303～305頁。但聯邦法院及英國並不採此分類，因為內、外部詐欺有時不易區分。

90 陳隆修，《國際私法管轄權評論》，台北，五南圖書公司，民國75年11月，初版，271～275頁。

Ginsburg, J.代表全體法官如此陳述[91]：「『一個地院是否必須先確立（自己之）管轄權然才可以不方便法院之理由駁回訴訟？』……我們認定一個地院有著裁量權去即時回應被告不方便法院之主張，並且不需要即時先處理任何其他門檻上之抗辯。特別是如果已決定無論如何外國法院是明顯的對案件的實體，是更合適的仲裁者，它沒有必要去解決其是否有著權力去判定訴因（主體管轄權）或對被告之對人管轄。」

美國最高法院認定不方便法院之行使為法院之裁量權[92]，並且定性其基本上是：「一個後續介入的法院地條款，為允許取代通常的法院地規則條款，於某些條件下，承審法院認為可以拒絕管轄。[93]」

另外聯邦法院除了於少數情形下會認定州或地區法院更是為方便之法院外，聯邦地院間案件之移轉是依據前述之28 U.S.C s.1404(a)。有趣的是美國最高法院陳述：「於聯邦法院之制度，國會將該法理成文化，而在當一聯邦姊妹法院是更為方便審判該訴訟之地時，去移轉而非駁回訴

91　127 S. Ct. 1184, 1188,
"This case concerns the doctrine of *forum non conveniens*, under which a federal district court may dismiss an action on the ground that a court abroad is the more appropriate and convenient forum for adjudicating the controversy. We granted review to decide a question that has divided the Courts of Appeals: "Whether a district court must first conclusively establish [its own] jurisdiction before dismissing a suit on the ground of *forum non conveniens*?" Pet. for Cert. i. We hold that a district court has discretion to respond at once to a defendant's forum non conveniens plea, and need not take up first any other threshold objection. In particular, a court need not resolve whether it has authority to adjudicate the cause (subject-matter jurisdiction) or personal jurisdiction over the defendant if it determines that, in any event, a foreign tribunal is plainly the more suitable arbiter of the merits of the case."

92　127 S. Ct. 1184, 1190,
"A federal court has discretion to dismiss a case on the ground of forum non conveniens when an alternative forum has jurisdiction to hear [the] case, and…trial in the chosen forum would establish…oppressiveness and vexation to a defendant…out of all proportion to plaintiff's convenience, or…the chosen forum [is] inappropriate because of considerations affecting the court's own administrative and legal problems. American Dredging Co. v. Miller, 510 U.S. 443, 447-448, 114 S. Ct. 981, 127 L. Ed. 2d 285 (1994) (quoting Piper Aircraft Co. v. Reyno, 454 U.S. 235, 241, 102 S. Ct. 252, 70 L. Ed. 2d 419 (1981), in turn quoting Koster v. (American) Lumbermens Mut. Casualty Co., 330 U.S. 518, 524, 67 S. Ct. 828, 91 L. Ed. 1067 (1947).

93　同上，"We have characterized forum non conveniens as, essentially, 'a supervening venue provision, permitting displacement of the ordinary rules of venue when, in light of certain conditions, the trial court thinks that jurisdiction ought to be declined,' American Dredging, 510, U.S., at 453, 114 S. Ct. 981, 127 L. Ed. 2d 285; cf. In re Papandreou, 139 F. 3d, at 255 (forum non conveniens 'involves a deliberate abstention from the exercise of jurisdiction')."

訟。[94]」故而判例上之「不方便法院」法學，不但適用於聯邦法院對外國法院，少數情形下適用於對州法院，更於聯邦地院間已有成文化之依據。將對州法院，更於聯邦地院間已有成文化之依據。將28 U.S.C s.1404(a)的視為「不方便法院」法學的成文化，相對於英國在對停止英國訴訟之「不方便法院」法學仍屬判例法是有趣的。但應注意的是英國法院允許送達境外之C.P.R. 1998, s.6.21（2A）規定法院須為「合適去提起請求之地」，是為「方便法院」成文化的一種形式，而且此規則早已將管轄權行使的基礎與限制融合在一起，個人認為這個規則是判例法、成文法融合之極致一法律邏輯一致性的要求與判例法達成正義的基本目的是融合在一起的。個人認為Sinochem除了一貫的美式違返外國人的平等權、訴訟權、財產權、及適當程序權外，亦是達到了法律邏輯與正義的目的一致的境界。

美國最高法院又引用判例法說：「當Steel Co.確認於處理之次序上管轄權之問題通常必須先於實體問題之決定，而Ruhrgas決定『管轄權爭點之次序』並無強制性。……於適當之情形下，Ruhrgas認定一個法院得基於沒有對人管轄權而駁回訴訟，不必先確立案件主體（實體、訴因）之管轄權。[95]」「Steel Co.及Ruhrgas皆認同一個聯邦法院有著空間去『拒絕對

---

94 127 S. Ct. 1184, 1190, 1191, "The Common-law doctrine of forum non conveniens 'has continuing application [in federal courts] only in cases where the alternative forum is abroad,' American Dredging, 510 U.S., at 449, n 2, 114 S. Ct. 981, 127 L. Ed. 2d 285, and perhaps in rare instances where a state or territorial court serves litigational convenience best. See 14D C. Wright, A. miller, & E. Cooper, Federal, Practice and Procedure §3828, pp 620-623, and nn 9-10 (3d ed. 2007). For the federal court system, Congress has codified the doctrine and has provided for transfer, rather than dismissal, when a sister federal court is the more convenient place for trial of the action. See 28 U.S.C. §1404(a)('For the convenience of parties and witnesses, in the interest of justice, a district court may transfer any civil action to any other district or division where it might have been brought.'); cf. §1406(a)('The district court of a district in which is filed a case laying venue in the wrong division or district shall dismiss, or if it be in the interest of justice, transfer such case to any district or division in which it could have been brought.'); Goldlawr, Inc. v. Heiman, 369 U.S. 463, 466, 82 S. Ct. 913, 8 L. Ed. 2d 39 (1962) (Section 1406(a) 'authorize[s] the transfer of [a] cas[e]… whether the court in which it was filed had personal jurisdiction over the defendants or not.')."

95 127 S. Ct. 1184, 1191, "While Steel Co. confirmed that jurisdictional question ordinarily must precede merits determinations in dispositional order, Ruhrgas held that there is no mandatory 'sequencing of jurisdictional issues.' 526 U.S., at 584, 119 S. Ct. 1563, 143 L. Ed. 2d 760. In appropriate circumstances, Ruhrgas decided, a court may dismiss for lack of personal jurisdiction without first establishing

一個案件之實體加以聽證時去選擇（管轄）門檻之理由。』……沒有對實體加以認定的駁回即是法院『完全不會進行』對訴因加以審判。因此一個地院基於裁量權之理由而拒絕審判依州法而來之請求時，並不需要首先去決定這些請求是否屬於其尚未下定論之管轄權範圍內。……同樣的一個聯邦地院在依Younger v. Harris拒絕審理當事人間是否存在著憲法第三條之案件或真實的問題前亦不需決定其是否有管轄權。[96]」其又引用第7巡迴法院而下結論：「只有在如果法院意圖對案件之實體下判決管轄權才是重要的。[97]」

「於作成不方便法院之決定時，使得其成為有關於非實體上、門檻之爭點，很簡單的重點就是：於解決不方便法院之提議時並不產生法院於實體上之『法律宣佈權力』之任何假設。[98]」法院雖然承認於決定不方便法院的因素會與「案件紛爭中的法律與事實爭點重大的重疊」[99]，但其他的門檻爭點亦是牽連到同樣的情況。「因此當於便利、公平、及司法經濟之

---

subject-matter jurisdiction. See id., at 578, 119 S. Ct. 1563, 143 L. Ed. 2d 760." Steel Co. v. Citizens for Better Environment, 523 U.S. 83, 118 S. Ct. 1003, 140 L. Ed. 2d 210 (1998); Ruhrgas AG v. Marathon Oil Co., 523 U.S. 574, 119 S. Ct. 1563, 143 L. Ed. 2d 760 (1990).

96 同上，"Both *Steel Co.* and *Ruhrgas* recognized that a federal court has leeway 'to choose among threshold grounds for denying audience to a case on the merits.' *Ruhrgas*, 526 U.S., at 585, 119 S. Ct. 1563, 143 L. Ed. 2d 760; *Steel Co*., 523 U.S., at 100-101, n 3, 118 S. Ct. 1003, 140 L. Ed. 2d 210. Dismissal short of reaching the merits means that the court will not 'proceed at all' to an adjudication of the cause. Thus, a district court declining to adjudicate state-law claims on discretionary grounds need not first determine whether those claims fall within its pendent jurisdiction. See Moor v. County of Alameda, 411 U.S. 693, 715-716, 93 S. Ct. 1785, 36 l. Ed. 2d 596 (1973). Nor must a federal court decide whether the parties present an Article III case or controversy before abstaining under Younger v. Harris, 401 U.S. 37, 91 S. Ct. 746, 27 L. Ed. 2d 669 (1971). See Eills v. Dyson, 421 U.S. 426, 433-434, 95 S. Ct. 1691, 44 L. Ed. 2d 274 (1975)."

97 127 S. Ct. 1184, 1191, 1192, "The principle underlying these decisions was well stated by the Seventh Circuit: '[J]urisdiction is vital only if the court proposes to issue a judgment on the merits.' *Intec USA*, 467 F. 3d, at 1041."

98 同上，1192, 1193, "The critical point here, rendering a *forum non conveniens* determination a threshold, nonmerits issue in the relevant context, is simply this: Resolving a *forum non conveniens* motion does not entail any assumption by the court of substantive 'law-declaring power.'."

99 同上，1192, "In that context, the Court observed that some factors relevant to *forum non conveniens*, notably what evidence will bear on the plaintiff's claim or on defense to the claim, 'will substantially overlap factual and legal issues of the underlying dispute.'" "Of course a court may need to identify the claims presented and the evidence relevant to adjudicating those issues to intelligently rule on a *forum non conveniens* motion. But other threshold issues may similarly involve a brush with 'factual and legal issues of the underlying dispute.'"

考慮之許可下，一個地院得依不方便法院之駁回而處理一個案件，而繞過主體及對人管轄之問題。[100]」

因此最高法院之結論為：「但是，如果一個法院已充分的準備好去決定其對訴因或被告是沒有管轄權，適當的途徑應是依該理由而去駁回。於過去的眾多案件中，管轄權『通常不會牽連到費力的探討』，並且同時司法經濟及通常尊重原告選擇法院的考量『因會迫使聯邦法院首先去處理（該些）爭點。』……但適當主體（訴因、實體）或對人管轄權是難以決定時，並且不方便法院的考量是重大的偏向駁回訴訟時，法院去選擇較沒有負擔的途徑是合適的。[101]」如Prof. Graveson所說當法律邏輯一致性之要求與判例法達成正義的目的有衝突時，法律邏輯一致性之要求應該退讓，本案之結論是符合Prof. Graveson的論述。但是本案更進一步的見證了-當舊有的法律邏輯不符合個案而被修改時，法院在達成正義的目的下是可以努力的塑造新的法律邏輯，這就是西方法學的自然正義[102]，更是中

---

[100] 同上，"A district court therefore may dispose of an action by a forum non conveniens dismissal, bypassing questions of subject-matter and personal jurisdiction, when considerations of convenience, fairness, and judicial economy so warrant."
另外因為中國法院已經正在處理該紛爭，故最高法院認為他們不需去決定是否不方便法院之決定須本著被告放棄於方便法院之管轄及時效之抗辯才得被作成，同上，1193, 1194, "here, however, Malaysia International faces no genuine risk that the more convenient forum will not take up the case... We therefore need not decide whether a court conditioning a forum non conveniens dismissal on the waiver of jurisdiction or limitations defenses in the foreign forum must first determine its own authority to adjudicate the case."

[101] 127 S. Ct. 1184, 1194, "If, however, a court can readily determine that it lacks jurisdiction over the cause or the defendant, the proper course would be to dismiss on that ground. In the mine run of cases, jurisdiction 'will involve no arduous inquiry' and both judicial economy and the consideration ordinarily accorded the plaintiff's choice of forum 'should impel the federal court to dispose of [those] issue[s] first.' *Ruhrgas*, 526 U.S., at 587-588, 119 S. Ct. 1563, 143 L. Ed. 2d 760. But where subject-matter or personal jurisdiction is difficult to determine, and *forum non conveniens* considerations weigh heavily in favor of dismissal, the court properly takes the less burdensome course."

[102] Price v Dewhurst (1837)8 Sim 279 at 302
SHADWELL V-C
"whenever it is manifest that justice has been disregarded, the court is bound to treat the decision as a matter of no value and no substance".但是於適用於外國判決時，英國判例法通常只是非常謹慎的將違反「自然正義」適用於外國法院的不引用適當的程序規則而已。但較近亦有判例法將「自然正義」的原則較為擴張，法院會考慮到程序上之瑕疵會構成違反英國法院實質正義的觀點。
Adams v Cape Industries plc [1990] Ch 433. "The expression 'contrary to natural justice' has, however, figured so prominently in judicial statements that it is essential to fix, if possible, its exact scope. When applied to foreign judgments it relates merely to alleged irregularities in the procedure adopted

國法學中的「道法自然」。

故而92重訴4號是以不方便法院法學為管轄權行使之基礎或限制，個人以為並不是重點，重點是那一個法院最能達成正義之目的。但92重訴4號有另一個盲點，屏東地院不應輕易的忽視原告被害人選擇侵權行為地及其住所地法院起訴之權利。美國最高法院即陳述：「於對抗原告所選擇的法院時，被告在主張不方便法院時通常會承受沈重的負擔。但是，當原告的選擇並非是在其家園時，對原告有利的推定『被適用時較為無力』，因為（原告）所選定的法院是合適的之假設於此情形下是『沒有那麼合理』。[103]」於92重訴4號中原告被害人以公法人之地位於侵權行為地之家園法院提起世紀之害石油污染訴訟，臺灣的法院卻以「不方便法院」而駁回訴訟。對照Sinochem案與個人前述早期之著作[104]，個人至此無言。

八、王道與不方便法院

美國之重視原告之利益或許為法律邏輯上之必然性，這亦就是前述英國早期採納「困擾性或壓迫性」法學之謹慎作風。但亦如前述隨著全球化的潮流所帶來不可避免的管轄權之擴張，法院亦不可避免的需要更多之裁量權以主持個案正義，故而英國現今所採納的是「方便與不方便法院」法學。而這個法學的重點即是在考慮所有當事人之利益下達成正義的目的。於Spiliada Maritime Corp v. Cansulex Ltd中，Lord Goff即陳述方便法院即是：「去辨別出案件可以在所有當事人的利益及達到正義的目的下而被

by the adjudicating court, and has nothing to do with the merits of the case. …… However, there is recent authority to the effect that are merely instances of a wider principle of natural justice, according to which the court has to consider whether there has been a procedural defect such as to constitute a breach of an English court's views of substantial justice." P M North, JJ Fawcett, Cheshire and North's Private International Law, 13th ed., pp, 450, 451. 14th ed., p. 564.

103 127 S. Ct. 1184, 1191, "A defendant invoking forum non conveniens ordinarily bears a heavy burden in opposing the plaintiff's chosen forum. When the plaintiff's choice is not its home forum, however, the presumption in the plaintiff's favor 'applies with less force,' for the assumption that the chosen forum is appropriate is in such cases 'less reasonable.' *Piper Aircraft Co.*, 454 U.S., at 255-256, 102 S. Ct. 252, 70 L. Ed. 2d 419."

104 陳隆修，《國際私法管轄權評論》，台北，五南圖書公司，民國75年11月，初版，170、171頁。

合適的審判法院[105]」。而不方便法院即是：「基本原則是法院之訴訟只能基於不方便法院而被停止，而其要件是法院能確認有其他有管轄權之法院存在，並且該法院是合適處理該訴訟之法院，亦即該訴訟可以為了正義的目的及所有當事人的利益，可以在該法院更合適的被加以審判。[106]」由固守傳統法律邏輯的尊重原告之合法利益，到順應全球化潮流的顧及所有當事人之利益，以達成個案正義的目的，這個英國法學的進化過程是令人敬佩的，更亦符合我們祖先「道法自然」的訓示。無論適用「困擾性或壓破性」、「方便法院」、或「不方便法院」之名稱，美國同僚或許應注意到英國母法放熱而不放光之進化。美國及其他同僚或許應少一點被所謂「歐洲革命」的光芒所暈眩，而多感受一點判例法母國法所輻射的熱能。

其實Sinochem的原告應知道[107]，美國法學所謂尊重原告之意願，常會僅限於美國原告之意願。對外國原告提起的外國訴因，美國法院是可能會以不方便法院而駁回[108]。美國這種違反訴訟法「以原告就被告」之作法，很明顯的是在扶持跨國企業以掠奪第三世界人民之資源。這是違反人權公約中之平等權、訴訟權、財產權、及生存權的「法律恐怖主義」、「掠奪性新殖民地主義」、及「岳不群法學」。

海牙1999年草約於22(1)及(2)條採用不方便法院（與英美法不同的

---

105 Spiliada Maritime Corp v. Cansulex Ltd [1987] 1 AC 460, at 480. "to identify the forum in which the case can be suitably tried for the interests of all the parties and for the ends of justice".

106 同上，476, "The basic principle is that a stay will only be granted on the ground of ground of forum non conveniens where the court is satisfied that there is some available forum having jurisdiction, which is the appropriate forum for trial of the action, i.e. in which the case may be tried more suitably for the interests of all the parties and the ends of justice."

107 127 S. Ct. 1184, 1189, "No significant interests of the United States were involved, the court observed, Fed. 27 Memo & Order, at 65a-67a; Apr. 13 Memo & Order, at 44a-47a, and while the cargo lad been loaded in Philadelphia, the nub of the controversy was entirely foreign: The dispute centered on the arrest of a foreign ship in foreign waters pursuant to the order of a foreign court. Feb. 27 Mrmo & Order, at 67a. Given the proceedings ongoing in China, and the absence of cause 'to second-guess the authority of Chinese law or the competence of [Chinese] courts,' the District Court granted the motion to dismiss under the doctrinr of *forum non conveniens*."或許法院應以不願與有管轄權的先繫屬法院造成可能不一致判決的理由駁回訴訟，會較沒有「重大的美國利益」為理由較好。

108 陳隆修，《國際私法管轄權評論》，台北，五南圖書公司，民國75年11月，初版，170頁，「但於Piper Aircraft Co. v. Reyno中，法院決定當原告為外國人，且訴因亦為外國訴因時，若法院地非為該外國損害發生地時，原告不可僅以法院地之法律對其比對外國法律較為有利為理由，去抗辯法院地為不方便法院之裁定。」102 S. Ct. 252 (1981).

是其不能違背專屬管轄條款之約定），其第3項特別規定：「於決定是否停止訴訟程序時，法院不能以國籍或慣居地為理由而歧視當事人。[109]」而2004年的ALl/UNIDROIT Principles of Transnational Civil Procedure於2.5條中規定：「當相較於其他更合適行使管轄權的法院，繫屬法院是明顯的不合適時，管轄權得被拒絕或程序得被停止。[110]」又不同於大陸法的絕對先繫屬優先，2.6條規定先繫屬法院若不能公平、有效、及迅速的處理案件，則後繫屬法院得接受或繼續處理案件[111]。但是如其註解P-2F所強調這個條文應與3.2條的反歧視平等原則一起被解釋[112]。第3.1條規定：「法院應確保訴訟當事人於主張或抗辯其權利時，應有平等待遇及合理機會。[113]」第3.2條規定：「平等對待之權利包含避免任何種類之非法歧視之避免，特別是基於居所或國籍之理由而來之歧視。法院應考慮到外國當

---

[109] Article 22 Exceptional circumstances for declining jurisdiction

1. In exceptional circumstances, when the jurisdiction of the court seised is not founded on an exclusive choice of court agreement valid under Article 4 or on Article 7, 8 or 12, the court may on application by a party, suspend its proceedings if in that case it is clearly inappropriate for that court to exercise jurisdiction and if a court of another State has jurisdiction and is clearly more appropriate to resolve the dispute. Such application must be made no later than at the time of the first defence on the merits.

2. The court shall take into account, in particular-

a) any inconvenience to the parties in view of their habitual residence;

b) the nature and location of the evidence, including documents and witnesses, and the procedures for obtaining such evidence;

c) applicable limitation or prescription periods;

d) the possibility of obtaining recognition and enforcement of any decision on the merits.

3. In deciding whether to suspend the proceedings, a court shall not discriminate on the basis of the nationality or habitual residence of the parties.

[110] Jurisdiction may be declined or the proceeding suspended when the court is manifestly inappropriate relative to another more appropriate court that could exercise jurisdiction.

[111] The court should decline jurisdiction or suspend the proceeding, when the dispute is previously pending in another court competent to exercise jurisdiction, unless it appears that the dispute will not be fairly, effectively, and expeditiously resolved in that forum.

[112] "This Principle should be interpreted in connection with the Principle of Procedural Equality of the Parties, which prohibits any kind of discrimination on the basis of nationality or residence. See Principle 3.2."

[113] 3.1 The court should ensure equal treatment and reasonable opportunity for litigants to assert or defend their rights.3.2 The right to equal treatment includes avoidance of any kind of illegitimate discrimination, particularly on the basis of nationality or residence. The court should take into account difficulties that might be encountered by a foreign party in participating in litigation. 又見3.4 Whenever possible, venue rules should not impose an unreasonable burden of access to court on a person who is not a habitual resident of the forum.

事人於參加訴訟時所可能遭遇之困難。[114]」其註解P-3B中又列舉了許多歧視之種類，但強調於「國際商業訴訟中基於國籍或居所之理由是個特別敏感的爭點」[115]。

海牙1999草約第22(3)條及ALI/UNIDROIT Principles of Transnational Civil Procedure第3.2條雖然將矛頭皆向以不方便法院之名而實施歧視非國民、（慣）居民之不平等待遇，這指的應是美國法院以法院地「公共利益」之名而拒絕外國原告提起外國訴因之違反人權公約之惡行。但為了保護跨國企業之利潤而踐踏第三世界人民的生存權、生命權、財產權、環境權、訴訟權、及平等權的，除了美國高超技巧的不方便法院法學外，歐盟布魯塞爾公約及規則第4條的禁止對內但得以對外之過度管轄亦是同樣的惡名昭彰，只是技術拙劣到令人啼笑皆非的目瞪口呆。由技術層次上而言，美國是巧取豪奪，歐盟明火執杖打家劫舍，相較之下日本是個抽冷子的地痞小混混[116]，但無論他們法律技術層級之不同，他們的法學皆是本於「利益」而來之「岳不群法學」。

故而個人一再重述二十一世紀全球化法學及新崛起中國式法學應本著「己所不欲，勿施於人」、「人溺已溺，人飢已飢」之中國式「王道」文化，亦唯有「王道」法學才是數千年來弱勢及二十一世紀第三世界人民的真正救贖。數千年來中華民族一再經戰火的蹂躪，但總能一再由廢墟中屢次重回世界舞台的中央，「王道」是千年不易最符合古今中外之「常識」，最能「達成正義的基本目的」，亦是最順乎「自然道法」。於中華

---

114 3.2 The right to equal treatment includes avoidance of any kind of illegitimate discrimination, particularly on the basis of nationality or residence. The court should take into account difficulties that might be encountered by a foreign party in participating in litigation.又見3.4 Whenever possible, venue rules should not impose an unreasonable burden of access to court on a person who is not a habitual resident of the forum.

115 P-3B Illegitimate discrimination includes discrimination on the basis of nationality, residence, gender, race, language, religion, political or other opinion, national or social origin, birth or other status, sexual orientation, association with a national minority. Any form of illegitimate discrimination is prohibited, but discrimination on the basis of nationality or residence is a particularly sensitive issue in transnational commercial litigation.

116 見陳隆修，《2005年海牙法院選擇公約評析》，台北，五南圖書公司，2009年1月，初版1刷，290、291頁。日本名古屋裁判所平成（ワ）1433與平成7（ワ）4179號華航名古屋空難判決。

民族再次崛起之際，做為一個資深的中華民族比較法的學生，個人於此鄭重的提醒大陸年輕同僚一個問題—近數十年來美國於不方便法院上偷雞摸狗的幫助跨國企業於第三世界掠奪利潤，但這些違反人權公約所取得的利益有阻止美國運勢的下滑嗎？數千年來中國的歷史已一再證明中國屢仆屢起，美國或過去的其他霸權有再次崛起的能力嗎？一個符合「天道」的法學其目的並不是在幫助其民族可以拓展霸權利益，而是在確保其子孫他日能由毀滅中再次浴火重生。中華民族的「王道」於數千年來一再透過我們數十億祖先的生命史證明了「王道」就是順天應人的「自然道法」，「王道」就是最符合人類數千年生活經驗的「常識」，亦就是「正義基本目的」的具體表徵。本於「自由貿易」、「比較經濟利益」而來的法學爭的是利益，本著「禮運大同」而來的中國「王道」法學，數千年來之傳統是爭千秋而不爭一世。

美國有些資深同僚[117]於討論「不方便法院」時喜歡引用、並且豔羨Lord Denning於The Atlantic Star[118]中膾炙人口之論述：「沒有任何到這些法院來要求正義的人會徒勞無功……到這裡來的權利並不只限於英國人。它及於任何友好的外國人。如果他期望去作這些行為，他可以要求我們法院的幫忙。如果你願意你可以稱呼這是『選購法院』，但如果法院是在英國，在貨物的品質及服務的速度上，這是一個去選購的好地方。」非常遺憾的這段暮鼓晨鐘的論述雖然為美國同僚所激賞，但並未能敲醒美國

[117] Walter W. Heiser, Forum non conveniens and choice of law: The impact of applying foreign law in transnational tort actions, 51 Wayne L. Rev. 1161, 1189 (2005).

[118] [1973] 1 Q.B. 364, 381-82 (C.A.). "No one who comes to these courts asking for justice should come in vain…. This right to come here is not confined to Englishmen. It extends to any friendly foreigner. He can seek the aid of our courts if he desires to do so. You may call this 'forum shopping' if you please, bur if the forum is England, it is a good place to shop in, both for the quality of the goods and the speed of service."這個論述是在採取「不方便法院」之前，但英國於此方面法學重心仍是於兼顧當事人之利益下達成正義之判決。

個人年輕時見到Lord Denning之肖像被置於美國有些法學院之禮堂正中。後來Lord Denning之回憶錄因陳述根據其經驗其不太相信被告為黑人時之黑人陪審團而不得不退休。經過數十年，個人認為種族平等不能淹滅沒有惡意之言論自由權。英國社會對一正直之法官過分無情，整個社會意圖遮掩社會經驗之事實亦過分矯情。故而個人相信中國「情」字法學是與人權公約相通的，於21世紀的全球化法學上個人再次認為「無情就是無義」。

以「利益」為基礎的法學方法論。

「沒有任何到這些法院來要求正義的人會徒勞無功……到這裡來的權利並不只限於英國人。它及於任何友好的外國人。」於92重訴4號中公法人代表二千三百萬人於損害行為發生地之自己家園法院要求正義，但卻被臺灣法院認為「不方便」去給予正義。這不是美國資本主義以「利益」為基礎之「不方便法院」，亦非英國以「正義」為基礎之「不方便法院」，更與1999海牙草約與2004 ALl/UNIDROIT Principles of Transnational Civil Procedure所禁止的相反-它所歧視的是法院地2,300萬國民與居民。請問臺灣屏東地院92重訴4號你所引用的「不方便法院」法學是哪一個國家、哪一個國際公約的法學？或著是哪一個星球的「不方便法院」？「爾俸爾祿民脂民膏，下民易虐上天難欺」。

又92重訴4號認為：「未按我國與挪威並無基於條約或協定之司法上判決相互承認，因此，縱使原告就繫屬本院之訴訟獲得終局之勝訴判決，也無法持之以向挪威法院為強制執行，及不能達到原告進行本訴訟（獲得實際受償）之目的。」判決是否能被加以執行的確是法院行使管轄權或不方便法院考量之一種因素。但挪威是聯合國及歐盟會員國之一，如果不承認依據聯合國油污染公約及布魯塞爾規則有管轄權的法院所作成的判決，那似乎有違常理。更何況依國際訴訟法之一般規則（國際慣例），侵權行為地法院是有著管轄權。即使台灣法院不具有管轄權，但被告的對案件訴因（實體）加以抗辯，亦使得台灣法院有著充分之管轄權。三十年前台灣民訴402(4)條對外國判決以為「無國際相互之承認者」，即為公法人格之不承認。後拙作中指出此處應限於司法之判決，才於2003年加以修正[119]。

---

119 現今改為「無相互之承認者」，仍未符合個人早期之建議：「最後，亦為最重要之點，即為我國所堅持之『對等待遇原則』似應被除去。蓋我國法院目前常誤解與我國無邦交之國家，即不承認我國之判決，故常遲而不承認該外國之判決。如前所述，此將國際公法與國際私法混淆之觀念，乃為錯誤之觀念。更何況我國經濟賴外貿以維生，我國不應自絕於國際社會，應改被動為主動，無論外國是否承認我國判決，皆應對該國判決加以承認方是。對等待遇理論於學理上已為一落伍之思想，我國應廢除此法律，進而採英國之『義務主義』，亦即債務人有義務清償其債務，及法院有主持正義之義務。如若不能，至少亦應採美國之『國際禮讓主義』，而不必理會外國是否承認我國之判決。」見陳隆修，《國際私法管轄權評論》，台北，五南圖書公司，民國75年11月，初版，315頁。

92重訴4號又似乎將時光倒流。

九、保護貿易利益法與跨國合作

大陸地區為世界第二經濟體，通常跨國企業皆不敢放棄這個市場。兩岸既已簽定經濟互助約定，大陸並且大氣的宣布「讓利」，則這自然順理成章的包含司法上之協助，任何台灣合乎衝突法規則的判決應在大陸得到執行上之助力，如此才能如歐盟一般的透過判決的承認以達成人、資金、貨品、服務流通之經濟合作之目的。

個人於第6屆兩岸國私研討會時強烈建議大陸採取英國The Protection of Trading Interests Act 1980，並認為應適用至台灣之廠商。台灣的電子廠商經常遭受美國與歐盟於貿易上不公平之掠奪與打壓，這種「保護貿易利益法」之宣示，不但是維護大中華區司法正義所必須，更是維護中國社會於二十一世紀高科技法學中聯合國1966年人權公約第1條生存權所必需。事實上各國對美國於反托辣斯之霸權主義皆紛紛採取不同之步驟以做為抗衡，個人認為「保護貿易利益法」為最名正言順之途徑。Cheshire and North[120]陳述其背景為：「這個法案的背景為英國對美國反托辣斯法於域外適用之不滿[121]。對於構成政治以及經濟、法律問題於外交上嘗試之解決辦法之失敗，導至法律上之戰爭。根據這個法律，對於影響到在英國之人之貿易利益的外國規範國際貿易的措失，國務卿是被給予寬廣的權利去應付[122]。」因為台灣與大陸所受到的不平等對待甚多，於不符合國際私法

---

120 P M North, JJ Fawcett, Cheshire and North's Private International Law, 13th ed, p.448, "The background to this Act is the United Kingdom resentment at the extra-territorial application of anti-trust laws by the United States. Diplomatic attempts at solving what is a political as well as an economic and legal problem failed and led to legal warfare. Under the Act, the Secretary of State is given wide powers to counter foreign measures for regulating international trade which affect the trading interests of persons in the United Kingdom." 14th ed., p. 561.

121 *See British Nylon Spinners Ltd v ICI Ltd* [1953] Ch 19, [1952] 2 All ER 780; *Re Westinghouse Electric Corpn Uranium Contract Litigation NDL Docket No 235* [1978] AC 547, [1978] 1 All ER 434.

122 1.-(1) If it appears to the Secretary of State-
(a) that measures have been or are proposed to be taken by or under the law of any overseas country for regulating or controlling international trade; and

無理的不承認中國法院之判決時自然是構成妨礙大中華區之貿易利益。包括挪威在內的每個國家都必須對有著龐大市場為後盾的中國判決加以謹慎的尊重。事實上英國1980年法律第2(2)條規定當一外國要求提供商業資訊而使得該外國侵犯英國管轄權、主權、安全及外交關係之行為是不被允許的，故而侵犯到大中華區之司法尊嚴自然不應被允許[123]，當於此種侵犯到大中華區貿易利益時，北京的國務院自應被授與英國Protection of Trading Interests Act 1980中相對的權力，以保護大中華地區的貿易利益[124]。事實上個人一向主張因為中國人之人均所得只有已開發國家的十分之一，故這已不是單純的經濟利益或國際法上的問題，這是1966年聯合國兩個人權公約中第1條[125]的生存權之問題。

另外第5條又規定於下列三種情形下外國判決不能被執行：(a)符合第3項的倍數賠償；(b)判決所依據的競爭法是根據第4項為國務卿所宣布是限制或扭曲公平競爭；或(c)上述(a)或(b)款判決中所作成之損害賠償對第三人提起要求賠償之判決[126]。(a)款中之拒絕執行倍數賠償之判決主要是針

(b) that those measures, in so far as they apply or would apply to things done or to be done outside the territorial jurisdiction of that country by persons carrying on business in the United Kingdom, are damaging or threaten to damage the trading interests of the United Kingdom,

The Secretary of State may by order direct that this section shall apply to those measures either generally or in their application to such cases as may be specified in the order.

123 (2) A requirement such as is mentioned in subsection (1)(a) or (b) above is inadmissible –

(a) if it infringes the jurisdiction of the United Kingdom or is otherwise prejudicial to the sovereignty of the United Kingdom; or

(b) if compliance with the requirement would be prejudicial to the security of the United Kingdom or to the relations of the government of the United Kingdom with the government of any other country.

124 1980年法律之序言說明："An Act to provide protection from requirements, prohibitions and judgments imposed or given under the laws of countries outside the United Kingdom and affecting the trading or other interests of persons in the United Kingdom."

125 International Covenant on Civil and Right; International Covenant on Economic, Social and Cultural Rights,

Article 1

1. All peoples have the right of self-determination. By virture of that right they freely determine their political status and freely pursue their economic, social and cultural development.
2. All peoples may, for their own ends, freely dispose of their natural wealth and resources without prejudice to any obligations arising out of international economic co-operation, based upon the principle of mutual benefit, and international law. "In no case may a people be deprived of its own means of subsistence."（引號為附加）

126 5. －(1) A judgment to which this section applies shall not be registered under Part II of the Administra-

對美國之反托辣斯法[127]。而這個禁止執行是包含判決中之所有部分，而非僅限於非損害賠償之部分。這與下述的第6條「抓回條款」僅限於超過損害部分之賠償額不同。

第5條只是個消極不執行的否定條款，更有爭議的是全世界著名的第6條積極「抓回條款」（claw-back provision）。第6(2)規定合格的被告可以對5(3)條外國數倍損害賠償勝訴的當事人起訴，要求返還已給付的超過外國作成判決法院認定為損害數額之賠償[128]。第6(1)條所規定的合格被告為：(a)英國及殖民地之公民；或(b)於英國或有責任地域組織而成之機構；或(c)於英國經商之人[129]。但第6(3)條規定於該外國法院作成判決時

---

tion of Justice Act 1920 or Part I of the Foreign Judgments (Reciprocal Enforcement) Act 1933 and no court in the United Kingdom shall entertain proceedings at common law for the recovery of any sum payable under such a judement. (2) This section applies to any judgment given by a court of an overseas country, being － (a) a judgment for multiple damages within the meaning of subsection (3) below; (b)a judgment based on a provision or rule of law specified or described in an order under subsection (4) below and given after the coming into force of the order; or (c) a judgment on a claim for contribution in respect of damages awarded by a judgment falling within paragragh (a) or (b) above. (3) In subsection (2)(a) above a judgment for multiple damages means a judgment for an amount arrived at by doubling, trebling or otherwise multiplying a sum assessed as compensation for the loss or damage sustained by the person in whose favour the judgment is given. (4) The Secretary of State may for the purpose of subsection (2)(b) above make an order in respect of any provision or rule of law which appears to him to be concerned with the prohibition or regulation of agreements, attangement to practices designed to restrain, distort or restrict competition in the carrying on of business of any description or to be otherwise concerned with the promotion of such competition as aforesaid.

127 Brirish Airways Board v Laker Airways Ltd [1985] AC 58 at 89 (per Lord DIPLOCK)

128 (2) Subject to subsections (3) and (4) below, the qualifying defendant shall be entitled to recover from the party in whose favour the judgment was given so much of the amount referred to in subsection (1) above as exceeds the part attributable to compensation; and that part shall be taken to be such part of the amount as bears to the whole of it the same proportion as the sum assessed by the court that gave the judgment as compensation for the loss or damage substained by that party bears to the whole of the damages awarded to that party.

129 (1) This section applies where a court of an overseas country has given a judgment for multiple damages within the meaning of section 5(3) above against –

(a) a citizen of the United Kingdom and Colonies; or

(b) a body corporate incorporated in the United Kingdom or in a territory outside the United Kingdom for whose international relations Her Majuesty's Government in the United Kingdom are responsible; or

(c) a person carrying on business in the United Kingdom,

(in this section referred to as a "qualifying defendant") and an amount on account of the damages has been paid by the qualifying defendant either to the party in whose favour the judgment was given or to another party who is entitled as against the qualifying defendant to contribution in respect of the damages.但不同於6(3)、(4)條，判例法認為第5條適用於一美國公司對另一美國公司所提起的反托辣

經常居住於該地之人或主要營業地為該地之組織不適用6(2)條[130]。第6(4)條規定6(2)條不適用於外國判決只是有關完全是於外國營業之情形[131]。第6(5)條規定本條文訴訟之請求，得適用於當被請求之被告不在英國法院地[132]。第6條不但創造了一個「抓回」訴因，並且對英美法所堅持的「所在」管轄基礎的要件亦加以退讓，因為這是立法之規定，故送達境外時亦不需法院之允許。但是這個管轄基礎應不能適用於歐盟國家。如果英國基於主權、管轄權、安全、及外交關係得以在對人訴訟之管轄基礎上加以退讓，大陸法於集體訴訟上似乎為了達成司法正義亦應適度的加以退讓[133]—法律邏輯一致性的要求應受限正義的基本目的，「道法自然」。

這種「保護貿易利益法」不只應適用於懲罰性賠償或不遵守國際私法的藐視大中華區之判決上，更應積極的採「抓回條款」而廣泛的適用於光怪離奇的國際貿易場合。較近台灣的友達、奇美皆被美國與歐盟以韓國廠商之自首而被處以百億以上之反托辣斯罰金[134]。首先個人必須嚴正的指出，反托辣斯法因對行為者之舉證不易，故歐盟與美國對此皆採「自首者從寬」之政策，藉此打擊反公平交易秘密約定。**但於訴訟法上若友達、奇**

斯訴訟，而該被指控之行為皆發生於美國，但因被告於英國有資產故原告於英國要求執行該美國判決。此事基於不執行外國刑法判決或公共政策之理由故而不執行外國判決，而非英國主權被侵犯之理由。British Airways Board v Laker Airways Ltd [1984] QB 142 at 161-163 (Parker J).

130 (3) Subsection (2) above does not apply where the qualifying defendant is an individual who was ordinarily resident in the overseas country at the time when the proceedings in which the judgment was given were instituted or a body corporate which had its principal place of business there at that time.

131 (4) Subsection (2) above does not apply where the qualifying defendant carried on business in the overseas country and the proccedings in which the judgment was given were concerned with activities exclusively carried on in that country.

132 (5) A court in the United Kingdom may entertain proceedings on a claim under this section notwithstanding that the person against whom the proceedings are brought is not within the jurisdiction of the court.

133 例如德國的Act on Model Case Proceedings in Disputes under Capital Markets Law (KapMuG)就仍受限於傳統管轄權邏輯之觀念，而無視於市場的需求。

134 中國時報，2000年12月11日，首版：「郭台銘語帶不平與憤怒意地說：『來溝通爭的不僅是法理，也求公平性。三星過去被處罰，但這個累犯這次做『抓耙仔』自首無罪，不知者（指台灣廠商）賣給韓國廠商卻被重罰，我問大家：這公平合理嗎？』郭台銘對歐盟提出的六點聲明，主要是質疑歐盟處分的案子，在時間點、計算基礎、法律程序、最後罰金結果上都有問題，同時也未給奇美電說明機會」。郭台銘「更強調，這是台韓的經濟戰爭」。但是應注意的是美國的托辣斯法只適用於效力發生於美國之行為，故而美國人一向強辯其判決只適用於美國之行為，故6(4)條應適用。

美不能充份參加韓國廠商之訴訟，那麼在相關韓國廠商之任何決定上對友達、奇美是完全沒有爭點禁反言之效果，這並不是訴訟法之萬國公法而已——這已是人權公約及憲法上基本問題。美國與歐盟肆無忌憚的作法以不只是侵犯大中華地區管轄權、主權、安全、及外交關係而已，這是侵犯到十三億中國人1966年聯合國兩個人權公約第1條生存權之問題。

第二，個人非常驚訝郭台銘董事長所控訴「未給奇美電說明機會」，這是明顯的違反訴訟法上給當事人充份抗辯機會的最高自然正義[135]。任何不給被告抗辯之行政、司法決定於全世界都不應被承認的，這是憲法及人權法之基本萬國公法普世價值。

第三，現今反托辣斯法的注重自首反而讓韓國有藉機打擊中國廠商之手段，韓國廠商所實施的是二十一世紀中新穎的不公平貿易手段。於兩岸簽定經濟合作後，大陸國務院應宣布這種作法妨礙大中華地區公平競爭的利益，而允許友達、奇美於大陸法院對韓國廠商的違反誠信原則而提起損害賠償之訴訟。UNIDROIT principles of International Commercial

[135] 因為實質正義可能於國際法上各國間基於自己的利益上之認定會有所爭執，故而英國判例法上通常謹慎的將「自然正義」之概念指向較為具體的程序正義。在Jacobson v Frachon (1927) 138 L.T. 386, 390, 392(CA)中，對於Lord Hanworth M.R.所使用的「自然正義原則」（"principles of natural justice."）Atkin L.J.解釋說："Those principles seem to me to involve this, first of all that the court being a court of competent jurisdiction, has given notice to the litigant that they are about to proceed to determine the rights between him and the other litigant; the other is that having given him that notice, it does afford him an opportunity of substantially presenting his case before the court."但是較近的Adams v Cape Industries Plc [1990] Ch. 433, at 564-566中，上訴法院認為違背自然正義（"breach of natural justice"）的抗辯應不只限於適當的通知及於外國法院的充分抗辯，其認為基本的問題是如Pemberton v Hughes [1899] 1 Ch. 781所陳述的，亦即程序上的瑕疵是否構成違背英國法院「實質正義」（"substantial justice"）之概念（"a breach of an English court's views of substantial justice"）。於Master v Leaver [2001] I.L.Pr. 387中，上訴法院認為德州法院嚴重的沒有遵守其評估損害之程序規則，導致其判決形成實質正義的拒絕。Dicey and Morris, the Conflict of Laws, 14th ed., p.634，認為「自然正義」與「實質正義」於此情形下是相通的。"The terms 'natural justice' and 'substantial justice' appear to be used interchangeably in this context."歐盟與美國不但於程序上違反「一事不再理」及「禁反言」之自然正義，於實質上其法律適用之結果亦剝奪中國人在人權公約上之生存權，故亦違反實質正義。對中國人而言歐盟與美國的反托辣斯法不只違憲，更是21世紀現實世界中由阿茲卡班地獄而來的佛地魔黑暗法則。Cheshire and North, 13th ed., p.452; 14th ed., p. 566，認為自然正義過分的寬廣可能造成不穩定，非程序上的不公平應交由公共政策來抗辯較好。個人認為21世紀之混亂中，唯一能確定的就只有法律邏輯應在正義目的下退讓。

Contracts 2004的1.7條[136]規定：「於進行國際貿易時每一當事人必須遵守誠信原則」；而1.8條[137]規定：「若一方當事人已造成他方當事人既有之理解，而他方當事人在對其不利下已經合理的依據此理解而加以作為，則該一方當事人之行為不可違反該理解。」韓國廠商這種違反誠信之行為不但違反2004年規則（UNIDROIT Principles（2004）），亦違反了幾乎所有文明國家的契約法。英國及歐盟的法律技術水平為世界所公認為最高之地區，豈有不知韓國廠商這種違反衡平法「乾淨手法則[138]」（clean-hands doctrine）之作法為違背誠信之作法。韓國廠商為中國廠商之天敵，採取敵對之他方之證詞，而嚴厲的處罰中國廠商，這是違反常識的「法律恐怖主義」、「掠奪式殖民地主義」。如前述歐美於反托辣斯法之認定上，已明目張膽的違反訴訟法上爭點禁止反言之基本規則，亦是違反人權法、憲法上之訴訟權、適當程序權、及財產權。如今採取敵對廠商之單方違背誠信證詞之作法，更是腥風血雨的踐踏大中華經濟區聯合國1966年兩個人權公約第1條的生存權。可笑的是WTO中信誓旦旦所宣誓的「自由貿易」、「比較經濟利益」，原來是「第一世界可以自由的霸凌第三世界的貿易」，「第一世界可以藉著比較第三世界高超的法律科學來攫取經濟利益」。而所謂的「諾貝爾和平獎」原來只是針對第三世界的落後司法人權，第一世界的「法律恐怖主義」、「掠奪式新殖民主義」是超乎1966年人權公約第1條第三世界人民之生存權上，「諾貝爾和平獎」是「諸法皆空自由自在」，是個「任我行加岳不群法學」的和平獎。第一世界的人

---

136 Article 1.7
(Good faith and fair dealing)
(1) Each party must act in according with good faith and fair dealing in international trade.
(2) The parties may not exclude or limit this duty.

137 Article 1.8
(Inconsistent Behavior)
A party connot act inconsistently with an understanding it has caused the other party to have and upon which that other party reasonably has acted in reliance to its detriment.

138 Black's Law Dictionary, 7th ed., p.244, "The principle that a party cannot seek equitable relief or assert an equitable defense if that party has violated an equitable defense if that party has violated an equitable principle, such as good faith. Such a party is described as having 'unclean hands.' – Also termed unclean-hands doctrine."

權法與諾貝爾和平獎是二十一世紀全球化法學中no law no heaven最終極之境界。

對抗美國的「法律霸權主義」、「帝國主義法學」，德國憲法法院除了不執行美國懲罰性賠償、拒絕送達美國法院訴訟之通知外，更高分貝的宣示：「若一個國家法院的訴訟是被以下列的形態與方式明顯地濫用：藉由公眾的壓力（可能是指集體訴訟）以及判決的風險去操控市場的參與者，這將可能抵觸德國憲法的規定[139]。」**如個人所一再論述，第一世界間的法律戰爭是於國際私法的規則內進行交戰，對第三世界的掠奪已是「諸法皆空自由自在」，更何況大中華地區的人均所得只有第一世界的十分之一。故而對德國是違反憲法的規定，對中國人而言是1966年兩個聯合國人權公約第1條的基本生存權之問題。「民為貴，社稷次之，君為輕」，大陸的國務院有義務在21世紀的法律戰爭中為中華經濟地區及所有全球第三世界的人民爭取1966年人權公約第1條之生存權。**

個人於此謹再次要求大陸必須即刻採納「保護貿易利益法」，以確保中華經濟區之司法權、主權、安全、外交關係，尤其應特別保障中國人之生存權。對韓國廠商違反誠信之不合理作法，基於貿易利益之保障，不必依賴契約法之保護，友達與奇美應可直接對其於大陸法院起訴（訴因）要求所有之損害賠償，而且不論其是否於大陸法院應皆具有管轄權（對人管轄基礎）。

以大陸目前之經濟實力或許難以對抗美國或歐盟，但英國1980年法律或許值得借鏡。該法之第7條[140]規定如若外國法規定對英國依第6條而作

---

139 “Werden Verfahren vor stattlichen Gerichten in einer offenkundig mißbräuchlichen Art und Weise genutzt, um mit publizistischem Druck und dem Risiko einer Verurteilung einen Marktteilnehmer grfügig zu machen, könnte dies deutsches Verfassungsrecht verletzen.” BVerfGE 108, 238 (248)以上中文翻譯感謝林更盛教授之幫助，個人自應負起任何可能之謬誤之責任。

140 7. －(1) If it appers to Her Majesty that the law of an overseas country provides or will provide for the enforcement in that country of judgments given under section 6 above, Her Majesty may by Order in Council provide for the enforcement in the United Kingdom of [judgments of any description specified in the Order which are given under any provision of the law of that country relating to the recovery of sums paid or obtained pursuant to a judgment for multiple damages within the meaning of section 5(3) above, whether or not that provision corresponds to section 6 above].

成之「抓回」判決加以執行，則英國會命令英國法院去執行與第5(3)條相似之外國相關倍數賠償「抓回」之判決，這表面上是個對等待遇的條款，但是因為5(3)條之範圍大於第6條（第5(3)條是包含真正損害在內之所有賠償），故而英國用心良苦是給予外國判決較大之空間（不限於第6條之僅限於超過損害部分之抓回）。由此可見已衰退的英國如何的期望與他國一起合作共同對抗美國法律帝國主義[141]，事實上眾所周知許多大英國協的會員國皆已採納這種「保護貿易利益法」。個人誠摯的認為如果大陸國務院不即刻採納判例法母國法的作法，並且與大英國協會員國攜手合作以對抗法律霸權主義，那是有違「天視自我民視，天聽自我民聽」之祖訓——而中國更喪失於二十一世紀中以王道法學領導全球化法學之契機。

事實上如屏東地院92重訴4號一般，許多台灣的法官會憂慮台灣判決於外國之執行性之問題。如果大陸能採納「保護貿易利益法」並將適用範圍及於大中華經濟區，那麼不但對台灣司法於反托辣斯上的執行性可以大幅的提高，並且北京政府亦可以在與大英國協正式的合作下，名正言順的在國際法及慣例法的框架下，維護大中華經濟區的管轄權、主權、安全、外交關係，尤其更能揭穿「霸權法律制度」、「法學帝國主義」隱藏在WTO及「諾貝爾和平獎」後面之「任我行及岳不群法學」，以確保大中華地區及全球第三世界等弱勢族群於聯合國1966年兩個人權公約第1條之基本生存權。

台灣人民在92重訴4號及友達、奇美案中遭受新時代中新形式的不平等條約之對待，這是二十一世紀中高科技的法律戰爭。於這種錯綜複雜的高科技戰爭中，法律霸權主義者經常以美式不方便法學、布魯塞爾規則第4條、反托辣斯法的「效力理論」、WTO的自由貿易、及諾貝爾和平獎的岳不?式帝國主義法學，來攫取任何可能的利益，而導致1966年兩個人權公約中第三世界的基本生存權被剝奪、踐踏。在這種詭異的岳不群法學及任我行法學的交相運作下，二十一世紀的中國式法學必須信守數千年來

141 例如the United Kingdom-Australia Agreement (1991)

「仁者無敵」之祖訓，反璞歸真正本清源，以「王道」的精神建立一個全球化的法學，帶領第三世界的弱勢人民走出第一世界的新殖民式法律戰爭，到達「禮運大同」的牛奶與蜂蜜之地。

第4章 全球化共同核心管轄基礎早已存在

一、對人管轄之基礎

92重訴字4號之運用不方便法院或許是受到美式「公共利益」不方便法院法學之迷惑，無論不方便法院或任何其他形式管轄權之運用，個人認為應以Lord Denning的論述為圭臬：「沒有任何到這些法院來要求正義的人會徒勞無功。」個人更認為無論任何法學皆應本著「常識」、「正義的目的」、「自然道法」為基礎，「天道無親，恆與善人」的王道法學是與「常識」、「正義的目的」相通的。而管轄權的行使自然亦應本著這個相通的基礎。於Connelly v. RTZ Corpn. plc[1]中，住所於蘇格蘭之原告，其於第一被告，為一英國公司，之南比亞子公司之南比亞鈾礦工作。於發現罹患癌症後，其於英國以過失之理由而告第一被告及第一被告之一英國子公司。其於南比亞無法得到任何經濟援助，但於英國其可得到貧民法律服務或與律師訂有條件的付費契約。英國最高法院拒絕被告停止訴訟之請求。雙方當事人皆同意南比亞為與案件有最密切關連之地。法院認為通常如果外國有著更明顯合適的管轄權法院，即使該外國法院對原告而言比英國法院於某些方面較為不利，原告仍應至該外國法院起訴。故而即使原告於該外國法院地無法取得貧民法律服務等經濟協助，而英國卻提供經濟援助，通常英國法院還是會停止英國訴訟程序[2]。但由於本案之性質與複雜

1 [1998] AC 854, HL.

2 本案如依歐盟Council Regulation No. 44/2001第19條，第一被告是否構成僱主之身分是個問題，故而可能不適用；至於1999 Hague Draft Convention on Jurisdiction第8條則不適用。故而於歐盟或海牙公約或許只能依被告之住所地或慣居地之基本管轄起訴。

性，如果原告沒有取得經濟援助則無法進行訴訟，故而法院認定如果原告被迫去合適的南比亞法院起訴，則於此特殊情形下實質的正義（substantial justice）無法被達成。個人以為這個案件應足以給美國不方便院及台灣不方便法院之不公義法學當頭棒喝－－即使是有著最真實密切關連的法院，於無法達成實質正義之情形下就會變成「不自然法院」。不但是不方便法院法學應以常識、正義的目的、自然道法為基本核心，管轄權及其他一切法學之行使亦應皆本著常識、正義的目的、自然道法為二十一世紀王道全球化法學的共同核心基本政策。

於二十一世紀商業全球化之潮流推動下，法學全球化是個自然不可避免的趨勢。從而各國司法管轄權與立法管轄權的直接或間接的對外拓展是個二十一世紀的自然寫實，而在這個趨勢中有趣的是經常立法與司法的適用基礎與適用的限制是混合在一起，因此經常伴隨著行政與司法上之寬裕的裁量權而一併被加以適用。例如於反托辣斯法的適用上是採納紛爭不斷的「效力理論」，而於跨國訴訟管轄權之適用上「禁訴令」與「不方便法院」所掀起之暴風雨亦充滿爭執。如果中國式王道法學無法於全球化法學發揮中流砥柱之「仁道」效力，可預見的是在逐漸加劇的二十一世紀法律戰爭中，十三億中國人及其他第三世界弱勢人民的基本生存權，將繼續會於第一世界的法律戰爭中淪為砲灰。無論是有關立法權的「效力理論」或管轄權的「禁訴令」及「不方便法院」，對判例法上傳統之管轄基礎加以追溯源頭是對這些二十一世紀法律戰爭上的問題加以釐清有助益的。

於Sirdar Gurdyal Singh v Rajah of Faridkote[3]中Lord Selborne說：「所有的管轄權應皆是地域性的」，「並且是extra territorium jus dicenti, impune non paretur……於一個對人屬性之訴訟中，被告無論於何種情

3 [1894] A.C. 670, 683-684 (PC), “All jurisdiction is properly territorial,” “and extra territorium jus dicenti, impune non paretur… In a personal action, … a decree pronounced in absentem by a foreign court, to the jurisdiction of which the defendant has not in any way submitted himself, is by international law an absolute nullity. He is under no obligation of any kind to obey it; and it must be regarded as a mere nullity by the courts of every nation, except (when authorised by special local legislation) in the country of the forum by which it was pronounced.”

形下皆未承認法院之管轄，而該外國法院卻作成缺席判決，於國際法上是個絕對無效的判決。被告是沒有任何義務去遵守該判決；並且除了在作成判決法院之國家外〈當該國有特別的當地法規允許時〉，該判決應僅是被每一個國家之法院視為無效。」故而於國際法上外國法院之判決不本於被告於該法院地之管轄基礎，是不會為英國判例法所承認的[4]。不過英國現加入歐盟，自應遵守布魯塞爾公約及規則，但對訂約國外之國家自然仍應適用判例法。

於Pemberton v Hughes[5]中Lord Lindley說：「如果一個外國法院所宣佈的判決是對在其管轄區域內之人，並且是其有管轄權去處理之事項，除非他們違反了英國實質正義的概念，英國法院是永遠不會去探究外國法院程序的合適性。」Dicey and Morris[6]認為：「這段話是指程序上之不規則」，但很明顯的當事人必須於外國管轄區內是先決要件。於對人管轄上判例法在John Russell & Co Ltd v Cayzer, Irvine & Co Ltd[7]中早已宣佈：「任何接到國王的命令（於現今英國稱為請求文件），並且於後來能被強迫去服從所作成判決的人，就是法院能對其有管轄權之人。」故而

---

4 於領頭案例*Buchanan v Rucker* (1808) 9 East 192, 194中，Tobago島的法院於被告從未到過該島，亦未接受其管轄，卻依該島法將訴訟通知釘於法院門口作為替代送達，Lord Ellenborough戲謔的問說：”Can the Island of Tobago pass a law to bind the rights of the whole world? Would the world submit to such an assumed jurisdiction?”恩師Prof. Graveson將這句話及小島的照片放於教材書的首頁。R.H. Graveson, Conflict of Laws, 7th ed.

5 [1899] 1 Ch. 781, 790 (CA), “If a judgment is pronounced by a foreign court over persons within its jurisdiction and in a matter with which it is competent to deal, English courts never investigate the propriety of the proceedings in the foreign court, unless they offend against English views of substantial justice.”

6 Dicey and Morris, the Conflict of Laws, 14th ed., pp. 633, 634, “This passage refers to irregularity in the proceedings, for it is clear that a foreign judgment, which is manifestly wrong on the merits or has misapplied English law or foreign law, is not impeachable on that ground. Nor is it impeachable because the court admitted evidence which is inadmissible in England or did not admit evidence which is admissible in England or otherwise followed a practice different from English law.” *See Jacobson v Frachon* (1927) 138 L.T. 386, 390, 393 (CA); *Adams v Cape Industries Plc* [1990] Ch. 433, 569 (CA); *De Cosse Brissac v Rathbone* (1861) 6 H. & N. 301 (the sixth plea); *Scarpetta v Lowenfeld* (1911) 27 T.L.R. 509; *Robinson v Fenner* [1913] 3 K.B. 835; *Boissière v Brockner* (1899) 6 T.L.R. 85.

7 [1916] 2 AC 298 at 302, HL, “whoever is served with the King’s writ [now called a claim form] and can be compelled consequently to submit to the decree made is a person over whom the courts have jurisdiction”

Cheshire and North[8]說：「英國判例法有關對人訴訟管轄權之規則上最顯著的特點就是他們純粹是程序上之性質。只要如果被告已被請求文件送達，任何人皆可主張或受到管轄。」判例法母法這種對人訴訟之核心管轄基礎自然亦為美國所承襲，於McDonald v Mabee[9]中Holmes J.說：「所在權力就是管轄之基礎」。

於Adams v Cape Industries Plc[10]中上訴法院認定被告未承認外國法院之管轄權時，外國法院之管轄權得依據被告所在於外國法院地而來：「只要其繼續身體所在於該國，其就享有該國法律上之利益，並應以接受該國法院程序徵召之方式，來顯示其接受該國法律之順與不順之全部。在沒有判例法顯示出相反之結論下，無論是永久性或暫時性及無論是否伴隨著居所而來[11]，我們會認定一個人自願的[12]出現於外國而短暫的所在於該地，根據我們國際私法的規則已經是足以給予該國法院地域管轄權。」

---

8 P M North, JJ Fawcett, Cheshire and North's Private International Law, 13th ed, p. 285, "The most striking feature of the English common law rules relating to competence in actions in personam is their purely procedural character. Anyone may invoke or become amenable to the jurisdiction, provided only that the defendant has been served with a claim form."14th ed., p. 353.

9 243 US 90at 91 (1917), "the foundation of jurisdiction is physical power".

10 [1990] Ch. 433 at p. 519, "So long as he remains physically present in that country, he has the benefit of its laws, and must take the rough with the smooth, by accepting his amenability to the process of its courts. In the absence of authority compelling a contrary conclusion, we would conclude that the voluntary presence of an individual in a foreign country, whether permanent or temporary and whether or not accompanied by residence, is sufficient to give the courts of that country territorial jurisdiction over him under our rules of private international law."

11 Dicey and Morris, the Conflict of Laws, 14th ed., p. 591, 592, "The older cases acknowledge that the residence of a defendant in the country at the time when proceedings are commenced gives that court jurisdiction over him at common law. The position is the same under the 1920 Act and the 1933 Act, except that the former requires 'ordinary residence'". *Schibsby v Westenholz* (1870) L.R. 6 Q. B. 155, 161; *Emanuel v Symon* [1908] 1 K.B. 302, 309 (CA).故而早期之判例法與現今之成文法是皆有以「居所」為法院管轄基礎之規定。於State Bank of India v Murjani Marketing Group Ltd, unreported, March 27, 1991 (CA).中，Sir Christopher Slade認為即使被告於訴訟時不在法院地，居所(in the sense of principal home)仍使得外國法院有充分管轄權。但如Dicey and Morris之結論，只是單純的居所而被告身體不在法院地(residence without presence)是否能構成管轄基礎，仍須由最高法院下結論："the issue remains open in the House of Lords."

12 對於被告被詐欺或脅迫進入外國法院地之管轄基礎是否成立，英國雖無直接判例法，但如被告不正當的被引誘進入英國管轄區，於合適情形下英國訴訟程序得被停止。*See Stein v Valkenhuysen* (1858) E. B. & E. 65 and *Watkins v North American Lands, etc., Co* (1904) 20 T.L.R. 534 (HL).美國Second Restatement, s. 82, comments b, d and f.認為原告參與脅迫或詐欺被告進入法院地時，法院雖有管轄權，但基於衡平理由應拒絕處理訴訟。Blandin v. Ostrander, 239 F. 700 (2d Cir. 1917).

「所在權力」管轄基礎是被以歐盟為首的大陸法認為是個「過度管轄」基礎，事實上於英美法其亦是有爭議的。Dicey and Morris[13]加以評述如下：「但是有些更舊的判例認為所在，而非居所，是個充分的管轄基礎[14]，並且以所在做為管轄基礎是為有些判例所加強，而這些判例認為對當地主權『短暫性效忠』是被告有著義務去順從當地法院判決的理由之一[15]。當被告僅是所在於相關之外國時這個理由仍是適用的。英國法院對於所在於英國之人之管轄權是亦為判例所支持的：於判例法上個別被告之短暫停留於英國會給予英國法院管轄權[16]，並且於此方面公司所在之標準是與公司於外國法院之管轄權於此方面相同的，雖然在後者是以居所之方式而非所在之方式被加以形容。但是如果當事人是外鄉人而訴因亦發生於相關國家之外，是否偶然的所在，而不同於居所，是個很好的管轄基礎是可能會受到懷疑。因為法院可能不會是方便法院，亦即不是最能恰當的去處理法律或事實的合適法院。」

同樣的Cheshire and North[17]認為由於請求文件在程序上之重要性這個

---

13 Dicey and Morris, the Conflict of Laws, 14th ed., p. 591, 592, "“But some of the older cases also suggest that presence, rather than residence, is a sufficient basis, and presence as a basis of jurisdiction is strengthened by those authorities which suggested that ‘temporary allegiance’ to the local sovereign was one of the reasons why a defendant might be under an obligation to comply with the judgment of its courts. For this reasoning is no less applicable where a defendant is merely present within the foreign country concerned. It is also supported by the authorities on the jurisdiction of the English court over persons present in England: the temporary presence of an individual defendant in England gives the English court jurisdiction at common law and the test for the presence of corporations in that context is the same as that for corporations in the context of the jurisdiction of foreign courts, although in the latter context it is described as residence rather than presence. It may be doubted, however, whether casual presence, as distinct from residence, is a desirable basis of jurisdiction if the parties are strangers and the cause of action arose outside the country concerned. For the court is not likely to be the forum conveniens, in the sense of the appropriate court most adequately equipped to deal with the facts or the law."

14 *Carrick v Hancock* (1895) 12 T.L.R. 59; *Herman v Meallin* (1891) 8 W.N. (NSW) 38; *Forbes v Simmons* (1914) 20 D.L.R. 100 (Alta); cf. *General Steam Navigation Co c Guillou* (1843) 11 M. & W. 377. *Contrast Australian Assets Co Ltd v Higginson* (1897) 18 L.R. (NSW) Eq. 189, 193.

15 *Schibsby v Westenholz* (1870) L.R. 6 Q.B. 155, 161; cf. *Sirdar Gurdyal Singh v Rajah of Faridkote* [1894] A.C. 670, 683-684 (PC).

16 *Colt Industries Inc v Sarlie* [1996] 1 W.L.R. 440 (CA); *Maharanee of Baroda v Wildenstein* [1972] 2 Q.B. 283 (CA).

17 P M North, JJ Fawcett, Cheshire and North's Private International Law, 13th ed., p. 287, "Not only is the justice of this exercise of power suspect, but in many cases it will be ineffective, for, in this example

理論於國內法是不可避免的，「但由於在管轄上沒有區分所在與居所於國際法上是不幸的。」不只「法院管轄權正義之行使會受到質疑」，並且於許多情形下由於判決的不會被外國法院的承認因而會「無法有效力」[18]。Cheshire and North[19]又認為：「除了於請求婚姻救濟之案件外，這個注重程序之方式即是意味著法院不會關心到有紛爭的當事人與英國之關係。兩個重要的後果因此而產生。首先，僅是請求文件的送達就會給予英國法院權力去審判案件，而該此案件卻可能是不合適在英國被審判的；例如被告可能是是一個只是正在通過英國之外國人，並且訴因與英國是沒有事實上之關連。對於這個問題以不方便法院為基礎去停止訴訟的寬廣、且彈性的裁量權之發展是個有效的解決方法。雖然法院有著權力去處理案件，這卻允許法院於不合適在此審判之情形下拒絕去審判案件……這種程序方式的第二種後果是第一種的相反。如果被告之所在並不在管轄區內，英國法

---

a judgment given in the action will be of no use to the claimant unless followed by proceedings in Japan for its enforcement, and a Japanese court can scarcely be expected to recognise a jurisdiction based on such flimsy grounds. This English doctrine is inevitable in domestic law because of the procedural significance of the claim form, but it is unfortunate from the point of view of private international law that no jurisdictional distinction is drawn between presence and residence."14th ed., p. 355.

18 The Foreign Judgments (Reciprocal Enforcement) Act 1933中，使用居所而非所在作為承認外國判決之管轄依據。

19 P M North, JJ Fawcett, Cheshire and North's Private International Law, 13th ed., p. 286, "This procedural approach has meant that, apart from cases where matrimonial relief is sought, the courts have not been concerned with the connection that the parties to the dispute have with England. Two important consequences stem from this. First, the mere service of a claim form will give the English courts power to try actions which may be inappropriate for trial in England; for example, the defendant may be a foreigner who is only in the course of passage through England and the cause of action may have no factual connection with England. The development of a wide, flexible discretion to stay actions on the basis of forum non conveniens is an effective solution to this problem. This allows courts, although competent to try the case, to refuse to do so where trial here would be inappropriate…. The second consequence of this procedural approach is the converse of the first. If the defendant is not present within the jurisdiction, the English courts are denied power to try actions in many cases in which it would be appropriate for trial to be held here, such as when a tort has been committed in English or when the defendant is domiciled, but not physically present, in England. This defect was recognized many years ago and was remedied by statute so as to give a discretionary power to the courts (now contained in Order 11 of the Rules of the Supreme Court, which is re-enacted in the Civil Procedure Rules) to authorise service of a claim form on a defendant abroad in certain cases. Another exception to the normal principle that the courts have no power to entertain an action against a defendant who is outside the jurisdiction was found to be necessary to deal with cases where the defendant submitted to the English court's jurisdiction.14th ed., p. 354.

院是被拒絕給予權力去處理案件，但是在許多情形下於當地審判卻是合適的，例如侵權行為是於英國被作成的，或被告身體所在雖不在英國但卻於英國有住所時。這個缺點於許多年前就被承認並且是被成文法（現今包含於Ord. 11, R.S.C.,而新修訂於C.P.R.[20]）所補救，以便給予法院裁量權去允許於某些情形下將請求文件送達給於外國之被告。」

故而在有著「所在權力」或被告承認法院管轄之情形下，英國法院雖有著管轄權，但若於訴因與法院無甚大關連或正義之需求下，英國法院是得以不方便法院而停止訴訟；而於訴因若與英國有著重大之關連及正義之需求下，英國法院得例外的將請求之文件送達境外之被告。**因而基於這個判例法的進化，個人較近建議[21]於行使民商管轄權時：各國仍得以既有的（國內）管轄規則為基礎（大陸法為國內民訴之管轄權規則；英美法仍為所在理論及送達境外之規則）。但訴訟之通知若於境內已適當的送達給被告，或於被告承認法院之管轄權時，於正義之需求下法院得以「不方便法院」原則為拒絕或停止訴訟裁量之依據（例如訴因與法院地沒有合理之牽連時）；而若法院欲送達通知至境外時，首先必須認知此為一種例外之過度管轄，其判決有可能不為外國法院所承認，應以「方便法院」原則來確認法院是否為合適、自然之管轄法院，以作為允許送達境外之適用標準（例如為了公平正義之目的或訴因與法院地有強烈牽連時）。**

雖然英美法於送達境內之所在理論，「如果當事人是外鄉人而訴因亦發生於相關國家之外，是否偶然的所在，而不同於居所，是個很好的管轄基礎是可能會受到懷疑的」，但是如果以不方便法院法則在正義的需求下或在訴因與法院地沒有強烈關連時，對管轄權之行使加以限制，則上述之問題就應會被加以和緩。大陸法的境內送達則因其國內民事訴訟法之管轄基礎侵權行為地、契約訂定地等，通常皆與法院地有著適度關連，故而過

20　CPR, Part 50 and Sch 1.

21　陳隆修、許兆慶、林恩瑋、李瑞生四人合著，《國際私法─管轄與選法理論之交錯》，台北，五南圖書公司，2009年3月，初版1刷，248頁；對於婚姻請求救濟之管轄基礎，個人建議於252頁。

度管轄之情形較為不明顯，但於複數國家皆有管轄權之國際複數訴訟時，不方便法院之適用是應較先繫屬優先原則能顧及個案正義。特別是如果其他國家與訴因的發生較法院地與訴因的發生有著明顯強烈的關連時[22]，硬性的先繫屬優先原則較可能會促成選購法院、否認之訴、規避法律等濫用訴訟程序之情形，並且較無法於特殊情形下顧及個案正義之司法基本目的。

二、境外送達為過度之例外管轄

至於境外送達上英國判例法長久以來就認為是過度或例外之管轄，並且有著一系列之判例法來規範裁量權之行使[23]。而成文法亦明確的規定法院允許送達境外時應謹慎的考慮一些因素。Civil Procedure Rules 1998, s. 6. 20 (3) (a)要求請求人與被告間「必須有一個真正的爭點合理的需要法院去審判」；s. 6. 21 (1)（b）規定原告必須以書面證明「其請求有著合理勝訴的機會」；而s. 6. 21 （2A）則明示「除非法院能同意法院地是個合適去提起請求之地，否則法院不會去允許送達境外」。故而在方便法院法則之相關判例法與成文法之交叉規範下，英國法是謹慎的避免對境外被告之人權與被告國家之主權加以侵犯。大陸法國內法及歐盟布魯塞爾規則第5條雖然於管轄權上接要求法院地與訴因有著關連，但對於境外與境內被告之送達並未加以區分，這是與一般常識上之認知及訴訟於實務上之困難不合的。對於境外被告加以送達、起訴，不但應注意到應訴被告之人

22 ALI/UNIDROIT Principles of Transnational Civil Procedure的2.1.2條規定法案地與當事人或系爭糾紛必須有「重大關連」，法院才能有對人管轄，但2.1.1條規定當事人亦可同意法院之管轄。當系爭事件的重大部分發生於法院地，或被告之慣居地是於法院地，或法人的登記成立地或主要營業地於法院地，或與案件爭點有關之財產是位於法院地，則「重大關連」是存在的。
2.1 Jurisdiction over a party may be exercised:
2.1.1 By consent of the parties to submit the dispute to the tribunal;
2.1.2 When there is a substantial connection between the forum state and the party or the transaction or occurrence in dispute. A substantial connection exists when a significant part of the transaction or occurrence occurred in the forum state, when an individual defendant is a habitual resident of the forum state or a jural entity has received its charter of organization or has its principal place of business therein, or when property to which the dispute relates is located in the forum state.

23 陳隆修，《國際私法管轄權評論》，台北，五南圖書公司，民國75年11月，初版，45-47頁。

權及其母國之尊嚴、主權之問題，更應務實的謹記法院判決於被告母國之執行性之問題。

歐盟布魯塞爾規則及大陸法管轄規則的不區分境外與境內被告，是違反「常識」，對境外當事人被告「不符合正義目的」，亦不符合二十一世紀現實生活經驗的「自然道法」，因此是「不合理」的作法。個人於論述契約法時就叨叨不休的一再喋喋重申：英美法客觀的合理性及大陸法主觀的誠信原則，應為所有契約法引為基礎的共同核心基本法理，亦是於個案上對抗實體法或程序法上所可能產生之不公正情形之警察原則。於二十一世紀全球化法學重視個案正義之趨勢下，個人並進而主張全球化法學，無論於人權法、憲法、實體法、程序法、國際法、國內法、侵權法、契約法、親屬繼承法及其他之一切所有法學，皆應以合理性、誠信原則、比例原則做為引以為基礎的共同核心基本法理與政策，並於個案上做為對抗實體法與程序法上所可能產生之不公正情形之警察原則。個人曾經不厭其煩的逐一列舉契約法上之相關條文以說明「合理性」為契約法的共同核心基本政策及警察原則，於國際民事訴訟法上ALI/UNIDROIT Principles of Transnational Civil Procedure第3條於規定當事人程序上之平等時，其comment P-3A[24]如此評述：「『合理性』的名詞是於整個（國際訴訟法）原則中皆被使用著，根據條文之內容其代表『比例的』、『顯著的』、『不過分』、或『公平』。其亦可意味著是獨斷的相反。合理性的概念並且排除過分技術性的法律辯論，並亦給予法院一系列之裁量權以便避免嚴苛、過分、或不合理的適用程序上之形式之情形。」

「合理性」的標準是符合「常識」、「判例法正義的目的」、及二十一世紀依據生活經驗而來的「自然道法」。依據「合理性」的標準，德、英、及大中華經濟圈是認定美國反托辣斯法於「效力理論」之適用

24 "The term 'reasonable' is used throughout the Principles and signifies 'proportional,' 'significant,' 'not excessive,' or 'fair,' according to the context. It can also mean the opposite of arbitrary. The concept of reasonableness also precludes hyper-technical legal argument and leaves a range of discretion to the court to avoid severe, excessive, or unreasonable application of procedural norms."

上，是「嚴苛、過分、不合理的適用程序上之形式」，並且是「過分技術性的法律辯論」。同樣的歐盟於國際管轄權上採「先繫屬優先」及不區分境內與境外請求文件之作法，於二十一世紀全球化市場之潮流中亦是「不合理」，不符合「常識」，不能達成「個案正義的目的」，違反二十一世紀生活經驗的「自然道法」。為了應付二十一世紀全球化世界的詭譎多變日新月異，各國法院不得不擴張其管轄基礎以便能於個別案中確保公平正義的結果，但是伴隨逐漸擴張的管轄基礎，自然「應給予法院一系列之裁量權以便避免嚴苛、過分、或不合理的適用程序上之形式」。故而在當被告於境內時，「以不方便法院為基礎去停止訴訟的寬廣、具彈性的裁量權之發展是個有效的解決方法」；但是當被告於境外時，「在許多情形下於當地審判卻是合適的」，故得依方便法院為基礎，「以便給予法院裁量權去允許於某些情形下將請求文件送達給於外國被告」。**因為送達境外之管轄權是屬於「過度」「例外」之管轄權，故而Civil Procedure Rules 1998之要件：(a)當事人間「必須有一個真正的爭點（事實或法律上）合理的需要法院去審判」；(b)原告必須以書面去證明「其請求有著合理勝訴的機會」；及最重要的(c)「法院地是個合適去提起請求之地」，必須成為全世界各法系於送達境外被告之考慮要件——亦即為對境外被告管轄權基礎之全球化法學。**

個人一再強調[25]「如同大自然之進化，經過長久歷史演進而來之判例法，經常亦屬於宇宙進化之一環，學術理論之創作最好不要逆天而行與判例法相抗衡」，是故於遵照黃進及趙相林雨教授之建議，於研究中國法學之大方向時，個人一再強烈的主張——「道法自然」應為所有中國法學及二十一世紀全球化法學之基礎。

大陸法（尤其歐盟）於跨國訴訟中故意藐視判例法母國法經歷千錘百鍊的進化結晶，粗暴的採取「先繫屬優先」法則，又昧於事實的不分被告

---

[25] 陳隆修，《2005年海牙法院選擇公約評析》，台北，五南圖書公司，2009年1月，初版1刷，94頁。於該處個人指出羅馬公約7(1)條與2005年海牙公約的以指定管轄法院地法為契約成立地法，為違反判例法之見證。

是否所在於境內之管轄權之行使，是「不合理」，不符合「常識」，又無視於「個案正義之目的」，尤其是藐視人類祖先於天地間所建立之「自然道法」。於Price v Dewhurst[26]中Shadwell V-C說：「無論何時只要正義很明顯的被忽視，法院就必須將判決視為沒有價值與沒有重要性。」歐盟為達行政之統一，以多數暴力蠻橫的藐視於全球化市場上法院需要寬廣的裁量權，與區分境內及境外被告於管轄權行使之區別，這是明顯的「忽視正義」之暴行。

布魯塞爾規則及公約的27至29條及21至23條，於相同訴因或相關訴訟上[27]歐盟皆採先繫屬優先。甚至於專屬管轄有平行（或複數）訴因時亦採納這個原則。硬性的先繫屬優先作法不但造成否認之訴之增加，鼓勵當事人先下手起訴以選購法院，這種機械式的作法更亦違反訴訟法上自然原告對自然被告於自然法院提起自然訴訟的「自然道法」[28]。對此Dicey and Morris評述這「是個有些粗糙的解決方法」[29]。另外對於歐盟固執的不區分被告於境內或境外管轄權之行使，ALI/UNIDROIT Principles of Transnational Civil Procedure於規定當事人間程序平等原則時，其第3.2條[30]之後半段規定：「法院應考慮到外國當事人於參加訴訟時可能會遭遇之問題。」事實上中國人於外國之訴訟，不但面臨簽證、語言、經濟、證據、

26 (1837) 8 Sim 279 at 302 “whenever it is manifest that justice has been disregarded, the court is bound to treat the decision as a matter of no value and no substance”.

27 於相同訴因以外之相關訴訟，會員國之法院有裁量權去決定是否採納先繫屬優先。

28 **或許所謂「自然原告」就是自認為權利受損之人，而「自然被告」就可能是其認為造成其損害之人。依英國判例法「自然法院」就是具有「最真實重大關連」之法院。而「自然訴訟」個人認為——無論是適用於國內或國際訴訟上——或許即應符合上述英國CPR 1998於法院許可下將訴訟通知送達境外之三要素：(a)真正的爭點；(b)合理勝訴之機會；(c)法院地是個合適去提起請求之地。事實上個人亦認為這三要件亦是法院可於決定國際訴訟及國內訴訟上，當事人是否有濫用程序之標準。**

29 Dicey and Morris, the Conflict of Laws, 14th ed., p. 489, “where, first, the proceedings involve ‘the same cause of action’ and, second, where the cause of action is not the same, but the actions are related. The Conventions adopt a somewhat crude solution to the problem of lis alibi pendens by requiring, in the first class of case, that any court other than the court first seised shall not exercise jurisdiction”. Dresser UK Ltd v *Falcongate Freight Management Ltd* [1992] Q.B. 502, 514 (CA).

30 3.2 The right to equal treatment includes avoidance of any kind of illegitimate discrimination, particularly on the basis of nationality or residence. The court should take into account difficulties that might be encountered by a foreign party in participating in litigation.

制度上之問題，於文化上亦常遭受西方強勢優越感之歧視[31]。除了第三世界人民於第一世界的法院訴訟會遭遇重大之險阻外，第一世界間亦常發生判決不被執行之困難，例如懲罰性賠償、集體訴訟判決、反托辣斯法之判決等美式判決，而大陸法的終身定期金賠償、違約金判決亦於英美法系遭受相同的對待。故而大陸法於國際管轄權之行使上不去區分被告知是否於法院地，不但漠視了現實生活之經驗與常識，更可能觸及了人權法所能允許的界線。

三、共同管轄基礎

英國判例法為「判例法之母國」（homeland of common law），於管轄權上美國同僚不虛心學習母法，胡天胡地的自以為有創意的建立了「最低限度關連點」（minimum contacts）標準，個人不客氣的評斷「最低限度關連製造最大程度之混亂」（minimum contacts have caused maximum chaos）。一些德裔的美國前輩同僚試圖引進大陸法「一般與特別管轄」（general and special jurisdictions）之國內法概念，但這些舉動於美國雖然發出令人暈眩的光芒，但並沒有產生熱能。事實上於訴因不一定須要與法院地有關連之一般管轄上，相對於大陸法的採住所（布魯塞爾

---

31 於陳隆修、許兆慶、林恩瑋、李瑞生四人合著，《國際私法-管轄與選法理論之交錯》，台北，五南圖書公司，2009年3月，初版1刷，232-236頁中，對於著名的台中地院94家訴字253號民事裁定，跨國監護權官司中個人以紐約訴訟費過分高昂，於當事人間造成正義之失衡，要求台灣法院再次審理該案，並評述如下：「另外阮母於紐約法院被認定為精神不穩定，於此國際公約已有斬釘截鐵之明文。海牙1996公約第25條及歐盟2201/2003規則第26條，明文規定有管轄權國家所作的事實認定應拘束被請求國（25條），及判決之實體於任何情形下皆不可再被重新審理（26條）。母愛乃附屬於小孩最佳利益下之至高天賦，正如Mckee所下之原則：國際禮誼於此至高原則下應退讓。個人於電視上觀阮母神智似十分清醒，全世界沒有任何鐵律可以恣意切斷母女間之神聖關連。由生活經驗上個人見過或許因我國文化較為包容，故而我國有些婦女所勇於表達情緒之偏差行為，為較為偏重理性之西方社會視為病態。固然文化不得做為偏差行為之藉口，個人所主張之實體法論認為應有人類文明共通之最低標準。但母愛為附屬於小孩最佳利益之至高原則，而且更如前述，於此至高公共政策之考量下，所有之國際公約皆允許我國法院不去承認或執行外國判決。故我國地院欲執行紐約判決前，應將阮母之精神狀態重新交付『我國』專家認定方是。」**聯合國1966年兩個人權公約之第1(1)條及歐盟2000年基本權利憲章第22條街信誓旦旦的保障各民族文化之發展，但做為一個資深的中國國際法的學生，個人於此正式提出嚴正的抗議：中國文化於西方法院並未得到充分的尊重，對中國人而言「正義有時很明顯的被忽視」。**

規則第2條[32]），英美法長久以來即採「所在權力」理論。而訴因須與法院地有一定關連之特別管轄，布魯塞爾規則第5條，英國送達境外的Civil Procedure Rules 1998, s. 6. 20，亦大致上皆有類似之規定。或許於一般及特別管轄上判例法與大陸法最大的差異在於：判例法於境內管轄（一般管轄）以不方便法院，而於境外管轄（特別管轄）以方便法院，為法院於適用管轄權時行使裁量權之依據或限制。而如ALI/UNIDROIT Principles of Transnational Civil Procedure第2.5條所規定，法院於其他法院更合適之情形下，得以不方便法院而停止訴訟。事實上於全球化市場之需求下，法院須同時擴展其管轄基礎及增加於個案主持正義之裁量權，故境內管轄之不方便法院與境外管轄之方便法院裁量權之行使，為二十一世紀必然之寫實，否則就形成「正義很明顯的被忽視」。

歐盟布魯塞爾規則（Council Regulation No. 44/2001）的第5條[33]或

---

[32] Article 2

1. Subject to this Regulation, persons domiciled in a Member State shall, whatever their nationality, be sued in the courts of that Member State.
2. Persons who are not nationals of the Member State in which they are domiciled shall be governed by the rules of jurisdiction asplicable to nationals of that State.

[33] Article 5

A person domiciled in a Member State may, in another Member State, be sued:

1.(a) in matters relating to a contract, in the courts for the place of performance of the obligation in question;

(b) for the purpose of this provision and unless otherwise agreed, the place of performance of the obligation in question shall be:

-- in the case of the sale of goods, the place in a Member State where, under the contract, the goods were delivered or should have been delivered,

-- in the case of the provision of services, the place in a Member State where, under the contract, the services were provided or should have been provided,

(c) if subparagraph (b) does not apply then subparagraph (a) applies;

2. in matters relating to maintenance, in the courts for the place where the maintemance creditor is domiciled or habitually resident or, if the matter is ancillary to proceedings concerning the status of a person, in the court which, according to its own law, has jurisdiction to entertain those proceedings, unless that jurisdiction is based solely on the nationality of one of the parties;

3. in matters relating to tort, delict or quasi-delict, in the courts for the place where the harmfull event occurred or may occur;

4. as regards a civil claim for damages or restitution which is based on an act giving rise to criminall proceedings, in the court seised of those proceedings, to the extent that that court has jurisdiction under its own law to entertain civil proceedings;

5. as regards a dispute arising out of the operatons of a branch, agency or other establishment, in the courts for the place in which the branch, agency or other establishment is situated;

許即為大陸法訴因須與法院地有關連之特別管轄之代表。其規定：住所於會員國之人得於其他會員國被訴：「1.(a)於有關契約之事項，於系爭義務履行地之法院；(b)為了本條文之目的及除非當事人另有同意，系爭義務之履行地應為：於貨品買賣之情形，依契約貨品已被移交或應被移交之地之會員國地，（或）於提供服務之情形，依契約服務已被提供或應被提供之地之會員國地，(c)如果(b)款不能適用則應適用(a)款；2.於有關扶養費之情形，被扶養權利人之住所地或慣居地之法院，或如果該事情是附屬於有關一個人身分之程序，則依據該法律，有管轄權去處理該程序之法院，除非該管轄權是只根據當事人之一之國籍而來；3.有關侵權或準侵權行為，損害行為發生地或可能發生地（歐盟這是包括損害行為地及損害效果發生地）；4.有關因基於引起刑事程序之行為而發生之損害賠償或恢復原狀，於依其法律該法院有管轄權去處理民事程序時，處理該刑事程序之法院；5.有關分行、代理、或其他機構之行為所引起之糾紛，該分行、代理或其他機構所在地之法院；6.於有關依法律、或依書面文件、或經由口頭但以書面證明，所產生之信託之立信託人、受託人、或受益人，信託住所地之會員國法院；7.有關貨物或運費之救助所請求報酬之付款之糾紛，於依系爭貨物或運費之所在地法律之法院：(a)該貨物或運費被扣押以清償該款項，或(b)該貨物或運費可被扣押，但保釋金或其他擔保已被提出；但本款只能適用於被告主張對該貨物或運費有著利益，或於救助時有這種利益。」

布魯塞爾公約[34]及規則第5條應是大陸法特別管轄（訴因與法院地須

---

6. as settler, trustee or beneficiary of a trust created by the operation of a statute, or by a written instrument, or created orally and evidenced in writing, in the courts of the Member State in which the trust is domiciled;
7. as regards a dispute concerning the payment of remuneration claimed in respect of the salvage of a cargo or freight, in the court under the authority of which the cargo or freight in question:
(a) has been arrested to secure such payment, or
(b) could have been so arrested, but bail or other security has been given;
provided that this provision shall apply only if it is claimed that the defendant has an interest in the cargo or freight or had such an interest at the time of salvage.

34 公約第5條見陳隆修，《國際私法管轄權評論》，台北，五南圖書公司，民國75年11月，初版，

有關連）中最具代表性的，事實上如果單就早期公約第5條而言，則更容易解讀。相對於規則第5條的特別管轄，或許英國Civil Procedure Rules 1998法院允許請求文件送達境外之s. 6. 20[35]最具有判例法之代表性。美國

12-14頁，於此不再贅述。

[35] 6.20 Service out of the jurisdiction where the permission of the court is required
In any proceedings to which rule 6.19 does not apply, a claim form may be served out of the jurisdiction with the permission of the court if—
(1) a claim is made for a remedy against a person domiciled within the jurisdiction.
(2) a claim is made for an injunction ordering the defendant to do or refrain from doing an act within the jurisdiction.
(3) a claim is made against someone on whom the claim form has been or will be served and –
(a) there is between the claimant and that person a real issue which it is reasonable for the court to try; and
(b) the claimant wishes to serve the claim form on another person who is a necessary or proper party to that claim.
(3A) a claim is a Part 20 claim and the person to be served is a necessary or proper party to the claim against the Part 20 claimant.
(4) a claim is made for an interim remedy under section 25(1) of the 1982 Act.
(5) a claim is made in respect of a contract where the contract –
(a) was made within the jurisdiction;
(b) was made by or through an agent trading or residing within the jurisdiction;
(c) is governed by English law; or
(d) contains a term to the effect that the court shall have jurisdiction to determine any claim in respect of the contract.
(6) a claim is made in respect of a breach of contract committed within the jurisdiction.
(7) a claim is made for a delaration that no contract exists where, if the contract was found to exist, it would comply with the conditions set out in paragraph (5).
(8) a claim is made in tort where –
(a) damage was sustained within the jurisdiction; or
(b) the damage sustained resulted form an act committed within the jurisdiction.
(9) a claim is made to enforce any judgment or arbitral award.
(10) the whole subject matter of a claim relates to property located within the jurisdiction.
(11) a claim is made for any remedy which might be obtained in proceedings to execute the trusts of a written instrument where –
(a) the trusts ought to be executed according to English law; and
(b) the person on whom the claim form is to be served is a trustee of the trusts.
(12) a claim is made for any remedy which might be obtained in proceedings for the administration of the estate of a person who died domiciled within the jurisdiction.
(13) a claim is made in probate proceedings which includes a claim for the rectification of a will.
(14) a claim is made for a remedy against the defendant as constructive trustee where the defendant's alleged liability arises out of acts committed within the jurisdiction.
(15) a claim is made for restitution where the defendant's alleged liability arises out of acts committed within the jurisdiction.
(16) a claim is made by the Commissioners of the Inland Revenue relating to duties or taxes against a defendant not domiciled in Scotland or Northern Ireland.
(17) a claim is made by a party to proceedings for an order that the court exercise its power under section 51 of the Supreme Court Act 1981 to make a costs order in favour of or against a person who

送達境外之長手法規（long arm statutes），因為總共有50州之法律，且交雜著最低限度關連點，故限於篇幅無法討論，但大致上亦相似[36]。於美國適當程序條款之規定下，若非居民被告於法院地之關連符合該條款之要求，則法院對其有管轄權。例如於法院地進行商業行為；於法院地發生侵權行為；於法院地有財產[37]；婚姻住所地於法院[38]；契約訂定地或履行地於

is not a party to those proceedings.

(17A) a claim is –

(a) in the nature of salvage and any part of the services took place within the jurisdiction; or

(b) to enforce a claim under section 153, 154 or 175 of the Merchant Shipping Act 1995(a).

(18) a claim is made under an enactment specified in the relevant practice direction.

36 見陳隆修，《國際私法管轄權評論》，台北，五南圖書公司，民國75年11月，初版，136-147頁。「依上述『最低限度關連點』理論，只要訴訟是基於被告與法院地有重大關係之行為，並且法院審理該訴訟並不違反傳統上公平及正義之原則時，則法院對非居民被告有管轄權。但以上乃為美國憲法有關適當程序條款之要求，各州仍須將此理論制成法規，以便州法院對非居民被告有管轄權，這些法規於美國稱為『長手法規』（long arm statutes）。沒有這些『長手法規』，無論非居民被告於法院地之活動為何，及與法院地之關連點（contacts）為何，州法院對其無管轄權。一般美國各州最常採用之長手法規，為伊利諾州所採用的長手法規。此類長手法規明文列舉各種特定之行為，如果行為人於法院地做成這些行為，則法院對於任何基於這些行為所引起之訴訟，對行為人有管轄權。另外加州於一九七〇年所通過之長手法規，並未列舉出各種特定之行為，其允許法院於憲法適當程序條款之範圍內，接受案件之管轄權，亦即美國憲法適當程序條款為其管轄權唯一之限制。故一般州法院欲依伊利諾州之長手法規主張管轄權時，除了必須符合該州長手法規之要求外，並須滿足憲法適當條款之要求；而加州法院欲依其長手法規主張管轄權時，只須滿足憲法適當條款之要求。例如前述之Cornelison v. Chaney案中，由於該貨車主偶而（occasional）從加州載貨或載貨至加州，雖車禍地為路途中之內華達州，加州法院亦主張對其有管轄權，並且認為此管轄基礎並不違背憲法上之適當程序條款，加州此種長手法規自然是給予法院甚大之自由，且甚具有彈性，但亦有不明確之缺點。」Ill. Rev. Stat, Ch. 110, § 17; 6 Cal 3d 143 (1976).

37 見陳隆修，《國際私法管轄權評論》，台北，五南圖書公司，民國75年11月，初版，144、145頁。「我國民事訴訟法第三條規定：『對於在中華民國現無住所或住所不明之人，因財產權涉訟者，得由被告可扣押之財產或請求標的所在地之法院管轄。被告之財產或請求標的如為債權，以債務人住所或該債權擔保之標的所在地，視為被告財產或請求標的之所在地。』作者推測或許本條之適用範圍僅限於國內案件，而不適用於國際案件。因為世界上各國似乎甚少以因被告於法院地有財產，而主張於與該財產無關之訴訟中，法院對其有對人訴訟管轄權。但美國之長手法規卻規定，因非居民被告於法院地擁有，使用或占有財產，因而引起訴訟，則法院對其有管轄權。例如由於非居民被告對其於法院地財產之使用或保管不週，因而使得法院地居民受傷，則法院對其有管轄權。有些法院對非居民被告於法院地有財產，因有關該財產而被提起契約不履行之訴，認為被告應接受法院之管轄權，於de Leo v. Childs中，原告建築師對於非居民財產所有人，提起有關重新改良於法院地之該財產之契約不履行之訴，法院判被告應接受其管轄。此管轄基礎無疑地亦為美國所首創，表面上看起來此管轄基礎似乎甚符合現代工商社會之需要，但事實上此管轄基礎似乎仍可由傳統之管轄基礎，如侵權行為地，損害發生地，契約訂定地及契約履行地等取代。」例如Mass Gen Laws ch 223A, § 3(e); Dubin v. City of Philadelphia, 34Pa, D. & C. 61 (1938) 304F. Supp 593 (D. Mass. 1969).又見150、151頁「訴訟與法院地之物無關」，現今國際法上通認若訴訟與法院地之財產無關之管轄為過度管轄，其判決不會被承認。

38 見陳隆修，《國際私法管轄權評論》，台北，五南圖書公司，民國75年11月，初版，146頁。「有些州之長手法規規定，於離婚或分居贍養費，小孩之扶養費及監護權之訴中，法院地若為

法院地。

英國之Civil Procedure Rules 1998, s. 6. 19為不需要法院許可即能送達境外被告之情形，這通常是指法律有明文規定之情形，例如符合布魯塞爾規則或保護貿易利益法。而s. 6. 20即為需法院允許才能送達給境外之被告之情形：「於6. 19規則不適用之任何程序中，在法院之許可下請求文件得被送達至境外，如果(1)請求是針對一住所於法院地之人要求其補償。(2)請求是要求作成禁止命令，命令被告於法院地作為或不作為某行為。(3)請求是針對請求文書已被送達或會被送達之人，並且(a)於請求人與被送達人間有一真正的爭點合理的需要法院去審理；並且(b)請求人希望對於該請求是個必須或合適當事人之其他人加以送達請求文件。（3A）該請求是屬於此規則20之請求，並且在對抗規則20之請求人之請求上該欲被送達之人是個必須或適合之當事人。(4)請求是1982年法律之25(1)條之暫時性救濟。(5)該請求是有關一契約，而該契約(a)是於法院地內被訂立；(b)是由或經由於法院地內居住或經商之代理人所訂立；(c)準據法為英國法；或(d)其中包含一個條款約定法院應有管轄權去決定有關契約之任何請求。(6)請求是有關於管轄區域內被違背的契約。(7)請求是有關契約不存在之確認，而如果該契約若被認為存在，其會符合第5項之條件。(8)當請求是以侵權行為而被提出時(a)損害是發生於管轄區內；或(b)損害是由於管轄區內之行為所導至。(9)請求是為了強制執行任何判決或仲裁判斷。(10)請求的整個主體（訴因、實體）是有關於管轄區域內之物。(11)一個請求的提出是為了於一個以書面建立的信託的執行程序中取得救濟，而(a)該信託應依英國法而被執行；且(b)請求文件被送達之人是信託之被信託人。(12)請求是為了於死亡時住所於管轄區域內之人之遺產處理程序中取得任何救濟。(13)請求是為了遺囑程序，而這包含遺囑修正

『婚姻住所地『（matrimonial domicile）則對被告有管轄權。此規定之目的是在保護被遺棄之一方，免得其必須去尋找另一方當事人。有些州有著較寬鬆之規定，只要於任何婚姻持續期間，夫妻有建立婚姻住所地於法院地，則法院對於因婚姻所引起之義務有管轄權，有些州則規定必須有一方當事人尚居住於法院地方可。』例如伊利諾州之Ill Rev Stat ch 110, §17(e);例如印第安納州之Ind. Rules of Trial Proc 44 (A) (7).

之請求。(14)請求是為了對被推定為信託人之被告而要求救濟之請求，而被告被主張之責任是基於管轄區域內之行為。(15)要求恢復原狀之請求，而被告被主張之責任發生於管轄區域內之行為。(16)請求是國稅局所提起，有關對住所非於蘇格蘭或北愛爾蘭被告之稅捐。(17)請求是由法院依1981年法院法第51條所行使的權力去作成命令之程序之當事人所提起，而該命令是對非為該程序之當事人之其他人有關費用之對其有利或不利之命令。（17A）請求是有關(a)發生於管轄區域內之財物救助之性質及任何部分之服務；或(b)去執行依1995(a)海商法153、154、或175條而來之請求。(18)根據有著明示相關實際規則之立法而來之請求。」

個人不厭其煩的將布魯塞爾規則特別管轄的第5條，及英國於法院允許下送達境外被告的C.P.R. 1998, s. 6. 20，逐一加以翻譯列出，乃是在說明兩者於大致上架構之相似之處。另外散見於各處一有甚多大致上略似之處，例如布魯塞爾規則第6(1)、(2)條之共同訴訟與C.P.R. 1998, s. 6. 20(3)、（3A）之英美法所謂之第三人訴訟。相信若比較法的同僚如可以逐一作更徹底的詳細比對，相同之處或許不限於「大致架構」而已。又更如布魯塞爾規則第2條以住所謂最基本的一般管轄基礎，一般總是認為相對上於英美法最為基本的一般管轄基礎（法院地與訴因不依定須有關連）應為「所在權力」，但事實上英國C.P.R. 1998, s. 6. 20(1)亦規定住所於管轄區內之被告得於法院允許下被送達至境外，而且這個管轄基礎亦符合大陸法一般管轄之概念（如了住所以外，法院地與訴因不一定需有關連）。而同樣主張「所在權力」之美國法，美國最高法院亦認為由憲法而言，住所係一充分之關連點[39]，故而亦符合大陸法一般管轄之概念（亦即

[39] 見陳隆修，《2005年海牙法院選擇公約評析》，台北，五南圖書公司，2009年1月，初版1刷。111～113頁。「即使被告不在於其住所之州內，住所地之法院對其亦有充分之對人訴訟管轄權。從憲法上之觀點而言，住所係一充分之關連點（sufficient contact）。因為當事人既於住所地享有許多權利，自然其亦應於住所地被起訴。而且即使訴之原因發生於他處，被告仍可能預期其會於住所地被起訴。何況於複雜之國際情形下，被告至少應有一處之法院對其有管轄權。」Milliken v. Meyer, 311 U.S. 457 (1940).「美國大部分州及第二新篇規定以起訴時被告之住所為準。有些州法規規定以訴訟原因發生時之住所為準，例如侵權行為人於行為後，但起訴前，搬至其他州。許多州皆承認這些法規。」Second Restatement § 29; Owens v. Superior Court,

除了住所外，訴因與法院地不再需要其他關連點）。**故而遠遠超乎一般人之觀念，除了於法院裁量權上之區別外，大陸法與英美法於一般管轄及特別管轄上可能不僅止於架構上大致相似——亦即除了於裁量權外，於國際管轄上或許一百多年來早已存在一個全球化的主流共同核心管轄規則。**

四、國王的新衣——「許多國家所行使的管轄權是相似的」

這種英美法與大陸法在國際管轄之隔閡，即使於英國加入歐盟後仍發生。於1984年Lord Diplock在Amin Rasheed Shipping Crop v Kuwait Insurance Co[40]中仍舊認為英國送達境外之管轄為「過度管轄」（exorbitiant furusdiction），因為：「依據一般之英國國際私法，除非有著條約規定應加以承認，他並非英國法院承認外國法院所擁有（之管轄權）。」

但於加入歐盟甚久之後英國資深同僚終於先後駭然發現他們所如履薄冰的境外過度管轄是為許多（或所有）大陸法所視為理所當然的。Prof. Collins[41]不平等的反擊如下：「但是非常遺憾的是過境管轄規則是否可以

52 Cal. 2d 822 (1959); Cooke v. Yarrington, 229 A. 2d 400 (N. J. 1972)「於憲法上居所亦構成適當之對人管轄權基礎。如果當事人與居所地有實質上重大的（substantial）關係，而法院主張管轄權為合理的（ressonable），則很多人認為居所地法院應有管轄權，第二新編亦認為是，例如軍人被派駐紮地之法院。但事實上大部分州皆於法律上將對居所實質上的要求，表面上冠以住所之名，例如內華達州以辦理『快速離婚』（quickee divorce）而聞名，其乃透過外人得以輕易取得當地住所之技巧，而達成外人可於當地離婚之目的。」Second Restatement § 30.荒謬的是歐盟雖以住所為管轄基礎，但並未對住所下定義，而是交由各國自行定義。

40 [1984] A.C. 50. 65, "it is one which under general English conflict rules, an English court would not recognize as possessed by any foreign court in the absence of some treaty providing for such recognition."

41 Lawrence Collins, Temporary Presence, Exorbitant Jruisdiction and the U.S. Supreme Court, Vol. 107, L.Q.R. 1991, pp. 10, 13, 14, "If there is a genuine dispute which has no connection with the forum, then the exercise of jurisdiction may be excessive if the defendant has no opportunity to contest its exercise under a forum non conveniens doctrine; this is perhaps why it is so regarded under the Brussels Convention régime, where forum non conveniens plays no part. But it is regrettable that the transient jurisdiction rule (as it is called in the United States) was branded as exorbitant by the Brussels Convention without regard to the effect of forum non conveniens, and even more regrettable that, under the influence of Lord Diplock, the English courts have come to regard it as established that the jurisdiction exercised under Order 11 is exorbitant. In *The Siskina* [1979] A.C. 210 at p. 254 he expressed the view that in several of the heads of Order 11 the jurisdiction exercised over foreigners was wider than that which was recognized in English law as being possessed by courts of foreign countries; these were exorbitant jurisdictions which ran counter to "to normal rules of comity among civilized nations"; see also Amin Rasheed Shipping Corpn. v. *Kuwait Insurance Co. Ltd.* [1984] A.C. 50 at p. 65. This view has

應用（如同現在於美國所稱呼的）是為布魯塞爾公約所冠以過度之名而未考慮到不方便法院之效力，以及更加令人遺憾的是，在Lord Diplock的影響下，英國法院將依Order 11而行使之管轄（境外送達）是過度管轄視為一個已經確立之概念。於The Siskina……中，其所表達之觀點為對外國人行使管轄權之Order 11中之數個項目（管轄基礎），是較英國法院所承認外國法院所擁有之管轄權為廣；這些是違反了「文明國家間所有的禮誼之正常規則」的過度管轄。……這個觀點為第一審……上訴審……及最高法院……的法官毫無疑問的接受。但這是謬誤的：傳統上英國法律只承認兩種外國法院之管轄基礎：所在及承認（管轄）。基於爭執的主體（訴因）與外國法院的關連而來的管轄基礎（例如於管轄區域內所發生的侵權行為）從來沒有因基於對等待遇或其他之基礎而被承認，這些是不被認為應構成外國判決被承認及執行之理由。但這不是因為這種管轄權的行使被視為過分及違反國際禮誼（因為大部分國家行使這種管轄），而是因為英國法院於執行外國判決上非常狹窄的方式。「過度管轄」的稱謂應是保留給真正不合理或過度的行使管轄之情形……並且Lord Diplock對Order 11過度及違反國際禮誼之完全不合道理之分類應被拒絕。」

事實上英國法院對外國特別管轄之無法承認，很可能主要的理由（或之一理由）為對於境外送達裁量權行使之無法規範，故而難以用國際禮誼之名而給予外國法院相對的對等待遇。這亦是於外國判決之承認上，

---

been accepted without question by judges at first instance (e.g. The Alexandros P. [1986] Q.B. 464 at p. 478), the Court of Appeal (e.g. Insurance Co. of Ireland v. *Strombus International Insurance* [1985] 2 Lloyd's Rep. 138 at p. 146) and the House of Lords (*The Spiliada* [1987] A.C. 460 at p. 481). But this is fallacious: traditionally English law has recognized only two bases of jurisdiction of foreign courts: presence and submission. Bases of jurisdiction based on the connection of the subject-matter of the dispute with the foreign forum (e.g. tort commited within its jurisdiction) have never been recongnised, on the basis of reciprocity or otherwise, as justifying the recognition and enforcement of foreign judgments. But this is not because such an exercise of jurisdiction is regarded as excessive and contrary to the comity of nations (for most countries exercise such a jurisdiction) but because of the very narrow approach of English courts to the enforcement of foreign judgents. The expression "exorbitant jurisdiction" should be reserved for the exercise of jurisdiction which is truly unreasonables or excessive (e.g. The Volvox Hollandia [1988] 2 Lloyd's Rep. 361 at p. 373; Deutsche Schachtbau v. *Shell International petroleum Co. Ltd.* [1990] A.C. 295 at pp. 341, 343-344), and the wholly unjustified categorisation by Lord Diplock of Order 11 as exorbitant and contrary to international comity should be rejected."

英國法院不採對等待遇或國際禮誼，而採義務主義理由之一。但尊敬的Prof Collins將這個邏輯的推演顛倒，反以承認外國判決的狹窄來說明境外送達的合理性，這是個有趣的說法。無論如何其在判例法國家中的論述「因為大部分國家行使這種管轄」，故而境外送達（特別管轄）並不是過度管轄——對英美法或全世界的大陸法的確是破天荒。或許更有趣的說法是：一百多年來英美法被自己鏡子裡的影像嚇著了，堅決的認為自己是過度管轄。於英國加入歐盟數十年後，英國同僚終於發現了大陸法國王新衣的真像——大陸法系原始、粗糙到不分境外與境內送達。

或許在全球化的市場上，英國法應拓展對外國判決承認的基礎。美國法於最低限度關連點驚慌失措的表現，同樣的可證明美國同僚亦受困於境內與境外送達之區別。但解決之道不在效法歐盟大陸法不分境內與境外管轄之不具常識、不切實際之作法，而在如英、美一般的於管轄權（境內及境外）之行使上以個案為依據的法院裁量權之行使。同樣的在對外國判決的承認基礎上亦應拓寬，並同樣的以裁量權之行使對個案於正義之需要時加以限制。事實上這種裁量權之行使於判決之承認上已發生——個人亦一再的舉美國成文法為例[42]，主張方便與不方便法院皆應成為二十一世紀承認外國判決之限制或基礎。

對於境外送達是違反了「文明國家間所有的禮誼之正常規則」之看法，不但Prof. Collins提出抗議，Dicey and Morris亦於英國加入歐盟數年後恍然大悟：「但是亦有論述認為依C.P.R., r. 6. 20而行使的管轄權並非是過度的，因為他與許多國家所行使的管轄權是相似的，而且於許多方面亦是和布魯塞爾規則與公約以及Lugano公約的條文於許多方面是相似

42　「美國的UNIFORM FOREIGN MONEY JUDGMENT RECOGNITION ACT，s. 4 (6), "in the case of jurisdiction based only on personal service, the foreign court was a seriously inconvenient forum for the trial of the action."故不方便法院亦可為不承認外國判決之理由，個人認為這是相當先進之思想，足以為全世界效法。特別是我國法院自二十多年前個人引進不方便法院後，現於國際管轄上經常以不方便法院作為管轄基礎或限制管轄權之依據。個人於此再誠摯的建議，效法美國該法規，不方便法院亦可堂而皇之的做為拒絕外國判決之理由。」見陳隆修，《2005年海牙法院選擇公約評析》，台北，五南圖書公司，2009年1月，初版1刷，255頁。

的[43]」。

故而個人一再主張正如於實體法之其他部門，於國際訴訟上「許多國家所行使的管轄權是相似的」，事實上在二十一世紀我們是已有一個管轄權之全球化共同核心存在——而且更驚人的是這個全球化的共同核心可能自有國際管轄之概念即早已存在。

但是英美法與大陸法於管轄權上仍在法院裁量權之行使上有著重大歧異，亦即大陸法並未接受境內與境外管轄在不方便法院與方便法院之行使。即使是有些英國同僚認為境外管轄是「大部分國家行使這種管轄」，個人還是認為基本上前述CPR 1998對送達境外之限制應為全球化之法學所適用，並且仍必須戒慎恐懼的認為境外管轄是基本上為「過度」或「例外」的管轄，而應以「方便法院」法學為限制或基礎。Dicey and Morris[44]對此點依判例法解釋的非常恰當：「過去的判例對4個主要之點加以強調[45]。首先，法院對於允許將文書送達給於英國境外之人應加以小心。這是因為經常有人認為送達至境外是對其他國家主權的一種干擾[46]，

43 Dicey and Morris, the Conflict of Laws, 14th ed., p. 364, 605, "But it is suggested that the jurisdiction exercised under CPR, r.6.20 is not exorbitant, since it is similar to the jurisdiction exercised by many countries, and is also in many respects similar to the rules in the Judgments Regulation and the 1968 and Lugano Conventions." "Although Lord Diplock was wrong to describe what is now CPR, r.6.20 as an exorbitant jurisdiction, he was certainly expressing the orthodox view on recognition of foreign judgments in cases where the debtor was neither within the foreign jurisdiction nor had submitted to it."

44 同上，pp. 364, 367, "Four cardinal points have been emphasised in the decided cases. First, the court ought to be cautious in allowing process to be served on a foreigner out of English. This has frequently been said to be because service out of the jurisdiction is an interference with the sovereignty of other countries, although today all countries exercise a degree of jurisdiction over persons abroad. Secondly, if there is any doubt in the construction of any of the heads of CPR, r.6.20, that doubt ought to be resolved in favour of the defendant. Thirdly, since the application for permission is made without notice to the defendant, a full and fair disclosure of all relevant facts ought to be made. Fourthly, the court will refuse permission if the case is within the letter but outside the spirit of the Rule." "The invocation of the principle of forum conveniens springs from the often expressed anxiety that great care should be taken in bringing before the English court a foreigner who owes no allegiance here."

45 See, especially for the first three points, *Societe Generale de Paris v Dreyfus Bros* (1885) 29 Ch.D. 239, 242-243; (1887) 37 Ch.D. 215, 224, 225 (CA); The Hagen [1908] P. 189, 201 (CA); Re Shintz [1926] Ch. 710, 716-717 (CA).

46 *The Siskina v Distos Compania Naviera SA* [1979] A.C. 210, 254; Amin Rasheed Shipping Corp v Kuwait Insurance Co Ltd [1984] A.C. 50, 65; and *see also The Alexandros P* [1986] Q.B. 464, 478; Insurance Co of Ireland v *Strombus Intrernational Insurance* [1985] 2 Lloyd's Rep. 138, 146 (CA); *Spiliada Maritime Corp v Cansulex Ltd* [1987] A.C. 460, 481; *Agar v Hyde* (2000) 201 C.L.R. 552, 570.

雖然今日對於域外之人所有的國家皆行使某種程度之管轄權。第二，如果對CPR, r. 6.20之項目之解釋有任何懷疑，該懷疑應以對被告有利之方式而被解決。第三，因為允許送達之申請是不須要對被告加以通知，故而（原告）對於相關之事實應給予完全而公平的陳述[47]。第四，如果案件是符合法律文字的規定，但超乎法律的精神，法院會拒絕允許（送達境外）[48]。」故而「雖然今日對於域外之人所有的國家皆行使某種程度之管轄權」，個人仍然堅決的信守「判例法經常為大自然進化之一環」，對於送達境外之管轄仍應如判例法一般將其視為「過度」或「例外」之管轄，並且前述CPR 1998之限制應為送達境外管轄行使之限制或基礎。

五、管轄基礎與裁量權之同步擴張

ALI/UNDROIT Principles of Transnational Civil procedure於2.1條規定對人管轄之基礎：第1項規定經由當事人之同意；第2項為「當法院地國與爭執中之行為或發生之事項或當事人有著重大之關連時。重大關連是存在於當一行為或發生事項的重大部分發生於法院地國，當個人被告之慣居地是於法院地國，或一法人於該地成立組織章程或該地為其主要營業地，或與紛爭有關之財產是位於法院地國。」這個條文雖沒有大陸法的「一般與特別管轄」，但於實質上是相似的[49]。「一般管轄」存在於自

---

[47] The Volvox Hollandia [1988] 2 Lloyd's Rep. 361, 372 (CA); Trafalgar Tours Ltd v Henry [1990] 2 Lloyd's Rep. 298 (CA); Newtherapeutics Ltd v Katz [1991] Ch. 226; The Olib [1991] 2 Lloyd's Rep. 108; ABCI v Banque Franco-Tunisienne [1996] 1 Lloyd's Rep. 485, affirmed [1997] 1 Lloyd's Rep. 531 (CA); ANCAP v Ridgley Shipping Inc [1996] 1 Lloyd's Rep. 570; Konamaneni v Rolls-Royce Industrial Power (India) Ltd [2002] 1 W.L.R. 1269; Marubeni Hong Kong and South China Ltd v Mongolian Government [2002] 2 All E.R. (Comm.) 873; BAS Capital Funding Crop v Medfinco Ltd [2003] EWHC 1798 (Ch.), [2004] 1 Lloy's Rep. 652. There is a continuing duty of disclosure after the order is made: Network Telecom (Europe) Ltd v Telephone Systems International Inc [2003] EWHC 2890 (Q.B.) [2004] 1 All E.R. (Comm.) 418.

[48] Johnson v Taylor Bros [1920] A.C. 144, 153; Rosler v Hibery [1925] Ch. 250, 259-260 (CA); George Monro Ltd v American Cyanamid Crop [1944] K.B. 432, 437, 442 (CA); Beck v Value Capital Ltd (No.2) [1975] 1 W.L.R. 6; affirmed [1976] 1 W.L.R. 572n. (CA).

[49] 通常英國同僚並沒有引用大陸法這個分類之習慣（至少到目前為止），但美國為一移民國家，有些德裔同僚喜歡介紹德國法制，「一般管轄與特別管轄」的觀念的確於美國國際管轄上為美國同僚所接受。但持平而論，在經過三、四十年英國於加入歐盟後英國同僚驚駭莫名的發

然人之慣居地及法人之成立地或主要營業地，至於「特別管轄」自然是與「重大關連」相似。故而規則2.1於實際上是與前述的全球化管轄權的共同核心一致，並且與前述布魯塞爾規則、美國與英國的管轄權規則於架構上是相似的。

其comment P-2B[50]陳述：「『重大關連』之標準是於國際法律糾紛上所普遍接受的。於行使這個標準時必須將實際的判斷與自制的因素考慮進去。這個標準排除僅是身體所在，這個基礎於美國是白話上被稱為『刺殺管轄』。僅以身體所在作為美國聯邦的管轄基礎是有著歷史的理由，但這是與現代國際紛爭不合的。『重大關連』的概念得被國際公約及各國法律所更明確的解釋。於所有的制度中這個概念的範圍可能不是一樣。」注釋P-2B所謂「重大關連之標準是於國際法律糾紛上所普遍接受的」，這是符合前述21世紀既有之全球化管轄權共同核心之現實。至於有關「於所有的制度中這個概念的範圍可能不是一樣的」，如果不將「實際的判斷與自制的因素考慮進去」，所有的判決皆一致，那麼或許電腦可以取代法

現，英國所視為戒慎恐懼的許多管轄基礎事實上是許多國家所執行的管轄基礎。「一般與特別管轄」之引入美國，經過近半世紀後或許可以被蓋棺論定——放光而不放熱。個人甚至認為這些德裔同僚於美國施放太多煙幕，阻撓了美國法制追隨英國母法之進化。可笑的是歷史一再重複，現在亦有一批歐裔同僚於全世界放「最重要關連」的煙幕，阻撓全世界於選法規則上「政策」之探討。Restatement (Third) of Foreign Relations Law § 421 (1987)，Reporters' Notes, 3. General and specific jurisdiction. Jurisdiction under Subsections (2)(a)-(e) and (h) is general jurisdiction to adjudicate, i.e., the jurisdiction is not limited to claims arising out of conduct or activity in the forum state. Jurisdiction under Subsection (2)(f), (i), (j), and (k) is sometimes called specific jurisdiction, i.e., the courts of the forum state have jurisdiction to adjudicate only with respect to claims arising out of a contact with the forum state. Whether jurisdiction under Subsection (2)(g) is general or specific depends on the scope of the consent. See von Mehren and Trautman, "Jurisdiction to Adjudicate: A Suggested Analysis," 79 Harv. L.Rev 1121 (1996); Hazard, "A General Theory of State-Court Jurisdiction," 1965 Sup.Ct.Rev. 241.

50 "The standard of 'substantial connection' has been generally accepted for international legal disputes. Administration of this standard necessarily involves elements of practical judgment and self-restraint. That standard excludes mere physical presence, which within the United States is colloquially called 'tag jurisdiction.' Mere physical presence as a basis of jurisdiction within the America federation has historical justification that is inapposite in modern international disputes. The concept of 'substantial connection' may be specified and elaborated in international conventions and in national laws. The scope of this expression might not be the same in all sytems. However, the concept does not support general jurisdiction on the basis of 'doing business' not related to the transaction or occurrence in dispute."以「經營商業」做為法人一般管轄之基礎，這種概念不但被批評，亦為甚多美國同僚懷疑其是否真正存在。

官。全球化法學或許在「重大關連」概念上一致，但各國，或甚至同一國之不同法院間，對「住所」，「慣居地」、「契約履行地」、或「侵權行為地」之認定上是經常會有不同之看法，這亦是人類社會進化之現象。

至於詮釋中所謂「身體所在」之管轄基礎「與現代國際紛爭不合」的看法，是長久以來美國與英國法制上既有的爭議。如前述一般英國同僚認為「所在權力」法學必須受到「不方便法院」法學的限制，個人完全認同。有趣的是美國法律協會的立場於此方面較近是有些變化，其1971年的Restatment （Secoond） of Conflict of Laws第28條[51]規定：「對於一個所在於其領域內之人，無論是永久性或暫時性，一個州得對其行使管轄權。」但正如英國同僚一般，對於「所在權力」於個案所可能造成的不正義，還是認為應交由法院之裁量權去避免任何可能的不正義。某comment (a)[52]如此論述：「以身體所在作為司法管轄基礎的規則，可能發生在被告與某一州沒有關係但卻被強迫去應訴之情形，而其與該州之關係只是於通過該州領土時被加以送達而已。亦有主張抗辯此規則是與司法管轄領域內所作為基礎的基本原則合理性不一致的（見24條）。但無論如何，這個規則所可能造成的困難，是被法院依82-84條的規則得拒絕行使其管轄權的事實而中和。」

其82條[53]規定：「當對被告或其財產所取得之司法管轄，是經由詐欺

51 "A state has power to exercise judicial jurisdiction over an individual who is present within its territory, whether permanently or temporarily."

52 "The rule that physical presence is a basis of judicial jurisdiction may result at times in a defendant being compelled to stand suit in a state to which he has no relationship other than the fact that he was served with process while passing through that state's territory. It can also be contended that the rule is inconsistent with the basic principle of resonableness which underlies the field of judicial jurisdiction (see § 24). In any event, the rule's potentialities for hardship, are mitigated by the fact that the court may refuse to exercise its jurisdiction under the rules of § § 82-84."

53 Restatmant (Second) of Conflict of Laws § 82 (1971), "A state will not exercise judicial jurisdiction, which has been obtained by fraud or unlawful force, over a defendant or his property."但有趣的是comment (f)認為這是法院裁量權之行使，於充分互信條款之拘束下，其他州法院必須承認其效力。"f. Fraud and force do not destroy jurisdiction of the state. Subject to rare exceptions, a state may exercise judicial jurisdiction over all persons and things within its territory. As stated in comments b-e, this jurisdiction is not usually exercised over a defendant who has been induced to enter the state by fraudulent misrepresentations, or through the use of unlawful force, or over a chattel whose owner has been induced by fraud to send it into the state or which has been brought into the state without the con-

或非法的武力而取得，該州不得行使管轄。」如前述這是與英國法一致的。83條[54]規定：「當於國際法或司法行政的需求之規定下，一個州不得行使管轄權。」例如因國際慣例法或條約，通常外國主權國家或其代表是有豁免權[55]。另外依慣例證人、律師、甚或當事人（有些州）亦被給予豁免權[56]。第84條[57]即為不方便法院條款：「如果對原告有著一個更合適的法院，並且法院對於審判該案件上是個嚴重的不方便之法院，法院不得行使管轄權。」其comment (a)[58]解釋：「美國憲法的第14及5修正案的適當程序條款及司法管轄於國際私法的規則只是建立一個州不得超越之最外部之界限。在這個界限內，跨界訴因之所有人通常有著寬廣的選擇到那一法

sent of the owner. These rules, however , are not jurisdictional. If a state chooses to exercise jurisdiction in any or all of these situations, its action will be recognized as valid in other states. When a judgment rendered under such circumstances is sought to be recognized or enforced in a second state, the courts of the latter state will look to the local law of the state of rendition. If under this law the judgment is impeachable for fraud or force, it will likewise be so impeachable in the second state. If, on the other hand, the judgment is immune from attack in the state of rendition, it will, as between States of the United States, be accorded the same effect elsewhere. This result is required by full faith and credit (compare § 115)."

54 Restatement (Second) of Conflict of Laws § 83 (1971), "A state will not exercise judicial jurisdiction when inaction on its part is required by international law or by the needs of judicial administration."

55 見comment (a)。州政府違反國際法之權力是受限於the supremacy clause of Aritcle VI of the Constitution.

56 Comment (b), "b. Needs of judicial administration. In order to encourage their appearance, it is customary for a state to grant immunity from service of process to non-residents whose presence it deems necessary for the proper conduct of a judicial proceeding. Such immunity is usually granted to witnesses and to lawyers and in some states to parites as well. The immunity ceases when the need for protectioin ends. It is lost, for example, when the person fails to leave the state within a reasonable time after his presence there has ceased to be necessary."

57 Restatement (Second) of Conflict of Laws § 84 (1971), "A state will not exercise jurisdiction if it is a seriously inconvenient forum for the trial of the action provided that a more appropriate forum is available to the plaintiff."

58 a. Rationale. The due process clauses of the Fifth and Fourteenth Amendments of the United States Constitution and the Conflict of Laws rules of judicial jurisdiction establish only the outermost limits beyond which a State may not go. Within these limits, the owner of a transitory cause of action will often have a wide choice of forums in which to sue. Some of these forums may have little relation either to the parites or to the cause of action, and suit in them may increase greatly the burden to the defendant of making a defense. On occasion, a plaintiff will bring suit in such a forum in the belief that he may there secure a larger or an easier recovery or in the hope that the inconvenience and burden of making a defense will induce the defendant to enter a compromise, to contest the case less strenuously, or to permit judgment to be entered against him by default. The rule has been developed that a court, even though it has jurisdiction will not entertain the suit if it believes itself to be a seriously inconvenient forum provided that a more appropriate forum is available to the plaintiff.

院起訴之權。這些法院有的可能與當事人或訴因沒有什麼關連，並且在那裡訴訟可能大幅增加被告提出抗辯的負擔。有時原告於這些法院起訴是因其相信，其於當地可以取得較大或較易的賠償或希望被告提出抗辯的負擔或不便利可以促使被告進入和解，較不會盡力的抗辯案件，或經由被告之缺席而達成對其不利之判決。」故而對於原告選購法院所可能對被告所造成之困擾性或壓迫性行為，美國與英國制度皆一致認為不方便法院法學所給予的法院裁量權，是保證個案正義的積極方法。而反觀大陸法硬式的先繫屬優先法則所可能造成的選購法院、否認之訴、困擾性或壓迫性訴訟，大陸法是幾乎一籌莫展，唯一的救贖或許可能是寄望於他國法院的對自己本國法院判決加以否認——這自然是對本國司法威嚴及主權的侮辱與侵犯，增加當事人之挫折與浪費社會司法資源，並且對正義的延宕。

但即使於有著不方便法院之限制下，美國法律協會於1988年又對第28條[59]加以修正如下：「除非一個人對於一個州的關係是如此的薄弱以致至這種管轄權的行使是不合理，該州對於所在於其域內之人是有權力去行使司法管轄。」以「合理性」做為管轄基礎或限制是美國判例法及法律協會所一再強調，這亦符合個人之主張。個人一再主張「合理性」（英美法）與「誠信原則」（大陸法）應為二十一世紀中所有法學引為基礎的基本原則，亦為於個案中對抗實體上或程序上所可能造成之不正義之警察規則。

第2新編24(1)條[60]規定：「如果一個人與一州之關係是能夠使得這種管轄的行使合理，則該州得對其行使司法管轄。」同樣法律學會（the American Law Institute）1987年的外交關係第3新編421(1)條[61]亦規定：

---

59 1988 Revision: "A state has power to exercise judicial jurisdiction over an individual who is present within its territory unless the individual's relationship to the state is so attenuated as to make the exercise of such jurisdiction unreasonable."

60 Restatement (Second) of Conflict of Laws § 24 (1971), (1) A state has power to exercise judicial jurisdiction over a person if the person's relationship to the state is such as to make the exercise of such jurisdiction reasonable.

61 Restatement (Third) of Foreign Relations Law § 421 (1987), (1) A state may exercise jurisdiction through its courts to adjudicate with respect to a person or thing if the relationship of the state to the

「如果一個州與一個人或物之關係是如此以使得管轄權之行使是合理，則該州得透過其法院對有關該人或物之審判而行使（司法）管轄權。」同樣1987年的第3新篇403(1)條[62]對於案件主體（實體、訴因）管轄權之限制亦如此規定：「即使依402條而來之管轄基礎之一是存在的，當於行使這種管轄是不合理時，一個州不得行使管轄權去規定法律於與其他州有關係之人或行為上。」而第2新編24條之comment (b)[63]更是明言合理性是「所有管轄規則中基本的原則」，並且舉例說明是美國最高法院一再引用之標準。故而「合理性」既已是美國法院於行使對人、對物、及對案件主體（實體、訴因、403條）管轄權之最基本原則，第2新編1988年28條之修正版事實上並不是創新。

對於「所在權力」最明顯的修正來自法律協會（the American Law Institute）1987年第3新編421 (2)(a)條[64]：「除了短暫性外，一個人或物

person or thing is such as to make the exercise of jurisdiction reasonable.

62 Restatement of the Law, Third, Foreign Relations Law of the United States, § 403, (1) Even when one of the bases for jurisdiction under § 402 is present, a state may not exercise jurisdiction to prescribe law with respect to a person or activity havng connections with another state when the exercise of such jurisdiction is unreasonable.

63 b. The basic principle. One basic principle underlies all rules of jurisdiction. This principle is that a state does not have jurisdiction in the absence of some reasonable basis for exercising it. With respect to judicial jurisdiction, this principle was laid down by the Supreme Court of the United States in Internaitonal Shoe Co. v. State of Washington, 326 U.S. 310 (1945). In that case, the Court stated that for jurisdiction to exist the exercise of jurisdiction by the State must be "reasonable, in the context of our federal system of government" and also that there must be "such minimum contacts" with the State as not to offend "traditional notions of fair play and substantial justice." More recent cases in which the Court has applied this standard are Hanson v. Denckla, 357 U.S. 235 (1958); McGee v. International Life Ins. Co., 355 U.S. 220 (1957); Perkins v. Benguet Consolidated Mining Co., 342 U.S. 437 (1952); Travelers Health Ass'n v. Virginia, 339 U.S. 643 (1950); Mullane v. Central Hanover Bank & Trust Co., 339 U.S. 306 (1950),"另外Restatement (Second) of Conflict of Laws § 28 (1971)的comment (b)亦有陳述："b. The requirement of reasonableness. In Shaffer v. Heitner, 433 U.S. 186 (1977), the Supreme Court rejected the notion that power derived from the mere presence of a thing in a State will always provide that State with a basis of jurisdiction to determine interests in the thing (see § § 59-68). Instead, the Supreme Court made clear that the principles of International Shoe Co. v. State of Washington, 326 U.S. 310 (1945), apply generally to questions of jurisdiction, whether over persons or things."

64 (2) In general, a state's exercise of jurisdiction to adjudicate with respect to a person or thing is reasonable if, at the time jurisdiction is asserted: (a) the person or thing is present in the territory of the state, other than transitorily.其comment (e)認為「刺殺管轄」依國際法通常是不能被接受的，故而單純「過境」是不能構成「所在」。於機場換機、由郵輪下船遊樂、或與訴的請求無關的逗留數日是不能購成(2)(a)款的「所在」，但比「居所」之構成較為短暫的停留是可以的。"e. Transitory presence. 'Tag' jurisdiction, i.e., jurisdiction based on service of process on a person only transitorily

是於一州之領域內」。但是第3新編421 (2)(a)條對「所在權力」管轄的修正為什麼（至少到現今）沒有被英國判例法所同步採納？答案在1971年第2新編28條之comment (c)[65]中：「由一個實際的角度而言，是否一個人短暫的停留於一個州會給予該州司法管轄的基礎，這個問題可能只是學術性的。這是因為一個訴訟只是基於這種短暫停留於一個州而沒有其他相關連之情形，可能會基於不方便法院之理由而被駁回或被移轉。」故而非常有趣的是美國法律協會（the American Law Institute）第2新編28條之comment (c)已經對第3新編421 (2)(a)於「所在權力」管轄之修正上，認為在「不方便法院」裁量權之行使下，應是否對「所在權力」加以修正「這個問題可能只是學術性的。」

「所在權力」的過度管轄在「不方便法院」的限制下變成一個「學術性」的問題，不只是法律協會第2新編28條之立場，這個立場更為斬釘截鐵旗幟鮮明的為ALI/UNIDORIT Principles of Transnational Civil Procedure所更為加強的公開立法。UNIDROIT Pinciples除了於有關對人訴訟的2.1條規定以當事人之同意及重大關連為主要的管轄基礎外，其於2.2條[66]中更加將「所在」、「國籍」、「物之所在」等三個一般認為過度之管轄基礎列為「必要管轄」：「當沒有其他之法院是可以合理的有效時，管轄權得基於下列基礎而被行使：2.2.1，被告於法院地之國籍或所在；或2.2.2，無論是爭執是否與該財產有關，被告之財產位於法院地，

---

in the territory of the state, is not generally acceptable under international law. 'Presence' in Subsection (2)(a) is satisfied by a less extended stay than is required to constitute residence, but it does not include merely transitory presence, such as while changing planes at an airport, coming on shore from a cruise ship, or a few days' sojourn unconnected with the activity giving rise to the claim."

65 c. Forum non conveniens. From a pragmatic standpoint, the question may be academic whether an individual's momentary presence in a state provides that state with a basis of judicial jurisdiction. This is because a suit based on such presence in the state without other affiliating circumstances would probably be dismissed or transferred on forum non conveniens grounds. See Comments a and c of § 84.

66 2.2 Jurisdiction may also be exercised, when no other forum is reasonably available, on the basis of :
2.2.1 Presence or nationality of the defendant in the forum state; or
2.2.2 Presence in the forum state of the defendant's property, whether or not the dispute relates to the property, but the court's authority should be limited to the property or its value.

但法院之權力只能限制於該財產或其價值內。」其comment P-2C[67]解釋如下：「原則2.2是包含『必要法院』之觀念——當沒有其他的法院是合理的可提供有效之管轄時，必要之法院就是於其時一個可以合適的行使管轄之法院。」無論是「身體所在」、「國籍」、或「與訴因無關之財產的所在」都通常為國際法上所認為之過度管轄，亦為歐盟布魯塞爾規則第3條[68]所明文禁止會員國間對會員國住民所行使之管轄權，及為海牙1999年草約（Hague Conference - preliminary draft Convention on judgments）18 (2)條[69]所特別列舉禁止之管轄權。**故而ALI/UNIDROIT Principles of Transnational Civil Procedure的第2.2條會將一般國際法上所認為可能為過度管轄之基礎列為預備的第2線最後之「必要管轄」基礎，或許是清楚而明白的證明本文前述之重點：於二十一世紀全球化浪潮之影響下，各國不得不擴張其管轄基礎[70]，但為了確保個案正義各國亦不得不給予其法**

67 P-2C Principle 2.2 covers the concept of "forum necessitatis" － the forum of necessity whereby a court may properly exercise jurisdiction when no other forum is reasonably available.

68 Article 3

1. Persons domiciled in a Member State may be sued in the courts of another Member State only by virtue of the rules set out in Sectins 2 to 7 of this Chapter.
2. In particular the rules of national jurisdiction set out in Annex I shall not be applicable as against them.

69 2. In particular, jurisdiction shall not be exercised by the courts of a Contracting State on the basis solely of one or more of the following –

a) the presence or the seizure in that State of property belonging to the defendant, except where the dispute is directly related to that property;
b) the nationality of the plaintiff;
c) the nationality of the defendant;
d) the domicile, habitual or temporary residence, or presence of the plaintiff in that State;
e) the carrying on of commercial or other activities by the defendant in that State, except where the dispute is directly related to those activities;
f) the service of a writ upon the defendant in that State;
g) the unilateral designation of the forum by the plaintiff;
h) proceedings in that State for declaration of enforceability or registratioin or for the enforcement of a judgment, except where the dispute is directly related to such proceedings;
i) the temporary residence or presence of the defendant in that State;
j) the signing in that State of the contract from which the dispute arises.

70 例如2.3 A court may grant provisional measures with respect to a person or to property in the territory of the forum state, even if the court does not have jurisdiction over the controversy.本條文給予法院權力去為了取得其他可能勝訴判決之賠償，而得對法院地之物加以假扣押（該物可能與該決之主體或聲明無關）。

院較為寬廣之裁量權。

如同前述，為了順應全球化的潮流，傳統上以嚴謹著名的英國判例法亦不得不將較符合法律邏輯的「困擾性」或「壓迫性」法學，更改為較寬鬆的「不方便法院」法學。個人希望年輕的大陸同僚能記住過去二十多年來我們所見證的國際法歷史上之進化——亦即在全球化之趨勢下，各國不得不擴張其管轄基礎，亦不得不給予其法院較寬廣之裁量權。而這亦是我們祖先所謂之「道法自然」。

六、全球化法學之共同核心—人權宣言與王道法學

UNIDROIT Principles 2.2 條的將過度管轄之基礎列為「必要法院」之後備管轄基礎，就是在全球化之需求下各國不得不擴張其管轄基礎之一種謹慎而務實的做法；而2.5條引用「不方便法院」法學即為不得不給予法院較寬廣裁量權以確保個案正義的做法。其2.5條[71]規定：「當相對於其他可以行使管轄權的更合適法院，承審法院是明顯的不合適時，管轄權得被拒絕或程序得被停止。」其comment P-2F[72]評論：「規則2.5中所認許的概念是與判例法規則中之不方便法院可以相比較的。於有些大陸法制度中，這個概念即為防止濫訴。」事實上禁止濫訴之概念於英美法是更為徹底的，於英國判例法上禁止濫訴與禁止反言經常是本於同一判例法而來。大陸法的禁止濫訴，或許於國際訴訟法上，可能與英國判例法之困擾性或

[71] 2.5 Jurisdiction may be declined or the proceeding suspended when the court is manifestly inappropriate relative to another more appropriate court that could exercise jurisdiction.但有趣的是規則2.6又畫蛇添足的在公平、有效、迅速的條件下，採納大陸法的先繫屬優先，這是徒增困擾的折衷式不必要手段。
2.6 The court should decline jurisdiction or suspend the proceeding, when the dispute is previously pending in another court competent to exercise jurisdiction, unless it appears that the dispute will not be fairly, effectively, and expeditiously resolved in that forum.

[72] P-2F The concept recognized in Principle 2.5 is comparable to the common-law rule of forum non conveniens. In some civil-law systems, the concept is that of preventing abuse of the forum. This principle can be given effect by suspending the forum proceeding in deference to another tribunal. The existence of a more convenient forum is necessary for application of this Principle. This Principle should be interpreted in connection with the Principle of Procedural Equality of the Parties, which prohibits any kind of discrimination on the basis of nationality or residence. See Principle 3.2.

壓迫性法學較可以相比較。故而如果合理的使用，不方便法院可以防止濫訴、避免選購法院、減少否認之訴（確認之訴）或規避法律等不誠信行為，這是由comment P-2F中可隱涵而推知。

但是針對美式的假「公共利益」之名而歧視第三世界弱勢人民之違反人權之作法，其又如此警告：「本規則應與當事人程序平等規則一起被解釋，而平等規則是禁止基於國籍或居所而來之任何歧視。」規則3.1條[73]如此規定：「法院應確保當事人間之公平對待及合理之機會去主張或抗辯其權利。」第3.2條規定所謂公平對待是包含應避免任何種類之非法歧視，特別是依據國籍或居所而來的歧視。但是對於這種近乎指名道姓的告誡，於保護美國跨國企業之利益下，美國法院仍然公開的以不方便法院之名而贊助美國企業於第三世界剝奪人權、摧殘環境[74]，並拒絕給予受害的第三世界人民聯合國人權宣言及兩個1966年人權公約中之訴訟權、財產權、生命權、適當程序權之最基本的應有之保護[75]。故而ALI/UNIDROIT Principles of Transtional Civil Procedure事實上已於法律上證明WTO所主張的「自由貿易」，於真實的世界中是擁有科技、資金、行銷的第一世界可以自由的壓榨第三世界；所謂的「比較利益」是擁有絕對優勢的第一世界是相較於第三世界有著絕對的比較經濟、法律、技術、行銷的壓倒性利益。對於諾貝爾和平獎的只是針對落後國家所附隨而來的落後司法人權，無視於第一世界的利用其絕對的法律、技術、經濟優勢，而剝奪第三世界人權公約之生存權[76]、生命權、財產權、訴訟權、環境權、及適當程序權，個人認為這是一種岳不群法學的終極表現。WTO與諾貝爾和平獎

---

73 3.1 The court should ensure equal treatment and reasonable opportunity for litigants to assert or defend their rights.

74 陳隆修，《2005年海牙法院選擇公約評析》，台北，五南圖書公司，2009年1月，初版1刷，304-306頁。

75 見舉世聞名的經典教科書案例In re Union Carbide Corp. Gas Plant Disaster, Bhopal, 634F. Supp. 842, 於該案中有超過20萬的印度人傷亡，但絕大部分超過20年仍未受到合理的賠償。

76 例如歐盟與美國先後對友達、奇美等課以上百億之反托辣斯罰款，見陳隆修，《智財法院97重附民1號》，載於〈國際私法：程序正義與實體正義〉，陳隆修、劉仁山、許兆慶合著，五南圖書出版公司，2011年9月，這是剝奪中國人生存權之暴行。

是二十一世紀中兩個藉著第一世界的絕對黑暗勢力的終極掠奪性新殖地主義，是岳不群法學巔峰的表現。

美國跨國企業經常會以低於美國環保法、勞工法、工業安全法等強行法之標準，於第三世界中經營工商業、開採自然資源，但對於第三世界中的受害者卻經常以「不方便法院」而拒絕其於美國起訴[77]。這種做法是違反1948年聯合國人權宣言25條1項[78]的規定：「每個人對於自己及其家人皆有權去要求健康及有益之合適的生活標準……」亦違反1966年聯合國兩個人權公約第1條第2項所揭櫫的「生存權」。對於美國跨國企業的於南美開採石油、礦產導致河川污染，使得沿岸之部落整族可能滅絕之情形，1992年聯合國於里約的環境發展宣言（Rio Declaration on Environment and Development）第13條[79]即規定：「有關污染被害人之損害賠償及責任與其他環境上之損害賠償，各國應發展其相關法律。對於因為在他們管轄區或控制區域內之行為導致在他們域外所發生之負面環境效果之損害賠償及責任，各國應以快速及更果決之態度以便合作發展此方面之國際法。」美國式的「不方便法院」是否踐踏第13條之規定事很明顯的，是否符合「岳不群法學」的要件亦是很明顯的。另外第5條[80]規定各國應將消除貧窮、減少生活水平差距視為「主要任務」；第6條[81]規定對於發展

77 Scott Holwick, Transnational Corporate Behavior and Its Disparate and Unjust Effects on the Indigenous, Cultures and the Environment of Developing Nations: Jota v. Texaco, a Case Study 11 COLO. J. INT'L ENVTL. L. & POL'Y 183, 209-212(2000).

78 "Everyone has the right to a standard of living adequate for the health and well-being of himself and of his family, including food, clothing, housing, and medical care and necessary social services, and the right to security in the event of unemployment, sickness, disability, widowhood, old age or other lack of livelihood in circumstances beyond his control."

79 Principle 13
States shall develop national law regarding liability and compensation for the victims of pollution and other environmental damage. States shall also cooperate in an expeditious and more determined manner to develop further international law regarding liability and compensation for adverse effects of environmental damage caused by activities within their jurisdiction or control to areas beyond their jurisdiction.

80 Principle 5
All State and all people shall cooperate in the essential task of eradicating poverty as an indispensable requirement for sustainable development, in order to decrease the disparities in standards of living and better meet the needs of the majority of the people of the world.

81 Principle 6
The special situation and needs of developing countries, particularly the least developed and those most

中國家，特別是最落後國家，之需求與情況「應被給予特別優先」。尤其第7條[82]後段白紙黑字的寫下：「在考慮已開發國家的社會對全球環境所造成之壓力及他們所掌握的技術及經濟資源，已開發國家承認於追逐國際永續發展上他們所承擔之責任。」做為一個第三世界的資深國際法的學生，個人很懷疑美國不方便法院、歐盟布魯塞爾規則第4條、海牙2005法院指定管轄公約是怎麼去「承擔責任」？第22條[83]則告誡第一世界及跨國公司如下：「原住民及其社會與其他當地社會於環境控制及發展上是有重要的地位，這是由於他們知識及傳統的作法。各國應承認及適度的幫助他們的認同、文化、及利益，並且於達成永續發展上幫助他們能有效的參加。」事實上國際公約對這種肆無忌憚的違反國際人權之惡劣行為，是有著管轄權上一定的共識，例如1999年海牙草約就於18條過度管轄之規定上，在第3項[84]中企圖授與國際管轄。

---

environmentally vulnerable, shall be given special priority. International actions in the field of environment and development should also address the interests and needs of all countries.

82 Principle 7
States shall cooperate in a spirit of global partnership to conserve, protect and restore the health and integrity of the Earth's ecosystem. In view of the different contributions to global environmental degradation, States have common but differentiated responsibilities. The developed countries acknowledge the responsibility that they bear in the international pursuit of sustainable development in view of the pressures their societies place on the global environment and of the technologies and financial resources they command.

83 Principle 22
Indigenous people and their communities and other local communities have a vital role in environmental management and development because of their knowledge and traditional practices. States should recognize and duly support their identity, culture and interests and enable their effective participation in the achievement of sustainable development.

84 Hague Conference – preliminary draft Convention on judgments (1999)
3. Nothing in this Article shall prevent a court in a Contracting State from exercising jurisdiction under national law in an action [seeking relief] [claiming damages] in respect of conduct which constitutes –
[Variant One:
[a] genocide, a crime against humanity or a war crime[, as defined in the Statute of the International Criminal Court]; or]
[b] a serious crime against a natural person under international law; or]
[c] a grave violation against a natural person of non-derogable fundamental rights established under international law, such as torture, slavery, forced labour and disappeared persons].
[Sub-paragraphs [b) and] c) above apply only if the party seeking relief is exposed to a risk of a denial of justice because proceedings in another State are not possible or cannot reasonably be required.]
Variant Two:
a serious crime under international law, provided that this State has established its criminal jurisdiction

有趣的是1999年的海牙草約的22條除了於第2項[85]列舉不方便法應考慮的事項外，於第3項[86]中亦特別規定：「於決定是否停止程序時，法院不能基於當事人之慣居地或國籍而加以歧視。」故而1999年海牙草約22(3)條與2004年ALI/UNIDROIT Principles of Transnational Civil Procedure第3條皆公開的禁止以不方便法院之名，而對被害人加以國籍或居所上之歧視。同樣的禁止亦應適用於歐盟布魯塞爾公約及規則第4條之歧視非歐盟住民之規定上。

如同聯合國1992里約宣言第7條所宣示「已開發國家的社會對全球環境所造成的壓力及他們所掌握的技術及經濟資源，已開發國家承認於追逐國際永續發展上他們所承擔之責任」，但WTO與諾貝爾和平獎似乎皆無視於此[87]。WTO繼續鼓勵已開發國家利用他們所掌握的技術、資金、與行銷，藉此於第三世界中「自由」的獲得「比較經濟利益」；而諾貝爾和平獎無視於第一世界的剝奪第三世界跨國企業的受害者之生命權、財產權、適當程序權、及訴訟權，而從頭到尾一昧的攻擊第三世界落後司法制度中所產生的人權問題，這是助紂為虐並剝奪第三世界循著階梯發展[88]的生

over that crime in accordance with an international treaty to which it is a party and that the claim is for civil compensatory damages for death or serious bodily injury arising from that crime.]

85 2. The court shall take into account, in particular –
a) any inconvenience to the parties in view of their habitual residence;
b) the nature and location of the evidence, including documents and witnesses, and the procedures for obtaining such evidence;
c) applicable limitation or prescription periods;
d) the possibility of obtaining recognition and enforcement of any decision on the merits.

86 3. In deciding whether to suspend the proceedings, a court shall not discriminate on the basis of the nationality or habitual residence of the paries.

87 例如於「智財院97重附民1號」中個人即指出美國與歐盟即極盡扭曲法律，對中國企業課以反辣斯法之重罰，這是違反中國人之生存權。

88 聯合國1966年經濟、社會、及文化權利公約第2(3)條即為「階梯理論」之代表，所謂"Ladder Theory"個人是指第三世界有著天賦人權去追隨第一世界的腳步——包括好及壞的過程－－而循序漸進，如果否認第三世界此種「階梯人權」，就是否認第三世界1966年兩個人權公約1(2)條之生存權。所謂「階梯理論」就是我們祖先的「自然道法」，亦是「常識」，亦是「基本正義」。"3. Developing countries, with due regard to human rights and their national economy, may determine to what extent they would guarantee the economic rights recognized in the present Covenant to non-nationals."尤其是於2008、2009全世界見證了美國跨國企業貪婪的藉自由市場之名而引起金融海嘯，事後美國更以貨幣寬鬆政策而於第三世界引起通貨膨脹，造成全世界的動盪。美國的跨國企業及政府以自由市場之名，不僅霸凌第三世界，更是剝奪了第三世界人民於人權公約第

存權，而更是違反兩千多年來「道法自然」之中國生活經驗。美國與歐盟不但猖狂的藐視國際私法禁止歧視外人之共同法理，更違反了1948年聯合國人權宣言25(1)條，1992年聯合國里約宣言13、5、6、7及22條，而最可怕的是他們明火執杖的剝奪第三世界人民1966年兩個人權公約第1(2)條之基本生存權[89]，這種作法是違反「常識」、「正義」、「自然道法」的逆天惡行。WTO與諾貝爾和平獎對這種第一世界的「掠奪性新殖民法學」及「岳不群法學」視而不見，他們對第三世界人民的苦難、所遭受的歧視所採取的是不聽、不說、不見三隻猴子哲學，或許WTO及諾貝爾和平獎應再增加一隻猴子——沒有天良。於美國、歐盟、WTO、及諾貝爾和平獎的黑暗利益共同體之煉獄中，第一世界所輪迴的是「人間道」，而第三世界人民所輪迴的是道不大、天不大、地不大、人更不大之「牲畜道」。這正亦是在黃進教授、趙相林教授提倡「中國式法學」後，個人有著「燃燒的慾望」認為「中國式法學」應以「王道」為核心基礎之道理（此點亦為黃進教授之共同主張）。**相對於WTO及諾貝爾和平獎的不聽、不說、不見，我們的祖先兩千多年來一向主張「不患寡而患不均」（里約宣言5條），「己所不欲勿施於人」（里約宣言7條），「禮運大同」之「仁道」（里約宣言6條），更重要的是「王道」是本於——「天視自我民視，天聽自我民聽」之天道。伴隨著大中華經濟圈之崛起，有著兩千多年生活經驗的中國王道思想，應成為二十一世紀所有的全球化法學及人權公約之最共同核心主流價值及警察原則。**

1條第2項之基本生存權。WTO與諾貝爾和平獎對這個滅絕第三世界基本生存權之滔天罪惡，照例採取不聽、不說、不見的三隻猴子哲學，故而個人一向主張WTO與諾貝爾和平獎這兩個岳不羣法學機構是有著第四隻猴子哲學——沒天良。

89 見「智財院97重附民1號」中所述歐美反托辣斯法及智慧財產法之適用於中國商人。

第5章 最低限度關連與境外送達

一、境外管轄為例外或過度之管轄

另外UNIDROIT Principles 3.2條又強調：「法院應考慮到外國當事人於參加訴訟時所可能遭遇之困難。」這種困難於第三世界之人民必須至第一世界應訴時更為明顯。例如個人年輕執業時就曾屢遇歐美當事人藉國家之優勢而欺凌台商之案例[1]，歷經歲月每個案件之血淚仍深植記憶之深處。第三世界人民所面臨之簽證、語言、文化、經濟、制度上之歧視，遠非UNIDROIT Principles第3條所謂的「公平對待」、「避免非法歧視」所能涵蓋。第三世界的人民是否能獲得司法正義，重點並非在其訴因是否符合正義，重點經常是在所選擇法院的正義、公平、便利性。但是3.2條所規定的「應考慮外國當事人所遭遇的困難」，固然明顯的適用於第三世界之人民，但於第一世界之訴訟當事人間亦是適用的。3.2條所見証的只不過是英國判例法上長久以來將送達境外之管轄視為「過度」、「例外」管轄之規則，而這個規則亦為成文法所加強。

UNIDROIT Principles為著順應全球化之潮流，的確是將各國之管轄基礎於有必要時加以擴大（必要管轄），並且於個案正義之需求下亦給予各國法院裁量權（不方便法院），而且其跳脫大陸法之盲點承認外國訴

1 見陳隆修，《比較國際私法》，台北，五南圖書公司，78年10月，初版，135、136頁；陳隆修，《國際私法管轄權評論》，台北，五南圖書公司，民國75年11月，初版，255、256頁。於該案中美國廠商已於日本大阪棉花協會仲裁及國貿局之協調中皆認定其棉花有瑕疵，但仍堅持至利物浦原棉協仲裁，中國商人因簽證及翻譯文件不及故而無法應訴，導致敗訴，個人當時花費甚大功夫才避免其工廠被加以執行拍賣。有資深同事因而戲謂個人「扶清滅洋」，但這亦是個人對2005年海牙公約如此極力反對之真正理由——21世紀的全球化法學若不考慮第三世界人民的真正苦難與正義，就不能為中國「王道」法學所接受。

訟當事人會遭受困難（第3.2條）。但如同個人所一再重述，聲名卓越的法院之判例法之演進經常是「自然道法」進化之一環。UNIDROIT Principles不應僅止於承認外國當事人之困難，應如英國判例法一般的承認境外管轄基本上是一種「過度」或「例外」之管轄，並且於當事人承認管轄或身體所在於法院（境內管轄）時，以「不方便法院」為管轄行使之基礎或限制；而對送達境外被告（境外管轄）時，以「方便法院」為管轄權行使之基礎或限制。UNIDROIT Principles這種隱晦式的承認「外國當事人之困難」是無法達成判例法確保個案正義的基本正義，亦無法於二十一世紀中明確的建立全球化國際管轄的規則。

如個人所一再重申[2]的是境外管轄基本上是「過度」或「例外」之管轄，而「方便法院」與「不方便法院」雖是一體之兩面，但尚不到融合之階段：「要注意的是訴訟之通知送達至外國基本上是一種過度（exorbitant）或例外（extraordinary）的管轄基礎[3]，經常冒著不被外國法院承認的風險，因而必須於非常謹慎之情形下方得行使此裁量權送達通知至境外[4]。基於方便法院之原則而將通知送達至境外，與基於不方便法院之原則於通知送達至境內後方停止訴訟，兩個裁量權行使的裁量因素、內容、甚至判例基本上皆相似，故而個人前述稱之為一體之兩面，但仍有相異之處。首先送達至境外基本上就被認為是過度管轄[5]，而於不方便法院之情況基本上法院是以有管轄權之後才去裁量是否停止管轄。另外於方便法院之情況下，舉證責任在於原告，並且於請求之階段因不須通知他方，故必須完全而且公平的陳述[6]；而於不方便法院的情況，至少於第一階段舉證在於主張不方便法院的被告[7]。」

---

2 陳隆修、許兆慶、林恩瑋、李瑞生四人合著，《國際私法—管轄與選法理論之交錯》，台北，五南圖書公司，2009年3月，初版1刷。203、204頁。

3 Spiliada Maritime Corpn v. Consulex Ltd [1987] AC 460 at 481.

4 Cordova land Co. Ltd., v. Victor Bro Inc [1966] 1 WLR 793 at 796.

5 The Spiliada [1987] AC 460 at 481.

6 Kuwait Oil Co. (KSC) v. Idemitsu Tankers KK, The Hida Maru [1981] 2 Lloyd's Rep 510.另外在對法律解釋有疑問時，應以對被告有利之方式解決。

7 The Spiliada, [1987] AC 460, at 474.

個人雖是最尊敬的恩師Prof. Graveson的忠誠信徒，並且堅信法律邏輯一致性的要求應受限於達成個案正義之基本目的，但在法律邏輯與個案正義兩者是如此一致之情形下，似乎沒有理由不將方便與不方便法院兩者之區別加以釐清。或許正如同區別不方便法院裁量權行使是管轄權行使之基礎或限制並不是絕對必要，硬是去區分方便與不方便法院裁量權行使於邏輯上之區別或許亦不是絕對必要。但正如UNIDORIT Principles 3.2條所確認的「外國當事人之困難」之原則，判例法長久以來即確認送達境外為對被告非常不利之不正當（unjustifiable）管轄，故只能於非常謹慎下才可將訴訟文書送達給境外之被告[8]。故而對於將方便法院與不方便法院兩個法學加以稍微釐清或許至少於目前仍是有必要的，因為方便法院法學所正面代表的核心意義是——送達境外之管轄基本上可能會是過度或例外之管轄，因為會對外國被告可能造成困難，故而僅能在極度謹慎下才能行使這種管轄。UNIDORIT Principles只是消極的承認「外國被告所遭遇之困難」，而不能積極的接受判例法歷經百多年時空淬鍊的「方便法院」法學，不但令人遺憾，且UNIDORIT Principles亦極可能因此而喪失領導全世界去建立一個真正符合現實生活經驗之全球化國際管轄法規之黃金機會。

如果不正視「境外管轄會對被告造成困難因而通常應是過度或例外管轄」之現實與常識，不但正義無法被達成，法律邏輯亦可能造成大混亂。如前述英國於對境內管轄採困擾性或壓迫性法學時即早已確立了送達境外是通常為例外性之管轄，而對於美國同僚長期的忽視英國母法，個人近期如此失望的評述[9]：「除了對抗歐盟的不平等條款外，有趣的是有些美國同僚甚至寄望透過國際公約或條約以終止美國於管轄法規上之亂象。個人長久以來即認為美國於管轄法規上不遵循英國母法，而自行創立一些觀念

8　陳隆修，《國際私法管轄權評論》，台北，五南圖書公司，民國75年11月，初版。45~48頁。The Hagen [1908] p. 189.

9　陳隆修，《2005年海牙法院選擇公約評析》，台北，五南圖書公司，2009年1月，初版1刷。288、289頁。

或引進大陸法（general and special jurisdictions），截至目前為止這些做法經常華而不實，徒增困擾。」

Prof. Clermont[10]說：「於民事案件上美國於地域管轄權之法律上是一團混亂。長久以來，這裡及外國，許多的評論者皆如此說。」於對美國管轄權上之「混亂」束手無策後，其寄望國際公約能解救美國法律[11]：「條約會直接改變於許多國際訴訟上之美國法，並且亦會促進有關國內訴訟之改革。」並說：「於合理的規範管轄權上，較以『最低限度關聯點』標準及『補救式的法律與事實的虛擬』來主宰美國管轄權的布魯塞爾公約是一種遠較成功的方式。」而同樣的Prof. Borchers[12]雖然認為若於無法訂定公約時，訂立雙邊條約是非常麻煩，但即使是條約「亦可能改進目前的『叢林法則』」。已故的Prof. Juenger更是直接挑明「最低限度關聯點」理論於美國所造成的混亂，使得美國無法於管轄權上對世界有所貢獻[13]：「但是如事實所證明，這種希望是不可能的。International Shoe及依其而衍生之判例除了於國內造成浩劫外，於國外和諧上亦造成無可跨越的障礙。因為我們自己家中是一團亂，我們沒有辦法對世界各地產生貢獻。」但是布魯塞爾公約及規則與其他公約（例如2005海牙法院選擇公約）真的能促進美國「國內訴訟之改革」？由英國加入歐盟後英國資深同僚之絕望看起

10 " The United States' law of territorial jurisdiction in civil cases is a mess. Many commentators, here and abroad, have said so for a long time." Kevin M. Clermont, Jurisdictional Salvation and The Hague Treaty, 85 Cornell L. Rev. 89 (1999)."

11 85 Cornell L. Rev. 89, 98, "The treaty directly would change the U.S. law in much of international litigation and might induce reform in regard to domestic litigation as well." "the Brussels convention is a far more successful effort at rationally regulating jurisdiction than the 'minimum contacts' test and the 'patchwork of legal and factual fictions' that dominate American jurisdiction."

12 "The fallback to signing the Lugano Convention would be to negotiate as many bilateral agreements as possible. Although this would be cumbersome, a few successful bilaterall agreements might pave the way for a multilateral agreement. Even if a multilateral agreement does not eventually result, some bilateral agreements would be an improvement over the current 'law of the jungle.'" Patrick J. Borchers, Comparing Personal Jurisdiction in the United States and the European Community: Lessons for American Reform, 40 Am J. Comp. L. 121, 153, 156 (1992).

13 "But, as matters stand, such hopes seem vain. Beyond the internal havoc they have caused, International Shoe and its progeny present formidable obstacles to international harmonization. Because our own house is in disarray, we are unable to render a contribution to the world at large." Friedrich K. Juenger, A Shoe Unfit for Globetrotting, 28 U.C. Davis L. Rev. 1027, 1044 (1994-1995).

來並非如此。對於英國法的即將被「消滅」，英國資深同僚的用詞可能比美國同僚抱怨「最低限度關連點」還傷感[14]。

對於「最低限度關連點」所造成的「一團混亂」、「叢林法則」、「浩劫」，個人戲謔的稱呼「最低限度關連點造成最大程度的混亂」（minimum contacts cause maximum chaos）。對於「布魯塞爾公約是一種遠較為成功的方式」的評語，心碎的英國母法資深同僚是可以給予這個評語很多切身之痛的經驗。寄望公約改善美國法的亂像或許是椽木求魚，個人如此評論[15]：「美國管轄規則有如狂奔之野馬，企圖以全世界之重量來減緩其速度。」包括美國同僚在內的許多國際法的資深同僚，對於美國管轄規則上（特別是最低限度關連點）之混亂，各自以富有創意的尖銳言語形容，彷彿作文比賽。事實上個人以為亂象的起源在於美國同僚的不遵守英國母法——區分境內送達與境外送達之分別。若非英國加入歐盟，這種二分式的國際管轄規則是質樸、合理的可以適應於全球化市場。美國最低限度關連點標準經過一連串判例法的演進，最後終於在Burnham v. Superior Court[16]中宣布，短暫過境管轄不受最低限度關連點之影響。故而或許可以這麼的說：「所在權力」基本上是不受影響，而「最低限度關連點」是通常適用於境外之被告。亦即反諷的是美國法院在看似一連串驚心動魄的創新後，返璞歸真的回到判例法母法簡單、合理的境外與境內管轄二分法。因此個人一再重覆絮絮嘮叨聲名卓越的法院歷經時空淬鍊而形成的判例法經常是大自然演進之一環，除非有確切的理由否則不應輕易違背它，是故「道法自然」。

事實上美國之管轄基礎基本上亦是本著英國在程序上之訴訟之通知得被加以送達而來，至於美國後來所自己創造的「最低限度關連點」則是判例法上有趣的演進（或突變？）。Restatement（Second）of Conflict

---

14 見陳隆修，《由歐盟經驗論中國式國際私法》，載於〈新世紀兩岸國際私法〉，五南圖書公司，2011年11月；又見「2005年海牙法院公約評析」，142-153頁。

15 陳隆修，《2005年海牙法院選擇公約評析》，台北，五南圖書公司，2009年1月，初版1刷。289頁。

16 495 U.S. 604 (1990).

of Laws § 28 (1971), comment (a)[17]說：「於判例法上身體所在於一個州是傳統的管轄基礎。這個管轄基礎所依據的是所在權力是管轄基礎的概念。在早期的判例法英國法院能對被告取得對人管轄唯一的方法就是使警長將其拘捕並將其帶至法院。最後，這個被告應被拘捕的規定被放棄，並且當被告於管轄區內被加以親自送達是被認定為已經足夠。即使被告只是短暫停留於該州亦是無關重要。其之所在於該州，即使只是一瞬間，已給予該州對其之司法管轄。」對於短暫過境管轄所可能產生與合理性之基本原則不一致之情形，如前述comment (a)認為法院得行使裁量權而拒絕管轄（如以不方便法院），因而所在權力規則所可能產生的困難是可以被緩和的[18]。故而美國法院對於「所在權力」所可能產生之困難，事實上亦是可以如英國法院一般行使裁量權（先前為困擾性或壓迫性法學）而拒絕管轄。美國法院既然可以不方便法院而於不合理之困難情形下去拒絕管轄，那麼為何又脫離（或忽視）母法而創造（或突變）了「最低限度關連點」，以致造成美國管轄規則上之「一團混亂」、「叢林法則」、及「浩劫」？

個人認為或許美國國際私法基本上是通常為適應美國各州之衝突而產生，於同文同種、同一國家、同一制度及社會上，美國同僚較易忽視對

[17] a. Physical power as the foundation of jurisdiction. Physical presence in the state was the traditional basis of jurisdiction at common law. This jurisdictional basis rested on the notion that the foundation of jurisdiction is physical power. At early common law the only way that an English court could obtain personal jurisdiction over a defendant was to have the sheriff arrest him and bring him into court. Eventually, the requirement that the defendant be arrested was abandoned and personal service of process on the defendant while he was within the jurisdiction was held to suffice. It was immaterial that the defendant was only temporarily in the state. His presence in the state, even for an instant, gave the state judicial jurisdiction over him. If at that time exercise of this jurisdiction was initiated by proper service of process, and if the individual was afforded a reasonable opportunity to be heard, a valid judgment might be entered against him even though he left the state immediately after the service of process (see § 26).

[18] " The rule that physical presence was a basis of judicial jurisdiction did result at times in a defendant being compelled to stand suit in a state with which he had no relationship other than the fact that he was served with process while passing through that state's territory. It might also be thought that the rule was inconsistent with the basic principle of reasonableness which underlies the field of judicial jurisdiction (see § 24). In any event, the rule's potentialities for hardship were mitigated by the fact that the court might refuse to exercise its jurisdiction under the rules of § § 82-84.

境外被告「所產生之困難」，因而忽視了英國母法「境外送達基本上是過度或例外管轄」之判例法。最低限度關連點已造成最大限度之混亂，或許美國同僚應返璞歸真的直視英國母法之區分境內與境外管轄，而對境外管轄基本上視為例外或過度管轄。對於「最低限度關連點」的回歸「不方便法院」法學的趨勢，Prof. Weintraub於評論Asahi Metal Industry v. Superior Court[19]時，便訝異的發現「最低限度關連點」與「不方便法院」的相似性[20]：「如此一來，通常與裁量權行使的不方便法院理論相關的一些概念便被提升至憲法的位階。」如果時光能倒流，或許美國同僚能將精力集中於英格蘭的困擾性或壓迫性法學、蘇格蘭的不方便法院、及送達境外的方便法院，則最低限度關連點不但不會「於國內造成浩劫，於國際和諧上亦造成無可跨越的障礙」，更進一步會「有辦法對世界各地產生貢獻」。

全世界在上個世紀中見證了二十世紀的世界霸主因為不遵循母法，因而陷入「一團混亂」、「浩劫」、「叢林法則」中，在無法駕御「最低限度關連點」之狂奔野馬時，居然狗急跳牆的企圖依賴不公不義的布魯塞爾公約為阻止其奔向地獄深淵的重量。布魯塞爾公約與規則的過度管轄因為侵害美國人之利益，故而許多美國同僚認為違反適當程序條款其判決不會於美國法院被承認[21]，而基於第三世界國際法學生之身分個人更進一步的指控[22]其違反聯合國人權公約及歐盟自己的人權公約。美國為二十世紀

---

19 480 U.S. 102(1987)

20 "Thus, concepts usually associated with the discretionary doctrine of forum non conveniens were elevated to consitutuinal status." Russell J. Weintraub, A Map Out of the Personal Jurisdiciton Labyrinth, 28 U.C. Davis L. Rev. 531, 539 (1994-1995).

21 Eugene F. Scoles, Peter Hey, Patrick J. Borchers, Symeon C. Symeonides, Conflict of laws, 3rd ed., p.1153, "One important feature of the Conventions is that they abolish nationally available exorbitant bases of jurisdiction in relations of member countries to each other but generalize the availability of all such bases in favor of domiciliaries of member states as against parties of third states. A resulting judgment is entitled to recognition in all member states. Thus, even when such a judgment would not be entitled to recognition in the United States, an American judgment debtor may be exposed to liability-through enforcement of the judgment against him-in any contracting state in which he has assets. This danger makes it particularly important that the United States conclude recognition conventions with foreign countries in order to guard against such problems." Arthur T. von Mehren, Recognition and Enforcement of Foreign Judgments: A New Approach for the Hague Conference, 57 Law & Contemp. Prob. 271, 279 (1994).

22 陳隆修，《2005年海牙法院選擇公約評析》，台北，五南圖書公司，2009年1月，初版1刷。147～149頁。

的霸主，其所以走入如此的「空亡」路並非時乖命舛，福禍無門唯自招之。無論是在有關選法規則或跨州管轄上，於憲法架構下美國最高法院之判例法經常是以平衡州際利益為主軸。任何以「利益」為主軸之法學，無論善意或惡意，經常或偶而會忽視實質正義的需求[23]。無論於選法規則或管轄規則上，「最低限度關連點」是以平衡州際利益為基礎，故而其可能違背常識、忽視個案正義的目的、及脫離自然道法。故而在黃進教授、趙相林教授提倡中國式國際私法下，個人一再主張中國式之「所有」法學應以「王道」為基礎，而不能以「利益」為基礎。對美國而言時光不能倒流，但對崛起的中華民族而言，我們必須體會「外國被告之困難」的「常識」，顧及外國被告「個案之正義」，遵循聲名卓越判例法所長久演進的「自然道法」。故而於二十一世紀之全球化管轄規則上，或許真正解決的方法在於遵循判例法長久以來所建立之規則——亦即應區分境外與境內管轄權假設基礎之不同，並分別以不方便及方便法院做為個案裁量權行使之基礎或限制。

二、Pennoyer v. Neff

Pennoyer v. Neff[24]通常是美國以「所在權力」（presence power）做為最基本管轄基礎的代表案例。於案中原告Neff主張其對一片位於奧勒岡之土地依美國法而擁有所有權；但被告Pennoyer亦主張於依奧州巡迴法院所作對原告不利之判決之執行程序中，其於警長處取得該土地之所有權。本案為有關該判決效力之問題。於奧州法院之訴訟中，Mitchell以Neff積欠律師費為由對Neff提起訴訟，而Neff於訴訟期間並非奧洲之居民，故未受到親自送達，並未出席訴訟；並且因未加以抗辯，故為缺席判決，而其只是受到公示送達（以刊登之假設送達）。

23 見陳隆修，《由歐盟經驗論中國式國際私法》，載於〈新世紀兩岸國際私法〉，五南圖書公司，2011年11月。
24 95 U.S. 714 (1877)

Justice Field代表大多數法官發表意見[25]：「每一個法院之權力是必須受限於其之所在地之州之地域範圍內。正如同本院已說過，任何權力的行使企圖超過這些界限是會被每一個其他法院視為非法僭越權力，並被以濫權而加以抗拒。……於對原告起訴之案件中（奧州判決），依判決而被拍賣之係爭財產並未被扣押，亦未被置於法院之管轄。它與案件的第一個關連是因執行而被徵收。因此它並非是根據任何判決而被處份，而是只為了執行與財產無關的對人判決，而該判決是針對一位於訴訟中未受到送達之非居民，並且其亦未出席訴訟。」

接著其又陳述兩個各州對人與物在管轄上建立已久之公法原則[26]：「事實上是，聯邦中之各州並非於每方面都是獨立的，許多原本屬於他們

---

25 95 U.S. 714, 720, "The authority of every tribunal is necessarily restricted by the territorial limits of the State in which it is established. Any attempt to exercise authority beyond those limits would be deemed in every other forum, as has been said by this court, in illegitimate assumption of power, and be resisted as mere abuse. D'Arcy v. Ketchum et al., 11 How. 165. In the case against the plaintiff, the property here in controversy sold under the judgment rendered was not attached, nor in any way brought under the jurisdiction of the court. Its first connection with the case was caused by a levy of the execution. It was not, therefore, disposed of pursuant to any adjudication, but only in enforcement of a personal judgment, having no relation to the property, rendered against a non-resident without service of process upon him in the action, or his appearance therein."

26 95 U.S. 714, 723, "And that they are sound would seem to follow from two well-established principles of public law respecting the jurisdiction of an independent State over persons and property. The several States of the Union are not, it is true, in every respect independent, many of the right and powers which originally belonged to them being now vested in the government created by the Constitution. But, except as restrained and limited by that instrument, they possess and exercise the authority of independent States, and the principles of public law to which we have referred are applicable to them. One of these principles is, that every State possesses exclusive jurisdiction and sovereignty over persons and property within its territory. As a consequence, every State has the power to determine for itself the civil status and capacities of its inhabitants; to prescribe the subjects upon which they may contract, the forms and solemnities with which their contracts shall be executed, the rights and obligations arising from them, and the mode in which their validity shall be determined and their obligations enforced; and also the regulate the manner and conditions upon which property situated within such territory, both personal and real, may be acquired, enjoyed, and transferred. The other principle of public law referred to follows from the one mentioned; that is, that no State can exercise direct jurisdiction and authority over persons or property without its territory. Story, Confl. Laws, c.2; Wheat. Int. law, pt. 2, c. 2. The several States are of equal dignity and authority, and the independence of one implies the exclusion of power from all others. And so it is laid down by jurists, as an elementary principle, that the laws of one State have no operation outside of its territory, except so far as is allowed by comity; and that no tribunal established by it can extend its process beyond that territory so as to subject either persons or property to its decisions. 'Any exertion of authority of this sort beyond this limit,' says Story, 'is a mere nullity, and incapable of binding such persons or property in any other tribunals.' Story, Confl. Laws, sect. 539."

的權力與權利現在是屬於憲法所產生的政府上。但是除非受限於憲法，他們仍擁有及行使獨立國家的權力，並且我們所提到的公法原則對他們是適用的。這些原則其中之一是，每一個州對在其領域中之人及物有著專屬管轄。……另外一個被提到之公法原則是隨著前述之原則而來；亦即，沒有任何州得對其領域外之人或物行使直接管轄及權力。……各州是具有相同的尊嚴及權力，一個州之獨立地位即暗示著排除其他所有之州。因此法學家們建立一下基本的原則，除非在禮誼所允許的程度內，一個州之法律不得於其領域外產生作用；並且其所建立的任何法院皆不得為了使得人或物歸屬於其判決中而將其程序延伸至領域外。『任何這樣的超過域外的行使權力，』Story這樣說，『僅是一種無效行為，並且對於在其他法院地之人或物是無法有拘束力的。』」

有趣的是Justice Field對於非居民於州內之財產得被本州公民以對該非居民求償而加以管轄，特別引用Justice Story之判決而加以論述[27]。美國這種所謂「準對物」之管轄或許於交通不便之早期有必要，但現今國際

[27] 95 U.S. 714, 723, 724, "So the State, through its tribunals, may subject property situated within its limits owned by non-residents to the payment of the demand of its own citizens against them; and the exercise of this jurisdiction in no respect infringes upon the sovereignty of the State where the owners are domiciled. Every State owes protection to its own citizens; and, when non-residents deal with them, it is a legitimate and just exercise of authority to hold and appropriate any property owned by such non-residents to satisfy the claims of its citizens. It is in virtue of the State's jurisdiction over the property of the non-resident situated within its limits that its tribunals can inquire into that non-resident's obligations to its own citizens, and the inquiry can then be carried only to the extent necessary to control the disposition of the property. If the non-resident have no property in the State, there is nothing upon which the tribunals can adjudicate." Picquet v. Swan, 5 Mas. 35, Mr. Justice Story, "Where a party is within a territory, he may justly be subjected to its process, and bound personally by the judgment pronounced on such process against him. Where he is not within such territory, and is not personally subject to its laws, if, on account of his supposed or actual property being within the territory, process by the local laws may, by attachment, go to compel his appearance, and for his default to appear judgment may be pronounced against him, such a judgment must, upon general principles, be deemed only to bind him to the extent of such property, and cannot have the effect of a conclusive judgment in personam, for the plain reason, that, except so far as the property is concerned, it is a judgment coram non judice." Boswell's Lessee v. Otis, 9 How. 336, Mr. Justice McLean, "Jurisdiction is acquired in one of two modes: first, as against the person of the defendant by the service of process; or, secondly, by a procedure against the property of the defendant within the jurisdiction of the court. In the latter case, the defendant is not personally bound by the judgment beyond the property in question. And it is immaterial whether the proceeding against the property be by an attachment or bill in chancery. It must be substantially a proceeding in rem."

上一般認為「物之所在地」之管轄只能限於與物有關之訴訟。最多只能如UNIDROIT Principles一般，如與該物無關，則「物之所在地」只能作為預備之第二線「必要管轄」。

另外Justice Field[28]又認為州得要求於其境內進行合夥、結社、或訂約之非居民指定代理人或代表人，以便對該相關行為之訴訟接受送達，並且如若在他們無法履行時，應指定得代為收受送達通知之應負責之公職人員，或其他方法。並且引用英國教科書目前仍廣為引用之Vallee v. Dumergue：「如果一個人已經同意接受訴訟程序的一個特定方式的通知，即使他可能事實上沒有收到程序的通知，其應受到任何遵守該特定方式的通知之判決的拘束，而這並未違反自然正義。」但Justice Field[29]最後下結論：「於目前之案件，並無這些特點，並且因此不需要考慮到對於執行非居民所訂契約之相關立法所可能產生之效力。本案之問題只是有關一個州所作成之金錢債務判決之效力，而該訴訟是針對其他州居民之一個單純契約上之問題，並且該外州居民並未受到送達，亦未出席訴訟。」故而其維持上訴審之判決，認定奧州法院之判決不具拘束力。這是因為美國最高法院[30]認為Neff於奧州之判決中既未受到親自送達亦未出庭答辯，而居民債

[28] 95 U.S. 714, 735, "Neither do we mean to assert that a State may not require a non-resident entering into a partnership or association within its limits, or making contracts enforceable there, to appoint an agent or representative in the State to receive service of process and notice in legal proceedings instituted with respect to such partnership, association, or contracts, or to designate a place where such service may be made and notice given, and provide, upon their failure, to make such appointment or to designate such place that service may be made upon a public officer designated for that purpose, or in some other prescribed way, and that judgments rendered upon such service may not be binding upon the non-residents both within and without the State. As was said by the Court of Exchequer in Vallee v. Dumergue, 4 Exch. 290, 'It is not contrary to natural justice that a man who has agreed to receive a particular mode of notification of legal proceedings should be bound by a judgment in which that particular mode of notification has been followed, even thought he may not have actual notice of them.'"

[29] 95 U.S. 714, 736 "In the present case, there is no feature of this kind, and, consequently, no consideration of what would be the effect of such legislation in enforcing the contract of a non-resident can arise. The question here respects only the validity of a money judgment rendered in one State, in an action upon a simple contract against the resident of another, without service of process upon him, or his appearance therein."

[30] 95 U.S. 714, 721, 722, "If, therefore, we were confined to the rulings of the court below upon the defects in the affidavits mentioned, we should be unable to uphold its decision. But it was also contended in that court, and is insisted upon here, that the judgment in the State court against the plaintiff was void for want of personal service of process on him, or of his appearance in the action in which it was

權人欲經由係爭土地取得賠償則必須直接提起對物訴訟（但如前述於現今這樣的訴訟可能會被歸類為過度管轄）。

本案是「所在權力」具有歷史意義之領頭案例，案中法院重申：「每一個法院之權力是必須受限於其之所在地之州之地域範圍內。……任何權力的行使企圖超越過這些界限是會被每一個其他法院視為非法僭越權力，並應被以濫權而加以抗拒。」「除非在禮誼所允許的範圍內，一個州之法律不得於其領域外產生作用」。但是最高法院亦謹慎的同意[31]「於本州所訂之契約可能只可以在他州執行，非居民亦可能擁有本州之財產，各州對本州之人及物所擁有管轄權之行使可能經常會影響到外州之人或物。因此各州透過如此去影響到外州之居民或物，是不會被合理的加以抗拒的。但是若企圖去給予其法律域外的效力，或去執行其法院在域外的管轄權，這種任何的對外州居民或物的直接施展權力，是會被當事人所住之州或物所在之州視為對該州獨立性之侵犯，並且被視為竊占主權而被抗拒。」

故而在一百三十多年前之領頭案例Pennoyer中，美國最高法院是如英國判例法般的遵循「所在權力」，並且對域外管轄是視為侵犯他州之主權而通常應加以禁止——亦即區分境內與境外管轄，而境外管轄是被視為「不正常」管轄。若以二十一世紀的術語，很可能域外管轄通常是被視為「過度」或「例外」管轄，只能於案件或當事人與法院地有「重大關連」時才能「間接」行使。

---

rendered and that the premises in controversy could not be subjected to the payment of the demand of a resident creditor except by a proceeding in rem; that is, by a direct proceeding against the property for that purpose."

[31] 95 U.S. 714, 723, "But as contracts made in one State may be enforceable only in another State, and property may be held by non-residents, the exercise of the jurisdiction which every State is admitted to possess over persons and property within its own territory will often affect persons and property without it. To any influence exerted in this way by a State affecting persons resident or property situated elsewhere, no objection can be justly taken; whilst any direct exertion of authority upon them, in an attempt to give ex-territorial operation to its laws, or to enforce an ex-territorial jurisdiction by its tribunals, would be deemed an encroachment upon the independence of the State in which the persons are domiciled or the property is situated, and be resisted as usurpation.

個人雖然認同Pennoyer對於域外管轄之禁誡，但認為於二十一世紀中「主權的被竊占」並非是全球化法學的重點。經過一百三十多年，全球化法學應有更高的進展，個人認二十一世紀全球化法學的重點應是在人權與個案正義，而非狹窄的強調土地主權。無論境內與境外送達皆應更強調個案正義的達成，故而境內與境外送達皆應分別以不方便與方便法院做為個案管轄權裁量行使之基礎或限制。這種本於Pennoyer為基礎之進化，才符合我們祖先所謂「天行健，君子以自強不息」，及「道法自然」。

三、International Shoe Co. v. Washington

(一)案件

International Shoe Co. v. Washington[32]是一般認為建立「最低限度關連點」（minimum contacts）之經典領頭案例。該案中之兩個問題為：(1)是否於14修正案適當程序條款之限制下，上訴人（為一德拉瓦公司）經由其於華盛頓州（被上訴人）之行為，使得在華盛頓州依法而對上訴人提起要求支付失業補償金之訴訟中，華盛頓州法院對上訴人有管轄權；及(2)華盛頓州之要求失業補償金是否符合適當程序條款。華盛頓州之上訴法院及最高法院皆維持行政機關之認定，判定州有權利向上訴人要求支付補償金。上訴人則抗辯華盛頓州法違反適當程序條款及憲法禁止對州際商業加以負擔之商業條款（the commerce clause）。

上訴人為一主要營業地於密蘇里州之德拉瓦公司，其於許多州皆有營業。其於華盛頓州雖沒有辦公室，但卻僱有十多位銷售員，有時這些銷售員會承租固定的展示間，但訂單之成立是由上訴人於密州決定。審判長Stone陳述最高法院之意見[33]，認為：「現在已經沒有必要再爭論，在行使

32　326 U.S. 310 (1945)

33　326 U.S. 310, 315, "For 53 Stat. 1391, 26 U.S.C. 1606(a), 26 U.S.C.A. Int.Rev.Code, 1606(a), provides that 'No person required under a State law to make payments to an unemployment fund shall be relieved from compliance therewith on the ground that he is engaged in interstate or foreign commerce, or that the State law does not distinguish between employees engaged in interstate or foreign commerce

商業權力時國會得明確的授權給各州，去規定州際商業或給予其負擔。」而於此方面國會已有明確之立法。

本案之重點在於[34]：「上訴人並且堅持其於州內之行為並不足以證明其之『所在』於當地，並且於其不在之情形下州法院是沒有管轄權，因此該州如使得上訴人去接受該訴訟之管轄是違反適當程序條款。」對於這個抗辯，Stone C.J.[35]代表法院提出不認同之意見，而其所提的意見即為日後被美國後輩同僚所視為「一團混亂」、「叢林法則」、「浩劫」的「最低限度關連點」：「歷史上法院作成對人訴訟判決的管轄權是本於他們對於被告人身的實際上權力而來。因此其於法院地域管轄區內之所在是法院於作成對其個人有拘束力之判決之必要條件。……但是現今capias ad respondendum[36]已經被訴訟的命令或其他形式的通知之親自送達所取代，適當程序只是要求，如果被告之所在不在法院地域內，為了使其受到對人判決之管轄，其必須與法院地有著某些最低限度關連點以至於訴訟的被提起不會違反『傳統上公平與實質正義的概念』。」如果「最低限度關連點」所造成的天搖地動之影響用台灣話表達那就是「驚動武林轟動萬教」，用北京話表達那就是「捲起千堆雪」，如果用個人之慣用語那就是「放出目

---

and those engaged in intrastate commerce.' It is no longer debatable that Congress, in the exercise of the commerce power, may authorize the states, in specified ways, to regulate interstate commerce or impose burdens upon it."

34 同上，"Appellant also insists that its activities within the state were nor sufficient to manifest its 'presence' there and that in its absence the state courts were without jurisdiction, that consequently it was a denial of due process for the state to subject appellant to suit. It refers to those cases in which it was said that the mere solicitation of orders for the purchase of goods within a state, to be accepted without the state and filled by shipment of the purchased goods interstate, does not render the corporation seller amenable to suit within the state."

35 326 U.S. 310, 316, "Historically the jurisdiction of courts to render judgment in personam is grounded on their de facto power over the defendant's person. Hence his presence within the territorial jurisdiction of court was prerequisite to its rendition of a judgment personally binding him. Pennoyer v. Neff, 95 U.S. 714, 733. But now that the capias ad respondendum has given way to personal service of summons or other form of notice, due process requires only that in order to subject a defendant to a judgment in personam, if he be not present within the territory of the forum, he have certain minimum contacts with it such that the maintenance of the suit does not offend 'traditional notions of fair play and substantial justice.'"

36 依照Black's Law Dictionary, 7th ed., p. 200,為命令警長拘捕被告以確保其出庭之意："A writ commanding the sheriff to take the defendant into custody to ensure that the defendant will appear in court."

眩神搖的光而沒放熱」。

Stone C.J.又說[37]：「因為公司人格是個假設……因而所謂『所在』或『身體所在』通常只是指公司代理人於州內之行為，而法院認為足夠滿足適當程序條款之規定。這些規定得經由公司於法院地之州內之關連點而使得其合理……一個遠離其『家鄉』或主要營業地之訴訟對公司所造成的『不方便的評估』於此方面是相關的。」接著又說[38]：「即使是未曾同意被訴或未曾授權給代理人去接受程序之送達，當公司於該地之行為不但是持續的且是有制度性的，並且造成被起訴之責任時，於此方面會構成『所在』於該州是從未被懷疑的。」事實上美國所有的同僚，七十年前與現今的同僚皆包含在內，皆應冷靜思考一個簡單的事實——英國母法[39]對於在法院地營業之外國公司如前所述是允許送達至境內之營業地的（限於與當地業務有關），而若契約訂定地、履行地或準據法為英國法亦可送達至境

---

37 326 U.S. 310, 316, 317, "Since the corporate personality is a fiction, although a fiction intended to be acted upon as though it were a fact, Klein v. Board of Tax Supervisors, 282 U.S. 19, 24, 51 S.Ct. 15, 16, 73 A.L.R. 679, it is clear that unlike an individual its 'presence' without, as well as within, the state of its origin can be manifested only by activties carried on in its behalf by those who are autorized to act for it. To say that the corporation is so far 'present' there as to satisfy due process requirements, for purposes of taxation or the maintenance of suits against it in the courts of the state, is to beg the question to be decided. For the terms 'present' or 'presence' are used merely to symbolize those activities of the corporation's agent within the state which courts will deem to be suffucuent to satisfy the demands of due process. L. Hand, J., in Hutchinson v. Chase & Gilbert, 2 Cir., 45 F.2d 139, 141. Those demands may be met by such contacts of the corporation with the state of the forum as make it reasonable, in the context of our federal system of government, to require the corporation to defend the particular suit which is brought there. An 'estimate of the inconveniences' which would result to the corporation from a trial away from its 'home' or principal place of business is relevant in this connection."

38 326 U.S. 310, 317, " 'presence' in the state in this sense has never been doubted when the activities of the corporation there have not only been continuous and systematic, but also give rise to the liabilities sued on, even thought no consent to be sued or authorization to an agent to accept service of process has been given,"

39 Civil Procedure Rules 1998, s. 6. 20,
(5) a claim is made in respect of a contract where the contract –
(a) was made within the jurisdiction;
(b) was made by or through an agent trading or residing wihtin the jurisdiction;
(c) is governed by English law; or
(d) contains a term to the effect that the court shall have jurisdiciton to determine any claim in respect of the contract.
(6) a claim is made in respect of a breach of contract committed within the jurisdiction.
(7) a claim is made for a declaration that no contract exists where, if the contract was found to exist, it would comply with the conditons set out in paragraph (5).

外，另外若契約透過境內之代理而訂定亦可送達境外。於母法有詳盡且確實的規定時，美國同僚為什麼要「燒盡午夜的油」去幻想出一個日後引起不斷爭議的學術理論，不遵守母國判例法就是不遵守「自然道法」。中國人對這種「空亡路」之「末路狂花」行徑通常以「鬼打牆」形容。

美國同僚這種詭異的行徑不僅是脫乎判例法母法的常軌，亦與大陸法長久以來習以為常的認知脫離。例如現今的布魯塞爾規則的第5條第1項[40]即規定契約履行地或買賣交貨地法院有管轄權；而第5項[41]又規定有關分行、代理、或其他機構之行為，該分行、代理、或其他機構之行為地法院有管轄權。而又如個人所一再強調大陸法之管轄基礎是不分境內或境外，故而皆可送達至境外之外國法人。美國最高法院在沒有迫切而明顯的理由下，竟然違背了聲名卓越的母法，又與歐洲大陸的其他文明國家的慣例脫離，於這麼大的動作下卻造成了半個世紀美國管轄法規的「浩劫」，美國同僚是否可以對目瞪口呆的其他同僚做一個說明？於美國同僚「燒盡午夜的油」去建立「最低限度關連點」後，個人只想知道所為何來？

另外有趣的是Stone C.J.說：「如果被告之所在不在法院地域內，為了使其受到對人判決之管轄，其必須與法院地有著某些最低限度關連點以致於訴訟的被提起不會違反『傳統上公平與實質正義的概念』。」故而「最低限度關連點」很明顯的指的是「被告之所在不在法院地域內」，因此應與英國母法一向對送達境外戒慎恐懼之判例法及成文法一致。但是其又接著說：「因而『所在』或『身體所在』通常只是指公司代理人於州內

---

40 1. (a) in matters relating to a contract, in the courts for the place of performance of the obligation in question;
(b) for the purpose of this provision and unless otherwise agreed, the place of performance of the obligation in question shall be:
— in the case of the sale of goods, the place in a Member State where, under the contract the goods were delivered or should have been delivered,
— in the case of the provision of services, the place in a Member State where, under the contract, the services were provided or should have been provided,
(c) if subparagraph (b) does not apply then subparagraph (a) applies.

41 5. as regards a dispute arising out of the operations of a branch, agency or other establishment, in the courts for the place in which the branch, agency or other establishment is situated.

之行為，而法院認為足夠滿足適當程序條款之規定。這些規定得經由公司於法院地之州內之關連點而使得其合理。」故而後段之論述是以「最低限度關連點」使的公司於域內之「所在」合理化。因而Stone C.J.對於「最低限度關連點」指的是「被告之所在不在法院地域內」，及「『所在』或『身體所在』通常只是指公司代理人於州內之行為」，故同時指向所在於域外及域內之行為，於邏輯上似乎有些困擾，難怪會對後來之判例法及學術理論上造成巨大之困擾。或許可以事後諸葛亮的加以整理歸納為，Stone C.J.所指的應是最低限度限制關連點是有關對域外被告在域內之行為是否得合理的構成對有關該行為之訴訟之管轄基礎。

但是如果對Stone C.J.的論述加以如此的詮釋，則使得最低限度關連點的創造變得沒有意義，因為如前所述無論英國母法或歐洲大陸法對此方面之管轄基礎長久以來皆有已建立之法律。**故而個人真誠的認為如果最低限度關連點欲「取代」英國母法對外送達或大陸法特別管轄之管轄基礎，那麼其自一出生便已失敗，並且其於美國管轄基礎上造成長久以來之「一團混亂」、「叢林法則」、及「浩劫」。但是如果最低限度關連點被加以適用的心態是，做為英國法境外送達或大陸法特別管轄行使之「輔助基礎行使之限制」，那或許是較為可被接受之一種方式。**

但是事實上做為英美法境外送達或大陸法特別管轄之輔助基礎或限制，在全球化法學之發展上早已有著方便法院或不方便法院之概念，「最低限度關連點」似乎為著維持法學發展之一貫性，或許仍應退居第二線之地位。如Stone C.J.自己在對「最低限度關連點」立下一個企圖開天闢地之論述時說：「一個遠離其『家鄉』或主要營業地之訴對公司所造成的『不方便的評估』於此方面是相關的。」故而Stone C.J.的論述已白紙黑字的證明「最低限度關連點」與對被告「所造成『不方便的評估』於此方面是相關的」。我們在這裡所應感到驚訝的是，為什麼Prof. Weintraub會遲至半個多世紀後才發現「不方便法院被提昇至憲法的位階」。Stone C.J.於創立「最低限度關連點」時便將其與「不方便法院」法學相提並論，或許可以這麼的說——「最低限度關連點」一出生便與「不方便法院」相連結。**或許個人可以更務實的這麼的主張——「最低限度關連點」只能做為「方便或不方便法院」裁量權行使的補助考量因素之一。而鑑於ALI/UNIDROIT Principles of Transnational Civil Procedure的以「重大關連」為管轄基礎，英國境外送達與大陸法特別管轄都亦有著「明確或特別」的關連點做為管轄基礎，美國式的「最低限度關連點」之要求皆已明顯的被滿足，故而除非有著更進一步的發展，否則其功能並不會明顯。**

Stone C.J.[42]又說：「我們對使得公司接受訴訟的管轄與那些不需要接受管轄的行為，所藉以劃下界限的標準，是很明顯的不能單純機械式的或以量計算。這個標準並不只是，如同有時被建議著，是否公司認為是合適去透過代理人去於他州取得利益之行為是或多或少之問題。……適當程序是否被滿足實際上是必須依據該行為之性質與品質的相較於適當程序條款的目的所欲確保的法律之公平而有秩序的行使。該條款並沒有設想對一與一個州沒有關連、連結、或關係之個人或公司，該州得對其作成有拘束力之對人判決。」又說[43]：「在採取這些標準下，替上訴人於華盛頓州所做的行為是既非不規則亦非偶然。於整個係爭的時間內他們是有制度及持

42 326 U.S. 310, 319 "It is evident that the criteria by which we mark the boundary line between those activities which justify the subjection of a corporation to suit, and those which do not, cannot be simply mechanical or quantitative. The test is not merely, as has sometimes been suggested, whether the activity, which the corporation has seen fit to procure through its agents in another state, is a little more or a little less. St. Louis S.W.R. Co. v. Alexander, supra, 227 U.S. 228, 33 S. Ct. 248, Ann.Cas, 1915B, 77; International Harvestor Co. v. Kentucky, supra, 234 U.S. 587, 34 S.Ct. 946. Whether due process is satisfied must depend rather upon the quality and nature of the activity in relation to the fair and orderly administration of the laws which it was the purpose of the due process clause to insure. That clause does not contemplate that a state may make binding a judgment in personam against an individual or corporate defendant with which the state has no contacts, ties, or relations. Cf. Pennoyer v. Neff, supra; Minnesota Commercial Men's Ass'n v. Benn, 261 U.S. 140, 43 S.Ct. 293."

43 326 U.S. 310, 320, "Applying these standards, the activities carried on in behalf of appellant in the State of Washington were neither irregular nor casual. They were systematic and continuous throughout the years in question. They resulted in a large volume of interstate business, in the course of which appellant received the benefits and protection of the laws of the state, including the right to resort to the courts for the enforcement of its rights. The obligation which is here sued upon arose out of those very activities. It is evident that these operations establish sufficient contacts or ties with the state of the forum to make it reasonable and just according to our traditional conception of fair play and substantial justice to permit the state to enforce the obligations which appellant has incurred there. Hence we cannot say the maintenance of the present suit in the State of Washington involves an unreasonable or undue procedure."

續性的。他們產生了一個巨額的州際貿易，而於過程中上訴人接受了利益及州法律的保護，這包含了訴之法院要求執行其權利之權利。於此所被起訴之義務是由於這些行為所引起的。很明顯的這些行為與法院地之州建立了足夠的關連點與連結，以至使得州去執行上訴人在當地所引起的義務，於根據我們傳統上公平與重大正義的概念下是合理及公正的。因此我們不能說於華盛頓州提起目前的訴訟是牽連到一個不合理或不適當之程序。」因此其之結論為[44]：「對於其銷售員於華盛頓州之行為所引起之義務之訴訟，上訴人已使得自己應接受管轄……建立其『所在』之行為使得其同樣的應接受州的課稅及為取得稅金而提起之訴訟。」

本案之所以日後會產生「叢林法則」的「一團混亂」，可能即為其於實際上是遵守判例法母法對境外送達加以謹慎之態度，但其卻未對這個判例法之傳統法律邏輯加以確認。反之，其庸人自擾的對域外之被告以其於域內之行為而假設其「所在」於域內，更糟糕的是其「鬼打牆」式的在沒有明顯迫切需要之情形下，脫離英國送達境外之母法而自創一個新的法學概念「最低限度關連點」。於英國母法送達境外之既有的傳統規則下，以一個比較法學生之地位，個人看不出最低限度關連點之功能性在那裡。而美國同僚之意見則有些已如前述。

(二)自然正義

另外有趣的是Black J.於贊同意見中則對「自然主義」概念之適用加以節制如下[45]：「目前所能辨認出之已被適用之標準應如下：適當程序的

44 326 U.S. 310, 321, “Appellant having rendered itself amenable to suit upon obligations arising out of the activities of its salesmen in Washington, the state may maintain the present suit in personam to collect the tax laid upon the exercise of the privilege of employing appellant’s salesmen within the state. For Washington has made one of those activities, which taken together establish appellant’s ‘presence’ there for purposes of suit, the taxable event by which the state brings appellant within the reach of its taxing power. The state thus has constitutional power to lay the tax and to subject appellant to a suit to recover it. The activities which establish its ‘presence’ subject it alike to taxation by the state and to suit to recover the tax.”

45 326 U.S. 310, 323, “The criteria adopted insofar as they can be identified read as follows: Due process does permit State courts to ‘enforce the obligations which appellant has incurred’ if it be found ‘reasonable and just according to our traditonal conception of fair play and substantial justice.’ And this in turn

確允許州法院去『執行上訴人所引起之義務』如果其是在『我們公平及實質正義的傳統概念下是合理及公正的』。而這個又接著意味著在『一個不方便的評估』下我們會『允許』一個州之行為，這會造成公司去面對一個不在其『家園』或主要營業地之訴訟之結果，我們認為要求其於其所營業之州接受訴訟之管轄是『合理的』。」又說[46]：「將自然正義[47]之概念加於憲法之特別禁令上，會對他們所包含的民主制度上之保障，例如言論、出版及宗教、與詢問律師之自由，產生重大之刪減。而這已發生。……因為這個自然法概念之適用，無論是以『合理』、『正義』、『公平原則』之名詞，使得法官成為這個國家之法律與執行上之最高仲裁者。……這個結果，我相信，會改變我們憲法所規定之政府的形式。我不能同意。」最後

means that we will 'permit' the State to act if upon 'an 'estimate of the inconveniences' which result to the corporation from a trial away from its 'home' or principal place of business', we conclude that it is 'reasonable' subject it to suit in a State where it is doing business."

46 326 U.S. 310, 325, 326, "There is a strong emotional appeal in the words 'fair play', 'justice', and 'reasonableness.' But they were not chosen by those who wrote the original Constitution or the Fourteenth Amendment as a measuring rod for this Court to use in invalidating State or Federal laws passed by elected legislative representatives. No one, not even those who most feared a democratic government, ever formally proposed that courts should be given power to invalidate legislation under any such elastic standards. Express prohibitions against certain types of legislation are found in the Constitution, and under the long settled practice, courts invalidate laws found to conflict with them. This requires interpretation, and interpretation it is true, may result in extension of the Constitution's purpose. But that is no reason for reading the due process clause so as to restrict a State's power to tax and sue those whose activities affect persons and businesses within the State, provided proper service can be had. Superimposing the natural justice concept on the Constitution's specific prohibitions could operate as a drastic abridgment of democratic safeguards they embody, such as freedom of speech, press and religion, and the right to counsel. This has already happened. Betts v. Brady, 316 U.S. 455, 62 S.Ct. 1252. Compare Feldman v. United States, 322 U.S. 487, 494-503, 64 S.Ct. 1082, 1085-1089, 154 A.L.R. 982. For application of this natural law concept, whether under the terms 'reasonableness', 'justice', or 'fair play', makes judges the supreme arbiters of the country's laws and practices. Polk Co. v. Glover, 305 U.S. 5, 17-18, 59 S.Ct. 15, 20, 21; Federal Power Commission v. Natural Gas Pipeline Co., 315 U.S. 575, 600, 62 S.Ct. 736, 750, note 4. This result, I believe, alters the form of government our Constitution provides. I cannot agree."

47 又如前述，因為基於對「正義」概念之可能產生之歧異，英國傳統判例將「自然正義」侷限於程序正義。但較近亦有判例法認為程序上重大的被違背之效果，亦可能產生「實質正義」被侵犯。但亦有英國同僚認為「自然正義」仍應只是指程序上之問題，有關「實質正義」之問題仍應在相關政策上去解決。Cheshire & North, 14th ed., pp.149, 566.而美國同僚對「實質正義」與「自然正義」之區分，似乎並不如此絕對涇渭分明。個人以比較法學生的角度去觀察，或許法律基本功夫的馬步仍應紮實，否則長久以後可能於正義之目的上會陷入走火入魔的歧途，例如不方便法院及最低限度關連點之適用上。

其引用[48]Mr. Justice Holmes於1930年之論述[49]作為結論：「對於第14修正案在刪減我所認為應是各州於憲法上之權利之被授與範圍之一直增加，我尚未恰當的表示我所感覺到超過焦慮的想法。如同現今的判例所代表的，如果這些州權利恰巧觸及本最高法院的大多數法官認為具備任何不受歡迎的任何理由，除了天空以外我幾乎見不到任何去限制使得這些州權利無效之權力。」

對於「因為這個自然法概念之適用，無論是以『合理』、『正義』、或『公平原則』之名詞，使得法官成為這個國家之法律與執行上之最高仲裁者」之爭議，或許自有成文法之歷史便已存在。台灣亦有資深民法同僚[50]引用德裔同僚Wilburg[51]之論述如下：「衡平者，乃在表示由嚴格的形式法到彈性法，由硬性的規則到個別精緻化的發展，不當得利請求權曾艱辛的藉助於衡平思想，成為一項法律制度。業經制度化的不當得利，已臻成熟，有其一定的構成要件及法律效果，正義與公平應該功成身退。」除非Prof. Wilburg之主文另有論述，否則單就這個論述而言是個無知到危險之主張。其之所以無知乃是因過去藉公平與正義而作成的衡平判決，的確是可以制度化或類型化，但天道莫測是中國人之古訓，西洋人亦認為上帝之道是神祕的，對於未來所可能發生之個案糾紛，無論是在以前或變幻莫測之二十一世紀，從來就沒有任何文明可以預測並事前就將其類型化。其之所以無知到危險乃是因為這個謬誤的論述可能侵犯到上個世紀人類文明所建立的各種人權公約中所保障的個別基本人權。

---

48 326 U.S. 310, 326, "True, the State's power is here upheld. But the rule announced means that tomorrow's judgment may strike down a State or Federal enactment on the ground that it does not conform to this Court's idea of natural justice.

49 "I have not yet adequately expressed the more than anxiety that I feel at the ever increasing scope given to the Fourteenth Amendment in cutting down what I believe to be the constitutional rights of the States. As the decisions now stand, I see hardly any limit but the sky to the invalidating of those rights if they happen to strike a majority of this Court as for any reason undesirable." Baldwin v. Missouri, 281 U.S. 586, 595, 50 S.Ct. 436, 439, 72 A.L.R. 1303.

50 王澤鑑，債權原理第2冊—不當得利，21-22頁，10版。

51 Wilburg, Die Lehre von der ungerechtfertigten Bereicherung nach öster – reichischem und deutschem Recht, 1934, S. 18.

對於Holmes J.及Black J.之論述，時間是最好的公證人，其母法英國判例法於半個世紀後在Castanho v. Brown & Root (U.K.) Ltd.[52]中，Lord Scarman在評述衡平法中之禁訴令時作了一個膾炙人口的陳述：「衡平法的寬度及靈活性是不可被類型化所破壞。」影響所及，幾乎於英國有關禁訴令之教科書或論文，皆必須唸上Lord Scarman這一段聖咒，然後才能小心翼翼的對禁訴令之類別加以遮遮掩掩的討論——這個情形很像中國人於祭典或開工時必須先上香向天地禱告。或許二十一世紀全球化法學之核心基本價值是在個案正義已被Lord Scarman的聖咒所附體。

對於「自然法概念」之「合理」、「正義」、「公平原則」之適用加以反對者，或者主張「正義與公平應功成身退」者，或許較近之Deutsche Schachtbau v. Shell International Petroleum Co., Ltd.[53]會是此方面給予當頭棒喝之最佳教科書案例，亦是現代社會中詭譎多變的國際貿易正義不能被類型化之預測所破壞之代表案例。於案中原告與被告雙方皆為外國公司，約定探測R'As al-Khaimah外海的油田，並約定若有糾紛應至日內瓦依據ICC的規則仲裁。後原告依條款至日內瓦要求仲裁，日內瓦的仲裁者認定被告應給付原告大筆賠償。但被告隨即於R'As al-Khaimah法院起訴，並基於詐欺而對原告取得解除契約及損害賠償之判決。雙方皆未出席對方所提出之救濟程序。原告於發現一英國公司因向被告購油而積欠被告金錢後，原告便要要求由英國公司所欠之錢取償，但被告即於R'As al-

52 "the width and flexibility of equity are not to be undermined by categorisation." [1981] A.C. 557, 573 (H.L.) (appeal taken from Eng.).

53 [1990] 1 A. C. 295 (CA), "where a court had to exercise its discretion whether or not to make a garnishee order absolute where the debtor was the subject of an order of a foreign court to pay his creditor, it would be inequitable to make such an order where payment by the garnishee would not necessarily discharge his liability and where there was therefore a real or substantial risk that he would be compelled by the legal process of the foreign court in effect to pay the attached debt twice over; and that where such a risk was shown it did not of itself matter whether or not the foreign court was exercising an exorbitant jurisdiction in making its order; that in relation to S. Ltd.'s debt there was a serious risk that the R'As al-Khaimah court judgment would be enforced in other neighbouring states where S. Ltd. carried on business notwithstanding its debt having been satisfied by the garnishee proceedings in England and, accordingly, it would not be equitable for the garnishee order to be made absolute and that, further, in the circumstances of the case it would not be right for the plaintiffs to pursue other methods of execution in respect of S. Ltd.'s indebtedness….."

Khaimah自己之法院取得對英國公司之判決，停止供應其石油並扣押其關係企業之船。後英國公司加入被告之抗辯要求停止仲裁判斷之執行及停止扣押其財產，但卻為英國高等法院所駁回。但有趣的是"double jeopardy"（雙重危險）雖較少發生於商業危害中，但英國最高法院卻據以駁回高等法院之判決。英國最高法院認為即使於依英國法外國法院過度行使管轄權之情形下，英國公司就算清償了它於英國被扣押之債務，它還是可能在R'As al-Khaimah鄰近它所營業的國家中，受到R'As al-Khaimah法院判決的強制執行。因此英國扣押程序的執行並不能解除英國公司之責任，它極有可能於外國法院再被起訴扣押一次，因此它有可能須清償債務兩次，所以是不符合衡平原則的。

這個案例是符合Cardozo J.所要求的「常識的限制」，Prof. Graveson所堅持的「判例法正義的目的」，及中國文化之「道法自然」。無論在那一個世代，但特別是在日新月異五光十色的二十一世紀，「衡平法的寬度及靈活性是不可以被類型化所破壞」。做為Prof. Graveson的學生及信徒，個人再度重申；「法律邏輯一致性的要求應受限於判例法達成正義的基本目的。」

又於該案中當事人並沒有選定主契約之準據法，他們所指定的仲裁地法被認定為仲裁條款之準據法，但並非為主契約之準據法。英國法院認可仲裁者所決定契約準據法應為「管轄契約關係之所被共同接受之法律原則」（accepted principles of law governing contractual relations）。對此Sir John Donaldson M.R.評述[54]：「這是昔日衡平法之功能。而卻是今日仲裁者得根據這樣子的條款恰當的去行使之作為。」依照衡平原則之公平正義之概念去解決契約糾紛已是近代社會中之一個無法抗拒之寫實。1985年之UNCITRAL Model Law on International Commercial Arbitration的28條第3、4項[55]即規定於當事人同意時，並於考慮貿易習慣下，得

54 同上，"That is what equity did in the old days. And it is what arbitrators may properly do today under such a clause as this."

55 Article 28

以「衡平善良原則」或「自發性接受協商」之方式去解決糾紛。其解釋報告（Explanatory Note）第35段說[56]：「它給予當事人去選擇應適用之實體法之自由，有鑑於許多國家的法律並沒有清楚的或完全的承認這個權利的事實，這是很重要的。另外，規定選擇『法律原則』而非『法律』，模範法在有關適用於糾紛之實體上之法律之指定給予當事人較大之選擇，例如他們得同意以國際法院所闡釋但卻尚未被納入任何國家之法律制度之法律原則為依據。」這段話指的是第1項，而其第36段[57]則是第3項之「衡平善良原則」加以補充解釋。

模範法的以「法律原則」、「衡平善良原則」、或「友好協商原

(1) The arbitral tribunal shall decide the dispute in accordance with such rules of law as are chosen by the parties as applicable to the substance of the dispute. Any designation of the law or legal system of a given State shall be construed, unless otherwise expressed, as directly referring to the substantive law of that State and not to its conflict of laws rules.
(2) Failing any designation by the parties, the arbitral tribunal shall apply the law determined by the conflict of laws rules which it considers applicable.
(3) The arbitral tribunal shall decide ex aequo et bono or as amiable compositeur only if the parties have expressly authorized it to do so.
(4) In all cases, the arbitral tribunal shall decide in accordance with the terms of the contract and shall take into account the usages of the trade applicable to the transaction.

有趣的是1985的模範公約又於2006年增訂2A條，條文中特別增加了自然法概念的「誠信原則」及「法學基本原則」，這是自CISG第7條以來盛行的實體法潮流。

Article 2A. International origin and general principles
(As adopted by the Commission at its thirtu-ninth session, in 2006)
(1) In the interpretation of this Law,regard is to be had to its international origin and to the need to promote uniformity in its application and the observance of good faith.
(2) Question concerning matters governed by this Law which are not expressly settled in it are to bo settled in conformity with the general principles on which this Law is based.

56 "It grants the parties the freedom to choose the applicable substantive law, which is important in view of the fact that a number of national laws do not clearly or fully recognize the right. In addition, by referring to the choice of 'rules of law' instead of 'law', the Model Law gives the parties a wider range of options as regards the designation of the law applicable to the substance of the dispute in that they may, for example, agree on rules of law that have been elaborated by an international forum but have not yet been incorporated into any national legal system."

57 36. According to article 28(3), the parties may authorize the arbitral tribunal to decide the dispute ex aequo et bono or as amiables compositeurs. This type of arbitration is currently not known or used in all legal systems and there exists no uniform understanding as regards the precise scope of the power of the arbitral tribunal. When parties anticipate an uncertainty in this respect, they may wish to provide a clarification in the arbitration agreement by a more specific authorization to the arbitral tribunal. Paragraph (4) makes clear that in all cases, i.e including an arbitration ex aequo et bono, the arbitral tribunal must decide in accordance with the terms of the contract and shall take into account the usages of the trade applicable to the transaction.

則」（ex aequo et bono or amiable compositeur）為仲裁之依據，亦為許多國家所採納。例如英國1996年之the Arbitration Act Section 46[58]採納如下：「(1) 仲裁庭處理糾紛時：(a) 應依當事人所選定適用於糾紛之實體之法律，或(b)如果當事人同意，應依當事人所同意或仲裁庭所決定之其他考量……(3)如果沒有這種選擇或同意，或者該糾紛不在其同意或選擇範圍內，仲裁庭應採用其認為合適之國際私法規則所決定之法律。」故而1996年之法如模範法46(1)(b)條允許當事人去選定一個不屬於任何國家之法律原則（如歐盟契約法原則），或商業習慣法（lex mercatoria），或依「衡平公正原則」（equity and fairness）去處理紛爭[59]。仲裁基本上是本於契約而來之法學概念，而所仲裁的實體內容亦更是通常有關契約（或由契約所延伸之不當得利）之糾紛。故而於二十一世紀中許多，或大部分，契約糾紛是得本於「法律原則」、「商業習慣法」、或「衡平正義原則」而被解決是不爭的國際寫實及生活經驗。「正義與公平應功成身退」是個與二十一世紀現實世界脫離的幻想，對Prof. Graveson的信徒而言更是褻瀆神明的邪惡思想。

但是對於公平正義及衡平原則之適用，是否真的如Holmes J.及Black J.所擔心的會「除了天空外幾乎沒有任何限制」？例如對於現代社會的傾向直接訴之衡平正義之概念以論斷仲裁糾紛，英國判例法於Bank Mellat v Helliniki Techniki SA[60]中即表示：「不能接受仲裁程序的與任何國家的國內法制度無關，而漂浮於超國界的蒼穹中。」雖然有些仲裁法的同僚強

---

58 (1) The arbitral tribunal shall decide the dispute-
(a) in accordance with the law chosen by the parties as applicable to the substance of the dispute, or
(b) if the parties so agree, in accordance with such other considerations as are agreed by them or determined by the tribunal⋯.
(3) If or to the extent that there is no such choice or agreement, the tribunal shall apply the law determined by the conflict of laws rules which it considers applicable.

59 The Report of the Departmental Advisory Committee on Arbitration Law (1997) 13 Arb. Int. 275, 310. 於Channel Tunnel Group Ltd. v. Balfour Beatty Construction Ltd.中，當事人約定建造橫跨英吉利海峽鐵路，契約中有加入準據法條款，要求契約之解釋必須符合英國與法國共有之原則，若於沒有共同原則時，則適用各國或國際間仲裁庭所適用之國際貿易法基本原則。[1993] A.C.334.

60 [1984] Q.B. 291, p.301, “does not recognise the concept of arbitral procedures floating in the transnational firmament, unconnected with any municipal system of law.”

烈的主張「仲裁的去地方化」（delocalised arbitration），但個人認為至今仍有許多國家是如英國一般，對於仲裁程序法（lex arbitri）還是會加以適度的監督。如較近個人所述[61]：「當事人可能會選擇主要仲裁機構之程序法（如UNCITRAL Arbitrational Rules, ICC Rules, or LCIA Rules）或某一國之程序法，現今一般而言雖皆承認當事人自主，但當事人自主仍須在仲裁地法強行規定之監督下進行[62]。而於當事人未明定時，通常仲裁地法決定其程序法，或補足其程序法上之缺陷[63]。另外仲裁地法亦有支援仲裁之功能，例如取得證據或給予保全命令等，另外如前述於仲裁者之決定超出仲裁契約之範圍或程序不適當時，仲裁地法院得給予救濟。最後仲裁地法給予仲裁判斷合法性，使其得以為其他國家所承認及強制執行[64]。」

各國國內法對仲裁監督的程度可能會是依仲裁於程序上是否符合自然正義，及其結果是否符合一般人於實質正義之觀念而定，亦即依仲裁是否符合「合理」、「正義」、或「公平原則」而定。但無論如何「仲裁的去地方化」而允許當事人以不屬於某國之法律（non-national rules）為依據，反而選擇以「天空為唯一限制」的法律原則、商業習慣法、或衡平正義為依據，是二十一世紀全球化法學進展到以個案正義為核心共同基本價值的表現，這就是個人所一再重申的「自然道法」的自然演進現象。對這個現象Dicey and Morris[65]評述：「這個潮流是『仲裁去地方

---

61 陳隆修，《2005年海牙法院選擇公約評析》，台北，五南圖書公司，2009年1月，初版1刷，68、69頁。

62 1996 Arbitration Act, sections 9.10.11.12.13.24.26.28.29.31.32.33.37 (2).40.43.56.60.66.67.68.70.71.72.73.74.75。另外如ICC Rules, art. 28(6)。

63 例如同上第12條給予法院權力去延展仲裁期限。

64 如紐約公約art.V (1)(e):
Article V 1.Recognition and enforcement of the award may be refused, at the request of the party against whom it is invoked, only if that party furnishes to the competent authority where the recognition and enforcement is sought, proof that:⋯..(e)The award has not yet become binding, on the parties, or has been set aside or suspended by a competent authority of the country in which, or under the law of which, that award was made.

65 Dicey and Morris, the Conflict of Laws, 14th ed., p.730, "This trend was another aspect of the development of 'delocalised arbitration', which saw the mandatory application of the choice of law rules of the forum as an unnecessary fetter on party autonomy,"這個趨勢已為國際主要之仲裁機構所接受，例

化』發展的另一面，這方面的發展認為法庭地選法規則的強行適用是對當事人自主原則加以不必要的束縛。」或許Dicey and Morris所陳述的只是仲裁上之現象，但美國衝突法選法規則的強調政策分析，羅馬I規則的強調強行法，歐盟契約法的以「誠信」為基本原則，美國UCC的以「合理性」為基本原則，美國法律協會（ALI）的以「合理性」為管轄基礎，而ALI/UNIDROIT Principles of Transnational Civil Procedure亦一再強調「合理性」的貫穿整個原則[66]。近幾十年來全球化法學所顯示的是偏向以實體政策分析為方法論，以「合理性」及「誠信原則」為基本法理之共同趨勢，而這些都指向一個二十一世紀文明進化的特徵——亦即人類文明已進化到二十一世紀全球化法學是注重在個案公平正義的達成。

於比較美國與英國同僚在司法裁量權上之差異時，Prof. Fentiman[67]說：「英國及美國法律學生共同皆有著一個對審判的認知，並且特別是於司法的角色上，這已深遠的影響到他們在國際私法程序上之觀點。雙方通常皆相信法官的地位並非是行政上的，而是審判性的——相信法官的工作並非僅是適用法律，而是去行使判斷。這已表現在判例法學生在國際私法

如International Chamber of Commerce Court of Arbitration (ICC) rules, art. 17(1); London Court of Internation Arbitration (LCIA) rules, art 22.3.

66 Comment:
P-3A The term “reasonable” is used throughout the Principles and signifies “proportional,” “significant,” “not excessive,” or “fair,” according to the context. It can also mean the opposite of arbitrary. The concept of reasonableness also precludes hyper-technical legal argument and leaves a range of discretion to the court to avoid severe, excessive, or unreasonable application of procedural norms.所應注意的是其規定應給法院相當裁量權。

67 Richard Fentiman, Choice of Law in Europe: Uniformity and Integration, 82 Tul. L. Rev. 2021, 2036, 2037, “English and American lawyers may also share a perception of adjudication, and in particulat of the judicial role, which profoundly affects their view of the conflicts process. Both generally share a belief that a judge’s role is not administrative, but adjudicatory – a belief that a judge’s task is not just to apply rules, but to exercise judgment. This is reflected in the common lawyer’s perception of the conflicts process. Of course, some cases are amenable to solution under canonical rules. But common lawyers assume that many or most conflicts cases are (or can be) too complex to submit to automatic regulation in that way. There may of course be situations which are subject to bright-line rules. But there will be others where choice-of-law norms should offer a principled infrastructure for what is at root an exercise in judicial discretion. …… Again, English judges are often reluctant to articulate precisely the grounds upon which they exercise discretion, in the conflict of laws as elsewhere. In some instances, this reflects a fear that by doing so their discretion will become limited, a particular concern if that discretion is to be exercised in the interests of justice.”

程序上之認知。當然的，依據成文法有些案件是已有答案。但判例法的學生是假設許多或大部分的衝突法案件是太過複雜以至無法以這種方式來自動的接受這些規則。當然的可能有些情況是可以接受這些明線規則的。但是亦有其他之情況下選法的形式規則只應做為行使司法裁量權的原則性架構之根源。……同樣的再一次，於國際私法上並如同於其他地方，英國法官經常不願意去表示其行使裁量權的確切理由。於有些情形下，這表示他們害怕如此作時他們的裁量權會受到限制，如果這個裁量權的行使是基於正義的利益時這個顧慮會受到特別的考量。」

如Black J.對「最低限度關連點」於適用上之評述：「在我們公平及實質正義的傳統概念下是合理及公正的」；「在『一個不方便的評估』下」；「要求其於所營業之州接受訴訟之管轄是『合理的』」。對於在境內營業之外國人加以有關該營業訴訟之境外送達，長久以來就是英國及大陸法之既有規範，故自然是「合理及公正的」。於現代化之社會中無論是對境內管轄或境外管轄，皆必須以正義為目的的行使方便或不方便法院裁量權之限制，這是二十一世紀全球化的自然需求。至於裁量權的行使是會以天空為唯一界限，這個問題是有自然法概念以來就有之問題，歷史上充滿著成功及失敗的案例。「合理性」的確是無法以一簡單的方程式去表達，亦無法被劃上一條數學的明線，但卻是六十億人每日賴以為生活經驗判斷之基準。

四、Shaffer v. Heitner

(一)案件

這個「最低限度關連點」標準，後來又於Shaffer v. Heitner[68]中再次被確認除了對人訴訟外亦應適用於準對物及對物訴訟中。亦即憲法適當程序條款（the Due Process Clause）要求被告、法院地、及訴訟間必須有

---

[68] 443 U.S. 186 (1977)，但海商案件因有特殊商業需求，例如船及船員可能離港甚久，故因而不適用。

著最低限度關連點，以使得法院於行使管轄權時，不會違反「傳統上公平原則及實質正義的概念」（traditional notions of fair play and substantial justice）。於案中被上訴人擁有一德拉瓦公司（主要營業地於亞歷桑那）之股票，其於德州法院對該公司、若干董事及行政人員提起訴訟。被上訴人宣稱個別被告因為違背職務，至使公司於奧勒岡遭受到鉅額之反托辣斯賠償。同時被上訴人亦根據德州法而對個別被告於公司之股份及權利而提出扣押之申請，這些個別被告並非德州之居民。被告主張根據International Shoe他們與德州並未有著充份關連點，因此要求取消送達及假扣押之命令。德州衡平法院拒絕被告（上訴人）之主張，認為該德州法之主要目的是以扣押來強迫非居民被告的親自出庭答辯對其提出之訴訟[69]。德州最高法院維持衡平法院之判決[70]。德州法院[71]認為訴訟是以準對物之程序而被提起，而準對物管轄是傳統上基於對法院地內之物之扣押而來，而並非基於被告與州間之關連點而來，故而拒絕上訴人於管轄權上之抗辯。德州法院之分析是本於有上百年歷史之Pennoyer v. Neff而來。但美國最高法院卻駁回德州最高法院之認定。

Marshall J.代表法院發言如下[72]：「正如我們所注意到的，依照Pen-

---

[69] 433 U.S. 186, 193, “The primary purpose of ‘sequestration’ as authorized by 10 Del. C. 366 is not to secure possession of property pending a trial between resident debtors and creditors on the issue of who has the right to retain it. On the contrary, as here employed, ‘sequestration’ is a process used to compel the personal appearance of a nonresident defendant to answer and defend a suit brought against him in a court of equity.”

[70] 433 U.S. 186, 195, “We hold that seizure of the Greyhound shares is not invalid because plaintiff has failed to meet the prior contacts tests of International Shoe.”

[71] 433 U.S. 186, 196, “The Delaware courts rejected appellant’s jurisdictional challenge by noting that this suit was brought as a quasi in rem proceeding. Since quasi in rem jurisdiction is traditionally based on attachment or seizure of property present in the jurisdiction, not on contacts between the defendant and the State, the courts considered appellants’ claimed lack of contacts with Delaware to be unimportant. This categorical analysis assumes the continued soundness of the conceptual structure founded on the centuryold case of Pennoyer v. Neff, 95 U.S. 714 (1878).”

[72] 433 U.S. 186, 198, 199, 200, “From our perspective, the importance of Pennoyer is not its result, but the fact that its principles and corollaries derived from them became the basic elements of the constitutional doctrine governing state-court jurisdiction. See, e. go., Hazard, A General Theory of State-Court Jurisdiction, 1965 Sup. Ct. Rev. 241 (hereafter Hazard). As we have noted, under Pennoyer state authority to adjudicate was based on the jurisdiction’s power over either persons or property. This fundamental concept is embodied in the very vocabulary which we use to describe judgments. If a court’s jurisdiction is based on its authority over the defendant’s person, the action and judgment are denominated “in

noyer州去審判的權利是依據其對人或物之管轄權力而來。這個基本的概念是包含於我們敘述判決所使用之語詞中。如果法院之管轄權是其對被告人身之權力而來，該訴訟及判決是被分類為『對人』，並且可以對原告有利的加諸義務於被告上。如果管轄權是根據法院對於境內之物而來，訴訟是被稱為『對物』或『準對物』。這種案件的判決之效力是限於支持該管轄權之物，並且不會對物之所有人加予對人之責任，這是因為其並未出現於法院之前。依Pennoyer的用詞，所有人只是『間接』的受到一個對物判決之影響，在法院得處理之物上其利益會有不利之影響。經由認定『法院之權力必須受限於其所在之州之地域界線，』……Pennoyer嚴格的限制對於居所不在法院地之被告之對人管轄的適當性。如果一個非居民被告不能於一個州被找到，他就不能於當地被起訴。相反的，因為物所在之州是被認為對該物有著專屬之主權，無論其所有人之所在為何對物訴訟仍得進行。的確的，因為一個州之程序不能超越其州界，於Pennoyer後本院認定適當程序並不要求當其財產牽涉到對物程序時，應對財產之所有人嘗試著給予任何親自之通知。……Pennoyer規則使得非居民被告之被起訴更為困難，故通常是對他們有利的。但是經由居民原告的能將被告任何位於原告之州之任何財產帶入法院，而取得對非居民被告的請求之滿足，這

personam" and can impose a personal obligation on the defendant in favor of the plaintiff. If jurisdiction is based on the court's power over property within its territory, the action is called "in rem" or "quasi in rem." The effect of a judgment in such a case is limited to the property that supports jurisdiction and does not impose a personal liability on the property owner, since he is not before the court. In Pennoyer' s terms, the owner is affected only "indirectly" by an in rem judgment adverse to his interest in the property subject to the court's disposition.

By concluding that "[t]he authority of every tribunal is necessarily restricted by the territorial limits of the State in which it is established," 95 U.S., at 720, Pennoyer sharply limited the availability of in perosnam jurisdiction over defendants not resident in the forum State. If a nonresident defendant could not be found in a State, he could not be sued there. On the other hand, since the State in which property was located was considered to have exclusive sovereignty over that property, in rem actions could proceed regardless of the owner's location. Indeed, since a State's process could not reach beyond its borders, this Court held after Pennoyer that due process did not require any effort to give a property owner personal notice that his property was involved in an in rem proceeding. See, e. g., Ballard v. Hunter, (1907); Arndt v. Griggs, 134 U.S. 316 (1890); Huling v. Kaw Valley R. Co., 130 U.S. 559 (1889).

The Pennoyer rules generally favored nonresident defendants by making them harder to sue. This advantage was reduced, however, by the ability of a resident plaintiff to satisfy a claim against a nonresident defendant by bringing into court any property of the defendant located in the plaintiff's State."

個利益是被減少的。」

又說[73]：「汽車的來到，伴隨著依據Pennoyer並非受到對人訴訟管轄之人於一些州所造成傷害之增加，司法管轄權力於地域上之限制必須被加以修改。正如為了配合跨州際上公司之行為之必須修改之現實，這個修改是以使用法律上之假設而使得Pennoyer所建立起之概念上之架構於理論上沒有被改變之方式而完成。」**美國法院之方式是以假設使用本州公路之駕駛人必須同意指定一個州之公職人員為送達接收之代理人。美國法院這種「修改」或「假設」是令人十分奇怪之作法，同樣的法律事實下，侵權行為地之法院依大陸法是對境內及境外之侵權行為人有管轄權的，而英國判例法母法亦於這種侵權行為之情況下，是可以對境外之侵權行為人加以送達的。美國法院這種「假設」是遺世獨立之行為，更是與其母法與歐陸文明國家完全不同之作法。在英國母法與其他歐陸文明國家長久以來既有明確的合理共同規則下，美國法院在沒有明顯而迫切的理由下，放棄文明世界公認的國際慣有規則，而自創一些日後可能產生紛擾的「假設」，個人實在看不出美國法院這些創意對個案正義或法學之穩定性有何助益。**

Marshall J.又做了下面著名的論述[74]：「因此，訴訟、法院地、及當事人間之關係成為對人管轄問題的主要考量，而非Pennoyer規則所依據的各州間主權互相的獨立性。這種與Pennoyer整個概念的脫離之直接效

[73] 433 U.S. 186, 202, "The advent of automobiles, with the concomitant increase in the incidence of individuals causing injury in States where they were not subject to in personam actions under Pennoyer, required further moderation of the territorial limits on jurisdictional power. This modification, like the accommodation to the realities of interstate corporate activities, was accomplished by use of a legal fiction that left the conceptual structure established in Pennoyer theoretically unaltered. Cf. Olberding v. Illinois Central R. Co., 346 U.S. 338, 340-341 (1953). The fiction used was that the out-of-state motorist, who it was assumed could be excluded altogether from the State's highways, had by using those highways appointed a designated state official as his agent to accept process. See Hess v. Pawloski, (1927). Since the motorist's "agent" could be personally served within the State, the state courts could obtain in personam jurisdiction over the nonresident driver."

[74] 433 U.S. 186, 204, "Thus, the relationship among the defendant, the forum, and the litigation, rather than the mutually exclusive sovereignty of the States on which the rules of Pennoyer rest, became the central concern of the inquiry into personal jurisdiction. The immediate effect of this departure from Pennoyer's conceptual apparatus was to increase the ability of the state courts to obtain personal jurisdiction over nonresident defendants."

果是，使得州法院對非居民被告取得對人訴訟管轄能力之增加。」在美國同僚受到這個有力的論述所感動，並且一再重覆引用這個論述時，作為同樣是英美法的學生，個人不得不煞風景的請美國同僚冷靜下來並且想一想——英國母法至今仍固守所在理論，但其對境外被告送達之作法與理論至今仍大致上未多加改變。美國同僚的熱血是否太容易沸騰？

在「Pennoyer之概念架構沒有被改變」之下，Marshall J.又說[75]：「於對物之管轄上之法律，同樣的亦沒有大改變。但是現在亦有主張認為Pennoyer對人訴訟部分之倒塌並未沒有減弱對物訴訟基礎上之判決。對於無論法院地與物之所有人及訴訟之爭點之關係為何，物之所在於該州皆給予該州管轄權去審判有關該物之權利之說法，下級法院已經提出甚好之理由對其加以懷疑。」又說[76]：「雖然本法院並未直接針對這個論點加以

[75] 433 U.S. 186, 205, "No equally dramatic change has occurred in the law governing jurisdiction in rem. There have, however, been intimations that the collapse of the in personam wing of Pennoyer has not left that decision unweakened as a foundation for in rem jurisdiction. Well-reasoned lower court opinions have questioned the proposition that the presence of property in a State gives that State jurisdiction to adjudicate rights to the property regardless of the relationship of the underlying dispute and the property owner to the forum. See, e. g., U.S. Industries, Inc. v. Gregg, 540 F.2d 142 (CA3 1976), cert. pending, No. 76-359; Jonnet v. Dollar Savings Bank, 530 F. 2d 1123, 1130-1143 (CA3 1976) (Gibbons, J., concurring); Camire v. Scieszka, 116 N. H. 281, 358 A. 2d 397 (1976); Bekins v. Huish, 1 Ariz. App. 258, 401 P.2d 743 (1965); Atkinson v. Superior Court, 49, Cal. 2d 338, 316 P.2d 960 (1957), appeal dismissed and cert. denied sub nom. Columbia Broadcasting System v. Atkinson, (1958). The overwhelming majority of commentators have also rejected Pennoyer's premise that a proceeding "against" property is not a proceeding against the owners of that property. Accordingly, they urge that the "traditional notions of fair play and substantial justice" that govern a State's power to adjudicate in personam should also govern its power to adjudicate personal rights to property located in the State. See e. g., Von Mehren & Trautman, Jurisdiction to Adjudicate: A Suggested Analysis, 79 Harv. L. Rev. 1121 (1966); Traynor, Is This Conflict Really Necessary?, 37 Texas L. Rev. 657 (1959); Ehrenzweig, The Transient Rule of Personal Jurisdiction: The "Power" Myth and Forum Conveniens, 65 Yale L. J. 289 (1956)."

[76] 433 U.S. 186, 206, "Although this Court has not addressed this argument directly, we have held that property cannot be subjected to a court's judgment unless reasonable and appropriate efforts have been made to give the property owners actual notice of the action. Schroeder v. City of New York, 371 U.S. 208 (1962); Walker v. City of Hutchinson, 352 U.S. 112 (1956); Mullane v. Central Bank & Trust Co., 339 U.S. 306 (1950). This conclusion recognizes, contrary to Pennoyer, that an adverse judgment in rem directly affects the property owner by divesting him of his rights in the property before the court. Schroeder v. City of New York, supra at 213; cf. Continental Grain Co. v. Barge FBL-585, 364 U.S. 19 (1960) (separate actions against barge and barge owner are one "civil action" for purpose of transfer under 28 U.S.C. 1404 (a)). Moreover, in Mullane we held that Fourteenth Amendment rights cannot depend on the classification of an action as in rem or in personam, since that is "a classification for which the standards are so elusive and confused generally and which, being primarily for state courts to define, may and do vary from state to state." 339 U.S., at 312."

評述，但是我們已經認定除非在合理及合適的努力下物之所有人被給予訴訟之確實通知，該物不能被置於法院判決之管轄權下。……與Pennoyer相反的，本法院之認定承認一個對物之所有人不利之對物判決會以剝奪其於法院前之物之權利之方式而直接受到影響。」因此Marshall J.[77]語出驚人的提出破天荒式的創見：「因此很明顯的，州法院於管轄權之法律上再也不能安穩的建立於Pennoyer所創立的基礎上。我們認為去考慮到International Shoe所創立的公平與實質正義的標準是否應被同樣的適用於對物及對人訴訟上的時間已經成熟。於對物訴訟管轄案件上去採用如同於對人訴訟管轄上所主張的『公平與實質正義』的相同標準是簡單而直接的。它的基礎是本於承認1971年第2新編國際私法56條之引言之主張『這個名詞『對一個物的司法管轄』是一種有關個人對物之利益之管轄權之習慣性簡略說法。』這種承認導致一個結論，亦即為了使得對物管轄之行使可以合理化，這個管轄基礎必須亦足以合理的行使『個人對物之利益之管轄權』。而去決定個人利益管轄權行使之是否符合適當程序條款之標準即為International Shoe中所闡釋的最低限度關連標準。」

但是Marshall J.於陳述對物管轄亦必須符合International Shoe的最低限度關連點標準後，隨即立刻小心翼翼的補充解釋[78]：「但是這個論述並

---

[77] 433 U.S. 186, 206, 207, "It is clear, therefore, that the law of state-court jurisdiction no longer stands securely on the foundation established in Pennoyer. We think that the time is ripe to consider whether the standard of fairness and substantial justice set forth in International Shoe should be held to govern actions in rem as well as in personam. The case for applying to jurisdiction in rem the same test of 'fair play and substantial justice' as governs assertions of jurisdiction in personam is simple and straightforward. It is premised on recognition that '[t]he phrase, 'judicial jurisdiction over a thing,' is a customary elliptical way of referring to jurisdiction over the interests of persons in a thing.' Restatement (Second) of Conflict of Laws 56, Introductory Note (1971). This recognition leads to the conclusion that in order to justify an exercise of jurisdiction in rem, the basis for jurisdiction must be sufficient to justify exercising' jurisdiction over the interests of persons in a thing.' The standard for determining whether an exercise of jurisdiction over the interests of persons is consistent with the Due Process Clause is the minimum-contacts standard elucidated in International Shoe."

[78] 433 U.S. 186, 207, 208, "This argument, of course, does not ignore the fact that the presence of property in a State may bear on the existence of jurisdiction by providing contacts among the forum State, the defendant, and the litigation. For example, when claims to the property itself are the source of the underlying controversy between the plaintiff and the defendant, it would be unusual for the State where the property is located not to have jurisdiction. In such cases, the defendant's claim to property located in the State would normally indicate that he expected to benefit from the State's protection of his in-

未忽視一個事實，亦即經由提供法院地州、被告、及訴訟間的關連點物之所在於一個州會顯示出管轄權之存在性。例如當對物之請求本身即為原告與被告間所存在紛爭之來源時，物之所在地之州若沒有管轄權時則是非常不尋常的。……因此看起來，現在是已經或得被以對物訴訟之方式而被提起之許多種類之訴訟之管轄權，是不會被州法院管轄權之主張必須滿足International Shoe標準之判決所影響。」事實上物之所在地法院為對物訴訟管轄之基礎，這是英國母法從以前至今從未變動的[79]，布魯塞爾規則22(1)條亦規定不動產所在地有專屬管轄；而於選法規則上，除了運送中之物難以認定其所在外，一般亦以物之所在地法來決定其物權[80]。美國最高法院這個謹慎的說法是國際間早已存在之事實。或許忠言逆耳，美國法院或許應該冷靜的回想，非常可能自有國際私法的歷史以來，以物之所在地做為管轄權之基礎及選法規則之連繫因素是國際上視為理所當然之常識——而這個常識之被全世界所接受是完全與較近創立之「最低限度關連點」無關的。美國同僚的將許多問題皆扯上「最低限度關連點」是否過分狂熱的有點「鬼打牆」？

對物訴訟雖不受影響，但最高法院認為有些準對物訴訟是受到影響的[81]：「但是對於Harris v. Balk所代表的準對物訴訟之種類及本案，接受

terest. The State's strong interests in assuring the marketability of property within its borders and in providing a procedure for peaceful resolution of disputes about the possession of that property would also support jurisdiction, as would the likelihood that important records and witnesses will be found in the State. The presence of property may also favor jurisdiction in cases, such as suits for injury suffered on the land of an absentee owner, where the defendant's ownership of the property is conceded but the cause of action is otherwise related to rights and duties growing out of that ownership. It appears, therefore, that jurisdiction over many types of actions which now are or might be brought in rem would not be affected by a holding that any assertion of state-court jurisdiction must satisfy the International Shoe standard."

79 陳隆修，《國際私法管轄權評論》，台北，五南圖書公司，民國75年11月，初版，30、31頁。

80 陳隆修，《比較國際私法》，台北，五南圖書公司，78年10月，初版，320-334頁。

81 433 U.S. 186, 208, 209, 'For the type of quasi in rem action typified by Harris v. Balk and the present case, however, accepting the proposed analysis would result in significant change. These are cases where the property which now serves as the basis for state-court jurisdiction is completely unrelated to the plaintiff's cause of action. Thus, although the presence of the defendant's property in a State might suggest the existence of other ties among the defendant, the State, and the litigation, the presence of the property alone would not support the State's jurisdiction. If those other ties did not exist, cases over which the State is now thought to have jurisdiction could not be brought in that forum." Harris v. Balk,

上述的分析會造成重大的改變。這些案件即為當做為州法院管轄基礎之物是完全與原告之訴因無關時。因此雖然被告之財產之所在於一個州可能顯示著被告、州、及訴訟間存在著其他關係，單獨的僅是物之所在並不會支持管轄權的成立。如果這些其他關係並不存在，一些現在州被認為有管轄權之案件則變為不可以在該法院被提起訴訟。」但法院又解釋說[82]：「在如同Harris及本案之案件中，物所扮演之唯一角色就是提供將被告帶至法院之基礎。的確，德州扣押程序所明示之目的就是去強迫被告親自出庭。在這些案件中，如果對被告對人管轄的直接主張會違反憲法，看起來這種間接管轄的主張亦會同樣的不被允許。」

法院又引用第2新編66條的註釋(a)[83]：「一個債務人不能經由便利性的將財產轉移至他不會受到對人訴訟管轄之地而得以避免支付其債務。」該第66條已因本案之判決於1988年被加以修正[84]。如修正後之註釋(a)

198 U.S. 215 (1905).

82 433 U.S. 186, 209, "Since acceptance of the International Shoe test would most affect this class of cases, we examine the arguments against adopting that standard as they relate to this category of litigation. Before doing so, however, we note that this type of case also presents the clearest illustration of the argument in favor of assessing assertions of jurisdiction by a single standard. For in cases such as Harris and this one, the only role played by the property is to provide the basis for bringing the defendant into court. Indeed, the express purpose of the Delaware sequestration procedure is to compel the defendant to enter a personal appearance. In such cases, if a direct assertion of personal jurisdiction over the defendant would violate the Constitution, it would seem that an indirect assertion of that jurisdiction should be equally impermissible."

83 Comment:

a. Rationale. A debtor should not be able to avoid payment of his obligations by the expedient of removing his assets to a place where he is not subject to an in personam suit. It is customary for states to provide by statute that tangible things within their territory may be sold and the proceeds applied to the payment of the owner's obligations. Such jurisdiction is commonly exercised through a proceeding begun by an attachment or by a bill in equity. A judgment rendered in such a proceeding is effective against interests in things which are within the state and against which the action is directed (see Comment c). Such a judgment does not impose a personal obligation upon the person against whom the claim is exercised if he is not personally subject to the jurisdiction of the state.

84 修正前原條文："A state has power to exercise judicial jurisdiction to apply to the satisfaction of a claim interests in a tangible thing that is subject to its judicial jurisdiction and belongs to the person against whom the claim is asserted, although the person himself is not subject to the jurisdiction of the state." 1998修正條文為：

(1) A state has power to exercise judicial jurisdiction to seize a tangible thing that is situated in the state, by attachment, sequestration, or similar procedure, in an action concerning a claim against the owner of the thing if:

(a) The court could properly exercise jurisdiction to adjudicate the claim under the rules stated in § §

說[85]：「正如所謂的『扣押管轄』，其理論的基礎之根據是一個州對於在境內之所有有形物有著完全的權力，並且對於在其法院之訴訟中所被主張之請求得扣押該物以便支付該請求。在起初，這個程序是給予當地債權人對於離開或不能被找到之債務人欲執行請求時之救濟，但是它已經通常被適用於為了執行於他處所引起之債務而可以針對從未到過州內之債務人身上。」但是如最高法院對扣押管轄所說[86]：「最多，其只是顯示所在之州，得經由合適之程序去扣押該物，以做為在符合International Shoe下而於法院被提起之訴訟的判決之保證。……充分互信條款終究使得一個州之對人判決得以有效的於所有的其他州被執行。」

Marshall J.代表法院下結論如下[87]：「『傳統上公平與實質正義之概

27-65; or

(b) The action is to enforce a judgment against the owner of the thing; or

(c) The action is properly in aid of other proceedings concerning the claim; or

(d) The exercise of such jurisdiction is otherwise reasonable.

(2) When a court undertakes to exercise jurisdiction as stated in Subsection (1), the owner of the thing may make an appearance to contest the court's jurisdiction over the thing without thereby submitting to the jurisdiction of the court.

85 "Jurisdiction is based on the fact that the thing is within the territorial limits of the state in which the court is located. 'Attachment jurisdiction,' as it may be called, is based on the theory that a state has comprehensive authority over all tangible things within its territorial limits and may seize such things for payment of claims asserted in actions in its courts. In origin, the procedure provided a remedy for local creditors attempting to enforce claims against obligors who had departed or could not be found, but it has also generally been made available against obligors who have never been in the state to enforce obligations that arose elsewhere."

86 433 U.S. 186, 210, "This justification, however, does not explain why jurisdiction should be recognized without regard to whether the property is present in the State because of an effort to avoid the owner's obligations. Nor does it support jurisdiction to adjudicate the underlying claim. At most, it suggests that a State in which property is located should have jurisdiction to attach that property, by use of proper procedures, as security for a judgment being sought in a forum where the litigation can be maintained consistently with International Shoe. See, e. g., Von Mehren & Trautman 1178; Hazard 284-285; Beale, supra, n. 18, at 123-124. Moreover, we know of nothing to justify the assumption that a debtor can avoid paying his obligations by removing his property to a State in which his creditor cannot obtain personal jurisdiction over him. The Full Faith and Credit Clause, after all, makes the valid in personam judgment of one State enforceable in all other States."

87 433 U.S. 186, 211, 212, "This history must be considered as supporting the proposition that jurisdiction based solely on the presence of property satisfies the demands of due process, cf. Ownbey v. Morgan, 256 U.S. 94, 111 (1921), but it is not decisive. 'Traditional notions of fair play and substantial justice' can be as readily offended by the perpetuation of ancient forms that are no longer justified as by the adoption of new procedures that are inconsistent with the basic values of our constitutional heritage. Cf. Sniadach v. Family Finance Corp., 395 U.S., at 340; Wolf v. Colorado, 338 U.S. 25, 27 (1949). The fiction that an assertion of jurisdiction over property is anything but an assertion of jurisdiction over the

念』可以輕易的因執行不符合時代的古老程式而被侵犯，正如同引用與我們憲法傳統上之基本價值不一致之新程序一般的被侵犯……對物管轄之主張並非是對該物所有人管轄之主張的虛構，是支持一個沒有得到現代社會實質合理的認可之古老程式。它的繼續被接受只會允許州法院去擁有對被告基本上不公平之管轄權。我們因此認定所有的州法院管轄權之主張應依照International Shoe及其後面所延續判例之所設下的標準去衡量。」

(二)對物訴訟

有關對物訴訟實際上是與物之所有人有關之論述於最低限度關連點理論被創造前，就由Holmes, C.J.於Tyler v. Judges of the Court of Registration一針見血的說[88]：「就如同所有的權利，所有的程序於事實上皆是對人的。……將其擬人化及以物為被告皆只是一種象徵而已，而並非是主要的事情。他們只是一些虛構，只是方便去表達程序上之性質及結果而已；並沒有其他意涵。」個人對於一百一十年前之社會架構可能是無法表

---

owner of the property supports an ancient form without substantial modern justification. Its continued acceptance would serve only to allow state-court jurisdiction that is fundamentally unfair to the defendant. We therefore conclude that all assertions of state-court jurisdiction must be evaluated according to the standards set forth in International Shoe and its progeny."

88 "If the technical object of the suit is to establish a claim against some particular person, with a judgment which generally in theory, at least, binds his body, or to bar some individual claim or objection, so that only certain persons are entitled to be heard in defense, the action is in personam…. If, on the other hand, the object is to bar indifferently all who might be minded to make an objection of any sort against the right sought to be established, and if any one in the world has a right to be heard on the strength of alleging facts which, if true, show an inconsistent interest, the proceeding is in rem…. All proceedings, like all right, are really against persons…. Personification and naming the res as defendant are mere symbols, not the essential matter. They are fictions, conveniently expressing the nature of the process and the result; nothing more." 175 Mass. 71, 76, 55 N. E. 812, 814 (Holmes, C. J.), appeal dismissed, 179 U.S. 405 (1900). Holmes, C. J.所定義之對人及對物訴訟為英國式之定義，見陳隆修，《國際私法管轄權評論》，台北，五南圖書公司，民國75年11月，初版，29頁，「英國法院將管轄權分為對人〈in perosnam〉與對物〈in rem〉兩種訟訴。對人之訴訟乃為其訴訟之目的在於解決當事人對於所爭執的標的物的權利與利益，而法院判決之效力只及於訴訟當事人間。對人訴訟的案件例如當事人之一方告他方契約不履行或侵權行為等。法院判決契約不履行或侵權行為之效力只及當事人之間。對物之訴訟乃為法院之判決決定一特定財產之權利及當事人之權利，該判決之效力不止於當事人間而已，並且及於所有與當事人或該特定財產有法律行為之人。例如有關房子所有權之訴訟。此外海商案件亦為對物之訴訟。海商訴訟可由於船或貨物於法院地而被提起。此種訴訟乃屬於標的「物」〈res〉位於法院地而引起，法院管轄權之主張很明顯地是基於其判決可被有效的強制執行。但是應注意的是被告之財產於法院地，並不能使法院對於被告有對人之管轄權。」

達意見，但對於Holmes, C. J.「沒有其他意涵」之論述或許另有意見。於海商訴訟中，Action in rem是請求人可以對船舶（船即為被告）請求而強制執行lien（抵押權）之權利，因為被告為船舶，故可以將訴訟之通知貼於船舶之外體上。[89]於早期交通、通訊不發達時，或許以「船舶為被告」之虛構在國際貿易及國際訴訟上是有著必要。於科技發達的21世紀中，特別是於有些美國律師事務所如同美國麥當勞的全球化連鎖性時，對物訴訟仍應將通知送達給所有權人是基本的憲法、人權法上之要求。

美國最高法院的認為對物訴訟「於事實上皆是對人的」、「只是一種象徵而已」，這種見解於英國加入歐盟後，對於英國這方面制度的不同，歐盟最高法院之見解亦與美國最高法院相似。在The Tatry[90]中，船東對貨主於荷蘭起訴，主張其對該貨物沒有責任。而後來貨主於英國扣押該船，以該船為被告提起對物訴訟（但若船東對該案提起辯護，英國法院對其亦有對人管轄權）。歐盟最高法院認定布魯塞爾公約的第21條[91]先繫屬優先之規定應被適用，因為第21條「相同訴因」與「相同當事人間」的名詞應有獨立的意義，而與各個訂約國的法律特色無關。故而訂約國對人訴訟與對物訴訟之區別與第21條之解釋無關[92]。不但是歐盟最高法院對於英國訴訟制度上對人與對物訴訟之區別認為應與歐盟管轄規則之適用無關，即使是英國最高法院自己亦認為對物訴訟於實際上是有著對人之效果。於

---

89 Civil Procedure Rules, Part 49, PD 49 F，para. 2.2a。又見陳隆修，《國際私法管轄權評論》，台北，五南圖書公司，民國75年11月，初版，226頁。

90 Case C- 406/92 [1994] E.C.R. I-5439.

91 Article 21
Where proceedings involving the same cause of action and between the same parties are brought in the courts of different Contracting States, anycourt other than the court first seised shall of its own motion stay its proceedings until such a time the jurisdiction of the court first seised is established.
Where the jurisdiction of the court first seised is established, any court other than the court first seised shall decline jurisdiction in favour of that court.

92 Case C-406/92 [1994] E.C.R. I-5439, para. 47, "In Article 21 of the Convention, the terms 'same cause of action' and 'between the same parties' have an independent meaning (see Gubisch Maschinenfabrik v Palumbo, cited above, paragraph 11). They must therefore be interpreted independently of the specific features of the law in force in each Contracting State. It follows that the distinction drawn by the law of a Contracting State between an action in personam and an action in rem is not material for the interpretation of Article 21."

Republic of India v India Steamship Co（No 2）[93]中，英國最高法院認為對物訴訟於實際上是對船東之訴訟，依s.34 Civil Jurisdiction and Judgment Act 1982[94]之規定，相同當事人對外國勝訴判決不得於英國對相同訴因再提起訴訟，故而外國判決中已決定之事情應有禁反言（estoppel）之適用。

非常有趣的是在Shaffer v. Heitner中美國最高法院引為論述主軸的「對物訴訟於事實上皆對人的」之概念，亦為歐盟最高法院及母法英國最高法院所採納——而很明顯的歐盟最高法院與英國最高法院之認定是與「最低限度關連點」無關的。與其將精力與注意力無謂的放在一個可有可無的創見上，不如直接的面對全球化的事實所必然引發的法學全球化之共同核心基本政策，而加以更腳踏實地的詳細探討。

至於扣押管轄是「通常被適用於為了執行於他處所引起之債務而可以針對從未到過州內之債務人身上」，但是如美國最高法院所說「如果對被告對人管轄的直接主張會違反憲法，看起來這種間接管轄的主張亦會被同樣的不被允許」。在全球化之潮流下外國判決之承認已不若早期為遙不可及之事情。而更為早期所不可想像之事為今日為著外國可能勝訴之判決，於財產所在地法院得提起假扣押、假處分之請求，已為有些國際公約所認為理所當然之事。布魯塞爾規則31條[95]規定，即使在其他會員國對案件之實體有著管轄權之情形下，仍得對會員國之法院依其規定而請求暫時性，包含保護性，之措施。而胎死腹中的1999海牙草約（Hague Conference -

93 [1998] AC 878.

94 Section 34: "No proceedings may be brought by a person in England and Wales or Northern Ireland on a cause of action in respect of which a judgment has been given in his favour in proceedings between the same parties, or their privies, in a court in another part of the United Kingdom or in a court of an overseas country, unless that judgment is not enforceable or entitled to recognition in England and Wales or, as the case may be, in Northern Ireland."

95 Article 31
Application may be made to the courts of a Member State for such provisional, including protective, measures as may be available under the law of that State, even if, under this Regulation, the courts of another Member State have jurisdiction as to the substance of the matter.

preliminary draft Convention on judgments）第13條[96]，除了規定對實體有管轄權法院及物之所在地法院得做成暫時性及保護性措施外，其他會員國法院亦得對訴訟中或可能被提起之實質請求做成暫時性保護措施，但其命令只能於域內被執行。而最具代表性的為2004年的ALI/UNIDROIT Principles of Transnational Civil Procedure 2.3條[97]：「即使對於爭執之糾紛法院沒有管轄權，一個法院仍得對法院地內之人或物做成暫時性之措施。」而其解釋報告P-2D[98]如此敘論：「2.3條承認一個國家得對位於境內之物行使假扣押或扣押之管轄權，而這種管轄之目的是例如為了保證將來可能之判決，即使該物並非該糾紛之標的或主體（實體）亦是如此。於有些法律制度有關位於域內之物之程序是稱為『準對物管轄』。2.3條是考慮到於這種案件下，所爭執的實體可能會於另一個法院中被審判。無形體之物之所在應依法院地所規定。」

對於保全處方之發展，個人不由得感嘆以前英國於加入歐盟前，判例法只能執行有關一確定數額之金錢債務（a definite sum of money）之外國判決[99]，且金額必須換入英國貨幣[100]。對於這種不符合市場需求及有違

---

[96] Article 13 Provisional and protective measures
1. A court having jurisdiction under Articles 3 to 12 to determine the merits of the case has jurisdiction to order any provisional or protective measures.
2. The courts of a State in which property is located have jurisdiction to order any provisional or protective measures in respect of that property.
3. A court of a Contracting State not having jurisdiction under paragraphs 1 or 2 may order provisional or protective measures, provided that –
a) their enforcement is limited to the territory of that State, and
b) their purpose is to protect on an interim basis a claim on the merits which is pending or to be brought by the requesting party.

[97] 2.3 A court may grant provisional measures with respect to a person or to property in the territory of the forum state, even if the court does not have jurisdiction over the controversy.

[98] P-2D "Principle 2.3 recognizes that a state may exercise jurisdiction by sequestration or attachment of locally situated property, for example to secure a potential judgment, even though the property is not the object or subject of the dispute. The procedure with respect to property locally situated is called 'quasi in rem jurisdiction' in some legal systems. Principle 2.3 contemplates that, in such a case, the merits of the underlying dispute might be adjudicated in some other forum. The location of intangible property should be ascribed according to forum law."

[99] 陳隆修，《國際私法管轄權評論》，台北，五南圖書公司，民國75年11月，初版，269-271頁。

[100] Sadler v. Rolins (1808) 1 Camp. 53.

公平正義的謹慎保守作法，個人年輕時還剴切的如此建議[101]：「英國只對外國有關一確定金錢債務之判決加以強制執行，固然可以適用於大部分案件，但此限制似乎過分狹窄。若外國法院判被告必須交付一於英國之動產則不能被強制執行，似乎不甚恰當，與不符合公平正義務之要求。台灣似乎應與歐洲判決公約一般，不只限於強制執行外國法院有關確定金錢債務之判決。」但是始料未及數十年後不但英國自加入歐盟後不得不執行其他非金錢債務之判決，而保全處分之執行更成為有些國際公約之必備條款。正如本書中個人所一再回首年輕時之建議，經常個人數十年前所提出之建議如若有過失之處，那就是時間經常證明個人早期之建議太過英國式的謹慎保守——但是個人還是感謝英國法律科學的血液基因，並且認為英國法律科學應是人類二十世紀文明之巔峰代表。對於跨國保全處分之能成為全球化法學之共同核心，無論是個人早期之建議、英國之接受跨國保全處分之請求、布魯塞爾規則31條、或ALI/UNIDROIT Principles of Transnational Civil Procedure 2.3條——個人於此再次請教美國最高法院，以上建議或法律之發展與掀起一片腥風血雨的「最低限度關連點」有何關連？

(三)物之所在為過度管轄及必要管轄之基礎

對於扣押管轄，如同Shaffer案中最高法院所表示「德州扣押程序所明示之目的就是去強迫被告親自出庭」，以及「做為在符合International Shoe下而於法院被提起之訴訟的判決之保證」。但是這兩個目的已在外國判決的較可能被承認下，及尤其是在跨國保全程序[102]已成為全球化法學

---

[101] 陳隆修，《國際私法管轄權評論》，台北，五南圖書公司，民國75年11月，初版，270、271頁。

[102] 民訴537條雖因審級關係而被取消，但個人年輕時對跨國保全程序之建議仍為現在本文所堅持，見陳隆修，《國際私法管轄權評論》，台北，五南圖書公司，民國75年11月，初版，153-155頁：「至於民事訴訟法第五二九條、第五三〇條及第五三七條，有關撤銷假扣押或假處分之命令而牽涉到本案管轄法院者，若台灣將這些法規亦適用於國際案件上，則很可能我國於此方面之法律為世界之最進步者。各國國際私法界似乎甚少〈或沒有〉論及此方面之法律關係者。例如民事訴訟法第五三七條規定；『由請求標的所在地之地方法院為假處分之裁定者，同時應定期間，命債權人向本案管轄法院聲請就假處分之當否為裁定。』『只要該外國本案法院願意接受』債權人之聲請，則作者認為本法規亦可適用於國際案件中。於國際案件中之債務人，自然應受到如同國內案件債務人之相同保護。但理論上，該外國本案法院之裁定不能拘束我國法

之共同核心政策後，這兩個目的已明顯的較不能成為扣押管轄之藉口。無論美國在準對物訴訟上之發展為何[103]，但與訴因無關之物之所在於法院地並不能構成該訴訟之管轄基礎，卻早已成為全球化法學之共同核心基本政策。事實上早期個人即對台灣民訴第3條[104]規定在台灣無住所之被告，以其可被扣押之財產所在做為因財產權訴訟之管轄基礎，在許多目前盛行的國際公約之前已對這個過度管轄提出如此建議[105]：「此管轄基礎於國際私法上可謂為已到了極端之管轄基礎。惟有美國之準對物訴訟之管轄基礎與台灣民訴第三條較有相似之處，然美國準對物訴訟之管轄基礎亦嚴格地限制於：(1)法院判決之範圍僅限於該標的物；(2)原告之請求與該標的物有關；及(3)必須符合『最低限度關連點』之要求。美國此以對物訴訟之管轄基礎，做為對人訴訟之管轄基礎，已為世界各國之最，故台灣民訴第三條若欲適用於國際案件上，似宜加修正。最根本之作法為台灣民事訴訟法似應增加對物訴訟之管轄基礎——亦即物之所在地法院對該物有管轄權。」

但是上述個人對台灣以對物管轄作為對人訴訟過度管轄基礎之建言並未被台灣所接受，對於台灣學術論文、國家考試、及司法判決的經常將此過度管轄視為天經地義之管轄，個人再度謙謙君子的按住火氣提醒台灣法

院，只有建議性。又如民事訴訟法第五二九條第一項規定：『本案尚未繫屬者，命假扣押之法院應依債務人聲請，命債權人於一定其間內起訴。』同樣的，於國際案件中債務人仍須受到與國內案件相同的保護。以上之建議，自然十分新潮與前進，但似乎並無不可之處。」另外於225頁中建議應接受跨國保全處分之請求：「於實務上，即使本訴訟發生於國外，台灣亦應准許財產地之法院，接受本訴訟原告之合理之請求，而對被告於法院地之財產加以保全處分方是。此規定於實務上對當事人甚為重要。」

103 見陳隆修，《國際私法管轄權評論》，台北，五南圖書公司，民國75年11月，初版，150-160頁。

104 第3條〈因財產權涉訴之特別審判籍〈一〉〉
I對於在中華民國憲無住所或住所不明之人，因財產權涉訴者，得由被告可扣押之財產或請求標的所在地之法院管轄。
II被告之財產或請求標的如為債權，以債務人住所或該債權擔保之標的所在地，視為被告財產或請求標的之所在地。

105 陳隆修，《國際私法管轄權評論》，台北，五南圖書公司，民國75年11月，初版，224、225頁。但於Burnham v. Superior Court, 495 U.S. 604(1990)後，個人發現對第(1)點現較少論及，或許是該案將最低限度關連點限制於被告不在法庭地內。另外歐洲人亦合理的批判，被告如果對實體加以答辯，則法院對該案之管轄經常就不限於標的物。

界及學術界如下[106]：「對於民訴第3條之評言很明顯的被忽略，此或許是因個人之建言完全以美國法為版本之故。衝突法為一國際法，沒有英美法與大陸法之分，無論於英國、美國或歐洲，任何不合時宜之作法皆會被時代的巨輪無情的輾過。事實上早期大陸法系如德[107]、奧[108]、等國亦有類似台灣民訴第3條之規定，國際私法界亦早有嚴苛之批評。例如經常被引用的例子為，一個外國旅客留一雙拖鞋於德國旅館，因留有財產於德國，故其所欠之十萬馬克債務可於德國被起訴[109]。台灣因政經及地理因素，於國際私法上經常歐美發生數十年後台灣才步其後塵，惟正因如此，所以更應將其經驗引為殷鑑」。

對於扣押管轄的以物之所在做為對人訴訟之過度管轄基礎，於國際上早已由學術上之撻伐，進入公約上之禁止階段。海牙會議1999年之草約18(2)(a)條[110]即將這個過度管轄列為禁止之第1項目：「(2)特別是，訂約國法院管轄權之行使不能只是依據下列之一個或數個管轄基礎——(a)被告於該國財產之所在或被扣押，但若該紛爭是直接與該財產有直接關連則為例外」。而歐盟早期的布魯賽爾公約及現今的布魯塞爾規則[111]皆於

---

106 陳隆修、許兆慶、林恩瑋、李瑞生四人合著，《國際私法-管轄與選法理論之交錯》，台北，五南圖書公司，2009年3月，初版1刷，179頁。但是如果現在個人再加以建言，則通常火辣的評語是「問台灣能有幾多野蠻無知之法學概念，恰似一江春水向東流」。這並非個人來日不多之故，而是個人三十年之謙忍，造成三十年正義之延宕。或許大陸同僚能參考這個台灣經驗——13億人可以等三十年嗎？

107 Art. 23. German Code of Civil Procedure.但的國現今要求必須有充除之關連點。BGH 2.7.1991, NJW 1991, 3092.

108 Para. 99, Austrian Jurisdiktionsnormen.

109 L.I. De Winter, Excessive Jurisdiction in Private International Law, 17 Int'l & Comp. L. Q. 706, 707 (1968).

110 Article 18 Prohibited grounds of jurisdiction

1. Where the defendant is habitually resident in a Contracting State, the application of a rule of jurisdiction provided for under the national law of Contracting State is prohibited if therer is no substantial connection between that State and the dispute.
2. In particular, jurisdiction shall not be exercised by the courts of a Contracting State on the basis solely of one or more of the following –

a) the presence or the seizure in that State of property belonging to the defendant, except where the dispute is directly related to that property.

111 Article 3

1. Persons domiciled in a Member State may be sued in the courts of another Member State only by virtue of the rules set out in Sections 2 to 7 of this Chapter.

第3條之附件一中禁止這個過度管轄。不但是國際公約或歐盟大陸法內部規則禁止這種過度管轄，事實上判例法的母法亦是沒有這種以物之所在做為對人管轄基礎。英國有關境外送達管轄基礎之Civil Procedure Rules 1998, s.6.20(10)[112]規定必須「請求之整個主體（實體）是有關位於境內之物」，法院才得允許通知被送達境外。故而以物（包括動產）之所在做為對人訴訟之管轄基礎，必須訴因與該物有關連（或應有直接關連）才不會於國際上被視為過度管轄。這種國際法上之共識早已為前輩同僚所提倡，更進而為歐盟布魯塞爾公約及規則所立法，為1999年海牙草約所明示，更重要的這亦是判例法母法於送達境外時所實施以久之法則。對於這個全球化的共同核心管轄規則的自然形成，個人請教美國同僚與美國最高法院——這個全球化共同核心管轄的形成與「最低限度關連點」有何關係？

---

2. In particular the rules of national jurisdiction set out in Annex I shall not be applicable as against them.

112 (10) the whole subject matter of a claim relates to property located within the jurisdiction.又見早期R.S.C., Ord 11, r 1(1)(i), "the claim is made for a debt secured in immovable property or is made to assert, declare or determine proprietary or possessory rights, or rights of security, in or over movable property, or to obtan authority to dispose of movable property, situate within the jurisdiction." Detusche National Bank v Paul [1898] 1 Ch 283.另外對於蘇格蘭及大陸法式之扣押管轄及美國之準對物訴訟，Cheshire and North直言：「英國法與這個理論保持距離，除非被告於英國時受到請求之通知或經由成文法規定所授予之權力被告於外國受到請求之通知，它堅持不可以對被告提起對人訴訟。」「但是實際上，被告於此地有財產及請求是有關該財產時，請求人通常是可能依11條去送達請求之通知至境外，或於境內找到一個合適的英國被告去加以送達。」P M North, JJ Fawcett, Cheshire and North's Private International Law, 13th ed., pp.323, 324, "A doctrine of arrestment ad fundandam jurisdictionem obtains in Scotland and in certain civil law countries under which an action may be brought against a person absent from the forum if movables situated there and belonging to him have been taken into the custody of the law at the instance of the claimant. The court can deal with a claim unconnected with the movables and deliver a personal judgment against the owner that will be wholly or partially satisfied by their sale. Another instance is the jurisdiction quast in rem that is recognised in the USA, which enables a personal claim against a defendant living abroad to be astisfied out of chattels owned by him but situated in the forum. Attachment of the chattels confers jurisdiction on the court of the situs, but any judgment that may be given is limited in its effect to the value of the property attached.
English law stands aloof from this doctrine. It insists that no action in personam will lie against a defendant unless he has been served with a claim form while present in England or unless by virtue of some statutory power a claim form has been served on him abroad……. If the claimant asserts some interest in or right to movables the position is very different. Although there is no separate basis of jurisdiction founded on the presence of movables in England, in practice, in cases where the defendant has assets here and the claim relates to those assets, it is often possible for the claimant either to serve a claim form out of the jurisdiction under Order 11 or to find a suitable English defendant upon whom a claim form can be served within the juisdiction." 14th ed., pp. 413, 414,對s.6.20(10)之說法更為保守。

(四)二十一世紀——管轄基礎與裁量權同步擴張

禁止過度管轄自然是二十世紀的重點，但個人以為二十一世紀全球化法學的重點是在確保個案正義。在這個崇高的目的下，不但應給予法院充分的裁量權，並且於必要時亦應擴大法院之必要管轄權。如同Shaffer法院所說：「汽車的來到，伴隨著依據Pennoyer並非受到對人訴訟管轄之人於一些州所造成傷害之增加，司法管轄權力於地域上之限制必須被加以修改。」這個論述是完全與個人前面引述Dicey and Morris之論述一致。Dicey and Morris認為隨著現代化之到來，法院不得不擴大其管轄權，並且於必要時應行使裁量權。個人並將這個論述作為英國法院放棄傳統上較謹慎之「困擾性或壓迫性」法學，而採納更且彈性之「不方便法院」法學之理由。個人並認為二十一世紀全球化管轄規則之趨勢為，法院不得不在確保個案正義下，擴大其必要之管轄權，並會被授予充分之裁量權行使範圍。個人認為這個二十一世紀全球化法學之代言人即為ALI/UNIDROIT Principles of Transnational Civil Procedure，其不但於2.5條採用「不方便法院」（其註解P-2F認為這種概念類似有些大陸法的防止濫用選擇法院），更與二十世紀末國際公約盛行的禁止「過度管轄」不同，其2.2條採用「必要管轄」之概念。其註解P-2C[113]認為「必要法院」之概念為「當

113 "Principle 2.2 covers the concept of 'forum necessitatis' – the forum of necessity whereby a court may properly exercise jurisdiction when no other forum is reasonably available."美國或許沒有明示「必要法院」之名詞，但這個「必要、預備管轄」之概念是充斥在American Law Institute之報告中。例如對於扣押管轄（物之所在為管轄基礎），見Restatement (Second) of Judgments, s. 8, comment (d), "Still another situation in which attachment jurisdiction may be appropriately exercised is that arising when a court in this country could not otherwise afford an adequate remedy to a plaintiff who should be allowed to sue here. Some foreign countries will not recognize some kinds of judgments rendered in this country, for example a judgment for taxes or penalties or a judgment based on contacts that the foreign country does not regard as a sufficient basis for in personam jurisdiction. In these situations, and perhaps others, it is the case both that a fully effective remedy should be available through the court systems of this country and that no such remedy is available in any single court. When that is the case, convenience of forum, which is the essence of the minimum contacts principle, should yield to remedial capability, which the rule of convenience ordinarily presupposes."以「身體所在」作為「必要法院」或「必要管轄」之概念，見Restatement of the Law, Second, Conflict of Laws, s. 28, comment (b), "Jurisdiction will be lacking, however, which the sole basis for its exercise is the momentary presence within the State of the individual involved unless the special circumstances of the case make its exercise reasonable. This might be so when jurisdiction could not conveniently be exercised over the individual in any other State of the United States. This might also be so when the objective of the action is to aid

沒有其他法院是合理的可被提起訴訟時，一個必要的法院就是一個得合適的行使管轄權之法院。」**因此個人認為UNIDROIT Principles的同時採納「不方便法院」，及將傳統上被列為過度管轄基礎之「所在」、「國籍」、及「物之所在」列為「必要管轄」之基礎[114]，即為全球化法學擴大法院管轄基礎並給予充分個案上之裁量權之代表。如個人較近所述[115]，於二十世紀的後半段歐盟與海牙會議忙著對過度管轄消極的加以撻伐及限制，倒不如積極的對過度管轄（特別是於境外管轄上）加以適度的合理規範。二十世紀後半段的重點或許是在禁止有些國家之法院藉由「過度管轄」而侵害到其他國家之主權及國際法之穩定性，但二十一世紀所形成之全球化法學之重點乃在確保個案正義以提高人類文明的層次。而於國際管轄上全球法學所賴以確保個案正義的，不外一面擴大法院之管轄基礎（例如必要管轄之設置），另一面則於需要之情形下給予法院充份裁量權[116]**

---

in the enforcement of a judgment obtained elsewhere, as when it is sought to enjoin the individual from disposing of his assets."另外以「住所」為例外之「必要法院」，見s.29, comment (b), "b. Unusual circumstances. Unusual circumstances, such as those mentioned in § 28, Comment b, might induce a court to hold that a person's purely technical domicil in a state affords a basis of jurisdiction even though such a finding of jurisdiction would not be made in the ordinary case. An example might be a situation where no other reasonably convenient forum would be available to the plaintiff in the United States."

[114] 2.2 Jurisdiction may also be exercised, when no other forum is reasonably available, on the basis of:
2.2.1 Presence or nationality of the defendant in the forum state; or
2.2.2 Presence in the forum state of the defendant's property, whether or not the dispute relates to the property, but the court's authority should be limited to the property or its value.

[115] 陳隆修、許兆慶、林恩瑋、李瑞生四人合著，《國際私法—管轄與選法理論之交錯》，台北，五南圖書公司，2009年3月，初版1刷，205頁。

[116] Shaffer案於美國掀起濤天巨浪，但於Burnham v. Superior Court, 495 U.S. 604(1990)被決定前，個人即與其時美國同僚不同，並不接受「所在權力」應被推翻，認為在達成個案正義之目的下，法院應有充分之管轄基礎及裁量權。如今時間還給個人一個公道，對於個人年輕時能與美國浪潮相抗衡，個人期望大陸同僚於創立中國式法學時，應記得中國文化對英雄出少年之寄望。見陳隆修，《國際私法管轄權評論》，台北，五南圖書公司，民國75年11月，初版，108-109頁。
「但是自Shaffer後，以「單一關連點」〈single contact〉為管轄權之依據，已被認為不構成充分之理由。故「短暫過境管轄權」〈transient jurisdiction〉的適用性於美國已受到懷疑。亦即若當事人皆非法院地之居民，且訴訟之原因〈cause of action〉亦與當事人之出現於〈present〉法院地無關，則法院是否有管轄權是值得懷疑。
美國法院本著英美法靈活而順應時勢之精神，為達成個案之公平正義，其豐富之創造力可能凌駕世界各國法院之上，但比起英國法院而言，其判例之穩定性則大為遜色。Shaffer一案之解釋及其是否能長久的保持其判例法之拘束力，實令人不敢輕易斷言。但英國基於當事人所在〈persence〉之管轄基礎，或者會被歐陸國家認為太廣泛，並且為歐洲判決公約所不採，Shaffer一案若能對此英美法傳統上之對人訴訟管轄基礎加以適當之限制，則未嘗不是一項折衷之提

（例如方便與不方便法院及防止濫訴）。二十世紀法學於此方面之重點在於禁止過度管轄，而二十一世紀全球化法學之重點則在如何恰當的行使裁量權，並於必要時利用這些被視為過度管轄[117]之基礎以確保個案正義。

如上個註解所述，個人自年輕時即對美國的「不默守英國成規」而感覺不安。「最低限度關連點」的造成美國法制的混亂是美國同僚的家務事，但這個理論的無助於全球化管轄規則是應該被加以重度譴責的。**其之所謂「最低限度關連點」之憲法最低限度要求，則因其只為「最低要求」故可輕易的為傳統的管轄基礎所輕易滿足，例如契約履行地、侵權行為地、不當得利地、代理人行為地等長久以來即為全世界國際法所共同接受、認可之管轄基礎。這個論點由上述個人仔細的逐一翻譯歐盟布魯塞爾規則第5條、英國送達境外的CPR 1998, s. 6.20，及UNIDROIT Principles 2.1.2條的「重大關連」管轄基礎可以印證。契約履行地、侵權行為地、不當得利地、代理人行為地等各國國內法特別管轄基礎不但為歐盟**

議，而可為各國所採用。

但實際上，作者仍傾向於傳統之英國理論，並認為美國較嚴謹之作法只應適用於範圍較窄之聯邦體系。於國際場合上，由於世界各國之國際私法無法統一，法院似乎仍應有適當之管轄基礎，並應有裁量權以決定其是否欲對某個案加以主持正義。應注意的是，美國理論之『所在權力』管轄權之基礎，不若英國之限制於對人訴訟，而及於對物訴訟。更尤其美國之準對物訴訟中，可以財產位於法院地，而對被告提起對人訴訟，此為美國所獨創之對人對物混合訴訟，其所賦予法院之管轄權未免太過於廣泛，故不得不以Shaffer限制之。故作者認為Shaffer之效力不應與對人訴訟之基礎有關，而應適用於準對物訴訟中，限制原告所提起之對人訴訟必須與被告於法院地之財產有關。總之，作者直覺上認為美國不默守英國成規，而獨創準對物訴訟，如今不得不以Shaffer來限制其發展。由此可見縱然富強如美國者，於法律學術上既要創新，又想求穩定，亦深感困難與迷惑。」

117 有些大陸法主張「特別分配」管轄，例如2004年比利時法典第11條：「於本法規定之外，當訴訟顯示與比利時有緊密連繫，而外國法律程序顯示不可能進行，或不能合理地要求訴訟得於外國提出者，比利時法院例外地有管轄權。」Art. 11. Nonobstant les autres dispositions de la présente loi, les juridiction belges sont exceptionnellement compétentes lorsque la cause présente des liens étroits avec la Belgique et qu'une procedure à l'étranger se révèle impossible ou qu'on ne peut raisonnablement exiger que la demande soit formée à l'étranger.以上翻譯引自林思緯，國際管轄權理論的法典法省思，財產法暨經濟法第4期，205頁。所謂與「比利時有緊密連繫」通常即可能符合傳統「重大管轄」之管轄基礎，故而「特別分配管轄」與「必要管轄」於此方面可能是不一致的。個人認為「方便與不方便法院」之重點是於正義之需求下，法院對於管轄權之行使得依此需要而加以裁量是較符合21世紀之作法。但「方便與不方便法院」之行使，仍須本著既有之管轄基礎，故「必要管轄」仍有需要。比利時這個「緊密關連」與法國判例法上在「剩餘管轄」之「某些關連」〈certains liens〉之要件上，於字面上似乎不完全一致。以上為個人與林教授之共同見解。法國判例見V. Civ. 1rc, 7 janv. 1982 *Rev. Crit.* DIP 1983.87, note Ancel; 16 avril 1985, Rev. crit. DIP 1986.694, note Batiffol.

及其他國際公約所接受，亦為英國對外送達之CPR 1998, s. 6.20及美國各州對外送達之長手法規[118]所共同接受與執行之共同管轄基礎，而這些人類文明社會長久以來之共同傳統上之管轄基礎，亦應滿足較近2004年之UNIDROIT Principles於2.1.2條中所規定的「重大（或實質）關連」之要求。這些傳統上全世界文明國家所共同接受之「重大（或實質）關連」之管轄基礎，自然是輕易的能滿足美國最高法院管轄規則上「最低」限度關連點之要求。 因此或許最低限度關連點只能與聯邦間州際憲政權力之劃分有關，對美國州際間國際私法上個案正義之追求無所助益。個人於此再次不客氣的直接請教美國最高法院——對於國際間傳統上盛行已久之「重大（實質）關連」管轄基礎之國際管轄規則上之全球化共同核心之存在，「最低限度關連點」與這個可能已存在數百年之共同核心有何關連？

針對傳統上之「重大（實質）關連」管轄基礎，「最低限度關連點」之要求，看起來似乎是傾向放寬管轄基礎之要件，但事實上Shaffer案卻是對「所在權力」及「扣押管轄」欲圖加以限制，這種作法認真而言是不甚符合邏輯。或許美國最高法院於潛意識中亦知道「最低限度」關連點不足以取代傳統上的「重大關連」管轄基礎，只是針對二十世紀中一般所詬病的「所在權力」及「扣押管轄」加以限制。如果美國最高法院意圖

---

[118] 陳隆修，《國際私法管轄權評論》，台北，五南圖書公司，民國75年11月，初版，136-147頁。另外，Restatement, Second, Conliclt of Laws § 27所規定的州對人司法管轄基礎亦是大致上類似：

(1) A state has power to exercise judicial jurisdiction over an individual on one or more of the following bases:

(a) presence
(b) domicil
(c) residence
(d) nationality or citizenship
(e) consent
(d) appearance in an acton
(g) doing business in the state
(h) an act done in the state
(i) causing an effect in the state by an act done elsewhere
(j) ownership, use or possession of a thing in the state
(k) other relationships to the state which make the exercise of judicial jurisdiction reasonable.

(2) The circumstances in which, and the extent to which, these bases are sufficient to support an exercise of judicial jurisdiction over an individual are stated in §§ 28-39.

如此，那麼實在沒有必要創設一個「鬼打牆法學」的最低限度關連點。二十世紀後半段國際私法界的全民運動就是一窩蜂的討伐「過度管轄」，美國最高法院其實只要名正言順的加入二十世紀的潮流即可。

至於「傳統上公平及實質正義的概念」的被引用，這個自然法的概念事實上亦是訴訟法上的共同核心。達成正義的目的是母法英國判例法於「方便與不方便法院」、「一事不再理」、「禁反言」、「禁止濫訴」、及限制「否認之訴」之核心概念，個人亦相信應為大陸法的「選購法院」、「誠信原則」、「禁止濫訴」、及「規避法律」上之核心概念。無論於實體法或程序法上[119]，這個自然法的概念長久以來都是實證法於判例運用中強而有力之武器。「傳統上公平與實質正義」的衡平概念，於國際訴訟上個人以為藉由現今之「方便與不方便法院」法學於許多地方皆可達成基本正義之目的。

或許「最低限度關連點」由實際上執行之效果而言可能近似「鬼打牆法學」，但或許由理想而言它可能是國際私法史上最羅曼蒂克的嘗試之一。或許於潛意識中美國最高法院企圖以「最低限度關連點」合理化傳統上之「重大（實質）關連」，排除「過度管轄」，並或許可能藉此給予法院較為彈性的裁量權。但傳統上之「重大關連」管轄基礎至少百年來皆為國內及過際訴訟法界所接受，而「過度管轄」之限制又為上世紀後半段所公認，至於有關彈性裁量權之給予先前已有「困擾性或壓迫性」法學，現又為「方便與不方便法院」法學所得以發揮功能。如果美國最高法院真的企圖以單一「最低限度關連點」法學來達成三種南轅北轍的目標，那就變

[119] 433 U.S. 186, 215, "But we have rejected the argument that if a State's law can properly be applied to a dispute, its courts necessarily have jurisdiction over the parties to that dispute. '[The State] does not acquire… jurisdiction by being the 'center of gravity' of the controversy, or the most convenient location for litigation. The issue is personal jurisdiction, not choice of law. It is resolved in this case by considering the acts of the [appellants].' Hanson v. Denckla, 357 U.S. 235, 254 (1958).對於美國法界及學界一再信誓旦旦的同意準據法的適用，不等於該州即享有管轄權。個人卻一再主張準據法的適用，即應為管轄權的重要考慮因素。這種情形見諸於英美法院經常以法院地為婚姻準據法、監護權之準據法上。又英國CPR 1998, s. 6.20亦規定契約準據法為英國法時得送達境外。另外於美國及英國之不方便法院之運用，準據法是否為法院是否為法院地法為一重要考量。

成國際法界的「唐吉軻德法學」。

五、Burnham v. Superior Court

(一)案件

於Shaffer後許多美國同僚懷疑，並或贊同，所在權力之基礎是否應被推翻。但1990年之Burnham v. Superior Court[120]則於驚濤駭浪中終於確定「最低限度關連點」只有適用於被告不在法院地而主張之管轄權基礎，而與於法院地受到送達之被告之管轄權無關。於案中上訴人Burnham先生與其太太住於紐澤西，於其太太搬至加利福尼亞前雙方同意女方會以「無法協調」而提出離婚之訴。但之後上訴人以「遺棄」而於紐州提起離婚之訴，可是並未將通知送達至其太太。女方隨後於加州提起離婚之訴。後來上訴人因商務旅行而去加州，並專程探視小孩，於渡完週末假期送還小孩時，收到女方於加州所提起離婚訴訟之通知。上訴人「特別出席」（a special appearance）加州法院，主張其只是為了商業及探視小孩短暫造訪加州，故加州法院缺乏對人管轄權而該送達應為無效。加州高等及上訴法院皆拒絕接受其與加州缺乏最低限度關連點並受到適當條款限制之抗辯。美國最高法院接受加州法院之見解。

Scalia J.代表其他三位大法官敘述法院之意見[121]：「這裡的問題是對於一個短暫停留於一個州之非居民加以親自送達，而訴訟是與其於該州之行為無關之訴訟中，14修正案之適當程序條款是否拒絕給予該州管轄權。」對於Pennoyer的「所在權力」International Shoe是認為只要不違反「傳統上公平與實質正義的概念」即符合適當程序條款。「我們認為這種脫離是可以被允許的，但應只限於是由於與缺席的被告於該州之關連所引起之訴訟而已。今日我們所必須決定的是當被告被送達時其身體所在於

---

[120] 495 U.S. 604 (1990).

[121] "The question presented is whether the Due Process Clause of the Fourteenth Amendment denies California courts jurisdiction over a nonresident, who was personally served with process while temporarily in that State, in a suit unrelated to his activities in the State."

該州時，是否適當程序要求被告與該州之關連以及訴訟間應有著同樣的牽連[122]。」

法院認為[123]：「於美國傳統上有關對人訴訟上所已最為堅定的被建立之原則即為一個州的法院對於身體所在於該州的非居民有著管轄權。早期所發展的見解是對於任何於州境內之個人每個州法院有著權力去將其強拖至法院，並且在經由合適的送達而對其取得管轄權後，無論其之造訪是如何的短暫，該州能保留對其不利判決之管轄權……」因此對於上訴人依據International Shoe的標準，主張在缺乏與法院地有著「持續而制度性」的關連時，非居民被告只能在與其於法院地之關連點有關之事情上受到判決，法院認為：「這個抗辯是根據對我們判例的完全誤解而來[124]。」

法院又說[125]：「但是於後面的年代卻見證了Pennoyer規則的減弱。於

---

122 "That criterion was first announced in Pennoyer v. Neff, supra, in which we stated that due process 'mean[s] a course of legal proceedings according to those rules and principles which have been established in our systems of jurisprudence for the protection and enforcement of private rights,' including the 'well-established principles of public law respecting the jurisdiction of an independent State over persons and property.' In what has become the classic expression of the criterion, we said in International Shoe Co. v. Washington, that a state court's assertion of personal jurisdiction satisfies the Due Process Clause if it does not violate 'traditional notions of fair play and substantial justice.' Since International Shoe, we have only been called upon to decided whether these 'traditional notions' permit State to exercise jurisdiction over absent defendants in a manner that deviates from the rules of jurisdiction applied in the 19th century. We have held such deviations permissible, but only with respect to suits arising out of the absent defendant's contacts with the State. The question we must decided today is whether due process requires a similar connection between the litigation and the defendant's contacts with the State in cases where the defendant is physically present in the State at the time process is served upon him."

123 Among the most firmly established principles of personal jurisdiction in American tradition is that the courts of a State have jurisdiction over nonresidents who are physically present in the State. The view developed early that each State had the power to hale before its courts any individual who could be found within its borders, and that once having acquired jurisdiction over such a person by properly serving him with process, the State could retain jurisdiction to enter judgment against him, no matte how fleeting his visit⋯.

124 "Despite this formidable body of precedent, petitioner contends, in reliance on our decisions applying the International Shoe standard, that in the absence of 'continuous and systematic' contacts with the forum, a nonresident defendant can be subjected to judgment only as to matters that arise out of or relate to his contacts with the forum. This argument rests on a thorough misunderstanding of our cases."

125 "Later years, however, saw the weakening of the Pennoyer rule. In the late 19th and early 20th centuries, changes in the technology of transportation and communication, and the tremendous growth of interstate business activity, led to an 'inevitable relaxation of the strict limits on state jurisdiction' over nonresident individuals and corporations⋯. Nothing in International Shoe or the cases that have followed it, however offers support for the very different proposition petitioner seeks to establish today: that a defendant's presence in the forum is not only unnecessary to validate novel, nontraditional as-

十九世紀末及二十世紀初，交通及通訊技術的改變，及州際商業行為的大量增加，造成一個對非居民個人及公司在州管轄權上嚴格之限制的不可避免的寬鬆情形。……但是International Shoe或根據其而來之判例們並未支持今日上訴人所企圖建立之非常不同之建議：被告於法院地之所在不只對於新奇、非傳統上管轄權之主張之有效性是為沒有必要的，而且其本身亦不足以構成管轄基礎。這個建議對我們於適當程序上的法理而言是同時在基礎及基本邏輯上不忠實的……」因此法院明確的再次維護傳統的「所在權力」規則如下[126]：「簡言之只是根據身體所在而來之管轄權就能符合適當程序，這是依據我們在法律制度上之繼續性的傳統之一，對於『傳統上公平與實質正義的概念』在適當程序上之標準的定義。這個標準之發展是與『身體所在』相比擬，並且如果說其現在可以被反過來對抗這個管轄權的試金石是會造成詭異的情形的。」

法院亦拒絕上訴人基於Shaffer而來之抗辯[127]：「請求人所抗辯的是太為超過，其主張Shaffer規則應是除非訴訟是基於一個人於州內之行為，否則該州對該個人缺乏管轄權。正如International Shoe一般，Shaffer所牽連的是對缺席被告之管轄權，而其所代表的只是一個建議，亦即當『最低限度關連點』是包含財產之所有權時，在做為身體所在之替代時，其必須如同其他之最低限度關連點般的與訴訟有關連。」並且認為上訴人對於Shaffer「所有的州法院管轄之主張應依International Shoe及其後來判決

---

sertions of jurisdiction, but is itself no longer sufficient to establish jurisdiction. That proposition is unfaithful to both elementary logic and the foundations of our due process jurisprudence…"

126 "The short of the matter is that jurisdiction based on physical presence alone constitutes due process because it is one of the continuing traditions of our legal system that define the due process standard of 'traditional notions of fair play and substantial justice.' That standard was developed by analogy to 'physical presence,' and it would be perverse to say it could now be turned against that touchstone of jurisdiction."

127 "It goes too far to say, as petitioner contends, that Shaffer compels the conclusion that a State lacks jurisdiction over an individual unless the litigation arises out of his activities in the State. Shaffer, like International Shoe, involved jurisdiction over an absent defendant, and it stands for nothing more than the proposition that when the 'minimum contact' that is a substitute for physical presence consists of property ownership it must, like other minimum contacts, be related to the litigation. Petitioner wrenches out of its context our statement in Shaffer that 'all assertions of state-court jurisdiction must be evaluated according to the standards set forth in International Shoe and its progeny.'…"

所規定之標準而被評量」之論述是與主文（判決）不合。又說[128]：「換言之，Shaffer並不是說對人訴訟管轄基礎（推定上應包括州內送達在內）之所有主張必須一視同仁，及必須受到International Shoe『最低關連點』分析的限制；而是假設性的『古代形式』之準對物訴訟及對人訴訟於實際上是相同的並且必須被加以相同的對待——其結果是準對物訴訟，亦即根據『物之所有權』關連點之對人訴訟之形式及於定義上是沒有伴隨著州內之親自被送達，必須滿足International Shoe之與訴訟有關連之要求。Shaffer規則之邏輯——無論一個特定關連的基礎是否有著一個獨立的拉丁名稱附著，對於對抗所有缺席之非居民之訴訟應被置於相同的憲法基準上——並無法被牽強的得到一個結論，亦即身體所在於法院地之被告應與缺席不在之被告被加以相同之對待……」

但是非常有趣的是法院坦白承認其基本概念上之與Shaffer不同，但其將問題交由國會，而不願做任何變動[129]：「但是持平而論，雖然我們今

128 "Shaffer was saying, in other words, not that all bases for the assertion of in personam jurisdiction (including, presumably, in-state service) must be treated alike and subjected to the 'minimum contacts' analysis of International Shoe; but rather that quasi in rem jurisdiction, that fictional 'ancient form,' and in personam jurisdiction, are really one and the same and must be treated alike – leading to the conclusion that quasi in rem jurisdiction, i.e., that form of in personam jurisdiction based upon a 'property ownership' contact and by definition unaccompanied by personal, in-state service, must satisfy the litigation-relatedness requirement of International Shoe. The logic of Shaffer's holding – which places all suits against absent nonresidents on the same constitutional footing, regardless of whether a separate Latin label is attached to one particular basis of contact – does not compel the conclusion that physically present defendants must be treated identically to absent ones…"

129 "It is fair to say, however, that while our holding today does not contradict Shaffer, our basic approach to the due process question is different. We have conducted no independent inquiry into the desirability or fairness of the prevailing in-state service rule, leaving that judgment to the legislatures that are free to amend it; for our purposes, its validation is its pedigree, as the phrase 'traditional notions of fair play and substantial justice' makes clear. Shaffer did conduct such an independent inquiry, asserting that 'traditional notions of fair play and substantial justice' can be as readily offended by the perpetuation of ancient forms that are no longer justified as by the adoption of new procedures that are inconsistent with the basic values of our constitutional heritage.' Perhaps that assertion can be sustained when the 'perpetuation of ancient forms' is engaged in by only a very small minority of the States. Where, however, as in the present case, a jurisdictional principle is both firmly approved by tradition and still favored, it is impossible to imagine what standard we could appeal to for the judgment that it is 'no longer justified.' While in no way receding from or casting doubt upon the holding of Shaffer or any other case, we reaffirm today our time-honored approach. For new procedures, hitherto unknown, the Due Process clause requires analysis to determine whether 'traditional notions of fair play and substantial justice' have been offended. But a doctrine of personal jurisdiction that dates back to the adoption of the Four-

日的認定並未與Shaffer相衝突，但是對於適當程序的問題上之基本概念是不一樣的。我們對於盛行的境內送達規則之公平性或妥適性並未進行獨立的調查，而將其交由會議去作判斷，以使議會能自由的去作修正；為了我們所需的目的下，如同『傳統上公平與實質正義的概念』之名詞本身就解釋得很清楚，其之歷史上之起源就使得其有效。而Shaffer確有進行這種獨立的調查，其主張『正如同採用與我們憲法傳統上之基本價值不一致之新程序一般，「傳統上之公平與實質正義之概念」可以明顯的被已經不再合理的古老程序之執行而被侵犯。』或許於當只有一個非常少數的州是採用這種『古老的程序之執行』時，這樣的主張是有效的。可是當如同於本案件中，一個管轄原則是同時被傳統所堅定的支持及在目前亦被認可著，這是無法想像我們能根據什麼標準去作成其『不再合理』之判斷。雖然於事實上並未從Shaffer或其他案件之判決中退縮或加以懷疑，我們今日卻再次確認一個我們已經被時間所證明之概念。截至目前為止我們幾乎不知道有任何新程序必須以適當程序之分析去決定『傳統上公平與實質正義的概念』是否被侵犯。但是一個對人訴訟之法則其日期是可以回溯至十四修正案被通過之時，並且至今是通常被遵守著，毫無疑問的符合這個標準。」

White J.對Scalia J.代表法院之論述作出贊同意見[130]：「即使沒有其他關連，允許法院去對非居民於法院地州內以親自送達而取得管轄之規則，

teenth Amendment and is still generally observed unquestionably meets that standard."

130 "The rule allowing jurisdiction to be obtained over a nonresident by personal service in the forum State, without more, has been and is so widely accepted throughout this country that I could not possibly strike it down, either on its face or as applied in this case, on the ground that it denies due process of law guaranteed by the Fourteenth Amendment. Although the Court has the authority under the Amendment to examine even traditionally accepted procedures and declare them invalid, there has been no showing here or elsewhere that as a general proposition the rule is so arbitrary and lacking in common sense in so many instances that it should be held violative of due process in every case. Furthermore, until such a showing is made, which would be difficult indeed, claims in individual cases that the rule would operate unfairly as applied to the particular nonresident involved need not be entertained. At least this would be the case where presence in the forum State is intentional, which would almost always be the fact. Otherwise, there would be endless, fact-specific litigation in the trial and appellate courts, including this one. Here, personal service in California, without more, is enough, and I agree that the judgment should be affirmed."

是於這個國家內非常廣泛的於過去及現在所被接受，因此無論於表面上或於本案之適用上，我皆不可能以其違反十四修正案所保障的法律上之適當程序去否定其適法性。」「這裡或其他地方並沒有證據顯示，做為一個基本法則這個規則在許多例子中是如此的獨斷及缺乏常識，以至於其應於每一個案件中被認定為違反適當程序。」「至少於所在於法院地之情形是故意的情形下應是如此，而通常幾乎皆是如此之情形。否則於第一審及上訴審，包含本案在內，會有著無盡止的特定事實之訴訟。在這裡即使是於沒有其他關連下，於加州之親自送達已是足夠，我同意判決應被加以維持。」

Brennan J.雖然認同判決，但其代表另外三位大法官對Scalia J.的論述並未完全認同，加以評述如下[131]：「我同意Scalia J.的意見，亦即十四修正案的適當程序條款在被告志願的所在於法院地州而被加以送達時，通常會允許該州法院對其行使管轄權。但是我並不認為有需要去決定，就只因為其『起源』於一個『非常長久以來就是這個土地於事實上之法律』之管轄規則，就自動符合適當程序法。雖然我同意於建立一個管轄規則是否符合適當程序之要件時歷史是個重要的因素，我不能承認它是唯一的因素，以至造成所有的傳統管轄規則皆永遠符合憲法的事情。不同於Scalia J.，我會行使一個『獨立的調查……去查明現在盛行的境內送達規則之公平性』。因此我只能同意於判決之部分。」Brennan J.又說[132]：「我相信

131 "I agree with JUSTICE SCALIA that the Due Process Clause of the Fourteenth Amendment generally permits a state court to exercise jurisdiction over a defendant if he is served with process while voluntarily present in the forum State. I do not perceive the need, however, to decide that a jurisdictional rule that 'has been immemorially the actual law of the land,' automatically comports with due process simply by virtue of its 'pedigree.' Although I agree that history is an important factor in establishing whether a jurisdictional rule satisfies due process requirements, I cannot agree that it is the only factor such that all traditional rules of jurisdiction are, ipso facto, forever constitutional. Unlike JUSTICE SCALIA, I would undertake an 'independent inquiry into the ⋯ fairness of the prevailing in-state service rule.' I therefore concur only in the judgment."其使用「過境管轄」名詞，並加以定義如下：" I use the term 'transient jurisdiction' to refer to jurisdiction premised solely on the fact that a person is served with process while physically present in the forum State."

132 "I believe that the approach adopted by JUSTICE SCALIA's opinion today -- reliance solely on historical pedigree -- is foreclosed by our decisions in International Shoe Co. v. Washington. In International Shoe, we held that a state court's assertion of personal jurisdiction does not violate the Due Process

今日Scalia J.之論述所採用之方式——完全依賴歷史之起源——是被我們於International Shoe之決定所終結。於International Shoe我們認定一個州法院在對人訴訟之主張如果符合『傳統上公平與實質正義之概念』則不會違反適當程序條款。於Shaffer，我們說『所有州法院管轄之主張必須依International Shoe及其後續判例所規定之標準而被衡量。』Shaffer批評性之見解即為所有之管轄規則，即使是古老的規則，必須符合適當程序於現代之觀念。對於『所在權力就是管轄權之基礎』及『對於其境內之人及物每一州皆擁有專屬管轄及主權』之宣示，我們在管轄權上之分析再也不會只是受限於這些宣示而已。……我同意這個方式並且繼續相信『於International Shoe中所發展之最低限度關連點分析……比起Pennoyer判決中所產生之法律及事實上假設之碎片式理論，代表著一個對州法院管轄權行使之遠較為合理之解釋』。」

(二)鬼打牆法學

但是令人訝異的是在Brennan J.根據International Shoe及Shaffer而對Pennoyer所代表的「所在權力」大肆加以強烈反對後，亦並且堅決的重申「所有州法院管轄之主張必須依International Shoe 及其後續判例所規定之標準而被衡量」，他的態度卻大為逆轉。於引用Story J.認為過境管轄之「創世紀是個神話」，並且認為其規則之歷史「起源」是受到懷疑的

Clause if it is consistent with 'traditional notions of fair play and substantial justice.' In Shaffer, we stated that 'all assertions of state-court jurisdiction must be evaluated according to the standards set forth in International Shoe and its progeny.' The critical insight of Shaffer is that all rules of jurisdiction, even ancient ones, must satisfy contemporary notions of due process. No longer were we content to limit our jurisdictional analysis to pronouncements that '[t]he foundation of jurisdiction is physical power,' and that 'every State possesses exclusive jurisdiction and sovereignty over persons and property within its territory.' While acknowledging that 'history must be considered as supporting the proposition that jurisdiction based solely on the presence of property satisfie[d] the demands of due process,' we found that this factor could not be 'decisive.' We recognized that '[t]raditional notions of fair play and substantial justice' can be as readily offended by the perpetuation of ancient forms that are no longer justified as by the adoption of new procedures that are inconsistent with the basic values of our constitutional heritage.' I agree with this approach and continue to believe that 'the minimum-contacts analysis developed in International Shoe··· represents a far more sensible construct for the exercise of state-court jurisdiction than the patchwork of legal and factual fictions that has been generated from the decision in Pennoyer v. Neff.'···"

之後，他又大迴轉的認為[133]：「過境管轄是與正當期待一致的，並且應該受到其是符合適當程序之強烈假設。」並加以如此的解釋[134]：「於拜訪法院地後，一個過境的被告事實上是已『利用』到該州所提供的重大利益。他的健康及安全是受到該州之警察、消防、及緊急醫療服務之保障；他可以自由的在該州的公路及水道旅行；他很可能亦享受到該州之經濟的果實。並且憲法第四條特權及豁免條款禁止州政府去經由拒絕被告其法律之保護或訴之其法院而對過境被告加以歧視。除了於不方便法院之限制外，一個外州原告得如州之公民般的利用州法院之情形下的使用州法院。如果沒有過境管轄，一個不均衡會發生：一個過境者會於法院地之州法院內有著原告權力之完全利益，但作為被告卻對州法院之權力享有豁免權。」最後Brennan J.對過境管轄加以合理化[135]：「對過境被告所可能產生之負擔是輕微的。『現代的交通及通訊已經使得一個被起訴之當事人在其居所地外之州去提起抗辯較為不困難。』被告已經至少旅行至法院地一次——這已如其在當地被加以送達的事實所證明——是一種於法院地之訴訟應可能

[133] "Regardless of whether Justice Story's account of the rule's genesis is mythical, our common understanding now, fortified by a century of judicial practice, is that jurisdiction is often a function of geography. The transient rule is consistent with reasonable expectations and is entitled to a strong presumption that it comports with due process. 'If I visit another State, … I knowingly assume some risk that the State will exercise its power over my property or my person while there. My contact with the State, though minimal, gives rise to predictable risks.'"

[134] "By visiting the forum State, a transient defendant actually 'avail[s]' himself, of significant benefits provided by the State. His health and safety are guaranteed by the State's police, fire, and emergency medical services; he is free to travel on the State's roads and waterways; he likely enjoys the fruits of the State's economy as well. Moreover, the Privileges and Immunities Clause of Article IV prevents a state government from discriminating against a transient defendant by denying him the protections of its law or the right of access to its courts. Subject only to the doctrine of forum non conveniens, an out-of-state plaintiff may use state courts in all circumstances in which those courts would be available to state citizens. Without transient jurisdiction, an asymmetry would arise: A transient would have the full benefit of the power of the forum State's courts as a plaintiff while retaining immunity from their authority as a defendant."

[135] "The potential burdens on a transient defendant are slight. '[M]odern transportation and communications have made it much less burdensome for a party sued to defend himself' in a State outside his place of residence. That the defendant has already journeyed at least once before to the forum – as evidenced by the fact that he was served with process there – is an indication that suit in the forum likely would not be prohibitively inconvenient. Finally, any burdens that do arise can be ameliorated by a variety of procedural devices. For these reasons, as a rule the exercise of personal jurisdiction over a defendant based on his voluntary presence in the forum will satisfy the requirements of due process."

不會過分的不方便之顯示。最後所發生的任何負擔可能會被各種的程序上之規定所減輕。基於這些理由，做為一個法規本於被告自願性的出現在法院地而行使的對被告之對人管轄是符合適當程序的要件。」

對Brennan J.的強烈意見Scalia J.只是繼續打傳統牌[136]：「依其自己的用語，如果一個州法院堅守著被通常所被適用及已經一直在美國所被適用之管轄規則則該標準已被滿足。」故而對適當程序條款上之「傳統上公平與實質正義的概念」是否應「符合適當程序於現代之觀念」，兩邊各有4位大法官持不同的意見。但是Stevens J.雖然同意案件之判決，並未加入討論。因為其認為上述大法官之討論[137]：「全部集合起來證明這的確是一個非常簡單的案件。」

無論是否於表面上是個簡單的案件，很明顯的兩派不同意見之大法官對於「所在權力」之是否「必須符合適當程序於現代之觀念」（個人認為可能通常應是指「最低限度關連點」）是有著對立之強烈意見。Scalia J.是忠實的傳統「所在權力」之支持者：「簡言之只是根據身體所在而來之管轄權就能符合適當程序，這是依據我們在法律制度上之繼續性的傳統之一，對於『傳統上公平與實質正義之概念』在適當程序上之標準的定義。」但是Brennan J.則對Scalia J.之論述直接加以正面挑戰：「我相信今日Scalia J.之論述所採用之方式——完全依賴歷史之起源——是被我們於International Shoe之決定所終結。」而對「所在權力」更是公開否認其之不可限制性：「對於『所在權力就是管轄權之基礎』及『對於其境內之人及物每一州皆擁有專屬管轄及主權』之宣示，我們在管轄權上之分析再也不會只是受限於這些宣示而已。」更令人吃驚的是Brennan J.居然暗示，或著已是十足的明示，「最低限度關連點」應凌駕，或者可能應取

136 "The 'contemporary notions of due process' applicable to personal jurisdiction are the enduring 'traditional notions of fair play and substantial justice' established as the test by International Shoe. By its very language, that test is satisfied if a state court adheres to jurisdictional rules that are generally applied and have always been applied in the United States."

137 "For me, it is sufficient to note that the historical evidence and consensus identified by JUSTICE SCALIA, the considerations of fairness identified by JUSTICE BRENNAN, and the common sense displayed by JUSTICE WHITE, all combine to demonstrate that this is, indeed, a very easy case."

代，「所在權力」之傳統管轄基礎：「我同意這個方式並繼續相信『於International Shoe中所發展之最低限度關連點分析……比起Pennoyer判決中所產生之法律及事實上假設之碎片式理論，代表著一個對州法院管轄權行使之遠較為合理之解釋』。」

在Brennan J.火力全開的主張International Shoe 中所發展之「最低限度關連點」可能應凌駕於Pennoyer所代表之「所在權力」後，他的結論是令人跌破眼鏡的。於合理化過境管轄後，其自以為聰明的對「所在權力」加以其自認為的適度「修正」：「基於這些理由，做為一個法規本於被告自願性的出現在法院地而行使的對被告之對人管轄是符合適當程序的要件。」換句話說在Brennan J.對Pennoyer的「所在權力」加以大肆批評，並加以「修正」後，Brennan J.與Scalia J.所代表的兩派法官皆認同以「所在權力」為基礎而「行使的對被告之對人管轄是符合適當程序之要件」。這兩派對「所在權力」管轄基礎行使之不同就只有表現於——Brennan J.要求非居民被告「自願性的出現在法院地」，而Scalia J.則遵守傳統的並未加以限制。但是Brennan J.真的有對「所在權力」加以修正嗎？Brennan J.派與Scalia J.派兩派大法官真的對「所在權力」管轄基礎之行使有歧異嗎？做為一個國際私法的同僚個人對美國最高法院於此說一聲——拜託（please）。

美國法律協會（The American Law Institute）早在本案之前已陳述一個為美國及全世界所有文明國家所共同承認之一個全球化法學之共同核心。其Restatement （Second） of Conflict of Laws § 82 （1971）規定[138]：「如果對一個被告或其財產之司法管轄權之取得，是經由詐欺或非法之暴力，則該州不能行使管轄權。」其comment (a)說[139]：「一個人不能被允許經由詐欺或非法暴力而取得利益。當原告可能是透過這種方法

[138] "A state will not exercise judicial jurisdiction, which has been obtained by fraud or unlawful force, over a defendant or his property."

[139] a. Rationale. A person is not permitted to profit from his use of fraud or unlawful force. A state will refuse to exercise such judicial jurisdiction as the plaintiff may obtain by such means over the defendant or his property.

而對被告或其物取得這種司法管轄權時，一個州得拒絕行使這種司法管轄。」其comments (b)及(c)規定被告或該物[140]於知悉後有合理機會下應盡速脫離該州。而comment (d)對非法暴力亦有類似規定。另外comment (e)[141]則規定原告不能在不衡平之情形下而經由第三人之詐欺或暴力而取得利益。但有趣的是comment (f)[142]認為於此種情況下法院通常不會行使管轄權，但這種權力之行使仍屬於法院之裁量權。最後comment (g)認為本82條通常是與刑事案件無關。事實上英國法亦規定法院不會對基於詐欺而來之管轄基礎行使管轄權，這是本文上述已論及之情形。

對於被告為原告所詐欺或強迫進入法院地，英美法院不會行使管轄權之規定個人早在本案發生之前即有論述[143]。另外基於同樣的法理，個人早期亦對英國法[144]與美國法[145]在詐欺之情形下，敗訴之當事人可對外國判決提起抗辯之情形加以論述。因為這個法理於訴訟實務上是甚為基本之議題，故個人較近於一事不再理之相關題目上亦有陳述[146]。強迫或詐欺於

140 而comment (c)對物之管轄有例外之規定："The exception is that judicial jurisdiction will usually be exercised over a chattel, even though it has been brought into the state without the owner's knowledge or consent, when recovery is sought for services rendered in repairing, preserving or storing the chattel in the state. So judicial jurisdiction will usually be exercised over a chattel to enforce a warehouseman's lien for services rendered in storing the chattel in the state."

141 e. Fraud or force of a third person. The rule of this Section is applicable when the fraud or force is practiced by a third person if his relationship to the plaintiff is such that it would be inequitable to allow the plaintiff to take advantage of the third person's action.

142 f. Fraud and force do not destroy jurisdiction of the state. Subject to rare exception, a state may exercise judicial jurisdiction over all persons and thing within its territory. As stated in Comments b-e, this jurisdiction is not usually exercised over a defendant who has been induced to enter the state by fraudulent misrepresentations, or through the use of unlawful force, or over a chattel whose owner has been induced by fraud to send into the state or which has been brought into the state without the consent of the owner. These rules, however, are not jurisdictional. If a state chooses to exercise jurisdiction in any or all of these situations, its action will be recognized as valid in other states. When a judgment rendered under such circumstances is sought to be recognized or enforced in a second state, the courts of the latter state will look to the local law of the state of rendition. If under this law the judgment is impeachable for fraud or force, it will likewise be so impeachable in the second state. If, on the other hand, the judgment is immune from attack in the state of rendition, it will, as between States of the United States, be accorded the same effect elsewhere. This result is required by full faith and credit (compare § 115).

143 陳隆修，《國際私法管轄權評論》，台北，五南圖書公司，民國75年11月，初版，110頁。Blandin v. Ostrander, 239 F. 700 (2d Cir. 1917).

144 陳隆修，《國際私法管轄權評論》，台北，五南圖書公司，民國75年11月，初版，272-275頁。

145 陳隆修，《國際私法管轄權評論》，台北，五南圖書公司，民國75年11月，初版，305頁。

146 陳隆修，《2005年海牙法院選擇公約評析》，台北，五南圖書公司，2009年1月，初版1刷，133

法律上無效或可抗辯性不只侷限於程序法，於實體法上亦經常為世界上之文明國家所共同接受。於2004年之Unidroit Principles of International Commercial Contracts的1.7條[147]即規定誠信原則的不可排除性；3.8條[148]規定契約得因詐欺而被撤銷；3.9條[149]規定契約得因脅迫而被撤銷；而其3.19條[150]規定有關詐欺及脅迫之規定為強行法，因此當事人自然不得違背。

故而無論是於程序法或實體法上，詐欺及脅迫行為之無效性、得撤銷性、或可抗辯性已是全世界文明國家於國內法及國際法上既有之核心共同基本價值。任何有著「不乾淨的手」之人不能據此而取得利益之衡平法，無論於程序法或實體法皆為全世界文明國家之共識及常識。Brennan J.對

頁。另外應注意的是2005年海牙法院選擇公約第9(d)條亦規定牽涉到程序上詐欺之外國判決得被拒絕承認。Article 9 Refusal of recognition or enforcement

Recognition or enforcement may be refused if-

d) the judgment was obtained by fraud in connection with a matter of procedure.另外布魯塞爾規則第35(3)條雖規定公序良俗不能適用於管轄規則，但一般認為詐欺得被承認為實體上之問題而依第34(1)條拒絕承認外國判決。

Article 34

A judgment shall not be recognised:

1. if such recognition is manifestly contrary to public policy in the Member State in which recognition is sought;

Article 35

3. Subject to the paragraph 1, the jurisdiction of the court of the Member State of origin may not be reviewed. The test of public policy referred to in point 1 of Article 34 may not be applied to the rules relating to jurisdiction.

[147] ARTICLE 1.7

(Good faith and fair dealing)

(1) Each party must act in accordance with good faith and fair dealing in international trade.

(2) The parties may not exclude or limit this duty.相同條文見歐盟契約法原則1:201條。

[148] ARTICLE 3.8 (Fraud)

A party may avoid the contract when it has been led to conclude the contract by the other party's fraudulent representation, including language or practices, or fraudulent non-disclosure of circumstances which, according to reasonable commercial standards of fair dealing, the latter party should have disclosed.又見歐盟契約法原則4:107條。

[149] ARTICLE 3.9 (Threat)

A party may avoid the contract when it has been led to conclude the contract by the other party's unjustified threat which, having regard to the circumstance, is so imminent and serious as to leave the first party no reasonable alternative. In particular, a threat is unjustified if the act or omission with which a party has been threatened is wrongful in itself, or it is wrongful to use it as a means to obtain the conclusion o the contract.見歐盟契約法原則4:108條。

[150] ARTICLE 3.19 (Mandatory character of the provisions)

The provisions of this Chapter are mandatory, except insofar as they relate to the binding force of mere agreement, initial impossibility or mistake.

於「所在權力」之「革命」居然是以在傳統規則上加個「自願性的出現在法院地」之條件為其革命性論述之基礎。請問Brennan J.——Pennoyer中所建立的「所在權力」管轄基礎可以允許對被告加以詐欺或脅迫而取得嗎？「所在權力」基礎之母法為英國判例法，請問美國最高法院你們的「常識」會允許你們去假設英國「所在權力」管轄基礎是准許對被告加以詐欺或脅迫而取得嗎？請問美國同僚，如果美國管轄基礎或契約權利——無論國內法或國際法——允許當事人以詐欺或脅迫取得利益，美國的法律秩序可以維持嗎？請問Scalia J.及Brennan J.你們對「所在權力」的解釋有任何差異嗎？請問美國最高法院可敬的同僚及全美國「所有」法律界之同僚冷靜的捫心自問——無論在國際法或國內法，亦無論在實體法或程序法，包括美國在內的全世界文明國家會有那一個國家會不顧法律與秩序的允許任何當事人經由詐欺或脅迫去取得利益？

自International Shoe以後「最低限度關連點」顯然在傳統的「所在權力」管轄基礎上掀起一片腥風血雨，故美國同僚有人形容其為「浩劫」或「叢林法則」。而Burnham則至少號稱在被告「有意」的進入法院地時兩派法官皆一致同意「所在權力」之管轄基礎是符合適當程序的[151]。個人戲稱「最低限度關連點」在International Shoe的崛起是個「鬼打牆法學」，如果因為有四位法官要求必須「自願性」的出現，故因此在Burnham因為

[151] 但是Patrick J. Borchers卻對英國母法的「所在權力」權力加以反對，認為其於憲法上沒有根源，是個「憲法上的滾草」。並認為過去數十年來如同滾草隨風而滾動，憲法在對人訴訟管轄權上是隨著最高法院的「幻想」而隨意一再改變。"In my view, however, personal jurisdiction is more of a constitutional tumbleweed. It has no original roots in the Constitution. The suggestion in Pennoyer that due process has anything to do with the territorial reach of state courts was ill-considered. The transformation of Pennoyer's collateral attack rationale to an all-ecompasing rationale in Menefee was similarly ill-considered. Further, this tumbleweed has not stayed in one spot long enough to grow any roots. The Court has listed a huge number of factors in its modern jurisdictional cases, but without ascribing any particular weight to any of the factors, preferring to throw several of them in the pot and then magically arriving at the result. Finally, the factors have not been consistent. In the space of twenty-nine years the Court has accepted, then rejected, then accepted, then rejected, and then accepted the 'federalism' or 'sovereignty' factor in the jurisdictional calculus. Like a tumbleweed, the consititional law of personal jurisdiction has been blown from place to place with the winds of whatever verbal formulation strikes the Court's fancy." The Death of the Constitutional Law of Personal Jurisdiction: From Pennoyer to Burnham and Back again, 24 U.C. Davis L. Rev. 19, 78 (1990-1991). Riverside & Dan River Cotton Mills v. Menefee, 237 U.S. 189 (1915).

於「所在權力」上達成一致的見解而消弭紛爭，那麼其紛爭的終止亦是個「鬼打牆法學」。「鬼打牆法學」的威力真是有趣的可怕。

(三)最低限度關連點只適用於境外送達

另外有趣的是兩派法官雖然勉強對「所在權力」達成表面上之互不侵犯協議，雙方於法學方法上卻公開叫陣似的不同。Brennan J.說：「不同於Scalia J.，我會行使一個『獨立的調查……去查明現在盛行的境內送達規則之公平性』。」而Scalia J.則先表態：「我們對於盛行的境內送達規則之公平性或妥適性並未進行獨立的調查，而將其交由議會去作判斷」。Scalia J.不但須面對Brennan J.於「所在權力」之公開質疑（甚或否定），其自己亦坦承其之基本概念亦是與Shaffer不同：「但是持平而論，雖然我們今日的認定並未與Shaffer相衝突，但是對於適當程序的問題上之基本概念是不一樣的。」因此任何外行人都可以看出在這個「簡單的案件」中，唯一簡單的事實是——美國最高法院的法官們對於「所在權力」及「最低限度關連點」的適用感到極度的焦慮與不安[152]。Burnham的整個案件之過程及結論是充滿著個人於英國判例法中所未曾見過的焦慮與不安。於這種焦躁的氛圍中所誕生的判例會給美國管轄權法規帶來平靜與祥和嗎？對於International Shoe之結果Scalia J.說：「我們認為這種脫離是可以被允許的（亦即脫離「所在權力」），但應只限於是由於與缺席的被告於該州之關連所引起之訴訟而已。」對於這種對境外被告之送達管轄，個人已一再陳述是可比擬於英國境外送達之C.P.R. 1998, s.6.20、大陸法之特別管轄、及UNIDROIT Principles 2.1.2條之「重大關連」管轄（行為之顯著部分發生於法院地），故而個人一再懷疑「最低限度關連

---

152 Patrick J. Borchers認為如同其他美國有關管轄權之案件，Burnham解決的問題比它挑起的問題還要少。有近半的法官的論述事實上是與Shaffer規則不一致的；而另一半（4位）雖號稱遵守Shaffer規則，但其實際上之結果是與最低限度關連標準不一致的。“Easy perhaps for justice Stevens, but as with so many other Supreme Court jurisdictional decisions, Burnham raised many more questions than it answered. Justice Scalia’s historical approach, which garnered three and one-half votes, was inconsistent with Shaffer. Jusrice Brennan’s opinion, which garnered four votes, paid homage to Shaffer, but its result inconsistent with the minimum contacts test.” 24 U.C. Davis L. Rev. 87 (1990-1991).

點」之必須存在性。The American Law Institute判決篇第5條[153]規定州與當事人之關係須能使得管轄權之行使為合理，而國際私法篇27條[154]之寬廣之對人管轄基礎，亦似乎皆滿足「最低限度關連點」之要求。

然而本案的問題是在：「這裡的問題是對於一個短暫停留於一個州之非居民加以親自送達，而訴訟是與其於該州之行為無關之訴訟中，14修正案之適當程序條款是否拒絕給予該州管轄權。」亦即Burnham法官們之焦慮是在於「所在權力」是否應受到「與法院地有著最低限度關連點以至訴訟的提起不會違反傳統上的公平與實質正義的概念」之限制。對於這個焦慮兩派法官中一派是擺明交由國會立法，一派是自作聰明的加上個「自願性」之莫須有條件。

對於傳統的「所在權力」之「公平性或妥適性」有必要交給「國會去作判斷」或加以一個莫須有的「自願性」條件嗎？如前所述自「最低限度關連點」之一出世其就與「不方便法院」連結[155]，對於傳統的「所在權

[153] Restatement (Second) of Judgments § 5 (1982)
A state may exercise jurisdiction over a person who has a relationship to the state such that the exercise of jurisdiction is reasonable. For relationships sufficient to support an exercise of such jurisdiction, see Restatement, Second, Conflict of Laws § § 27-32, 35-44, 47-52.

[154] Restatement, Second, Conflict of Laws § 27
(1) A state has power to exercise judicial jurisdiction over an individual on one or more of the following bases:
(a) presence
(b) domicil
(c) residence
(d) nationality or citizenship
(e) consent
(f) appearance in an action
(g) doing business in the state
(h) an act done in the state
(i) causing an effect in the state by an act done elsewhere
(j) ownership, use or possession of a thing in the state
(k) other relationships to the state which make the exercise of judicial jurisdiction reasonable.
(2) The circumstances in which, and the extent to which, these bases are sufficient to support an exercise of judicial jurisdiction over an individual are stated in § § 28-39.但是「所在」、國籍及「物之所在」做為對人管轄基礎，一般國際上是認為過度管轄。

[155] 326 U.S. 310, 317, "Those demands may be met by such contacts of the corporation with the state of the forum as make it reasonable, in the context of our federal system of government, to require the corporation to defend the particular suit which is brought there. An 'estimate of the inconveniences' which would result to the corporation from a trial away from its 'home' or principal place of business is rel-

力」之「公平性或妥適性」事實上依「不方便法院」法則加以衡量是較為可接受之作法。以「不方便法院」法則來對「所在權力」之過度管轄加以節制，如前述已為英國法界、美國法律協會自己（認為過境管轄是個「學術性」問題[156]）、及UNIDROIT Principles 2.2及2.5條所公開的認可之作法。如果「所在權力」之母法英國判例法對「所在權力」之可能過度管轄之情形，可以依「不方便法院」而加以節制，同為判例法之美國最高法院並未加以解釋為何英國母法不能適用於美國。這又是一個不遵循享有崇高聲譽之判例法之不良示範，這不是「道法自然」之作風。這亦是個人一再認為Burnham中之辯論及其「自願性」之折衷法則是個「鬼打牆法學」之故。

坦白說個人覺得Burnham之辯論及結論皆是嚴重失焦，其重點不應放在非居民被告是否「自願性」的所在於法院地，或非居民被告於該州之行為是否與訴訟有關。兩派法官皆承認非居民被告所在，或自願性的所在，於法院地是可以滿足14修正案的適當程序的，亦即居民或非居民被告皆能於法院地內被親自給予送達而受到法院之管轄——那麼「最低限度關連點」或「傳統上公平與實質正義的概念」基本上只成為適用於對境外被告加以送達之標準。因此做為一個英國法的同僚個人不得不善意的提醒美國最高法院的同僚及其他所有的美國同僚，不好意思，近七十年來你們的重點可能有點失焦了——應如英國母法一般，重點是在公開的承認送達境外被告通常是一種「例外」或「過度」之管轄。

如White J.之贊同意見所說：「即使沒有其他關連，允許法院去對非居民於法院地內以親自送達而取得管轄之規則，是於這個國家內非常廣泛的於過去及現在所被接受，因此無論於表面上或於本案之適用上，我皆不

---

evant in this connection."

156 Restatement (Second) of Conflict of Laws § 28 (1971), comment (c),
c. Forum non conveniens. From a pragmatic standpoint, the question may be academic whether an individual's momentary presence in a state provides that state with a basis of judicial jurisdiction. This is because a suit based on such presence in the state without other affiliating circumstances would probably be dismissed or transferred on forum non conveniens grounds.

可能以其違反十四修正案所保障的法律上之適當程序去否定其適法性。」因此既然對法院地內之非居民（包含居民）得以親自送達而取得對其之管轄權，那麼「所在權力」之管轄基礎（自然應排除「非自願性」之所在）是理所當然的符合十四修正案所保障之適當程序條款——亦即對非居民（及居民）被告「所在權力」之管轄基礎（排除「非自願性」之所在）是符合適當程序條款的，而且應注意的是這種管轄基礎是不需要有其他關連的。如果於法院地內之送達（所在權力）是符合十四修正案之適當程序條款，那麼International Shoe中所主張的「與法院地有著最低限度關連點以至訴訟的提起不會違反傳統上公平與實質正義的概念」自然是只是有關對法院地外之被告已送達之標準。

六、全球化管轄規則

(一)全球化管轄規則之務實建議

事實上如果美國同僚及最高法院冷靜的回溯六十六年前International Shoe的用語是[157]：「如果被告之所在不是於法院地域內，為了使被告受到對人判決之管轄適當程序條款只是要求，其與法院地有著若干最低限度關連點以至訴訟的提起不會違反傳統上公平與實質正義的概念。」故而這個「最低限度關連點」所設立之目的，白紙黑字的顯示其只是針對境外之被告（亦即境外送達）而已。更且如這段話之前文所同樣白紙黑字的顯示，International Shoe是重申Pennoyer之「所在權力」的：「因此其（被告）之所在於法院管轄地域內，對於作成對其有屬人拘束力之判決是個先決必

[157] 326 U.S. 310, 316, "Historically the jurisdiction of courts to render judgment in personam is grounded on their de facto power over the defendant's person. Hence his presence within the territorial jurisdiction of court was prerequisite to its rendition of a judgment personally binding him. Pennoyer v. Neff, 95 U.S. 714, 733. But now that the capias ad respondendum has given way to personal service of summons or other form of notice, due process requires only that in order to subject a defendant to a judgment in personam, if he be not present within the territory of the forum, he have certain minimum contacts with it such that the maintenance of the suit does not offend 'traditional notions of fair play and substantial justice."

要條件。」因此「最低限度關連點」的「創世紀」白紙黑字的顯示：「所在權力」管轄基礎是對人訴訟的先決要件；「最低限度關連點」之標準只是適用於法院地外之被告。但是Shaffer法院對於上述白紙黑字的規則卻又故意的如此宣示[158]：「我們因此下個結論，亦即所有州法院管轄權的主張必須依International Shoe及其後續判決所立下之標準而被評量。」Shaffer法院這個故意搞曖昧的宣示，造成Burnham案中之Brennan J.派法官改革性的挑戰「所在權力」之權威，並主張：「對於『所在權力就是管轄權之基礎』及『對於其境內之人及物每一州皆擁有專屬管轄及主張』之宣示，我們在管轄權上之分析再也不會只是受限於這些宣示而已。」又說：「於International Shoe中所發展之最低限度關連點分析……比起Pennoyer判決中所產生之法律及事實上假設之碎片式理論，代表著一個對州法院管轄權行使之遠較為合理之解釋。」但是在Brennan J.派如此磨刀霍霍的對「所在理論」提出如此殺氣騰騰的指控後，他們又雷大雨小（根本是一滴雨都沒有）的跟傳統派的法官以「自願性的所在」做為妥協[159]。以「自願性」的出現在法院地做為條件如個人所述是個莫須有的條件，是個極度彆扭的障眼法。

近七十年來美國法院對「所在理論」的改革最後又回歸原點，如果這是一齣法學進化的大戲，那麼它就是歹戲拖棚。它的改革過程雖然喧嘩熱鬧，雖然美國同僚或許覺得過程驚濤駭浪血脈賁張，但不爭的事實是其又

---

[158] 433 U.S. 186, 212, "We therefore conclude that all assertions of state-court jurisdiction must be evaluated according to the standards set forth in International Shoe and its progeny."

[159] Patrick J. Borchers認為Pennoyer之死亡是過分被誇張，而於Burnham最高法院維持了「刺殺管轄」的合憲性；Scalia J.則沿用判例法採納了Pennoyer「寬廣的論述」。"The tumbleweed's next and more recent stop on its aimless journey was Burnham v. Superior Court. As it turned out, the reports of Pennoyer's death were greatly exaggerated. In Burnham the Court upheld the constitutionality of tag jurisdiction. ⋯... Like Asahi, Burnham produced a unanimous result with splintered reasoning. Justice Scalia announced the judgment of the Court, but only the Chief Justice and Justice Kennedy joined his opinion in full. Scalia began with a brief review of the effect of judgments entered without jurisdiction. Consistent with the Court's approach since Menefee, Scalia adopted the expansive view of Pennoyer that extra-jurisdictional judgments are both viod in the judgment-rendering court and not entitled to recognition in other courts." 24 U.C. Davis L. Rev. 78-80 (1990-1991). Asahi Metal Indus. Co. v. Superior Court, 480 U.S. 102 (1987).

回到英國母法「所在權力」的傳統法學原點。如果這是一齣戲對於看戲的所有外國同僚而言，或許只能對其回到原點的結果目瞪口呆要求退錢，或許再加一句台灣話——裝肖的。

對於傳統的所在權力理論英國法界亦早已承認其可能會造成過度管轄之後果，並且如前述一般是認為「不方便法院」法學是經常可以用來避免不正義的後果。而且如一再重述的，這種將所在權力與不方便法院結合使用之作法並非為英國母法所特有，亦為美國法律協會及UNIDROIT Principles所承認。給予法院適度或充分的裁量權以便於個案主持正義，是一種英美法與大陸法皆不得不有之警察原則。英國於採納不方便法院之前是採用「困擾性」或「壓迫性」法學，而與全世界的認知相反的，大陸法或許不那麼死硬。UNIDORIT Principles於2.5條的comment[160]中，將英美法的不方便法院與大陸法的「禁止濫訴」（「濫選法院」）相提並論。故而美國最高法院顯然是應有著足夠的學識與常識去知道英美法院所具有的裁量權可以讓他們於個案中保障正義的執行。那麼這二十世紀的霸主在二十世紀中所展現出來對所在權力的高度焦慮是為什麼？為什麼英國母法信守所在權力更為長久，個人卻從未見出這樣高度的焦慮與不安？

個人認為答案在於英國法學一向視境外送達為「過度」或「例外」之管轄。個人於比較英、美兩國判例法後，認為個人於大學時期即受到師長諄諄告誡的「境外送達經常是過度或例外之管轄，必須於謹慎之情形下才得行使」之法學基本原則普遍較未為美國同僚所注重。個人以為「不方便法院」及「困擾性或壓迫性」法學只是一部分解答，其適用範圍只及於境內送達（至少於英國）。個人以為這個嚴重的美國症狀之主要原因在於，因為美國是個聯邦，故美國法學比較起英國母法較不注重境外送達之過度性或例外性。而英國法學遠在採納不方便法院及Burnham案作成前即早已在傳統上對境外送達皆加以謹慎之態度。例如個人早期之著作即大幅的評

160 P-2F The concept recognized in Principle 2.5 is comparable to the common-law rule of forum non conveniens. In some civil-law systems, the concept is that of preventing abuse of the forum.

述英國法院對境外送達之謹慎作法[161]，而個人這種論述是在英國採納不方便法院及美國Burnham判決之前。

做為一個外國同僚個人認為自Pennoyer及International Shoe以來，這個美國不安與焦慮應由兩方面加以分析：一個是所在權力的可能過度管轄之後果，一個是「自願性」的所在於法院地即可符合適當程序條款。對於前者，亦即「所在權力」之「公平性或妥適性」是否應交付「國會去作判斷」或加上一個彆扭的「自願性」條件之問題，英國母法是將這個問題交付「困擾性或壓迫性」或「不方便法院」法學處理。至於有關「自願性」的所在即可構成符合適當程序條款之結果，則變成「與法院地有著最低限度關連點以至訴訟的提起不會違反傳統上公平與實質正義的概念」之標準只能適用於送達境外被告之情形，而這亦即是對境外送達加以「公平性或妥適性」的規範——這個情形又同樣的回到英國母法一向所主張的對境外送達應謹慎而小心之傳統作法，現在英國判例法稱之為「方便法院」法學。

對於美國正式的將「最低限度關連點」侷限於境外送達，而英國正式的命名對境外送達應謹慎的限制於「方便法院」之情形，當幾年前個人「發現」這個現象後，喜悅之情如同個人26歲時「發現」實體法方法論一般，個人自覺涯中第2次登上學術界的天堂。個人再次重述[162]天堂之美景如下：「或許是無論於英國方便法院原則之公開確認，或美國於Burnham對短暫過境管轄之確認，至今皆不滿二十年，個人甚為訝異的發現國際私法界有一個驚天動地的新潮流又鋪天蓋地的席捲而來，而全世界仍然白目的視而不見——英國與美國皆不約而同的對送達至境外加以重新規範，英國以『方便法院』原則而美國以『最低限度關連點』原則為裁量權行使之規範。雖然學理與名稱不同，但基本精神乃是將送達至境外的過度管轄權加以適度合理的規範，如前述歐盟與海牙會議數十年來忙著對過度

161 陳隆修，《國際私法管轄權評論》，台北，五南圖書公司，民國75年11月，初版，45～48頁。

162 陳隆修、許兆慶、林恩瑋、李瑞生四人合著，《國際私法—管轄與選法理論之交錯》，台北，五南圖書公司，2009年3月，初版1刷，204、205頁。

管轄消極的加以撻伐及限制，然而最近不到二十年來英國及美國卻不約而同的以不同的手段積極的對送達至境外加以制度化及合理化。或許歐陸國家應擺脫消極禁止的態度，而積極的去制度化境外送達。個人不知是否有其他衝突法的同僚注意到英、美此處異曲同工之創見，如若是沒有，那麼如同個人近三十年前於實體法方法論一般，於此處管轄權理論驚濤駭浪般澎湃洶湧的新趨勢中，本文很榮幸的於此為衝突法管轄權歷史作一個大時代潮流的新見證。國際私法的江山如此的多嬌，難怪60、70年代的前輩美國選法革命論者直以生死相許。」

另外個人又論及[163]：「基於最低限度關連點而來的美國各州之長手法規」（long arms statute），乃是規定各州對非居民被告基於其法院地相關之行為而引起之對人訴訟管轄權，其與英國之R.S.C. Order 11, rule 1 (1)（即現今之C.P.R. 1998, s.6.20）之規定性質上相近，台灣民訴第1章第1節管轄規則篇亦有甚多類似之規定」。現今英國同僚於加入歐盟後亦發現英國送達境外之C.P.R. 1998, s.6.20已為甚多大陸法國家之管轄規則及歐盟布魯賽爾公約及規則第5條中所執行。而個人更發現上述英美法及大陸法之國內或國際管轄規則亦符合UNIDROIT Principles 2.1條「重大〈實質〉關連」之管轄基礎[164]。因此個人情不自禁的宣布全球化法學國際

---

163 陳隆修、許兆慶、林恩瑋、李瑞生四人合著，《國際私法—管轄與選法理論之交錯》，台北，五南圖書公司，2009年3月，初版1刷，205頁。

164 The American Law Institute判決篇第4條亦規定在地域管轄上聯邦與州法院必須與該案件有著關連。

§ 4. Constitutional And Legislative Determinants Of Territorial Jurisdiction

(1) A state court may exercise territorial jurisdiction over persons in an action if:

(a) The state has a relationship to the action or the parties thereto stated in §§ 5 to 8; and

(b) The exercise of jurisdiction is not impermissible under federal law, the law of the state itself, or other applicable restriction.

(2) A federal court may exercise jurisdiction over persons in an action if:

(a) The court has a territorial jurisdictional relationship to the action prescribed by statute or rule of court; and

(b) The exercise of jurisdiction is not impermissible under federal law or other applicable restriction.另外又見Restatement, Second, Conflict of Laws § 27

(1) A state has power to exercise judicial jurisdiction over an individual on one or more of the following bases:

(a) presence

(b) domicil

管轄之共同核心於基本概念上早已長久存在。的確，契約履行地、侵權行為地、或不當得利地等「重大關連」之管轄基礎，不但符合「最低限度關連點」之要求，其存在之普遍性及長久性更是符合「傳統上」公平與實質正義之概念。因此基於這個全球化管轄基礎之共同核心，及對境外被告國家主權之尊重、訴訟實務上之困難、判決於境外之執行性、及特別是基於UNIDORIT Principles 3.2條對境外被告之人權考量，個人謙卑的提出下列建議[165]以便作為二十一世紀全球化法學民事訴訟管轄權之共同核心基礎：**各國仍得以既有的管轄規則為基礎（英美法為「所在權力」及境外送達之規則，大陸法通常為國內民訴之管轄規則），但訴訟之通知若於境內已適當的送達給被告，或於被告承認法院之管轄權時，法院得以「不方便法院」法則為拒絕或停止訴訟裁量之依據（例如於正義之需求下或訴因與法院地沒有合理之牽連時）；而若法院欲送達通知至境外時，首先必須認知此為一種例外之過度管轄，其判決有可能不為外國法院所承認，應以「方便法院」原則來確認法院是否為合適、自然之管轄法院，以作為允許送達境外之適用標準（例如為了公平正義之目的或訴因與法院地有強烈牽連時）。**

如前述個人之所以提出這樣的建議，事實上並非個人之創見。個人只是依據英國之現況而將英國目前所適用之法學推廣至其他法律制度而已，如前所述英國法長久以來就於不同之名詞下給予法院裁量權以便於個案下

(c) residence
(d) nationality or citizenship
(e) consent
(f) appearance in an action
(g) doing business in the state
(h) an act done in the state
(i) causing an effect in the state by an act done elsewhere
(j) ownership, use or possession of a thing in the state
(k) other relationships to the state which make the exercise of judicial jurisdiction reasonable.
(2) The circumstances in which, and the extent to which, these bases are sufficient to support an exercise of judicial jurisdiction over an individual are stated in §§28-39.

165 陳隆修、許兆慶、林恩瑋、李瑞生四人合著，《國際私法—管轄與選法理論之交錯》，台北，五南圖書公司，2009年3月，初版1刷，248頁。婚姻管轄之建議，249-252頁。

主持主義。如Cheshire and North[166]所說：「現在已經見證了去允許請求文件的被送達至境外的裁量權是依據方便法院的基礎而被行使。而於有些特定的情形下，亦有著依據不方便法院（例如當英國不是審判的合適法院時）去停止訴訟的裁量權。」這個自十九世紀[167]中期以來就為英國所執行之法學，經過百多年來時空之淬鍊，除非有著明顯而迫切之相反證據，否則個人認為其應可適用於今日全球化社會。

如前所述全球化的現代社會讓我們很驚訝的發現，原來自始至終全世界無論於國內或國際管轄上，UNIDROIT Principles 2.1條式的「重大（實質）關連」管轄早已存在於大部分之文明國家。而又如Shaffer法院[168]所說，汽車的產生伴隨著外來的人於州內所造成的傷害，促使「管轄權力於地域上之限制的應被加以改革」。如前述英國同僚亦同意於現代化之社會中，法院須擴大其管轄權，並以裁量權來確保個案之公平正義。而又如前述，這個擴大法院之必要管轄權並給予法院裁量權之趨勢[169]，又於

---

[166] P M North, JJ Fawcett, Cheshire and North's Private International Law, 13th ed., p.334, "It has already been seen that the discretionary power to allow service of a claim form out of the jurisdiction is exercised on the basis of forum conveniens. There is also a discretion to stay actions on the basis of forum non conveniens (ie where England is not the appropriate forum for trial) in certain specific situations." 又見14th ed., p.426,相同之論述: "It has already been seen that the discretionary power to allow service of a claim form out of the jurisdiction is exercised on the basis of forum conveniens. There is also a general discretionary power to stay actions on the basis of forum non conveniens (ie where the clearly appropriate forum for trial is abroad)."

[167] 陳隆修，《國際私法管轄權評論》，台北，五南圖書公司，民國75年11月，初版，45頁。

[168] 433 U.S. 186, 202, "The advent of automobiles, with the concomitant increase in the incidence of individuals causing injury in States where they were not subject to in personam actions under Pennoyer, required further moderation of the territorial limits on jurisdictional power. This modification, like the accommodation to the realities of interstate corporate activities, was accomplished by use of a legal fiction that left the conceptual structure established in Pennoyer theoretically unaltered."

[169] 於面對外國判決之承認與執行時，加拿大最高法院亦作出同樣的論述，La Forest J., Morguard Investments Ltd. v. De Savoye, [1990] 3 S.C.R. 1077, at p. 1098: The world has changed since the above rules [concerning the recognition and enforcement of foreign judgments] were developed in 19th century England. Modern means of travel and communications have made many of these 19th century concerns appear parochial. The businesss community operates in a world economy and we correctly speak of a world community even in the face of decentralized political and legal power. Accommodating the flow of wealth, skills and people across state lines has now become imperative. Under these circumstances, our approach to the recognition and enforcement of foreign judgments would appear ripe for reappraisal.

於Pro Swing Inc. v. Elta Golf Inc., 2006 Can. Sup. Ct. LEXIS 52; 2006 SCC 52; [2006] S.C.J. No. 52中，La Forest J.的論述一再的被引用，見McLachlin C.J., para. 78: In Hunt v. T&N plc, [1993] 4

UNIDROIT Principles之2.2條（必要管轄）及2.5條（不方便法院）中再次被確認。

如Marshall J.又於Shaffer[170]中所說：「雖然可能會有建議認為應允許對物管轄權去避免International Shoe標準所既有之不穩定性，及確保原告會有一法院。……但是我們相信International Shoe之公平標準可以輕易的適用於大部分之案件上。並且當依International Shoe一個特定法院之管轄權之存在是不清楚時，為了簡化訴訟而去避免管轄問題的代價可能就是去犧牲『公平與實質正義』。這個代價太高。」二十一世紀的全球化法學之核心價值在尊重人權確保個案正義，這個價值顯現在UNIDORIT Principles第3條[171]的於當事人間確保程序平等條款上，其中第2項後半段所規定的對外國被告之困難應加以考慮之法則更是英國法學自十九世紀中期以來之寫實及個人對全球化管轄規則建議之核心。Marshall J.所說：「為了

S.C.R. 289, La Forest J. futher described rigidity in this area of the law as resting on an "outmoded conception of the world that emphasized sovereignty and independence, often at the cost of unfairness" (pp. 321-22). The common law must evolve in a way that takes into account the importance social and economic forces that shape commercial and other kinds of relationships.

亦即於今日的全球化法學中，犧牲公平性以強調主權與獨立性是「過時的」，判例法是隨著社會與經濟的發展而進化的—判例法的這種方法論是符合中國文化2500年來一貫之「道法自然」傳統哲學。

170 433 U.S. 186, 211, "It might also be suggested that allowing in rem jurisdiction avoids the uncertainty inherent in the International Shoe standard and assures a plaintiff of a forum……. We believe, however, that the fairness standard of International Shoe can be easily applied in the vast majority of cases. Moreover, when the existence of jurisdiction in a particular forum under International Shoe is unclear, the cost of simplifying the litigation by avoiding the jurisdictional question may be the sacrifice of 'fair play and substantial justice.' That cost is too high."

171 第1項為確保當事人間公平及合理之對待及機會。第2項為禁止基於國籍及居所而非法歧視。第3項為禁止因為國籍及居所而須繳保證金。第4項為管轄規則不能使得非居民難以利用法院。

ALI/UNIDORIT Principles of Transnational Civil Procedure

3. Procedural Equality of the Parties

3.1 The court should ensure equal treatment and reasonable opportunity for litigants to assert or defend their rights.

3.2 The right to equal treatment includes avoidance of any kind of illegitimate discrimination, particularly on the basis of nationality or residence. The court should take into account difficulties that might be encountered by a foreign party in participating in litigation.

3.3 A person should not be required to provide security for costs, or security for liability for pursuing provisional measures, solely because the person is not a national or resident of the forum state.

3.4 Whenever possible, venue rules should not impose an unreasonable burden of access to court on a person who is not a habitual resident of the forum.

簡化訴訟而去避免管轄問題的代價可能就是去犧牲『公平與實質正義』。這個代價太高。」這個論述可能會為許多同僚所接受，UNIDORIT Principles 2.2條的「必要管轄」及2.5條的「不方便法院」或許就是這種論述的實踐。而2.5條之comment P-2F將「不方便法院」與大陸法的「濫用程序」（濫選法院）相比擬，可見號稱死硬的大陸法管轄規則亦有著以彈性裁量權來確保個案正義之習慣與傳統。

事實上於彈性裁量權方面，大陸法除了「禁止濫用程序」外，近來迫於全球化的壓力，亦不得不於國際公約之潮流下，捲旗繳械的對「不方便法院」豎起白旗而接受「不方便法院」之適用。除了1999年海牙草約曾企圖引進「不方便法院」外，國際上最著名的例子，為海牙1996 Convention on Jurisdiction, Applicable Law, Recognition, Enforcement and Co-operation in Respect of Parental Responsibility and Measures for the Protection of Children的第8條規定於處理有關未成年兒童之父母責任時，在小孩最佳利益下有管轄權之法院得將案件移轉至其他合適之法院[172]。在1996海牙公約採納不方便法院的影響下，歐盟亦於Council Regulation（EC）No 2201/2003 concerning jurisdiction and the recognition and enforcement of judgments in matrimonial matters and the matters of parental responsibility第15條中規定，在小孩最佳利益下得將有關

[172] Article 8
1 By way of exception, the authority of a Contracting State having jurisdiction under Article 5 or 6, if it considers that the authority of another Contracting State would be better placed in the particular case to assess the best interests of the child, may either – request that other authority, directly or with the assistance of the Central Authority of its State, to assume jurisdiction to take such measures of protection as it considers to be necessary, or – suspend consideration of the case and invite the parties to introduce such a request before the authority of that other State.
又見explanatory report by Paul Lagarde, paragraph 55, "Paragraph 2 mentions, finally, ' a State with which the child has a substantial connection'. This formulation, the flexibility of which goes very well with the underlying theory of forum non conveniens which inspires Article 8, encompasses and exceeds the three preceding cases mentioned, which are only illustrations. It will permit, according to the case and always as a function of the child's best interests, the possible jurisdiction, for example of the authorities of the State of the former habitual residence of the child, or of the State in which members of the child's family life who are willing to look after him or her."
見陳隆修、許兆慶、林恩瑋、李瑞生四人合著，《國際私法—管轄與選法理論之交錯》，台北，五南圖書公司，2009年3月，初版1刷，194～196頁。

父母責任之案件移轉到較合適之法院[173]。更有趣的是在有牽涉到歐盟以外之國家時，2007年9月於漢堡所開的the 17th Session European Croup for Private International Law之結論為：建議歐盟給予會員國於對非會員國時，在決定會員國法院之管轄權時應有裁量權[174]。正如歐盟在號稱大陸法

---

[173] Article 15
Transfer to a court better placed to hear the case
1.By way of exception, the courts of a Member State having jurisdiction as to the substance of the matter may, if they consider that a court of another Member State, with which the child has a particular connection, would be better placed to hear the case, or a specific part thereof, and where this is in the best interests of the child:
(a) stay the case or the part thereof in question and invite the parties to introduce a request before the court of that other Member State in accordance with paragraph 4; or
(b) request a court of another Member State to assume jurisdiction in accordance with paragraph 5.
又見Aude Fiorini, *The Codification of Private International Law in Europe – Could the Community Learn from the Experience of Mixed Jurisdictions?* 23 Tul. Eur. & Civ. L.F. 89, 106 (2008), "Even in Europe, what could be described as a watered down form of forum non conveniens has been included in a largely civilian instrument on jurisdiction, recognition and enforcement, albeit in family law matters, Council Regulation(EC) No 2201/2003 of 27 November 2003 concerning jurisdiction and the recognition and enforcement of judgments in matrimonial matters and the matters of parental responsibility (the 'Brussels IIa Regulation')。"

[174] 後於2008年9月於Bergen則對漢堡會議之決議提出詳細規則：
Article 23 bis
"1. A court of a Member state seised of proceedings over which it has jurisdiction under this Regulation, and with regard to which the parties have given exclusive jurisdiction to a court or the courts of a non-member State under an agreement complying with the conditions laid down by Article 23, shall not hear the proceedings unless and until the chosen court has declined jurisdiction.
It shall stay the proceedings as long as the chosen court has not been seised or, if it has been seised, has not declined jurisdiction. It shall decline jurisdiction once the chosen court has given a judgment entitled to recognition under the law of the State of the court seised.
Nevertheless, it may hear the proceedings if it appears that:
(a) the chosen court will not give judgment within a reasonable time;
(b) the chosen court will give a judgment which will not be entitled to recognition under the law of the State of the court seised.
[2. The choice by the parties of a court of a non-member State shall have no effect if all other elements relevant to the situation at the time of the choice are located in the same Member State]"
Article 24 bit:
"Where no court of a Member State has jurisdiction under this Regulation, a person may be sued before the courts of a Member State with which the claim has a sufficient connection, especially by reason of the presence of property in the territory of that State, if the right to a fair trial so requires, in particular:
(a)if proceedings in a non-Member State are shown to be impossible; or
(b)if it could not reasonably be required that the claim should be brought before a court of a non-Member State; or
(c)if a judgment given on the claim in a non-Member State would not be entitled to recognition in the State of the court seised under the law of that State and such recognition is necessary to ensure that the rights of the claimant are satisfied."
Article 30 bis:

不採用「禁反言」（甚至連「一事不再理」知名此都儘可能不使用）之情形下，布魯塞爾規則第34(3)及(4)條有關外國判決之承認時仍不能不牽涉及此概念。歐盟及其他大陸法在既有的禁止濫用程序之裁量權基礎上，適度的採用「不方便法院」法學是全球化下不得不然之趨勢。或許較為務實的建議是，歐盟裁量權之行使可由先前較為謹慎的「困擾性」或「壓迫性」法學之英國先例而開始。

(二)最低限度關連癌細胞的擴散

台灣、大陸、及日本等法制，由於給予法院適當的裁量權行使基礎，故依國際標準通常是可被歸類為採納「不方便法院」之制度。但是日本的名稱非常詭異，日本同僚稱為「特別情事」原則[175]，而且更有趣的是有些同僚認為此原則可能是參考「最低限度關連點」而來。**如果是參考**

"In the case of lis pendens or related actions as understood in Article 27 and 28, when the claim is pending before the courts of a non-member State, the court of a Member State seised second may stay the proceedings before it until the court seised first gives judgment, if it appears that judgment will be given within a reasonable time and that it will be subject to recognition under the law of the Member state in question. It shall decline jurisdiction once the court seised first has given a judgment entitled to recognition under the law of that Member State."

Proposed Amendment of Regulation 44/2001 in Order to Apply it to External Situations, Bergen, 21 September 2008。見http://www.gedip-egpil.eu/documents/gedip-documents-28EN.htm.

這種規則自然違反UNIDROIT Principles第三條當事人程序平等之規定。

175 見蔡華凱，國際裁判管轄總論之研究，中正法學集刊17期，22-28頁，「最判昭56・10・16判時1020號9頁。【事實】馬來西亞國內線班機在飛往吉隆坡途中，因劫機事件而墜毀在馬來西亞境內，機上乘客和機組人員無一生還。罹難乘客中有日本國籍者一名，其家屬向日本法院以馬來西亞航空為被告，基於旅客運送契約之債務不履行提起損害賠償請求訴訟。馬來西亞航空在日本東京雖有營業所，惟該名罹難之日本乘客係在馬來西亞國內購買該國內線機票，與被告法人位於日本東京之營業所之業務毫無關聯。又此事件係屬國內之航空事件，無華沙公約之適用。

【要旨】

(1)『…按一國之裁判權係其主權之作用之一，裁判權所及範圍原則上與主權所及範圍同一，故被告為總公司設在外國之外國法人時，除了該法人主動服從之外，原則上日本之裁判權不及於該外國法人。惟其例外為，對於與我國領土一部之土地有關之事件或被告與我國有任何法的關聯性之訴訟事件，不問被告的國籍、所在如何，要其服從我國之裁判權難謂不當。而關於處理例外情形之範圍，無直接規定國際裁判管轄之法規，亦無國際社會一般承認之明確國際法上的原則可資依據的現狀之下，依據期待當事人間的公平、裁判的正當、迅速之理念，依法理決之可謂為相當。』」

最判平9・11・11判時1626號74頁，「我國民訴法所規定之任何裁判籍位於我國國內時，原則上，對於在我國法院所提起之訴訟事件，讓被告服於我國的裁判權並無不當，惟在我國進行裁判，認為有違期待當事人間的公平、裁判的正當與迅速等理念之特別情存在時，應否定我國的國際裁判管轄」。

「最低限度關連點」而來，那麼日本同僚就應特別注意到這個法學只適用在對於境外之被告加以送達之訴訟，請問「特別情事」原則對境內送達將以何種法理取代？如果「特別情事」是本於「不方便法院」那麼日本同僚並未解釋清楚。如果「特別情事」是脫離「最低限度關連點」而為一自創法學，那麼殷鑑不遠，自International Shoe脫離母法自創「最低限度關連點」以來，美國於這方面之法規即成為「浩劫」，最後又「鬼打牆」的回到「所在權力」之母法原點。英國自十九世紀中期以來即嘗試著以裁量權之行使而對境外被告加以送達，而從二十多年前才正式引用「方便與不方便法院」。同時違背美國與英國兩國聲名卓越法院百多年進化所累積的人類祖先的生活經驗，很明顯的不是「道法自然」之行為。做為同樣屬於法律學落後的「法學第三世界」的國際法學生，個人必須誠摯的請日本同僚冷靜的思考——全球化的世界會給日本同僚一百五十年的時間去發展一個獨創的理論嗎？

為著配合交通、資訊、金融、貿易的全球化，於1984年時英國法院已準備放棄長久以來所堅守的較為嚴謹、較為符合法律邏輯的「困擾性」或「壓迫性」法學，而採納較為寬鬆的「不方便法院」法學，於The Abidin Daver中Lord DIPLOCK氣勢恢宏的宣布[176]：「司法的自大應為司法的禮誼所取代。」「最低限度關連點」的「創世紀」及其紛爭於「目前」的停止，個人皆認為是個「神話」，亦是「鬼打牆」。對於「鬼打牆」法學於海外的沿續或其突變種，個人再已沒任何語文的能力可以形容。對於管轄基礎的正視境內與境外之區別，不但「合理」，亦符合人類的「常識」與生活經驗，更是本於英美判例法至少百多年的進化結果，亦為2004年UNIDROIT Principles第3條所默認之全球化法學共同核心。對於境內與境外管轄分別以「不方便及方便法院」為基礎及限制，是二十一世紀全球化管轄規則為了確保個案正義而不得不向我們人類共同祖先擷取其進化經

[176] [1984] AC 398, 411, "judicial chauvinism has been replaced by judicial comity"

驗之自然結果。雖然在評論Spiliada Maritime Corpn v Cansulex Ltd.[177]之採用「方便與不方便法院」兩種法學時，Cheshire and North說[178]：「由這個案件中很清楚的可以見到相同的基本標準是適用於有關停止訴訟之案件（即不方便法院），正如同適用於將請求文件送達於境外時所行使的裁量權一般。」雖然是適用「相同的基本標準」，但是舉證責任並不完全相同，尤其是對送達境內與境外管轄權有無之假設基礎之不同，更是為兩個法學最重要之區別。無論所使用之名詞為何，個人衷心期盼日本同僚以「最重要關連點」為殷鑑，而儘量引用英國自十九世紀中期以來所累積之生活經驗與智慧。

177 [1987] AC 460.

178 P M North, JJ Fawcett, Cheshire and North's Private International Law, 13th ed., p.335, "that the English discretion to stay was indistinguishable from the Scottish doctrine of forum non conveniens. This view has been endorsed by the House of Lords in the leading case on stays of action, Spiliada Maritime Corpn v Cansulex Ltd. It is clear from this case that the same basic criterion applies in cases involving stays of action as in cases involving the exercise of the discretion to serve a claim form out of the jurisdiction." 又見14th ed., pp. 426, 427.

第6章 美國法一「濫用程序」的掠奪式新殖民地主義

無論是「公平、正當、與迅速」、「傳統上公平與實質正義」、或「方便與不方便法院」之「當事人利益及正義的目的」都是自然法的概念，他們的確無法用一個簡單的方程式表達，亦無法劃上一條明線，但在大英帝國協以一百多年的歷史經驗為依據後，天空不會是他們唯一的界限，「方便與不方便法院」法學在許多方面其判例的累積已相當程度的成為一種精準的科學[1]。但是美國所使用的「不方便法院」法學為什麼會為1999年海牙草約22(3)條及UNIDROIT Principles 3.2條所公開禁止其基於國籍或住所而來之歧視行為呢？而個人於較近著作之結論亦如此的論述「這種邪派理論」[2]：「美國法院於『不方便法院』之發展上，造成人類國際私法歷史上最黑暗的紀錄。」這個二十世紀的霸主為什麼會在其霸業即將結束的二十一世紀留下這樣野蠻不光彩的紀錄？即將再度成為21世紀霸主的中華民族必須認真的探其究竟。

---

1 Kekewich J.認為公共政策無法被給予定義，亦不能輕易的被解釋。Davies v. Davies (1887) 36 Ch D 359 at p. 364, "Public policy does not admit of definition and is not easily explained".而更早期著名的論述即為Burrough J.所說的公共政策：「是一匹極度脫韁的野馬，當你騎上牠之後你永遠不會知道牠會載你到那裡。」但是後來Lord Denning MR卻如此的回答：「但是如果一個好人騎在馬鞍上，這匹野馬是可被加以控制的。」Richardson v. Mellish (1824) 2 Bing 229 at p. 252, "is a very unruly horse, and when once you get astride it you never know where it will carry you." *Enderby Town Football Club v. Football Association* [1971] Ch. 591 at p. 606H, "With a good man in the saddle, the unruly horse can be kept in control".

2 陳隆修，《2005年海牙法院選擇公約評析》，台北，五南圖書公司，2009年1月，初版1刷，306頁。

一、Gulf Oil Corporation v. Gilbert

(一)案件

或許1947年的Gulf Oil Corporation v. Gilbert[3]是「不方便法院」法學在蘇格蘭式以「正義為目的」及美國式對第三世界採「掠奪式新殖民地法學」之死亡交叉點。本案之問題為紐約聯邦地院是否有著固有權力去依不方便法院而拒絕案件，及若是有權力時該權力於本案是否被濫用。於案中原告被上訴人為維吉尼亞州人，其於紐約地院提告。其主張被告上訴人違反維州法而有過失的交付其汽油，以致引起倉庫之爆炸，故要求依侵權行為而提出損害賠償之請求。上訴人為賓夕法尼亞之公司，於紐約及維州皆有登記營業及指定送達代收人。於地院上訴人主張不方便法院，宣稱維州是較為合適之審判地，因為被上訴人居住於該地而上訴人於該地營業，訴訟之所有相關事情於該地發生，大部分證人住於該地，並且當地之州及聯邦法院皆可對上訴人取得管轄權。聯邦地院依據Erie Railroad Co. v. Tompkins[4]適用紐約法院地法之不方便法院法則，要求將案件交付維州法院，因此駁回訴訟。上訴巡迴法院不認同應適用紐約法，並對聯邦法院的適用不方便法院採取較嚴格之看法。最高法院的大多數法院不認同上訴法院對不方便法院所採取之嚴格觀點，並駁回其判決。對於聯邦地院駁回原告之訴訟並命其回到其原來社區之法院起訴，最高法院認為地院並未逾越其權力或裁量權之範圍。

Jackson J.代表法院作成判決。其認為[5]最高法院無論用什麼文字形

---

3 330 U.S. 501 (1947); 91 L.Ed. 1055; 67 S. Ct. 839.

4 304 U.S. 64, 58 S. Ct. 817, 82 L. Ed. 1188, 114 A. L. R. 1487.

5 330 U.S. 501, para. 7, This court, in one form of words or another, has repeatedly recognized the existence of the power to decline jurisdiction in exceptional circumstances. As formulated by Mr. Justice Brandeis the rule is: 'Obviously, the proposition that a court having jurisdiction must exercise it, is not universally true; else the admiralty court could never decline jurisdiction on the ground that the litigation is between foreigners. Nor is it true of courts administering other systems of our law. Courts of equity and of law also occasionally decline, in the interest of justice, to exercise jurisdiction, where the suit is between aliens or nonresidents, or where for kindred reasons the litigation can more appropriately be conducted in a foreign tribunal.' Canada Malting Co., Ltd., v. Paterson Steamships. Ltd., 285 U.S. 413, 422, 423, 52 S. Ct. 413, 415, 76 L. Ed. 837. 又para. 8, We later expressly said that a state court 'may

容，已經一再承認於「特殊情形」下是存在著去拒絕管轄之權力。並引用Mr. Justice Brandeis所建立的規則說明：「很明顯的，法院有管轄權就必須行使的建議是不見得永遠是正確的……並且在正義的利益下，有時法律及衡平法院會拒絕行使管轄權，這種情形是產生在訴訟是於外國人或非居民間發生時，或基於類似之理由該訴訟可以更合適的於一個外國法院被提起時。」

Jackson J.又說[6]：「不方便法院原則很簡單的就是一個法院得抗拒加於其身上之管轄權，即使是管轄權是依一般管轄條款之規定而來時亦是一樣。這些條款必須以一般性的方式而被規定，並且通常會給予原告去選擇法院的機會，以便其被確保至少有地方去提起救濟之請求。但是這種開放的方式可能會去允許那些不只要求正義，而或許是正義混雜一些騷擾的行動。有時原告可能受到誘惑去訴之在對手最不方便之地方強行訴訟之策略，即使是對他自己會有些不方便亦會如此。」這個美國有關不方便法院的經典案例說明了無論英美法或大陸法的一般管轄條款是經常給予原告多重選擇之機會，而原告有時會利用這種機會去困擾或壓迫對方。歐盟於布魯塞爾規則的一般管轄（住所）及特別管轄（第5條）經常重疊交叉之情形下，仍然不顧一切的以先繫屬優先，對於一個經常強調禁止規避法律[7]、選購法院、濫用訴訴程序之法律制度而言，這是非常不可思議的。但令人更感憤慨的（而且是極度憤慨）是歐盟Council Regulation No. 2201/2003第3條[8]的對離婚、分居、或結婚無效管轄的幾乎全面解放，過

---

in appropriate cases apply the doctrine of forum non conveniens.'

6　同上，para. 11,
The principle of forum non conveniens is simply that a court may resist imposition upon its jurisdiction even when jurisdiction is authorized by the letter of a general venue statute. These statutes are drawn with a necessary generality and usually give a plaintiff a choice of courts, so that he may be quite sure of some place in which to pursue his remedy. But the open door may admit those who seek not simply justice but perhaps justice blended with some harassment. A plaintiff sometimes is under temptation to resort to a strategy of forcing the trial at a most inconvenient place for an adversary, even at some inconvenience to himself.

7　見陳隆修、許兆慶、林恩瑋、李瑞生四人合著，《國際私法—管轄與選法理論之交錯》，台北，五南圖書公司，2009年3月，初版1刷，213頁。

8　Article 3

去有著嚴格專屬管轄，現在已變為複數專屬管轄。更糟糕的是依歐盟之慣例，其第19條[9]亦採先繫屬優先原則。這種作法自然有時會導致欲提起離婚訴訟之一方「在對手最不方便之地方強行訴訟之策略」。尤其在歐盟至今尚無法確立婚姻法之統一規則或統一選法規則[10]下，這種作法是對婚姻

General jurisdiction

1. In matters relating to divorce, legal separation or marriage annulment, jurisdiction shall lie with the courts of the Member State

(a) in whose territory:

- the spouses are habitually resident, or
- the spouses were last habitually resident, insofar as one of them still resides there, or
- the respondent is habitually resident, or
- in the event of a joint application, either of the spouses is habitually resident, or
- the applicant is habitually resident if he or she resided there for at least a year immediately before the application was made, or
-the applicant is habitually resident if he or she resided there for at least six months immediately before the application was made and is either a national of the Member State in question or, in the case of the United Kingdom and Ireland, has his or her "domicile" there;

(b) of the nationality of both spouses or, in the case of the United Kingdom and Ireland, of the "domicile" of the both spouses.

2. For the purpose of this Regulation, "domicile" shall have the same meaning as it has under the legal systems of the United Kingdom and Ireland.

9 Article 19

Lis pendens and dependent actions

1. Where proceedings relating to divorce, legal separation or marriage annulment between the same parties are brought before courts of different Member States, the court second seised shall of its own motion stay its proceedings until such time as the jurisdiction of the court first seised is established.
2. Where proceedings relating to parental responsibility relating to the same child and involving the same cause of action are brought before courts of different Member States, the court second seised shall of its own motion stay its proceedings until such time as the jurisdiction of the court first seised is established.
3. Where the jurisdiction of the court first seised is established, the court second seised shall decline jurisdiction in favour of that court.

In the case, the party who brought the relevant action before the court second seised may bring that action before the court first seised.

10 陳隆修、許兆慶、林恩瑋、李瑞生四人合著，《國際私法—管轄與選法理論之交錯》，台北，五南圖書公司，2009年3月，初版1刷，239、240頁。「個人還是一向基於家事一體之觀念，認為父母責任案件應通常以離婚法院做為第一優先法院較妥。但如若離婚法院欲成為第一優先管轄法院，先決要件是離婚法院保有舊式『真正』專屬管轄。對於歐盟近來於沒有統一選擇法規下，幾乎全面式開放離婚管轄基礎，個人認為會增加選購法院與跛腳婚姻之機率。歐陸國家早期於身分行為上過分注重選法規則，而忽視專屬管轄法院對於其法院地法適用之必然性，個人覺得這是歐陸文明過去（或現在仍是）發展史之一大謬誤。然而眼睜睜的看著於身分行為管轄權之專屬性上，或許歐陸國家又正在締造一次歷史上的錯誤。

離婚案件之管轄基礎，現已為國際上紛擾不斷之多頭馬車。多年苦思之結果，個人主張應以被告配偶之慣居地（或住所）為專屬管轄法院。並且依英美法長久之傳統，經常專屬管轄地法應是世上唯一與該身分行為有著真正最親密關連之準據法。」

弱勢一方極度不利——而這麼多年來歐盟卻享有保護婦女及幼兒之假象。

對付這種濫用程序英美法向來是以「困擾性或壓迫性」或「不方便法院」法學來確保當事人間程序上之自然正義。Jackson J.又說[11]：「許多州是以給予法院裁量權去基於許多理由而去改變審判地點之方式以應付審判地之濫用，例如證人的便利性及正義的目的。聯邦法並無明示之標準以便指引地院去行使其權力。但這是一個非常古老的問題，它影響到法院的行政程序及當事人之權利，並且英國及這個國家的判例法皆同時創造出應付它之技術及標準。」事實上對於濫用審判地（選購法院）大陸法是較英美法更為偏重的，早期英國法是較為尊重原告之利益的[12]，故而大陸法的不若英美法的公開認可法院裁量權之必要性是相當的自我矛盾。並且個人有點訝異的是於1947年法院即認為英美的判例法「已同時創造出應付它（裁量權）之技術及標準」。個人是無法斷定1947年之情況，但如前述個人認為六十多年來英國於「方便與不方便法院」之「技術及標準」已到達一定的成熟與穩定性。

Jackson J.又說[13]：「對於請求救濟的拒絕或允許所必須或構成合理之情形，還好很聰明的並沒有任何嘗試去企圖將其分類。這個法學交給原告所選擇的法院許多裁量權，並且經驗並未顯示有著強烈的司法傾向去放棄自己的管轄權以致造成許多的濫用程序。」正如Lord Scarman所說的[14]：

---

11 330 U.S. 501, para. 12,
Many of the states have met misuse of venue by investing courts with a discretion to change the place of trial on various grounds, such as the convenience of witnesses and the ends of justice. The federal law contains no such express criteria to guide the district court in exercising its power. But the problem is a very old one affecting the administration of the courts as well as the rights of litigants, and both in England and in this country the common law worked out techniques and criteria for dealing with it.

12 陳隆修、許兆慶、林恩瑋、李瑞生四人合著，《國際私法—管轄與選法理論之交錯》，台北，五南圖書公司，2009年3月，初版1刷，313頁。

13 330 U.S. 501, para. 13,
Wisely, it has not been attempted to catalogue the circumstances which will justify or require either grant or denial of remedy. The doctrine leaves much to the discretion of the court to which plaintiff resorts, and experience has not shown a judicial tendency to renounce one's own jurisdiction so strong as to result in many abuses.

14 Castanho v. Brown & Root (U.K.) Ltd., [1981] A.C. 557, 573 (H.L.), "the width and flexibility of equity are not to be undermined by categorisation."

「衡平法的寬度及彈性是不能被類別所破壞。」企圖將裁量權硬性類別化是有可能會傷害到未來之個案正義。但是如前述美國裁量權是如英國（或蘇格蘭）法制一般，其行使的基礎是「正義的目的[15]」，並引用英國判例法[16]為論述之依據，為什麼自1947年本案後會有「經驗顯示有著強烈的司法傾向去放棄自己的管轄權以致造成許多（對外國人）的濫用程序」？美國法院基於國籍或居所之理由而對第三世界的受害者加以歧視之情形，不但為個人怒髮衝冠的一再指責，亦如前述為1999年海牙草約第22(3)條及2004年UNIDROIT Principles第3.2條所公開禁止。為什麼英國母法之判例法是以「正義為目的」之法學，自1947年後於美國法院會變成「濫用程序」的「掠奪性新殖地法學」？

(二)公共利益與法律恐怖主義

於1947年Jackson J.即提出對「不方便法院」法學所應加以考量之因素的經典論述[17]：「如果欲將對於造成既定結果所必須的因素的份量及結合去加以敘述或預測是有困難的，但是對那些應該被加以考慮的去將其陳列出來並無困難。一個應考量的利益，並且這個利益可能會是最應優先的，就是訴訟者之私人利益。其他重要的考量為證據來源接近的相對容易性；不情願出庭證人強迫程序的可供利用性，及取得願意出庭證人之費

---

15 Spiliada Mar. Corp. v. Cansulex Ltd., [1987] A.C. 460, 465 (H.L.) (appeal taken from Eng.)見陳隆修、許兆慶、林恩瑋、李瑞生四人合著，《國際私法-管轄與選法理論之交錯》，台北，五南圖書公司，2009年3月，初版1刷，195-215頁。

16 Logan v. Bank of Scotland, (1906) 1 K.B. 141; cf. La Socie te du Gaz de Paris v. La Socie te Anonyme de Navigation 'Les Armateurs Francais.' (1926) Sess.Cas. (H.L.) 13.

17 330 U.S. 501, para. 14,
If the combination and weight of factors requisite to given results are difficult to forecast or state, those to be considered are not difficult to name. An interest to be considered, and the one likely to be most pressed, is the private interest of the litigant. Important considerations are the relative ease of access to sources of proof; availability of compulsory process for attendance of unwilling, and the cost of obtaining attendance of willing, witnesses; possibility of view of premises, if view would be appropriate to the action; and all other practical problems that make trial of a case easy, expeditious and inexpensive. There may also be questions as to the enforcibility of a judgment if one is obtained. The court will weigh relative advantages and obstacles to fair trial. It is often said that the plaintiff may not, by choice of an inconvenient forum, 'vex,' 'harass,' or 'oppress' the defendant by inflicting upon him expense or trouble not necessary to his own right to pursue his remedy. But unless the balance is strongly in favor of the defendant, the plaintiff's choice of forum should rarely be disturbed.

用；如果地點的視察對於訴訟是有必要的，視察的可能性；及使得案件之審判能夠簡單、快速、及便宜之所有其他之實際問題。另外可能有關之問題為取得判決後之強制執行問題。為了能達成公平的審判法院會衡量相關的益處及障礙。通常是認為原告不得經由選擇一個不方便的法院去加諸被告費用或依其權利去要求救濟之不必要之麻煩，以『困擾』、『騷擾』、或『壓迫』被告。但是除非是考量的平衡是強烈的對被告有利，原告所選擇的法院是應極少被干擾的。」這個論述很明顯的與英國母法先前的「困擾性或壓迫性」主義一般，禁止原告對被告造成「困擾或壓迫」之行為。另外本案中美國最高法院認為「原告所選擇的法院是應極少被干擾的」，這與早期英國法院極度尊重當事人原告之利益事一致的[18]。即使現在採用「不方便法院」法學，個人較近亦如此論述[19]：「故而第一階段是被告必須證明除了英國法院外，還有其他有管轄權的法院很明顯的（clearly or distinctly）較英國法院合適。除了要有其他有管轄權之法院外，該法院必須很明顯的較英國法院合適，只是證明英國法院不是合適或不是自然的法院並不符合要件。所謂『明顯的合適』之要件，事實上於英國採納不方便法院之前，英國已有自然法院（natural forum）之概念。」

---

18 見陳隆修，《國際私法管轄權評論》，台北，五南圖書公司，民國75年11月，初版，84頁。「因為英國法院於訴訟會造成困擾（vexation）或壓迫（oppression）之情形下，為避免造成不正當（unjust）的後果，可以命令停止（stay）或駁回（dismiss）當事人於英國之訴訟，甚至可以禁止（injunction）當事人於國外起訴或繼續進行國外之訴訟，或強制執行國外之判決。此種管轄上之權力為英法院之自由裁量權（discretionary power），法院必須很謹慎地使用此種權力。法院必須於當事人之一方，若繼續進行其於法院地或法院外之訴訟，會很明顯地對他方當事人造成困擾或壓迫，或著濫用法院之訴訟程序時才可使用此種權力。另一要件為法院欲停止訴訟之進行時，必須不能對原告造成不公平（injustice）之現象。而上述兩要件之舉證責任在於被告。」

19 陳隆修、許兆慶、林恩瑋、李瑞生四人合著，《國際私法-管轄與選法理論之交錯》，台北，五南圖書公司，2009年3月，初版1刷，208頁。另外於209頁中如此敘述：「總之所謂『明顯的合適』的概念，事實上與前述方便法院一般，法院不但會注意當事人居住或經商之地，證人的便利性及花費，還有交易之準據法等。至於當事人若有指定管轄法院及提起否認債權之訴時，學理上亦與前述方便法院一致。」「當事人若提出否認之訴時，英國法院因怕會與其他國家之法院發生管轄之衝突，故通常會允許停止訴訟之請求，但於Smyth v. Behbehani (1999) Times, 9 April, CA中，為了使得類似的訴訟可同時一起被處理，在正義的需求下，否認之訴被允許提起。」另外210頁：「但是除了於第一階段被告須證明有明顯的更合適的有管轄權的外國法院外，於第二階段法院必須考慮到是否為了正義的需求，停止訴訟之請求應被駁回，此時原告須證明其於英國提起訴訟之正當性。故而第二階段的舉證責任在於原告」。

個人認為或許Jackson J.於下面之論述是美國判例法於裁量權上與母法英國判例法上於裁量權在行使上之分水嶺[20]：「公共利益之因素在適用這個法理上亦占有著地位。當訴訟是被堆積在一個擁塞的中心而不是在其起源處被解決，則對法院會造成行政上之困難。陪審團的義務是一種負擔，而若訴訟是與社區無關這種負擔不應加諸在該社區的人民身上。若是於牽涉及許多人之事情之訴訟，審判應以他們的觀點及可接觸的範圍內進行是合乎道理的，而不應是於一個遙遠角落的國家進行，而他們只能經由報告而知道該訴訟。當地是有個利益去使得當地的紛爭於家園之地解決。另外並且有一種合適性是存在著，亦即在審判不同州籍之案件時，應於對案件準據法之州法較為熟悉之法院中審理，而不是使得其他地方之法院去解決衝突法及對其陌生之法律之問題。」如前述準據法是否為法院地法為英、美兩國不方便法院法學所應考慮之重點，而於英國的CPR 1998, s.6.20(5)(c)中契約準據法為英國法甚至是訴訟通知送達境外之一種管轄基礎（方便法院）。但是使美國「不方便法院」法學與英國於此方面之裁量權不同的是在美國法院於「公共利益」上之考量，這是英國母法所沒有的。

基於「公共利益」之考量，後續的美國案例經常以「法院案件擁塞」、「人民沒有義務當陪審員」、或「訴訟程序耗費人民稅金」為理由，而拒絕第三世界人民於當地受到美國跨國公司傷害之請求。這種以「公共利益」去拒絕外國請求者基於外國訴因而對美國被告所提起的請求

20 330 U.S. 501, para. 15,
Factors of public interest also have place in applying the doctrine. Administrative difficulties follow for courts when litigation is piled up in congested centers instead of being handled at its origin. Jury duty is a burden that ought not to be imposed upon the people of a community which has no relation to the litigation. In cases which touch the affairs of many persons, there is reason for holding the trial in their view and reach rather than in remote parts of the country where they can learn of it by report only. There is a local interest in having localized controversies decided at home. There is an appropriateness, too, in having the trial of a diversity case in a forum that is at home with the state law that must govern the case, rather than having a court in some other forum untangle problems in conflict of laws, and in law foreign to itself.

是有道理嗎[21]？對於美國法院基於「公共利益」所行使的拒絕管轄之裁量權，個人基於第三世界法律學生之身分，於此謹代表13億中國人質問美國法院——請問美國跨國公司在第三世界所榨取的大量「利益」及資源是否為美國投資者及美國政府所受益？所謂的「公共利益」就只有避免「法院程序的擁塞」與「人民加入陪審團的負擔」而已嗎？美國跨國公司在第三世界造成環境汙染，侵害當地人民身體、健康、生命，及甚至造成種族滅絕之暴行[22]，因而所獲得的巨額利益及所產生之稅收難道不屬於美國社會的「真實性公共利益」？美國於「不方便法院」上所賴以行使裁量權之「公共利益」理論，一方面幫助美國以WTO及自由貿易之名於第三世界憑藉著資金、技術、行銷之絕對優勢大肆掠奪自然資源及獲取高額商業利潤，一方面卻又拒絕給予第三世界之被害者到美國法院要求正義，因此個人習慣性的稱美國「不方便法院」法學對第三世界人民所實施的是「法

21 類似之案情亦發生於英國之Lubbe v. Cape PLC, [2000] 1 W.L.R. 1545 (H.L.)。於該案中被告英國母公司之南非子公司於南非開採石棉礦，其被主張其子公司於南非未遵守安全規則故造成死傷，三千多請求者中只有一人為英國公民及居民，其餘皆為南非公民與居民。被告不方便法院之主張為一審所接受，二審亦認為南非為明顯的合適法院。最高法院採納Spiliada及Connelly之原則，認為請求人若沒有法律扶助或律師抽成制，則無法起訴，拒絕美式公共利益之考量，允許訴訟之進行。Lord Bingham (Lubbe v. Cape PLC, [2000] 1 W.L.R. 1545, 1561 (H.L.))認為公共利益是與當事人的利益及正義的目的無關："public interest considerations not related to the private interests of the parties and the ends of justice have no bearing on the decision which the court has to make. Where a catastrophe has occurred in a particular place, the fact that numerous victims live in that place, that the relevant evidence is to be found there and that site inspections are most conveniently and inexpensively carried out there will provide factors connecting any ensuing litigation with the Court exercising jurisdiction in that place. These are matters of which the Spiliada test takes full account."又認為（at 1559）如果在「更合適的」南非法院進行訴訟會等同於「正義的拒絕」："if these proceedings were stayed in favour of the more appropriate forum in South Africa the probability is that the plaintiffs would have no means of obtaining the professional representation and expert evidence which would be essential if these claims were to be justly decided. This would amount to a denial of justice. In the special and unusual circumstances of these proceedings, lack of the means, in South Africa, to prosecute these claims to a conclusion, provides a compelling ground, at the second stage of the Spiliada test, for refusing to stay the proceedings here."而Lord Hope (Lubbe v. Cape PLC, [2000] 1 W.L.R. 1545, 1561)則採用「司法自尊與政治上之責任或利益不能被適用」之原則 ("questions of judicial amour propre and political interest or responsibility have no part to play.")其認為蘇格蘭判例已於此方面一再證明這個原則，La Societe du Gaz de Paris v. La Societe Anonyme de Navigation "Les Armateurs Francaise", 1926 Sess. Cas. 13, 21 (H.L. 1925) (appeal taken form Scot.) "Obviously the Court cannot allege its own convenience, or the amount of its own business, or its distaste for trying actions which involve taking evidence in French, as a ground for refusal⋯." (Lord Sumner)

22 陳隆修，《2005年海牙法院選擇公約評析》，台北，五南圖書公司，2009年1月，初版1刷，294、295、304-306頁。

律恐怖主義」（“legal terrorism”）或「掠奪性新殖民主義」（“predatory neocolonialism”）。

於Jackson J.做成論述後近65年，個人對其精闢之論述是深感佩服的。雖然對於「公共利益」之詮釋Jackson J.可能是與英國作法不同[23]，但個人以為問題不在於其對「公共利益」之強調，而在後續判決之行使方式。對於Gulf Oil Corp.於「公共利益」之詮釋，英國法院傳統上之看法卻是相反的，個人較近如此論述[24]：「相對於美國一般之看法，英國法院傳統上對外國人於英國訴訟，卻認為是無形的外匯收入[25]，並且對英國司法名譽之提升有益。」相對於英國母法之傳統作法，美國「不方便法院」於「公共利益」上之操作，已為舉世公認對弱勢第三世界人民造成莫大傷害之作法。Justice Jackson之論述或許是甚為符合邏輯，並應值得贊許，但如個人最近於評析Hilton v. Guyot[26]時，對Justice Gray於一百多年前引用其時英國判例法之論述如此的敘述[27]：「雖然Hilton已不為許多州所遵守，但不可否認的上述Justice Gray的法律邏輯是氣勢磅礡無懈可擊。個

---

[23] 在較近於Lubbe v Cape plc, [2000] 1 WLR 1545, 1567中，Lord Hope重申不方便法院之基本原則仍在於當事人之利益及正義的目的。這個基本原則並不允許將公共利益之因素加以考慮，並且即使是這個因素應被加以考慮，英國法院並不合適去進行這種諮詢。因此其認為無論如何的基於公共利益或公共政策，該訴訟是應於外國進行，如果不能證明在所有當事人之利益及正義之目的下，案件是可以更合適的在外國法院審理，則英國法院仍應行使管轄權（"however desirable it may be on grounds of public interest or public policy that the litigation should be conducted elsewhere and not in the English Courts."）相反的，如果所有當事人之利益及正義之目的要求英國法院停止訴訟，無論公共利益或公共政策是如何的要求必須於英國審理，英國法院仍會允許停止訴訟（" if the interests of all the parties and the ends of justice require that the action in this country should be stayed, a stay ought to be granted however desirable it may be on grounds of public interest or public policy that the action should be tried here."）[2000] 1 W.L.R. at 1566, 1567。因此Lord Hope在Lubbe中是明示的拒絕美式「公共利益」之運作。故而Piper Aircraft Co. v. Reyno, 454 U.S. 235 (1981)中之「公共利益」論述是被拒絕的。

[24] 陳隆修、許兆慶、林恩瑋、李瑞生四人合著，《國際私法-管轄與選法理論之交錯》，台北，五南圖書公司，2009年3月，初版1刷，215頁。個人又如此論述：「但現在英國最高法院認為司法上之自大，應為司法禮誼所取代，故這方面之作法可能有待觀察。但事實上甚多商會或仲裁中心皆位於英國，以個人從事律師業務之經驗，實務上商業習慣與需求會淹沒任何看似完美的新理論。」

[25] Camilla Cotton Oil Co v. Granadex SA [1976] 2 Lloyd’s Rep 10 at 14.

[26] 159 U.S. 113, 16 S, Ct. 139, 40 L. Ed. 95 (1895).

[27] 陳隆修，〈97台上2376號〉，陳隆修、宋連斌、許兆慶著，《國際私法—國際程序法新視界》，五南出版，2011年，第116頁。

人以為Justice Gray精闢的分析是令人衷心懾服的，如果由法律邏輯而言似乎於其時是沒有缺陷。對這個領頭案例美國同僚自然有著不少評論，但似乎並沒有以其所本的母法英國法之觀點而加以評價。雖然Justice Gray所闡述的法律邏輯近乎完美，但它卻與其母法近年來之發展背道而馳。Hilton案顯示法律邏輯無論如何的嚴謹及無懈可擊——它仍可能無法通過時間終極的考驗。Hilton案赤裸裸的給我們上一課：法律的重心不在嚴謹的法學邏輯，而在有效的執行正義。如果法律的重心在無懈可擊的邏輯分析，那麼如Hilton案所顯示的，它可能通不過時間的終極考驗。」個人其時引用最尊敬的恩師Prof. Graveson的論述做為結論，而該結論似乎同時亦可於此處被加以適用：「……邏輯並非判例法之最高價值。英國國際私法於要求實質正義之基本目地上會給予邏輯一致性之政策必要之限制[28]。」

的確自然法的概念，無論是程序上之自然正義或是實體上之實質正義，我們不得不於司法程序開始及結果時一再重覆背誦這個經咒，否則就容易走入歧途。但事實上在國際訴訟上，於複數訴訟（平行訴訟）時英國判例法Lopez v Chavarri於一百多年前即對法院之選定下個萬世不移之基礎論調[29]：「是否正義的真正利益是將問題於此審判或將其交付外國法院最能被達成。」因此在「正義的直正利益」之核心基礎下，於國際訴訟上當面對複數訴訟時，不但歐盟助長選購法院鼓勵濫訴之先繫屬優先死硬原則不能被加以合理化，美國法院對第三世界弱勢被害者加以歧視之「公共利益」之不當運作更應被視為非法。

歐盟的迷思在於布魯賽爾公約及規則第2條之一般管轄（住所）及第5條之特別管轄皆符合傳統上「重大（實質）關連之要求」，故大陸法通常認為在有管轄權法院皆具有「重大關連」之情形下，法院不需要行使不方便法院之裁量權。但是在二十一世紀全球化的現代商業社會中，經常

28　R.H. Graveson, Conflict of Laws, p. 79 (7th ed. 1974).

29　Lopez v Chavarri [1901] W.N. 115, 116, “whether the true interests of justice would be best served by trying the question here, or leaving it to the foreign tribunal”.

對同一訴因會有著數個法院皆具有「重大關連」之管轄權，而第一個先繫屬之法院不見得是最符合所有當事人利益及正義目的之法院。因此先繫屬優先原則不但可能會破壞當事人和解之機會而鼓勵當事人先發動訴訟，更可能會造成自然被告去選購法院及對自然原告造成困擾或壓迫之濫用訴訟之情形（包括否認之訴之提出）。於Shaffer中Marshall J.即公開表示為了簡化管轄權問題而去犧牲自然法上公平正義之概念，「代價太高了」[30]：「並且，當一個特定法院依International Shoe其管轄權之存在是不清楚時，以迴避管轄問題來簡化訴訟的代價可能是犧牲了『公平與實質正義』。這個代價是太高。」很清楚的，以死硬簡單的先繫優先原則來處理21世紀全球化世界的跨國訴訟——「代價太高了」。

同樣的意見亦展現在Dicey and Morris對布魯賽爾公約的評語上[31]：「在第一類之案件中，以要求除了第一個繫屬的法院外其他任何法院皆不得行使管轄，公約在解決複數訴訟之問題上是採取一個有些粗糙的方法。」先繫屬優先原則或許是過分粗糙，其簡單化之代價或許太高。但是美國之「不方便法院」於「公共利益」之運作上更是危害及第三世界受害者1966年人權公約之訴訟權、財產權、及第2條之基本生存權。個人一再強調聲名卓越的法院所長久累積的判例就是「自然道法」，對於歐盟的「先繫屬優先原則」及美國的「公共利益」之操作所帶來之負面效果，個人以一百多年前Lopez v Chavarri所立下之順天應人之標準來加以回覆——「是否正義的真正利益最能被達成」。

---

30 433 U.S. 186, 211, "It might also be suggested that allowing in rem jurisdiction avoids the uncertainty inherent in the International Shoe standard and assures a plaintiff of a forum. We believe, however, that the fairness standard of International Shoe can be easily applied in the vast majority of cases. Moreover, when the existence of jurisdiction in a particular forum under International Shoe is unclear, the cost of simplifying the litigation by avoiding the jurisdictional question may be the sacrifice of 'fair play and substantial justice.' That cost is too high."

31 Dicey, Morris and Collins, 14th ed., p.489, "The Conventions adopt a somewhat crude solution to the problem of lis alibi pendens by requiring, in the first class of case, that any court other than the court first seised shall not exercise jurisdiction." Dresser UK Led v Falcongate Freight Management Ltd [1992] Q.B. 502, 514 (CA).

(三)沒有人到這些法院來要求正義會徒勞無功

對於歐盟及美國，個人希望Lord Denning如暮鼓晨鐘的論述能有著醍醐灌頂之效果[32]：「沒有人到這些法院來要求正義會徒勞無功……這個到這裡來的權力並不只侷限於英國人。它拓展至任何友好的外國人。如果他願意如此做，他可以要求我們法院的幫助。如果你願意你可以稱這是『選購法院』，但如果法院是在英國，同時在貨的品質及服務的速度上，它是一個選購的好地方。」相對於Lord Denning這個大義領凜然氣勢磅礴的論述，迷信於「重大關連」管轄基礎的歐盟同僚必須體認「以迴避管轄問題來簡化訴訟的代價可能是犧牲了『公平與實質正義』，這個代價是太高。」故而在目前二十一世紀全球化法學（包含國際管轄在內）之重心是在追求個案正義下，歐盟同僚必須認真思考以機械式的先繫屬優先原則來迴避管轄權於裁量權上之行使，「這個代價是太高」[33]。而美國同僚慣

32 "No one who comes to these courts asking for justice should come in vain···. This right to come here is not confined to Englishmen. It extends to any friendly foreigner. He can seek the aid of our courts if he desires to do so. You may call this 'forum shopping' if you please, but if the forum is England, it is a good place to shop in, both for the quality of the goods and the speed of service." The Atlantic Star, [1973] 1 Q.B. 364, 381-82 (C.A.).但是於House of Lords中Lord Reid卻對Lord Denning這個磅礡雄偉的論述，認為過分屬於「舊時代的好日子」："the good old days, the passing of which many may regret, when inhabitants of this island felt an innate superiority over those unfortunate enough to belong to other races." The Atlantic Star, [1974] 1 A.C. 436, 478 (H.L. 1973) (appeal taken from Eng.)

33 如果全面性的指控大陸法於自然程序正義上完全忽視個案正義或許是一種太過嚴重的控訴。正如英國法大陸法亦禁止濫用程序，另外對「選購法院」（這裡指於不適當的法院提起訴訟）雖不能以「不方便法院」而去避免，但是可以於承認及執行外國判決階段間接的去處理。個人認為這是時間與司法資源的浪費與拖延，並可能侵犯及國際禮誼之和諧。P M North, JJ Fawcett, Cheshire and North's Private International Law, 13th ed., pp. 268, 269, "civil law jurisdictions, when faced with the same problem of forum shopping abroad, deal with it in an indirect way at the stage of recognition and enforcement of the foreign judgment obtained in an inappropriate forum for trial." 14th ed., p.334.有趣的是在Gulf Oil Corp. v. Gilbert作成前5年，Jackson, J.對於選購法院、困擾性或壓迫性法則、及不方便法院中的公共利益作如此有趣的論述Miles v. Ill. Cent. R.R. Co., 315 U.S. 698, 706 (1942): "The judiciary has never favored this sort of shopping for a forum. It has sought to protect its own good name as well as to protect defendants by injunctions against the practice of seeking out soft spots in the judicial system in which to bring particular kinds of litigation. But the judges, with lawyerly indirection, have not avowed the interest of the judiciary in orderly resort to the courts as a basis for their decision, and have cast their protective doctrines in terms of sheltering defendants against vexatious and harassing suits. This judicial treatment of the subject of venue leads Congress and the parties to think of the choice of a forum as a private matter between litigants, and in cases like the present obscures the public interest in venue practices behind a rather fantastic fiction that a widow is harassing the Illinois Central Railroad."於英國Lord Diplock曾表達類似之公共政策，MacShannon v. Rockware Glass Ltd., 1978 A.C. 795 (H.L.): "that the administration of justice within the United

性的以「公共利益」來行使「不方便法院」的裁量，他們必須捫心自問在這樣的裁量權之行使下，「是否資本主義的掠奪性真正利益最能被達成」[34]，或者是「是否正義的真正利益最能被達成」？

(四)天道無親恆與善人—全球化法學

如同前述所謂「不方便法院」的「conveniens」指的並不是「便利」之意思[35]，而所謂自然原告對自然被告於「自然法院」提起自然之訴訟，所謂「自然法院」當然不是「資本主義之利益被達成之法院」，亦不完全是「具有重大關連管轄基礎之法院」，而應是「正義的真正利益最能被達成之法院」。二十一世紀全球化法學於國際管轄——這自然包含裁量權之行使——之心與靈魂（heart and soul）是在於「是否正義的真正利益

Kingdom should be conducted in such a way as to avoid any unnecessary diversion to the purposes of litigation, of time and efforts of witnesses and others which would otherwise be spent on activities that are more productive of national wealth or well-being. Many a mickle makes a muckle; and if it were to become the common practice to bring Scottish industrial injury cases in England, the total waste of time and effort would be substantial."

34 "Simultaneously, substantial groups of foreign citizens are suffering from manufacturing and environmental disasters caused by American corporations and their subsidiaries. The number of injured individuals is becoming too large to ignore and their injuries too grave to disregard. Yet U.S. courts continue to dismiss these cases, basing their decision on forum non conveniens. The docrine considers a set of public and private factors but excludes social and moral factors from the balance. Neither the public nor private factors consider the social and moral responsibility that accompany the expanding global economy. Forum non conveniens should be a fluid doctrine capable of weighing dominant economic and social trends. Factoring moral and social responsibility into the forum non conveniens balance would reduce the number of plaintiffs injured by American corporations who are unable to bring their claims. By leaving moral and social responsibility out of the forum non conveniens analysis, American courts are enabling the exploitation of foreign citizens within the framework of the globalized economy." Leah Nico, From local to global: Reform of forum non conveniens needed to ensure justice in the era of globalization, 11 Sw.J.L.& Trade Am. 345 (2005).

35 於早期採「困擾性」或「壓迫性」法學時，Lord Justice Scott即說只是便利因素的平衡並不能剝奪原告於英國起訴之利益，故必須對被告造成不公正（困擾、壓迫、或濫用程序），及停止訴訟不會對原告造成不公正，才可停止訴訟，而舉證責任在被告。

"(1) A mere balance of convenience is not a sufficient ground for depriving a plaintiff of the advantages of prosecuting his action in an English court if it is otherwise properly brought. The right of access to the King's court must not be lightly refused.

(2) In order to justify a stay two conditions must be satisfied, one positive and the other negative:

(a) the defendant must satisfy the court that the continuance of the action would work an injustice because it would be oppressive or vexatious to him or would be an abuse of the process of the court in some other way; and

(b) the stay must not cause an injustice to the plaintiff. On both, the burden of proof is on the defendant." St. Pierre v. S. Am. Stores (Gath & Chalves) Ltd., [1936] 1 K.B. 382, 398 (Eng. C.A. 1935).

最能被達成」。個人經常舉Connelly v. RTZ Corpn. plc[36]為例，最密切關連地之法院不見得永遠是「最能達成正義之真正利益」的法院。如Lord Goff於Spiliada Maritime Corpn v. Cansulex Ltd中所說的[37]：「如果有著其他可供起訴之法院而該法院對於該訴訟之審判是表面上明顯的為更合適時，除非由於正義要求停止訴訟之請求是不可以被允許之情形下，否則通常停止之請求會被允許。」故而由Connelly或Spiliada所顯示與案件最具有密切關連之地之法院或明顯的更為合適之法院雖然通常是自然原告對自然被告順理成章應該提起自然之訴之法院（亦即通常表面上可能直覺的會認定為自然法院），於例外之可能情形下，他們的所謂表面上之自然管轄權應在個案正義之要求下退讓[38]。亦即真正的自然法院（不同於表面上合適之自然法院）是在自然正義程序及實質正義的要求下，於國際複數訴訟中「正義的真正利益最能被達成」之法院。這亦是中國式法學「道法自然」的詮釋之一種。

因此如果與案件具有最密切關連之地之法院及表面上為明顯的更合適法院，於個案「實質正義」（substantial justice）的要求下，其管轄權應退讓給「正義的真正利益最能被達成」之法院，則該後者法院才是符合自

36 [1998] AC 854, HL.見陳隆修、許兆慶、林恩瑋、李瑞生四人合著，《國際私法—管轄與選法理論之交錯》，台北，五南圖書公司，2009年3月，初版1刷，210頁。

37 The Spiliada [1987] AC 460 at 476. Lord Goff: "… if there is some other available forum which prima facie is clearly more appropriate for the trial of the action, it will ordinarily grant a stay unless there are circumstance by reason of which justice requires that a stay should nevertheless not be granted."

38 於Connelly v. RTZ Corp. PLC, 1998 A.C. 854, 872 (H.L. 1997)中英國最高法院雖然認為："if a clearly more appropriate forum overseas has been identified, generally speaking the plaintiff will have to take that forum as he finds it, even if it is in certain respects less advantageous to him than the English forum."但是請求者若於外國法院會受到不公正之對待，英國法院不會允許訴訟停止之請求。例如外國司法之不獨立，訴訟可能會拖延10年才會受到審判，或過低之賠償等，皆構成正義之拒絕。The Abidin Daver, 1 A.C. 398, 411 (H.L. 1984); The Vishva Ajay, 2 Lloyd's Rep. 558, 560 (Q.B. 1989); BMG Trading Ltd. v. A.S. McKay, 1998 I.L. Pr. 691 (Eng. C.A.).而後來在Lubbe v. Cape PLC, [2000]1 W.L.R. 1545, 1554 (H.L.)中，正如以前所發生於Connelly, 1998 A.C. at 874中，請求者於原來外國「合適法院」，由於缺乏外國法律貧民扶助或律師抽成制度，故無法起訴。英國最高法院將這個「私人利益」放置於整個分析的重點。嚴格而論，由於涉及英國法律扶助，故「公共利益」的分析對英國是不利的。於經過Connelly案後，英國政府對於外國人申請法律扶助去對英國公司起訴之情形，於2000年修改法律扶助辦法，但仍保留交換律師抽成制度。Access to Justice Act 1999, c. 22, 4-10 (Eng.); Conditional Fee Agreements Regulations, (2000) SI 2000/692. 見C.G.J. Morse, Not in the Public Interest? Lubbe v. Cape PLC, 37 Tex. Int'l L.J. 541, 549, 550 (2002).

然正義之自然法院。個人一再認為Connelly v. RTZ Corpn. plc[39]案充分證明於特殊情形下，即使與案件具有最密切關連之法院因為無法達成「實質正義」[40]，因此不能符合自然法院之核心要件。如果相較於英國判例法於裁量權上一百多年來之經驗，在國際複數訴訟上，美國「公共利益」之運作[41]，及歐盟本於「重大關連管轄」而來之先繫屬優先法則，或許有時無法於個案上達成「實質正義」之要求，因此即使是具有「重大關連管轄」或「最密切關連管轄」之法院，亦不應該被認為是永遠符合「自然法院」之要件。二十一世紀全球化法學在國際管轄上，無論是英國式的「方便與不方便法院」，美國式的「最低限度關連點」與「不方便法院」，及大陸法的「禁止濫用訴訟程序」，這些裁量權法學行使的心與靈魂都應是在於「是否正義的真正利益最能被達成」[42]。而對這個二十一世紀全球化國際管轄法規於裁量權之心與靈魂，我們中國文化早在近二千多年前即領先宣示「天道無親恆與善人」。「不患寡患不均」之「禮運大同」「王道」法律哲學與二十一世紀全球化法學於國際管轄法規裁量權行使[43]之心與靈魂

39 [1998] AC 854, HL. 見陳隆修、許兆慶、林恩瑋、李瑞生四人合著，《國際私法—管轄與選法理論之交錯》，台北，五南圖書公司，2009年3月，初版1刷。210、211頁。

40 事實上在Lubbe, [2000]1 W.L.R. at 1558, 1559, 1560中，南非法院雖為Lord Bingham所認為是「更為合適之法院」（"the more appropriate forum"），但是由於南非當時尚未有完整的集體訴訟法規，故其認為於南非進行訴訟，會構成「正義的拒絕」（This would amount to a denial of justice）。

41 有趣的是由於法制的不完備，許多第三世界的政府皆認為訴訟若於當地進行是與當地的公共利益無關。在Lubbe v. Cape PLC中，南非政府於第三審時介入，認為被告與南非沒有關連，更於南非沒有財產，故公共利益指向應於英國進行訴訟。Peter Muchlinski, Corporations in Internatinoal Litigation: Problems of Jurisdiction and the United Kingdom Asbestos Cases, 50 Int'l & Comp. L.Q.1, 21 (2001); C. G. J. Morse, Not in the Public Interest? Lubbe v. Cape PLC, 37 Tex. Int'l L.J. 541, 552 (2002).相同的在舉世震驚且傷害更達數十倍以上的In re Union Carbide Corp. Gas Plant Disaster at Bhopal, India in Dec. 1984, 634 F. Supp. 842 (S.D.N.Y. 1986), affd, 809 F.2d 195 (2nd Cir. 1987), cert. denied, 484 U.S. 871 (1987).案件中，印度政府亦表明其司法無法承受數十萬請求之能力，但美國法院仍堅守「逆向帝國主義」法學。個人基於比較法學之立場，請教WTO及諾貝爾和平獎——美國沒有進行「保護貿易主義」嗎？美國法院沒有侵犯第三世界人權公約中所保障的訴訟權、財產權、生命權嗎？更重要的1966年人權公約第1(2)條中第三世界的生存權沒有被踐踏嗎？相較之下在Lubbe中約7500個請求者取得兩千一百萬英鎊的和解金。37Tex. Int'l L.J. 541, 557.

42 調查顯示於英美若案件以不方便法院而被停止，則訴訟甚少在其他法院再被提起。David W. Robertson, Forum Non Conveniens in America and England: A Rather Fantastic Fiction, 103 Law Q. Rev. 398 (1987).

43 在Airbus Indus. G.I.E. v. Patel, [1999] 1 A.C. 119, 141 (H.L. 1998)中，Lord Goff公開宣示不方便法院法學「可被視為最文明之法學原則之一」〈"can be regarded as one of the most civilised of legal

是相配合的。

二、Piper Aircraft Co. v. Reyno

(一)案件

如果Gulf Oil Corporation v. Gilbert[44]案可說是正式的定立下美國不方便法學之定義與基礎，則Piper Aircraft Co. v. Reyno[45]可謂是美國法院光明正大理直氣壯的以不方便法院之名，而拒絕給予外國原告基於外國訴因而來之請求之濫觴[46]。於案中一小型商用包機於蘇格蘭墜毀，駕駛與5名乘客立即死亡，他們皆為蘇格蘭公民及居民。原告被上訴人代表5名乘客之遺產而對被告上訴人於加州法院提起不當死亡之訴訟。被告為一於賓夕法尼亞製造飛機之公司及一於俄亥俄製造螺旋槳之公司。飛機於英國登記並為英國公司所擁有及經營。死亡乘客之繼承人及最近家屬皆為蘇格蘭人，而事故之調查是由英國官方所進行。基於無過失責任或過失責任原告要求被告損害賠償，蘇格蘭法並不承認無過失責任。原告承認其於美國提告是因美國法於責任、訴訟資格、及損害賠償上是較蘇格蘭法對原告有利。後被告要求將訴訟移至加州聯邦法院，再後又根據28 U.S.C. § 1404(a)[47]而被移至賓州聯邦法院。賓州地院准許被告之請求，以不方便法院而駁回訴訟。法院依據Gilbert之標準[48]，而「分析影響到當事人便利

---

principles"〉。

44 330 U.S. 501 (1947).

45 454 U.S. 235 (1981).

46 對這種現象加以批評之評論見Jacqueline Duval-Major, Note, One-Way Ticket Home: The Federal Doctrine of Forum Non Conveniens and the International Plaintiff, 77 Cornell L. Rev. 650 (1992); John R. Wilson, Note, Coming to America to File Suit: Foreign Plaintiffs and the Forum Non Conveniens Barrier in Transnational Litigation, 65 Ohio St. L.J. 659 (2004). 又見Ronald A. Brand & Scott R. Jablonski, Forum Non Conveniens: History, Global Practice, and Future Under the Hague Convention on Choice of Court Agreements 58 (2007).

47 Section 1404(a) provides:
"For the convenience of parties and witnesses, in the interest of justice, a district court may transfer any civil action to any other district or division where it might have been brought."

48 454 U.S. 235, 236, Syllabus, "The District Court granted petitioners' motion to dismiss the action on the ground of *forum non conveniens*. Relying on the test set forth in *Gulf Oil Crop. v. Gilbert*, 330 U.S. 501, and analyzing the 'private interest factors' affecting the litigants' conenience and the 'public inter-

之『私人利益因素』及影響到法院便利之『公共利益因素』，正如同Gilbert所定下之標準，地院認定蘇格蘭是合適之法院。」但是上訴法院更改其判決，認定地院於進行Gilbert之分析時已經濫用裁量權，並且當另一個法院之法律是較原告所選之法院之法律不利時，訴訟之駁回是會被自動禁止的。美國最高法院認同地院之決定而更改高院之判決。

Justice Marshall代表法院作成判決。首先其注意到地院認為另一有管轄權之法院存在於蘇格蘭，兩個被告皆同意接受蘇格蘭法院之管轄，並且若時效屆至他們同意拋棄時效之抗辯[49]。英美法院於行使停止訴訟之裁量權前，會經常要求被告承認外國管轄、拋棄時效利益（現歐盟契約法原則14:601條[50]已接受英美法當事人得同意更改時效之作法）、承認外國法院之判決、提出外國判決執行之擔保金、或承認審判前調查庭所作成之證據。這是台灣民訴182之2條[51]及大陸於實行不方便法院所應注意的。

死者之家屬另外於蘇格蘭對駕駛、飛機經營商、及所有人另外提起訴訟。地院唯恐美國被告無法加入蘇格蘭第三當事人被告，因此認為「如果相關的所有的證人之可供利用之證據整個案件是呈現在一個陪審團前，對於所有的當事人是會更公平及花費較少」[52]。地院亦擔心由於美國採無過

---

est factors' affecting the forum's convenience, as set forth in *Gilbert*, the District Court concluded that Scotland was the appropriate forum. However, the Court of Appeals reversed, holding that the District Court had abused its discretion in conducting the *Gilbert* analysis and that, in any event, dismissal is automatically barred where the law of the alternative forum is less favorable to the plaintiff than the law of the forum chosen by the plaintiff."

49 454 U.S. 242, "It began by observing that an alternative forum existed in Scotland; Piper and Hartzell had agreed to submit to the jurisdiction of the Scottish courts and to waive any statute of limitations defense that might be available."

50 Section 6: Modification by Agreement
ARTICLE 14:601: AGREEMENTS CONCERNING PRESCRIPTION
(1) The requirements for prescription may be modified by agreement between the parties, in particular by either shortening or lengthening the periods of prescription.
(2) The period of prescription may not, however, be reduced to less than one year or extended to more than thirty years after the time of commencement set out in Article 14:203.

51 見陳隆修、許兆慶、林恩瑋、李瑞生四人合著，《國際私法—管轄與選法理論之交錯》，台北，五南圖書公司，2009年3月，初版1刷。229、230頁。

52 454 U.S. 243, "[I]t would be fairer to all parties and less costly if the entire case was presented to one jury with available testimony from all relevant witnesses."

失責任，而蘇格蘭採過失責任，因而會造成不一致之判決[53]。布魯賽爾規則的第6(1)條[54]有著共同訴訟之規定，而第28條[55]亦有著避免相關訴訟造成不一致判決之規定。故而聯邦地院之作法並未與其他文明國家之慣例在表面上會有脫節之處。但真正的問題似乎不在這裡。依個人所主張的實體法方法論，真正的問題在於產品的無過失責任在任何文明國家都是一種公共政策之問題，而如前述英國法院在有關英國公共政策時是經常不會將案件交付無法執行該政策之外國法院的。例如歐盟的羅馬II（Rome II）的第16條即規定無論非契約責任之準據法為何，法院地強行法之適用是不會被禁止的[56]。做為一個死忠的實體法論者，個人認為這個案件的重點不在法院於管轄權上裁量權之行使，而在於其公共政策（產品之無過失責任政策）被執行之強度（是否適用於外國消費者之保護上）。

上訴法院認為被告之無法追加蘇格蘭第三被告是一種「負擔但不是不公平」[57]。上訴法院又認為「如果它會導致對原告不利的準據法適用的

---

53 Footnote 7,
"The District Court explained that inconsistent verdicts might result if petitioners were held liable on the basis of strict liability here, and then required to prove negligence in an indemnity action in Scotland. Moreover, even if the same standard of liability applied, there was a danger that different juries would find different facts and produce inconsistent results."

54 Article 6
A person domiciled in a Member State may also be sued:
1. Where he is one of a number of defendants, in the courts for the place where any one of them is domiciled, provided the claims are so closely connected that it is expedient to hear and determine them together to avoid the risk of irreconcilable judgments resulting from separate proceedings.

55 Article 28
1.Where related actions are pending in the courts of different Member States, any court other than the court first seised may stay its proceedings.
……………
3.For the purposes of this Article, actions are deemed to be related where they are so closely connected that it is expedient to hear and determine them together to avoid the risk of irreconcilable judgments resulting from separate proceedings.

56 REGULATION (EC) No 864/2007 OF THE EUROPEAN PARLIAMENT AND OF THE COUNCIL of 11 July 2007 on the law applicable to non-contractual obligations
Article 16
Overriding mandatory provisions
Nothing in this Regulation shall restrict the application of the provisions of the law of the forum in a situation where they are mandatory irrespective of the law otherwise applicable to the non-contractual obligation.

57 454 U.S. 244, "The Court of Appeals gave little weight to the fact that Piper and Hartzell would not be

改變，法院會決定駁回訴訟會自動的被禁止。」[58]但美國最高法院認為：「只是經由證明於另一個替代法院所適用之實體法是比起現在法院所適用之法是對原告為較不利，原告即可挫敗基於不方便法院而要求駁回訴訟之請求，上訴法院這種認定是不對的。於探詢不方便法院之適用時，實體法可能之改變通常不應被給予決定性或甚至重大的份量。[59]」

(二)Conveniens不是指「便利」

但是更有趣的是最高法院說[60]：「的確，藉由認定不方便法院的諮詢之中心重點是便利性，Gilbert默示的承認不能僅因一個法律上不利之改變之可能即可禁止駁回之請求。依據Gilbert，當訴訟是於原告所選定之法院舉行時會對被告及法院產生重大負擔，並且原告是無法給予任何有關便利之明確理由以支持其選擇時，駁回訴訟是通常會是合適的。但是，如果對於法律不利的改變之可能性是給予重大的份量時，即使是所選定法院之審判地是明顯的不便利時駁回訴訟之要求仍可能被禁止。」**另外又說[61]：「當家園地之法院被選定時，去假設這個選擇是便利的是為合理**

able to implead potential Scottish third-party defendants, reasoning that this difficulty would be 'burdensome' but not 'unfair,' 630 F.2d 162."上訴法院並且認為由於賓州與蘇格蘭皆採用一事不再理原則，故判決不一致之情形不太會發生（註9）。

58 454 U.S. 246, "In other words, the court decided that dismissal is automatically barred if it would lead to a change in the applicable law unfavorable to the plaintiff." "[I]t is apparent that the dismissal would work a change in the applicable law so that the plaintiff's strict liability claim would be eliminated from the case. But ··· a dismissal for forum non conveniens, like a statutory transfer, 'should not, despite its convenience, result in a change in the applicable law.' Only when American law is not applicable, or when the foreign jurisdiction would, as a matter of its own choice of law, give the plaintiff the benefit of the claim to which she is entitled here, would dismissal be justified." 630 F.2d 163-164.

59 454 U.S. 247, "The Court of Appeals erred in holding that plaintiffs may defeat a motion to dismiss on the ground of forum non conveniens merely by showing that the substantive law that would be applied in the alternative forum is less favorable to the plaintiffs than that of the present forum. The possibility of a change in substantive law should ordinarily not be given conclusive or even substantial weight in the forum non conveniens inquiry."

60 454 U.S. 249, "Indeed, by holding that the central focus of the forum non conveniens inquiry is convenience, Gilbert implicitly recognized that dismissal may not be barred solely because of the possibility of an unfavorable change in law. Under Gilbert, dismissal will ordinarily be appropriate where trial in the plaintiff's chosen forum imposes a heavy burden on the defendant or the court, and where the plaintiff is unable to offer any specific reasons of convenience supporting his choice. If substantial weight were given to the possibility of an unfavorable change in law, however, dismissal might be barred even where trial in the chosen forum was plainly inconvenient."

61 454 U.S. 255, 256, "When the home forum has been chosen, it is reasonable to assume that this choice

的。但是當原告是外國人時，這個假設就是非常的沒有那麼合理。因為任何不方便法院的諮詢之中心目的就是去確保審判是便利的，一個外國原告的選擇是較不值得順服的。」但是「不方便法院的諮詢之中心重點是便利性」這個論述是正確的嗎？請允許個人再次引用Dicey and Morris 的教科書如下[62]：「不方便法院法學，亦即所謂其他法院是更『合適』指的就是為了正義的目的是更適合」。故而所謂「合適」的自然法院指的就是為了正義的目的更適合之意思。彷彿這樣還不夠明確，其又於註解中引用判例法而更白紙黑字的明確宣示[63]：「conveniens不是指『便利』」。於確立「方便與不方便法院」法學之領頭案例Spiliada中，Lord Goff宣示[64]所謂「合適法院」就是能更妥善的處理所有當事人之利益及正義之目的之法院。因此個人於此請求美國同僚注意，你們判例法的母法鏗鏘有力的宣布「conveniens不是『便利』，因此「不方便法院的諮詢中心的重點是便利性」是與母法之判例法不合的。

---

is convenient. When the plaintiff is foreign, however, this assumption is much less reasonable. Because the central purpose of any forum non conveniens inquiry is to ensure that the trial is convenient, a foreign plaintiff's choice deserves less deference."

62 Dicey and Morris, the Conflict of Laws, 14th ed., p.465, "The doctrine of *forum non conveniens*, i.e. that some other forum is more 'appropriate' in the sense of more suitable for the ends of justice, was developed by the Scottish courts in the nineteenth century, and was adopted (with some modifications) in the United States."

63 同上，"*Conveniens does not mean* 'convenient': see *The Atlantic Star* [1974] A.C. 436, 475; *GAF Corp v Amchem Products Inc* [1975] 1 Lloyd's Rep. 601, 607; *Spiliada Maritime Crop v Cansulex Ltd* [1987] A.C. 460, 474-475.

64 Spiliada Maritime Crop v. Cansulex Ltd [1987] 1 AC460, at 480, "to identify the forum in which the case can be suitably tried for the interests of all the parties and for the ends of justice"
Spiliada Maritime Crop v. Cansulex Ltd [1987] 1 AC460, at 476, "The basic principle is that a stay will only be granted on the ground of forum non conveniens where the court is satisfied that there is some available forum having jurisdiction, which is the appropriate forum for trial of the action, i.e. in which the case may be tried more suitably for the interests of all the parites and the ends of justice."但是在Spiliada Mar. Corp v. Cansulex Ltd.的「不方便及方便法院」原則確立之前，英國法院已累積了一些前置判例。例如於The Atlantic Star, [1974] 1 A.C. at 478 (H.L.)中對「困擾性或壓迫性」給予更開放之解釋。及Lord Justice Scott於MacShannon v. Rockware Glass Ltd., 1978 A.C. 795, 812 (H.L.)中對停止訴訟所立下之要件："In order to justify a stay two conditions must be satisfied, one positive and one negative: (a) the defendant must satisfy the court that there is another forum to whose jurisdiction he is amenable in which justice can be done between the parties at substantially less inconvenience or expense, and (b) the stay must not deprive the plaintiff of a legitimate personal or juridical advantage which would be available to him if he invoked the jurisdiction of the English court."

個人認為任何「方便與不方便法院」法學之重點若不是以正義為目的，就不是「道法自然」之行為。「外國原告之選擇較不值得順服」之論述就是這種謬誤理論之產物，它不但違反UNIDROIT Principles第3條禁止歧視之規定，亦違反1999海牙草約第22(3)條禁止歧視之規定，更是違反所有人權公約中的生存權、財產權、及訴訟權。因此個人於此再唸一次經咒——方便與不方便法院的心與靈魂在於「正義的真正利益是否最能被達成」[65]。這個儀式性的經咒不得不一再被重覆朗誦，否則第三世界無法驅逐美國「掠奪性新殖民地主義法學」的邪靈。「正義的真正利益是否最能被達成」的經咒，是今日全球化下保護第三世界對抗第一世界資本主義及自由貿易主義邪靈的金鋼經，是全球化法學中對第三世界人民救苦救難的大悲咒，是對WTO及諾貝爾和平獎這些岳不群機構加以降魔伏妖佛法無邊的金鋼杵、降魔杖。

但是固執的堅守死硬的先繫屬優先原則的大陸法必須注意到最高法院所說的[66]：「我們已經說過我們不會去立下一個規定裁量權之死硬規則，並且『每一個案件是根據其事實而來』。如果主要的重心只是被置於任何一個因素上，不方便法院便會失掉其大部分之靈活性，而使其不具有如此之價值。」這個有關裁量權的靈活性之必要性，是與Lord Scarman在Castanho v. Brown & Root （U.K.） Ltd.[67]中所說的「衡平法的寬度及靈活度是不可以被類別化所破壞」，在政策上是一致的。

通常有趣的是Marshall J.又說[68]：「上訴法院的方法不只是與不方便

65 Lopez v Chavarri [1901] W.N. 115, 116, "whether the true interests of justice would be best served by trying the question here, or leaving it to the foreign tribunal".

66 454 U.S. 249, 250, "And in *Williams v. Green Bay & Western R. Co.,* 326 U.S. 549, 326 U.S. 557 (1946), we stated that we would not lay down a rigid rule to govern discretion, and that '[e]ach case turns on its facts.' If central emphasis were placed on any one factor, the *forum non conveniens* doctrine would lose much of the very flexibility that makes it so valuable."

67 [1981] A.C. 557, 573 (H.L.), "the width and flexibility of equity are not to be undermined by categorisation."

68 454 U.S. 251, "The Court of Appeals' approach is not only inconsistent with the purpose of the *forum non conveniens* doctrine, but also poses substantial practical problems. If the possiblilty of a change in law were given substantial weight, deciding motions to dismiss on the ground of forum non conveniens would become quite difficult. Choice of law analysis would become extremely important, and the courts

法院法學之目的不一致，並且於實際上造成重大之困難。如果法律可能之改變是被給予重大之份量，那麼基於不方便法院之理由而去決定駁回之請求則會變成非常困難。」因為法院必須去決定選法規則及確定外國法院所適用之法律。最後又必須去比較各國法院所適用法律所給予當事人之權利、救濟、及程序，而就只能於另一法院與被選定之法院所適用之法律對原告一樣有利時才能駁回訴訟。而不方便法院法學被設立之部分原因就是去幫助法院去避免進行複雜的比較法工作，這就是Gilbert中所說的公共利益因素。

對於Marshall J.於1981年本於Gilbert去避免法院「去解決國際私法及自己所不熟悉法律之問題」之論述，或許是於某些程度上是正確的。但如Cardozo J.所說：「法學上的概念很少被執行至邏輯的極限」。這個避免「實際上重大困難」的「公共利益」之法學概念，還是應適度的受到「正義的真正利益」的限制。Marshall J.在1977年Shaffer[69]中已是先對自己在1981年之論述給予一個斬釘截鐵之明確答案：「為了簡化訴訟而去避免管轄問題之代價可能是會犧牲『公平原則與實質正義』。這個代價太高了。」

至於有關聯邦地院間之移轉，如前述美國最高法院於Van Dusen v. Barrack[70]中認為s. 1404(a)之移轉不應造成準據法之改變。這是因為最高法院認為下級法院：「強烈的傾向保護原告以對抗移轉所可能帶來州適用

---

would frequently be required to interpret the law of foreign jurisdictions. First, the trial court would have to determine what law would apply if the case were tried in the chosen forum, and what law would apply if the case were tried in the alternative forum. It would then have to compare the rights, remedies, and procedures available under the law that would be applied in each forum. Dismissal would be appropriate only if the court concluded that the Law applied by the alternative forum is as favorable to the plaintiff as that of the chosen forum. The doctrine of forum non conveniens, however, is designed in part to help courts avoid conducting complex exercise in comparative law. As we stated in Gilbert, the public interest factors point towards dismissal where the court would be required to 'untangle problems in conflict of laws, and in law foreign to itself.' 330 U.S. at 330 U.S. 509."

69 433 U.S. 186, 211, "Moreover, when the existence of jurisdiction in a particular forum under International Shoe is unclear, the cost of simplifying the litigation by avoiding the jurisdictional question may be the sacrifice of 'fair play and substantial justice.' That cost is too high."這個論述是直接關於最低限度關連點，但或許應適用於所有管轄問題上。

70 376 U.S. 612 (1964).

法上不利的改變之危險。[71]」故而Marshall J.說s.1404(a)是[72]：「雖然該條文是依據不方便法院而訂定，……但它是被意圖成為判例法之修正，而非為判例法之成文法。……地院依s. 1404(a)是被給予較多裁量權去移轉，而依不方便法院去駁回相較之下是較少的。……這個條文是被設計為『聯邦內務管理規則』，以便允許於一個統一的聯邦間較為容易去改變審判地點。法院擔心如果審判地點的改變伴隨著法律的改變，當事人會利用寬鬆的移轉標準而去選購法院取得不公平的利益。」因此不方便法院的駁回訴訟雖然於他州可能造成準據法的改變，但s. 1404(a)聯邦地院間之移轉是不會造成準據法的變更。但是或許如一般美國訴訟法[73]所習慣區分的「主體（實體）管轄」（subject matter jurisdiction）與「地域（土地）管轄」（territorial jurisdiction），s.1404(a)與「主體管轄」通常可能是較有關聯邦制度內務管理規則，故於國際法上或許經常只構成一些單純的學術性問題而已。

---

[71] 376 U.S. 630, "strongly inclined to protect plaintiffs against the risk that transfer might be accompanied by a prejudicial change in applicable state laws."

[72] 454 U.S. 253, 254, "Although the statute was drafted in accordance with the doctrine of forum non conveniens, see Revisor's Note, H.R.Rep. No. 308, 80th Cong., 1st Sess., A132(1947); H.R.Rep. No. 2646, 79 th Cong., 2d Sess., A127 (1946), it was intended to be a revision, rather than a codification of the common law. Norwood v. Kirkpatrick, 349 U.S 29 (1955). District courts were given more discretion to transfer under § 1404(a) than they had to dismiss on grounds of *forum non conveniens*……. Barrack concluded that Congree could not have intended a transfer to be accompanied by a change in law. Id. at 376 U.S. 622. The statute was designed as a 'federal housekeeping measure,' allowing easy change of venue within a unified federal system. Id. at 376 U.S. 613. The Court feared that, if a change in venue were accompanied by a change in law, forum-shopping parties would take unfair advantage of the relaxed standards for transfer. The rule was necessary to ensure the just and efficient operation of the statute."

[73] Restatement (Second) of Judgment § 1 (1982),
Comment:
a. Rationale. A fundamental element of procedural fairness is that a tribunal presuming to adjudicate a controversy have legal authority to do so. One aspect of the question of authority is whether the tribunal is empowered to adjudicate the type of controversy that is presented. This is conventionally referred to, and is referred to herein, as the question of subject matter jurisdiction. See s.11. Another aspect of the question concerns the authority of the tribunal in relation to that of tribunals created by political sovereigns of territorially coordinate authority, such as the states in our federal system and nations in the international community. This is referred to as the question of territorial jurisdiction. See ss. 4 to 9. Authority in the latter respect, unlike that regarding subject matter jurisdiction, may be conferred simply by a party's submission to the court by litigating on the merits. See s.10.

(三)逆向選購法院及逆向不方便法院主義

有趣的是於本案Marshall J.又如此不放心的加以保留的說[74]：「當然，如果另一個法院所提供的救濟是如此明顯的不合適或令人不滿意，以至形成根本上沒有救濟，那麼法律上不利之改變可能被給予重大的份量；地院可能認定駁回會不符合正義之利益。但是於這些案件中，蘇格蘭法院所提供的救濟並不在這些類別內。雖然死者的遺族或許不能依據無過失責任，並且雖然他們可能得到的損害賠償額或許較少，他們被剝奪任何救濟或被加以不公平對待的危險是不存在的。」有關產品責任的過失或無過失責任，於大部分之文明國家皆是屬於重大的政策。歐盟的羅馬II規則（Rome II）第5條[75]準據法順序依序為被害人慣居地（銷售地）、取得產品地（銷售地）、或損害發生地（銷售地），其政策就是本於在今日高科技的社會中，應將產品責任的風險加以分散，並藉此保護消費者、刺激創

---

[74] 454 U.S 254, 255, "We do not hold that the possibility of an unfavorable change in law should never be a relevant consideration in a *forum non conveniens* inquiry. Of course, if the remedy provided by the alternative forum is so clearly inadequate or unsatisfactory that it is no remedy at all, the unfavorable change in law may be given substantial weight; the district court may conclude that dismissal would not be in the interests of justice. In these cases, however, the remedies that would be provided by the Scottiish courts do not fall within this category. Although the relatives of the decedents may not be able to rely on a strict liability theory, and although their potential damages award may be smaller, there is no danger that they will be deprived of any remedy or treated unfairly."

[75] Article 5
Product liability
1. Without prejudice to Article 4(2). The law applicable to a non-contractual obligation arising out of damage caused by a product shall be:
(a) the law of the country in which the person sustaining the damage had his or her habitual residence when the damage occurred, if the product was marketed in that country; or, failing that.
(b) the law of the country in which the product was acquired, if the product was marketed in that country; or, failing that,
(c) the law of the country in which the damage occurred, if the product was marketed in that country.
However, the law applicable shall be the law of the country in which the person claimed to be liable is habitually resident if he or she could not reasonably foresee the marketing of the product, or a product of the same type, in the country the law of which is applicable under (a), (b) or (c).
2. Where it is clear from all the circumstances of the case that the tort/delict is manifestly more closely connected with a country other than that indicated in paragraph 1, the law of that other country shall apply. A manifestly closer connection with another country might be based in particular on a pre-existing relationship between the parties, such as a contract, that is closely connected with the tort/delict in question.

造力[76]。如果美國法院認為其對美國所生產之物品沒有利益那就是不合常理。對於地院認為與蘇格蘭之關係為是「壓倒性」的，最高法院認為[77]：「這種定性是有些誇張。特別是有關證據來源取得的比較容易性的問題上，私人利益指向雙方。如被上訴人所強調，有關發動機及飛機的測試、製造、及設計的記錄皆位於美國。如果審判是在這裡舉行，對於其無過失及過失責任理論之相關證據來源她會較能取得。」基本上美國最高法院是已存在著不受理外國人本著外國訴因對美國被告所提起之訴訟之心態。事實證明自本案後，於美國跨國企業在第三世界所造成的災害中，有許多「外國法院所提供的救濟是如此明顯的不合適或令人不滿意，以致形成根本上沒有救濟」，美國法院仍舊駁回訴訟。就如同本案一般[78]，現今美國的跨國企業已經得到美國法院之強力背書，經常以「不方便法院」請求駁回訴訟之策略，而對第三世界之受害者進行「逆向選購法院」[79]〈reverse

[76] 見其Recital 20, "The conflict-of-law rule in matters of product liability should meet the objectives of fairly spreading the risks inherent in a modern high-technology society, protecting consumers' health, stimulating innovation, securing undistorted competition and facilitating trade. Creation of a cascade system of connecting factors, together with a foreseeability clause, is a balanced solution in regard to these objectives. The first element to be taken into account is the law of the country in which the person sustaining the damage had his or her habitual residence when the damage occurred, if the product was marketed in that country. The other elements of the cascade are triggered if the product was not marketed in that country, without prejudice to Article 4(2) and to the possibility of a manifestly closer connection to another country."

[77] 454 U.S. 257, "In analyzing the private interest factors, the District Court stated that the connections with Scotland are 'overwhelming'. 479 F.Supp. at 732. This characterization may be somewhat exaggerated. Particularly with respect to the question of relative ease of access to sources of proof, the private interests point in both directions. As respondent emphasizes, records concerning the design, manufacture, and testing of the propeller and plane are located in the United States. She would have greater access to sources of proof relevant to her strict liability and negligence theories if trial were held here."

[78] Footnote 19, "We recognize, of course, that Piper and Hartzell may be engaged in reverse forum-shopping. However, this possibility ordinarily should not enter into a trial court's analysis of the private interests. If the defendant is able to overcome the presumption in favor of plaintiff by showing that trial in the chosen forum would be unnecessarily burdensome, dismissal is appropriate – regardless of the fact that defendant may also be motivated by a desire to obtain a more favorable forum."

[79] Professor Juenger認為「選購法院」是有著「一個壞名聲」("has a bad name.") Friedrich K. Juenger, Forum Shopping, Domestic and International, 63 Tul. L. Rev. 553(1989).但是於p.570中其又認為有些是可以被允許的，因為這些行為於法律上或道德上並非可受譴責的："Not all forum shopping merits condemnation. Some clearly does, such as the 'pennoyering' of casual travelers and, worse yet, the kidnapping of hapless children. But can anyone blame the solicitors who retained American attorneys, instead of the barristers with whom they normally deal, to litigate the Paris air-crash cases? Far from doing anything legally or morally reprehensible, the solicitors simply served their clients well."

forum-shopping〉。

當一個文明國家的法院有意的在產品責任上淡化風險的分散及保護消費者的全球化共同核心基本政策，並且公開的為跨國企業為了規避責任所採取的「逆向選購法院」之行為加以背書時，做為一個終生的國際法學生，個人理解到這已超出國際法學之範圍——這是一個二十世紀的唯一霸主赤裸裸的展現出其逆天而行不可一世之暴力法學，中國文化自古稱之為「霸道」法學。

最高法院又說[80]：「地院承認通常對原告所選定之法院是存在著一個有利之強烈假設，這個假設只能於公與私的利益因素清楚的指向於另一個法院審理時才能被超越。但現在已是被認定，當原告或有利益的真正當事人是外國人時，這個假設被適用時是較無力道的。地院的區分居民或公民原告及外國原告是充分的有道理的。在Koster中，法院表示當原告選擇家園之法院時，原告之選擇法院應受到較大之尊重。……當家園之法院被選擇時，去假定該選擇是便利的是為合理的。但是當原告是外國人時，這個假設就非常的沒有合理性。因為任何不方便法院的諮詢之中心目的就是去確保該審判是便利的，一個外國原告的選擇是較不值得尊重。」美國最高法院這種基於國籍及居所而來之歧視，已經激起包括第一世界在內之所有其他國家之強烈反對，故於1999年之Hague Conference - preliminary

---

又見Friedrich K. Juenger, Jurisdiction, Choice of Law and the Elusive Goal of Decisional Harmony, in Law And Reality, Essays on National and International Procedural Law in Honour of Cornelis Carel Albert Voskuil 137 (M. Sumampouw et al. eds., 1992); Friedrich K. Juenger, What's Wrong with Forum Shopping?, 16 Sydney L. Rev. 5, 10 (1994).

80 454 U.S. 255, 256, "The District Court acknowledged that there is ordinarily a strong presumption in favor of the plaintiff's choice of forum, which may be overcome only when the private and public interest factors clearly point towards trial in the alternative forum. It held, however, that the presumption applies with less force when the plaintiff or real parties in interest are foreign. The District Court's distinction between resident or citizen plaintiffs and foreign plaintiffs is fully justified. In Koster, the Court indicated that a plaintiff's choice of forum is entitled to greater deference when the plaintiff has chosen the home forum. 330 U.S. at 330 U.S. 524. When the home forum has been chosen, it is reasonable to assume that this choice is convenient. When the plaintiff is foreign, however, this assumption is much less reasonable. Because the central purpose of any forum non conveniens inquiry is to ensure that the trial is convenient, a foreign plaintiff's choice deserves less deference." Koster v. Lumbermens Mut. Cas. Co., 330 U.S. 518 (1947).

draft Convention on judgments第22(3)條及2004年的ALI/UNIDROIT principles of Transnational Civil Procedure第3條這兩個國際公約中斬釘截鐵白紙黑字的禁止基於國籍或居所而來之歧視。

對於「因為任何不方便法院諮詢之中心目的就是去確保該審判是便利的」之錯誤論述，個人再次引用聲名卓越法院之判例法來證明其走火入魔——「conveniens並非便利之意」[81]。

另外對於最高法院所說的：「地院的區分居民或公民原告及外國原告是充分的有道理的。」個人卻認為可能是沒有道理的。請問美國最高法院如何去面對「actor sequitur forum rei」這個國內及國際訴訟法上最基本之法理？原告至被告處之法院起訴是個自然的萬國公法[82]。於一般管轄上，英美法經常是以被告之所在為基礎（所在權力），大陸法的布魯塞爾公約及規則第2條是以被告之住所為基礎，而海牙草約第3條是以被告之慣居地為基礎[83]。又即使在送達境外之管轄上，英國C.P.R. 1998, s.

---

81 "Conveniens does not mean 'convenient': see *The Atlantic Star* [1974] A.C. 436, 475; *GAF Corp v Amchem Products Ins* [1975] 1 Lloyd's Rep. 601, 607; *Spiliada Maritime Corp v Cansulex Ltd* [1987] A.C. 460, 474-475." Dicey and Morris, the Conflict of Laws.14th ed., p. 465.

82 美國the American Law Institute的Restatement (Second) of Conflict of Laws (1971)之29及30條亦承認對於住所或居所（非不合理之情形下）於州內之人，州法院有著司法管轄權。

§29. Domicil (1988 Revision)

A state has power to exercise judicial jurisdiction over an individual who is domiciled in the state, except in the highly unusual case where the individual's relationship to the state is so attenuated as to make the exercise of such jurisdiction unreasonable.

§30. Residence

A state has power to exercise judicial jurisdiction over an individual who is a resident of the state unless the individual's relationship to the state is so attenuated as to make the exercise of such jurisdiction unreasonable.

又見29條之註解(a)及(d)。

a. Rationale. Except in a highly unusual situation, a person will in the nature of things have a sufficiently close relationship to the state of his domicil to make that state a fair and reasonable forum for the maintenance there of an action against him. So much was recognized by the Supreme Court in Milliken v. Meyer, 311 U.S. 457 (1940). This basis of jurisdiction assures the existence of a place in which a person is continuously amenable to suit.

d. Necessity for statute. Domicil was not generally recognized as a basis of judicial jurisdiction at common law. When the question has arisen, the courts have usually held themselves without authority under their local law to exercise jurisdiction on bases not recognized at common law unless authorized to do so by statute. Due process does not prevent retroactive application of such a statute to claims that arose prior to its enactment. See McGee v. International Life Insurance Co., 355 U.S. 220 (1957).

83 Article 3 Defendant's forum

6.20(1)[84]及美國的相關判例[85]，被告的住所皆構成一個可能的過度管轄基礎。這種以原就被之國際法及訴訟法之萬國公法亦是為美國所遵守的，如果以較近時髦的說法，這即是自然原告對自然被告於自然法院提起自然訴訟。如果美國最高法院承認美國被告是經常「逆向選購法院」，那麼美國法院的操作不方便法院就是一種「逆向不方便法院」法學。

(四)逆向帝國主義

最高法院認為[86]「蘇格蘭在這個訴訟中有著一個非常強烈的利益」，「如同於Gilbert中所說的當地存在著一個利益，以使得當地的紛爭於家園中被決定」。「被上訴人之抗辯中主張美國公民有著一個利益去確保美

---

1. Subject to the provisions of the Convention, a defendant may be sued in the courts of the State where that defendant is habitually resident.
2. For the purposes of the Convention, an entity or person other than a natural person shall be considered to be habitually resident in the State –

a) where it has its statutory seat,
b) under whose law it was incorporated or formed,
c) where it has its central administration, or
a) where it has its principle place of business.

84 (1) a claim is made for a remedy against a person domiciled within the jurisdiction.

85 陳隆修，《國際私法管轄權評論》，台北，五南圖書公司，民國75年11月，初版，111頁。「即使被告不在於其住所之州內，住所地之法院對其亦有充分之對人訴訟管轄權。從憲法上之觀點而言，住所係一充分之關連點（sufficient contact）。因為當事人既於住所地享有許多權利，自然其亦應於住所地被起訴。而且即使訴之原因發生於他處，被告仍可能預期其會於住所地被起訴。何況於複雜之國際情形下，被告至少應有一處之法院對其有管轄權。」Milliken v. Meyer, 311 U.S. 457(1940).又見Restatement, Second, Conflict of Law §27

(1) A state has power to exercise judicial jurisdiction over an individual on one or more of the following bases:
(a) presence
(b) domicil
(c) residence
(d) nationality or citizenship

86 454 U.S. 260, 261, "Scotland has a very strong interest in this litigation. The accident occurred in its airspace. All of the decedents were Scottish. Apart from Piper and Hartzell, all potential plaintiffs and defendants are either Scottish or English. As we stated in Gilbert, there is 'a local interest in having localized controversies decided at home.' 330 U.S at 330 U.S. 509. Respondent argues that American citizens have an interest in ensuring that American manufactures are deterred from producing defective products, and that additional deterrence might be obtained if Piper and Hartzell were tried in the United States, where they could be sued on the basis of both negligence and strict liability. However, the incremental deterrence that would be gained if this trial were held in an American court is likely to be insignificant. The American interest in this accident is simply not sufficient to justify the enormous commitment of judicial time and resources that would inevitably be required if the case were to be tried here."

國製造商會被嚇阻去生產有瑕疵之產品，並且如果Piper及Hartzell是在美國被審判的話會有額外的嚇阻效果被產生，亦即於美國他們可以同時被以過失及無過失責任之基礎而被起訴。但是如果這個審判是在一個美國法院進行所可能得到的增加的嚇阻是應該會是不重要的。如果這個案件是於此進行審判，那麼不可避免的須要投入龐大的司法資源與時間，很簡單的在這個事故中美國的利益不足以合理化這種投入。」在英國於不方便法院之考量上，一般是認為法院所考慮的主要因素為當事人（私的）利益與正義的（公的）利益。現今由於困擾性或壓迫性法學轉向不方便法院法學，英國法院對原告利益之解釋較為嚴格[87]。對於英國判例法上之私人利益個人如此論述[88]：「傳統上所認為的利益有個人的、司法上的及程序上的利益。有關個人的利益之情形，例如：原告居住於法院地。司法上的利益則通常為英國之實體法對當事人較為有利情形，例如：英國的選法規則會使得原告取得快速之判決。而對原告較為通常發生之利益則為程序上的情形，例如：原告可以取得其請求權之完全擔保，較快的訴程序，較高的損害賠償金額，利息的給付，費用的賠償，或較長的消滅時效。」但是如個人所一再重述，如Connelly v. RTZ Corpn. plc[89]所顯示，於特殊情形下實質正義（substantial justice）的考量應超越其他表面上更為合適之考量。

---

87 Cheshire and North, Private International Law, 13th ed. P. 345, "At one time great weight was attached to this factor, and if the claimant obtained a substantial advantage from trial in England the courts were unlikely to grant a stay of the English proceedings. The House of Lords in the Spiliada case sought to reduce the weight given to the advantage to the claimant when exercising the discretion to stay. Hence the principle that the mere fact that the claimant has a legitimate personal or juridical advantage in proceedings in England cannot be decisive." 14th ed., p.437.見陳隆修、許兆慶、林恩瑋、李瑞生四人合著，《國際私法-管轄與選法理論之交錯》，台北，五南圖書公司，2009年3月，初版1刷。213、214頁。Spiliada Maritime Corpn v. Cansulex Ltd [1987] AC 460 at 482.

88 陳隆修、許兆慶、林恩瑋、李瑞生四人合著，《國際私法-管轄與選法理論之交錯》，台北，五南圖書公司，2009年3月，初版1刷。212頁。Power Curber International Ltd v. National Bank of Kuwait SAK [1981] 1 WLR 1233 at 1240.又見212、213頁：「事實上甚至於採納不方便主義之前，英國法院已對原告之利益設下限制。首先：該利益必須為真實的，客觀上可證明的。於Marshannon中原告於取得法律意見後，真誠的認為他們可於英國訴訟程序中取得利益，在沒有客觀之證據下，英國法院認定他們無法於英國訴訟中取得利益。第二：於英國取得的利益必須與於外國取得的利益相比較。例如：於英國對物訴訟得扣船之利益與於外國法院取得擔保金之利益相較，並不被認為有利益。第三：該利益必須為合法，故自然不能故意去困擾被告。」The Abidin Daver [1984] AC 398 at 410; Rockware Glass Ltd. v. MacShannon [1978] AC 795 at 812.

89 [1998] AC 854, HL.

美國為世界第一大國，其農工商之產品由飛機、麥當勞、至可口可樂行銷至世界每一角落，其金融及服務業亦經常操控世界市場。「很簡單的在這個事故中美國的利益不足以合理化這種（司法）投入」——很簡單的是個神話。在全球化的市場下，無論是第一世界還是第三世界都必須在全球化的「商業潮流」（stream of commerce）中「一起游泳或下沉」（swim or sink together）。沒有任何有關產品責任的契約可以規避瑕疵擔保責任或無過失責任，亦沒有任何有關產品所造成的傷害可以規避其侵權行為責任。這些基本常識是不必等待法學的全球化即早已存在。利益與責任是如影隨形的，美國的跨國企業在全球化的「商業潮流」中所獲取的巨大利益，自然使得他們必須與其產品的受害人「一起游泳或下沉」。中國人吃芝麻一定掉屑，這是什麼法學又要吃芝麻又不掉屑？

如歐盟羅馬II規則Recital 20所說，產品責任的最核心目的即在分散風險，以保護消費者、刺激創造力、保障公平競爭、及促進貿易。故而保障跨國企業「逆向選購法院」[90]及「取得更有利之法院」，藉以減輕個別

[90] 在Lubbe v. Cape PLC, [2000] 1 Lloyd's Rep. 139,161中，上訴法院之認定雖為最高法院所不採納，但Lord Justice Pill於上訴審中卻企圖引用惡名昭彰的In re Union Carbide Corp. Gas Plant Disaster at Bhopal, India in Dec. 1984, 634 F. Supp. 842 (S.D.N.Y. 1986), aff'd, 809 F.2d 195 (2nd Cir. 1987), cert. denied, 484 U.S. 871 (1987)中Judge Keenan之論述："In the court's view, to retain this litigation in this forum, as plaintiffs request, would be yet another example of imperialism, another situation in which an established sovereign inflicted its rules, its standards and values on a developing nation. This Court declines to play such a role. The Union of India is a world power in 1986, and its courts have the proven capacity to mete out fair and equal justice. To deprive the Indian judiciary of the opportunity to stand tall before the world and to pass judgment on behalf of its own people would be to revive a history of subservience and subjugation from which India has emerged."這種駭人聽聞的岳不羣論述，被具有純正謙謙英國君子血統的恩師Prof. Morse諷刺性的稱呼為一個「特別的紫色言詞」（a particularly purple passage;過分高尚的言詞；台灣話叫「蓋高尚」），甚至挑明其為「逆向帝國主義」："While disagreeing with the use of the expression 'imperialism,' Lord Justice Pill thought that this 'general approach' appeared 'apt in the context of personal injury litigation such as the present. These personal injury actions concern operations conducted in South Africa and are concerned with their effect on persons employed and resident there.' In other words, perhaps , South Africa was the 'origin' or 'home' of this litigation as it was the country with which the litigation has the 'most real and substantial connection.' Whether Lord Justice Pill's derivation actually reflects what Judge Keenan (in more grandiose terms) actually meant must be open to question. For Judge Keenan, India had an obligation to throw off the colonial yolk, to stand tall, and to hear the Bhopal litigation because of its strong interest in so doing; this conclusion is slightly peculiar given that the Union of India was, in fact, seeking to have the trial before an American court. From another perspective, Judge Keenan might be thought to be patronizing, or as engaging in what one might call 'reverse imperialism.'" C. G. J. Morse,

企業之損害賠償責任，並不是二十一世紀全球化法學於產品責任之共同核心主流政策。對於過失及無過失責任的「額外嚇阻效果」，「如果這個審判是在一個美國法院進行所可能得到的增加的嚇阻是應該會是不重要的」，這種論述是與產品責任在全球化法學的共同核心政策——包括美國自己的國內政策在內——相違背。美國在農工商產品、高科技產品、及金融服務業，經常是藉著行銷的獨占而幾乎壟斷市場，進而攫取龐大的利益。但是在被害人依「以原就被」的傳統訴訟法規則到被告家園的法院要求跨國企業負起全球化法學共同核心的產品責任時，美國法院卻說出這樣的神話——「很簡單的在這個事故中美國的利益不足以合理化這種（司法）投入」。美國憲法所膨風出來的「商業潮流」、「一起游泳或下沉」的泡泡，都被這個以「資本主義」及「自由貿易」為基礎的「神話法學」所徹底刺破。本著Piper Aircraft Co. v. Reyno的「神話法學」，我們可以正確的去解讀WTO的「自由貿易」及「比較經濟利益」就是——經濟力量比較強勢地區的資本家可以自由的在經濟弱勢地區攫取比較高的利益，而經濟弱勢地區的受害者無法在經濟強勢地區要求資本家負起責任。

事實上受到這個資本主義及自由貿易主義所創造的「神話法學」所荼毒的亦不限於極低度開發國家。1998年美國跨國企業本著「金融自由流通」的概念於東南亞攫暴利而造成亞洲金融風暴，而2009年更變本加厲的造成全世界金融海嘯。所有全世界的受害者皆無能力到美國求償，所有的美國跨國企業皆受到這個「神話法學」的保護[91]。美國法院的「神話法

Not in the Public Interest? Lubbe v. Cape PLC, 37 Tex. Int'l L.J. 541, 551, 552 (2002).

91 為了保護投資大眾、維持市場之穩定、促進國家金融市場之成長，通常各國皆視其相關之金融法規為強行法。美國投資銀行、保險業者、及信評公司於2008、2009年所操作的過度槓桿投資高風險行為，皆有抵觸各國相關金融法規之處，這是很明顯的違反羅馬I規則第9(3)條契約不得違反履行地強行法之全球化法規。但是受阻於美國法學帝國主義的霸權法律而使得全球的消費投資大眾皆無法得到實質的損害賠償。

就以歐盟而言，事實上歐盟早於金融風暴之前，便明確的要求投資公司必須誠實、公正、及專業的促進市場的完整。見DIRECTIVE 2004/39/EC OF THE EUROPEAN PARLIAMENT AND OF THE COUNCIL of 21 April 2004 on markets in financial instruments,

Article 25

Obligation to uphold integrity of markets, report transactions and maintain records.

1. Without prejudice to the allocateion of responsebilities forenforcing the provisions of Directive

學」不但違反「以原就被」及一般管轄的訴訟法共同核心，亦違反產品責任及保護投資消費者於實體法上之共同核心。這個「神話法學」不但違反實體法及程序法上之全球化共同核心，亦違反了幾乎所有文明國家憲法及人權公約中所保障的訴訟權、財產權、生命權、平等權、及適當程序權，更應特別指出的是它違反了聯合國1966年兩個人權公約第1條2項中之生存權。第2項[92]規定：「在他們自己的目的下，所有的人得自由的處分他們的自然財富及資源，但不得違反基於國際法與互利原則而來的國際經濟合作所產生的任何義務。無論於何種情形下，沒有任何人得被剝奪其賴以

2003/6/EC of the European Parliament and of the Council of 28 January 2003 on insider dealing and market manipulation (market abuse) (1), Member States shill ensure that appropriate measures are in place to enable the competent authority to monitor the activities of investment firms to ensure that they act honestly, fairly and professionally and in a manner which promotes the integrity of the Market.
並且亦規定資訊必須以合理的術語而對大眾達成透明化。
Article 44
Pre-trade transparency requirements for regulated markets
1. Member States shall, at least, require regulated markets to make public current bid and ofter prices and the depth of trading interests at those prices which are advertised through their systems for shares admitted to trading. Member States shall require this information to be made available to the public on reasonable commercial terms and on a continuous basis during normal trading hours.
而第9條及37條更要求投資公司管理人必須有著好聲譽及經驗以確保健全及謹慎之管理。
Article 9
Persons who effusively direct the business
1. Member States shall require the persons who effectively direct the business of an investment firm to be of sufficiently good repute and sufficiently experienced as to ensure the sound and prudent management of the investment firm.
Article 37
Requirements for the management of the regulated market
1. Members States shall require the persons who effectively direct the business and the operations of the regulated market to be of sufficiently good repute and sufficiently experienced as to ensure the sound and prudent management and operation of the regulated market. Member States shall also require the operator of the regulated market to inform the competent authority of the identity authority of the identity and any other subsequent changes of the persons who effectively direct the business and the operations of the regulated market.
故而21世紀的全球化法學已有充分的法學科技去防止金融風暴的發生，只是人性對於資本主義所帶來的財富假象之渴望，遠大於追求司法正義的決心。個人真誠的認為我們祖先二千多年來的「不患寡患不均」之王道精神，應為21世紀全球化法學最核心的共同基本政策—而這或許就是黃進教授所主張的「中國法學革命」之真正特色。

92 2. All peoples may, for their own ends, freely dispose of their natural wealth and resources without prejudice to any obligations arising out of international economic co-operation, based upon the principle of mutual benefit, and international law. In no case may a people be deprived of its own means of subsistence.

生存之依據。」很明顯的，在1998年及2009年美國跨國企業以金融自由之名所引起的金融風暴，已違反了「自然財富之處分不得違反互利原則下國際經濟合作所產生之義務」，對第三世界人民而言這更是「剝奪其賴以生存之依據」。美國法院違反實體法與程序法在全球化法學的共同核心，允許跨國企業「逆向選購法院」以躲避其產品責任，這是一種「逆向不方便法院」（reverse forum non conveniens）之行使。對這違反「傳統上公平與實質正義」的「逆向不方便法院」神話法學[93]，個人再次重申——這是一個二十世紀的唯一霸主赤裸裸的展現出逆天而行不可一世之暴力法學，中國文化自古稱之為霸道法學。

跨國企業的藉著「霸權法律制度」或「法律帝國主義」以攫取自由市場上的暴力之行為，除了表現在「逆向不方便法院」之行使外，另外又表現在其母國於反托辣斯法過分的擴張適用，及商標專利法的專制執行上。這種優勢經濟力量與優勢法律科學之結合，不但扭曲了自由市場自由貿易

---

93 於Footnote 18中，美國最高法院列舉了5個外國原告為何如「飛蛾撲火」般的向美國法院提告之原因。1.通常各州給予無過失責任之保護；2.美國可能有50個州之法律可選擇；3.於美國民事案件可交由陪審團；4.律師抽成制度，並且不必替贏的一方付律師費；5.有著案件審判前調查庭。"First, all but 6 of the 50 American States – Delaware, Massachusetts, Michigan, North Carolina, Virginia, and Wyoming – offer strict liability. 1 CCH Prod. Liability Rep. § 4016 (1981). Rules roughly equivalent to American strict liability are effective in France, Belgium, and Luxembourg. West Germany and Japan have a strict liability statute for pharmaceuticals. However, strict liability remains primarily an American innovation. Second, the tort plaintiff may choose, at least potentially, from among 50 jurisdictions if he decides to file suit in the United States. Each of these jurisdictions applies its own set of malleable choice of law rules. Third, jury trials are almost always available in the United States, while they are never provided in civil law jurisdictions. G. Gloss, Comparative Law 12 (1979); J. Merryman, The Civil Law Tradition 121 (1969). Even in the United Kingdom, most civil actions are not tried before a jury. 1 G. Keeton, The United Kingdom: The Development of its Laws and Constitutions 309 (1955). Fourth, unlike most foreign jurisdictions, American courts allow contingent attorney's fees, and do not tax losing parties with their opponents' attorney's fees. R. Schlesinger, Comparative Law: Cases, Text, Materials 275-277 (3d ed. 1970); Orban, Product Liability: A Comparative Legal Restatement – Foreign National Law and the EEC Directive, 8 Ga.J.Int'l & Comp.L. 342, 393 (1978). Fifth, discovery is more extensive in American than in foreign courts. R. Schlesinger, *supra*, at 307, 310, and n. 33."首先審判前調查庭為英美法所有共有，英國是認為這是一個好制度。至於民事案件是否須經常動用到不相干之人做為陪審員，這是美國應檢討的。而陪審團亦的確較容易給予高額賠償金。至於律師抽成制度雖然有可能鼓勵訴訟，但亦為保護弱勢之一種制度。而有關產品的無過失責任，這已是全球化法學的趨勢。事實上即使歐洲同僚亦不見得能掌握美國法學，美國同僚之觀點或許太過主觀。以個人在台灣之經驗，第三世界的人對於在美國訴訟是有恐懼感的，面對著許多困難，他們所以願意冒險至美國訴訟，最大的理由就是當地法院沒有辦法給予充分救濟——而這正是「方便與不方便法院」法學之核心目的。

的真正公平性，對第三世界而言，第一世界已違反1966年人權公約第1(2)條的「互利原則下國際經濟合作之義務」，並剝奪第三世界「賴以生存之依據」。WTO對這種妨礙真正公平貿易之行為從未加以禁止，而諾貝爾和平獎亦對第一世界違反1966年人權公約第1(2)條之義務並剝奪第三世界生存權之邪惡暴行視而未見。故而WTO與諾貝爾和平獎是第一世界黑暗勢力終極掠奪性新殖民地主義法學之執行組織，是岳不群法學巔峰的表現。

在註解19中美國最高法院說[94]：「當然的我們承認Piper and Hartzell（被告）可能在操作逆向選購法院（reverse forum-shopping）。但是這個可能性通常不應於地院[95]在分析私人利益時被加以考慮。如果被告可以經由證明審判於被選定的法院舉行會造成不必要的負擔，則就可以超越對原告有利的假設，那麼駁回訴訟就是合適的——無論於事實上被告之動機可能亦是在於企圖取得一個更有利的法院。」當美國跨國企業在全世界造成金融海嘯，或在第三世界為了掠奪自然資源而造成環境污染或種族滅絕，或其產品在第三世界造成傷亡時，外國被害人本著外國訴因依訴訟法的基本原則到跨國企業的家園（住所、居所）法院起訴時，美國最高法院脫離英國母法的宣示：「美國的利益不足以合理化這種司法投入」。但是

---

[94] Footnote 19, "We recognize, of course, that Piper and Hartzell may be engaged in reverse forum-shopping. However, this possibility ordinarily should not enter into a trial court's analysis of the private interests. If the defendant is able to overcome the presumption in favor of plaintiff by showing that trial in the chosen forum would be unnecessarily burdensome, dismissal is appropriate – regardless of the fact that defendant may also be motivated by a desire to obtain a more favorable forum. *Cf. Kloechner Reederei und Kohlenhandel v. A/S Hakedal*, 210 F.2d 754, 757 (CA2) (defendant not entitled to dismissal on grounds of *forum non conveniens* solely because the law of the original forum is less favorable to him than the law of the alternative forum), *cert. dism'd by stipulation*, 348 U.S. 801 (1954)."

[95] 454 U.S. 257, "The *forum non conveniens* determination is committed to the sound discretion of the trial court. It may be reversed only when there has been a clear abuse of discretion; where the court has considered all relevant public and private interest factors, and where its balancing of these factors is reasonable, its decision deserves substantial deference."「不方便法院」通常主要是由地院來行使裁量權，這亦為英國判例法所認同。於Spiliada Mar. Corp. v. Cansulex Ltd., [1987] A.C. 460, 465中，Lord Templeman說這個問題「最主要是第一審法官的問題」（"pre-eminently a matter for the trial judge"），只能依法官的經驗，而沒有引用判例法，於「數小時內而非數日內」（"in hours and not days"）解決。這是因為第一審法官較上訴審法官接近事實，因此有較好的地位去決定問題。

當肇事的美國企業「事實上之動機可能亦是在於取得一個更有利的法院」時，美國最高法院又說：「這個可能性通常不應於地院在分析私人利益時被加以考慮。」最尊敬的恩師Prof. Graveson說「法律邏輯一致性的政策必須受限於實現正義的概括性目的」，而相反的是很明顯的在替美國跨國企業的「逆向選購法院」加以背書時，美國最高法院所行使的「逆向不方便法院」[96]神話法學所信仰的是資本主義的「法律邏輯一致性的政策必須受限於跨國企業實現利益的概括性目的」。中國人沒有那麼高雅精緻的法學傳統，我們很粗俗的稱這種現象為人嘴兩片皮——兩片皮法學。

(五)聯合國人權宣言與禮運大同

聯合國1948年的Universal Declaration of Human Rights的序言[97]要求各會員國維持友好關係及尊重人類的價值、尊嚴、平等與促進生活水準、社會進步，美國的「逆向不方便法院」法學顯然是違反聯合國之人權宣言。另外其25條1項[98]又規定：「每個人對於自己及其家人皆有權去要求符合健康及有益之適當的生活標準」。

對於第一世界之跨國企業在第三世界中大肆開採石油、礦產、設立污染性工業，導致環境破壞河川污染，以至傷害到當地居民，甚至沿岸部落遭受到種族滅絕之威脅，1992年聯合國的Rio Declaration on Environ-

---

96 「方便及不方便法院」法學之核心是「正義的利益」，見陳隆修、許兆慶、林恩瑋、李瑞生四人合著，《國際私法—管轄與選法理論之交錯》，台北，五南圖書公司，2009年3月，初版1刷。197、208頁，亦即「正義的目的及所有當事人之利益」。但美國最高法院於此卻與英國判例法相反，是以美國企業利益為核心政策，故是一種「逆向法學」。

97 Preamble
Whereas it is essential to promote the development of friendly relations between nations. Whereas the peoples of the United Nations have in the Charter reaffirmed their faith in fundamental human rights, in the dignity and worth of the human person and in the equal rights of men and women and have determined to promote social progress and better standards of life in larger freedom.

98 Article 25
1. Everyone has the right to a standard of living adequate for the health and well-being of himself and of his family, including food, clothing, housing and medical care and necessary social services, and the right to security in the event of unemployment, sickness, disability, widowhood, old age or other lack of livelihood in circumstances beyond his control.而這個25條1項之規定很明顯的近似我們傳統的「禮運大同」思想，故應為21世紀全球化法學之核心基礎。

ment and Development第13條[99]規定：「有關污染被害人之損害賠償及責任與其他環境上之損害賠償，各國應發展其相關法律。對於因為在他們管轄區或控制區域內之行為導致在他們域外所發生之負面環境效果之損害賠償及責任，各國應以快速及更果決之態度以便合作發展此方面之國際法。」第5條[100]規定各國應將消除貧窮、減少生活水平差距視為「主要任務」；第6條[101]規定發展中國家，特別是最落後國家，之需求與情況「應被給予特別優先」。第7條[102]後半段又規定：「在考慮已開發國家的社會對全球環境所造成之壓力及他們所掌握的技術及經濟資源，已開發國家承認於追逐國際永續發展上他們所承擔之責任。」對於弱勢之原住民第22條[103]規定如下：「原住民及其社會與其他當地社會於環境控制及發展上是有重要的地位，這是由於他們的知識及傳統的作法。各國應承認及適度的幫助他們的認同、文化、及利益，並且於達成永續發展上幫助他們能有效

99 Principle 13
States shall develop national law regarding liability and compensation for the victims of pollution and other environmental damage. States shall also cooperate in an expeditious and more determined manner to develop further international law regarding liability and compensation for adverse effects of environmental damage caused by activities within their jurisdiction or control to areas beyond their jurisdiction.

100 Principle 5
All States and all people shall cooperate in the essential task of eradication poverty as an indispensable requirement for sustainable development, in order to decrease the disparities in standards of living and better meet the needs of the majority of the people of the world.第5及6條近似「不患寡患不均」之中國思想。

101 Principle 6
The special situation and needs of developing countries, particularly the least developed and those most environmentally vulnerable, shall be given special priority. International actions in the field of environment and development should also address the interests and needs of all countries.

102 Principle 7
States shall cooperate in a spirit of global partnership to conserve, protect and restore the health and integrity of the Earth's ecosystem. In view of the different contributions to global environmental degradation, States have common but differentiated responsibilities. The developed countries acknowledge the responsibility that they bear in the international pursuit of sustainable development in view of the pressures their societies place on the global environment and of the technologies and financial resources they command.

103 Principle 22
Indigenous people and their communities and other local communities have a vital role in environmental management and development because of their knowledge and traditional practices. States should recognize and duly support their identity, culture and interests and enable their effective participation in the achievement of sustainable development.

的參加。」

聯合國這些人權、環保公約白紙黑字的記錄著美國「逆向不方便法院」法學，血淚斑斑的迫害第三世界受害者於憲法、人權公約上之平等權、訴訟權[104]、財產權、生命權。事實上第一世界、WTO、及諾貝爾和平獎憑藉著第一世界於科技、經濟、行銷、資金、及法律科學的優勢，迫害第三世界人民的惡行罄竹難書。例如台灣社會在反托辣斯法及智慧財產權上所受到的壓迫，就是歐盟及美國藐視他們於國際經濟上所應合作之義務及中國人民基本生存權之殘酷事實，而這是1966年聯合國兩個人權公約所於開宗明義的第1(2)條所列為應優先禁止之惡行。

如果一幅畫勝過千句言語，那麼一顆正義的心勝過一千個人權公約。無論「方便與不方便法院」法學之邏輯一致性為何，必要時應如Connelly v. RTZ Corpn. plc[105]案所顯示，於特殊情形下實質正義（substantial justice）的達成應超越其他考量，亦即「方便與不方便法院」法學的心與靈魂在於「是否正義的真正利益最能被達成[106]」——而個人認為

---

[104] 歐盟1950年人權公約第6(1)條規定："In the determination of his civil rights and obligations or of any criminal charge against him, everyone is entitled to a fair and public hearing within a reasonable time by an independent and impartial tribunal established by law."但是Lord Bingham認為第6條不會視Spiliada為違反這個人權條款（Spiliada, 1 A.C. 460），故於實際上他亦是據此而認定Lubbe之結果（Lubbe, [2000] 1 W.L.R. 1545）是符合公約的，反而停止訴訟會造成對原告構成「正義之拒絕」，故會違反公約。（Lubbe, [2000] 1 W.L.R. 1545, 1561）如於Connelly v. RTZ Corp. PLC, 1998 A.C. 854 (H.L. 1997)中所顯示的，如果因為經濟或其他原因以致請求者不能於其他另一個法院請求，則構成正義的拒絕，Lubbe案亦顯示同樣的結果。個人近年來之所以聲嘶力竭的指控美國「逆向不方便法院」法則違反人權公約，乃是其肆無忌憚的違反ALI/UNIDROIT Principles of Transnational Civil Procedure第3條的公平保護條款，對外國居民構成「正義之拒絕」之非法情形。如恩師所說：「於是否訴訟當事人間有著平等的立足點之問題上，特別是由於跨國公司於外國之行為所引起的人身傷害請求權上，人權問題可能會發生。這個因素反映了當事人相較上之私人利益，並且再加強了於英國不方便法院之諮詢上，私人利益超越其它因素之看法。」" Human rights issues might also arise in relation to the question of whether parties to litigation are on an equal footing, particularly in the context of personal injury claims against multinational companies that arise out of the activities of those companies in foreign countries. This factor reflects the comparative private interests of the parties and reinforces the view that in the English forum non conveniens inquiry, private interests dominate." C.G.J. Morse, Not in the Public Interest? Lubbe v. Cape PLC, 37 Tex. Int'l L.J. 541, 555 (2002).

[105] [1998] AC 854, HL.

[106] Lopez v Chavarri [1901] W.N. 115, 116, "whether the true interests of justice would be best served by trying the question here, or leaving it to the foreign tribunal".如最尊敬的恩師Prof. Morse對於Lubbe v. Cape PLC, [2000] 1 W.L.R. 1545 (H.L.)案之結果所加以之評論：「很難相信這個結果是對任何合

這亦是中國思想下二十一世紀全球化法學的心與靈魂。

如前述德國同僚認為禁訴令的行使構成法律戰爭，而英國同僚則認為美國反托拉斯法的行使導致法律戰爭。個人則認為美國法院「逆向不方便法院」法學之行使[107]並非是一個戰爭，而是以第三世界為殺戮戰場的對第三世界人民展開一連串違反人權公約的大屠殺（holocaust）。WTO則提供這些違反人權的酷行充分之平台與工具，諾貝爾和平獎則在旁邊大聲吆喝，故意將違反人權的施暴者渲染成既有秩序的慈悲和平維護者。因此個人認為對抗這種「逆向不方便法院」法學最名正言順之作法是仿效大英國協——亦即在遵守過去三十年來先進國家之國際慣例下--去採用保護貿易利益法[108]：「這個法案的背景為中國對美國逆向不方便法院法學適用之不滿。對於構成政治以及經濟、法律問題於外交上嘗試之解決作法之失敗，

法之公共利益是有害的。」"it was reported in The Times of London on January 15, 2002, that some 7500 claimants had settled their claims against Cape PLC for ￡ 21 million. It is hard to believe that this outcome is inimical to any legitimate public interest." 37 Tex. Int'l L.J. 541, 557.

[107] 英國的Civil Procedure Rules 1998, Rule 1.1即開宗明義的於第1條之第1項規定程序法則的「超越性目的」("Overriding Objective")就在於幫助法院去「公正」的處理案件：

(1) These Rules are a new procedural code with the overriding objective of enabling the court to deal with cases justly.

(2) Dealing with cases justly includes, so far as practicable –

(a) ensuring that the parties are on an equal footing;

(b) saving expense;

(c) dealing with the case in ways which are proportionate –

(i) to the amount of money involved;

(ii) to the importance of the case;

(iii) to the complexity of the issues; and

(iv) to the financial position of each party;

(d) ensuring that it is dealt with expeditiously and fairly; and

(e) allotting to it an appropriate share of the court's resources, while taking into account the need to allot resources

而(2)(a)中「確保當事人間公平的地足點」(ensuring that the parties are on an equal footing)就是大陸法所謂「武器平等」之近義，亦是ALI/UNIDROIT Principles of Transnational Civil Procedure第3條所謂的「公平保護」條款之內涵，這些都是明顯的站在美國〔逆向不方便法院」法學之對立面。

[108] P M North, JJ Fawcett, Cheshire and North's Private International Law, 13th ed., p.448, "The background to this Act is the United kingdom resentment at the extra-territorial application of anti-trust laws by the United States. Diplomatic attempts at solving what is a political as well as an economic and legal problem failed and led to legal warfare. Under the Act, the Secretary of State is given wide powers to counter foreign measures for regulating international trade which affect the trading interests of persons in the United Kingdom." 14th ed., p. 561.

導致法律上之戰爭。根據這個法律，對於影響到在中國之人之貿易利益的外國規範國際貿易的措施，國務院是被給予寬廣的權利去應付[109]。」正如美國法院在適用「逆向不方便法院」法則以維護跨國企業之利益，所有的第一世界國家皆經常在WTO及諾貝爾和平獎的交叉掩護下，挾著優勢科技、經濟、行銷，藉著複雜的法律科學技術[110]，而對第三世界加以霸凌獲取利益。以目前看來，保護貿易利益法的成立，是二十一世紀中十三億中國人帶領全世界第三世界的人民，要求第一世界遵守1966年人權公約第1(2)條「互利原則下國際經濟合作之義務」，及爭取第三世界最基本的「生存之依據」，之順乎國際慣例法之天賦人權。

---

[109] 1.-(1) If it appears to the Secretary of State-
(a) that measures have been or are proposed to be taken by or under the law of any overseas country for regulating or controlling international trade; and
(b) that those measures, in so far as they apply or would apply to things done or to be done outside the territorial jurisdiction of that country by persons carrying on business in the United Kingdom, are damaging or threaten to damage the trading interests of the United Kingdom,
The Secretary of State may by order direct that this section shall apply to those measures either generally or in their application to such cases as may be specified in the order.

[110] 2004年ALI/ UNIDROIT Principles of Transnational Civil Procedure的第3條是有關當事人之平等保護條款，其註解中說明「合理性」是於整個2004年之規則中皆被貫穿使用。而所謂「合理性的概念是並且排除過分高度技術性的法律論述」，以及「避免嚴重、過分、或不合理的適用程序上之方式」。2004年的規則亦採不方便法院法學，這個規則的3.2條本就在禁止美式不方便法院之適用。這個註解又在禁止「逆向不方便法院」之「過分高度技術性的法律論述」，及避免程序上「過分、不合理」之適用。P-3A The term “reasonable” is used throughout the Principles and signifies “proportional,” “significant,” “not excessive,” or “fair,” according to the context. It can also mean the opposite of arbitrary. The concept of reasonableness also precludes hyper-technical legal argument and leaves a range of discretion to the court to avoid severe, excessive, or unreasonable application of procedural norms.

第7章 禁止訴訟命令—雞同鴨講

一、The European Court of Unification

在國際訴訟上所可能產生平行訴訟（parallel proceedings）或複數訴訟（multiple proceedings）之問題，歐盟之布魯塞爾公約（Brussels Convention）21、22條或布魯塞爾規則（Brussels Regulation）27、28條是以大陸法國內法所謂的「先繫屬優先原則」（lis pendens）為依據，而英美法則通常是以「不方便法院」來停止法院地之訴訟，或作成「禁止訴訟命令」，禁止當事人於國外起訴或繼續進行國外之訴訟，或強制執行國外之判決[1]。「不方便法院」是法院行使自己之裁量權而停止自己之訴訟程序。但禁訴令之作成是要求當事人停止外國之訴訟程序，因此會間接的干擾到外國司法主權，有可能進而產生糾紛。

對於先繫屬優先的鼓勵當事人先下手選購法院，因此可能會違反自然原告於自然法院對自然被告提起自然訴訟之原理，個人近年來一再批評[2]，於此不再贅述。至於英式的「不方便法院」法學，在Spiliada[3]、Connelly[4]、Lubbe[5]等領導判例之適用下，為Lord Goff所高調的宣示[6]：「可被視為最文明之法學原則之一」。但是這個「最文明的法學原則之

1 見陳隆修，《國際私法管轄權評論》，台北，五南圖書公司，民國75年11月，初版，84頁。
2 見陳隆修，《2005年海牙法院選擇公約評析》，台北，五南圖書公司，2009年1月，初版1刷，105、106頁。又見拙作，《歐盟經驗論中國式國際私法之建立》，高雄大學法學論叢6卷2期，2011年，23-34頁。
3 Spiliada Mar. Corp. v. Consulex Ltd., [1987] 1 A.C. 460, 460 (H.L. 1986) (appeal taken from Eng.).
4 Connelly v. RTZ Corp. PLC, 1998 A.C. 854, 872 (H.L. 1997) (appeal taken from Eng.).
5 Lubbe v. Cape PLC, [2000] 1 W.L.R. 1545 (H.L.) (appeal taken from Eng.).
6 Airbus Indus. G.I.E. v. Patel, [1999] 1 A.C. 119, 141 (H.L. 1998), "can be regarded as one of the most civilised of legal principles".

一」，較近在Owusu v. Jackson[7]中卻為歐盟最高法院所嚴格的禁止英國法院之適用此理論在布魯塞爾公約之相關條文上[8]：「即使於沒有其他訂約國法院的管轄權有問題或程序與其他任何訂約國皆無連繫因素時，布魯塞爾公約仍然禁止訂約國之法院，基於某一非訂約國之法院是為較合適處理訴訟之法院，而拒絕行使公約第2條所給予之管轄權。」歐盟法院認為「預測性」及「穩定性」是布魯塞爾公約之基礎[9]：「不方便法院原則於有關外國法院是否為進行該訴訟更合適的法院之問題上，給予繫屬法院寬廣的裁量權，故而其之適用會破壞布魯塞爾公約所規範的管轄規則之預測性，特別是第2條之規則之預測性，並且因而會破壞做為公約基礎的法律穩定性原則。」因此即使英國法院認為非訂約國之法院為更合適之法院，並且英國判決於非訂約國執行時會有困難，歐盟法院仍認為英國法院不能適用不方便法院[10]。

個人認為在Owusu案中，正如在許多牽涉到英美法特色之案件類型中，歐盟法院所奉守的大姆指原則是法律之一致性，而非個案正義之達成[11]：「另外，因為不方便法院原則就只有少數的會員國承認，於布魯塞

---

7 C-281/02, [2005] ECR I-1383.見陳隆修，《歐盟經驗論中國式國際私法之建立》，高雄大學法學論叢6卷2期，2011年，39-41頁。

8 Owusu v. Jackson, para. 45. "the Brussels Convention precludes a court of a Contracting State from declining the jurisdiction conferred on it by Article 2 of that convention on the ground that a court of a non-Contracting State would be a more appropriate forum for the trial of the action even if the jurisdiction of no other Contracting State is in issue or the proceedings have no connecting factors to any other contracting State."

9 Id, para. 41, "Application of the forum non conveniens doctrine, which allows the court seised a wide discretion as regards the question whether a foreign court would be a more appropriate forum for the trial of an action, is liable to undermine the predictability of the rules of jurisdiction laid down by the Brussels Convention, in particular that of Article 2, and consequently to undermine the principle of legal certainty, which is the basis of the Convention."

10 歐盟法院於此案之決定引起許多英國同儕之不滿。見Trevor C. Hartley, The European Union and the Systematic Dismantling of the Common Law of Conflict of Laws, 54 I. C. L. Q，813，827 (2005); Adrian Briggs, The Death of Harrods: Forum Non Conveniens and the European Court, 121 L.Q.R. 535, 535 (2005); Richard Fentiman, Civil Jurisdiction and Third States: Owusu and After, 43 Common Mkt. L. Rev. 705, 713-18 (2006).

11 Case C-281/02. *Andrew Owusu v N.B. Jackson, trading as 'Villa Holidays Bai-Inn Villas' and others*, para. 43, "Moreover, allowing forum non conveniens in the context of the Brussels Convention would be likely to affect the uniform application of the rules of jurisdiction contained therein in so far as that doctrine is recognized only in a limited number of Contracting States, whereas the objective of the

爾公約的規範下，如果允許這個原則的適用，有可能會影響到公約管轄規則適用的一致性，而公約的目的正是在排除破壞性的國內法規，並建立共同的法規。」因此如果只是消極的企圖以不方便法院之名而將案件交由非訂約國之法院去行使管轄權都無法被歐盟法院認可，積極的企圖以禁訴令去間接的干擾其他國家管轄權之行使怎麼有可能得到歐盟法院之祝福？

在Turner v. Grovit[12]中，原告為住所在英國之英國人，其受僱於一西班牙跨國集團之英國子公司，其工作地點先後為倫敦及西班牙。於1998年原告於英國勞工法院對該英國子公司提起訴訟，而法院准予其損害賠償之請求。於稍後西班牙跨國集團亦於西班牙對英國原告於職業上之行為提起訴訟。於1999年英國上訴法院認為於西班牙之訴訟是為了困擾原告於英國之訴訟，是基於「惡意」（bad faith）而提起之訴訟，故准予原告之請求，對該集團、其子公司、及其總裁發給禁訴令，禁止他們於西班牙或其他地方對原告提起或繼續有關該僱傭契約之訴訟。然而歐盟法院卻判決歐盟之管轄公約[13]：「應被解釋為，一個於一訂約國法院訴訟程序中之當事人，是不應被該國法院給予禁止該當事人於其他訂約國法院提起或繼續訴訟之令命，即使該當事人之目的是本於惡意的想阻礙該法院地原來既有的訴訟亦同。」

雖然英國法院及學界秉持判例法的傳統，認為禁訴令是意圖減少各國間相衝突判決之可能性，並且可以避免平行訴訟（或複數訴訟）之發

Brussels Convention is precisely to lay down common rules to the exclusion of derogating national rules."

12 Case C-159/02, Gregory Paul Turner v. Felix Fareed Ismail Grovit, Harada Ltd. & Changepoint SA, [2004] ECR I-3565.又見陳隆修，《歐盟經驗論中國式國際私法之建立》，高雄大學法學論叢6卷2期，2011年，23-39頁。

13 "The Convention of 27 September 1968 on Jurisdiction and the Enforcement of Judgments in Civil and Commercial Matters, as amended by the Convention of 9 October 1978 on the accession of the Kingdom of Denmark, Ireland and the United Kingdom of Great Britain and Northern Ireland, by the Convention of 25 October 1982 on the accession of the Hellenic Republic and by the convention of 26 May 1989 on the accession of the Kingdom of Spain and the Portuguese Republic, is to be interpreted as precluding the grant of an injunction whereby a court of a Contracting State prohibits a party to proceedings pending before it from commencing or continuing legal proceedings before a court of another Contracting State, even where that party is acting in bad faith with a view to frustrating the existing proceedings."

生，對達成歐盟布魯賽爾公約之目的是有助益的。但歐盟法院並不接受這種英國論述而加以反駁如下[14]：「首先，就同一訴訟於不同國家被提起，或相關連的訴訟於不同國家被提起時，公約所規定的特別制度會被這種方法的被引用而變得無效。第二，它可能會造成衝突，而該種衝突公約並無規範。即使一訂約國已作成禁止命令，其他訂約國法院仍可能作成判決的可能性是不能被排除的。同樣的，兩個引用這種方法的訂約國的法院，可能發給相衝突的禁止命令的可能性亦不能被排除。」或許歐盟法院的反駁並非全無道理，如前述英美法國家間的「反禁止訴訟命令」[15]，甚或偶有「反反禁止訴訟命令」[16]的司法上「禁止命令戰爭」（battle of injunctions）是已發生過之事實。

另外歐盟法院於*Kongress Agentur Hagen GmbH v Zeehagbe BV*[17]中，認為只要不傷害公約的有效性，程序問題與公約無涉。歐盟法院認定：「應該被強調的是，公約的目的不是在統一程序規則，而是決定歐盟內有關民商事件糾紛的法院管轄權，及幫助判決的被執行……此外，於有關程序規則上，法院一向認為必須引用各國法院所適用的該國規則（特別是參閱，於有關複數訴訟之概念，1984年6月7號之判決……及，有關執行外國法院之條件，1985年7月2號之判決……，及1988年2月4號之判

---

14 Para. 30
"The argument that the grant of injunctions may contribute to attainment of the objective of the Convention, which is to minimize the risk of conflicting decisions and to avoid a multiplicity of proceedings, cannot be accepted. First, recourse to such measures renders ineffective the specific mechanisms provided for by the Convention for cases of lis alibi pendens and of related actions. Second, it is liable to give rise to situations involving conflicts for which the Convention contains no rules. The possibility cannot be excluded that, even if an injunction had been issued in one Contracting State, a decision might nevertheless be given by a court of another Contracting state. Similarly, the possibility cannot be excluded that the courts of two Contracting States that allowed such measures might issue contradictory injunctions."

15 有關英美法院間之"anti-anti-suit injunction"，見British Airways Board v. Laker Airways, [1985] AC 58 [House of Lords, 1984]; Laker Airways Ltd. v. Sabena, Belgian World Airlines, 731 F.2d 909 (D.C. Cir. 1984).

16 有關"anti- anti-anti-suit injunction"，見Cf. Smith Kline French Laboratories Ltd v Bloch [1983] 1 W.L.R. 730 (CA). Shell UK Exploration and Production Ltd v Innes, 1995 S.L.T. 807; General Star International Indemnity Ltd v Stirling Cooke Browne Reinsurance Brokers Ltd [2003] EWHC 3 (Comm.), [2003] I.L.Pr. 314; National Australia Bank Ltd v Idoport [2002] NSWSC 623.

17 Case 365/88，[1990] ECR I-1845。

決……）。但應注意的是，各國程序規則的適用不可以妨礙到公約的有效性。」[18]故而雖然英國政府認為禁訴令只是在保護英國訴訟程序的完整，因此完全只是有關英國的程序法規而已，於Turner v. Grovit中歐盟法院還是認為禁訴令實際上會有限制適用公約管轄規則的效果，因此會妨礙到公約的有效性[19]。「至於被告包含其求助於其他會員國法院管轄權在內之被批評之行為，有關認定該行為是濫用程序之判決，事實上亦是暗示著對於其他會員國法院提起訴訟合適性的評估。這種評估是與互信原則相衝突的，而正如本判決24至26段所指出的，這種互信是本公約的基礎，並且除了不適用本案件在內之特殊情形外，是禁止任何法院去審核其他會員國法院之管轄權。」[20]

歐盟法院於複數訴訟時所謂的「特別制度」、「公約的有效性」，只不過是「粗糙」而「原始」的先繫屬優先原則而已，這種鐵血作風自然

---

[18] 同上，paras. 17, 19, 20, "It should be stressed that the object of the Convention is not to unify procedural rules but to determine which court has jurisdiction in disputes relating to civil and commercial matters in intra-Community relations and to facilitate the enforcement of judgments….. Moreover, the Court has consistently held that, as regards procedural rules, reference must be made to the national rules applicable by the national court (see in particular, as regards the concept of lis alibi pendens, the judgment of 7 June 1984 in Case 129/83 *Zelger v Salinitri* [1984] ECR 2397, and, as regards the conditions for the enforcement of a foreign judgment, the judgments of 2 July 1985 in Case 148/84 *Deutsche Genossenschaftsbank v Brasserie du Pêcheur SA* [1985] ECR 1981, and of 4 February 1988 in Case 145/86 Hoffmann v Krieg [1988] ECR 645).
It should be noted, however, that the application of national procedural rules may not impair the effectiveness of the Convention."

[19] Case C-159/02, [2004] ECR I-3565, para. 29, "Even if it were assumed, as has been contended, that an injunction could be regarded as a measure of a procedural nature intended to safeguard the integrity of the proceedings pending before the court which issues it, and therefore as being a matter of national law alone, it need merely be borne in mind that the application of national procedural rules may not impair the effectiveness of the Convention (Case C-365/88 Hagen [1990] ECR I-1845, paragraph 20). However, that result would follow from the grant of an injunction of the kind at issue which, as has been established in paragraph 27 of this judgment, has the effect of limiting the application of the rules on jurisdiction laid down by the Convention."

[20] "In so far as the conduct for which the defendant is criticized consists in recourse to the jurisdiction of the court of another Member State, the judgment made as to the abusive nature of that conduct implies an assessment of the appropriateness of bringing proceeding before a court of another Member State. Such an assessment runs counter to the principle of mutual trust which, as pointed out in paragraphs 24 to 26 this judgment, underpins the Convention and prohibits a court, except in special circumstances which are not applicable in this case, from reviewing the jurisdiction of the court of another Member State."

引起一些英國同僚的不滿[21]。做為一個狂熱的實體法方法論之擁護者，個人必須提醒歐盟法院保護弱勢員工是過去百年來之法學共同核心。歐盟自己的羅馬I（Rome I）號規則第8條即規定僱佣契約不得違反相關之強行法[22]，而其recital 35又再次強調強行法只能於對受僱者有利之情形下才得被違背[23]。而於*Turner v. Grovit*中，依歐盟自己的布魯塞爾規則20條，受僱者「只能」於其住所地（亦即英國）被其僱主起訴[24]。英國法院所作只不過依判例法的程序規則去執行歐盟及全世界所共同接受之主流核心價值而已，而事實上西班牙法院自己（甚或包含歐盟法院本身）才是布魯塞爾規則第20條之違背者。

對於歐盟法院的忽視全球化法學共同核心政策所代表的「傳統上公平與實質正義的概念」，卻一再強調「公約管轄規則適用的一致性」，

---

21 Aude Fiorini, *The Codification of Private International Law in Europe – Could the Community Learn from the Experience of Mixed Jurisdictions?* 23 Tul. Eur. & Civ. L.F. 89, 103 (2008), "For example, despite the discussions which had taken place in the seventies during the negotiation of the first accession convention, the text and framework of the instrument did not provide clear responses to the debate whether all discretion was to be excluded. The European Court of Justice has though resisted all attempts to safeguard traditional common law devices or countenance flexible solutions when applying the instrument. In particular, the Luxembourg court has adopted a very civilian attitude, privileging adherence to dogma over efficiency and commercial sense, rejecting the recourse to anti-suit injunctions even where these would have been used to support and protect deficient conventional mechanisms and extending the refusal to allow the exercise of discretion by English judges even in international cases having no other connection with another contracting State."
"In this way the ECJ has extended the civilian influence of the instrument well beyond its exclusively intra-European remit."

22 1. An individual employment contract shall be governed by the law chosen by the parties in accordance with Article 3. Such a choice of law may not, however, have the result of depriving the employee of the protection afforded to him by provisions that cannot be derogated from by agreement under the law that, in the absence of choice, would have been applicable pursuant to paragraphs2, 3 and 4 of this Article.

23 (35) Employees should not be deprived of the protection afforded to them by provisions which cannot be derogated from by agreement or which can only be derogated from to their benefit.

24 Article 20
1. An employer may bring proceedings only in the courts of the Member State in which the employee is domiciled.
2. The provisions of this Section shall not affect the right to bring a counter-claim in the court in which , in accordance with this Section, the original claim is pending.
Article 21
The provisions of this Section may be departed from only by an agreement on jurisdiction:
1. which is entered into after the dispute has arisen; or
2. which allows the employee to bring proceedings in courts other than those indicated in this Section.

個人最近認為「歐盟法院」（European Court of Justice）並非是個court of justice，它的正名應為European Court of Unification[25]。因為歐盟公約（the Treaty Establishing the European Community）第2條[26]明示公約之任務為建立一個共同市場及經濟聯盟，其第65條則規定：「於遵照67條及內部市場所需要的適當功能性下，對於跨境界有影響的民事司法合作範圍的措施，應包含：改進及簡化……(b)各會員國有關國際私法及管轄權方面所適用法規上相容性的促進……」[27]而第220條又規定：「歐盟法院及第一審法院，各自於其管轄權範圍內，應確保於解釋及適用本條約時本法應會被遵守。」[28]故而很明顯的，歐盟法院設立之目的是在以法院之名，而忠誠的執行歐盟公約第2條建立共同市場，第65及220條所賦予的政治及行政責任。與各文明國家之court of justice之目的是在解決當事人之私人糾紛與確保正義的判決不一樣，歐盟法院的任務是在確保各國法律

25　見陳隆修，《歐盟經驗論中國式國際私法之建立》，高雄大學法學論叢6卷2期，2011年，21、22頁。

26　Article 2
The Community shall have as its task, by establishing a common market and an economic and monetary union and by implementing common policies or activities referred to in Articles 3 and 4, to promote throughout the Community a harmonious, balanced and sustainable development of economic activities, a high level of employment and of social protection, equality between men and women, sustainable and non-inflationary growth, a high degree of competitiveness and convergence of economic performance, a high level of protection and improvement of the quality of the environment, the raising of the standard of living and quality of life, and economic and social cohesion and solidarity among Member States.

27　Article 65
Measures in the field of judicial cooperation in civil matters having cross-border implications, to be taken in accordance with Article 67 and in so far as necessary for the proper functioning of the internal market, shall include:
Improving and simplifying:
(a) – the system for cross-border service of judicial and extrajudicial documents,
Cooperation in the taking of evidence,
the recognition and enforcement of decisions in civil and commercial cases, including decisions in extrajudicial cases;
(b) – promoting the compatibility of the rules applicable in the Member States concerning the conflict of laws and of jurisdiction;
(c) – eliminating obstacles to the good functioning of civil proceedings, if necessary by promoting the compatibility of the rules on civil procedure applicable in the Member States.

28　Article 20
The Court of Justice and the Court of First Instance, each within its jurisdiction, shall ensure that in the interpretation and application of this Treaty the law is observed.

的相容性〈一致性〉，及負責促進歐盟建立的條約被各國遵守，故事實上它是個負有崇高政治及行政使命的行政機關。它的法源不是憲法三權分立下應就個案主持正義解決私人紛爭的court of justice，故而它是個以法院為名之行政機構，它的唯一任務是統和歐盟的法律，及剷除與大部分國家不同的國家的法律，故而它的正名應是European Court of Unification[29]。這個所謂的「歐洲法律革命」（European legal revolution），不但他們所設計的法律是為了能服務統合的目標[30]，連為現代文明社會最後人性堡壘的法院亦淪落為統合的行政機構。相對之下1998年英國的Civil Procedure Rules開宗明義的一開始即於Rule 1.1中宣示[31]「新程序規則的超越性目標是在幫助法院公平的去處理案件」。相較歐盟法院與英國法院的「超越性目的」"Overriding Objective"，難怪英國同僚不留情面的「認為歐盟法院應該為自己感覺可恥」[32]。

二、少數民族之司法文化人權

有60位法國同僚對於羅馬I規則的較沒有給予法國法有關保護性強行

---

29 其他英國同僚認為歐盟法院是個具有較多行政功能之機構。見Richard Fentiman, *Choice of law in Europe: Uniformity and Integration*, 82 TUL. L. REV. 2021, 2045, 2046 (2008). "*Owusu* suggests that the Community conflicts regime is ultimately the servant of European intergration-the principle of instrumentalism. The Community regime is not an end in itself (a better private international law), but a means to an end (European integration). The enterprise is not to achieve the optimal result, judged from the perspective of the private international lawyer. ……It is tempting to suggest, however that the Court of Justice rejected judicial discretion in OWUSU, not because European integration required it, but because they adopted a more administrative, less adjudicatory, view of the judicial role."

30 Ralf Michaels, *The New European Choice-of-Law Revolution,* 82 Tul. L. Rev. 1607, 2049, (2008), "In a teasing sense, recent developments in Europe have no significance for conflicts lawyers, even (counter intuitively) those in Europe itself. They are, however, of the first importance to students of the European polity and the science of international relations. Ultimately, enactments such as the Rome I and Rome II regulations are instruments in the service of European integration. The agenda they promote is not the design of optimal rules for choice of law, but rules which serve that homogenizing project."

31 These Rules are a new procedural code with the overriding objective of enabling the court to deal with cases justly.

32 A. Briggs, *The Impact of Recent Judgments of the European court on English Procedural Law and Practice*, 124 Zeitschrift Fur Schweizerisches Recht 231 et seq. (2005). "The European Court has had an impact on the law and practice of English courts which is far from benign and which fully deserves the description of a menace to the morality of commercial litigation. It is difficult to avoid the sense that it should be ashamed of itself."

規則的適用空間，因此曾聯名寫信給其時的席哈克總統[33]，抗議：「國家立法者並沒有被給予裁量權去評估正義及社會功能性之需求……並且這個對民主制度的侮辱，是伴隨著對憲政國家體制同樣清楚的背叛。」類似的看法與邏輯，於1977年時在美國最高法院的Shaffer v. Heitner亦為Marshall J.所說[34]：「經由避免管轄問題以簡化訴訟的代價可能就是會犧牲『公平與實質正義』。這個代價是太高了。」個人最近亦如此論述[35]：「個人一向認為強行立法通過一些死硬式的法規以達到判決一致性的目的，是在摧毀每個案件中之糾紛，而非解決每個案件中之糾紛。如此盲目的要求一致性的判決，是明顯的侵害人民的訴訟權及財產權。每個國家的憲法都有保障人民訴訟的權利及財產權，難怪有些法國同僚認為歐盟盲目一致性的要求是違憲的。聯合國的人權宣言（Universal Declaration of Human Rights）第8條規定：『於憲法或法律所保障的基本權利受侵犯時，每個人有權力要求各國有管轄權之法院給予有效的救濟[36]。』」「另

---

33 "First, it constitutes a very serious attack on democracy, since it strips national legislators of all powers. As they are left without any discretion to assess the requirements of justice and social usefulness, and are only authorized to take note of what the least demanding among them requires, national legislators lose their very raison d' être…"
And this insult to democracy comes along with an equally clear contradiction of the constitutional state. Indeed. Art. 65 of the EC Treaty authorizes the European Union to take measures in the area at issue here (i.e. the conflict of laws) only for the purpose of 'promoting the compatibility' of national solutions, and thus refuses to grant the EU the power to standardize national solutions, that is, to make them identical (as the preparatory work so clearly and unequivocally confirms). The initiative currently under way therefore constitutes a manifest excess of jurisdiction – which , considering its extent, outdoes in seriousness all of the abuses of power that, alas, have become a habit for Community authorities…
For not much longer will the undersigned law professors be able to accept to disgrace themselves, in both their writings and their teachings, by pretending to consider as such what obviously is not law."
該封公開信請參閱網頁如下：http://comparativelawblog.blogspot.com/2007/01/open-letter-french-private.html. 但法國學者意見較為分歧，更多人聯名反對此公開信，認為太過誇張，並因此展開論戰。

34 433 U.S. 186, 211, "Moreover, when the existence of jurisdiction in a particular forum under International Shoe is unclear, the cost of simplifying the litigation by avoiding the jurisdictional question may be the sacrifice of 'fair play and substantial justice.' That cost is too high."

35 見陳隆修，《歐盟經驗論中國式國際私法之建立》，高雄大學法學論叢6卷2期，2011年，17、18頁。

36 "Everyone has the right to an effective remedy by the competent national tribunals for acts violating the fundamental rights granted him by the constitution or by law."

外17條第2項則規定：『任何人皆不得武斷得被剝奪財產權[37]。』而歐盟自己的人權及基本自由保護（羅馬）公約（Convention for the Protection of Human Rights and Fundamental Freedoms）亦有著相對應的條款，其第6條第1項規定：『於決定其民法上之權利義務，或對其之任何刑事指控時，每個人皆有權利要求依法所設立之公正而獨立之法院於一段合理之時間內舉行一個公平而公開之審判。』[38]」

不同於大陸法的法國體系，傳統上以個案正義為「超越性目的」的英國司法訴訟體系，自然對歐盟規則及歐盟法院之判決會有著除了上述憲法及人權公約上之問題外，有著更多的疑慮。方便及不方便法院法學與禁訴令之作成為英國法在處理國際複數訴訟時，「公正的解決案件」之主要依據。這兩種法律原理是否應被適用於21世紀之全球化法學中，應以其適用之結果是否能符合「傳統上公平與實質正義之概念」為依據，亦即以「正義的真正利益是否最能被達成」為「超越性的目的」。如若只是一味的強調法律或「公約的目的」是在建立「統一的規則」[39]，則被違反的

37 "2.No one shall be arbitrarily deprived of his property."相關條文請參閱1966年的International Covenant on Civil and Political Rights 第2條3項(a)、(b)款：
3.Each State Party to the present Covenant undertakes:
(a) To ensure that any person whose rights or freedoms as herein recognized are violated shall have an effective remedy, notwithstanding that the violation has been committed by persons acting in an official capacity;
(b) To ensure that any person claiming such a remedy shall have his right thereto determined by competent judicial, administrative or legislative authorities, or by any other competent authority provided for by the legal system of the State, and to develop the possibilities of judicial remedy;

38 "In the determination of his civil rights and obligations or of any criminal charge against him, everyone is entitled to a fair and public hearing within a reasonable time by an independent and impartial tribunal established by law."相關條文參閱2000年的Charter of fundamental rights of the European union，第47條：Right to an effective remedy and to a fair trial
"Everyone whose rights and freedoms guaranteed by the law of the Union are violated has the right to an effective remedy before a tribunal in compliance with the conditions laid down in this Article.
Everyone is entitled to a fair and public hearing within a reasonable time by an independent and impartial tribunal previously established by law. Everyone shall have the possibility of being advised, defended and represented.
Legal aid shall be made available to those who lack sufficient resources in so far as such aid is necessary to ensure effective access to justice."

39 例如於*Benincasa v. Dentalkit Srl*中，C-265/98 [1997] E.C.R. I-3767, para. 25, "A jurisdiction clause, which serves a procedural purpose, is governed by the provisions of the Convention, whose aim is to establish uniform rules of international jurisdiction."

可能不只上述的憲法及人權公約上之規定而已。個人最近又如此主張[40]：「歐盟Charter of Fundamental Rights of the European Union（2003/C 364/01）的序文開宗明義的宣示：『經由建立聯盟的公民權，及創造自由、安全及正義的空間，歐盟將個人置於其活動之中心[41]。』歐盟於此昭告全世界，其立國之宗旨及社會之基石為一創造正義的空間及以個人為國家制度之中心；但是歐盟法院於所有的判決中卻一再信誓旦旦的強調於互信原則下法律一致性的必要性。很明顯的歐盟於其基本權利憲章中對歐盟人民及全世界所宣誓的崇高信念，與在實務上其最高法院藐視個案正義強調法律一致性之真正行為並不相符，而且可說是南轅北轍。難道歐盟是世界法律學中之岳不群？」

2000年的歐盟基本權利憲章又如此的揭示著[42]：「於尊重歐洲人民之文化及傳統的多元性，會員國之國家認同性，及會員國之國家性、區域性及地方性之公家單位之組織下，歐盟致力於這些共同價值的保存及發展……」除了序言外，這個尊重文化、傳統的多元性及國家的認同性又於22條[43]中再次被重申。尊重文化、傳統的多元性並非只是歐洲新興民族的「超越性目的」，它早已是全世界人權法的核心之一。聯合國1948年人權宣言第27(1)條[44]即規定對人類文化、藝術、及科學進步利益之保護；

40 見陳隆修，《歐盟經驗論中國式國際私法之建立》，高雄大學法學論叢6卷2期，2011年，33頁。

41 “It places the individual at the heart of its activities, by establishing the citizenship of the Union and by creating an area of freedom, security and justice.”

42 “The Union contributes to the preservation and to the development of these common values while respecting the diversity of the cultures and traditions of the peoples of Europe as well as the national identities of the Member States and the organization of their public authorities at national, regional and local levels...”

43 Article 22
Cultural, religious and linguistic diversity
The Union shall respect cultural, religious and linguistic diversity.

44 1. Everyone has the right freely to participate in the cultural life of the community, to enjoy the arts and to share in scientific advancement and its benefits.

聯合國1966年經濟、社會、及文化權利公約於序文[45]及第15(1)(a)條[46]亦再次明文規定。而聯合國1966年公民及政治公約除了於序文中有同樣規定外，做為歐洲新興聯盟中之少數民族[47]，英國民族應依公約27條[48]要求歐盟公約及歐盟法院尊重其聲名卓越之司法文化。

因此在二十一世紀的全球化法學中，「方便及不方便法院」法學及「禁訴令」是否有適用之必要，如果如歐盟法院般以建立「統一的規則」為主要的標準，可能在憲法及人權法上另有著非常大的問題。「方便及不方便法院」法學及「禁訴令」於21世紀全球化法學中是否有存在及適用的需要，應視其通常被加以適用之後果是否能符合「傳統上公平與實質正義的概念」而定——亦即這兩個英美法傳統上在複數訴訟時所適用的法學，是否能幫助法院去確認「正義的真正利益是否最能被達成」之地。

三、充分互信v.消滅英國判例法

儘管如前述歐盟Charter of Fundamental Rights of the European Union之序文冠冕堂皇大言不慚的對全世界宣示「其將個人放置於其活動之心中」（It places the individual at the heart of its activities），但於國際複數訴訟時，其又以「國際民商衝突管轄規則之統一」為目的（objectives of unification of the rules of conflict of jurisdiction in civil and commercial matters）。以歐盟法院為其司法發言人之歐盟完全無視於在

---

45 "Recognizing that, in accordance with the Universal Declaration of Human Rights, the ideal of free human beings enjoying freedom from fear and want can only be achieved if conditions are created whereby everyone may enjoy his economic, social and cultural rights, as well as his civil and political rights."

46 Article 15
1. The States Parties to the present Covenant recognize the right of everyone:
(a) To take part in cultural life;

47 這種成為少數民族的悲哀，早已為英國同僚所感嘆，見J. Beatson, *Has the Common Law a Future*?, 56 Cambridge L.J. 291, 295 (1995). "we will become the Louisiana, or give our relationship with the European Union, the Quebec, of Europe."

48 Article 27
In those States in which ethnic, religious or linguistic minorities exist, persons belonging to such minorities shall not be denied the right, in community with the other members of their group, to enjoy their own culture, to profess and practice their own religion, or to use their own language.

國際訴訟上（包含不方便法院與禁訴令），「心與靈魂應在正義的真正利益是否最能被達成」。對於這種言行不一的法學，個人最近命名為「岳不群法學」[49]。

或許「岳不群法學」還是太過保守的說法，較近歐盟法院甚至公開的對不適用於布魯塞爾規則的範圍，亦命令英國法院應不得作成禁訴令。於*Allianz SpA, Generali Assicurazioni Generali SpA, v West Tankers Inc.*[50]，中，Erg石油公司承租West Tankers之船，並於意大利與自己之碼頭碰撞，Erg在對保險公司取得理賠後，對不足之部分於倫敦對West Tankers提起不足部分之仲裁。傭船契約準據法為英國法，並有包含於倫敦仲裁之條款。保險公司於給付賠償後代位Erg之權利於意大利對West Tankers起訴。West Tankers於倫敦起訴，要求保險公司依約定去仲裁，並要求英國法院禁止保險公司於意大利進行訴訟：英國最高法院認為根據Regulation No 44/2001,Art. 1 (2) (d)[51]，所有仲裁的事項均被排除在公約之適用範圍外[52]。並且認為禁訴令會防止仲裁判斷與各國法院判決之衝突，而且如果各會員國能採用禁訴令，會使得歐盟於國際仲裁上比起紐約、百慕達及新加坡有競爭力[53]。歐盟法院認為[54]布魯塞爾規則之適用範圍，必須完全依據訴訟程序的實體（或主體）而定[55]。更明確的說其於規則範圍內之地

---

49 見最近拙作，《歐盟經驗論中國式國際私法之建立》，高雄大學法學論叢6卷2期，2011年。

50 [2009] EUECJ C-185/07，又見陳隆修，《歐盟經驗論中國式國際私法之建立》，高雄大學法學論叢6卷2期，2011年，70-75頁。

51 Article 1(1) and (2)of that regulation provides:
-1. This Regulation shall apply in civil and commercial matters whatever the nature of the court or tribunal. It shall not extend, in particular, to revenue, customs or administrative matters.
2. The Regulation shall not apply to: ...(d) arbitration.'

52 Para.16。

53 Para.17。

54 Para.22。

55 Case C-190/89 *Marc Rich and Co. AG v Società Italiana Impianti* PA [1991] ECR I-3855, para.26, "Those interpretations cannot be accepted. In order to determine whether a dispute falls within the scope of the Convention, reference must be made solely to the subject-matter of the dispute. If, by virtue of its subject-matter, such as the appointment of an arbitrator, a dispute falls outside the scope of the Convention, the existence of a preliminary issue which the court must resolve in order to determine the dispute cannot, whatever that issue may be, justify application of the Convention."

位，並非由其性質而決定，而是由其要保護的權利之性質而決定[56]。法院認為基於仲裁條款（包括條款之效力）而去對義大利法院主張沒有管轄權的抗議，仍屬於規則之範圍內，並且完全是由意大利法院根據規則之第1(2)(d)及5(3)條去決定該抗議是否成立及自己之管轄權[57]。法院認為：「在主訴訟程序中之禁訴令，是違反了法院在布魯塞爾公約中所建立之大原則，亦即根據應適用之法規，由各繫屬法院去決定其是否對面前之糾紛有管轄權……我們應記住44/2001號規則，除了與目前的主要程序無關的幾個有限例外之情形外，並不允許會員國法院之管轄權被另一會員國法院重新再檢驗……[58]」「這種禁訴令是違反了互信，而這種互信是會員國間應給予其他法律制度及機構的，並且44/2001號規則的管轄制度是根據這樣的互信而來。[59]」事實上44/2001號規則很明白的將仲裁排除在規則外，但歐盟法院則鐵了心要消滅英國的禁訴令：「但是，即使這些程序沒有涵

---

[56] Case C-391/95 *Van Uden* [1998] ECR I-7091, Para.33, "However, it must be noted in that regard that provisional measures are not in principle ancillary to arbitration proceedings but are ordered in parallel to such proceedings and are intended as measures of support. They concern not arbitration as such but the protection of a wide variety of rights. Their place in the scope of the Convention is thus determined not by their own nature but by the nature of the rights which they serve to protect (see Case C-261/90 Reichert and *Kockler v Dresdner Bank* [1992] ECR I-2149, paragraph 32)."

[57] Para.27, "It follows that the objection of lack of jurisdiction raised by West Tankers before the Tribunale di Siracusa on the basis of the existence of an arbitration agreement, including the question of the validity of that agreement, comes within the scope of Regulation No 44/2001 and that it is therefore exclusively for that court to rule on that objection and on its own jurisdiction, pursuant to Articles 1(2)(d) and 5(3) of that regulation."

[58] Para.29, It follows, first, as noted by the Advocate General in point 57 of her Opinion, that an anti-suit injunction, such as that in the main proceedings, is contrary to the general principle which emerges from the case-law of the Court on the Brussels Convention, that every court seised itself determines, under the rules applicable to it, whether it has jurisdiction to resolve the dispute before it (see, to that effect, Gasser, paragraphs 48 and 49). It should be borne in mind in that regard that Regulation No 44/2001, apart from a few limited exceptions which are not relevant to the main proceedings, does not authorize the jurisdiction of a court of a Member State to be reviewed by a court in another Member State (Case C-351/89 *Overseas Union Insurance and Others* [1991] ECR I-3317, paragraph 24, and Turner, paragraph 26). That jurisdiction is determined directly by the rules laid down by that regulation, including those relating to its scope of application. Thus in no case is a court of one Member State in a better position to determine whether the court of another Member State has jurisdiction (*Overseas Union Insurance and Others*, paragraph 23, and Gasser, paragraph 48).

[59] Para.30, "such an anti-suit injunction also runs counter to the trust which the Member States accord to one another' s legal systems and judicial institutions and on which the system of jurisdiction under Regulation No 44/2001 is based (see, to that effect, *Turner,* paragraph 24)."

蓋在44/2001號規則之範圍內，他們仍可能會有破壞規則有效性的後果，亦即於民商事件上國際私法管轄權規則統一目標的達成及於這些事情上判決之自由流動。這是因為這些程序阻止了其他會員國的法院依據44/2001號規則去行使他們的管轄權。[60]」

因此無論仲裁是否含蓋在布魯塞爾規則之範圍內，為了「國際民商衝突管轄規則統一目標的達成」，禁訴令是被視為「可能會有破壞規則有效性的後果」，因此英國法院是被禁止對其他會員國法院作成禁訴令。做為一個法律學生個人對歐盟法院的邏輯百思不解——如果「其要保護的權利之性質」（訴訟程序的主體）沒有涵蓋在公約或規則之範圍內，他們如何去破壞公約或規則的有效性？原來歐洲人所有自吹自擂的「歐州法律革命」[61]（European legal revolution）是效法中國人的文化大革命——無法無天。

正如在Owusu案中英國法院被禁止以不方便法院之名將案件於事實上移轉給非會員國之法院一般[62]，於West Tankers中歐盟法院真正的理由可能是禁訴令與不方便法院原則就只有少數會員國承認，而「公約的目的正是在排除破壞性的國內法規，並建立共同的法規」。如前述事實上歐盟公約第65(b)條只是是要求國際私法及管轄權的「相容性」而已，並非「建立共同的法規」。事實上於1995年時恩師Prof. C. G. J. Morse即於風暴尚未形成前即對充滿憧憬的美國同僚，給予暮鼓晨鐘般的警世真言。最尊敬的恩師於其時即質疑歐盟法律及判決統一之協調性（harmonization）對

60 Para. 24, "However, even though proceedings do not come within the scope of Regulation No 44/2001, they may nevertheless have consequences which undermine its effectiveness, namely preventing the attainment of the objectives of unification of the rules of conflict of jurisdiction in civil and commercial matters and the free movement of decisions in those matters. This is so, inter alia, where such proceedings prevent a court of another Member State from exercising the jurisdiction conferred on it by Regulation No 44/2001."

61 Ralf Michaels, *The New European Choice-of-Law Revolution*, 82 Tul. L. Rev. 1607 (2008).

62 Case C-281/02. Andrew Owusu v N.B. *Jackson, trading as 'Villa Holidays Bai-Inn Villas' and others, para.*43, "Moreover, allowing forum non conveniens in the context of the Brussels Convention would be likely to affect the uniform application of the rules of contained therein so far as that doctrine is recognized only in a limited number of Contracting States, whereas the objective of the Brussels Convention is precisely to lay down common rules to the exclusion of derogating national rules."

共同市場建立之必要性：「這些無疑的是很堂皇的情操。但於這些法律被作成時並無證據被提出來以支持他們，並且自他們被作成至今亦無任何詳實的證據來支持他們。判決的自由流動（被承認）對共同市場的有效運作是很重要的概念，或許應該仍是一個應被懷疑的概念[63]。」或許恩師之懷疑是完全站得住腳的，並且是有充分的證據來支持其論點的。在Sun Oil Co. v. Wortman[64]中，美國最高法院即白紙黑字的認為規定聯邦法院應遵守所在地州法的Erie案，是為了建立判決可預測的一致性；而充分互信條款並非為了建立一致性，是為確認各州立法權的限制範圍[65]。換言之，有

---

63 C. G. J. Morse, *International Shoe v. Brussels and Lugano: Principles and Pitfalls in the Law of Personal Jurisdiction,* 28 U.C. DAVIS L. REV. 999,1002 (1995).“These are undoubtedly grandiloquent sentiments. But no evidence was offered to support them at the time they were made, and no hard evidence to support them has emerged since. The notion that the free movement of judgments is fundamental to the effective working of a common market must, perhaps, remain a suspect one.”

64 486 U.S. 717; 108 S. Ct. 2117; 100 L. Ed. 2d 743; 1988 U.S. LEXIS 2723; 56 U.S.L.W. 4601; 101 Oil & Gas Rep. 1.

65 同上，726, 727, “In the context of our Erie jurisprudence, see Erie R. Co. v. Tompkins, 304 U.S. 64, 82 L. Ed. 1188, 58 S. Ct. 817 (1938), that purpose is to establish (within the limits of applicable federal law, including the prescribed Rules of Federal Procedure) substantial uniformity of predictable outcome between cases tried in a federal court and cases tried in the courts of the State in which the federal court sits. See Guaranty Trust, supra, at 109; Hanna v. Plumer, 380 U.S. 460, 467, 471-474, 14 L. Ed. 2d 8, 85 S. Ct. 1136 (1965). The purpose of the substance procedure dichotomy in the context of the Full Faith and Credit Clause, by contrast, is not to establish uniformity but to delimit spheres of state legislative competence.” 歐盟布魯塞爾公約及規則是被稱為「歐洲的充份互信條款」，但相對於美國之「充份互信條款」並不意圖建立一致性，反而是尊重各州之立法權，歐盟之意圖消滅英美法是甚為反諷而低級。更有趣的是Erie（見陳隆修、許兆慶、林恩瑋，《台灣財產法暨經濟法研究叢書（十三）-國際私法：選法理論之回顧與展望》，台灣財產法暨經濟法研究協會發行，2007年1月，初版，194頁）案之目的是尊重各州之法律及判決，卻被認為是可以促進統一，歐盟何時才能進化為文明之國家？

事實上亦有美國同僚注意到歐盟之鐵血政策意圖消滅英國判例法，進而達到法律之統一，並促成內部市場發達之作法是美國經驗不合的。見George A. Bermann, Rome I: A Comparative View,於Rome I Regulation: The law Applicable to Contractual Obligations in Europe edited by Franco Ferrari, Stefan Leible, pp. 354, 355: “The United States, due to its long and incrementally accomplished federalism, is simply less intent than the European Union on pursuing market integration through legislative action. Achievement of a market without internal borders simply is not and has not for some time been an overriding political objective. While the processes of conscious union-building within the EU are undoubtedly plagued with controversy, the subject itself remains a major preoccupation. The United States by contrast has developed over time the sense that formal unification of commercial law is simply not essentiall to the survival of either the American market or American federalism.” “We may conclude then that a leavening of differences among the contract laws of the States through Restatements of Contracts, combined with a leavening of differences among the conflicts of law rules of the States through Restatements of Conflict of Laws, has struck Americans as the better recipe for coherence than the legal federalization of either the one or the other body of law. It is thought better to leave some ‘breathing

著200年以上的聯邦共同市場的建立，其基礎是大部分（於聯邦法及程序法之限制內）本於尊重各州的立法——而非如歐盟般的決定消滅英國法。共同市場的有效性及互信是本於「充分互信」各州之法律而來，而非本於「排除破壞性的國內法規」而來。

於兩岸已簽訂經濟合作條約後，個人於此提出雄霸二十世紀的美國共同市場的經驗鐵證——必須充分互信各個單獨經濟體的文化及法律制度才能促進共同市場的繁榮。於評論數個歐盟法院對英國法之判決時（特別是Owusu）恩師Prof. Trevor C. Hartley不由得感嘆[66]：「這個判決的特點在於，即使與歐盟的利益無關，卻仍然粗魯的堅持英國判例法必須被消滅，這對英國的法界人士會造成最大的困難。看起來似乎歐盟法院中大陸法系的法官，認為他們是有著確定的權利，去將拆毀英國判例法當成是一個目標。另外（歐盟法院）將事實上的考慮完全忽略也是令人不安的。」就個人所知最尊敬的恩師這個「摧毀判例法」的感嘆，普遍為英、美的國際法同僚所深為注目。個人亦藉勢而大聲指責第一世界及其附庸打手機構WTO及諾貝爾和平獎的剝奪第三世界1966年兩個聯合國人權公約第1(2)條生存權之「岳不群法學」。

四、2005年海牙公約——聖靈叫人活

另外有趣的是很少有最高法院的案例會如West Tankers一般，赤裸裸的顯示第一世界的「岳不群法學」。個人之所以反對2005年海牙法院選

space' both in substantive state contract law and in state conflicts lae than to establish a federal law strait jacket in either."

66 Trevor C. Hartley, *The European Union and the Systematic Dismantling of the Common Law of Conflict of Laws,*54 I.C.L.Q, 813, 828 (2005). "The crass insistence that common law rules must be abolished even where no Community interest is at stake is the feature of this judgment that will cause most difficulty for lawyers in England. It seems that the continental judges on the European Court want to dismantle the common law as an objective in its own right. The brushing aside of all practical considerations is also disturbing."又見Trevor C. Hartley, *Unnecessary Europeanization under the Brussels Jurisdiction and Judgments Convention: The Case of the Dissatisfied Sub-Purchaser*, 18 E.L. REV. 506 (1993).其認為歐盟法院判例法過分「不必要的歐盟化（unnecessary Europeanization），會造成「不穩定及混亂」（uncertainty and confusion），另外又會造成各國法院須經常請求歐盟法院給予答案，但歐盟法院以前之決定並不合適目前個案之情形。

擇公約乃是於其5(1)[67]、6(a)[68]、及9(a)[69]條等主要條文[70]中，公約不但以被選定之法院為唯一管轄法院，並以其法律為指定管轄條款效力之準據法。如同Dicey與Morris於評論第9條a款之以被指定法院地法為依據時，一針見血的說：「一個有這樣內容的規定，在有關承認外國判決的判例法上是沒有直接的相似決定的。[71]」做為Prof. Graveson的忠誠教徒，個人對法學邏輯並非十分執著，但對「判例法實現正義的目的」個人是十分堅持。個人反對2005年海牙公約的對優勢議價者之主導地位的一面倒的保護，這是剝奪弱勢者——特別是第三世界的人——人權公約所保障的平等權、訴訟權、財產權、適當程序權中所涵蓋之保障。英國1998年之Civil Procedure Rules, Rule 1.1[72]中「公平處理案件」之「超越性目的」及「確保當事人立足點平等」的人類有史以來訴訟法（包括國內及國際訴訟）之文明規範，皆被2005年海牙公約以高度法律科技加以徹底的破壞。2005年海

---

67 Article 5

1. The court or courts of a Contracting State designated in an exclusive choice of court agreement shall have jurisdiction to decide a dispute to which the agreement applies, unless the agreement is null and void under the law of that State.
2. A court that has jurisdiction under paragraph 1 shall not decline to exercise jurisdiction on the ground that the dispute should be decided in a court of another State.

68 Article 6

A court of a Contracting State other than that of the chosen court shall suspend or dismiss proceedings to which an exclusive choice of court agreement applies unless –

a) the agreement is null and void under the law of the State of the chosen court;

69 Article 9

Recognition or enforcement may be refused if –

a)the agreement was null and void under the law of the State of the chosen court, unless the chosen court has determined that the agreement is valid;

70 但是公約對中間保全處分並未禁止或允許，而保持開放態度。

Article 7

Interim measures of protection are not governed by this Convention. This Convention neither requires nor precludes the grant, refusal of termination of interim measures of protection by a court of a Contracting State and does not affect whether or not a party may request or a court should grant, refuse or terminate such measures.故其對禁訴令之作成是保持開放之態度。

71 Dicey and Morris, the Conflict of Laws, 14th ed., p. 566, footnote 1, "a rule in these terms has no direct counterpart in the common law on the recognition of judgments"

72 (1) These Rules are a new procedural code with the overriding objective of enabling the court to deal with cases justly.

(2) Dealing with cases justly includes, so far as practicable –

(a) ensuring that the parties are on an equal footing;

牙法院選擇公約是個典型的「岳不群公約」。

2005年海牙公約號稱要成為司法上的聯合國紐約仲裁公約（Convention on the Recognition and Enforcement of Foreign Arbitral Awards），意圖與紐約公約平行。但紐約公約的2(3)條卻是如此規定[73]：「當訴訟是有關當事人於本條文之範圍內所訂之約定，並且繫屬於訂約國之法院時，在當事人之一方請求下，應命令當事人去仲裁，除非法院認為該約定是無效、不適用或無法被履行。」因此很明顯的兩個「號稱」平行的國際公約在其「主要」（或「骨幹」）條款上，對弱勢是否給予最後一線生機是南轅北轍的。事實上無論仲裁條款或指定專屬管轄條款，皆不折不扣的為契約法的範圍。而如同訴訟法，契約法的共同核心價值亦是在保護當事人間「立足點之平等」——只是契約法於英美較常以「合理性」為「基本政策」（超越性政策），而大陸法以「誠信原則」為強行法。

亦如同美國法律協會（the American Law Institute）的Restatement (Second) of Judgments, s. 84, comment (a)所說[74]：「仲裁是紛爭當事人間透過契約所允許的一種解決法律紛爭的一種方法。」至於專屬法院管轄條款，無論其附屬於契約之一部分或為一個單獨獨立之約定，皆很明顯的是屬於契約之一種。既然是屬於契約就應受到契約法上強行法規或強行政策之拘束。於國際私法上強行法的代表法規之一或許就是羅馬Ｉ（Rome

---

73 3. The court of a Contracting State, when seized of an action in a matter in respect of which the parties have made an agreement within the meaning of this article, shall, at the request of one of the parties, refer the parties to arbitration, unless it finds that the said agreement is null and void, inoperative or incapable of being performed. 1985年的模範公約第8(1)條亦有類似規定：
Article 8. Arbitration agreement and substantive claim before court
(1) A court before which an action is brought in a matter which is the subject of an arbitration agreement shall, if a party so requests not later than when submitting his first statement on the substance of the dispute, refer the parties to arbitration unless it finds that the agreement is null and void, inoperative or incapable of being performed.

74 a. Scope. Arbitration is a method of determining legal disputes that is authorized by contract between the parties to the dispute. There are forms of dispute-resolution procedure that are called "arbitration" but which are made obligatory by law instead of being prescribed by contract, for example, some proceedings in "no fault" insurance schemes. These procedures might perhaps better be regarded as adjudication before specialized tribunals. See s. 83.

I）規則第9條[75]的對強行法加以定義、法院地強行法的超越性、及對履行地法的尊重。而其recital 23亦規定[76]：「有關與被視為較弱勢之當事人所訂之契約，那些當事人應受到較一般規則對他們的利益有好處的國際私法規則的保護。」至於強行法於實體契約法代表之一，或許就是Unidroit Principles of International Commercial Contracts 2004。其第3章有關契約的效力之部分幾乎全部皆被視為強行法[77]，故為當事人所不能藉著強勢

---

[75] Article 9 Overriding mandatory provisions

1. Overriding mandatory provisions are provisions the respect for which is regarded as crucial by a country for safeguarding its public interests, such as its political, social or economic organisation, to such an extent that they are applicable to any situation falling within their scope, irrespective of the law otherwise applicable to the contract under this Regulation.
2. Nothing in this Regulation shall restrict the application of the overriding mandatory provisions of the law of the forum.
3. Effect may be given to the overriding mandatory provisions of the law of the country where the obligations arising out of the contract have to be or have been performed, in so far as those overriding mandatory provisions render the performance of the contract unlawful. In considering whether to give effect to those provisions, regard shall be had to their nature and purpose and to the consequences of their application or non-application.

[76] (23) As regards contracts concluded with parties regarded as being weaker, those parties should be protected by conflict-of-law rules that are more favourable to their interests than the general rules.

[77] Article 3.1 (Matters not covered)
These Principles do not deal with invalidity arising from
(a) lack of capacity;
(b) immorality or illegality.
Article 3.19 (Mandatory character of the provisions)
The provisions of this Chapter are mandatory, except insofar as they relate to the binding force of mere agreement, initial impossibility or mistake.
又例如美國2004年新版的統一商法1-302條即規定誠信原則、合理性、及適當注意性與勤奮性皆為強制性規定。See U.C.C 1-302:
1-302, VARIATION BY AGREEMENT
(a)Except as otherwise provided in subsection (b) or elsewhere in [the Uniform Commercial Code], the effect of provisions of [the Uniform Commercial Code] may be varied by agreement.
(b)The obligations of good faith, diligence, reasonableness, and care prescribed by [the Uniform Commercial Code] may not be disclaimed by agreement. The parties, by agreement, may determine the standards by which the performance of those obligations is to be measured if those standards are not manifestly unreasonable. Whenever [the Uniform Commercial Code] requires an action to be taken within a reasonable time, a time that is not manifestly unreasonable may be fixed by agreement.
而更有趣的是如後述，即使於非契約上之義務，歐盟2007年羅馬II之序言要點31即規定，於認定當事人間合意之存在時，應有某些強行之限制以保護弱勢之一方。
(31) To respect the principle of party autonomy and to enhance legal certainty, the parties should be allowed to make a choice as to the law applicable to a non-contractual obligation. This choice should be expressed or demonstrated with reasonable certainty by the circumstances of the case.
Where establishing the existence of the agreement, the court has to respect the intentions of the parties. Protection should be given to weaker parties by imposing certain conditions on the choice.

地位而加以改變。

因此無論是依紐約公約2(3)條、歐盟羅馬I規則、及Unidroit Principles（2004），對弱勢者加以保護及契約之效力這些有關公平正義之事項，並非強勢當事人所得以主導的——而這正是2005年海牙公約的阿奇里斯腳踝（heel of Achilles）。

2005年海牙公約不顧訴訟法要求「當事人間立足點平等」（武器平等），亦不顧契約法「保護弱勢當事人」之強行基本政策，一昧順服強勢當事人所選定之法院地及該地之法律，這個公開的秘密應早已為第一世界的各個法系所深知。他們的各別最高法院之判決中，如歐盟法院之West Tankers[78]，英國最高法院之The Sennar（No.2）[79]，及美國最高法院之The Bremen[80]，皆已充分的證明了於個案正義之需求下，管轄條款之效力應適時的退讓。於較近的West Tankers案中，為了消滅英國法劇除禁訴令，歐盟法院公開的引用紐約公約第2(3)條[81]：「這個結論是受到紐約公約第2(3)條所支持的，根據該規定，有關當事人所訂定之仲裁條款範圍內之訴訟所繫屬的會員國法院，在當事人一方之請求下，應命令當事人去仲裁，除非法院認定該條款是無效、不適用、或無法被履行。」故而為了消滅禁訴令，為了歐盟法律的統一適用，及給歐盟人民「他所應享有的司法保護的形式」，歐盟法院始終都知道[82]：「當事人之一方只要依賴該條款就可避免訴訟程序，而申請人，他認為該條款是無效、不適用、或不能被

---

78 [2009] EUECJ C-185/07。

79 [1985] 1 WLR 490 at 500。

80 407 U.S. 1（1972）。

81 Para.33, “This finding is supported by Article II(3) of the New York Convention, according to which it is the court of a Contracting State, when seised of an action in a matter in respect of which the parties have made an arbitration agreement, that will, at the request of one of the parties, refer the parties to arbitration, unless it finds that the said agreement is null and void, inoperative or incapable of being performed.”

82 Para. 31, “Lastly, if, by means of an anti-suit injunction, the Tribunable di Siracusa were prevented from examining itself the preliminary issue of the validity or the applicability of the arbitration agreement, a party could avoid the proceedings merely by relying on that agreement and the applicant, which considers that the agreement is void, inoperative or incapable of being performed, would thus be barred from access to the court before which it brought proceedings under Article 5(3) of Regulation No 44/2001 and would therefore be deprived of a form of judicial protection to which it is entitled.”

履行，則將會被禁止依44/2001規則第5(3)條去法院提出訴訟，並因此而會被剝奪他所應享有的司法保護的形式。」請問歐盟、英國、及美國，你們的最高法院一向皆秉持著當事人仲裁條款（及於指定管轄條款）之效力，必須符合人民「應享有的司法保護的形式」、「公平正義」、或「合理性」之要件才具有效力，如果對自己的人民是適用這樣的法則，為什麼對第三世界人民在2005年海牙公約所適用的法則卻完全不一樣？難道繼WTO及諾貝爾和平獎後，第一世界的岳不群法學機構又多了一個2005年海牙公約？

在當事人訂有仲裁或專屬管轄條款時，美國、英國、及歐盟最高法院，都嚴守著契約法保護弱勢及訴訟法要求當事人立足點平等之基本法學政策，而分別要求必須「合理」、符合「公平正義」及不能剝奪人民「應享有的司法保護的形式」；但是在2005年海牙公約卻又搖身一變，美、英、及歐盟皆不約而同的對第三世界強調優勢當事人所指定的管轄條款之有效性、穩定性、及特別是獨立性，所可能帶來之促進商業之利益。對指定管轄或仲裁條款效力之單一議題上，第一世界可以藉著高法律科技，對內給予人民「應享有的司法保護的形式」，對外可以「摧毀禁訴令」及拓展自由市場的法律穩定性，「岳不群法學」的應用已到達巔峰。

但是做為第三世界的法律學生，個人必須提醒第一世界ALI/UNIDROIT Principles of Transnational Civil Procedure第3條當事人程序平等條款之註解P-3A[83]中，規定所謂整個原則中皆被貫穿使用之「合理

---

83 P-3A "The term 'reasonable' is used throughout the Principles and signifies 'proportional,' 'significant,' 'not excessive,' or 'fair,' according to the context. It can also mean the opposite of arbitrary. The concept of reasonableness also precludes hyper-technical legal argument and leaves a range of discretion to the court to avoid severe, excessive, or unreasonable application of procedural norms."
又聖經新約哥林多後書第3章：「你們明顯是基督的信、藉著我們修成的。不是用墨寫的、乃是用永生上帝的靈寫的。不是寫在石版上，乃是寫在心版上。我們因基督所以在上帝面前纔有這樣的信心。並不是我們憑自己能承擔什麼事、我們所能承擔的、乃是出於上帝。他叫我們能承擔這新約的執事。不是憑著字句、乃是憑著精意。因為那字句是叫人死、精意是叫人活。」「精意或作聖靈」
對2005年海牙公約「嚴厲、過分、不合理」條款的適用，對第三世界弱勢之商人、社會所可能造成之毀滅性傷害，第一世界可能必須摸著良心重新再唸一次：「因為那字句是叫人死，聖靈是叫人活」。

性」，是排除「過分技術性的法律論述」，並且應避免「程序法形式上過分嚴苛之適用」。註解P-3A這個論述，個人以為這是我們中國人祖先二千多年前所謂「道法自然」的「王道」法學。

五、國際禮誼要求足夠的利益與關連

因此對於英國法院所作成之禁訴令，上述歐盟法院偏向政治性的意見個人以為並不具有甚大的法學參考價值。於全球化訴訟法之觀點，禁訴令是否有存在之價值，還是應以其是否能達成正義的真正利益為評斷。於面對國際複數訴訟時，英國法是以「方便及不方便法院」法學而大陸法通常是以「先繫屬優先」法則為依據，而除此之外英美法又多一個「禁訴令」之衡平救濟。無論是「不方便法院」或「先繫屬優先」之適用，於其他法系皆有著反對之意見。禁訴令雖然只是禁止當事人於外國法院提起訴訟，並非直接命令外國法院如何進行訴訟，但其後果還是可能間接的干擾到外國訴訟之進行，因此經常於大陸法被視為對本國管轄權具有敵意之干涉。因此在Airbus Industrie GIE v. Patel中Lord Goff說[84]：「通常的基本規則

84 [1991] 1 AC 119 at 138, "As a general rule, before an anti-suit injunction can properly be granted by an English court to restrain a person from pursuing proceedings in a foreign jurisdiction in cases of the kind under consideration in the present case, comity requires that the English forum should have a sufficient interest in, or connection with, the matter in question to justify the indirect interference with foreign court which an anti-suit injunction entails."同樣的亦有美國上訴巡迴法院認為禁訴令只能於維護法院之管轄權及保護重要的國家政策時才能作成。Quaak v. Klynveld Peat Marwick Goerdeler Bedrijfsrevisoren, 361 F. 3d 11, 17 (1st Cir. 2004)。而所謂「國家政策」指的可能是支持仲裁之政策。見Paramedics Electromedicina Comercial v. GE Med. Sys. Info. Techs., 369 F.3d 645, 653, 654 (2d Cir. 2004), "Federal policy strongly favors the enforcement of arbitration agreements⋯ The federal policy favoring the liberal enforcement of arbitration clause⋯applies with particular force in international disputes⋯ We need not decide categorically whether an attempt to sidestep arbitration is alone sufficient to support a foreign anti-suit injunction, because 'there is less justification for permitting a second action,' as here, 'after a prior court has reached a judgment on the same issues.' "對於Federal Arbitration Act (FAA)之通過，美國最高法院是有著期待。Dean Witter Reynolds, Inc. v. Byrd, 470 U.S. 213, 220 (1985), "passage of the Act was motivated, first and foremost, by a congressional desire to enforce agreements into which parties had entered, and [that the court] must not overlook this principal objective when construing the statute, or allow the fortuitous impact of the Act on efficient dispute resolution to overshadow the underlying motivation".
Scherk v. Alberto-Culver Co., 417 U.S. 506, 516-17 (1974), "A parochial refusal by the courts of one country to enforce an international arbitration agreement would not only frustrate these purposes, but would invite unseemly and mutually destructive jockeying by the parties to secure tactical litigation ad-

是，在如目前所被考慮之本案件之類型中，在英國法院許可去合適的作成禁訴令以限制一個人於外國法院提起訴訟程序前，國際禮誼要求英國法院與係爭之問題必須有著一個充足的利益，或足夠的關係，以使得禁訴令所帶來的間接的干擾外國法院之後果為合理。」

事實上由於國際禮誼的牽制，不只英國法院要求必須於十分謹慎下才可作成禁訴令，有些美國法院亦有著同樣保守之態度。例如於Quaak v. Klynveld Peat Marwick Goerdeler Bedrijfsrevisoren中，聯邦第一巡迴法院即說[85]：「作成一國國際禁訴令是一個『應該在小心及極度自制下才能作成』之步驟。」在著名的Laker Airways v. Sabena, Belgian World Airlines中，哥倫比亞巡迴法院[86]說：「因此，只有在最迫切之情形下，一個法院才有裁量權去作成禁訴令。」於China Trade & Dev. Corp. v. M.V. Choong Yong中，第二巡迴法院說[87]：「一個禁止外國訴訟的命令應該『極少被使用』，並且『只能謹慎而極度克制』下才能被允許。」自然亦有些法院直接引用國際禮誼，例如Athina Invs. Ltd. v. Pinchuk[88]就認為禁訴令之作成必須考慮到「法院於國際禮誼上之重大利益」，並且「如同事實所顯示的是，本法院沒辦法想像有任何一天國際禮誼會不存在之情形。」於Empresa Generadora de Electricidad ITABO, S.A. v. Corporacion Dominicana de Empresas Electricas Estatales中，紐約地院引用第二

vantages."
Gilmer v. Interstate/Johnson Lane Corp., 500 U.S. 20, 25 (1991), "These provisions manifest a 'liberal federal policy favoring arbitration agreements.' "

85 361 F.3d 11, 17, 18(1st Cir. 2004), "Issuing an international antisuit injunction is a step that should 'be taken only with care and great restraint.' " (citing Canadian Filters (Harwich) Ltd. v. Lear-Siegler, Inc., 412 F.2d 577, 578 (1st Cir. 1969).

86 731 F.2d 909, 927 (D.C. Cir. 1984), "Thus, only in the most compelling circumstances does a court have discretion to issue an anti-suit injunction." 又說禁訴令會有效的限制外國法院之管轄權，故只能在保護法院的管轄或防止當事人規避法院地之公共政策時才能作成，"effectively restricts the foreign court' s ability to exercise jurisdiction", "necessary to protect the jurisdiction of the enjoining court, or to prevent the litigant' s evasion of the important public policies of the forum".

87 China Trade & Dev. Corp. v. M.V. Choong Yong, 837 F.2d 33, 36 (2d Cir. 1987), "An anti-foreign-suit injunction should be 'used sparingly' , and should be granted 'only with care and great restraint.' "

88 443 F. Supp. 177, 182 (D. Mass. 2006), "nevertheless be weighed against the forum' s substantial interest in international comity", "on the facts as they stand right now, this Court can envision no scenario under which comity would not carry the day".

巡迴法院說[89]：「作成禁訴令可能是不合適的，因為『禮誼原則於作成外國禁訴令之決定中是占很大分量的。』」

但是個人覺得相較之下，地理上遠離歐洲之美國同僚似乎遠不若英國法院的將「禮誼」視為例行必唸經咒。Daniel Tan說[90]：「在美國令人感覺困擾的趨勢是，法院已經開始用禮誼做為一個實質的因素去拒絕禁訴令之救濟。」在Allendale Mut. Ins. Co. v. Bull Data Sys.中，第七巡迴法院[91]說：「國際禮誼所唯一會牽扯到的顧慮完全只是理論上而已，而這是不應超越過申請禁訴令者切實而有說服力的所顯現出之損害，這種損害在禁訴令如果被拒絕下，相較起如果禁訴令被允許下對方所可能產生的傷害是無法彌補。」在Kaepa, Inc. v. Achilles Corp.中，第五巡迴法院[92]說：

---

89 05 Civ. 5004 (RMB), 2005 U.S. Dist. LEXIS 14712, at 27 (S.D.N.Y. Jul. 18, 2005), "Even assuming arguendo that Plaintiff showed irreparable harm, an anti-suit injunction might be inappropriate because 'principles of comity weigh heavily in the decision to impose a foreign anti-suit injunction.' " (quoting Paramedics Electromedicina Comercial v. GE Med. Sys. Info. Techs., 369 F.3d 645, 654-55 (2d Cir. 2004).

90 Daniel Tan, Enforcing International Arbitration Agreements in Federal Courts: Rethinking the Court's Remedial Powers, 47 Va. J. Int'l L. 545, 594 (2007), "The disturbing trend in the United States is that the courts have started using comity as a substantive factor to deny antisuit relief. Fear of infringing comity so influenced the courts that the First Circuit Court of Appeals in Quaak elevated comity into a pivotal role in the antisuit analysis. This is not helpful. Unless the courts are prepared to give the remedy up altogether, any profitable development must seek to answer the crucial question of when antisuit relief would be available despite the concerns of comity. An approach where comity, the natural limiter on any such relief, plays a major role, casts no light on this all-important question."又見Daniel Tan, Anti-Suit Injunctions and the Vexing Problem of Comity, 45 Va. J. Int'l L. 283, 309-312 (2005); Steven R. Swanson, Antisuit Injunctions in Support of International Arbitration, 81 Tul. L. Rev. 395, 429-40 (2006); George A. Bermann, The Use of Anti-suit Injunctions in Internatonal Litigation, 28 Colum. J. Transnat'l L., 589, 629 (1990); Trevor C. Hartley, Comity and the Use of Antisuit Injunctions in International Litigation, 35 Am. J. Comp. L. 487 (1987);Richard W. Raushenbush, Note, Antisuit Injunctions and International Comity, 71 Va. L. Rev. 1039 (1985); Eric Roberson, Comment, Comity Be Damned: The Use of Antisuit Injunctions Against the Courts of a Foreign Nation, 147 U. Pa. L. Rev. 409, 421-33 (1998); Laura M. Salava, Comment, Balancing Comity with Antisuit Injunctions: Considerations Beyond Jurisdiction, 20 J. Legis. 267 (1994).

91 Allendale Mut. Ins. V. Bull Data Sys., 10 F.3d 425, 431-33 (7th Cir. 1993), "When every practical consideration supports the injunction, it is reasonable to ask the opponent for some indication that the issuance of an injunction really would throw a monkey wrench, however small, into the foreign relations of the United States… The only concern with international comity is a purely theoretical one that ought not trump a concrete and persuasive demonstration of harm to the applicant for the injunction, if it is denied, not offset by any harm to the opponent if it is granted."

92 Kaepa, Inc. v. Achilles Corp., 76 F. 3d 624, 627 (5th Cir. 1996), "We decline, however, to require a district court to genuflect before a vague and omnipotent notion of comity every time that it must decide whether to enjoin a foreign action. In the instant case, for example, it simply cannot be said that the

「但是我們拒絕去要求，每一次地方法院必須去決定是否禁止一外國訴訟時，應對模糊而無所不能的禮誼概念加以屈服。」如前述雖然英國政府認為禁訴令只是在保護英國訴訟程序之完整，但於*Turner v. Grovit*[93]中歐盟法院還是認為禁訴令會妨礙公約的有效性（因為其於實際上會有限制適用公約管轄規則的效果）。歐盟法院又說互信是布魯塞爾公約的基礎，因此禁止任何法院去審核其他會員國法院之管轄基礎。故而有些美國同僚及有些美國法院忽視國際禮誼之作法，是與歐盟大陸法及母法英國判例法之主流不合的[94]。

grant of the antisuit injunction actually threatens relations between the United States and Japan. First, no public international issue is implicated by the case: Achilles is a private party engaged in a contractual dispute with another private party. Second, the dispute has been long and firmly ensconced within the confines of the United States judicial system."

93 Turner v. Grovit Case C-159/02, [2004] ECR I-3565, para. 29.

94 加拿大最高法院認為外國法院管轄權之取得，若是違反加拿大國際私法有關不方便法院法學，並造成當事人間之不公正之後果，那麼便可做成禁訴令。由於外國法院的不遵守禮誼，故其決定不能基於禮誼而被尊重。見AMCHEM PRODUCTS INC. v. BRITISH COLUMBIA, [1993] 1 S.C.R. 897; 1993 S.C.R. LEXIS 32, Sopinka J., "The result of the application of these principles is that when a foreign court assumes jurisdiction on a basis that generally conforms to our rule of private international law relating to the forum non conveniens, that decision will be respected and a Canadian court will not purport to make the decision for the foreign court. The policy of our courts with respect to comity demands no less. If, however, a foreign court assumes jurisdiction on a basis that is inconsistent with our rules of private international law and an injustice results to a litigant or 'would-be' litigant in our courts, then the assumption of jurisdiction is inequitable and the party invoking the foreign jurisdiction can be restrained. The foreign court, not having, itself, observed the rules of comity, cannot expect its decision to be respected on the basis of comity."又說：It has been suggested that by reason of comity, anti-suit injunctions should either never be granted or severely restricted to those cases in which it is necessary to protect the jurisdiction of the court issuing the injunction or prevent evasion of an important public policy of the domestic forum. See Richard W. Raushenbush, "Antisuit Injunctions and International Comity" (1985), 71 Va. Law Rev. 1039.

這個案件是加拿大最高法院允許德州法院對英屬哥倫比亞院的當事人作成反禁訴令（anti-anti-suit injunctions）之案件。其引述Lord Goff, SNI Aerospatiale v. Lee Kui Jak, [1987] 3 All E.R. 510, 519, 522, "First, the jurisdiction is to be exercised when the 'end of justice' require it… Second, where the court decides to grant an injunction restraining proceedings in a foreign court, its order is directed not against the foreign court but against the parties so proceeding or threatening to proceed… Third, it follows that an injunction will only be issued restraining a party who is amenable to the jurisdiction of the court against whom an injunction will be an effective remedy… Fourth, it has been emphasized on many occasions that, since such an order indirectly affects the foreign court, the jurisdictions is one which must be exercised with caution…." "In the opinion of their Lordships, in a case such as the present where a remedy for a particular wrong is available both in the English (or, as here, the Brunei) court and in a foreign court, the English (or Brunei) court will, generally speaking, only restrain the plaintiff from pursuing proceedings in the foreign court if such pursuit would be vexatious or oppressive. This presupposes that, as a general rule, the English or Brunei court must conclude that it provides the natu-

「國際禮誼」或許是一個鬆散的概念，於Schibsby v Westenholz[95]中Lord Blackburn於確立英國的「義務主義」時即稱「禮誼主義」是鬆散性質的。稍後在Hilton v. Guyot[96]中Justice Gray即說[97]：「禮誼是，而且向來就一定是，不確定的；它是一定必須根據不同的情況而來，而這些情況是不能被簡化成任何確定的原則；沒有國家會接受其他國家的法律來干擾自己的法律以致造成自己公民的傷害；是否外國法會造成傷害必須根據外國法被要求執行之國家之情況，她的法律、她的政策、及她的制度特點之特別性質；於國際私法上那一種應優先是通常有疑問的。」但即使如此其還是連續兩次引用Wheaton如下[98]：「但是國際間之一般禮誼、功能及便利性，已經於大部分文明國家間建立一個慣例，經由該慣例有管轄權的外國法院之最後判決是互惠的被執行。」國際禮誼或許的確是個虛無飄渺的

---

ral forum for the trial of the action, and further, since the court is concerned with the ends of justice, that account must be taken not only of injustice to the defendant if the plaintiff is allowed to pursue the foreign proceedings, but also of injustice to the plaintiff if he is not allowed to do so. So, as a general rule, the court will not grant an injunction if, by doing so, it will deprive the plaintiff of adnantages in the foreign forum of which it would be unjust to deprive him."

95 (1870) L.R. 6 Q.B. 155, 159, "if the principle on which foreign judgments were enforced was that which is loosely called 'comity.' We could hardly decline to enforce a foreign judgment given in France against a resident in Great Britain under circumstances hardly, if at all, distinguishable from those under which we, *mutatis mutandis*, might give judgment against a resident in France; but it is quite different of the principle be that which we have just laid down."

96 159 U.S. 113, 16 S, Ct. 139, 40 L. Ed. 95 (1895).

97 159 U.S. 113, 164, 165, "that comity is, and ever must be, uncertain; that it must necessarily depend on a variety of circumstances which cannot be reduced to any certain rule; that no nation will suffer the laws of another to interfere with her own to the injury of her citizens; that whether they do or not must depend on the condition of the country in which the foreign law is sought to be enforced, the particular nature of her legislation, and the character of her institutions; that in the conflict of laws it must often be a matter of doubt which should prevail; and that, whenever a doubt does exist, the court, which decides, will prefer the laws of its own country to that of the stranger,"

98 159 U.S. 113, 166, 214, "Mr. Wheaton said: 'There is no obligation, recognized by legislators, public authorities, and publicists, to regard foreign laws; but their application is admitted only from considerations of utility and the mutual convenience of States – ex comitate, ob reciprocam utilitatem.' 'The general comity, utility and convenience of nations have, however, established a usage among most civilized States, by which the final judgments of foreign courts of competent jurisdiction are reciprocally carried into execution.' Wheaton' s International Law, (8th ed.) §§79, 147."

159 U.S. 113, 163, 164, " 'Comity.' in the legal sense, is neither a matter of absolute obligation, on the one hand, nor of mere courtesy and good will, upon the other. But it is the recognition which one nation allows within its territory to the legislative, executive or judicial acts of another nation, having due regard both to international duty and convenience, and to the rights of its own citizens or of other persons who are under the protection of its laws."

鬆散概念，但它最基本的起點基礎應就是互惠[99]。美國這些擂著戰鼓的禁訴令愛用者，或許自恃美國國勢的兵強馬壯，但如若碰到國勢幾乎旗鼓相當的歐盟去拒絕執行其判決時，在當事人空有勝訴判決而不能執行其權利時，則或許傳統的禮誼概念就會被重新加以考慮。早期個人之拙作即強調判決的有效性[100]，這是或許源自英國法根深蒂固的認為不能被執行的權利即不能被視為存在之傳統概念。事實上美國最高法院[101]亦認為契約之權力若沒有救濟之方法即於法律上不能被視為存在。

如前述英國即使是尚未採納「不方便法院」法學前，對境外被告之送達是採戒慎小心之態度，並視其通常是為不正當的（unjustifiable）[102]，現今更正式的規定必須於「方便法院」之情形下才可送達境外之被告。對禁止被告於外國法院進行訴訟之行為，自然應是更加以戒慎恐懼。如前述美國同僚因為沒有公開的承認境外送達是一種過度管轄，故而於「最低限度關連點」上造成甚多的無謂紛擾。個人以為同樣的盲點又出現在有些美國同僚對禁訴令之態度上。事實上正如美國法律協會（American Law Institute）亦本著英國母法而來，一再強調的衡平救濟是於法律救濟

99 見陳隆修，〈97台上2376號〉，陳隆修、宋連斌、許兆慶著，《國際私法—國際程序法新視界》，五南出版，2011年，122-125頁，「禮誼與過度管轄」。

100 見陳隆修，《國際私法管轄權評論》，台北，五南圖書公司，民國75年11月，初版，27、28頁。台灣的同僚雖常接受這個概念，但卻忽略了身分行為之例外性，見33頁。又基於兒童最佳利益之超越性考量，本於國家為parens patriae之地位，英國法院仍會對不在英國之兒童行使管轄權，見陳隆修、許兆慶、林恩瑋、李瑞生四人合著，《國際私法-管轄與選法理論之交錯》，台北，五南圖書公司，2009年3月，初版1刷，216、217頁。

101 "Nothing can be more material to the obligation than the means of enforcement. Without the remedy the contract may, indeed, in the sense of the law, be said not to exist, and its obligation to fall within the class of those moral and social duties which depend for their fulfilment wholly upon the will of the individual. The ideas of validity and remedy are inseparable, and both are parts of the obligation, which is guaranteed by the Constitution against invasion. The obligation of a contract 'is the law which binds the parties to perform their agreement.' " Von Hoffman v. City of Quincy, 71 U.S. 535, 552 (1867) (quoting Sturges v. Crowninshield, 17 U.S. 122 (1819)).

102 見陳隆修，《國際私法管轄權評論》，台北，五南圖書公司，民國75年11月，初版，45-47頁。The Hagen (1908) p.189.

不足下才可作成[103]。其第一新編契約篇第358(1)條規定[104]：「無論是以肯定（命令作為）或否定（禁止作為）之命令方式，如果損害賠償之救濟是不足之情形下，一個契約特別履行方式之命令是會被作成，以便對付已經違約或威脅著將要違約之當事人。」而第二新編契約篇第359(1)條亦有類似規定[105]：「如果損害賠償是足以保護受害當事人所期待的正當利益，特別履行或禁止的命令是不會被作成的。」這些規定是與英國判例法於許多方面是一致的，而美國判例法亦是如此規定。於Gen. Universal Sys. v. lee中，第五巡迴法院說[106]：「就只有在受損之當事人不能由損害賠償的法律救濟而取得完全的賠償或損害賠償不能被正確的確認時，特別履行的衡平法救濟就通常只能於該種情形下才能被加以適用。」於Lucente v. IBM Corp.中，第二巡迴法院[107]說：「在特別履行的『不尋常』衡平救濟命令被作成前，申請救濟的當事人必須證明法律上之補救是不完整的，並且不

103 判例法通常是以損害賠償為典型之救濟，而衡平法是有關道德及防止不符合良心之行為，見加拿大最高法院Pro Swing Inc. v. Elta Golf Inc., 2006 Can. Sup. Ct. LEXIS 52; 2006 SCC 52; [2006] S.C.J. No. 52, para. 22, Deschamps J.: [22] At common law, the typical remedy is an award for damages however, a wide range of equitable remedies are available, and they take various forms. Their commonality is that they are awarded at the judge' s discretion. Judges do not apply strict rules, but follow general guidelines illustrated by such maxims as "Equity follows the law", "Delay defeats equities", "Where the equities are equal the law prevail", "He who comes to equity must come with clean hands" and "Equity acts *in personam*" (H.G. Hanbury and J. Martin, *Modern Equity* (17th ed. 2005), at paras 1-024 to 1-036, and D. C. F. Spry, *The Principles of Equitable Remedies: Specific Performance, Injunctions, Rectification and Equitable Damages* (6th ed. 2001), at p. 6). The application of equitable principles is largely dependent on the social fabric. As Spry puts it: …the maxims of equity are of significance, for they reflect the ethical quality of the body of principle that has tended not so much to the formation of fixed and immutable rules, as rather to a determination of the conscionability or justice of the behavior of the parities according to recognized moral principles, this ethical quality remains, and its presence explains to a large extent the adoption by courts of equity of broad general principles that may be applied with flexibility to new situations as they arise. [p. 6]

104 Restatement of Contracts §358(1) (1932), "A decree for the specific performance of a contract, either in the form of an affirmative or of a negative order, will be granted against a party who has committed a breach, or is threatening one, if the remedy in damages would not be adequate."

105 Restatement (Second) of Contracts §359(1) (1981), "Specific performance or an injunction will not be ordered if damages would be adequate to protect the expectation interest of the injured party."

106 Gen. Universal Sys. v. Lee, 379 F. 3d 131, 153 (5th Cir. 2004), "Specific performance is an equitable remedy that is normally available only when the complaining party cannot be fully compensated through the legal remedy of damages or when damages may not be accurately ascertained."

107 Lucente v. IBM Corp., 310 F.3d 243, 262 (2d Cir. 2002), "Before the 'extraordinary' equitable remedy of specific performance may be ordered, the party seeking relief must demonstrate that remedies at law are incomplete and inadequate to accomplish substantial justice."

足以達成實質正義。」

但是或許是美國於此方面之法規較為不明顯，Daniel Tan建議於強迫當事人履行仲裁條款上美國法院應採國內法之衡平救濟[108]。英國的the Supreme Court Act 1981, s. 37(1)規定[109]：「高院〔類似地院〕得以命令（無論是中間或最後）而作成禁止命令……而這是在所有案件中對法院而言顯現出正義及便利去行使時皆可以。」又英國the Arbitration Act 1996, s. 44規定為了支持仲裁，法院得作成禁止命令[110]：「(1)除非當事人另有同意，為了仲裁程序之目的及相關事情，正如同為了法律程序之目的及相關事情時，法院有著相同權力去為下列事項而作成命令。(2)這些事項為……(e)給予一個中間禁止命令……」

但事實上美國的the Federal Arbitration Act （FAA）的第3條[111]亦規定在仲裁條款一方當事人之申請下，法院得停止訴訟程序直至仲裁依約定被履行為止。而第4條[112]則更直接規定美國聯邦地院在一方當事人之申請

108 47 Va. J. Int' l L. 545, 560, "Even so, because the court is relying on its well-established equitable powers to provide specific relief, the general law of remedies must delineate the court' s power to compel arbitration. Domestic law has developed rules to govern the scope and availability of contractual remedies. For example, established principles of equity dictate that the power to compel specific performance be limited to situations where common law damages would be inadequate to vindicate the breach. This rule traces its origins to the rule that the common law courts will typically award common law damages as the default remedy and will not award equitable remedies unless damages are inadequate. In the absence of compelling private international law considerations, the courts ought to follow these domestic remedial principles in deciding whether to compel arbitration."

109 Section 37(1) of the Supreme Court act 1981, "The High Court may by order (whether interlocutory or final) grant an injunction …‥ in all cases in which it appears to the court to be just and convenient to do so."

110 Section 44 of the Arbitration Act 1996, "(1) Unless otherwise agreed by the parties, the court has for the purposes of and in relation to arbitral proceedings the same power of making orders about the matters listed below as it has for the purposes of and in relation to legal proceedings. (2) Those matters are: (e) the granting of an interim injunction …."

111 "If any suit or proceeding be brought in any of the courts of the United States upon any issue referable to arbitration under an agreement in writing for such arbitration, the court in which such suit is pending, upon being satisfied that the issue involved in such suit or proceeding is referable to arbitration under such an agreement, shall on application of one of the parties stay the trial of the action until such arbitration has been had in accordance with the terms of the agreement…" 9 U.S.C. § 3 (2000).

112 "[a] party aggrieved by the alleged failure, neglect, or refusal of another to arbitrate under a written agreement for arbitration may petition any United States district court … for an order directing that such arbitration proceed in the manner provided for in such agreement." 9 U.S.C. § 4 (2000).

下，得命令不履行仲裁約定之一方依約定去仲裁。因此於Moses H. Cone Mem'l Hosp. v. Mercury Constr. Corp.[113]中，美國最高法院認為FAA規定了兩個平行的規則去執行仲裁條款：一個是停止訴訟，一個是強制命令去仲裁。

六、符合正義及便利下可作成禁止令命

另外the American Law Institute第2新編國際私法篇的第53條亦規定[114]：「一個州對於受到其司法管轄權所拘束之人，得行使司法管轄權去命令該個人於其他州內去作某行為或不能去作某行為。」如同英國母法一般，因為禁止命令之作成是一種對人訴訟，故美國法律協會53條亦規定須先有對人管轄權後，法院才能作成禁止命令。另外又如英國的the Supreme Court Act 1981, s. 37(1)一般，必須於符合正義及便利下才可作成禁止命令。其comment (b)規定[115]：「於正義及便利之考量下要求這種救濟之時，一個人得被命令去於其他州作某種行為。法院之不願去作成這種命令最主要是由於(1)擔心去不當的干涉其他州之事情，及(2)要被告去服

---

[113] 460 U.S. 1, 22 (1983), "The Act provides two parallel devices for enforcing an arbitration agreement: a stay of litigation in any case raising a dispute referable to arbitration, 9 U.S.C. § 3, and an affirmative order to engage in arbitration, § 4."

[114] Restatement (Second) of Conflict of Laws § 53 (1971)
§ 53. Decree To Be Carried Out In Another State
A state has power to exercise judicial jurisdiction to order a person, who is subject to its judicial jurisdiction, to do an act, or to refrain from doing an act, in another state.

[115] Comment:
b. When jurisdiction exercised. A person will be ordered to do an act in another state when this relief is required by the demands of justice and convenience. The reluctance of the courts to issue such orders stems primarily from (1) the fear of interfering unduly with the affairs of the other state and (2) the possible difficulty or enforcing obedience to an order that defendant do an act in a place beyond the effective control of the court. Because of the first factor, the defendant will not, except on extremely rare occasions, be ordered to do an act which violates the law of the other state (see Comment d); nor will a decree be issued which calls for continuing supervision by the court of the defendant's activities in that state. Contrariwise, there is greater likelihood of the defendant's being ordered to do an act in another state if the court has some means at its disposal of insuring compliance with the decree, as by requiring the defendant to post a bond or to act in the other state through the medium of an agent. The situation dealt with in § 54 is a clear example of this latter sort and is an instance where relief is frequently granted.

從在法院無法有效控制地區去作某個行為之命令之強制執行性可能是有困難的。因為第1個因素，除非在極端不尋常之情形下，被告是不會被命令去作違反其他州法律之行為……；當被告在該州之行為需要法院持續性的監督時，該種命令亦不會被作成。」但是法院可以要求被告提出擔保，以確保命令的被執行。

另外其comment (c)[116]又說：「比較起命令於其他州做某種行為，法院顯示出較有意願去禁止於其他州做某種行為。這是因為這種禁止命令可以在不擾亂其他州目前既有的狀態下而被執行，而且因為通常被告只要繼續停留在作成命令之法院之州即可符合命令之條件。於個案中法院是有著寬廣的裁量權以決定是否應作成禁止命令，並且法院是依據自己州法院所發展及理解的衡平原則而來。通常當有些受到威脅的行為會導致原告受到無可挽救的損害，或公平及便利的需求要求如此時，這種救濟就會被許可[117]。」如Daniel Tan所說[118]：「因為在這兩種救濟中強制命令是被視為較沈重的，比起禁止命令法院通常較不願去作成強制命令。」這種英國判例法[119]的概念是普遍亦盛行於美國法院[120]。但是因為禁止訴訟命令會間接

[116] c. Enjoining acts in another state. The courts have shown greater readiness to enjoin action in another state than to order an act to be done there. This is because such an injunction may be carried out without disturbing the physical status quo in the other state and because the defendant may ordinarily comply with its terms simply by remaining in the state whose court issues the decree. A court has broad discretion in deciding whether such an injunction should be issued in a given case and will be guided by principles of equity as developed and understood by the courts of its own state. Generally speaking, such relief will be granted whenever acts are threatened which would subject the plaintiff to irreparable damage or when the demands of fairness and convenience so require.

[117] N. Cal. Power Agency v. Grace Geothermal Corp., 469 U.S. 1306, 1306 (1984), "A party seeking an injunction from a federal court must invariably show that it does not have an adequate remedy at law." Beacon Theatres, Inc. v. Westover, 359 U.S. 500, 506-07 (1959), "The basis of injunctive relief in the federal courts has always been irreparable harm and inadequacy of legal remedies."

[118] This is especially true since mandatory injunctions are regarded as the more onerous of the two remedies, and courts are generally less inclined to issue mandatory rather than prohibitory injunctions. 47 Va. J. Int'l L. 545, 583.

[119] Lumley v. Wagner, 42 Eng. Rep. 687 (1852).

[120] Int'l Equity Invs., Inc. v. Opportunity Equity Partners, 441 F. Supp. 2d 552, 561 (S.D.N.Y. 2006), "Mandatory injunctions are those that disturb the status quo, while prohibitory injunctions preserve it." Griffin v. Oklahoma Natural Gas Corp., 37 F.2d 545, 549 (10th Cir. 1930), "An injunction against the breach of a contract is a negative decree of specific performance. The power and duty of a court of equity to grant such injunction is broader than its power and duty to grant a decree of specific performance,

的干擾到外國法院之訴訟程序，故個人認為國際禮誼應優先於這個英美法的法律邏輯。

或許因為英美皆認為禁訴令只得於正義及便利之需求下方得作成，法律協會第2新編國際私法篇84條不方便法院條文之comment (h)這樣解釋[121]：「有時一個法院得對其有著對人管轄權之人，禁止該個人去於法院認為不合適之法院提起訴訟。法院所依據以作為給予這種救濟的命令之因素是與法院考慮是否以不方便法院為理由去駁回一個案件之因素是一樣的（見comment(c)）。這種禁止命令就只有在極端的情形下才會被准予。」而comment (c)如此敘述[122]：「法院是否保留訴訟要看兩個最重要的因素。他們是(1)因為是應由原告去選擇訴訟之地，故除了有重大的理由外，其所選之法院不應被改變，及(2)除非對原告有著另外一個合適之法院，否則訴訟不應被駁回。因為第2個因素之故，如果被告無法受到其他州之管轄，則無論法院地是多麼的不合適，訴訟仍應受到審理。」

美國法律協會84條註釋h與c的直接將不方便法院與禁訴令連接在一

---

since an injunction to restrain acts in violation of a lawful contract will be granted, even when specific performance would be denied because of the nature of the contract." Nat'l Marking Mach. Co. v. Triumph Mfg. Co., 13 F.2d 6, 9 (8th Cir. 1926), "An injunction against the breach or the continuance of a breach of a contract is a negative decree of specific performance, and the power and duty of a court of equity to grant such an injunction is even greater, under the rules, principles, and practices in equity, than its power and duty to grant decrees of specific performance. A court of equity may issue its injunction to prevent a violation, or the continuance of a violation, of a contract in cases in which it would not decree specific performance thereof."

121 The American Law Institute, Restatement (Second) of Conflict of Laws § 84 (1971),
Comment:
h. Injunction against suit in inappropriate forum. On occasion, a court may enjoin a person over whom it has personal jurisdiction from bringing suit in what the court deems to be an inappropriate forum. The factors which determine the award of such relief are the same as those a court considers in deciding whether to dismiss a case on forum non conveniens grounds (see Comment c). Injunctions of this sort are only granted in extreme circumstances.

122 c. Factors to be considered. The two most important factors look to the court's retention of the case. They are (1) that since it is for the plaintiff to choose the place of suit, his choice of a forum should not be disturbed except for weighty reasons, and (2) that the action will not be dismissed unless a suitable alternative forum is available to the plaintiff. Because of the second factor, the suit will be entertained, no matter how inappropriate the forum may be, if the defendant cannot be subjected to jurisdiction in other states. The same will be true if the plaintiff's cause of action would elsewhere be barred by the statute of limitations, unless the court is willing to accept the defendant's stipulation that he will not raise this defense in the second state.

起是個危險的作法，前者是推掉自己之管轄案件，後者是間接禁止外國法院之管轄案件，這又是個忽視國際禮誼的壞習慣。更重要的是這個論述與英國判例法的事實不合。註釋c中第2個因素所陳述之情形即為英國同僚所謂「單一法院案件」（single forum cases），於討論是否當事人之訴訟行為構成不公正、不合公理之行為（unconscionable conduct）時，個人曾如此論述[123]：「而不合公理之情形則常發生於僅有一個法院有管轄權之情形。通常於僅有一個管轄法院之情形，法院對是否做成禁止訴訟命令會更謹慎。所謂不合公理指的是違反英國衡平法之情形，通常是被告有抗辯權或不應被起訴之情形。」雖然於著名的British Airways Board v. Laker Airways Ltd.[124]中，Laker Airways對其他航空公司於英國並無訴因存在，但於美國卻可依反托辣斯法而起訴，雖然英國不執行美國懲罰性賠償（於商業方面）[125]，英國最高法院還是拒絕作成禁止Laker Airways於美國起訴其他英國航空公司之命令。但於同事件之Midland Bank plc v Laker Airways Ltd[126]中，英國上訴法院卻認定Laker Airways對銀行（Midland Bank）於美國所提的反托辣斯訴訟為不公正的行為，並允許作成限制Laker Airways於美國提起訴訟之命令。該銀行之業務發生於英國並以英國法為依據；該銀行從未接受美國之反托辣斯法或美國之司法管轄；而且於英國並未有訴因發生。故而於單一法院之案件中，英國法院雖然是會較為謹慎，但於外國法院之請求者在外國所提之訴訟是輕率、困擾性的，並且很明顯的會失敗時，則會構成不公正之情形，在這種例外之情形下英國法院則會作成禁訴令[127]。但當事人會於美國程序中遭受到審判前之事實調查這種事情本身並不會構成不公正[128]。故而英國判例法顯示即使在只有單一法院之案件中，在特殊情形下英國法院還是有可能作成禁訴令。個人以

---

123 陳隆修、許兆慶、林恩瑋、李瑞生四人合著，《國際私法—管轄與選法理論之交錯》，台北，五南圖書公司，2009年3月，初版1刷，246頁。
124 [1985] AC 58, [1984] 3 All ER 39, HL.
125 見前述之the Protection of Trading Interests Act 1980, s. 5.
126 [1986] QB 689, C.A.
127 [1986] QB 689 at 700, 702, 710, 712-713.
128 [1986] QB 689 at 714.

為Midland Bank的意義不但彰顯了美國反托辣斯強行法規「效力理論」的適用界線，於程序法上亦證明禁訴令不只適用於國際平行訴訟上，如果在正義之需求下亦可適用於單一法院之案例——這更證明了全球化跨國訴訟之管轄規則在二十一世紀中，其心與靈魂是在「正義的真正利益是否最能被達成」。

另外亦有同僚認為英國的衡平法理論只是有對人訴訟之效果[129]，故而禁訴令對大陸法並非是難以接受。於Webb v. Webb[130]中歐盟法院認為原告依衡平法去要求被告被信託人去交付土地，該訴訟並非是以決定有關法國土地之權利為目的之對物訴訟。因此，「衡平法是有關執行個人義務的對人訴訟」，是故大陸法不應有執行上之困難。但是歐盟法院的將交付土地權利（權狀）與物權行為本身的分開，不只是其對英國衡平法上有這種見解，美國法亦持相同概念。美國法律協會第2新編國際私法篇102條規定[131]：「一個有效的判決，其內容是非給付金錢而是行使某種作為之命

---

129 Daniel Tan, 47 Va. J. Int' l L. 545, 592, 593, "Rightly so. Equity operated in personam to enforce a personal obligation."

130 Case C-294/92, Webb v. Webb, 1994 E.C.R. I-717, "An action for a declaration that a person holds immovable property as trustee and for an order requiring that person to execute such documents as should be required to vest the legal ownership in the plaintiff does not constitute an action in rem within the meaning of Article 16(1) of the Convention of 27 September 1968 on Jurisdiction and the Enforcement of Judgments in Civil and Commercial Matters."

131 Restatement of the Law, Second, Conflict of Laws §102 Enforcement of Judgment Ordering or Enjoining Act
A valid judgment that orders the doing of an act other than the payment of money, or that enjoins the doing of an act, may be enforced, or be the subject of remedies, in other states.
但見comment (c), "In opposition to these arguments and in support of the view that the enforcement of such a sister State decree lies in the discretion of the forum is the argument made §449 of the original Restatement of this Subject that the granting or denying of equitable relief, other than an order for the payment of money, is a matter of discretion and that '[t]he decision by one court to give specific relief … will not limit another court and thus exclude the use of the discretion of the second court.' Also the enforcement of a judgment ordering or enjoining the doing of an act might on occasion require continuing supervision by the enforcing court or be otherwise onerous."又Restat 2d of Conflict of Laws, §103, comment (a)認為第102條不屬於充分互信條款之範圍："The rule of this Section is not concerned with the enforcement of sister State judgments that order the doing of an act other than the payment of money or that enjoin the doing of an act. As stated in §102, the enforcement of such judgments may not be required by full faith and credit." "Full Faith and Credit shall be given in each State to the public Acts, Records, and judicial Proceedings of every other State. And the Congress may by general Laws prescribe the Manner in which such Acts, Records and Proceedings shall be proved, and the Effect thereof." Art. IV, s. 1. "Such Acts, records and judicial proceedings or copies thereof, so authenticated,

令，或禁止某種作為之命令，得於其他州被執行，或作為救濟之主體（實體）。」在美國憲法充分互信條款（the full faith and credit clause（Art. IV, §1））及國會的補充立法（28 U.S.C. §1738）下，各州之司法決定（"judicial proceedings"）應受到充分互信的尊重。其comment (d)特別對不動產（土地）之交付規定如下[132]：「對於位於其他州土地交付之命令提供了符合本條文規則範圍內判決之共同案例。」與英美法不同的是大陸法通常對物權與債權之區分是涇渭分明的，故於此問題上對大陸法是不構成困擾的，更不應與禁訴令的執行有關連。無論是ALI/UNIDROIT Principles of Transnational Civil Procedure的2.3條，布魯塞爾規則的31條，或2005年海牙法院選擇公約的7條（**其不排除保全處分**），大陸法慣行的保全處分已為大部分國際公約所採納。英國法過去在國際法上對保全處分的限制[133]不應與禁訴令的應存在與否有關連。

七、禁訴令於美國聯邦間之效力

無論是否有國際禮誼的因素存在，於國際訴訟上禁訴令是否應被其他國家之法院所接受，最直接的解答就是觀察美國聯邦間禁訴令被尊重的程度。因為第2新編國際私法102條的comment (g)[134]說只要外國的裁判是

---

shall have the same full faith and credit in every court within the United States and its Territories and Possessions as they have by law or usage in the courts of such State, Territory or Possession from which they are taken." 28 U.S.C. s.1738.

132 *d. Orders to convey land.* Orders to convey land situated in another State provide a common instance of judgments falling within the scope of the rule of this Section. Such orders may be issued to enforce a pre-existing obligation of the defendant, such as when the defendant is ordered by a decree of specific performance to fulfill his contract to convey land. Such orders may also be issued in situations where there is no pre-existing obligation, such as when a court in providing for the support of a wife following a divorce orders the husband to convey to her certain of his lands. The rule of this Section is applicable in both of these situations.

133 見陳隆修，《國際私法管轄權評論》，台北，五南圖書公司，民國75年11月，初版，269-271頁。

134 Restatement of the Law, Second, Conflict of Laws §102, comment g, "A valid decree rendered in a foreign nation that orders or enjoins the doing of an act will usually be recognized in the United States (see §98). That is to say, such a decree will usually be given the same res judicata effect in the United States that it enjoys in the nation of its rendition. So far as enforcement is concerned, it can safely be said that a valid foreign nation decree that orders the payment of money will usually be enforced in the

「符合正義與善良道德的基本原則」，美國法院「通常於外國判決符合第98條註釋c所規定之要件時，會給予外國判決如同姊妹州之判決相同程度的尊重。」但是如前述第102條之強制命令或禁止命令並不在充分互信條款範圍內，故外國法院於非金錢給付之類似衡平救濟自然亦不會在充分互信之範圍內。

美國憲法的充分互信條款是個重要的聯邦政策，如同Mr. Justice Stone在Milwaukee Country v. M.E. White Co.[135]中說：「充分互信條款的真正目的就是在改變各州做為獨立外國主權國家的地位，這些個別國家有著自由得以去忽視其他國家法律或司法程序所創造出來的義務，而使得他們成為一個單獨國家的完整部分，在這個完整的國家內無論其來源為何州，一個救濟可以被要求附著在一個正當的義務上。」故而大中華經濟圈的同僚應該非常注意到美國與歐盟的不同：如前述歐盟的互信是建築在消滅少數不同的法律制度，以取得公約的有效性及一致性；而美國的充分互信[136]是建築在尊重各國的法律及判決上，以便無論義務的來源為那一個州

United States. Existing authority does not warrant the making of any definite statement as to the enforcement of decrees that order the doing of other kinds of acts or that enjoin the doing of an act. American courts, however, have usually given the same measure of respect to judgments rendered in foreign nations, which meet the requirements stated in §98, Comment c, that they give to judgments rendered in sister States. It can therefore be assumed that a decree rendered in a foreign nation which orders or enjoins the doing of an act will be enforced in this country provided that such enforcement is necessary to effectuate the decree and will not impose an undue burden upon the American court and provided further that in the view of the American court the decree is consistent with fundamental principles of justice and of good morals."

[135] 296 U.S. 268, 276-7 (1935), "The very purpose of the full faith and credit clause was to alter the status of the several states as independent foreign sovereignties, each free to ignore obligations created under the laws or by the judicial proceedings of the others, and to make them integral parts of a single nation throughout which a remedy upon a just obligation might be demanded as of right, irrespective of the state of its origin."又見Estin v. Estin, 334 U.S. 541, 546 (1948)，美國最高法院認為充分互信條款是"substituted a command for the earlier principles of comity and thus basically altered the status of the States as independent sovereigns."

[136] Sun Oil Co. v. Wortman, 486 U.S. 717, 726, 727, "In the context of our Erie jurisprudence, see Erie R. Co. v. Tompkins, 304 U.S. 64, 82 L. Ed. 1188, 58 S. Ct. 817 (1938), that purpose is to establish (within the limits of applicable federal law, including the prescribed Rules of Federal Procedure) substantial uniformity of predictable outcome between cases tried in a federal court and cases tried in the courts of the State in which the federal court sits. See Guaranty Trust, supra, at 109; Hanna v. Plumer, 380 U.S. 460, 467, 471-474, 14 L. Ed. 2d 8, 85 S. Ct. 1136 (1965). The purpose of the substance procedure dichotomy in the context of the Full Faith and Credit Clause, by contrast, is not to establish uniformity

皆可被加以救濟。美國的作法自然符合人權公約中尊重文化的多元姓，亦是符合「道法自然」的中國哲學。

雖然美國最高法院於Eire R. Co. v. Tompkins[137]中規定，在應適用之聯邦法之限制下（包含聯邦程序法），聯邦法院應適用所在地州法律以「建立聯邦法院與州法院間判決之可預測性及重大一致性」。而第2新編國際私法篇95條之註釋g又說[138]：「在憲法之限制下，作成判決之州之當地法決定是否，及到什麼程度，在相同當事人間，或他們的關係人（權利接收人）間，在後來不同請求或不同訴因之訴訟所牽連的爭點上是有既判力的。」但是在Baker v. General Motors Corp.[139]中，在一密蘇里聯邦法院之訴訟中，原告請求一被密西根州法院禁止於牽連到通用汽車公司之訴訟中作證之證人出席，該證人與通用已達成和解並取得和解金。密州聯邦地院允許該證人出庭作證，但巡迴法院卻更改地院之判決，不允許該證人作證。美國最高法院卻認為證人於密州法院之作證不會侵犯到聯邦充分互信之政策，將案件發回更審。

Ginsburg J.替最高法院作成判決。首先，其認為判例法對於充分互信在法律與判決上是不同的。即使是法院自己依法不須處理該外州判決之訴訟，仍是應給予該外州判決充分互信；充分互信條款並未要求一個州在其有權力立法之範圍內去以他州之法律來取代自己之法律[140]。「但是於判決

but to delimit spheres of state legislative competence."歐盟布魯塞爾公約及規則是被稱為「歐洲的充份互信條款」，但相對於美國之「充份互信條款」並不意圖建立一致性，反而是尊重各州之立法權，歐盟之意圖消滅英美法是甚為反諷而低級。更有趣的是Erie（見陳隆修、許兆慶、林恩瑋，《台灣財產法暨經濟法研究叢書（十三）—國際私法：選法理論之回顧與展望》，台灣財產法暨經濟法研究協會發行，2007年1月，初版，194頁）案之目的是尊重各州之法律及判決，卻被認為是可以促進統一，歐盟何時才能進化為文明之國家？

137 Eire R. Co. v. Tompkin, 304 U.S. 64, 82 L. Ed. 1188, 58 S. Ct. 817 (1938).

138 Restatement, Second, Conflict of Laws §95, comment (g) (1971), "the local law of the State where the judgment was rendered determines, subject to constitutional limitations, whether, and to what extent the judgment is conclusive as to the issues involved in a later suit between the parties, or their privies, upon a different claim or cause of action."

139 522 U.S. 222 (1998).

140 522 U.S 222, 232 (1998), "Our precedent differentiates the credit owed to laws (legislative measures and common law) and to judgments. 'In numerous cases this Court has held that credit must be given to the judgment of another state although the forum would not be required to entertain the suit on which the judgment was founded,' *Milwaukee County*, 296 U.S., at 277. The Full Faith and Credit Clause

上充分互信之義務則要求甚高。一個州的最後判決，如果是對判決中之人及主體有裁判權之法院所作成，則應於聯邦之土地上所被承認。這是於請求及爭點排除（一事不再理）之目的上皆適用，亦即作成判決州之判決取得全國性之效力。[141]」又最高法院之判例顯示並不允許各州以游移不定的公共政策為理由，去拒絕給予外州判決充分互信，「即使外州判決所表現出具有敵意的政策……亦被命令去接受。[142]」

---

does not compel 'a state to substitute the statutes of other states for its own statutes dealing with a subject matter concerning which it is competent to legislate.' *Pacific Employers Ins. Co. v. Industrial Accident Comm'n*, 306 U.S. 493, 501 (1939); see *Phillips Petroleum Co. v. Shutts*, 472 U.S. 797, 818-819 (1985)."又見Restat 2d of Conflict of Laws, § 117.

§ 117 Original Claim Contrary to Public Policy of State Where Enforcement of Judgment Is Sought

A valid judgment rendered in one State of the United States will be recognized and enforced in a sister State even though the strong public policy of the latter State would have precluded recovery in its courts on the original claim.其comment (b)說："As between States of the United States, the rule of this Section is one of constitutional law. Provided that the judgment is valid (see § 92), full faith and credit requires that it be recognized and enforced in a sister State even though the original claim is contrary to the strong public policy of the sister State. Fauntleroy v. Lum, 210 U.S. 230 (1908)."又見Larry Kramer, Same-Sex Marriage, Conflict of Laws, and the Unconstitutional Public Policy Exception, 106 Yale L. J. 1965, 1980 (1997), "The central object of the Clause was, in fact, to eliminate a state' s prideful unwillingness to recognize other states' law or judgments on the ground that these are inferior or unacceptable."

141 同上，Regarding judgments, however, the full faith and credit obligation is exacting. A final judgment in one State, if rendered by a court with adjudicatory authority over the subject matter and persons governed by the judgment, qualifies for recognition throughout the land. For claim and issue preclusion (res judicata) purposes, in other words, the judgment of the rendering State gains nationwide force. See *e.g., Matsushita Elec. Industrial Co. v. Epstein*, 516 U.S. 367, 373 (1996); *Kremer v. Chemical Constr. Corp.*, 456 U.S. 461, 485 (1982); see also Reese & Johnson, The Scope of Full Faith and Credit to Judgments, 49 Colum. L. Rev. 153 (1949).其註5對美式禁反言解釋如下："'Res judicata' is the term traditionally used to describe two discrete effects: (1) what we now call claim preclusion (a valid final adjudication of a claim precludes a second action on that claim or any part of it), see Restatement (Second) of judgments ss. 17-19 (1982); and (2) issue preclusion, long called 'collateral estoppel' (an issue of fact or law, actually litigated and resolved by a valid final judgment, binds the parties in a subsequent action, whether on the same or a different claim), see id., s.27. On use of the plain English terms claim and issue preclusion in lieu of res judicata and collateral estoppels, see *Migra v. Warren City School Dist. Bd. Of Ed.*, 465 U.S. 75, 77, n. 1 (1984)."美國最高法院於此認為傳統的一事不再理是包含請求排除及爭點排除原則。

142 同上，"A court may be guided by the forum State' s 'public policy' in determining the law applicable to a controversy. See *Nevada v. Hall*, 440, U.S. 410, 421-424 (1979). But our decisions support no roving 'public policy exception' to the full faith and credit due judgments. See Estin, 334 U.S., at 546 (Full Faith and Credit Clause 'ordered submission … even to hostile policies reflected in the judgment of another State, because the practical operation of the federal system, which the Constitution designed, demanded it.'); *Fauntleroy* v. *Lum,* 210 U.S. 230, 237 (1908) (judgment of Missouri court)"

但是Ginburg J.又說[143]：「但是充分互信並不表示於執行判決上之時間、方式、及機構，各州應採納其他州之措施。排除效力（禁反言）是隨同姊妹州之判決可跨過州界，但執行之方式並沒有；這些方式仍然是在法院地法公平的控制下。[144]」更重要的其又宣示[145]：「命令去作某行為或不作為時，當他們宣稱去完成某種專屬於其他州的職權內之公行為時，或去干擾到一個訴訟而該下達命令之州對該事情並沒有權力時，該命令會於其他姊妹州被拒絕執行。因此一個姊妹州之命令是有關位於其他州土地之所有權時，是被認定為無法移轉所有權……雖然對於外州訴訟之當事人間，這個命令可能的確對他們的權利與義務是有排除效力的被加以認定」[146]。

143 522 U.S. 222, 234 (1998), "Full faith and credit, however, does not mean that States must adopt the practices of other States regarding the time, manner, and mechanisms for enforcing judgments. Enforcement measures do not travel with the sister state judgment as preclusive effects do; such measures remain subject to the evenhanded control of forum law. See *McElmoyle ex rel. Bailey v. Cohen*, 13 Pet. 312,325 (1839) (judgment may be enforced only as 'laws [of enforcing forum] may permit'); see also Restatement (Second) of Conflict of Laws s. 99 (1969) ('The local law of the forum determines the methods by which a judgment of another state is enforced.')"

144 如英國國協一般，美國聯邦法院及州際法院間亦有著類似登記執行判決制度，見註釋8："Congress has provided for the interdistrict registration of federal-court judgments for the recovery of money or property. 28 U.S.C. s. 1963 (upon registration, the judgment 'shall have the same effect as a judgment of the district court of the district where registered and may be enforced in like manner'). A similar interstate registration procedure is effective in most States, as a result of widespread adoption of the Revised Uniform Enforcement of Foreign Judgments Act, 13 U.L.A. 149 (1986). See id., at 13 (Supp. 1997) (Table) (listing adoptions in 44 States and the District of Columbia).

145 522 U.S. 222, 234 (1998), "Orders commanding action or inaction have been denied enforcement in a sister State when they purported to accomplish an official act within the exclusive province of that other State or interfered with litigation over which the ordering State had no authority. Thus, a sister State' s decree concerning land ownership in another State has been held ineffective to *transfer title*, see *Fall* v. *Eastin*, 215 U.S. 1 (1909), although such a decree may indeed preclusively adjudicate the rights and obligations running between the parties to the foreign litigation, see, e.g., Robertson v. Howard, 229 U.S. 254, 261 (1913) ('[I]t may not be doubted that a court of equity in one State in a proper case could compel a defendant before it to convey property situated in another State.')"

146 但亦有對此判決加以批評者，見Patrick J. Borchers, Baker v. General Motors: Implications For Inter-Jurisdictional Recognition of Non-traditional Marriages, 32 Creighton L. Rev. 147, 178, 179 (1998), "Thus, to the extent that Baker makes any change in the scope of existing full-faith–and-credit law, it narrows – not expands – the duties of courts with regard to each others' decree. One might fairly wonder, therefore, what it is that the proponents of same-sex marriage like in the decision. Undoubtedly, the language that is seen as helpful is the Court' s statement that there is no 'roving' public policy exception to the enforcement of judgments. This language' s superficial appeal is produced only, however, by confusion of the credit due judgments and the credit due laws. Recall that the question of the recognition of a sister state' s marriage license is a choice-of-law question; no judgment is involved. The Court' s 'public policy' language in Baker is actually quite unhelpful from the standpoint of the pro-

因此根據上面的論述最高法院明確的決定外州的禁訴令不能拘束於本州所進行的訴訟[147]：「即使在符合適當程序條款下以作為限制當事人行為之命令，有關在其他地方所進行訴訟之禁訴令....於事實上是對有關於該法院的訴訟所進行的第二個法院的訴訟是不能控制的。……又見E. Scoles & P. Hay, Conflict of Laws s. 24.21. p.981 （2d ed. 1992）（陳述禁訴令『並未處理，因此並未有排除效力於，[有關第二個法院]的訴訟之實體上』）。無論如何，對於該禁止命令之違反的處罰，通常是由作成禁止命令的法院所行使。」通常違反禁訴令是會被法院判予藐視法院[148]，因為甚少因此而被拘禁，故若當事人於法院地沒有財產則較難執行該命令。

因此法院之結論為[149]：「總之，在一個案件中所牽涉之人及訴因皆超

---

recognition arguments, because it specifically reaffirms the authority of states to use 'public policy' to apply their own law – a position directly contrary to the narrow argument. The Court' s language in Baker is also unhelpful to the expansive argument because of its clear reaffirmation of the fundamentally different nature of the full-faith-and-credit obligations of courts towards each others' laws and judgments."

[147] 522, U.S. 222, 236 (1998), "And antisuit injunctions regarding litigation elsewhere, even if compatible with due process as a direction constraining parties to the decree, see Cole v. Cunningham, 133 U.S. 107 (1890), in fact have not controlled the second court' s actions regarding litigation in that court. See, e.g., James v. *Grand Trunk Western R. Co*., 14 Ill. 2d 356, 372, 152 N.E. 2d 858, 867 (1958); see also E. Scoles & P. Hay, Conflict of Laws s. 24.21, p.981 (2d ed. 1992) (observing that antisuit injunction 'does not address, and thus has no preclusive effect on, the merits of the litigation [in the second forum]'). Sanctions for violations of an injunction, in any event, are generally administered by the court that issued the injunction. See, e.g., Stiller v. Hardman, 324 F. 2d 626, 628 (CA2 1963) (nonrendition forum enforces monetary relief portion of a judgment but leaves enforcement of injunctive portion to rendition forum)."

[148] 見Paramedics Electromedicina Comercial, Ltda. v. G.E. Med. Sys. Info. Techs., Inc., 369 F. 3d 645 (2d Cir. 2004), paras. 48, 36,

48. A party who violates an injunction entered by the district court faces the threat of both civil and criminal contempt. See Timken Roller Bearing Co. v. United States, 341 U.S. 593, 604, 71 S.Ct. 971, 95 L. Ed. 1199 (1951) (Reed, J., concurring); Universal City Studios, Inc. v. N.Y. Broadway Int' l Corp., 705 F. 2d 94, 96 (2d Cir. 1983). Criminal contempt is typically imposed "to punish the violation and vindicate the court' s authority." *Universal City Studios*, 705 F. 2d at 96.

36. A party may be held in civil contempt for failure to comply with a court order of "(1) the order the contemnor failed to comply with is clear and unambiguous, (2) the proof of noncompliance is clear and convincing, and (3) the contemnor has not diligently attempted to comply in a reasonable manner." *King v. Allied Vision, Ltd*., 65 F.3d 1051, 1058 (2d Cir. 1995). It need not be established that the violation was willful. *Donovan v. Sovereign Sec. Ltd*., 726 F. 2d 55, 59 (2d Cir. 1984).

[149] 522 U.S. 222, 240, "In sum, Michigan has no authority to shield a witness from another jurisdiction' s subpoena power in a case involving persons and causes outside Michigan' s governance. Recognition, under full faith and credit, is owed to dispositions Michigan has authority to order. But a Michigan decree cannot command obedience elsewhere on a matter *the Michigan court lacks authority to resolve.*

乎密西根之管轄外，密西根是沒有權力去保護一個證人以避免其受到其他管轄區召喚之權力。依充分互信條款，承認之義務必須根據密西根有權力去裁決所下的命令而來。但是在密西根法院缺乏權力去解決的事情上，密西根的命令不能要求其他地方去服從這個命令。」

最高法院這個認定是與第2新編國際私法篇的103條相呼應的[150]：「如果會牽連到對姊妹州重要利益的不當的干擾，因而充分互信的國家政策並不要求對聯邦中之州所作成之判決之承認或執行，則這種判決並不需於這個姊妹州中被承認或執行。」因此第103條依據Baker案的邏輯而言，所謂「會牽連到對姊妹州重要利益的不當干擾」，就是「命令去作某行為或不做為時，當他們宣稱去完成某種專屬於其他州的職權內之公行為時，或去干擾到一個訴訟而該下達命令之州對該事情並沒有權力時」，在這些情形下，「該命令會於其他姊妹州被拒絕執行」。因此禁訴令是「會牽連到對姊妹州重要利益之不當干擾」，而於該州中並不需要被「承認或執行」。

103條的comment (b)又說明充分互信之極少數例外如下[151]：「但是在

See Thomas v. Washington Gas Light Co., 448 U.S. 261, 282-283 (1980) (plurality opinion) ('Full faith and credit must be given to [a] determination that [a State' s tribunal]) had the authority to make; but by a parity of reasoning, full faith and credit need not be given to determinations that it had no power to make.')"

[150] Restatement of the Law, Second, Conflict of Laws (1988 Revisions)
§ 103 Limitations on Full Faith and Credit
A judgment rendered in one State of the United States need not be recognized or enforced in a sister State if such recognition or enforcement is not required by the national policy of full faith and credit because it would involve an improper interference with important interests of the sister State.

[151] Restatement of the Law, Second, Conflict of Laws (1988 Revisions), § 103, comment (b), "Regard must be had in a federal nation for the needs of each individual State. Almost invariably, the federal policy of full faith and credit will outweigh any interest that a State may have in not recognizing or enforcing a sister State judgment. So, for example, full faith and credit requires that a valid judgment rendered in a State of the United States be recognized and enforced in a sister State even though action on the original claim could not have been maintained in the sister State because it would be contrary to its strong public policy (see § 117). There will be extremely rare occasions, however, when recognition of a sister State judgment would require too large a sacrifice by a State of its interests in a matter with which it is primarily concerned. On these extremely rare occasions, the policy embodied in full faith and credit will give way before the national policy that requires protection of the dignity and of the fundamental interests of each individual State. So, full faith and credit does not require a State to recognize a sister State injunction against suit in its courts on the ground that it is an inconvenient forum. This is

極度例外之情形下，當去承認一個姊妹州的判決會要求另一個州在與其有著最主要關連的事情上，太大的犧牲其利益。在這些極度例外之情況，在要求保護各個州之基本利益及尊嚴之國家政策前，充分互信所包含的政策必須讓步。因此充分互信並不要求一個州去承認姊妹州基於其為一個不方便法院為理由而對於其法院所進行之訴訟所作成之禁訴令。這是因為在管轄權之限制下，一個州應被允許去自己決定其法院應審判什麼案件，而不必聽令於其他州。同樣的一個州得採用自己的消滅時效而去拒絕執行一個姊妹州的判決（見118條，註釋c）。於姊妹州之一方缺席離婚判決上，最高法院亦曾經認定，被請求承認之州並未被禁止去重新檢驗有關住所是否在於作成判決之州之問題，而這個『證明』是由作成判決法院所提供，並且該法院據以作成原告配偶在判決時住所於其地域之決定，而且因此其有著管轄權去作離婚判決。」另外聯邦的Defense of Marriage Act是因夏威夷最高法院通過認同同性婚姻[152]，故而對此加以回應，給予各州權力保留不認同同性婚姻之權力，但最高法院尚未就此法案的合憲性作出決定。

於尊重離婚自由價值下，美國是以原告配偶之住所為離婚管轄基礎[153]，法院認為離婚訴訟是對物訴訟（action in rem），婚姻的關係是res（物），故而住所地即是物之所在地。如此自然為造成「單方離婚」（ex parte divorce），亦即被告不出席因而對其無對人管轄（personal jurisdiction）之離婚判決，但此種離婚判決仍有效[154]。即使原告被原住所

because a State, subject to jurisdiction limitations, should be permitted to decide for itself, and without dictation from another State, what cases its courts will hear. Similarly, a State may apply its local statute of limitations to refuse enforcement to a sister State judgment (see §118, Comment c). The Supreme Court has also held that, in the case of sister State ex parte divorce decrees, the court of the State where recognition is sought is not foreclosed from reexamining the question of domicil in the State of rendition by the fact that 'warrant' could be found in the record of the rendering court for its conclusion that the plaintiff spouse had been domiciled within its territory at the time of the decree, and that it thus had jurisdiction to render the divorce. Williams v. North Carolina, 325 U.S. 226 (1945)."

152 Baehr v. Miike, 1996 WL 694235 (Hawaii Cir. Ct. 1996), aff'd 950 P.2d 1234 (Hawai'i 1997), prior opinion 80 Haw. 341, 910 P. 2d 112 (Hawaii 1996).

153 Williams v. North Carolina, 317 U.S. 287 (1942)

154 除非被告配偶住所地法院基於該州保護居民之利益，而以該州住所的定義去重新認定原告是否為作成判決之州之居民，如果不構成住所於作成判決之州，則該判決得不予承認，但先決條件是被告不得出席外州法院。Williams v. North Carolina, 325 U.S. 226 (1945).

地法院禁止於新住所地提起離婚之訴訟，該離婚判決仍為有效[155]。但是對這種「單方離婚」（一方缺席），因為被告配偶之州得重新以該州之定義去認定原告是否為作成判決之州之居民，並且採「分割式離婚」（divisible divorce）[156]，故對弱勢配偶還是有可能加以保護，故個人認為問題並不大。這種「分割式離婚割式離婚」本為英國國內案件之作法，美國卻將其適用於跨州案件。英國法院先是於若當事人國外住所地法院允許之前提下會加以承認[157]，現則於跨國案件中可以依法而對已被宣布離婚之配偶加以財產上之救濟[158]。「分割式離婚」於英美法之進化過程是甚為有趣，這亦是個人於作為比較法的學生一輩子後，深信「道法自然」之故。個人真誠的認為「分割式離婚」[159]，既可以保障離婚自由的人權價值，但又可同時顧及弱勢一方之實際上經濟人權，不但應為二十一世紀中國法學（包含國際及國內法）之內容，更應為二十一世紀全球化法學（包含國際及國內法）之共同核心。

另外對於「一個州得採用自己的消滅時效而去拒絕執行一個姊妹州的判決」，個人認為美式之作法過分複雜的喪失社會生活的真實性[160]。大

[155] Keck v. Keck, 290 N.E. 2d 385 (Ill. 1972).

[156] Estin v. Estin, 334 U.S. 541 (1948).單方離婚因為沒有對人管轄權，因此不能給予對人訴訟（action in personam）之救濟，例如不能給予贍養費、扶養費或轉移財產。換言之，只能為離婚目的有管轄權，但不能為其他目的有管轄權，故而已被其他州之法院判決離婚之妻子可以於其住所地法院繼續請求給付先前分居判決的扶養費，這稱為「可分割之離婚」（divisible divorce）。即使婚姻於其他州之法院被有效的終止後，缺席配偶仍可事後於其住所地法院請求贍養費（alimony）。Vanderbilt v. Vanderbilt, 354 U.S. 416 (1957), 因為贍養費之請求為personal right.

[157] Wood v. Wood [1957] 2 W.L.R. 826.

[158] The Matrimonial and Family Proceedings Act 1984, Part III.

[159] 陳隆修、許兆慶、林恩瑋、李瑞生四人合著，《國際私法—管轄與選法理論之交錯》，台北，五南圖書公司，2009年3月，初版1刷，192、193頁。

[160] Restat 2d of Conflict of Laws, § 118 Statute of Limitations

(1) A valid judgment rendered in a State of the United States will be enforced in a sister State although action on the original claim was barred by the statute of limitations of the sister State at the time when the judgment was rendered.

(2) A valid judgment rendered in a State of the United States may be denied enforcement in a sister State if suit on the judgment is barred by the sister State' s statute of limitations applicable to judgments. 又見其comment (c)更為複雜："If under the local law of the State of rendition the effect of this revival is to create a new judgment, then suit on this judgment may not be held barred under full faith and credit in the sister State. The contrary will be true, however, if the effect of the revival in the State of rendition is not to create a new judgment but rather to prolong the effective life of

陸法一向視消滅時效為實體法，故應依案件之應適用法律（準據法）而定[161]，而非如英美法傳統上的視為程序法而依法院地法。英國為了加入羅馬公約於契約上有關時效之規定，於加入前即已修法[162]而將傳統上視為程序法的消滅時效規定應為實體事項[163]。美國同僚或許應認真的思考，一個在美國長久以來造成甚多紛擾，甚至必須經由最高法院以釋憲之方式來加以處理之問題，當世界潮流已如此明顯時，是否應加入英國法而追隨潮流？

八、依國際慣例而回應杜新麗教授

早期歐盟的布魯塞爾公約是被戲稱為歐洲版的充分互信條款，有趣的是在禁訴令上無論是美版的充分互信條款或是歐版布魯塞爾公約或規則，皆不賦予外國法院之禁訴令充分互信的效果。**雖然如前述歐盟與美國皆致力於判決之統一，但其手段卻是南轅北轍。歐盟法院認為[164]：「公約的目**

---

the original judgment. The Supreme Court of the United States may review the determination of the court in the sister State to determine whether this court has correctly applied the local law of the State of rendition in ascertaining the effect of the revival. Union National Bank v. Lamb, 337 U.S. 38 (1949)."又見Catlett v. Catlett, 412 P. 2d 942 (OKl. 1966).

161 見羅馬I規則12(1)(d):
Article 12
Scope of the law applicable
1.The law applicable to a contract by virtue of this Regulation shall govern in particular:
……………
(d) the various ways of extinguishing obligations, and prescription and limitation of actions;

162 The Foreign Limitation Periods Act 1984.

163 見陳隆修、許兆慶、林恩瑋，《台灣財產法暨經濟法研究叢書（十三）—國際私法：選法理論之回顧與展望》，台灣財產法暨經濟法研究協會發行，2007年1月，初版，117頁。於1984年之the Foreign Limitation Periods Act中，section 2(1)有保留裁量權給予法院去拒絕採用過長或過短的外國消滅時效。另外section 2(2)中又對當事人不知所適用的外國準據法禁止的情況下，而同意延長消滅時效，因而所造成的不適當的困擾，法院得以違反公共政策為由不去適用該準據法。另外對消滅時效的起算、暫停計算，權利人對時效的遲延是否有過失等，皆有詳細規定。但個人發現英國國際私法界對大陸法自然債務之觀念甚為混淆不清。因為依大陸法權利人雖仍享有請求權，但債務人卻有抗辯權。嚴格而言，由英國法之觀點，權利人不但於實體上仍享有權利，於程序法上其時效之利益亦尚在。

164 Case C-281/02. Andrew Owusu v N.B. Jackson, trading as 'Villa Holidays Bai-Inn Villas' and others, para. 43, "Moreover, allowing forum non conveniens in the context of the Brussels Convention would be likely to affect the uniform application of the rules of jurisdiction contained therein in so far as that doctrine is recognized only in a limited number of Contracting States, whereas the objective of the Brussels Convention is precisely to lay down common rules to the exclusion of derogating national rules."

的是在排除破壞性的國內法規，並建立共同的法規。」但美國最高法院卻逆向的宣示[165]聯邦法院應適用所在地之州法以求得判決的統一及可預性，並且充分互信條款是在確認各州之立法權。有二千多年歷史的中國式法學應向二百多年歷史的法學學習，還是向五十多年歷史的法學學習，相信答案是很清楚的。

有趣的是儘管這兩個聯邦的法學政策完全相異，但雙方對待外國法院之禁訴令卻是驚人的相似。即使是當今兩個聯盟皆有著不同版本的充分互信條款，但雙方的邏輯卻是一致。美國第2新編國際私法篇的103條之註釋說[166]：「一個州應被允許去自己決定其法院應審判什麼案件，而不必聽令於其他州。」而歐盟法院亦是於不同場合一再宣示[167]：「並且，應該注意到無論在什麼案子中，不可能會有第2繫屬的法院比起第1繫屬的法院有著較好的地位去決定後者是否有管轄權。」故而無論是否同意美國或歐盟的法律邏輯，不爭的事實是：這兩個有著充分互信條款或公約的聯盟，對於其他成員法院所作成的禁訴令並未給予充分互信。

---

165 Sun Oil Co. v. Wortman 486 U.S. 717, 726, 727, "In the context of our Erie jurisprudence, see Erie R. Co. v. Tompkins, 304 U.S. 64, 82 L. Ed. 1188, 58 S. Ct. 817 (1938), that purpose is to establish (within the limits of applicable federal law, including the prescribed Rules of Federal Procedure) substantial uniformity of predictable outcome between cases tried in a federal court and cases tried in the courts of the State in which the federal court sits. See Guaranty Trust, supra, at 109; Hanna v. Plumer, 380 U.S. 460, 467, 471-474, 14 L. Ed. 2d 8, 85 S. Ct. 1136 (1965). The purpose of the substance procedure dichotomy in the context of the Full Faith and Credit Clause, by contrast, is not to establish uniformity but to delimit spheres of state legislative competence."

166 Restatement of the Law, Second, Conflict of Laws (1988 Revisions), § 103, comment (b), "This is because a State, subject to jurisdictional limitations, should be permitted to decide for itself, and without dictation from another State, what cases its courts will hear."

167 Case C-351-89, *Overseas Union Insurance Limited and Others v New Hampshire Insurance Company*, [1991] ECR I-3317, para. 23, 24.
23-Moreover, it should be noted that in no case is the court second seised in a better position than the court first seised to determine whether the latter has jurisdiction. Either the jurisdiction of the court first seised is determined directly by the rules of the Convention, which are common to both courts and may be interpreted and applied with the same authority by each of them, or it is derived, by virtue of Article 4 of the Convention, from the law of the State of the court first seised, in which case that court is undeniably better placed to rule on the question of its own jurisdiction.
24-Moreover, the cases in which a court in a Contracting State may review the jurisdiction of a court in another contracting State are set out exhaustively in article 28 and the second paragraph of Article 34 of the Convention.

即使判例法母國法之英國法院亦未必能接受其他國家法院對其訴訟程序所下之禁訴令。如Daniel Tan所說[168]：「這並不是說判例法法院他們自己本身是會去作成禁訴令的，可是當一個禁訴令是對他們的程序所作成時是會完全給予諒解的。」於General Star International Indemnity Ltd. v. Stirling Cooke Brown Reinsurance[169]中，Judge Langley如同歐盟法院與美國法律協會的第2新編一般，認為管轄權之問題應由繫屬之法院所決定，而並非由當事人間接的於其他法院之訴訟所決定，因此其對首先作成禁訴令的紐約法院之訴訟當事人再作成一個禁訴令。Judge Langley這個英國法院應決定自己管轄權範圍之論述，亦為其他英國法院所引述[170]。

杜新麗教授在兩岸第4屆國私會議（於西安）提出中國法院應如何面對外國禁訴令之問題，個人於此回應如下：**大中華地區之法院如果不承認外國法院之禁止訴訟命令之效力，並不會違反美國聯邦、歐盟、及英國目前所盛行之判例法，故而不給予外國禁止訴訟命令充分互信，於目前並不會違反國際慣例。**

---

[168] 47 Va. J. Int'l L. 545, 589, "But a major hindrance towards realizing the full utility of the antisuit devices is the hostility that courts dish out when they are on the receiving end of an antisuit order – especially civilian courts that are less familiar with the remedy. This is not to say that common law courts who themselves issue antisuit orders are entirely sympathetic when one is directed at their proceedings."

[169] [2003] EWHC 3, para. 16 (Eng. Q.B.).

[170] Tonicstar Ltd v. Am. Home Assurance Co., [2004] EWHC 1234, para. 13 (Eng. Q.B.), "It seems to me that AHA have tried to hijack the decision which is presently before this court, namely whether the arbitration clause is apt to embrace the disputes between the parties, and, if so, where its seat should be … The effect of their conduct is to seek to pre-empt this court from reaching its own decision on the arbitration questions. AHA no doubt hoped that their tractic would lead to an earlier determination by the New York Court which would then be invited to restrain the English Court form considering the issue; or at the least, arguing that the decision of the New York court was final and binding as between the parties. The essential facts in this case are sufficiently close to the facts in the case of General Star … to make what Langley J held in that case worth citing as appropriate in this case too."

第8章 中國思想下的禁止訴訟命令

一、契約的平衡性與訴訟法立足點平等

於目前若大中華經濟區之法院對外國法院所作成之禁訴令[1]沒有信心或不清楚之情形，遽然不加以承認其效力是不違背國際間既有的習慣及大部分文明國家間盛行的判例法。但是個人以為中國式的國際私法欲於五十年後成為全球化法學之基礎，自然不應僅只於追隨國際慣例法。如前述國際訴訟法在二十一世紀全球化法學之心與靈魂是在於正義的真正利益是否最能被達成，而這亦正是中國「王道」精神之所在。

在China Trade & Dev. Corp. v. M.V. Choong Yong[2]中，聯邦第二巡迴法院更改地院所下之永久禁訴令。於案中中國商人委託韓國船商由美國運送黃豆至中國。後中方主張黃豆進水而於加州扣押韓方之船，韓方提供保釋金及答應承認紐約地院之管轄，以換取船隻之釋放。但於紐約調查程序中，韓方卻於韓國法院提起確認債權不存在之訴。

地院對禁訴令作成之要件為巡迴法院所引用。首先，「對於這種禁止

---

1 自1821起英國法院已行使管轄權去限制外國法院之程序或停止國內之訴訟。見Leach V.-C., Bushby v. Munday (1821), 5 Madd. 297, 56 E.R. 908, at p. 307 and p. 913, "Where parties Defendants are resident in England, and brought by subpoena here, this Court has full authority to act upon them personally with respect to the subject of the suit, as the ends of justice require; and with that view, to order them to take, or omit to take, any steps and proceedings in any other Court of Justice, whether in this country, or in a foreign country."
故無論是停止國內之訴訟（不方便法院）或限制當事人於外國之程序（禁訴令），其起源皆是在於「正義的目的之需求下」。例如其又說："the substantial ends of justice would require that this Court should pursue its own better means of determining both the law and the fact of the case", at p. 308 and p. 913.但是在「司法的自大應被司法的禮誼所取代」的今日英國法學，這句話應會被加以適度的修正。

2 China Trade & Dev. Corp. v. M.V. Choong Yong, 837 F. 2d 33 (2d Cir. 1987).

令法院說明應有兩個門檻要件：(1)在兩件事情上當事人是相同的；及(2)作成命令法院之案件之解決方法對被禁止之訴訟必須是有決定性的。[3]」「當這些門檻的要件被滿足後，於決定上述訴訟是否應被禁止前，五個因素應被加以考慮：(1)下禁止令之法院之政策的被挫敗；(2)外國的訴訟是困擾性的；(3)對作成命令法院之對物或準對物管轄造成威脅；(4)另外一個法院的程序會違反其他的衡平考量；或(5)於不同案件中對同一爭點加以裁判，會造成遲延、不方便、費用、不一致、或一個判決速度之競爭。[4]」

第二巡迴法院重申[5]：「禁止令只是針對當事人，而非直接對外國法院之事實，並不會減少對國際禮誼原則應有的尊重之需要……因為這種命令有效的限制一個外國主權國家法院的管轄權……因此一個對外國訴訟之禁訴令『只能於謹慎及極度自制』下才能被給予。」法院又引用判例

3 837 F2d 33, para. 8, "the court articulated two threshold requirements for such an injunction: (1) the parties must be the same in both matters, and (2) resolution of the case before the enjoining court must be dispositive of the action to be enjoined."

4 同上，paras. 9, 10,
9
When these threshold requirements are met, five factors are suggested in determining whether the foregoing action should be enjoined: (1) frustration of a policy in the enjoining forum; (2) the foreign action would be vexatious; (3) a threat to the issuing court's in rem or quasi in rem jurisdiction; (4) the proceedings in the other forum prejudice other equitable considerations; or (5) adjudication of the same issues in separate actions would result in delay, inconvenience, expense, inconsistency, or a race to judgment.
10
American Home Assurance, 603 F. Supp. at 643. See also Garpeg, Limited v. United States, 583 F. Supp. 789 (S.D.N.Y. 1984).

5 同上，para. 13, The power of federal courts to enjoin foreign suits by persons subject to their jurisdiction is well-established. U.S. v. Davis, 767 F.2d 1025, 1038 (2d Cir. 1985); Laker Airways. Ltd. v. Sabena Belgian World Airlines, 731 F.2d 909, 926 (D.C. Cir. 1984). The fact that the injunction operates only against the parties, and not directly against the foreign court, does not eliminate the need for due regard to principles of international comity, Peck v. Jenness, 48 U.S. (7 How.) 612, 625, 12 L.Ed. 841 (1849), because such an order effectively restricts the jurisdiction of the court of a foreign sovereign, U.S. v. Davis, 767 F.2d at 1038. Therefore, an anti-foreign-suit injunction should be "used sparingly", U.S. v. Davis, 767 F.2d at 1038, and should be granted "only with care and great restraint." Canadian Filters (Harwich) v. Lear-Siegler, 412 F.2d 577, 578 (1st Cir. 1969); see Laker v. Sabena, 731 F.2d at 927; Compagnie Des Bauxites De Guinea v. Insurance Co. of N. Am., 651 F.2d 877, 887 (3rd Cir. 1981). See also Garpeg Ltd., 583 F. Supp. at 798.

法說[6]：「對於同一對人請求之平行訴訟，通常是應被允許去同時進行，至少是直至一個判決可以在另一個判決中被主張一事不再理的時候。」又說[7]：「在適當的考慮到禮誼之利益下，我們認為American Home Assurance Corp.中所建議的兩個因素，於決定Ssangyong（韓商）是否應被禁止其於韓國之訴訟是有著較大的意義：(a)是否外國訴訟威脅到作成命令法院之管轄權，及(b)是否作成命令法院的強烈公共政策受到外國訴訟的威脅。」法院作成結論[8]：「於允許禁訴令時地院所依賴的衡平原則，並不足以克服國際禮誼所要求的自制及謹慎。因為韓國的訴訟對地院的管轄權及本法院的任何重要公共政策皆不構成威脅，我們認定地院所給予禁訴令的行為是濫用程序。」

坦白說個人認為第二巡迴法院的結論可能是基於非法律理由。或許法院認為一個台商及韓商間之紛爭不值得美國法院去危害與韓國法院間之禮誼，亦即美國沒有充分的利益去間接的干擾到韓國法院之程序[9]。

---

6 同上，para. 14, Concurrent jurisdiction in two courts does not necessarily result in a conflict. Laker v. Sabena, 731 F.2d at 926. When two sovereigns have concurrent in personam jurisdiction one court will ordinarily not interfere with or try to restrain proceedings before the other. Donovan v. City of Dallas, 377 U.S. 408, 412, 84 S. Ct. 1579, 1582, 12 L.Ed. 2d 409 (1964), citing Princess Lida of Thurn and Taxis v. Thompson, 305 U.S. 456, 466, 59 S. Ct. 275, 280, 83 L.Ed. 285 (1939); Laker v. Sabena, 731 F.2d at 926-27; Compagnie des Bauxites v. Insurance Co. of N. Am., 651 F.2d at 887. "[P]arallel proceedings on the same in personam claim should ordinarily be allowed to proceed simultaneously, at least until a judgment is reached in one which can be pled as res judicata in the other," Laker v. Sabena, 731 F.2d at 926-27, citing Colorado River Water Conservation District v. United States, 424 U.S. 800, 817, 96 S. Ct. 1236, 1246, 47 L. Ed. 2d 483 (1976).

7 同上，para. 16, Having due regard to the interests of comity, we think that in the circumstances of this case two of the other factors suggested in American Home Assurance Corp. take on much greater significance in determining whether Ssangyong should be enjoined from proceeding in its Korean action: (A) whether the foreign action threatens the jurisdiction of the enjoining forum, and (B) whether strong public policies of the enjoining forum are threatened by the foreign action. See Laker v. Sabena, 731 F.2d at 927, 937.

8 同上，para. 24, The equitable factors relied upon by the district court in granting the anti-suit injunction are not sufficient to overcome the restraint and caution required by international comity. Because the Korean litigation poses no threat to the jurisdiction of the district court or to any important public policy of this forum, we conclude that the district court abused its discretion by issuing the injunction. Reversed.

9 但是於後續之Ibeto Petrochemical Industries Limited v. M/t Beffen A/s, 475 F3d 56 (2d Cir. 2007)中，第二巡迴法院大致上支持地院之判決，禁止當事人繼續於奈及利亞所率先提出之訴訟，而靜待倫敦之仲裁結果。其認為聯邦有強烈支持仲裁之政策，其所引用之標準即為上述China Trade之標準。但法院強調應考慮所有其他之因素，而非只是法院之管轄權及公共政策。見para. 41。

由案件之判決文中個人看不出依國際通用之管轄規則，韓國法院是如何對一個契約訂定地及履行地皆不在韓國的臺灣當事人有著適當的管轄基礎？如果韓國法院的被告是美國人，美國法院不會認定韓國法院沒有管轄權或過度管轄嗎？

於解除加州之扣押程序中，韓商雖未保證在韓國不會另起訴訟，但已答應出席紐約之訴訟及放棄抗辯不方便法院之權利。個人認為這是違背禁反言之衡平精神（inequitable）。如個人較近[10]一再引用之著名英國判例Carl-Zeiss-Stiftung v Rayner & Keeler Ltd （No 2）[11]11Lord Guest就陳述禁反言是基於訴訟必須有終結及正義要求當事人不得於相同訴因上被困擾兩次。而Lord Upjohn更於此案中說出千古名言[12]：「並非所有的禁反言皆是令人憎惡的，其必須被適用來行使正義，而非不正義，並且我認為禁反言原則之適用於後面案件之情形中，必須謹記這個超越性考量。」而2004年的ALI/ UNIDROIT Principles of Transnational Civil Procedure s. 28.3除了重申爭點禁反言須以執行正義為超越性考量外，其comment

---

41 In the China Trade case, we found that the factors having "greater significance" there were threats to the enjoining forum's jurisdiction and to its strong public policies. Id. at 36. Finding no such threats, we determined that the equitable factors of that case were "not sufficient to overcome the restraint and caution required by international comity." Id. at 37. Some courts and commentators have erroneously interpreted China Trade to say that we consider only these two factors. *See, e.g., Gau Shan Co. Ltd. v. Bankers Trust Co.*, 956 F.2d 1349, 1353 (6th Cir. 1992); Edwin A. Perry, *Killing One Bird with One Stone: How the United States Federal Courts Should Issue Foreign Antisuit Injunctions in the Information Age*, 8 U. MIAMI BUS. L. REV. 123, 142-43 (Winter 1999).
雖然支持地院基於仲裁條款而下禁訴令，第二巡迴法院仍然作成如下警誡性之結論，見para. 43。
43 The foregoing having been said, we reiterate our understanding that due regard for principles of international comity and reciprocity require a delicate touch in the issuance of anti-foreign suit injunctions, that such injunctions should be used sparingly, and that the pendency of a suit involving the same parties and same issues does not alone form the basis for such an injunction. See China Trade, 837 F.2d at 36.

10 陳隆修，〈97台上2376號〉，陳隆修、宋連斌、許兆慶著，《國際私法—國際程序法新視界》，五南出版，2011年，76-109頁。

11 [1967] 1 AC 853, [1966] 2 All ER 536, [1966] 3 WLR 125, [1967] RPC 497.

12 "All estoppels are not odious but must be applied so as to work justice and not injustice, and I think that the principle of issue estoppel must be applied to the circumstances of the subsequent case with this overriding consideration in mind."

P-28C亦認為衡平禁反言就是大陸法的「誠信原則」[13]。韓商的作法是否符合衡平正義及誠信原則相信是很清楚的。

另外韓國商人所提起的是國際訴訟上一般認為應該儘量避免的否認之訴[14]（確認之訴）。美國法律協會第2新編判決篇33條的註釋c亦認為對於確認之訴[15]：「法院應傾向拒絕訴訟如果其他救濟……是明顯的存在，並且會有著更廣的一事不再理效力。」

由判決書中個人認同Bright J.之反對意見，韓商於韓國法院提起相同當事人相同爭點之訴訟是企圖對台商造成困擾及壓迫[16]：「韓國之訴訟可

---

13 "A broader scope of issue preclusion is recognized in many common-law systems, but the more limited concept in Principle 28.3 is derived from the principle of good faith, as it is referred to in civil-law systems, or estoppel in pais, as the principle is referred to in common-law systems."
28.3 The concept of issue preclusion, as to an issue of fact or application of law to facts, should be applied only to prevent substantial injustice.

14 見陳隆修，《歐盟經驗論中國式國際私法之建立》，高雄大學法學論叢6卷2期，2011年，27、28頁。

15 Restatement of the Law, Second, Judgments, § 33, comment (c), "A litigant's seeking a declaratory remedy when he could have maintained a conventional action for coercive relief often signifies that he is in a quandary not only as to what his rights and duties are, but also as to how to secure their adjudication. Allowing piecemeal litigation in such a circumstance is comparable to the option to 'split' recognized by § 26(1)(e). And the opposing party can generally counter the effort to split either by objecting to the declaratory proceeding or by counterclaiming in such a way, including a request of his own for declaratory relief, as to get the whole controversy determined at once. In any event the court whose discretion is invoked by a declaratory action has means of preventing abuse. The court should lean toward declining the action if another remedy, such as a coercive action on an existing claim, is plainly available and would have wider res judicata effects. And as an aid in the sound exercise of discretion, the court may appropriately require the plaintiff to indicate the nature of the issues or claims, related to the subject of the action, that could be presented for adjudication but are not incorporated in the complaint. Also, whether or not a claim has accrued, the court may reject a second declaratory action after judgment in the first if the matters sought to be declared could well have been raised in the first."
而comment (b), "If a non-appearing party were not concluded as to matters declared by the judgment, a defendant might abort all possible effects of the declaratory action by simply defaulting. On the other hand, the fact that one of the parties does not wish to litigate at a particular stage of a controversy may be a factor militating against entertainment of the action, especially where the proceeding involves the consequence of future action as distinguished from a dispute over present interests in property or present status. In any event a court should not make a declaration upon default on the basis of the pleadings alone but should require the plaintiff to present enough evidence to warrant the granting of declaratory relief. Such an examination of the evidence can be regarded as an aspect of the preliminary determination, required by the declaratory relief statutes, that there is a genuine controversy between the parties."

16 837 F2d 33, paras. 43, 44.
43 The Korean action may serve only as a harassment to plaintiff and will multiply legal proceedings. Should the Korean courts absolve Ssangyong of responsibility for the cargo loss, that judgment, for want of personal jurisdiction over the ship or the parties or for other reasons, may not affect the ac-

能只是達成對原告困擾之目的，並且會造成複數訴訟。如果韓國法院解除Ssangyong（韓商）於貨物損失上之責任，因為缺乏對船、當事人、或其他原因之對人訴訟之管轄權，該判決不會影響到紐約南方地院之程序……當對解決一個商業訴訟並不會牽連至國家間之禮誼原則時，在訴訟費用極度高昂之今日我個人認為法院有個明確之責任去防止一個當事人，跳到地球另一邊的法院去對在這個國家之法院正在進行之審判，產生困擾、混亂、及複雜的效果。尤其是當法院已經處理這個案件幾達兩年，並已經對當事人取得對人管轄及對請求的主體（實體）亦已取得管轄後，這是特別有道理的。」

故而在相同當事人相同爭點之訴訟，於有管轄權之法院進行兩年之久後，被告突然又於其母國對原告沒管轄權之法院，提起否認之訴。韓商之作法很明顯的違背訴訟法「自然原告於自然法院對自然被告提起自然訴訟」之原則，而是一種貨真價實的選購法院之行為。其間接的違背承認紐約法院管轄權之作法，同時違反了英美法衡平禁反言及大陸法誠信原則之精神，很明顯的對台商構成困擾或壓迫性之行為。於當事人有著相當的議價能力及充分之經驗下，個人以為禁訴令的給予是符合21世紀全球化法學以維護個案正義為超越性考量之共同核心。如果美國欲維持禁訴令之制度，本案應是一個教科書案例。

於Paramedics Electromedicina Comercial v. GE Medical Systems Information Technologies[17]中，一巴西經銷公司與一美國威斯康辛製藥公司訂兩個附有仲裁條款之經銷契約。於發生糾紛後美商要求向美洲商務仲

---

tion of the Southern District of New York in its proceeding. Should the courts of Korea find liability, the plaintiff may, nevertheless, be required to proceed with a full trial in New York, or the case in the Southern District of New York may already have been concluded.

44 It seems to me that in this day of exceedingly high costs of litigation, where no comity principles between nations are at stake in resolving a piece of commercial litigation, courts have an affirmative duty to prevent a litigant from hopping halfway around the world to a foreign court as a means of confusing, obfuscating and complicating litigation already pending for trial in a court in this country. This is especially true when that court has been processing the case for almost two years and has acquired personal jurisdiction over the parties and subject matter jurisdiction over the claim.

17 Paramedics Electromedicina Comercial v. GE Med. Sys. Info. Techs. 369 F.3d 645(2d Cir. 2004).

裁協會（“IACAC”）提起仲裁程序，而10日後巴西商人於巴西法院提起訴訟，於所有主張中，其首先主張「該契約缺乏『契約上之平衡性』，依巴西法是不能被執行」[18]。巴西商人於紐約法院提訴要求停止仲裁程序，而美商反訴要求禁止巴商於巴西之訴訟並強迫其去仲裁。紐約聯邦地院認為仲裁條款有效，並給予禁訴令。後巴西公司及其總裁因未服從法院之命令，被罰每日一千及五千美元不等。後上訴法院維持地院之判決，但要求再次考慮罰金之數額。

上訴第二巡迴法院重申China Trade之門檻條件及其他因素[19]。另外又引用聯邦仲裁法及最高法院之判例說明[20]：「聯邦政策強力的贊同執行仲裁條款。」第二巡迴法院又引用自己先前之判例Smith/Enron Cogeneration Ltd. P'ship v. Smith Cogeneration Int'l Inc.中之論述，這個論述個人相信不但為美國同僚之一般看法，亦可能為許多英國同僚之看法[21]：「在聯邦強力的贊同仲裁之政策下，我們過去曾說在一個寬鬆的仲裁約定之存在下，應去仲裁的假設只能在有明確的保證仲裁條款不會受到涵蓋於所爭執的範圍的解釋下才能被加以推翻。……對於是否一個特別的請求是屬

---

18 同上，para. 8. On May 23, 2002, Tecnimed filed its complaint with the Porto Alegre court, naming as defendants GEMS-IT and GE Brasil, and alleging, inter alia: (i) that the Agreement lacked "contractual equilibrium" and were unenforceable under Brazilian law.

19 同上，para. 20. An anti-suit injunction against parallel litigation may be imposed only if: (A) the parties are the same in both matters, and (B) resolution of the case before the enjoining court is dispositive of the action to be enjoined. *China Trade*, 837 F.2d at 35. Once past this threshold, courts are directed to consider a number of additional factors, including whether the foreign action threatens the jurisdiction or the strong public policies of the enjoining forum. Id. at 36.

20 同上，para. 27, "Federal policy strongly favors the enforcement of arbitration agreements. See 9 U.S.C. § 2; *Moses H. Cone Mem'l Hosp. v. Mercury Constr. Corp.*, 460 U.S. 1, 24-25, 103 S. Ct. 927, 74 L.Ed. 2d 765 (1983).

21 198 F. 3d 88, 99 (2d Cir. 1999), "We have stated previously that in light of 'the strong federal policy in favor of arbitration, the existence of a broad agreement to arbitrate creates a presumption of arbitrability which is only overcome if it may be said with positive assurance that the arbitration clause is not susceptible of an interpretation that covers the asserted dispute. Doubts should be resolved in favor of coverage.' Worldcrisa Corp. v. Armstrong, 129 F.3d 71, 74 (2d Cir. 1997) (citations and internal quotation marks omitted). We stated in Genesco that when we consider 'whether a particular claim falls within the scope of the parties' arbitration agreement, we focus on the factual allegations in the complaint rather than the legal causes of action asserted. If the allegations underlying the claims 'touch matters' covered by the parties' … agreements, then those claims must be arbitrated, whatever the legal labels attached to them.' 815 F. 2d at 846 (citation omitted)."

於當事人之仲裁條款，我們所注意的是當事人所抱怨的事實上之主張，而非所主張的法律上之訴因。如果該請求的主張『觸碰』到當事人之……約定，那麼無論在其上所貼上之法律標籤為何，那些請求必須被加以仲裁。」

因此在「聯邦強力的贊同仲裁之政策下」，美國（及英國）的法院經常傾向作成禁訴令。這種情況亦通常適用於管轄條款上。即使是仲裁的約定是「寬鬆的」，還是有著「應去仲裁的假設」，必須有著「明確的保證」「才能被加以推翻」。又如果「請求的主張觸碰到當事人之約定」，「那麼無論在其上所貼上之標籤為何，那些請求必須被加以仲裁。」作為一個主張王道的法律學生，個人所認同的是「不患寡患不均」之中國二千多年來之一貫政策。聯邦法院這種主張市場弱肉強食的資本主義法學政策，所捍衛的是跨國企業追逐市場利益下的穩定，並非是「正義的真正利益是否最能被達成」。

巴西商人所主張『該契約缺乏「契約上之平衡性」依巴西法是不能被執行的』。相較於英美法固守十九世紀資本主義而來的強調「商業的功效」之法學政策，大陸法一般是較為傾向社會主義。巴西法律或許是真正的有著這個政策。如前述，即使是注重「商業功效」的資本主義發源地英國之法制，其C.P.R. 1998, r.1.1即規定訴訟程序法之超越性考量為「公正」的處理案件，而「公正」的第一要件即為「確保當事人間立足點的平等」。在本案介於跨國藥廠與當地經銷商間，欲保持「契約的平衡性」及「當事人間立足點之平等」，唯一的辦法就是將平衡點傾向經銷商，以確保「真正」立足點之平等。

二、應享有的司法保護的形式

羅馬I規則的序言23[22]即揭櫫了現代契約法上對於「較弱勢」之當事

22 (23) As regards contracts concluded with parties regarded as being weaker, those parties should be protected by conflict-of-law rules that are more favourable to their interests than the general rules.

人，應給予「較一般規則對他們的利益有利」的「保護」。第4條(1)(f)款規定於當事人未有效的選定準據法時，應以「經銷商之慣居地法」為依據[23]；同樣的情形亦顯示在(1)(e)款保護加盟店之規定。更為直接的即為引起英國法界同僚議論紛紛的強行法概念。相較羅馬公約第7條，規則第9條即較明確，其規定法院地強行法不得被違背，另外本案履行地巴西法之強行法應被加以慎重的考慮[24]。即使是有關非契約責任的羅馬II規則，亦規定對當事人事後之訂約應「給予弱勢當事人保護」[25]。因此即使是——而且個人真誠的認為應該是——該仲裁約定因「缺乏契約上之平衡性」而不能被巴西執行，巴西法是符合世界潮流而在保護「正義的真正利益的被達成」。經常依據仲裁條款而作成禁訴令的英國、美國法院，可能是違反「訴訟法上立足點平等」及「契約法上平衡性」的掠奪性新殖民主義法學的偽善資本主義的幫兇及法學帝國主義的先驅。

美國法律協會第2新編判決篇84條的註釋(a)說[26]：「仲裁是紛爭中當事人以契約方式授權來解決紛爭之一種方法。」美國最高法院亦一再重申這個看法。於First Options of Chicage, Inc. v. Kaplan最高法院說[27]：「仲

---

23 (f) a distribution contract shall be governed by the law of the country where the distributor has his habitual residence;

24 Recital 27,
(37) Considerations of public interest justify giving the courts of the Member States the possibility, in exceptional circumstances, of applying exceptions based on public policy and overriding mandatory provisions. The concept of overriding mandatory provision's should be distinguished from the expression 'provisions which cannot be derogated from by agreement' and should be construed more restrictively.

25 Recital 30,
(31) To respect the principle of party autonomy and to enhance legal certainty, the parties should be allowed to make a choice as to the law applicable to a non-contractual obligation. This choice should be expressed or demonstrated with reasonable certainty by the circumstances of the case. Where establishing the existence of the agreement, the court has to respect the intentions of the parties. Protection should be given to weaker parties by imposing certain conditions on the choice.

26 Restat 2d of Judgments, s. 84, comment (a), "Arbitration is a method of determining legal disputes that is authorized by contract between the parties to the dispute. There are forms of dispute-resolution procedure that are called 'arbitration' but which are made obligatory by law instead of being prescribed by contract, for example, some proceedings in 'no fault' insurance schemes. These procedures might perhaps better be regarded as adjudication before specialized tribunals. See s. 83."

27 First Options of Chicago, Inc. v. Kaplan, 514 U.S. 938, 943 (1995), "Arbitration is simply a matter of contract between the parties; it is a way to resolve those dispute – but only those disputes – that the par-

裁只是當事人間之一種契約；它只是解決這些糾紛之一種方法——但只限於這些糾紛——意即當事人同意交付仲裁。」亦更早曾於Prima Paint Corp. v. Flood & Conklin Mfg. Co.中說[28]：「仲裁約定得如其他契約般而被執行，但並不會超過這個。」故而如果仲裁條款是屬於一般的契約條款，自然應受到一般契約法上之禁制，例如錯誤、詐欺、脅迫、議價能力不相當、誠信及合理性原則之限制。而於國際法上自然亦應受到法院地或履行地強行法之限制。

仲裁條款應受到契約法共通核心原則之制約是受到聯合國紐約仲裁公約第2條第3項所認同的，其規定[29]：「當訴訟是有關當事人於本條文之範圍內所訂之約定，並且繫屬於訂約國之法院時，在當事人之一方請求下，應命令當事人去仲裁，除非法院認為該約定是無效，不適用或無法被履行。」故而與2005年海牙選擇法院公約及美國法院強力的仲裁條款效力之假設不一致，紐約公約規定於「約定是無效、不適用、或無法被履行」時，仲裁條款是可不被執行的。美國聯邦仲裁法（FAA）至少於表面上亦採這個契約法的原則，其第2條規定[30]仲裁條款「除了於法律或衡平法上所存在可以撤銷任何契約之理由外，應是有效、不可撤銷、及得被執行。」

---

ties have agreed to submit to arbitration."

28 Prima Paint Corp. v. Flood & Conklin Mfg. Co., 388 U.S. 395, 404 n. 12 (1967), "Arbitration agreements [can be] as enforceable as other contracts, but not more so." MCI Telecomms. Corp. v. Exalon Indus., 138 F.3d 426, 428-29 (1st Cir. 1998), "There is no general legal duty to arbitrate private commercial disputes; instead, such proceedings are strictly the product of voluntary contractual obligation."; Son Shipping Co. v. De Fosse & Tanghe, 199 F.2d 687, 689 (2d Cir, 1952), "Arbitration clauses should be treated like any other contract provisions."

29 3. The court of a Contracting State, when seized of an action in a matter in respect of which the parties have made an agreement within the meaning of this article, shall, at the request of one of the parties, refer the parties to arbitration, unless it finds that the said agreement is null and void, inoperative or incapable of being performed.

30 9 U.S.C. §2.
Section 2. Validity, irrevocability, and enforcement of agreements to arbitrate
A written provision in any maritime transaction or a contract evidencing a transaction involving commerce to settle by arbitration a controversy thereafter arising out of such contract or transaction, or the refusal to perform the whole or any part thereof, or an agreement in writing to submit to arbitration an existing controversy arising out of such a contract, transaction, or refusal, shall be valid, irrevocable, and enforceable, save upon such grounds as exist at law or in equity for the revocation of any contract.

更為有趣而值得全世界同僚——特別是迷信仲裁條款有效之假設之美國同僚——所應注意的是，歐盟法院為了「消滅英國判例法」，而禁止英國法院依當事人之仲裁條款對一方當事人於義大利所提起之訴訟下禁訴令。於Allianz SpA, Generali Assicurazioni Generali SpA, v West Tankers Inc.[31]中，英國最高法院認為根據Regulation No 44/2001,Art. 1 (2)(d)，所有仲裁的事項均被排除在公約之適用範圍外。並且認為禁訴令會防止仲裁判斷與各國院判決之衝突，而且如果各會員國能採用禁訴令，會使得歐盟於國際仲裁上比起紐約、百慕達及新加坡有競爭力。歐盟法院認為布魯塞爾規則之適用範圍，必須完全依據訴訟程序的實體（或主體）而定。更明確的說其於規則範圍內之地位，並非由其性質而決定，而是由其要保護的權利之性質而決定。法院認為基於仲裁條款（包括條款之效力）而對意大利法院主張沒有管轄權的抗議，仍屬於規則之範圍內，並且完全是由意大利法院根據規則之第1(2)(d)及5(3)條去決定該抗議是否成立及自己之管轄權。法院認為：「在主訴訟程序中之禁訴令，是違反了法院在布魯塞爾公約中所建立之大原則，亦即根據應適用之法規，由各繫屬法院去決定其是否對面前之糾紛有管轄權....我們應記住44/2001號規則，除了與目前的主要程序無關的幾個有限例外之情形外，並不允許會員國法院之管轄權被另一會員國法院重新再檢驗……[32]」「這種禁訴令是違反了互信，而這種互信是會員國間應給予其他法律制度及機構的，並且44/2001號規

---

31 [2009] EUECJ C-185/07. 又見陳隆修，《歐盟經驗論中國式國際私法之建立》，高雄大學法學論叢6卷2期，2011年，70-75頁。

32 Para.29, It follows, first, as noted by the Advocate General in point 57 of her Opinion, that an anti-suit injunction, such as that in the main proceedings, is contrary to the general principle which emerges from the case-law of the Court on the Brussels Convention, that every court seised itself determines, under the rules applicable to it, whether it has jurisdiction to resolve the dispute before it (see, to that effect, *Gasser*, paragraphs 48 and 49). It should be borne in mind in that regard that Regulation No 44/2001, apart from a few limited exceptions which are not relevant to the main proceedings, does not authorize the jurisdiction of a court of a Member State to be reviewed by a court in another Member State (Case C-351/89 *Overseas Union Insurance and Others* [1991] ECR I-3317, paragraph 24, and *Turner*, paragraph 26). That jurisdiction is determined directly by the rules laid down by that regulation, including those relating to its scope of application. Thus in no case is a court of one Member State in a better position to determine whether the court of another Member State has jurisdiction (*Overseas Union Insurance and Others, paragraph* 23, and Gasser, paragraph 48).

則的管轄制度是根據這樣的互信而來。[33]」

事實上44/2001號規則很明白的將仲裁排除在規則外，但歐盟法院則鐵了心要消滅英國的禁訴令：「但是，即使這些程序沒有涵蓋在44/2001號規則之範圍內，他們仍可能會有破壞規則有效性的後果，亦即於民商事件上國際私法管轄權規則統一目標的達成及於這些事情上判決之自由流動。這是因為這些程序阻止了其他會員國的法院依據44/2001號規則去行使他們的管轄權。[34]」

但是讓個人感覺最驚訝的是，2005年海牙選擇法院公約硬性的以被指定法院為唯一有管轄權之法院，包括契約無效、不成立、或得被撤銷在內之所有問題都必須至被指定法院地去訴訟。如此不但對弱勢一方不公，而且明顯的違背紐約公約2(3)條之規定。歐盟雖然加入了2005年海牙公約，歐盟最高法院卻於West Tankers中白紙黑字的認同紐約公約2(3)條，用以剷除英國禁訴令制度[35]：「這個結論是受到紐約公約第2(3)條所支持的，根據該規定，有關當事人所訂定之仲裁條款範圍內之訴訟所繫屬的會員國法院，在當事人一方之請求下，應命令當事人去仲裁，除非法院認定該條款是無效、不適用、或無法被履行。」而其認同紐約公約2(3)條及反對英美法禁訴令之理由則陳述如下[36]：「最後，如果經由一個禁訴令，而

---

33 Para.30, “such an anti-suit injunction also runs counter to the trust which the Member States accord to one another’s legal systems and judicial institutions and on which the system of jurisdiction under Regulation No 44/2001 is based (see, to that effect, *Turner*, paragraph 24).”

34 Para. 24, “However, even though proceedings do not come within the scope of Regulation No 44/2001, they may nevertheless have consequences which undermine its effectiveness, namely preventing the attainment of the objectives of unification of the rules of conflict of jurisdiction in civil and commercial matters and the free movement of decisions in those matters. This is so, inter alia, where such proceedings prevent a court of another Member State from exercising the jurisdiction conferred on it by Regulation No 44/2001.”

35 Para.33, “This finding is supported by Article II(3) of the New York Convention, according to which it is the court of a Contracting State, when seised of an action in a matter in respect of which the parties have made an arbitration agreement, that will, at the request of one of the parties, refer the parties to arbitration, unless it finds that the said agreement is null and void, inoperative or incapable of being performed.”

36 Para. 31, “Lastly, if, by means of an anti-suit injunction, the Tribunable di Siracusa were prevented from examining itself the preliminary issue of the validity or the applicability of the arbitration agreement, a party could avoid the proceedings merely by relying on that agreement and the applicant, which considers that the agreement is void, inoperative or incapable of being performed, would thus be barred from

使得Tribunable di Siracusa（義大利法院）不能去檢驗仲裁條款的適用性或效力等先決問題，當事人之一方只要依賴該條款就可避免訴訟程序，而請求人，其認為該（仲裁）條款是無效、不適用、或不能被履行，則將會被禁止依44/2001規則第5(3)條去法院提出訴訟，並因此而會被剝奪他所應享有的司法保護的形式。」

無論歐盟法院認同紐約公約5(3)條之真正動機為何，但不爭之事實是其白紙黑字的判決為「請求人，其認為（管轄或仲裁）該條款是無效、不適用、或不能被履行，則將會被禁止依44/2001規則第5(3)條去法院提出訴訟，並因此而會被剝奪他所應享有的司法保護的形式。」無論歐盟法院這個論述之動機是否為了消滅禁訴令，個人認同這個論述本身所代表的契約法、訴訟法上給予弱勢「所應享有的司法保護的形式」。

事實上個人是認同契約中之管轄條款及仲裁條款的。個人認為這些條款的確能幫助提昇司法的穩定性，因而促進商業的效能——但是個人一向反對因司法的穩定或商業的利益而違反個案正義。正如契約上所有之部門一般，管轄及仲裁條款皆必須受到人類文明長久以來所建立之契約法的規範所限制。亦即管轄條款、仲裁條款、及英美法對此二條款如影隨形的禁訴令，皆必須受到對一般契約法之限制。或者至少很明確的可以指出這些限制的最低標準：亦即羅馬規則I第9條所規定之強行法，英國稱為超越性考量，而美國稱為基本政策。

美國法律協會第2新編國際私法篇第90條規定[37]：「對於違反法院地強烈之公共政策之外國訴因之執行，法院得拒絕接受。」而於此方面美國

---

access to the court before which it brought proceedings under Article 5(3) of Regulation No 44/2001 and would therefore be deprived of a form of judicial protection to which it is entitled."

[37] Restat 2d of Conflict of Laws, § 90
§ 90 Action Contrary to Public Policy
No action will be entertained on a foreign cause of action the enforcement of which is contrary to the strong public policy of the forum.但美國最高法院認為欲行使此抗辯時，法院地必須與當事人或該行為有合理關連，Home Ins. Co. v. Dick, 281 U.S. 397 (1930).又如果只是法律之不同亦不能行使此抗辯。

同僚最經常喜歡唸的咒語就是Judge Cardozo所說的[38]：「會違反到某些正義的基本原則，某些盛行的道德觀念，某些於公益上根深蒂固的傳統」。而很明顯的傳統上錯誤、詐欺、脅迫、無經驗等自然皆屬於這些強烈公共政策。另外現代社會中保護消費者、加盟者、經銷商、勞工、保單持有人等新社會正義觀念之形成，亦成為全球化法學之共同核心政策，管轄條款、仲裁條款、及附隨的禁訴令皆應受到這些全球化政策的限制。

較近個人於拙作中[39]，為了顯示2005年海牙公約對管轄條款的有效性加以機械式的承認之不符合公平公平正義，除了重申國際法上對法院地及履行地的強行法必須加以尊重外，另外又舉例說明契約或管轄條款之存在、成立、或效力於實務上是經常產生問題。例如當事人之沈默、契約無對價、錯誤、詐欺、脅迫、合併條款、額外附加條款、標準格式契約、相衝突條款、當事人之同意及合法性等問題，都可能對案件之結果有著決定性的影響。**而在這些問題上，如果當事人間有著相當的議價能力，自然可以傾向「應去仲裁的假設」，並且「如果觸碰到約定，那些請求必須被加以仲裁」。但是如果是一般人、小商人、或第三世界之人民與大企業發生糾紛，那麼「契約之平衡性」及訴訟程序上「立足點之平等」很明顯的應是傾向弱者。如ALI/ UNIDROIT Principles of Transnational Civil Procedure第3.2條後半段規定[40]：「法院應考慮到外國當事人於參加訴訟時所可能遭遇的困難。」於二十一世紀之全球化法學中，無論是契約法或訴訟法皆必須確保弱勢者，尤其是對第三世界之人民，「所應享有的司法保護之形式」——亦即「契約法上之平衡性」及「訴訟法上『真正』立足點之平等」。**

38 "would violate some fundamental principle of justice, some prevalent conception of morals, some deep-seated tradition of the commonweal." Loucks v. Standard Oil Co. of New York, 224 N. Y. 99, 111, 120 N.E. 198, 202 (1918).

39 陳隆修，《2005年海牙法院選擇公約評析》，台北，五南圖書公司，2009年1月，初版1刷，55-122頁。

40 "The court should take into account difficulties that might be encountered by a foreign party in participating in litigation."

三、誠信、合理性、強行法等基本原則

Unidroit Principles of International Commercial Contracts 2004除了於1.4條[41]規定應適用法律（例如羅馬I規則之第9條強行法）之強行法不得被違背外，又於1.7條[42]規定：「(1)於國際貿易上每個當事人必須依誠信及公平交易而行事。(2)當事人不得限制或排除這些責任。」事實上the UNIDROIT Principles （2004）中充滿著當事人所不能違反的強行法規。尤其3.19條更是直接將有關契約效力第三章的大部分規則視為強行法，另外條文中亦充斥著保護弱勢之條款，如4.6條[43]、5.1.7條2項[44]、3.10條1項[45]等。例如3.10條1項即規定不能有重大不平衡如下：「(1)如果於訂定契約時，契約或條款不公平的給予其他當事人過分的利益，他方當事人得使得契約或其中之個別條款為無效。於所有因素中，應特別考慮到，(a)其他當事人不公平的取得第一當事人之利益是基於下列之事實，第一當事人之須依賴他人、經濟困頓、急迫、無遠見、無知、無經驗、或無議價能力，及(b)契約之性質及目的。」或許這些要求「契約平衡性」的契約法共同核心超越性政策，會使得強烈支持仲裁條款、管轄條款、及附隨禁訴令的超越性效力之資本主義及WTO既得利益者，能夠再次回想一年

---

41 Article 1.4 (Mandatory rules)
Nothing in these Principles shall restrict the application of mandatory rules, whether of national, international or supranational origin, which are applicable in accordance with the relevant rules of private international law.

42 Article 1.7 (Good faith and fair dealing)
(1)Each party must act in accordance with good faith and fair dealing in international trade.
(2)The parties may not exclude or limit this duty.

43 Article 4.6 (Contra proferentem rule)
If contract terms supplied by one party are unclear, an interpretation against that party is preferred.

44 (2) Where the price is to be determined by one party and that determination is manifestly unreasonable, a reasonable price shall be substituted notwithstanding any contract term to the contrary.

45 Article 3.10 (Gross disparity)
(1) A party may avoid the contract or an individual term of it if, at the time of the conclusion of the contract, the contract or term unjustifiably gave the other party an excessive advantage, Regard is to be had, among other factors, to
(a) the fact that the other party has taken unfair advantage of the first party's dependence, economic distress or urgent needs, or of its improvidence, ignorance, inexperience or lack of bargaining skill, and
(b) the nature and purpose of the contract.

級時上契約法課程的基本精神。

聯合國1980的國際貨物買賣公約（CISG）雖然只是有關商業契約，但其第7(1)條亦規定誠信原則如下[46]：「於解釋本公約時，應注意其國際性質，及其適用時需促進統一性，及遵循國際貿易中之誠信原則。」而歐盟契約法原則[47]更是充滿著強行法及誠信、合理性原則。其1:103條第2項[48]規定：「如果根據相關的國際私法規則（例如羅馬I第3(3)條），無論契約準據法為何，應適用之國際法、超國家法、及國家之強行法應被加以適用，則他們應被給予效力。」另外15:101條[49]則規定：「契約於違反歐盟會員國間所承認之法律基本原則之範圍內是無效的。」其註釋B則將此範圍包含歐洲公約及人權公約[50]。而其註釋D更是認為無論當事人之知識及意圖，違反這些基本原則一定使得契約無效[51]。

---

46 Article 7
(1) In the interpretation of this Convention, regard is to be had to its international character and to the need to promote uniformity in its application and the observance of good faith in international trade.
(2) Questions concerning matters governed by this Convention which are not expressly settled in it are to be settled in conformity with the general principles on which it is based or, in the absence of such principles, in conformity with the law applicable by virtue of the rules of private international law.

47 見the Commission of European Contract Law, Principles of European Contract Law, edited by Ole Lando and Hugh Beale (2000).

48 Article 1:103: Mandatory Law
(1) Where the law otherwise applicable so allows, the parties may choose to have their contract governed by the Principles, with the effect that national mandatory rules are not applicable.
(2) Effect should nevertheless be given to those mandatory rules of national, supranational and international law which, according to the relevant rules of private international law, are applicable irrespective of the law governing the contract.

49 Article 15:101: Contracts Contrary to Fundamental Principles
A contract is of no effect to the extent that it is contrary to principles recognised as fundamental in the laws of the Member States of the European Union.

50 B. Contrary to Principles Recognised as Fundamental in the Laws of the Member States
The formulation of Article 15:101 is intended to avoid the varying national concepts of immorality, illegality at common law, public policy, *ordre public* and *bonos mores*, by invoking a necessarily broad idea of fundamental principles of law found across the European Union, including European Community law. Guidance as to these fundamental principles may be obtained from such documents as the EC Treaty (e.g. in favour of free movement of goods, services and persons, protection of market competition), the European Convention on Human Rights …… and the European Union Charter on Fundamental Rights.

51 D. No Discretion
Unlike the position in Article 15:102, the judge or arbitrator is given no discretion to determine the effects of a contract which is contrary to European fundamental principles of law: such a contract is to be given no effect at all. The intentions and knowledge of the parties are irrelevant.

歐盟契約法原則1:201條規定誠信原則如下[52]：「(1)每個當事人必須遵守誠信及公平交易原則。(2)當事人不得排除這個責任。」英美法常用的合理性標準則規定於1:302條[53]。1:201條誠信原則之註釋A如此論述[54]：「這個條文是貫穿整個契約原則中之基本原則。於契約中對當事人責任之執行、履行、及成立誠信及公平交易原則是皆被要求的，同樣的於契約中當事人權利之行使亦是被要求的。」另外與the UNIDROIT Principles

---

而有關違反1:103條強行法之效力如下

Article 15:102: Contracts Infringing Mandatory Rules

(1) Where a contract infringes a mandatory rule of law applicable under Article 1:103 of these Principles, the effects of that infringement upon the contract are the effects, if any, expressly prescribed by that mandatory rule.

(2) Where the mandatory rule does not expressly prescribe the effects of an infringement upon a contract, the contract may be declared to have full effect, to have some effect, to have no effect, or to be subject to modification.

(3) A decision reached under paragraph (2) must be an appropriate and proportional response to the infringement, having regard to all relevant circumstances, including:

(a) the purpose of the rule which has been infringed;

(b) the category of persons for whose protection the rule exists;

(c) any sanction that may be imposed under the rule infringed;

(d) the seriousness of the infringement;

(e) whether the infringement was intentional; and

(f) the closeness of the relationship between the infringement and the contract.

52 Article 1:201: Good Faith and Fair Dealing

(1) Each party must act in accordance with good faith and fair dealing.

(2) The parties may not exclude or limit this duty.

53 Article 1:302: Reasonableness

Under these Principles reasonableness is to be judged by what persons acting in good faith and in the same situation as the parties would consider to be reasonable. In particular, in assessing what is reasonable the nature and purpose of the contract, the circumstances of the case and usages and practices of the trades or professions involved should be taken into account.

54 A. Good Faith and Fair Dealing

This Article sets forth a basic principle running through the Principles. Good faith and fair dealing are required in the formation, performance and enforcement of the parties' duties under a contract, and equally in the exercise or a party's rights under the contract.

B. Not Confined to Specific Rules

The concept is, however, broader than any of these specific applications. It applies generally as a companion to Article 1:104 on Usages. Its purpose is to enforce community standards of decency, fairness and reasonableness in commercial transactions, see Article 1:108 on Reasonableness. It supplements the provisions of the Principles, and it may take precedence over other provisions of these Principles when a strict adherence to them would lead to a manifestly unjust result. Thus, even if the non-performance of an obligation is fundamental because strict compliance with the obligation is of the essence of the contract under Article 8:103, a party would not be permitted to terminate because of a trivial breach of the obligation.另見2:104條。

3.10條不公平利益條款相類似之條款亦規定於原則4:109條中[55]。另外4:110條1項又規定[56]：「如果在違反誠信及公平交易之要求下，一個契約條款並非個別洽商而成，又對契約當事人之權利義務產生重大之不平衡，以致造成當事人之損害，於考慮契約之應履行之性質，契約之所有其他條款，及訂約時之情形，該當事人得主張該條款無效。」另外同樣的5:103條亦有規定[57]：「當非個別洽商而成之契約條款之意思是有爭議時，對於提供該些條款之當事人較為不利之解釋是應較為受到認同。」事實上在現實生活中，無論個人或小商人在面對管轄或仲裁條款時，經常就是這些條款所欲保護之對象。故而若禁訴令隨著這些受到嚴厲監督之管轄或仲裁條款而來，自然容易被以國際禮誼之名而被拒絕，但真正的理由可能是在契約法維持契約平衡的基本公平正義之誠信理念。

即使是在二十世紀資本主義大本營的美國，上述國際上要求契約平衡的誠信原則亦是在一個程度上被遵循的。美國2004年的統一商法

---

55 Article 4:109: Excessive Benefit or Unfair Advantage
(1) A party may avoid a contract if, at the time of the conclusion of the contract:
(a) it was dependent on or had a relationship of trust with the other party, was in economic distress or had urgent needs, was improvident, ignorant, inexperienced or lacking in bargaining skill, and
(b) the other party knew or ought to have know of this and, given the circumstances and purpose of the contract, took advantage of the first party's situation in a way which was grossly unfair or took an excessive benefit.

56 Article 4:110: Unfair Terms not Individually Negotiated
(1) A party may avoid a term which has not been individually negotiated if, contrary to the requirements of good faith and fair dealing, it causes a significant imbalance in the parties' rights and obligations arising under the contract to the detriment of that party, taking into account the nature of the performance to be rendered under the contract, all the other terms of the contract and the circumstances at the time the contract was concluded.
(2) This Article does not apply to:
(a) a term which defines the main subject matter of the contract, provided the term is in plain and intelligible language; or to
(b) the adequacy in value of one party's obligations compared to the value of the obligations of the other party.
本條款是將the EC Council Directive 93/13 on Unfair Terms in Consumer Contracts (1993)之規定加以推廣，因為商業契約的廣泛，不似1993年之指令，本條款不列出所禁止之黑名單。

57 Article 5:103: Contra Proferentem Rule
Where there is doubt about the meaning of a contract term not individually negotiated, an interpretation of the term against the party which supplied it is to be preferred.

（U.C.C.）的1-301條f項[58]即規定當事人之約定不可以違反本應適用法律之基本政策。亦即於當事人若無選法時，本應適用法律之強行法不得被違背[59]。有趣的是其註釋9說[60]：「首先，在適用當事人所選定的其他管轄區之法律會違反法院地之基本政策時，法院有時會拒絕適用該法律，即使該法律並不會違反於當事人契約沒選法時應適用之國家或州法律之基本政策時亦會如此。」**因此非常有趣的是美國之the Uniform Commercial Code與歐盟的羅馬規則I第9(2)條皆不約而同的承認法院地之「基本政策」、「強行法」、或「超越性考量」得於必要時超越其他相關連國家之法律[61]。如果在這種情形下國際私法還不算有著全球化法學的共同核心，**

---

58 (f) An agreement otherwise effective under subsection (c) is not effective to the extent that application of the law of the State or country designated would be contrary to a fundamental policy of the State or country whose law would govern in the absence of agreement under subsection (d).

59 其comment 6評述："Rather, the difference must be contrary to a public policy of that jurisdiction that is so substantial that it justifies overriding the concerns for certainty and predictability underlying modern commercial law as well as concerns for judicial economy generally. Thus, application of the designated law will rarely be found to be contrary to a fundamental policy of the State or country whose law would otherwise govern when the difference between the two concerns a requirement, such as a statute of frauds, that relates to formalities, or general rules of contract law, such as those concerned with the need for consideration."而Judge Cardozo於Loucks v. Standard Oil Co. of New York, 120 N.E. 198 (1918)中之論述又再次被引用如下："Our own scheme of legislation may be different. We may even have no legislation on the subject. That is not enough to show that public policy forbids us to enforce the foreign right. A right of action is property. If a foreign statute gives the right, the mere fact that we do not give a like right is no reason for refusing to help the plaintiff getting what belongs to him. We are not so provincial as to say that every solution of a problem is wrong because we deal with it otherwise at home. Similarity of legislation has indeed this importance; its presence shows beyond question that the foreign statute does not offend the local policy. But its absence does not prove the contrary. It is not to be exalted into an indispensable condition. The misleading word 'comity' has been responsible for much of the trouble. It has been fertile in suggesting a discretion unregulated by general principles. …… The courts are not free to refuse to enforce a foreign right at the pleasure of the judges, to suit the individual notion of expediency or fairness. They do not close their doors, unless help would violate some fundamental principle of justice, some prevalent conception of good morals, some deep-rooted tradition of the common weal." 120 N.E. at 201-02 (citations to authorities omitted). 事實上英美法並沒有「強行法」之名詞，因為每個被通過之法律本就應於不同程度、不同場合上被執行。「強行法」可能受歐盟羅馬公約所影響。

60 "First, a forum will occasionally decline to apply the law of a different jurisdiction selected by the parties when application of that law would be contrary to a fundamental policy of the forum jurisdiction, even if it would not be contrary to a fundamental policy of the State or country whose law would govern in the absence of contractual designation. Standards for application of this doctrine relate primarily to concepts of sovereignty rather than commercial law and are thus left to the courts."

61 如果根據歐洲人較習慣之排列編序，那麼或許統一商法1-301條f項是與歐盟契約法1:103條2項是大略上為同一級，例如羅馬I的3(3)條即是。

那就有些奇怪。更奇怪的是在繫屬法院得基於自己的基本政策，而去適用自己的強行法，以超越其他相關的法律，已成為一個全球化公認的國際私法共同核心下，為何還有些資本主義的信徒（既得利益者）仍可以睜眼瞎說仲裁條款與管轄條款的超越性？不但禁訴令的愛好者必須三思，2005年海牙選擇法院公約的鼓吹者或許更應將其一年級時的契約法教科書再次複習。

統一商法1-302條(b)項亦規定[62]：「（統一商法）中所規定的誠信、勤勞、合理性、及注意等義務不得以約定而加以放棄。」其註釋中陳述[63]：「契約自由原則的個別例外是規定於統一商法的其他部分，而一般的例外是規定於此處。」另外統一商法又不厭其煩的再次於1-304條中重申[64]：「（統一商法）內之每個契約或責任在其執行或履行時，皆被賦予誠信之義務。」而更有趣的是其註釋1亦說明[65]：「這個條文所規定的基本原則貫穿了整個統一商法。這個原則就是於商業交易中在履行或執行所

而統一商法1-301條註釋9法院地之基本政策則可能是與羅馬I規則的公序良俗條款（21條）及9(2)條法院地之強行法是屬於同一級數的更強力之強行法。

以上兩個強弱政策級數的分類是依在羅馬規則上歐洲同僚慣用之分列，見recital 27。但個人現今以為歐盟契約法原則15:101條更應屬於超越前二級之超強第三級。

但是上述為大陸法之慣性分列法。個人真正認為每一種被通過之法律皆應被執行，只是依個別場合之不同，其執行之程序與強度皆不同而已。

62 U.C.C. § 1-302

§ 1-302. VARIATION BY AGREEMENT

(a) Except as otherwise provided in subsection (b) or elsewhere in [the Uniform commercial Code], the effect of provisions of [the Uniform Commercial Code] may be varied by agreement.

(b) The obligations of good faith, diligence, reasonableness, and care prescribed by [the Uniform Commercial Code] may not be disclaimed by agreement. The parties, by agreement, may determine the standards by which the performance of those obligations is to be measured if those standards are not manifestly unreasonable. Whenever [the Uniform commercial Code] requires an action to be taken within a reasonable time, a time that is not manifestly unreasonable may be fixed by agreement. ……

63 "This principle of freedom of contract is subject to specific exceptions found elsewhere in the Uniform Commercial Code and to the general exception stated here."

64 U.C.C. s.1-304

1-304. OBLIGATION OF GOOD FAITH

Every contract or duty within [the Uniform Commercial Code] imposes an obligation of good faith in its performance and enforcement.

65 1. This section sets forth a basic principle running throughout the Uniform Commercial Code. The principle is that in commercial transactions good faith is required in the performance and enforcement of all agreements or duties.

有的約定或責任時，誠信原則皆被要求應加以遵守。」

做為比較法的學生，我們或許有些訝異，但又會理所當然的發現，統一商法1-304條的註釋1與歐盟契約法原則1:201條的註釋A，皆認為誠信原則是「基本原則貫穿了整個統一商法」或「貫穿整個契約的原則中之基本原則」。故而契約法上議價能力的平衡性與附隨而來於訴訟程序上立足點之平等，以及ALI/UNIDROIT Principles of Transnational Civil Procedure的3.2條所規定對第三世界人民參加外國訴訟之困難必須加以考慮，這些很明顯的應屬於歐盟契約法原則15:101條「契約違反歐盟會員國（事實上應為全世界）間所承認之法律基本原則之範圍內是無效的。」主張管轄條款、仲裁條款、及附隨而來之禁訴令、以及2005年海牙選擇法院公約所代表之契約條款之效力應超越一切全世界目前所公認的既有契約法共同核心基本原則的人，請問他們憑什麼可以超越這些全球化法學的共同核心強行法、基本政策、及超越性考量？

2005年海牙選擇法院公約是排除自然人之消費契約，但如果比較統一商法2A-106條[66]之規定，仍是甚為有趣而明顯的對比。該條文對消費租賃契約之準據法條款及指定法院管轄條款，皆有嚴格的限制，這些強行條款的適用，自然是預期對弱勢消費者能給予契約上之平衡及訴訟程序上立足點之平等之保護。其立法理由為[67]：「有一個真實性的危險存在於，出租人會誘使承租人去同意一個管轄區其所適用之法律對消費者沒有有效的

---

[66] U.C.C. §.2A-106
LIMITATION ON POWER OF PARTIES TO CONSUMER LEASE TO CHOOSE APPLICABLE LAW AND JUDICIAL FORUM
(1) If the law chosen by the parties to a consumer lease is that of a jurisdiction other than a jurisdiction in which the lessee resides at the time the lease agreement becomes enforceable or within 30 days thereafter or in which the goods are to be used, the choice is not enforceable.
(2) If the judicial forum chosen by the parties to a consumer lease is a forum that would not otherwise have jurisdiction over the lessee, the choice is not enforceable.

[67] "There is real danger that a lessor may induce a consumer lessee to agree that the applicable law will be a jurisdiction that has little effective consumer protection, or to agree that the applicable forum will be a forum that is inconvenient for the lessee in the event of litigation. As a result, this section invalidates these choice of law or forum clauses, except where the law chosen is that of the state of the consumer's residence or where the goods will be kept, or the forum chosen is one that otherwise would have jurisdiction over the lessee."

保護之準據法，或去同意一個指定之法院，而該法院對承租人而言在訴訟時是不方便的。」強勢之跨國企業在其霸權的母國之支持下，不公平的由弱勢第三世界之人民、企業上奪取鉅額利益，這是國際貿易舞台上經常表演的黑色戲劇。例如在環保、反托辣斯法、專利權的誇張適用、不方便法院等情形，全世界皆習以為常。但是有趣的是在美國國內所發生的「真實性危險」，於國際貿易上對第三世界弱勢人民、企業，在仲裁條款、管轄條款、附隨的禁訴令、及2005年海牙公約上，就突然變得「非真實性危險」，這是怎麼回事？難道第一世界跟第三世界是處在異次元世界？

四、王道法學與不患寡患不均

個人必須很誠懇的對那些仍主張仲裁條款、管轄條款、附隨之禁訴令、及2005海牙選擇法院公約具有超越性效力之同僚——特別是英美法的同僚，隨著二十一世紀全球化法學的形成，契約自由及契約促進市場效能之基本政策已受到大幅度之限制。伴隨著十九世紀資本主義而興起注重自由市場的法學，對於今日注重個案正義的全球化法學而言已是正式進入歷史時光隧道的昨日黃花。相對於有著近二千五百年的中國文化，十九世紀英國本著自由市場資本主義而興起的英式契約法只是曇花一現，它或許在十九世紀有著功能及貢獻，但在二十一世紀注重人權、環保、及個案正義之浪潮下，它早該鞠躬謝幕。於剛逝去的二十世紀我們見識了萬馬奔騰氣勢非凡的美國「選法革命」[68]，及於世紀末號稱的「歐洲法學革命」。隨著大中華經濟區的躍上舞台，個人認同黃進、趙相林教授所主張的中國式國際私法會於二十一世紀誕生。而黃進教授與個人皆一起認為中國式法學應本於二千多年來的「王道」精神。在二十一世紀鋪天蓋地而來的全

68 見Symposium, Choice of Law: How it Ought to Be, 48 Mercer L. Rev. 639, 653 (1977)；但是亦有人認為「利益說」是「智慧上破產」（“intellectually bankrupt”），Patrick J. Borchers, Professor Brilmayer and the Holy Grail, 1991 Wis. L. Rev. 465.466 (1991)。相對於60、70年代的同僚，個人寧願認為90年代的同僚「能力上破產」。個人認為60、70年代的同僚開了門，個人才能返回二千年前中國式法學的殿堂。

球化法學之浪潮中，「禮運大同」應成為中國式法學之基本政策，契約法應回歸「不患寡患不均」[69]之「傳統上公平與基本正義之概念」。在中國「王道」之思想下，二十一世紀全球化法學之心與靈魂在於「是否正義的真正利益最能被達成」。故而本於十九世紀資本市場主義而來注重市場效能的契約法，在二十一世紀「中國法學革命」（事實上應是中國法學「復興」（renaissance; resurrection））之思潮下成為野蠻、不合時宜的「掠奪性新殖地法學」。

在二十一世紀全球化法學中，仲裁條款、管轄條款、附隨之禁訴令、及2005年海牙法院公約，皆應受到契約法平衡性、訴訟法立足點平等的嚴厲審核。我們不要忘了仲裁及管轄條款之效力於一百多年前還是被認為侵犯法律公權力之運作，因而是被認為無效的，相較之下美國法於這方面的起步是較晚的。世界貿易組織（World Trade Organization, WTO）的Agreement on Trade-Related Aspects of Intellectual Property Rights（TRIPS）即使是在擎著自由貿易的旗幟下，基於地球村彼此互相牽扯必須共同面對不可預測的災害疾病，仍不得不在第31(b)條[70]規定各會

---

69 又見道德經：「自勝者強，知足者富」；「甚愛必大費，多藏必厚亡」；「最莫大於多欲，禍莫大於不足，咎莫大於欲得」。又見聖經路加福音第18章：「不可姦淫、不可殺人、不可偷盜、不可作假見證、當孝敬父母。那人說，這一切我從小都遵守了。耶穌聽見了，就說，你還缺少一件，要變賣你一切所有的，分給窮人，就必有財寶在天上，你還要來跟從我。他聽見這話，就甚憂愁，因為他很富足。耶穌看見他就說，有錢財的人進上帝的國，是何等的難哪。駱駝穿過鍼的眼，比財主進上帝的國，還容易呢。」

70 Article 31
Other Use Without Authorization of the Right Holder
Where the law of a Member allows for other use of the subject matter of a patent without the authorization of the right holder, including use by the government or third parties authorized by the government, the following provisions shall be respected:
…………………
(b) such use may only be permitted of, prior to such use, the proposed user has made efforts to obtain authorization from the right holder on reasonable commercial terms and conditions and that such efforts have not been successful within a reasonable period of time. This requirement may be waived by a Member in the case of a national emergency or other circumstances of extreme urgency or in case of public non-commercial use. In situations of national emergency or other circumstances of extreme urgency, the right holder shall, nevertheless, be notified as soon as reasonably practicable. In the case of public non-commercial use, where the government or contractor, without making a patent search, knows or has demonstrable grounds to know that a valid patent is or will be used or for the government, the right holder shall be informed promptly;

員國得於緊急情形下，未經權利人之同意，得強制使用其專利權之主體（實體）。即使是號稱二十世紀唯一超強之美國，仍有不得不行使這個強制授權的緊急情況。同樣防止專利權濫用的條款，亦出現於Paris Convention for the Protection of Industrial Property的5(a)(2)條[71]的強制授權條款，以防止專屬專利權之濫用。這些條款在二十一世紀的全球化法學，固然可以稱為地球村同舟共濟條款；但在二千多年前，中國式法學不但稱之為「不患寡患不均」政策，更稱之為「王道」之「禮運大同」基本政策、超越性考量、及最強行之法。

五、衡平法不可類別化

美國聯邦第二巡迴法院於China Trade & Dev. Corp. v. M.V. Choong Yong[72]中，立下對於外國法院提起訴訟當事人之禁訴令之標準。其所立下的兩個門檻要件，及要件滿足後之各種考慮因素（特別是保護法院之管轄權及法院地之強烈公共政策），為許多後續法院所引用[73]。這個標準的內容看起來言之有物，又甚為周到多元。但由英國母法一直對禁訴令之類別，無論於學術上或判例法上，皆無法給予較一致性之定義，上述美國聯

(c) the scope and duration of such use shall be limited to the purpose for which it was authorized, and in the case of semi-conductor technology shall only be for public non-commercial use or to remedy a practice determined after judicial or administrative process to be anti-competitive;

71 (2) Each country of the Union shall have the right to take legislative measures providing for the grant of compulsory licenses to prevent the abuse which might result from the exercise of the exclusive rights conferred by the patent, for example, failure to work.

(3) Forfeiture of the patent shall not be provided for except in cases where the grant of compulsory licenses would not have been sufficient to prevent the said abuses. No proceedings for the forfeiture or revocation of a patent may be instituted before the expiration of two years from the grant of the first compulsory license.

72 837 F. 2d 33, 35-36 (2d Cir. 1987).

73 例如Ibeto Petrochemical Industries Limited v. M/t Beffen A/s, 475 F3d 56 (2d Cir. 2007) paras. 35, 36.
35 Pursuant to the China Trade test,
36 [a]n anti-suit injunction against parallel litigation may be imposed only if: (A) the parties are the same in both matters, and (B) resolution of the case before the enjoining court is dispositive of the action to be enjoined. China Trade, 837 F. 2d at 35. Once past this threshold, courts are directed to consider a number of additional factors, including whether the foreign action threatens the jurisdiction or the strong public policies of the enjoining forum. Id, at 36.

邦第二巡迴法院之標準亦可能只可作為軟性參考，而非硬性的條件。畢竟Lord Scarman膾炙人口的論述是於英國廣被唸誦著[74]：「衡平法的寬度及靈活性是不可被類別化所破壞。」

相較於美國法院，英國法院於審理案件所行使的權力中（the Court's Case management Powers），是明白的規定有著作成禁訴令之裁量權，其Civil Procedure Rules, 3.3規定[75]：「除非有著規定或另外其他之立法，法院得在當事人之申請下或主動行使其權力。」而the Supreme Court Act 1981之Section 37(1)規定[76]：「第一審法院得經由命令（無論是中間或最後）而給予禁止命令……這是於所有的案件中法院認為是公平及方便如此作時皆可以的。」另外於仲裁上Section 44 of the Arbitration Act 1996規定[77]：「(1)除非當事人另有同意，為了及相關仲裁程序之目的，正如同於為了及相關法律程序之目的，法院對於下列事項有著相同的權力去給予命令。(2)這些事項為：……(e)給予一個中間命令……」

如較近之Cheshire and North所說[78]：「那是有可能將給予禁訴令之案件分成許多類別，而每個類別包含著許可禁訴令的更多明確的標準。但是

---

74 Castanho v. Brown & Root (U.K.) Ltd., [1981] A.C. 557, 573 (H.L.) (appeal taken from Eng.), "the width and flexibility of equity are not to be undermined by categorisation."

75 Civil procedure Rules, 3.3 Court's power to make order of its own initiative
(1) Except where a rule or some other enactment provides otherwise, the court may exercise its powers on an application or of its own initiative.

76 "The High Court may by order (whether interlocutory or final) grant an injunction ⋯ in all cases in which it appears to the court to be just and convenient to do so."

77 Section 44 of the Arbitration Act 1996, entitled "Court powers exercisable in support of arbitral proceedings", provides:
"(1) Unless otherwise agreed by the parties, the court has for the purposes of and in relation to arbitral proceedings the same power of making orders about the matters listed below as it has for the purposes of and in relation to legal proceedings.
(2) Those matters are:
……
(e) the granting of an interim injunction ⋯"

78 Cheshire, North & Fawcett, Private International Law, 14th ed., pp. 457, 458, "It is possible to divide up the cases where an injunction has been granted into various categories, and each category contains more specific criteria for the grant of an injunction. However, neither the judges in the leading cases nor writers are able to agree on what these categories are. This is partly because different attempts at categorization emphasize different things: some focus on the conduct of the party to be restrained; others on the right of the applicant to complain."

無論是作出領導判例的法官或作者們皆無法同意這些類別應是什麼。這有可能部分原因是在於去嘗試不同的類別的重點是在於不同的事情上：有些注重被禁止當事人之行為；有些是在請求者所要求的權利。」例如於South Carolina Co v. Assurantie NV[79]中，之分類為：侵犯到當事人不可於外國被訴之法律上或衡平上之權利；於外國提起訴訟是不公正的；在正義的利益下有著其他更合適的法院。而個人先前著作[80]所引用之Airbus Industrie GIE v. Patel[81]則分成三種：於外國之訴訟是構成困擾性或壓迫性時；於外國之訴訟是不公正時；於外國之訴訟是違反契約之約定時。但較近於Turner v Grovit[82]中Lord Hobhouse是對作成命令的要件較為注重，而非注重於分類。這個要件即為被禁止之當事人有著不當之行為，而對這行為申請者有權利去請求及有著合法的利益去要求防止。對最高法院於Turner中之決定，上訴法院[83]將其解釋為分成兩種類別：(1)被制止之當事人之行為是不公正的（unconscionable）；(2)於外國所提起之程序是違反契約的約定。但如Lord Scarman[84]所說的，於「正義的目的」（the ends of justice）之需求下，新的類別是可被引進的。

禁訴令與不方便法院（先前為困擾性或壓迫性法學）為英國法於處理國際平行訴訟時重要之法學理論，前者為有關停止外國程序，後者為

79 South Carolina Co v Assurantie NV [1987] AC 24 at 40, HL, invasion of a legal or equitable right not to be used abroad; bringing of the proceedings abroad would be unconscionable; there is another forum which is more appropriate in the interests of justice. 又見Cheshire and North, 14th ed., p. 458.

80 見陳隆修、許兆慶、林恩瑋、李瑞生四人合著，《國際私法—管轄與選法理論之交錯》，台北，五南圖書公司，2009年3月，初版1刷，244-246頁；North and Fawcett, Private International Law, 13th ed., pp. 359-373.

81 Airbus Industrie GIE v Patel [1999] 1 AC 119, HL, vexation or oppression, breach of an agreement, unconscionability.

82 [2001] UKHL 65, [2002] 1 WLR 107; followed in *Glencore International AG v Exter Shipping Ltd* [2002] EWCA Civ 528 at [42], [2002] 2 All ER (Comm) 1. 見Cheshire and North, 14th ed., pp.455-476.

83 *Sabah Shipyard (Pakistan) Ltd v Islamic Republic of Pakistan* [2002] EWCA Civ 1643 at [39]; [2003] 2 Lloyd's Rep 571, CA; *Royal Bank of Canada v Cooperative Centrale Raiffeisen-Boerenleenbank BA* [2004] EWCA Civ 7 at [8], [2004] 1 Lloyd's Rep 471; *Seismic Shipping Inc v Total EP UK plc (The Western Regent)* [2005] EWCA Civ 985 at [44]-[46]. [2005] 2 Lloyd's Rep 359; *OT Africal Line Ltd v Magic Sportwear Corpn* [2006] EWCA Civ 710 at [63], [83], [2005] 2 Lloyd's Rep 170.

84 Castanho v Brown and Root (UK) Ltd [1981] AC 557 at 573.

有關停止法院地之程序。於這兩方面英國早已有成文法[85]。個人早期如此論述[86]：「因為英國法院於訴訟會造成困擾（vexation）或壓迫（oppression）之情形下，為避免造成不正當（unjust）的後果，可以命令停止（stay）或駁回（dismiss）當事人於英國之訴訟，甚至可以禁止（injunction）當事人於國外起訴或繼續進行國外之訴訟，或強制執行國外之判決。此種管轄上之權力為英法院之自由裁量權（discretionary power），法院必須很謹慎地使用此種權力。法院必須於當事人之一方，若繼續進行其於法院地或法院外之訴訟，會很明顯地對他方當事人造成困擾或壓迫，或者濫用法院之訴訟程序時才可使用此種權力。另一要件為法院欲停止訴訟之進行時，必須不能對原告造成不公平（injustice）之現象。而上述兩要件之舉證責任在於被告。」通常英、美兩國之同僚一般皆認為於平行訴訟時，禁訴令與不方便法院是法院賴以解決這方面問題之主要法理。但個人認為即使於採納不方便法院之前，對所在於境外之被告英國已立法[87]認為在極度謹慎下，英國法院有裁量權送達給境外之被告，這是國際訴訟非常重要的一個法理。個人認為美國最低限度關連點就是不能體會境外送達應本於方便法院而來，才會造成「鬼打牆」現象。

至於禁訴令是否會造成違反1950年歐盟基本自由及人權保障公約中第6條之訴訟權[88]，判例法[89]認為第6條並非是有關當事人應於何處行使公平及公開之審判程序，而是有關當事人之權利必須於根據本條文之規定下，在某處之法院舉行審判之規定。如同Cardozo J.所說[90]：「但實際上

---

85 Supreme Court of Judicature (Consolidation) Act 1925, s. 41, proviso (a).

86 見陳隆修，《國際私法管轄權評論》，台北，五南圖書公司，民國75年11月，初版，84頁。

87 見陳隆修，《國際私法管轄權評論》，台北，五南圖書公司，民國75年11月，初版，45-48頁。

88 Article 6 – Right to a fair trial
In the determination of his civil rights and obligations or of any criminal charge against him, everyone is entitled to a fair and public hearing within a reasonable time by an independent and impartial tribunal established by law.

89 OT Africa Line Ltd v Hijazy (The Kribi) [2001] 1 Lloyd's Rep 76 at [41]-[44].

90 Boris N. Sokoloff v. The national City Bank of New York
239 N.Y. 158, 165, "Juridically, a government that is unrecognized may be viewed as no government at all, if the power withholding recognition chooses thus to view it. In practice, however, since, juridical conceptions are seldom, if ever, carried to the limit of their logic, the equivalence is not absolute, but is

因為法學的概念很少被執行至邏輯的極限，而是受制於自我設限的常識及公平原則的限制」。而最尊敬的恩師Prof. Graveson亦說[91]：「邏輯並非判例法的最高價值。英國國際私法實現正義的概括性目的給予邏輯一致性的政策必要的限制。」個人認為這種論述是中國文化二千多年「道法自然」之意[92]。故而「方便與不方便法院法學」及「禁訴令」是否違背人權公約及憲法上所規定的訴訟權、財產權、平等權、及適當程序權，並非以其法律邏輯本身而定，應視其適用之結果是否違反契約法之平衡性及訴訟法立足點平等之要求而定。

Cheshire and North[93]於禁訴令之原則上因為新增判例法之故，比起舊版多了新判例法之解釋原則。首先如美國法一般，禁訴令並非針對外國法院，而是針對正提起或威脅提起外國訴訟之當事人[94]，故屬於對人訴訟，因而法院對被禁止之當事人必須有對人之管轄。對於不服從命令之當事人

---

subject to self-imposed limitations of common sense and fairness, as we learned in litigations following our Civil War."

Cardozo J.這個論述是有關內戰中之政府之行為之效力，又見p.164, "It would be hazardous, not the less, to say that a rule so comprehensive and so drastic is not subject to exceptions under pressure of some insistent claim of policy or justice."

91 R.H. Graveson, Conflict of Laws, p.79 (7th ed. 1974), "The acceptability of this solution rests in the fact that logic is not the highest value in the common law. The necessary limits on the policy of logical consistency are imposed by the general purpose of positive justice of English private international law. An English court may thus uphold the legitimacy of children as the subsidiary question and declare null and void the marriage of their parents as the principal question, using different systems of conflict of laws for the purpose. Common law judges regard rules as tools, not as fetters, to promote, not prevent, the fulfillment of their function." In Hashmi v. Hashmi [1972] Fam. 36.

92 ALI/ Unidroit Principles of Transnational Civil Procedure第3條當事人訴訟程序之平等，其註釋對「合理性」之說明，特別是在於排除過分技術性之論述及「過分」「嚴重」之後果，這種說明符合「道法自然」之概念。

P-3A The term "reasonable" is used throughout the Principles and signifies "proportional," "significant," "not excessive," or "fair," according to the context. It can also mean the opposite of arbitrary. The concept of reasonableness also precludes hyper-technical legal argument and leaves a range of discretion to the court to avoid severe, excessive, or unreasonable application of procedural norms. 又見新約哥林多後書第3章：「你們明顯是基督的信、藉著我們修成的。不是用墨寫的、乃是用永生上帝的靈寫的。不是寫在石版上，乃是寫在心版上。我們因基督所以在上帝面前纔有這樣的信心。並不是我們憑自己能承擔什麼事、我們所能承擔的、乃是出於上帝。他叫我們能承擔這新約的執事。不是憑著字句、乃是憑著精意。因為那字句是叫人死、精意是叫人活。精意或作聖靈」

93 Cheshire, North and Fawcett, 14th 2d., pp, 455-476.

94 *Donohue v Armco Inc* [2001] UKHL 64, [2002] 1 All ER 749, 757; *Turner v Grovit* [2001] UKHL 65 at [23], [2002] 1 WLR 107; *Société Nationale Industrielle Aérospatiale v. Lee Kui Jak* [1987] AC 871, 892.

固然可以給予藐視法院之處罰，但是當事人若不在法院地，或者於法院地沒有足夠之財產，則該命令不容易被執行。法院必須有著對人管轄權才能使得命令生效[95]，該管轄權可能基於當事人之接受管轄[96]，或與法院地有著足夠的關連使得法院可以行使這個權力[97]，例如當事人違背應於法院地履行之管轄或仲裁條款[98]。另外如果依C.P.R. 1998, r. 6.20法院得對境外被告加以送達時，法院即有權力禁止其於外國提起訴訟[99]。

六、充足的利益或關連

禁訴令雖然形式上是針對當事人，只是其實際上卻會有間接的影響到外國法院之訴訟之效果。故而國際禮誼會要求必須於謹慎之情形下，方得作成禁訴令[100]，這是與許多美國法院相似的。而且與前述美國聯邦第二巡迴法院所說的大致相同，於一個法院訴訟越深入進行越久，法院就越有禁止當事人於他處就相同當事人相同訴因再提起訴訟之正當性。但反過來說，外國訴訟進行越久，就越應給予國際禮誼上之尊重[101]。但無論如何如同Lord Goff於Airbus Industrie GIE v Patel中所說的名言[102]：「通常，就

95 *Castanho v. Brown & Root* (U.K.) Ltd., [1981] A.C. 557, HL; *Midland Bank Plc v Laker Airways Ltd* [1986] Q.B. 689; *Bank of Tokyo Ltd v Karoon* [1987] AC 45 n at 59, CA; *Société Nationale Industrielle Aérospatiale v. Lee Kui Jak* [1987] AC 871, 892; *Donohue v Armco Inc*, supra, at 757; *Turner v Grovit, supra*, at [23].

96 *Glencore International AG v Exter Shipping Ltd* [2002] EWCA Civ 528 at [52], [2002] 2 All ER (Comm) 1, See also *Royal Exchange Assurance Co Ltd v Compaňia Naviera Santi SA, The Tropaioforos* [1962] 1 Lloyd's Rep 410; *Castanho v. Brown & Root (U.K.) Ltd*, supra.

97 Castanho v Brown and Root (UK) Ltd [1981] AC 557.

98 Tracomin SA v Sudan Oil Seeds Co Ltd (Nos 1 and 2) [1983] 1 WLR 1026.

99 Royal Exchange Assurance Co Ltd v Compania Naviera Santi SA, The Tropaioforos [1962] 1 Lloyd's Rep 410.

100 *British Airways Board v Laker Airways Ltd* [1985] AC 58 at 95 (per Lord Scarman), HL; *South Carolina Insurance Co v Assurantie NV* [1987] AC 24 at 40, HL (per Lord Brandon); Airbus Industrie GIE v Patel [1999] 1 AC 119 at 133, HL; *Sabah Shipyard (Pakistan) Ltd v Islamic Republic of Pakistan* [2002] EWCA Civ 1643 at [40]; [2003] 2 Lloyd's Rep 571, CA.

101 *Royal Bank of Canada v Cooperative Centrale Raiffeisen-Boerenleenbank BA* [2004] EWCA Civ 7 at [50], "Considerations of comity grow in importance the longer the foreign suit continues and the more the parties and the Judge have engaged in its conduct and management."
例如在屏東地院92重訴4號裁定中，臺灣或北京法院就應該對保險人於挪威所提之否認之訴加以禁訴令。

102 "As a general rule, before an anti-suit injunction can properly be granted by an English court to restrain

目前之案件所考慮到之一般案件之種類中，在英國法院得合適的許可一個禁訴令以禁止一個人於外國法院提起訴訟程序前，國際禮誼要求英國法院與系爭之問題須有著充足的利益，或關係，以使得禁訴令所產生的間接的干擾到外國法院訴訟之進行之後果合理化。」雖然於「通常」之情形下應給予外國法院「禮誼」之考量，但Lord Goff則認為於例外之情形下禁訴令之作成卻不必考慮給予外國法院禮誼之尊重[103]：「例如於當外國所行使的管轄之行為是如此以致其被剝奪通常所應被予的禮誼之尊重。」

依據Turner v Grovit[104]法院作成命令之權力是根據被告應被禁止的不當行為，而對這行為申請人（原告）有權利去請求，並且有著合法的利益去要求制止[105]。系爭的行為必須符合英國判例法所謂的「不公正」[106]（unconscionable）。禁訴令基本上是一種針對不當行為之救濟措施[107]，亦即一種給予禁止命令以對抗不公正之行為而藉以保護衡平上或法律上之權利[108]。但是有些資深英國同僚[109]認為於Turner v Grovit中，Lord Hobhouse

---

a person from pursuing proceedings in a foreign jurisdiction in cases of the kind under consideration in the present case, comity requires that the English forum should have a sufficient interest in, or connection with, the matter in question to justify the indirect interference with foreign court which an anti-suit injunction entails." Airbus Industrie GIE v Patel [1999] 1 AC 119 at 138.

103 同上，at 140, "for example where the conduct of the foreign state exercising jurisdiction is such as to deprive it of the respect normally required by comity".

104 [2001] UKHL 65, [2002] 1 WLR 107.

105 [2001] UKHL 65, at [24].

106 同上；但這是根據判例法而來，見British Airways Board v Laker Airways Ltd [1985] AC 58 at 81 (per Lord DIPLOCK).

107 Turner v Grovit [2001] UKHL 65 at [24].

108 Glencore International AG v Exter Shipping Ltd [2002] EWCA Civ 528 at [42], [2002] 2 All ER (Comm) 1; *OT Africa Line Ltd v Magic Sportwear Corpn* [2005] EWCA Civ 710 at [63] and [83], [2005] 2 Lloyd's Rep 170.

109 Cheshire, North and Fawcett, pp. 464, 465, Lord Hobhouse in *Turner v Grovit* has caused some confusion by referring to the need for the *applicant* to have a legitimate interest in making his application and interpreting *Airbus Industrie GIE v Patel* as being a case where the applicant had no such interest. According to Lord Hobhouse, what this case shows is that the necessary legitimate interest of the applicant must be the existence of proceedings in England which need to be protected by the grant of a restraining order. This misunderstands the reasoning in the case where the concern was with England's interest Moreover, whilst the two different tests in relation to the relevant interest lead to the same result in a case like *Airbus Industrie GIE v Patel*, the legitimate interest of the applicant test causes real problem in single forum cases.

要求申請人必須有合法的利益，這是與Airbus Industrie GIE v Patel[110]中Lord Goff所要求的英國的充足利益不一致，已造成混亂。並且這兩種有關利益的不同標準，雖然於Airbus Industrie GIE v Patel中造成相同的結果，亦即英國沒有足夠的利益與關連，及申請人沒有合法的利益，但申請人之利益標準會於單一法院之案件中造成困擾。甚至在前述之Midland Bank plc v Laker Airways Ltd[111]中，申請人的利益標準被這些資深的評論員形容為「攪混了一池春水」[112]。因為於該案中申請人於英國並未有訴訟程序，故並無合法的利益需要禁訴令之保護，但英國法院依Lord Goff之論述是仍有足夠的權益去給予禁訴令。

美國法院所謂「聯邦政策」可能近似英國法院之「國家利益」。或許衡平法的寬度及靈活性不可被類別化所破壞，故或許在正義及便利之情形下，國家「或」個人之利益都足以作成禁訴令。於「正義之真正利益」下，國家亦有著利益去確保個人不於外國被濫訴之私人利益，故私人利益與國家利益並不一定不相容。

畢竟禁止訴訟命令之作成，無論是依成文法或判例法，皆須以正義之目的為依據。如Lord Goff於Société Nationale Industrielle Aérospatiale v. Lee Kui Jak[113]所說的，亦為Turner v Grovit中Lord Hobhouse再次引用：「正義的基本原則」[114]（“the basic principle of justice”）。

---

[110] [1999] 1 AC 119, HL.

[111] [1986] QB 689, CA, Distinguished in Barclays Bank plc v Homan [1993] BCLC 680 at 688, 692; [1993] BCLC 680 at 705, CA.

[112] Cheshire, North and Fawcett, pp. 468, 469, “Lord Hobhouse in Turner v Grovit has muddied the waters by introducing the requirement that the applicant has a legitimate interest in seeking to prevent the wrongful conduct and that where there was unconscionable conduct for some non-contractual reason, the necessary legitimate interest of the applicant must be the existence of proceedings in England which need to be protected by the grant of a restraining order. There were no such English proceedings in the Midland Bank case. However, Lord Hobhouse was not referring to single forum cases and his words should not be taken as limiting the right to grant an injunction in such cases. He was thinking of Airbus Industrie GIE v Patel and seems not to have understood the concern in that case that England should have an interest. Looking at that requirement, what Lord Goff’s comments (in Airbus Industrie GIE v Patel) in relation to the Midland Bank case show is that the requisite interest of the English forum can still be shown even where there are no proceedings in England which need to be protected.”

[113] [1987] AC at 893.

[114] Turner v Grovit [2001] UKHL 65 at [24].

依照上訴法院對最高法院於Turner v Grovit[115]中之分類，禁訴令分成2類：(1)當事人應被制止之行為是不公正的（unconscionable）；(2)於外國所提之訴訟是違反契約之約定的。但是一般的共識是同意給予禁訴令之權力並不侷限於有限度的分類，而且如Lord Scarman[116]所說於正義目的之需求下，應可加入新的類別[117]。但是個人近年來之主張是與英國及美國之主流意見（至少於禁訴令上）水火不容的。相對於一百多年前將管轄及仲裁條款視為違背法律公權力之運作而無效（美國之發展相對上較晚），近年來卻每每試圖將這兩個條款於國際貿易上提昇至近乎聖牛之地位，而企圖規避契約法共同核心政策之限制。個人並非反對管轄或仲裁條款，但是在WTO所揭櫫的自由貿易下，資本、技術優勢之一方必然會對第三世界大肆掠奪，因此管轄或仲裁條款之成立及效力必須受到傳統契約法之制約。如果不分青紅皂白一昧的支持資本優勢者所主導的管轄或仲裁條款之效力，更甚而給予禁訴令，那麼法院之作為就是實足「不公正」之行為。這種支持第一世界資本家所主導之管轄條款或仲裁條款全面性效力之作法，不但是違反人類良心之「不公正」行為，亦明顯的違反契約法「平衡性」原則，及違反訴訟法要求「確保當事人間立足點平等」之基本要件。尤其更違反了我們祖先二千多年來「不患寡患不均」之「王道」文化，這種違反常識、正義、人權公約之作法，不是二十一世紀全球化法學所可以接受的內容。這種作法不能達成正義的真正利益，是個沒有心與靈魂的法學，是以資本主義為基礎的帝國主義法學。

對於Turner v Grovit之分類，Cheshire and North[118]又將及加以更詳細之區別。這或許是其他相信衡平法不可類別化之同僚所不認同的，但或許重點是在案件之特點，而非其類別。Lord Scarman[119]在British Airways

---

115 [2001]UKHL 65, [2002] 1 WLR 107; Glencore International AG v Exter Shipping Ltd [2002] EWCA Civ 528 at [42], [2002] 2 All ER (Comm) 1.

116 Castanho v Brown and Root (UK) Ltd [1981] AC 557 at 573.

117 又見British Airways Board v Laker Airways Ltd [1985] AC 58 at 81, HL; Société Nationale Industrielle Aérospatiale v. Lee Kui Jak [1987] AC 871 at 892.

118 Cheshire, North and Fawcett, pp. 459-475.

119 *British Airways Board v Laker Airways Ltd* [1985] AC 58 at 95, “The power of the English court to

Board v Laker Airways Ltd中說：「如果於外國法院所提起的訴訟之情形是如此的不公正，以致依照我們『寬廣及靈活』的衡平法原則，是可以被認為侵犯了申請者之衡平權利，那麼英國法院許可禁止令之權力是存在的。[120]」故而第一類別是當事人被禁止的行為是不公正的。而在這個類別下又分兩個小類別。

第一小類別是於外國之訴訟對他方當事人構成困擾性或壓迫性（vexatious or oppressive）之訴訟。在這個小類別中，由於外國法院的不合適性使得被告有權利不在該外國法院被訴[121]。第二小類別為屬於其他的不公正行為。當事人不應於外國被訴之權利，並非基於外國法院之不合適性，而是由於該訴訟行為本身的不合適性[122]。這些小類別雖然不同，但Cheshire and North[123]認為可稱之為基於「困擾性」或「壓迫性」之理由（vexation or oppression）而給予禁訴令。英國甚早就有判例[124]，亦有成文法[125]，在原告之訴若構成困擾性或壓迫性之訴訟，或濫用司法程序（abuse of the process of the court），則法院可以停止或駁回當事人於英國之訴訟，甚至可以禁止當事人於外國起訴或繼續進行國外之訴訟。故於英國法院改採「不方便法院」前，長久以來「困擾性」或「壓迫性」法學就是英國法院停止自己之訴訟程序，或禁止當事人於外國之訴訟程序之主要依據。比起較為寬廣的「不方便法院」，「困擾性」或「壓迫性」法學自然遠較為嚴謹及能充份保護當事人之訴訟權。事實上個人認為如果當事人之行為已構成「困擾或「壓迫性」，則自然為了「所有當事人之利

---

grant the injunction exists, if the bringing of the suit in the foreign court is in the circumstances so unconscionable that in accordance with our principles of a 'wide and flexible' equity it can be seen to be an infringement of an equitable right of the applicant."

120 Airbus Industrie GIE v. Patel [1999] 1 AC at 134 (per Lord Goff), HL; Midland Bank Plc v Laker Airways Ltd [1986] QB 689 at 701, 711-712.

121 Turner v Grovit [2001] UKHL 65 at [25].

122 同上。

123 Cheshire, North and Fawcett, p. 459.

124 見陳隆修，《國際私法管轄權評論》，台北，五南圖書公司，民國75年11月，初版，84-96頁所引述之英國案例。

125 Supreme Court of Judicature (Consolidation) Act 1925, s. 41, proviso (a).又見The Supreme Court Act 1981, s. 37.

益及正義之目的」[126]，通常亦應符合較為寬鬆的「不方便法院法學」之要件。事實上於Gulf Oil Corp. v. Gilbert[127]中，美國最高法院是將困擾性及壓迫性做為考慮因素之一，以決定是否停止法院地之訴訟。

在間接的干擾到外國法院訴訟程序時，仍是應以較為嚴謹的困擾性或壓迫性標準為依據。於South Carolina Insurance Co v Assurantie NV[128]中，英國最高法院就認為不公正的行為是包含「困擾性或壓迫性之行為」。於Airbus Industrie GIE v Patel[129]中，Lord Goff就認為基於管轄權的寬廣原則而適用的禁訴令須於正義之目的有需求時才能行使。於*Turner v Grovit*[130]中，Lord Hobhouse認為「困擾性」及「壓迫性」就是譴責不公正行為的另一說法，但這些說法並非為這種定義之限制，他亦是強調「正義的基本原則」（“the basic principle of justice”）。個人雖然反對將仲裁及管轄條款的成立與效力提昇至不受契約法共同基本政策的限制，但如若是因「不公正」、「困擾性」、或「壓迫性」行為而法院作成禁訴令，個人是認同的。因為個人相信全世界大部分的文明國家皆有禁止濫訴之政策，故而個人認為若基於禁止濫訴所作成之禁訴令並不會違反全球化法學的共同核心。但是濫訴之標準各國可能還需時間去達成一致的看法。至於英國法院則長久以來就有自己有關正義的看法[131]。

於這個小類別中有一種情況是，在可以起訴之法院中是包括英國法院在內。而如前述英國法院長久以來是基於困擾性或壓迫性之理由，去行使

126 不方便法院之要件尚需有其他更合適之法院，見Spiliada Maritime Corpn v. Cansulex [1987] AC 460 at 476, “The basic principle is that a stay will only be granted on the ground of ground non conveniens where the court is satisfied that there is some available forum having jurisdiction, which is the appropriate forum for trial of the action, i.e. in which the case may be tried more suitably for the interests of all the parties and the ends of justice.”

127 330 U.S. 501 at 508, “The court will weigh relative advantages and obstacles to fair trial. It is often said that the plaintiff may not, by choice of an inconvenient forum, ‘vex,’ ‘harass,’ or ‘oppress’ the defendant by inflicting upon him expense or trouble not necessary to his own right to pursue his remedy. But unless the balance is strongly in favor of the defendant, the plaintiff’s choice of forum should rarely be disturbed.”

128 [1987] AC 24, “conduct which is oppressive or vexatious”.

129 [1999] 1 AC 119 at 133, HL.

130 Turner v Grovit [2001] UKHL 65 at [24].

131 Barclays Bank plc v Homan [1993] BCLC 680 at 687 (Hoffmann J); [1993] BCLC 680 at 705, CA.

權力限制當事人於外國之訴訟[132]。過去判例法曾認為停止英國程序與限制外國的程序之法理應是一致的[133]。但如前述全球化的浪潮造成法院須有更寬廣的管轄基礎及更自由的裁量空間，嚴謹的「困擾性」或「壓迫性」法學不得不於停止法院地之訴訟上，在Spiliada Maritime Corpn v. Cansulex Ltd[134]中正式退讓給較為寬鬆的「不方便法院」。但是於Société Nationale Industrielle Aérospatiale v Lee Kui Jak[135]中，大英國協最高法院（the Privy Council）認定在Spiliada後，將限制外國訴訟之標準與停止英國訴訟之標準，如以前一般視為相同是不對的。因為如此會違反禮誼原則，及忽視了禁訴令只能於正義之目的有需求時才能被許可之基本要件。於該案中Lord Goff說[136]：「在如同本案件之情形下，當對一個不當行為之救濟是同時存在於……英國法院及外國法院時，……英國法院一般而言，通常只會於如果這種訴訟會構成困擾性或壓迫性時才會禁止原告於外國法院提起這種程序。」如Cheshire and North評論[137]：「這個舊名詞（困擾性或壓迫性）因而與自然法院的現代名詞結合。根據Lord Goff[138]，前提必須通常是英國法院先認為其為合適審判的自然法院，然後才會採取現代的困擾性或壓迫性標準。」一般是認為英國法院較不願在外國法院決定其管轄權前就許可禁訴令[139]。又因困擾性或壓迫性法學之要件是較不方便法院嚴

132 Cohen v Rothfield [1919] 1 KB 410.
133 Castanho v Brown & Root (UK) Ltd [1981] AC 557 a5 574 (per Scarman).
134 [1987] AC 460.
135 [1987] AC 871.
136 Société Nationale Industrielle Aérospatiale v. Lee Kui Jak [1987] AC 871 at 896. "in a case such as the present where a remedy for a particular wrong is available both in the English ⋯ court and in a foreign court, the English ⋯ court will, general speaking, only restrain the plaintiff from pursuing proceedings in the foreign court if such pursuit would be vexatious or oppressive."
137 Cheshire, North and Fawcett, p.460, "This old terminology was then combined with the modern terminology of the natural forum. According to Lord Goff, the vexation or oppression test that is now being adopted generally presupposes that the English court has first concluded that it provides the natural forum for trial."
138 Société Nationale Industrielle Aérospatiale v. Lee Kui Jak [1987] AC 871 at 896.
139 Amchem Products Inc v Workers' Compensation Board (1993) 102 DLR (4th) 96 at 118 (per Sopinka J); Deaville v Aeroflot [1997] 2 Lloyd's Rep at 67; Pan American World Airways Inc v Andrew 1992 SLT 268.

格，僅是法院地為自然法院並不能滿足這個要件[140]。必須能證明如若當事人被允許於外國進行訴訟會對被告構成不正義之情形才可滿足要件。因為法院最大的考量為正義之目的，故外國訴訟中原告的利益亦需被加以考量，如Société Aérospatiale中所說[141]：「如果禁訴令的許可會剝奪原告於外國法院之利益，而這會構成不公正的剝奪其權利，法院不會許可禁訴令。」

Société Nationale Industrielle Aérospatiale v. Lee Kui Jak[142]是一般被認為有關困擾性或壓迫性之行為而給予禁訴令許可之案件[143]。「死者為婆羅洲之居民，因被告法國公司所造之直昇機掉於婆羅洲而死亡。該直昇機是由一馬來西亞公司所操作。因法國公司於德州有營業，故死者之遺孺於德州及婆羅洲起訴告法國及馬來西亞公司。法國公司要求原告停止德州之訴訟，大英帝國協最高法院發給禁止訴訟之命令。英國法院為自然法院並不足以構成禁止於外國訴訟之理由，必須該外國訴訟對被告造成困擾或壓迫方可。首先要求被告於不同之法院去答辯，已構成不公正之情形[144]。另外法國公司無法對馬來西亞公司於德州求償，必須於婆羅洲另外起訴，對其亦不公平。此外原告於德州訴訟所取得之證據及專家之證詞等利益，因被告法國公司同意亦可於婆羅洲適用，故原告被禁止於德州訴訟，對其並無不公正之情形。另外如個人早期所言[145]，訴訟雖然相同，但相同當事人之原告或被告之地位於不同國家不同時，法院應對停止訴訟之進行更為謹慎[146]，此觀點亦為本案所採。值得注意的是，歐盟及海牙會議之lis pendens對此方面則並未有所區分。法院認為外國訴訟之原告被迫於英國訴訟

---

140 Cadre SA v Astra Asigurari SA [2005] EWHC 2626 (comm.) at [13], [2006] 1 Lloyd's Rep 560.

141 Société Nationale Industrielle Aérospatiale v. Lee Kui Jak [1987] AC 871 at 896, "the court will not grant an injunction if, by doing so, it will deprive the plaintiff of advantages in the foreign forum of which it would be unjust to deprive him."

142 [1987] AC 871.

143 陳隆修、許兆慶、林恩瑋、李瑞生四人合著，《國際私法—管轄與選法理論之交錯》，台北，五南圖書公司，2009年3月，初版1刷，245頁。

144 SCOR v. Eras EIL (No. 2) [1995] 2 ALL ER 278.

145 陳隆修，《國際私法管轄權評論》，台北，五南圖書公司，民國75年11月，初版，86、87頁。

146 E I Du Pont & Co v J C Agnew [1988] 2 Lloyd's Rep 240.

當被告，故應特別加以考慮[147]。個人則持老式看法，外國原告有權利依外國法而取得其合法之利益。」

於認定是否形成「困擾性」或「壓迫性」之標準時，所應注意的因素為當事人之利益、與另一個法院之關連、國際禮誼之規範、及禁止外國程序前所應有之戒慎[148]。如前述美國聯邦第二巡迴法院於反對意見所陳述，英國法院通常亦認為要求被告同時於兩個不同法院應訴可能等同於重大不公平[149]。重大不公平之情形亦包括當事人不能合適的準備其案件、外國法院被誤導、或當事人被迫去增加付出與案件無關之費用[150]；當被告於外國不能得到公平審判時[151]；當於外國之請求是基於惡意而提起時，或是一定會失敗時[152]；或是外國訴訟之被提起是為了防止其他法院之接受管轄而沒有其他之正當理由[153]。而違反專屬管轄條款之約定本身近來於英美法已被視為困擾性或壓迫性行為[154]，這是個人所反對的。雖然平行訴訟可能會產生相衝突之判決，或者競相取得判決以先產生一事不再理之效力[155]，但如同前述美國聯邦第二巡迴法院英國法院亦認為平行訴訟本身並非即構成困擾性或壓迫性之訴訟[156]。如果有足夠的關連及理由於外國提起訴訟，則不構成困擾性或壓迫性[157]。

---

147 *Cohen v Rothfield* [1919] 1 KB 410 at 414; *Hemain v Hemain* [1988] 2 FLR 388, 390.

148 *Metall und Rohstoff AG v ACLI Metals (London) Ltd* [1984] 1 Lloyd's Rep 598.

149 *SCOR v Eras EIL (No 2)* [1995] 2 All ER 278; *Advanced Portfolio Technologies Inc v Ainsworth* [1996] FSR 217; *FMC Corpn v Russell* 1999 SLT 99 at 102; *General Star v Stirling Cooke* [2003] EWHC 3 (Comm), [2003] IL Pr 19; *Albon v Naza Motor Trading Sdn Bhd (No 4)* [2007] EWHC 1897 (Ch), [2007] 2 Lloyd's Rep 420.

150 *FMC Corpn v Russell* 1999 SLT 99 at 102.

151 *Al-Bassam v Al-Bassam* (2004) EWCA Civ 857.

152 *SCOR v Eras EIL (No 2)* [1995] 2 All ER 278; *Shell International Petroleum Co Ltd v Coral Oil Co Ltd (No 2)* [1999] 2 Lloyd's Rep 606. See also *Trafigura Beheer BV v Kookmin Bank Co (No 2)* [2006] EWHC 1921 (Comm) at [51], [52], [2007] 1 Lloyd's Rep 669.

153 *Cadre SA v Astra Asigurari SA* [2005] EWHC 2626 (Comm) at [18], [2006] 1 Lloyd's Rep 560.

154 *Sohio Supply Co v Gatoil (USA) Inc* [1989] 1 Lloyd's Rep 588.

155 Seismic Shipping Inc Total E&P UK plc (The Western Regent) [2005] EWCA Civ 985 at [44].

156 Société Nationale Industrielle Aérospatiale v. Lee Kui Jak [1987] AC 871, 894.

157 Donohue v Armco Inc [2001[UKHL 64, [2002] 1 All ER 749 at [20] (per lord Bingham, Lords Mackay and Nicholls concurring), [45] (per Lord Hobhouse), Kornberg v Kornberg (1991) 76 DLR (4th) 379, Pan American World Airways Inc v Andrews 1992 SLT 268; Through Transport Mutual Insurance Association (Eurasia) Ltd v New India Assurance Co Ltd [2004] EWCA (Civ) 1598 at [96].

至於所謂當事人合法利益，個人以為與以前個人之論述[158]近似，故不再贅述。或許是採納不方便法院法學之故，如個人以前之論述[159]，現在較高之損害賠償額取得之利益似乎不若以前般的受到尊重[160]。而於Société Aérospatiale中，原告如果是不能證明德州的關連性，原告的欲取得美式的懲罰性賠償甚至會被認為是困擾性或壓迫性的證據[161]。而又如以前所述，律師抽成制及審判前事實調查庭並不能被視為合法之利益[162]。律師抽成制固然會鼓勵訴訟，但亦經常對弱勢之訴訟權有著甚大之保障，故個人認為不可一概而論。

英國法院於「自然法院」（natural forum）概念之形成是在不方便法院法學被正式採納之前[163]。於有關國家利益上，英國最高法院（House of Lords）於Airbus Industrie GIE v. Patel[164]中即認為，若英國法院是解決紛爭的自然法院，則就不會存在著有違反國際禮誼之情形。因為這已經給予英國充分的利益及關連，以致於在這個問題上可以給予禁訴令而合理的去間接的干擾到外國程序。

另外在這個第一小類別中還有一種情況是，於外國尚有具有管轄權之法院，但英國並沒有。於這種情況下通常英國法院是可能不會允許作成禁訴令。於Airbus Industrie GIE v. Patel[165]中，被告及其他被告們是英國居民，他們於印度之一場空難中死亡及受傷。他們或其家屬欲於德州對原告空中巴士提訴，但空中巴士於印度法院取得禁訴令，禁止被告們於印度外對原告提訴。由於禁訴令之作成必須本於對人管轄之基礎而來[166]，而被

---

158 陳隆修、許兆慶、林恩瑋、李瑞生四人合著，《國際私法—管轄與選法理論之交錯》，台北，五南圖書公司，2009年3月，初版1刷，211-215頁。

159 同上，202頁。

160 The Spiliada, [1987] AC 460 at 482-484.

161 [1987] 1 AC 871 at 899.

162 Simon Engineering plc v Butte Mining plc [1996] 1 Lloyd's Rep 104 n at 110-111; Simon Engineering plc v Butte Mining plc (No 2) [1996] 1 Lloyd's Rep 91 at 98-100; following Smith Kline & French Laboratories Ltd v Bloch [1983] 1 WLR 730, CA.

163 Rockware Glass Ltd v. MacShannon [1978] AC 795.

164 Airbus Industrie GIE v. Patel [1999] 1 AC 119 at 134, 138-139 (per Lord Goff), HL.

165 [1999] 1 AC 119, HL.

166 The Tropaioforos [1962] 1 Ll.R 410. 亦即被禁止之當事人必須於法院地受到送達，或接受法院之

告卻居住於英國，故印度禁訴令無法於英國生效。空中巴士要求英國法院執行印度禁訴令，或替代性的請求作成英國法院自己之禁訴令。因為案件不屬於布魯塞爾或Lugano公約，故一審Colman J[167]認為依英國判例法之傳統只能執行金錢債務之判決，並拒絕給予禁訴令。但上訴法院卻許可禁訴令[168]。後英國最高法院（the House of Lords）又撤銷禁訴令的給予。雖然印度法院是個自然法院，但卻無法對英國居民下達禁訴令，而英國法院又可以有效的禁止當事人於德州提起一個可被視為困擾性及壓迫性之訴訟。另外德州於其時尚未採取不受國際禮誼所尊重的「不方便法院」法學[169]（這裡指的應是美式「不方便法院」，英國於其時採納「不方便法院」已有十三年）。英國最高法院認為英國並沒有充分的利益或關連去作成禁訴令，以便間接的干擾外國法院程序之進行，若於此情形下作成禁訴令可能會與禮誼不一致。但依實體法論之觀點而言，真正的問題可能是在印度過低之賠償及美國懲罰性高度賠償間取得一個平衡，以達成真正正義之目的。

七、充足的利益或關連—大衛的魔術

在*Turner v Grovit*[170]中Lord Hobhouse認為會有其他「不公正的行為」（unconscionable conduct）造成當事人於外國有不被訴之權利，這不是基於外國法院的不合適或違背契約的約定，而是由於行為本身所引起。判例法傳統上並不願意對「不公正行為」下定義[171]，基本上它只是指違反英國的衡平法規則[172]而已，何謂「不公正」是不可能完全的被確切的加以定

管轄（submission），或即使不在法院地但依CPR Rule 6.20英國法院得將通知送達至域外。

167 [1996] ILPr. 465.

168 [1997] 2 Ll.R 8 CA.

169 事實上於作成判決時德州正採取不方便法院法學。

170 Turner v Grovit [2001] UKHL 65 at [25].

171 South Carolina Insurance Co v Assurantie NV [1987] AC 24 at 41, HL.

172 Barclays Bank plc v Homan [1993] BCLC 680 at 687 (Hoffmann J); [1993] BCLC 680 at 705, CA.

義[173]。於*British Airways Board v Laker Airways Ltd*[174]中，Lord Diplock認為不公正之行為應包含依照英國法一個人有權利不被起訴之抗辯，例如衡平禁反言、承諾、選擇、放棄、消滅時效屆至等。於South Carolina Insurance Co v Assurantie NV[175]中英國最高法院認為不公正之行為不只包括困擾性或壓迫性行為，並且包括「干擾法院適當程序」之行為（conduct "which interferes with the due process of the court"），這種行為有時亦被稱為濫用程序（abuse of precess）。*Turner v Grovit*[176]是被認為有關濫用程序之案件，因為其對英國法院進行中之程序產生不公正之後果。於該案中[177]，原告Mr. Turner為一住所於英國之英國人，於1990年受僱於一西班牙跨國集團之英國子公司，替其於倫敦從事兌換外幣之工作，於1997年原告主動要求對換至西班牙工作。於1998年3月原告於倫敦勞工法庭對該英國子公司提起訴訟，宣稱其可能為不法行為之受害者，公司等於對其造成不公平之解聘，英國法院准予其損害賠償之請求。於1998年7月該西班牙跨國集團於西班牙法院對Mr. Turner於職業上之行為，提起訴訟要求損害賠償。1999年5月英國上訴法院准予原告之要求，對該集團、其子公司、及集團總裁發給禁訴令，禁止他們於西班牙或其他地方對原告提起或繼續有關該僱傭契約之訴訟。上訴法院認為於西班牙之訴訟，是為了困擾原告於英國勞工法庭所提起之訴訟，是基於惡意（bad faith）而提起之訴訟。

英國最高法院認同上訴法院基於下列事實而給予禁訴令[178]：(1)申請人是英國程序中之當事人；(2)被告是惡意的於其他國家提起訴訟以阻礙英國程序；(3)法院認為欲保護申請人於英國程序中之合法利益須對被告給

---

173 Glencore International AG v. Exter Shipping Ltd [2002] EWCA Civ 528 at [42], [2002] 2 All ER (Comm) 1.

174 [1985] AC 58, 81.

175 [1987] AC 24, HL.

176 *Turner v Grovit* [2001] UKHL 65 at [24], [2002] 1 WLR 107.

177 見陳隆修，《歐盟經驗論中國式國際私法之建立》，高雄大學法學論叢6卷2期，2011年，23-39頁。

178 *Turner v Grovit* [2001] UKHL 65 at [29].

予禁訴令。英國最高法院[179]並對此問題交付歐盟最高法院（Court of Justice），詢問對於惡意阻撓英國程序之當事人於其他會員國提起程序時，給予禁訴令是否會與公約不一致？歐盟法院判決歐盟之管轄公約[180]：「應被解釋為，一個於一訂約國法院訴訟程序中之當事人，是不應被該國法院給予禁止該當事人於其他訂約國法院提起或繼續訴訟之命令，即使該當事人之目的是本於惡意的想阻礙該法院地原來既有的訴訟亦同。」

歐盟法院連續對英國法制的不方便法院及禁訴令作出「消滅英美法」的判決（截至目前為止較著名的有四個），自然引起全世界法界驚訝。歐盟法院於實質上是個執行歐盟法制統一的行政機構，或許不必給予太多注目與心思。但由實體法論而言，羅馬I第9條規定強行法，第8條[181]則規定個別僱傭契約之強行法。布魯塞爾規則第18至21條則是充滿著對受僱者之保護，第20條[182]更明定僱主只能於受僱者之家園對其提起訴訟，英國法院於本案之實質作法是合乎歐盟於管轄規則及實體選法規之強行政

---

[179] [2001] UKHL 65, [2002] 1 WLR 107, "to grant restraining orders against defendants who are threatening to commence or continue legal proceedings in another Convention country when those defendants are acting in bad faith with the intent and purpose of frustrating or obstructing proceedings properly brought before the English courts?"

[180] Case C-159/02, Gregory Paul Turner v. Felix Fareed Ismail Grovit, Harada Ltd. & Changepoint SA, [2004] ECR I-3565. "The Convention of 27 September 1968 on Jurisdiction and the Enforcement of Judgments in Civil and Commercial Matters, as amended by the Convention of 9 October 1978 on the accession of the Kingdom of Denmark, Ireland and the United Kingdom of Great Britain and Northern Ireland, by the Convention of 25 October 1982 on the accession of the Hellenic Republic and by the convention of 26 May 1989 on the accession of the Kingdom of Spain and the Portuguese Republic, is to be interpreted as precluding the grant of an injunction whereby a court of a Contracting State prohibits a party to proceedings pending before it from commencing or continuing legal proceedings before a court of another Contracting State, even where that party is acting in bad faith with a view to frustrating the existing proceedings."

[181] Article 8 Individual employment contracts

1.An individual employment contract shall be governed by the law chosen by the parties in accordance with Article3. Such a choice of law may not, however, have the result of depriving the employee of the protection afforded to him by provisions that cannot be derogated from by agreement under the law that, in the absence of choice, would have been applicable pursuant to paragraphs 2, 3 and 4 of this Article.

[182] Article 20

1. An employer may bring proceedings only in the courts of the Member State in which the employee is domiciled.
2. The provisions of this Section shall not affect the right to bring a counter-claim in the court in which, in accordance with this Section, the original claim is pending.

策。而更重要的是禁訴令的作成，個人以為重點並非在保護歐盟規則的一致性，或保護英國的司法程序不受阻礙，而是在「達成正義的真正利益」。全球化法學於二十一世紀勞工法之共同核心基本政策是在保護勞工與受僱人，於本案禁訴令之作成是符合這個全球化法學之共同核心，亦符合「不患寡患不均」之中國核心政策，因此於本案個人是認同禁訴令之作成。

於Airbus Industrie GIE v Patel中，個人已本於實體法論而認為真正的問題是在美國超額的懲罰性賠償及印度可能過低之賠償（個人推測），而於國際案件中這兩種情況可能皆不符合一般所同意的公平正義的解答。**Lord Goff的要件為英國必須有充分的利益或關連才能給予禁訴令，事實上是與達成正義的解決方法無關的。或許我們可以說這是禁訴令上英國版的利益說與最重要關連說的再次結合——或者我們乾脆說英國禁訴令版的「最低限度關連點」。而對於正宗的美版「最低限度關連」，於選法規則上個人是認為是實體政策的障眼法，於管轄規則上個人是認為是「鬼打牆」法學。或許禁訴令的是否給予應慎重的考慮到所牽連的實體政策，亦即考慮到全球化法學政策中之個案正義。**

另外在所謂的「單一法院案件」（single forum cases）中指的並非僅是被禁止進行程序的法院是唯一有管轄權之法院，而是包含該法院是請求人唯一能有訴因（勝訴之機會）之法院[183]。於引起國際矚目及國際糾紛的教科書案例（反托辣斯及國際私法）British Airways Board v Laker Airways Ltd.[184]中，一家英國航空公司加入英國航空公會，其他航空公司依公會規章而聯合訂定票價。依英國法該英國航空公司對其他航空公司並無訴因存在，但其他航空公司之行為卻違反美國反托辣斯法。英國最高法院拒絕作成禁止該英國航空公司於美國起訴之命令。法院認為該美國訴訟並非基於英國票價而起訴，而是基於違反美國法律。雖然美國反托辣斯法

[183] Barclays Bank plc v Homan [1993] BCLC 680 at 698, CA.

[184] [1985] AC 58 HL又見陳隆修、許兆慶、林恩瑋、李瑞生四人合著，《國際私法-管轄與選法理論之交錯》，台北，五南圖書公司，2009年3月，初版1刷，245、246頁。

的多重損害賠償之判決無法於英國被執行，英國法院裁量權之行使並未受到影響。因為美國是該英國航空公司唯一可以取得救濟之國家，法院認為其他有數個可供利用法院之案件應與本案分開，並且對本案並無助益[185]。於這種單一法院案件中，對於是否作成禁訴令通常法院是有著「非常必要」（very necessary）去小心謹慎的[186]。雖然公會及其他航空公司主張該航空公司既然加入公會，就對會員依公會之規則訂定票價不能反對。但法院仍認為於美國提起程序之行為並非不公正之行為，因為該航空公司於美國之訴訟並非基於票價，而是基於其他航空公司之違反美國法律[187]。有趣的是美國倍數損害賠償之判決於英國因為1980年保護貿易法之通過是不能被執行[188]，但法院對此點似乎不加以考慮。

事實上保護貿易法著名的特色並不是在於拒絕執行，而是對於在美國已付之超額損害賠償是可以回到英國法院全數「抓回」。但或許正如德國跨國企業一般，通常英國跨國企業亦是於美國有資產且經營業務，故「抓回」理論似乎無用武之地。個人與黃進教授曾論及保護貿易法，但我們皆同意該法應以國力為後盾。至於本案所牽連之實體法共同核心主流價值是非常明顯的——契約之履行是不能違反當地合乎情理之法律。這不但是法律，亦是常識。羅馬I規則9(3)條[189]明文規定得對履行地之強行法之效力加

---

[185] [1985] AC 58, at 80, 85.

[186] 同上，at 95.

[187] [1985] AC 58, at 84-85.

[188] Protection of Trading Interests Act 1980, s 5.本案有趣之處為國務卿根據該法之第2及3條發佈命令，禁止其他兩家航空公司去遵守美國反托辣斯法及提供有關美國訴訟之資料及證據。本案有趣之處為對於美國之訴訟，行政與司法部門之觀點是不同的。Lord Diplock認為申請禁訴令之航空公司必須能證明他們已有著一個訴因存在以致禁訴令可成為一種救濟手段，或者他們已有著法律上或衡平上之權利不應於外國法院以外國訴因而被起訴，例如基於契約（如英國法院管轄條款）或他方當事人不公正的行為（如禁反言、選擇、放棄、或時效等依英國法有著抗辯之理由），因為法院許可作成禁訴令之權力只限於這些情況。而其他航空公司並沒有這種訴因或權利。The Siskina [1979] AC 210, 256 HL.有趣的是Lord Diplock認為行政部門對the Protection of Trading Interests Act 1980的解釋是根據錯誤的觀念。因為美國法院將美國法律適用於發生於美國之行為上並沒有侵犯英國的主權（sovereignty），故而英國公共政策並未受到侵犯。但行政部門認為美國違反條約。有關於公平競爭法世界上許多國家採「效力理論」，但由本案可見其效力是同時產生於英美兩國。個人認為最主要還是要達成主流共識，亦即可接受行為之界限。

[189] 3. Effect may be given to the overriding mandatory provisions of the law of the country where the obligations arising out of the contract have to be or have been performed, in so far as those overriding mandatory provisions render the performance of the contract unlawful. In considering whether to give effect

以尊重。遠在2008年羅馬I之前，個人早期即已強調這個國際法規[190]。個人近年來在全球化法學之觀點下，更發現這已不單純是國際法之常規，亦已是實體契約法之重要內容，例如Unidroit Principles of International Commercial Contract 2004的7.2.2條[191]即白紙黑字的規定於「法律或事實不能」之下得不履行義務。**故契約之履行不能違反履行地合理之法律已是全球化法學之共同核心基本政策，該航空公司之依據美國履行地法之合法行為自然不能被視為不公正之行為，反而他方之行為才是違反全球化法學之不公正行為。請問Lord Goff契約不得違反履行地法之全球化法學與「英國充分的利益或關連」有何必要的連接性？**

與*British Airways Board v Laker Airways Ltd*相關連的即為前述之*Midland Bank plc v Laker Airways Ltd*[192]，兩個案件皆基於相同的紛爭。但前者禁訴令之申請是被拒絕的，於後者該航空公司之破產管理人卻被給予禁訴令，禁止其於美國對兩家英國銀行提起反托辣斯訴訟。在Airbus Industrie GIE v. Patel中，Lord Goff認為英國法院必須與該系爭問題有著充分的利益或關連才能作成禁訴令。對*Midland Bank*案件Lord Goff[193]認為相關之交易行為最主要皆是屬於英國性質，故是符合這個要件，而*British Airways Board*卻不符合這個要件。但是對這種解決方式並非所有英國同僚皆認同，亦有提出質疑者[194]。事實上在反托辣斯法上許多國家是

---

to those provisions, regard shall be had to their nature and purpose and to the consequences of their application or non-application.

190 見陳隆修，《國際私法契約評論》，台北，五南圖書公司，民國75年2月，初版，80、81頁。

191 Article 7.2.2 (Performance of non-monetary obligation)
Where a party who owes an obligation other than one to pay money does not perform, the other party may require performance, unless
(a) performance is impossible in law or in fact;
(b) performance or, where relevant, enforcement is unreasonably burdensome or expensive;
(c) the party entitled to performance may reasonably obtain performance from another source;
(d) performance is of an exclusively personal character, or
(e) the party entitled to performance does not require performance within a reasonable time after it has, or ought to have, become aware of the non-performance.

192 [1986] QB 689, CA.

193 Airbus Industrie GIE v. Patel [1999] 1 AC 119 at 138 (per Lord Goff), HL.

194 J. G. Collier, Conflict of Laws, 3rd ed., p. 105, "It can be said that though the House's decision put an end to a conflict between the English and the United States courts, it hardly answers the objection to

採「效力理論」，而根據這個理論其他英國航空公司及英國銀行之行為，對於英國及美國之市場及消費者皆產生嚴重之後果。並且無論是於英國或美國反托辣斯法或保護消費者法毫無疑問的皆屬於歐盟的所謂強行法。而根據羅馬I規則9(1)[195]條強行法之定義為：「強行法就是被一個國家認為在為了保護其公共利益方面，例如其政治、社會或經濟制度上是非常重要的法律，無論是依本規則該契約應適用之法律為何，只要是符合他們之範圍內他們重要到皆應被加以適用。」這種法規或許英美法沒有直接之論述，但相對之概念可被稱為「超越性考量」或「基本政策」。而且無論是英美法或大陸法（羅馬規則9(2)條），法院地之強行政策或考量是不能被超越的。故而無論英國法院或美國法院對航空公司或銀行的行為，對其牽連到反托辣斯法及消費者之利益，是皆有著「充足的利益或關連」的。如果真有區別，那就是銀行之行為屬於間接性的。但反托辣斯法之核心困難即為所有跨國公司之秘密協定皆發生於外國，意定外國法為準據法，而且不接受產生效力國家之管轄。如果不同意個人之論述，可以請教臺灣一些被嚴厲的指控、打壓之企業。反托辣斯法是超乎這些傳統的考量，而專注在效力（effect）的產生[196]。這些跨國銀行如果不知道他們的行為會於美國產

allowing one British company to sue two other British companies in a foreign court when it could not do so here. Nor foes it give much weight to the argument, based on public policy, against making the executive and the courts appear to be speaking with different voices on a matter which affects relations with another state."

[195] Article 9 Overriding mandatory provisions

1. Overriding mandatory provisions are provisions the respect for which is regarded as crucial by a country for safeguarding its public interests, such as its political, social or economic organisation, to such an extent that they are applicable to any situation falling within their scope, irrespective of the law otherwise applicable to the contract under thus Regulation.
2. Nothing in this Regulation shall restrict the application of the overriding mandatory provisions of the law of the forum.

[196] 但是即使是依傳統的國際私法，行為雖發生於外國，但「間接」的效果發生於損害發生地，通常還是會以損害發生地法為依據，故英國最高法院之論述是違背國際法與常識的，見羅馬II規則第4(1)條。

Article 4 General rule

1. Unless otherwise provided for in this Regulation, the law applicable to a non-contractual obligation arising out of a tort/delict shall be the law of the country in which the damage occurs irrespective of the country in which the event giving rise to the damage occurred and irrespective of the country or countries in which the indirect consequences of that event occur.

另外依美國Restatement of the Law, Third, Foreign Relations Law of the United States, § 402之

生效力，那就是非常奇怪的不專業。如果換成是台灣銀行，很可能會被歐盟及美國處以鉅額罰金。

如果完全遵照於Airbus Industrie GIE v. Patel中Lord Goff之標準，事實上英國及美國於兩個案件中皆有著充分的利益或關連。如全世界所矚目的，這兩個案件充滿著司法與政治的衝突。個人認為禁訴令的作成還是應回歸二十一世紀全球化法學的共同核心——正義的真正利益是否最能被達成。而在這兩個案件中，英美兩國法院所應確認的應是該其他航空公司與英國銀行直接或間接的行為是否傷害了交易的公平性，違反了禮運大同反資本主義的暴利商業詐欺手段。正如於所有反托辣斯案件中，欲辨認出所被宣稱之秘密協定是最困難的部分，而英國法院卻技巧的避開這個核心困難。「充足的利益或關連」或許正如「利益說」與「最重要關連說」一般，是一種避開實體政策的障眼法理論，是一種柿子挑軟的規避手段，是國際私法的大衛虛幻魔術法學。

依判例法顯示英國法院給予禁止訴訟命令裁量權行使之基本原則為「當為了避免不公正而合適」[197]（where it is appropriate to avoid injustice）去行使時，或當外國程序是「違反衡平及正直的良心時」[198]（contrary to equity and good conscience）。而如前述於Société Industrielle Aérospatiale v Lee Kui Jak[199]中，大英國協最高法院（the Privy Council）

---

(1)(c)，即使行為發生於外國，只要於美國產生重大效力，美國各州法仍可適用，而依該402條英國法亦可適用，故而兩國皆有「充足的利益」。所謂「充足的利益或關連」可能如「利益說」與「最重要關連說」一般，經常是實體政策之障眼術。

§ 402 Bases of Jurisdiction to Prescribe

Subject to § 403, a state has jurisdiction to prescribe law with respect to

(1)(a) conduct that, wholly or in substantial part, takes place within its territory;

(b) the status of persons, or interests in things, present within its territory;

(c) conduct outside its territory that has or is intended to have substantial effect within its territory;

(2) the activities, interests, status, or relations of its nationals outside as well as within its territory; and

(3) certain conduct outside its territory by persons not its nationals that is directed against the security of the state or against a limited class of other state interests.

同樣的效力理論又見第2新編國際私法27(1)(i)條之規定。

197 Castanho v Brown & Root (UK) Ltd [1981] AC 557, 573.

198 Carron Iron Co v Maclaren (1855) 5 H.L.C. 416, 439.

199 [1987] A.C. 871.

認為禁訴令所適用之原則，不應與於Spiliada Maritime Corpn v Cansulex Ltd[200]中所發展出來的不方便法院（forum non conveniens）法則一致。因為如果兩個法則一致的話，若於外國法院與英國法院對於「自然法院」（the natural forum）之觀點不一致之情形下，經由禁訴令之許可，英國法院會對於案件之解決可能產生自我攬權之現象，而這可能是「與國際禮儀不合」及「忽視禁訴令只能在正義的目的之要求下才能被允許之基本要件」[201]。在Société Nationale Industrielle Aérospatiale v. Lee Kui Jak[202]中，法院認為通常英國法院需要為自然法院，才能給予禁訴令制止於外國程序中困擾性或壓迫性之行為。於Airbus Industrie GIE v. Patel[203]中，這個要件更被提昇至一般性的規則。但是英國法院自一百多年前就故意不對這些名詞給予一個完全性或限制性之定義[204]，較近法院又認為「衡平法的寬度及靈活性不能被類別化所破壞」[205]。Cheshire and North對於「國家利益」與「私人利益」之區別似乎過分執著，由大處而言國家是有著利益去維護私人合法之利益。過分執著於類別化之要件可能沈淪至迷惑於類別化之皮相，而「忽視禁訴令只能在正義的目的之要求下才能被允許之基本要件」，及「為了避免不公正而合適」之情形下才能行使這個裁量權。

八、禁止濫用程序

無論是稱為「侵犯當事人不於外國被訴之法律或衡平上之權利」、「不公正之行為」、「困擾性或壓迫性」、「妨礙法院的正當程序」[206]、

---

200 [1987] A.C. 460.

201 “be inconsistent with comity”, “disregard the fundamental requirement that an injunction will only be granted where the ends of justice so require.” [1987] A.C. 460, 495 (Lord Goff).

202 [1987] A.C. 871, 896.

203 Airbus Industrie GIE v. Patel [1999] 1 A.C. 119.

204 McHenry v Lewis (1882) 22 Ch. D. 397, 407-408 (CA); Re Connelly Bros Ltd [1911] 1 Ch. 731. 746 (CA).

205 “the width and flexibility of equity are not to be undermined by categorisation”, Castanho v Brown & Root (UK) Ltd A.C. 557, 573. cf. Soc Nat Ind Aérospatiale v Lee Kui Jak [1987] A.C. 871, 982 (PC).

206 在Seismic Shipping Inc v Total E & P UK plc [2005] EWCA Civ. 985, [2005] 2 All E.R. (comm.) 515中，於一個海商請求，英國法院雖然作成賠償額之限制，但法院認為不能因為不能確認外國法院是否會承認英國之命令之有效性即作成禁訴令。由實體法論而言海商之國際公約經常不一

或更通常為「濫用程序」（abuse of the process），這都代表了法院追求個案正義的決心，禁訴令只有在追求個案正義的目的下才具有正當性。雖然英國嚴格的限制濫用程序於有關程序上之自然正義上，但於二十一世紀全球化法學的廣泛概念下，自然正義與實質正義已無法再嚴守十九世紀單純社會的單純界線。美國與日本於管轄權上之「最低限度關連」與日式的「不方便法院」即為程序上自然正義與實質正義概念混和之代表。如果禁止濫訴的概念——無論被定位為自然或實質正義——為許多文明國家所接受，那麼可能禁訴令之被作成及應否被其他國家所接受，皆應本著「禁止濫訴」這個全球化法學的共同核心。

英美法——特別是英國法長久之傳統——經常會制止當事人之濫用程序，但大陸法並非沒有這概念。於ALI/ UNIDROIT Principles of Transnational Civil Procedure之第2.5條之comment P-2F[207]中，有趣的將停止或駁回訴訟之方法，比喻為英美法之不方便法院法學及大陸法的防止濫選法院之法學。而且更有趣的是註釋中闡明本2.5條應與第3條的當事人程序上公平條款一起被解釋，特別是應去防止可能發生3.2條基於國籍、居所、及外地人參加訴訟之困難而來的歧視之情形。無論濫用程序是於那一個法系是以那一種名詞被稱呼，其為二十一世紀全球化管轄規則之核心概念是個不爭之事實，而其核心之目的則是在確認「正義的真正利益在那裡最能被達成」——故而禁訴令之行使與是否應被其他國家所接受，應在這個全球化管轄規則之核心目的下被檢驗。

衡平法的靈活性既然不能被類別化所破壞，濫用訴訟程序自然於全球化法學中亦不能被類別化所破壞，即使於任何一個國家之制度內亦不應被類別化。濫用程序之範圍雖然無法限制，但於美國通常被舉之例子為美

致，很難認定世界上會有一致之意見，故不宜輕易作成禁訴令。

207 P-2F The concept recognized in Principle 2.5 is comparable to the common-law rule of forum non conveniens. In some civil-law systems, the concept is that of preventing abuse of the forum. This principle can be given effect by suspending the forum proceeding in deference to another tribunal. The existence of a more convenient forum is necessary for application of this Principle. This Principle should be interpreted in connection with the Principle of Procedural Equality of the Parties, which prohibits any kind of discrimination on the basis of nationality or residence. See Principle 3.2

國聯邦民事訴訟法（FRCP）的Rule 11(b)，其規定[208]呈交法院之主張於已經過合理之查詢後，當事人必須真誠的相信：「(1)其並非為了不適當之目的而被提出，例如去困擾（他方）、造成不必要的遲延、或不必要的增加訴訟之費用；(2)主張、抗辯、及其他法律上之辯論是目前法律所許可的，或為了延伸、改進、或推翻現有法律的非輕率之辯論，或為了建立新法律；(3)對於事實上之抗辯是有著證據上之支持，或如果是特別的被確認出來時，會在更進一步的調查或查詢之合理的機會後將可能有支持的證據；及(4)於有證據之支持下事實上之抗辯是可被拒絕的或，如果特別的被確認出來時，其是合理的基於信念或缺乏資訊之故。」Rule (c)[209]規定對於違反Rule (b)之情形法院對於律師、事務所、或當事人得給予合適之處罰，法院並得主動命令當事人證明行為之理由。

---

208 (b) Representations to the Court.

By presenting to the court a pleading, written motion, or other paper – whether by signing, filling, submitting, or later advocating it – an attorney or unrepresented party certifies that to the best of the person's knowledge, information, and belief, formed after an inquiry reasonable under the circumstances:

(1) It is not being presented for any improper purpose, such as to harass, cause unnecessary delay, or needlessly increase the cost of litigation;

(2) the claims, defenses, and other legal contentions are warranted by existing law or by a nonfrivolous argument for extending, modifying, or reversing existing law or for establishing new law;

(3) the factual contentions have evidentiary support or, if specifically so identified, will likely have evidentiary support after a reasonable opportunity for further investigation or discovery; and

(4) the denials of factual contentions are warranted on the evidence or, if specifically so identified, are reasonably based on belief or a lack of information.

209 (c) Sanctions.

(1) In General.

If, after notice and a reasonable opportunity to respond, the court determines that Rule 11(b) has been violated, the court may impose an appropriate sanction on any attorney, law firm, or party that violated the rule or is responsible for the violation. Absent exceptional circumstances, a law firm must be held jointly responsible for a violation committed by its partner, associate, or employee.

…………….

(3) On the Court's Initiative.

On its own, the court may order an attorney, law firm, or party to show cause why conduct specifically described in the order has not violated Rule 11 (b)

(4) Nature of a Sanction.

A sanction imposed under this rule must be limited to what suffices to deter repetition of the conduct or comparable conduct by others similarly situated. The sanction may include nonmonetary directives; an order to pay a penalty into court; or, if imposed on motion and warranted for effective deterrence, an order directing payment to the movant of part or all of the reasonable attorney's fees and other expenses directly resulting from the violation.

即使是一向重視判例法的英國法制，亦於其民事訴訟法規CPR rule 3.4(2)中規定[210]：「法院得排除案件之陳述，如果對法院而言它顯示出：(a)該案件之陳述並未表達抗辯對方之請求，或提出請求，之任何合理的理由；(b)該案件之陳述是濫用法院之程序，或是可能造成公平正義的處理該訴訟程序的障礙……」而如美國FRCP, Rule 11 (c)(3)，英國的CPR rule 3.3亦規定[211]法院得依申請或主動行使其權力，對於濫用程序的制止是不只侷限於審判的過程中確保程序上的自然正義，更重要的是希望能達成公平正義的實質結果。因為如同前述，雖然自然正義是侷限於程序上之正義，但較近的判例法顯示程序上重大的瑕疵亦會構成實質上之不正義[212]。因此有關濫用程序上的問題，或許不應單純視為程序上有關自然正

[210] Civil Procedure Rules
3.4 Power to strike out a statement of case
"(1) In this rule and rule 3.5, reference to a statement of case includes reference to part of a statement of case.
(2) The court may strike out a statement of case if it appears to the court –
(a) that the statement of case discloses no reasonable grounds for bringing or defending the claim;
(b) that the statement of case is an abuse of the court's process or is otherwise likely to obstruct the just disposal of the proceedings …."

[211] Civil Procedure Rules, 3.3 Court's power to make order of its own initiative
(1)Except where a rule or some other enactment provides otherwise, the court may exercise its powers on an application or of its own initiative.

[212] 英國上訴法院於*Adams v Cape Industries plc*, [1990] Ch 433 at 564中，認為美國德州聯邦地院並未依法而個別的估量各個原告之損害，而只平均估量206個原告之損害，又被告因未出席而無法得知其評估之方法，故而亦無法於原審法院請求救濟。因此程序上之瑕疵（自然正義之違反）已構成「英國法院所認為的實質正義的違反」，"a breach of an English court's view of substantial justice".
但Cheshire and North, 14th ed., p. 566,認為："The use of the concept of substantial injustice in relation to the recognition and enforcement of foreign judgments creates new uncertainty over the ambit of the defence of natural justice. Cases of procedural unfairness which do not involve a lack of due notice or opportunity to be heard would be better dealt with under the defence of public policy."其之觀點可能受到英國加入歐盟法學之影響。傳統上判例法對於「違反英國實質正義概念」（"which offends against English ideas of substantial justice", Middleton v Middleton [1967] P 62 at 69）的外國離婚是有權力去拒絕承認的。但自加入歐盟後，歐盟法規並未明文基於實質正義得拒絕承認外國離婚判決。可是歐盟法規仍允許會員國基於自然正義（Brussels II bis, Art 22(b); Family Law Act 1986, s 51(3)(a)）及公共政策（Brussels II bis, Art 22(a); Family Law Act 1986, s 51(3)(c)）之理由而去拒絕承認外國離婚判決。
對於由實質正義的概念轉向公共政策的概念，Lord Simon於Vervaeke v Smith [1983] 1 AC 145 at 164中，認為兩個概念於實質上應是相同的。而英國的Law Commission亦認為法院於處理兩個概念的方式是相同的（Law Com No 137 (1984), para 2.26）。道德經32章：「道常無名」。新約哥林多後書第3章：「因為那字句是叫人死，精意（聖靈）是叫人活。」Shadwell V-C認為：「無論何時只要正義很明顯的被忽略，法院就必須將該判決視為沒有價值與實質上不存在。」Price

義之問題，其亦牽涉到實質正義上自然法之概念。

九、程序自然正義與自然法實質正義的結合

於二十一世紀全球化法學中，程序自然正義與實質正義上自然法概念的結合之全球化趨勢，個人以為最明顯的例子或許為ALI/UNIDROIT Principles of Transnational Civil Procedure的28.3條[213]的規定爭點禁反言只能適用於防止重大的不正義上。另外更有趣的是其comment P-28C[214]是將大陸法自然法概念的「誠信原則」與英美法程序自然正義之爭點禁反言相提並論——故而二十一世紀全球化法學之重點是在實質政策之共同核心，而非各法律制度於邏輯上之區別。

事實上在英國判例法之發展史上，禁止濫用程序、一事不再理、及禁反言是有著密切關連的[215]。於Henderson v Henderson[216]中Sir James Wigram早在1843年即宣布：「除了於特殊情形下，一事不再理之主張不但適用於事實上當事人要求法院去作成之意見及宣布之判決之問題上，並且適用於屬於案件之主體之每一問題上，而這些問題是當事人於其時在合理的勤奮下應會提出來的。[217]」亦即「當一個特定的問題成為於一個有管

---

v Dewhurst (1837) 8 Sim 279 at 302, "whenever it is manifest that justice has been disregarded, the court is bound to treat the decision as a matter of no value and no substance".二十一世紀全球化法學之心與靈魂在個案正義，而不是20世紀所產生的法律邏輯是否能於二十一世紀仍保有一致性。而這或許就是羅馬公約與規則於強行法上雖然一團混亂但仍被堅持下去的真正核心政策。

213 28.3 The concept of issue preclusion, as to an issue of fact or application of law to facts, should be applied only to prevent substantial injustice.

214 "Some legal systems, particularly those of common law, employ the concept of issue preclusion, sometimes referred to as collateral estoppel or issue estoppel. The concept is that a determination of an issue as a necessary element of a judgment generally should not be reexamined in a subsequent dispute in which the same issue is also presented. Under Principle 28.3, issue preclusion might be applied when, for example, a party has justifiably relied in its conduct on a determination of an issue of law or fact in a previous proceeding. A broader scope of issue preclusion is recognized in many common-law systems, but the more limited concept in Principle 28.3 is derived from the principle of good faith, as it is referred to in civil-law systems, or estoppel in pais, as the principle is referred to in common-law systems.

215 見陳隆修，〈97台上2376號〉，陳隆修、宋連斌、許兆慶著，《國際私法—國際程序法新視界》，五南出版，2011年，92-98頁。

216 [1843] 3 Hare, 99; [1844] 6 Q.B. 288.

217 "The plea of *res juducata* applies, except in special cases, not only to point upon which the Court was actually required by the parties to form an opinion and pronounce a judgment, but to every point which

轄權法院的訴訟及審判中之主體，法院要求訴訟當事人去提出他們整個案件，（除了於特殊情形下）對於有關抗辯主體的一部分應可以被提出來，但只因為疏忽、不小心或甚至意外而忽略他們案件之一部分，而未被提出，則不允許相同當事人再次提出相同的訴訟主體。[218]」一般是認為這個論述適用於一事不再理、禁反言、及濫用程序（abuse of the process）上，這種情形令人想起中國話的「萬流歸宗」、「反璞歸真」。

Somervell LJ於Greenhalgh v Mallard中說：「那些爭點或事實明顯的是構成訴訟主體之一部分，並且是很明顯的可以在以前可以被提出，如果一個有關他們的新程序可以再被提起就會形成對法院程序的濫用。[219]」Lord Diplock在Hunter v Chief Constable of the West Midlands Police中說：「雖然與其程序規則之實際適用並沒有不一致，但仍然會對訴訟當事人造成明顯的不公平，或者於思考正確的人間造成正義的實施會有不名譽之情形下，任何法院皆一定要有此種既存的主動權去防止這種不當的運用其程序之行為。濫用程序可能發生於非常不同的情形；會上訴到本院（最高法院）一定是非常特別的。我認為如果本院若藉此機會去陳述任何會被認為去限制或訂定這種情形之種類之事情是很不智的，而這些情形是法院有義務（我拒絕裁量權之名詞）去行使這個有益的權力的。[220]」Lord

properly belonged to the subject of litigation, and which the parties, exercising reasonable diligence, might have brought forward at the time." [1843] 3 Hare, 99, 115.

218 "In trying this question I believe I state the rule of the Court correctly when I say that, where a given matter becomes the subject of litigation in, and of adjudication by, a Court of competent jurisdiction, the Court requires the parties to that litigation to bring forward their whole case, and will not (except under special circumstances) permit the same parties to open the same subject of litigation in respect of matter which might have been brought forward as part of the subject in contest, but which was not brought forward, only because they have, from negligence, inadvertence, or even accident, omitted part of their case." [1843] 3 Hare, 99, 114, 115.

219 [1947] 2 All ER 255, 257, "issues or facts which are so clearly part of the subject-matter of the litigation and so clearly could have been raised that it would be an abuse of the process of the court to allow a new proceeding to be started in respect of them."

220 "inherent power which any court of justice must possess to prevent misuse of its procedure in a way which, although not inconsistent with the literal application of its procedural rules, would nevertheless be manifestly unfair to a party to litigation before it, or would otherwise bring the administration of justice into disrepute among right-thinking people. The circumstances in which abuse of process can arise are very varied; those which give rise to the instant appeal must surely be unique. It would, in my view, be most unwise if this House were to use this occasion to say anything that might be taken as limiting

Bingham在Johnson v Gore Wood & Co中解釋這種權力之使用情形：「於RSC Ord. 18, r. 19中可發現這種權力之一種表現，這使得法院在任何階段之程序中，去駁回任何顯示不合理的訴因或防禦之主張，或其為不名譽、輕率或困擾性，或是其可能濫用法院之程序。現在於CPR r. 3.4亦有相同之權力。[221]」因此如Lord Diplock所說的濫用程序是不能被「限制或訂定這種情形之種類」，其目的是為了避免「明顯的不公平」或「造成正義的實施會有不名譽之情形」。而同樣的在Johnson v Gore Wood & Co中，Lord Bingham亦說[222]：「由於我們無法將所有可能濫用的形式皆廣泛

---

to fixed categories the kinds of circumstances in which the court has a duty (I disavow the word discretion) to exercise this salutary power." [1982] AC 529, 536.

221 [2002] 2 AC 1, "One manifestation of this power was to be found in RSC Ord 18, r. 19 which empowered the court, at any stage of the proceedings, to strike out any pleading which disclosed no reasonable cause of action or defence, or which was scandalous, frivolous or vexatious, or which was otherwise an abuse of the process of the court. A similar power is now to be found in CPR r 3.4."

222 在Johnson v Gore Wood & Co [2002] 2 AC 1中，Lord Bingham亦認為「濫訴之形式無法表列，亦無法組成死硬的規則」，但「對於保證正義的利益卻是很重要」。

"But Henderson v Henderson abuse of process, as now understood, although separate and distinct from cause of action estoppel and issue estoppel, has much in common with them. The underlying public interest is the same: that there should be finality in litigation and that a party should not be twice vexed in the same matter. This public interest is reinforced by the current emphasis on efficiency and economy in the conduct of litigation, in the interests of the parties and the public as a whole. The bringing of a claim or the raising of a defence in later proceedings may, without more, amount to abuse if the court is satisfied (the onus being on the party alleging abuse) that the claim or defence should have been raised in the earlier proceedings if it was to be raised at all. I would not accept that it is necessary, before abuse may be found to identify any additional element such as a collateral attack on a previous decision or some dishonesty, but where those elements are present the later proceedings will be much more obviously abusive, and there will rarely be a finding of abuse unless the later proceeding involves what the court regards as unjust harassment of a party. It is, however, wrong to hold that because a matter could have been raised in earlier proceedings it should have been, so as to render the raising of it in later proceedings necessarily abusive. That is to adopt too dogmatic an approach to what should in my opinion be a broad, merits-based judgment which takes account of the public and private interests involved and also takes account of all the facts of the case, focusing attention on the crucial question whether, in all the circumstances, a party is misusing or abusing the process of the court by seeking to raise before it the issue which could have been raised before. As one cannot comprehensively list all possible forms of abuse, so one cannot formulate any hard and fast rule to determine whether, on given facts, abuse is to be found or not. Thus while I would accept that lack of funds would not ordinarily excuse a failure to raise in earlier proceedings an issue which could and should have been raised then, I would not regard it as necessarily irrelevant, particularly if it appears that the lack of funds has caused by the party against whom it is sought to claim. While the result may often be the same, it is in my view preferable to ask whether in all the circumstances a party's conduct is an abuse than to ask whether the conduct is an abuse and then, if it is, to ask whether the abuse is excused or justified by special circumstances. Properly applied, and whatever the legitimacy of its descent, the rule has in my view a valuable part to play

的加以表列，故而我們亦無組成任何死硬的規則……這個規則是於保證正義的利益之目的下一個很重要的部分。」

個人以為在Hunter v Chief Constable of the West Midlands Police中Lord Diplock所說的有著特別的意義：「雖然與其程序規則之實際適用並沒有不一致，但仍然會對訴訟當事人造成明顯的不公平，或者於思考正確的人間造成正義的實施會有不名譽之情形下，任何法院皆一定要有此種既存的主動權去防止這種不當的運用其程序之行為。……而這些情形是法院有義務（我拒絕裁量權之名詞）去行使這個有益的權利的。[223]」故有關濫訴第一要點是為了「防止不公正」、「實施正義」。而第二要點即其「形式無法表列，亦無法組成死硬的規則」。第三要點即其超越訴訟程序中當事人主義之進行，法院有「責任、義務（非為法院之裁量權）去行使這個有益的權力」。第四點為「即使與程序規則之實際適用並無不一致之處」，但會對當事人造成「明顯的不公或不正義」之情形下，「任何法院皆一定要有此種既存的主動權去防止這種不當的運用其程序之行為」。故而很明顯的程序上自然正義的規定，有時在正義的需求下，應以個案正義的自然法概念為其適用之基礎及限制。很明顯的二十一世紀全球化法學於管轄權上之規則——包含衡平法上的禁訴令及各國之禁止濫訴——的心與靈魂就在個案正義是否能被達成。

雖然禁止濫訴亦是不能被類別化所破壞，但個人以為英國之Civil Procedure Rules, Rule 1[224]或許是個值得參考的指標：「(1)這些規則是一

---

in protecting the interests of justice."

[223] [1982] AC 529, 536.

[224] (1) These Rules are a new procedural code with the overriding objective of enabling the court to deal with cases justly.
(2) Dealing with cases justly includes, so far as practicable –
(a) ensuring that the parties are on an equal footing;
(b) saving expense;
(c)dealing with the case in ways which are proportionate –
(i) to the amount of money involved;
(ii) to the importance of the case;
(iii) to the complexity of the issues; and
(iv) to the financial position of each party;

個新的程序上法規，而其超越性目的是在使得法院能公正的處理案件。(2)於儘可能的範圍內，公正的處理案件包含——(a)確保當事人之立足點平等[225]；(b)節省費用；(c)以符合比例之方式去處理案件——(i)所牽連金額之數量；（ii）案件之重要性；（iii）爭點之複雜性；及（iv）各個當事人財產之情況[226]；(d)確保案件公平及迅速的被處理；及(e)於考慮分配資源之需要性下，給予案件法院資源合適之配額。[227]」雖然這個規則是指示法院公正的處理案件，而非針對當事人之濫用程序。但由於濫用程序是無法被表列，故或許妨礙法院公正的處理案件之超越性目的即可能是類似或接近濫用程序。尤其過去二十世紀在WTO及其唱和組織諾貝爾和平獎的強勢運作下，所謂的「自由市場」完全是掠奪性帝國資本主義之市場，全球化產生了極端的貧富不均。故而二十一世紀的全球化管轄規則應特別重視「當事人立足點之平等」及「當事人之財產狀況」。

聯合國高峰會於1992年Rio Declaration on environment and Devel-

(d) ensuring that it is dealt with expeditiously and fairly; and
(e) allotting to it an appropriate share of the court's resources, while taking into account the need to allot resources.

225 當事人立足點平等於21世紀貧富不均的全球化世界是非常重要的一點。個人亦因此而反對2005年海牙公約與英美於管轄條款及仲裁條款的超約性考量。個人認為管轄及仲裁條款應受到程序法立足點平等及契約法平衡性的約束。

226 個人曾於拙作陳隆修、許兆慶、林恩瑋、李瑞生四人合著，《國際私法—管轄與選法理論之交錯》，台北，五南圖書公司，2009年3月，初版1刷，235、236頁中評論其時轟動台灣社會之中美混血兒童監護權案。個人淺見後為台北地院95年度監字第84號民事裁定所採，見陳隆修，《2005年海牙法院選擇公約評析》，台北，五南圖書公司，2009年1月，初版1刷，151、152頁，可是對於陳隆修、許兆慶、林恩瑋、李瑞生四人合著，《國際私法—管轄與選法理論之交錯》，台北，五南圖書公司，2009年3月，初版1刷，235、236頁中強烈的主張應以當事人財力不平等而要求法院重審已為外國所判定之監護權，「個人感到非常遺憾」的是兩岸年輕同僚雖認同個人觀點，但似乎皆未注意到此點。道大、天大、地大、人亦大。個人自詡為終生的法律學生，故個人自詡亦為很大。當事人財力的不平等，不但有違程序上之自然正義，更不符合自然法的精神，亦違反中國禮運大同之王道精神。21世紀全球化訴訟法必須遵守立足點真正平等的超越性政策。作為一個法律學生，個人與此論述在此一起立下投名狀。立足點平等於21世紀全球化訴訟法上相同的精神亦表現在集體訴訟法上，其號稱是現代社會（第三世界）平民的大衛對抗哥萊亞巨人的跨國企業之彈弓。

227 英國判例法是反對美式「公共利益」之不方便法院。

opment中之第5條[228]宣示決心欲「降低生活水平之差距」，第6條[229]則又規定「開發中國家之特別環境及需要應被給予特別優先」。聯合國高峰會又後續於2002年之Johannesburg declaration on Sustainable Development之14條[230]公開宣示：「全球化的利益及代價並未平均分配，面對這個挑戰開發中國家遭遇著特別的困難」。而第15條[231]則承認：「我們有著加深全球化不平均之危險，除非我們行動的方式能由基本上改變他們的生活，貧窮世界可能失去對我們仍舊深信的民主制度及他們的代表之信心，而視他們的代表只不過是會發聲的管樂器及發亮的鐃鈸。」於聯合國高峰會連續對全球化所產生貧富不均的負面效果加以作成正式宣言後，作為法律學生的我們對全球化法學於二十一世紀之發展，自然應以這些宣言為全球化法學之基礎原則及警察原則。全球化法學無論是於實體法或程序法自然皆應以這些宣言為核心共同政策。故於全球化管轄規則之禁訴令或禁止濫訴上自然亦應以此些宣言為共同核心——亦即必須去確保當事人立足點之平等及避免貧富差距所產生之不公正。

故無論是於契約法上之要求平衡性原則，於訴訟法上要求立足點平等及避免當事人貧富不均所產生之不公正，及最重要的聯合國數次高峰會針對「全球化的利益及代價並未平均分配」，因而要求「降低生活水平之差距」，以上這些實體法、訴訟法、及聯合國高峰會宣言不但是二十一世紀

---

228 Principle 5
All States and all people shall cooperate in the essential task of eradicating poverty as an indispensable requirement for sustainable development, in order to decrease the disparities in standards of living and better meet the needs of the majority of the people of the world.

229 Principle 6
The special situation and needs of developing countries, particularly the least developed and those most environmentally vulnerable, shall be given special priority. International actions in the field of environment and development should also address the interests and needs of all countries.

230 Globalization has added a new dimension to these challenges. The rapid integration of markets, mobility of capital and significant increases in investment flows around the world have opened new challenges and opportunities for the pursuit of sustainable development. But the benefits and costs of globalization are unevenly distributed, with developing countries facing special difficulties in meeting this challenge.

231 We risk the entrenchment of these global disparities and unless we act in a manner that fundamentally changes their lives the poor of the world may lose confidence in their representatives and the democratic systems to which we remain committed, seeing their representatives as nothing more than sounding brass or tinkling cymbals.

全球化法學的共同核心基本政策，更是中華民族二千五百年來我們祖先的「不患寡患不均」「禮運大同」的「王道」思想。故個人對率先提倡中國式法學的黃進、趙相林教授於此再次鄭重回應——二十一世紀的全球化法學不但應本著聯合國高峰會之宣言，更應本著中國歷經數千年戰火災難經由我們祖先之血淚生活經驗所千錘百鍊凝聚而成之「不患寡患不均」「禮運大同」之「王道」文化為核心基礎。中國二千五百年來屹立不搖的「王道」文化既然與現代聯合國高峰會的屢次正式宣言一致，二十一世紀全球化法學以中國思想為基礎原則，及為於個案上對抗實體法或程序法所可能產生之不公正之警察原則，自然是水到渠成順理成章。

十、對禁訴令之建議

(一)禁止濫用程序為全球化共同核心

對於濫用程序台灣民訴249之(2)、(3)條規定法院可以直接駁回甚至處以罰鍰[232]。另外449之1條及495之1條亦有類似規定，故三級之法院皆有此權力。而日本民事訴訟法303條[233]亦有濫用程序之禁止規定。

於德國雖然似乎沒有如英美法之濫用程序，但或許如德國同僚所

232 II原告之訴，依其所訴之事實，在法律上顯無理由者，法院得不經言詞辯論，逕以判決駁回之。

III前項情形，法院得處原告新臺幣六萬元以下之罰鍰。

233「高等法院，依前條第一項之規定駁回上訴時，若認定上訴人係以拖延訴訟為目的而提起訴訟者，得命上訴人繳交上訴費用10倍以下之金額。

依前項規定所為之裁判，必須揭載於判決主文。

依第一項所為裁判，經判決變更時，失其效力。

最高法院，駁回上訴時，得變更依第一項規定所為之裁判。

第一八九條之規定，準用於依第一項規定所為之裁判。」以上翻譯為蕭淑芬副教授所提供，特此感謝，但個人自負謬誤之責。又見如下判決：最高裁昭和53年7月10日第一小法廷判決（昭和52年(オ)第1321號社員總會決議不存在確認請求事件）；札幌高裁昭和41年9月19日決定（昭和41年(ラ)第32號移送申立卻下決定に對する即時抗告事件）；名古屋地裁昭和40年9月30日決定（昭和35年(ワ)第178號借地權確認等請求事件）；札幌高裁昭和51年11月12日決定（昭和51年(行ス)第3號裁判官忌避申立卻下決定に對する即時抗告申立事件）；最高裁昭和63年1月26日第3小法廷判決（昭和60年(オ)第122號損害賠償請求事件）。以上感謝蔡華凱教授提供，但個人自負謬誤之責。

說[234]：「於德國民事訴訟法，『合法的利益去提起訴訟』[235]是一般被認為程序上之先決要件，該要件之缺乏會使得訴訟沒有訴因而被駁回[236]。這個『合法的利益去提起訴訟』是先假設原告同時具有一個有效的訴因及一個誠實信用之意圖以便其夠資格得到程序上及法律上之保護，並且會考慮到其他因素例如便利性及有效性等[237]。就只有在於社會及社區之容忍限制範圍內法律之保護才會被允許。『濫用程序』造成這種保護之喪失及原告被拒絕『合法的利益去提起法律訴訟』[238]。當評量原告之『合法的利益去提起法律訴訟』，法院是參考司法程序的目的並因此而行使類似早期英美法『濫用程序』法學之標準。[239]」又說[240]：「如果在另一方面而言若產生濫用制度，既有的法理及程序上的原則，例如『缺乏合法的利益去提起法律訴訟』的法理及BGB第242條『誠實信用』的要求，給予（法院）足夠的工具去補救這種情況，而不必依賴司法上一般性的裁量權法理。[241]」這個

[234] Alexander Reus, A Comparative View of the Doctrine of Forum Non Conveniens in the United States, the United Kingdom, and Germany, 16 Loy. L.A. Int'l & Comp. L.J. 455, 498, 499 (1994), "In German civil procedure, the 'legitimate interest to take legal action' is a commonly acknowledged procedural prerequisite, the lack of which leads to a dismissal for nonsuit. This 'legitimate interest to take legal action' presupposes both a valid cause and a good-faith intention on the part of the plaintiff to qualify for procedural and legal protection, and takes into account considerations such as expediency and effectiveness.

Legal protection is only granted within the limits tolerated by society and community. An 'abuse of process' results in the loss of such protection and in the denial of the plaintiffs 'legitimate interest to take legal action.' When evaluating the plaintiff's 'legitimate interest to take legal action.' Courts refer to the purpose of the judicial process and thereby engage in a test that resembles the 'abuse of process' approach of early Anglo-American law."

[235] Klinkhardt, 7 Munchener Kommentar Zum BGB art. 22 EGBGB n. 202 (1983)' OLG Zweibrucken, 1973 FamRZ 479; Jayme, 1984 IP Rax 124; Heldrich Palandt, Kommentar zum BGB art. 22 EGBGB n. 4(c)(bb) (51st ed. 1992).

[236] Rosenberg & Schwab, Zivilprozessrecht 93IV (14th ed. 1986); Thomas & Putzo, ZPO-Kommentar pre 253m (18th ed. 1993); Hartmann et al., ZPO-Kommentar at Grundz. 253 (5A) (50th ed.1992).

[237] Rosenberg & Schwab, supra note 276, 93 IV(1).

[238] BGH, 1976 GRUR 257; 1 Ekkehard Schumann et al., Kommentar zur ZPO pre 253 n. 118 (20th ed.1984).

[239] 或許此處指的是先前英國「困擾性」或「壓迫性」濫訴。

[240] 16 Loy. L.A. Int'l & Comp. L.J. 455, 510, "If, on the other hand, an abuse of the system should occur, existing doctrines and procedural principles, such as the doctrine of 'lacking legitimate interest to take legal action' and the 'good faith' requirement of Section 242 of the BGB, provide sufficient tools to remedy the situation without resorting to a general discretionary doctrine of the judiciary."

[241] BGH, 1983 NJW 1269, at 1270.

所謂的「合法利益」或許有些類似美國法上所謂「地位」（standing）之概念[242]，而並非為有關管轄權之問題[243]：「但是有理論上及法理上的問題以致反對於『缺乏合法的利益去提起法律訴訟』時去拒絕管轄——這個法理不能於管轄階段被採用。依據對『缺乏合法的利益去提起法律訴訟』之嚴格解釋，其適用更可能導致沒有訴因的被駁回而非沒有國際管轄權。」

雖然這個德國理論是有關實體上之判決，而非有關管轄權之階段[244]。但是於全球化法學之觀點下，目前似乎我們是可以滿意於有著一個禁止濫用程序的共同核心基本政策的存在，而不必拘泥於各個法系是以程序自然正義之方式來達成，或以實體法上自然法之概念來達成。如前述全球化法學於此方面最明顯的將程序上自然正義與自然法之概念結合的為ALI/UNIDROIT Principles of Transnational Civil Procedure（2004）。其2.5條之註釋P-2F中是將大陸法的濫選法院與英美法的不方便法院相提並論，而這些法理皆必須依第3條的當事人程序公平條款而被加以解釋，尤其特別應注意的是第3條的解釋是以自然法概念之「合理性」為基礎。而28.3條的註釋P-28C更是明白的將英美法程序上的「衡平禁反言」與大陸法自然法概念的「誠信原則」相比擬。故只要是能防止當事人濫用司法程序困擾對方，無論是以「不公正行為」、「困擾性」、「壓迫性」、「一事不再理」、「禁反言」、「濫用程序」等程序上自然正義之名稱，

---

242 見Black's Law Dictionary, 7th ed., p. 1413, standing, n. A party's right to make a legal claim or seek judicial enforcement of a duty or right. To have standing in federal court a plaintiff must show (1) that the challenged conduct has caused the plaintiff actual injury, and (2) that the interest sought to be protected is within the zone of interests meant to be regulated by the statutory or constitutional guarantee in question. 又見16 Loy. L.A. Int'l & Comp. L.J. 455, 491.

243 16 Loy. L.A. Int'l & Comp. L.J. 455, 502, "Yet, there is a theoretical and dogmatic objection to declining jurisdiction according to the doctrine of 'lacking legitimate interest to take legal action' – this doctrine cannot be applied at the jurisdictional stage. According to a strict interpretation of the doctrine of 'lacking legitimate interest to take legal action,' its application would more likely lead to a dismissal for nonsuit than to a lack of international jurisdiction."

244 16 Loy. L.A. Int'l & Comp. L.J. 455, 510, "The doctrine of 'lacking legitimate interest to take legal action' theoretically applies in areas covered in the United States by forum non conveniens, and somehow resembles the 'abuse of process' version of the doctrine. These doctrines cannot be fairly compared with each other, however, due to the limited applicability of the doctrine of 'lacking legitimate interest to take legal action.' That doctrine is restricted to decisions on the merits, in order to prevent the courts from denying a plaintiff access to a proceeding at the jurisdictional stage."

或是於實體法上以「誠信原則」、「合理性」、「合法利益」等自然法之概念，於全球化法學之概念下皆是有著共同的核心基本政策。

故而在全球化法學的概念下，禁訴令隨著全球化經濟市場的擴展，亦可視為全球化法學日益拓展之一個環節。若外國法院所作成禁訴令之基礎為當事人於程序上的濫用程序違反自然正義，或其之行為違反誠信原則的自然法概念[245]，則為了達成當事人間之公平正義，在符合法院地法濫用程序或誠信原則之既有標準下，自然可以執行外國法院之禁訴令。但是外國禁訴令之作成基礎若不符合法院地既有的濫用程序自然正義之標準，亦不符合法院地既有的實體上誠信原則之自然法概念，自然可以不承認外國法院所作成之禁訴令。因為美國聯邦各州間、歐盟會員國內、及英國法院於傳統上皆沒有承認外國法院所作成之禁訴令之義務，故中國法院若不承認外國（通常是英美法）法院所做之禁訴令，自然不會違反國際禮誼及既有的國際慣例[246]。

---

245 ALI/UNIDROIT Principles of Transnational Civil Procedure 的第11條可為全球化法學於禁止濫訴上之代表，該條文規定當事人及其律師對法院及其他當事人之行為，必須符合誠信及道德上之標準，並應避免程序上之濫用。

11. Obligations of the Parties and Lawyers

11.1 The parties and their lawyers must conduct themselves in good faith in dealing with the court and other parties.

11.2 The parties share with the court the responsibility to promote a fair, efficient, and reasonably speedy resolution of the proceeding. The parties must refrain from procedural abuse, such as interference with witnesses or destruction of evidence.

11.3 In the pleading phase, the parties must present in reasonable detail the relevant facts, their contentions of law, and the relief requested, and describe with sufficient specification the available evidence to be offered in support of their allegations. When a party shows good cause for inability to provide reasonable details of relevant facts or sufficient specification of evidence, the court should give due regard to the possibility that necessary facts and evidence will develop later in the course of the proceeding.

11.4 A party's unjustified failure to make a timely response to an opposing party's contention may be taken by the court, after warning the party, as a sufficient basis for considering that contention to be admitted or accepted.

11.5 Lawyers for parties have a professional obligation to assist the parties in observing their procedural obligations.

Comment:

P-11D It is a universal rule that the lawyer has professional and ethical responsibilities for fair dealing with all parties, their lawyers, witnesses, and the court.

246 Story J.甚早以前就說：「如果一個文明的國家欲尋求其自己法院的判決於其它地方被認定為有效，他們應該公正的注意到其他文明國家的權利及慣例，及於行使正義時各國及國際共同的原則。」"If a civilized nation seeks to have the sentences of its own courts held of any validity

(二)契約條款不能被違反之神話法學

另外一個英美法院下禁訴令之理由（或許最常引為依據之理由），即為當事人違反契約條款而於外國起訴，例如專屬管轄條款及仲裁條款。個人近幾年已一再重申所有的契約條款皆應受到契約基本核心政策之制約，以防止契約上之不平衡。專屬管轄條款的超越性已為2005年海牙公約所大力提倡，並為個人近年來所極力反對，個人視這種管轄及仲裁條款超越性之法學為對第三世界的掠奪性新殖民主義法學。是違反契約法基本強行政策及人權公約的帝國主義法學，是司法霸權主義的終極表現。

個人以上激烈的指控是有著白紙黑字的證據。如個人最近所述[247]：「硬性的命令弱勢一方去強勢一方所指定之法院應訴或提訴，怎麼會是對第三世界人民『平等、衡平、及互利』之作法？2005年海牙公約及2008年鹿特丹規則不但違反了人類文明於契約法數百年來所發展出的保護弱勢之普世價值[248]，亦違反了風行於全世界半世紀的紐約公約第2(3)條、1985年模範公約第8(1)條、漢堡規則第21條、及聯合國自己的ALI/UNIDROIT Principles of Transnational Civil Procedure第2.4條。另外如前述亦違反了這些提倡這個『新不平等條約』的主要國家自己最高法院日積月累千錘百鍊之判例法，如歐盟法院之West Tankers[249]，英國最高法院之The Sen-

elsewhere, they ought to have a just regard to the rights and usages of other civilized nations, and the principles of public and national law in the administration justice" Bradstreet v. Neptune Ins. Co., 3 Summer, 600, 608.

247 陳隆修，《歐盟經驗論中國式國際私法之建立》，高雄大學法學論叢6卷2期，2011年，94、95頁。

248 例如美國2004年新版的統一商法1-302條即規定誠信原則、合理性、及適當注意性與勤奮性皆為強制性規定。See U.C.C 1-302:
1-302. VARIATION BY AGREEMENT
(a) Except as otherwise provided in subsection (b) or elsewhere in [the Uniform Commercial Code], the effect of provisions of [the Uniform Commercial Code] may be varied by agreement.
(b) The obligations of good faith, diligence, reasonableness, and care prescribed by [the Uniform Commercial Code] may not be disclaimed by agreement. The parties, by agreement, may determine the standards by which the performance of those obligations is to be measured if those standards are not manifestly unreasonable. Whenever [the Uniform Commercial Code] requires an action to be taken within a reasonable time, a time that is not manifestly unreasonable may be fixed by agreement.
而更有趣的是如後述，即使於非契約上之義務，歐盟2007年羅馬II之序言要點31即規定，於認定當事人間合意之存在時，應有某些強行之限制以保護弱勢之一方。

249 [2009] EUECJ C-185/07。

nar（No.2）[250]，及美國最高法院之The Bremen[251]。」

而對第三世界的弱勢人民而言，主張禁訴令的必要性及2005年海牙選擇法院公約的強行性之英美同僚有義務去回答英國Civil Jurisdiction and Judgment Act 1982, s. 32[252]之規定。其(1)(a)款雖然規定違反契約之約定不於所約定國家之法院解決紛爭，而於外國法院起訴之外國判決不應被承認與執行。但其第2項則規定：「於(1)(a)款所述之契約之約定是非法、無效、不能被執行或不能被履行時，且原因是不能歸責於提起已被作成判決之訴訟之當事人時，第(1)項之規定不適用。」第(3)項則規定有關第(1)或(2)項之任何問題，於決定外國法院所作之判決是否應被承認或執行上，英國法院不受外國法院之拘束。對於這的32條(2)、(3)項白紙黑字的規定，英美法的同僚於對外作成禁訴令或於2005年海牙選擇法院公約時，面對第三世界時或許可能集體得到失憶症。於仲裁條款上，或許同樣的集體暫時失憶症亦發生於對英國Arbitration Act 1996的第9條(4)項[253]上。這個規定與聯合國紐約公約的第2(3)條及1985模範公約第8(1)條一致。

但有趣的是英國仲裁法第7條[254]規定即使主契約被宣稱為無效、已被

---

250 [1985] 1 WLR 490 at 500。

251 407 U.S. 1 (1972)。

252 32. – (1) Subject to the following provisions of this section, a judgment given by a court of an overseas country in any proceedings shall not be recognized or enforced in the United Kingdom if –
(a) the bringing of those proceedings in that court was contrary to an agreement under which the dispute in question was to be settled otherwise than by proceedings in the courts of that country; and
(b) those proceedings were not brought in that court by, or with the agreement of, the person against whom the judgment was given; and
(c) that person did not counterclaim in the proceedings or otherwise submit to the jurisdiction of that court.
(2) Subsection (1) does not apply where the agreement referred to in paragraph (a) of that subsection was illegal, void or unenforceable or was incapable of being performed for reasons not attributable to the fault of the party bringing the proceedings in which the judgment was given.
(3) In determining whether a judgment given by a court of an overseas country should be recognized or enforced in the United Kingdom, a court in the United Kingdom shall not be bound by any decision of the overseas court relating to any of the matters mentioned in subsection (1) or (2).

253 (4) On an application under this section the court shall grant a stay unless satisfied that the arbitration agreement is null and void, inoperative, or incapable of being performed.

254 另外其第7條又規定仲裁條款之獨立性如下：
7. Unless otherwise agreed by the parties, an arbitration agreement which forms or was intended to

撤銷、非法[255]、或被違背而已解除[256]，該仲裁條款仍應被視為獨立，故仍應依仲裁條款之準據法去決定應否交付仲裁。這種仲裁條款之效力獨立於（或分開於）主契約效力之作法亦為其他仲裁機構所採，例如著名的ICC規則8.4條規定[257]「仲裁者如果認為仲裁條款有效，其不能因為主契約是被主張為無效或不存在而停止管轄權。即使是主契約本身是不存在或無效，其應繼續有管轄權去決定當事人之權利及仲裁他們的請求和主張。」聯合國1985年的模範仲裁公約第16(1)條[258]雖然有著類似規定，但其16(3)[259]條給予當事人上訴至法院之機會。這個「獨立性」原則亦為2005年海牙的選擇法院公約3(d)條所採，但法院之上卻沒有再上訴之機構。這種獨立性之法理已為一般判例法視為順理成章之事[260]。於Bremer Vulkan[261]

---

form part of another agreement (whether or not in writing) shall not be regarded as invalid, nonexistent or ineffective because that other agreement is invalid, or did not come into existence or has become ineffective, and it shall for that purpose be treated as a distinct agreement.這個獨立性（或分開性）又為2005年海牙選擇法院公約第3(d)條所採如下：

d) an exclusive choice of court agreement that forms part of a contract shall be treated as an agreement independent of the other terms of the contract. The validity of the exclusive choice of court agreement cannot be contested solely on the ground that the contract is not valid.

這種將契約條款之效力與整個契約效力硬是分開之作法是違反一般人之常識。這種將例外視為常規之奇怪作法完全是資本主義者之掠奪性作風，對弱勢者不利。如ALI/UNIDROIT Principles of Transnational Civil Procedure之comment P-3A所論述，「過分技術性之法律論述」是「不合理」的，亦即不公平的。這種論述之平衡點完全倒向資本主義。

255 Dalmia Dairy Industries Ltd. v. National Bank of Pakistan. [1978] 1 Lloyd's Rep 223 (CA).

256 Black Clawson International Ltd. v. Papierwerke Waldhof-Aschaffenburg AG [1981] 2 Lloyd's Rep. 446.

257 Art. 8.4: "shall not cease to have jurisdiction by reason of any claim that the contract is null and void or allegation that it is inexistent provided that he upholds the validity of the agreement to arbitrate. He shall continue to have jurisdiction, even though the contract itself may be inexistent or null and void, to determine the respective rights of the parties and to adjudicate their claims and pleads."

258 (1) The arbitral tribunal may rule on its own jurisdiction, including any objections with respect to the existence or validity of the arbitration agreement For that purpose, an arbitration clause which forms part of a contract shall be treated as an agreement independent of the other terms of the contract. A decision by the arbitral tribunal that the contract is null and void shall not entail ipso jure the invalidity of the arbitration clause.

259 (3) The arbitral tribunal may rule on a plea referred to in paragraph (2) of this article either as a preliminary question or in an award on the merits. If the arbitral tribunal rules as a preliminary question that it has jurisdiction, any party may request, within thirty days after having received notice of that ruling, the court specified in article 6 to decide the matter, which decision shall be subject to no appeal; while such a request is pending, the arbitral tribunal may continue the arbitral proceedings and make an award.

260 陳隆修，《2005年海牙法院選擇公約評析》，台北，五南圖書公司，2009年1月，初版1刷，63-65頁。

261 Bremer Vulkan Schiffbau und Maschinenfabrik v. South India ShippingCorporation, [1981] Lloyd'

中Lord Diplock說：「於本案中造船契約，除了仲裁條款外，已經停止執行之效力；當事人履行主要義務之時間已過去。在另一方面，造船契約其他條款上第二次義務的存在與範圍於當事人間如果繼續有紛爭，則仲裁條款應繼續有執行之效力。仲裁條款中之附隨約定並不完全符合雙方或單方或假設契約『如果』應如何之類之契約定性。這是當或如果一特殊事件發生時，當事人間已經同意各自應該作之行為之約定。」

依常理而言整個契約無效但其中之一個條款卻奇蹟式的仍為有效，這種例外或許會有，但肯定不是經常發生。這種企圖將例外硬拗成常規，是一種指鹿為馬之行為，並不符合人類的生活經驗，很明顯的法院促進「商業功效」的資本主義功利心態又是這種變態法學的主要原因。ALI/UNIDROIT Principles of Transnational Civil Procedure的第3條是規定保護當事人程序上公平之條款，其註釋P-3A[262]中特別強調種個規則充滿著

s Rep. 253, at 260, "in the instant case the shipbuilding agreement, apart from the arbitration clause, has ceased to be executory; the time for performance of the parties' primary obligations under it was past. The arbitration clause on the other hand would continue to remain executory so long as there were outstanding any dispute between the parties as to the existence or extent of their secondary obligations under the other clauses of the shipbuilding agreement. The collateral agreement contained in the arbitration clause does not fit readily into a classification of contracts that are synallagmatic on the one hand or unilateral or 'if' contracts on the other. It is an agreement between the parties as to what each of them will do if and when ever there occurs an event of a particular kind."

[262] P-3A The term "reasonable" is used throughout the Principles and signifies "proportional," "significant," "not excessive," or "fair," according to the context. It can also mean the opposite of arbitrary. The concept of reasonableness also precludes hyper-technical legal argument and leaves a range of discretion to the court to avoid severe, excessive, or unreasonable application of procedural norms.
但是在這種促進「商業效能」及仲裁及管轄條款效力「獨立」之氛圍下，當事人，尤其是若是之外國人，欲舉證條款無效、不成立、不存在、或已被撤銷是很困難的。通常舉證整個契約無效是不足夠的，必須是以證明該條款本身為無效或可撤銷才可以。如Cheshire, North and Fawcett, 14th ed., pp. 448, 449所說：
"However, a claimant can escape from a foreign exclusive jurisdiction clause by showing that it is void and therefore of no effect. It will only be in rare cases that the claimant will succeed in establishing this. It is not enough to show that part of the agreement between the parties is void, if the foreign choice of jurisdiction clause is still left intact. Neither it appears will it necessarily be enough for the claimant to show that the whole agreement of which the jurisdiction agreement is a part is void. There is support for the idea that a jurisdiction agreement (whether foreign or English) should be regarded as severable from the main contract in which the jurisdiction agreement is contained (in a clause). This is on the basis that the parties, when nominating a court to settle their disputes, may well have expected this court to try the issue of the validity of the main contract. This draws an analogy with the position in relation to arbitration agreements, which can be void or voidable only on grounds which relate directly to the arbitration agreement. Applying this analogy, where it is argued that there never was a main contract at all (eg

「合理性」的要求，而合理性的概念是「排除過分技術性的法律辯論」。將例外性的個案硬拗成全球化法學的硬規則，其目的就只有在促進跨國企業所期望的商業穩定性。做為法律學生我們所服務的是個案正義的利益，而非商業的利益。仲裁條款及管轄條款仍是契約法之一環，仍應受到契約平衡性要求之制約及訴訟法立足點平等之限制。

對於管轄條款之效力英國判例法是長久以來有著一致的看法[263]：「當事人若於契約中有指定專屬或非專屬[264]法院時，無論被指定之法院為英國或外國法院，英國法院之立場皆一致，亦即認為通常該被指定之法院為合適之法院。故如被指定之法院為外國法院時，除非有堅強之理由否則英國法院不會送達訴訟之通知至外國[265]。如果被告於英國境內時，英國法院亦通常會停止訴訟之進行，例如個人早期討論過之The Eleftheria[266]。但如早期亦經討論過為「正義且合適」（just and proper）之例外情形下，英國法院會繼續該訴訟之進行[267]。Brandon J.於The Eleftheria之意見後來又於The El Amria[268]中再重申一次如下：(1)當原告違反契約應將爭執交付外國法院之約定而於英國法院起訴，假定英法院有管轄權，而被告要求停止訴訟時，英國法院有裁量權去決定是否停止訴訟。(2)除非有相當強的理由，否則應停止訴訟。(3)原告應負起證明此相當強的理由的責任。(4)於行使裁量權時法院應考慮到個案中之所有情況。(5)於第(4)款之規定下應特別考慮下面情況：(a)案件事實的爭點的證據在那個國家或那個國家較

---

because of forgery), that will also be an attack on the validity of the jurisdiction agreement contained within the main contract. In contrast, an argument that the main contract can be rescinded because it was procured by bribery may affect the main contract but does not undermine the jurisdiction agreement."又見陳隆修，《2005年海牙法院選擇公約評析》，台北，五南圖書公司，2009年1月，初版1刷，46-54頁，特別是47頁有關聯邦巡迴法院之論述。

263 見陳隆修、許兆慶、林恩瑋、李瑞生四人合著，《國際私法—管轄與選法理論之交錯》，台北，五南圖書公司，2009年3月，初版1刷，198-200頁。

264 過去如果是專屬管轄條款，英國法院對於當事人欲違反該條款，要求會比非專屬條款來得高。Evans Marshall and Co Ltd v. Bertola SA [1973]1 WLR 349（要求繼續英國之訴訟），Mackender v. Feldid AC [1967]2 *OB 590*（要求通知送達至外國）。

265 *Evans Marshall & Co Ltd v. Bertola SA[1973]1 All ER 992*。

266 [1970] P94.

267 *The Fehmarn* [1958] 1 All ER 333

268 *Aratra Potato Co. Ltd v. Egyptian Navigation Co.*, The El Amria [1981] 2 Lloyd's Rep. 119, CA.

容易取得，比較英國與外國法院的便利性與訴訟之費用。(b)是否該外國法院之法律會被適用，如果被適用，是否會與英國法有重大不同[269]。(c)當事人是否與這些國家有密切關連。(d)被告是否真正的希望於外國審判，或只是希望取得程序上的優勢。(e)原告若於外國起訴是否會遭受到下列的不利：(i)他們的請求會沒有擔保；（ii）沒有辦法強制執行取得之判決（iii）遭受到英國所沒有的時效的限制；（iv）因為政治、種族、宗教及其他的理由而無法公平的受到審判[270]。」因此很明顯的英國法院之判例法顯示，傳統上對於管轄條款的效力之認定上，通常英國法院並不如於作成禁訴令或於2005年海牙選擇法院公約時一般的具有超越性之效力。其實同樣或更明顯的情形更出現在歐盟最高法院的West Tankers[271]及美國最高法院的The Bremen[272]中，而不可否認的這三個不同國家最高法院之判例都是國際上著名的案例。依常識而言一個學術理論要違反三個聲名卓越最高法院長久以來的領頭判例，其「合理性」證明可能是困難。

個人一再重申通常在符合契約法平衡性及訴訟法立足點平等之情形

---

269 *Spiliada Maritime Corpn. v. Cansulex Ltd.* [1987] AC 460.

270 英國最高法院於The Sennar (No.2) [1985] 1 WLR 490 at 500中確認這些原則。"The principles established by the authorities can, I think, be summarized as follows:(1)Where plaintiffs sue in England in breach of an agreement to refer disputes to a foreign court, and the defendants apply for a stay, the English court, assuming the claim to be otherwise within its jurisdiction, is not bound to grant a stay but has a discretion whether to do so or not.(2)The discretion should be exercised by granting a stay unless strong cause for not doing so is shown.(3)The burden of proving such strong cause is on the plaintiffs.(4)In exercising its discretion the court should take into account all the circumstances of the particular case.(5)In particular, but without prejudice to (4),the following matters, where they arise, may properly be regarded:(a)In what country the evidence on the issues of fact is situated, or more readily available, and the effect of that on the relative convenience and expense of trial as between the English and foreign courts.(b)Whether the law of the foreign court applies and, if so, whether it differs from English law in any material respects.(c)With what country either party is connected, and how closely.(d)Whether the defendants genuinely desire trial in the foreign country, or are only seeking procedural advantages. (e)Whether the plaintiffs would be prejudiced by having to sue in the foreign court because they would:(i)be deprived of security for their claim;(ii)be unable to enforce any judgment obtained;(iii)be faced with a time bar not applicable in England; or(iv)for political, racial, religious or other reasons be unlikely to get fair trial."另外於New Hampshire Insurance Co v. Phillips Electronics North America Corpn [1998] IL Pr 256, CA,英國法院認為法律問題與事實問題若分屬於不同之合適法院，兩者應合併於同一法院審理較好，而應以合適處理事實問題之法院優先。

271 [2009] EUECJ C-185/07.

272 The Bermen v. Zapata Off-shore Co., 407 U.S. 1 (1972).

下，個人並不反對仲裁條款及管轄條款等正常商業契約，但即使是較為注重「商業功效」的英美法院亦不見得完全支持這些條款之效力。The Hollandia[273]案為一般教科書上引為當事人之專屬管轄條款無效之案例，個人以為或許亦可成為羅馬公約或規則上所強調法院地強行法或公共政策之範例。於案中即使載貨證券中有規定應於荷蘭訴訟之專屬管轄條款，但原告貨主仍主張被告運送人違反契約要求損害賠償，並於英國提起對物訴訟。運送人依據該專屬管轄條款要求法院停止訴訟程序。因為根據the Hague-Visby Rules任何使得運送人之責任低於該規則之契約條款皆為無效，荷蘭法院所適用之荷蘭法對於運送人之責任是低於該規則之規定，因此該專屬管轄之條款會間接的降低運送人之責任。又因該規則已成為英國法[274]，故最高法院認為該專屬管轄條款為無效[275]。

另外傳統上英國判例法是通常視送達給境外之被告為「過度」或「不尋常」之情形。但於Evans Marshall and Co Ltd v. Bertola SA[276]中，即使契約中有約定外國法院為專屬管轄條款，英國法院仍決定允許將訴訟之通知送達給於外國之外國被告。於該案中，原告英國酒商與第一被告，西班牙造酒商，簽訂一個原告為第一被告於英國之獨家賣酒代理契約，並且同意任何糾紛應至西班牙法院處理。原告後來宣稱第一被告指定第二被告，另一英國商人，為代理人。原告於英國法院對兩個被告提出假處分及損害賠償之請求。因為主張之內容是有關於英國賣酒，主要證人於英國，第二被告為英國人而其中之一主張為兩個被告之企圖破壞契約，西班牙訴訟程序較英國慢，而且西班牙法院不允許假處分，故而英國上訴法院基於上述特殊情形，允許將訴訟之通知送達境外。全球化法學於管轄規則之心與靈魂在於個案正義之真正利益是否最能被達成。雖然通常送達境外之管

[273] [1983] 1 AC 565, [1982] 3 AllER 1141. 又見The Benarty [1984] 2 Lloyd's Rep 244，亦屬同樣海牙威士比規則之案件，但該案是以船所裝載噸位計算損害，而非以包裝的貨件計算，故符合規則，法院允許停止英國之程序。

[274] 見the Schedule of the Carriage of Goods by Sea Act 1971, Art III, para 8.

[275] 但見Baghlaf Al Zafer v PNSC [1998] 2 Lloyd's Rep 229 at 238, CA,如若被告願放棄外國法院最低責任額之保障，則管轄條款之效力仍會受到承認。

[276] [1973] 1 All ER 992, [1973] 1 WLR 349.

轄可能是構成「過度」或「不尋常」之管轄，只能於特殊情形下為之[277]，而當事人專屬管轄之約定亦應受到尊重，但於Evans Marshall and Co Ltd v. Bertola SA中法院為了「公正的處理案件之超越性目的[278]」，仍不得不送達給境外之外國被告而不受當事人間管轄條款的約束。故而2005年海牙選法公約的支持者及禁訴令之主張者或許必須接受一個事實——法院公正的處理案件之目的於判例法之傳統上是超越當事人契約上管轄條款之拘束力。個人曾經形容「最低限度關連點」的相關爭議過程為「鬼打牆」法學，或許由於故意藐視判例法長久演進的經驗，主張2005年海牙選擇法院公約及禁訴令中管轄條款之超越性的同僚亦陷入「鬼打牆迷思」。

至於有關當事人基於專屬管轄條款而請求法院作成禁訴令卻被拒絕之案例，較近亦發生於Donohue v Armco Inc[279]中。該案是有關於買賣股份之契約中包含著英國法院有專屬管轄之條款。原告於英國法院提出請求要求禁止被告於紐約提起訴訟程序。但於英國程序之被告確有著相當強之理由，足以取代申請人原告要求履行契約義務之通常既有之權利，因而原告要求禁止於紐約提起訴訟之請求為法院所拒絕。這是因為於紐約程序中之有些其他被告，他們於英國程序中有可能亦是共同請求者，而他們間有些人並未簽訂專屬管轄條款。法院之所以拒絕作成禁訴令之主要理由為，如果禁訴令被允許的話訴訟可能在被告以及原告請求人與其他共同請求者之間部分於紐約及部分於英國一起被進行[280]。因為將整個案件交給一個能處理所有爭執中之問題之單一法院，亦即紐約法院，是最能達成正義的利益[281]。

於Donohue中Lord Bingham認為一個當事人可能會由於拖延或其他

277 見陳隆修，《國際私法管轄權評論》，台北，五南圖書公司，民國75年11月，初版，45-47頁。

278 Civil Procedure Rules 1998, Rule 1.1,
(1)There Rules are a new procedural code with the overriding objective of enabling the court to deal with cases justly.

279 [2001] UKHL 64, [2002] 1 All ER 749.

280 Donohue v Armco Inc [2001] UKHL 64 at [33] (per Lord Bingham) and [75] (per Lord Scorr).

281 同上，at [34].

不公正之行為而失去其請求衡平救濟之權利[282]。因此愈晚申請禁訴令愈有被拒絕之理由，同樣的自願接受外國之管轄亦是拒絕之正當理由。特別是當外國程序已進行相當時間後，尤其是於申請停止外國程序而已失敗後，皆構成拒絕禁訴令申請之正當理由[283]。如Cheshire and North所說[284]：「於檢驗兩部門『禁訴令及停止訴訟』之許多判例後，Lord Bingham之結論為，當紛爭只是介於兩個訂約當事人間，而並未牽扯到其他當事人之利益時，通常專屬管轄條款是會被給予效力[285]。相對的，當除了訂專屬管轄條款之當事人外尚有其他當事人之利益是被牽連著，或者相關連之紛爭尚包含著不是該條款內容範圍內之請求理由時，可能會產生平行訴訟及判決不一致之危險時，英國法院可能拒絕給予一個禁訴令（或依案情拒絕停

---

282 同上，at [24].

283 Society of Lloyd's v White (No 1) [2002] IL Pr 10; Advent Capital plc v GN Ellinas Importers-Exporters Ltd [2003] EWHC 3330 at [26]-[44], [2004] IL Pr 23; cf Akai Pty Ltd v People's Insurance Co Ltd [1998] 1 Lloyd's Rep 90 at 107-108; DVA v Voest Alpine [1997] 2 Lloyd's Rep 279 at 288, CA.

284 Cheshire, North and Fawcett, 14th ed., p. 471, "After examining many of the authorities from both areas, Lord Bingham concluded that, where the dispute is between two contracting parties, and the interests of other parties are not involved, effect will in all probability be given to the exclusive jurisdiction clause. In contrast, the English court may well decline to grant an anti-suit injunction (or a stay as the case may be) where the interests of parties other than the parties bound by the exclusive jurisdiction clause are involved or grounds of claim not the subject of the clause are part of the relevant dispute so that there is a risk of parallel proceedings and inconsistent decisions. The principle that applies in cases of fourm non conveniens that, where there is a clause providing for the exclusive jurisdiction of the English courts, the courts should refuse to pay regard to matters of convenience that were foreseeable at the time the contract was concluded, has been applied in the present context."於Donohue v Armco Inc [2001] UKHL 64 at [24]中，Lord Bingham公開的宣示當事人於證明有強烈的理由下，契約上的專屬管轄條款是可以被違背的，法院亦有著裁量權去決定是否停止英國訴訟程序、作成禁訴令、或其他合適的程序上之命令："If contracting parties agree to give a particular court exclusive jutistiction to rule on claims between those parties, and a claim falling within the scope of the agreement is made in proceedings in a forum other than that which th parties have agreed, the English court will ordinarily exercise its discretion (whether by granting a stay of proceedings in England, or by restraining the prosecution of proceedings in the non-contractual forum abroad, or by such other procedural order as is appropriate in the circumstances) to secure compliance with the contractual bargain, unless the party suing in the non-contractual forum (the burden being on him) can show strong reasons for suing in that forum."
英國判例法於此方面的裁量權之行使已近兩百年，這已接近中國人所謂「自然道法」的境界。對於the House of Lords於領導判例Donohue v Armco Inc中斬釘截鐵的宣示，不知2005年海牙選擇法院公約的鼓吹者及禁訴令的狂熱者，如何面對這個聲名卓越的法院所呈現的白紙黑字的事實？

285 Donohue v Armco Inc [2001] UKHL 64 at [25]. See Horn Linie GmbH Co v Panamericana Formas e Impresos SA (The Hornbay) [2006] EWHC 373 (Comm), [2006] 2 Lloyd's Rep 44.

止訴訟）。[286]」故而除了契約法平衡性及訴訟法立足點平等之要求外，即使在滿足這些實體法及程序法上基本核心政策之要求下，在一般的商業契約中之專屬管轄條款，仍有可能為了避免「產生平行訴訟及判決不一致之危險」，英國法院可能拒絕給予一個禁訴令或依案情拒絕停止英國程序。故而2005年海牙選擇法院公約及禁訴令之支持者或許應該面對一個事實——自他們誕生之日起一百多年來當事人的選法條款、管轄條款、及仲裁條款的超越性自始至終都是神話。至少在可預見的將來這三個條款的超越性不可能出現在上帝所創造的人間，這種資本主義夢寐以求的幻境就只可能出現在資本主義者的天堂中——地獄。

286 同上，at [27].

第9章 結論——全球化之管轄規則

一、全球化法學下的禁訴令

(一)英國法院過度之信心

另外Cheshire and North[1]又認為在因當事人之專屬管轄條款之被違反而作成禁訴令禁止當事人於外國之程序，與因違反外國法院專屬管轄條款而停止英國之程序，所應考慮的因素是相關的，亦即上述Brandon J.於The Eleftheria中之論述。但是對於以「不方便法院」而停止英國程序與因外國法院專屬管轄條款而停止英國程序，個人先前如此評述[2]：「英美法對於專屬管轄法院之排他性並非如歐盟及海牙規則般為硬性的，英美法院還是有discretionary power去決定是否停止法院之訴訟，法院以類似『不方便法院主義』之考量基準去決定其裁量權。但英國認為這兩個理論還是有些不同之處。首先，如有外國專屬管轄條款時，英法院會傾向停止訴訟；而於『不方便法院』時，如若訴訟是適當的於英國被提起時，該訴訟通常應被允許進行。第二，於外國專屬管轄條款時，舉證責任在原告去證明訴訟不應停止；而『不方便法院』時，第一階段於證明『外國自然法

1 Cheshire, North and Fawcett, 14th ed., pp. 471, "These principle apply in both the contexts of an injunction restraining foreign proceedings brought in breach of an exclusive jurisdiction clause providing for trial in England and of a stay of English proceedings brought in breach of an exclusive jurisdiction clause providing for trial abroad. The matters that might properly be regarded by the court when exercising its discretion in the latter context are equally relevant in the former context. It follows that the matters listed by Brandon J in *The Eleftheria*, set out earlier in this chapter when discussing stays of action, should be considered when exercising the discretion to grant an injunction. This is not intended to be an exhaustive list."

2 陳隆修、許兆慶、林恩瑋、李瑞生四人合著，《國際私法-管轄與選法理論之交錯》，台北，五南圖書公司，2009年3月，初版1刷，154頁，註60。

院』時，舉證責任在被告。」

判例法經常認為因為違反專屬管轄條款與違反仲裁條款而給予禁訴令是通常沒有差別[3]。於Tracomin SA v. Sudan Oil Seeds Ltd (No. 2)[4]中，瑞士買方與蘇丹賣方雖訂有英國仲裁條款，但買方卻於瑞士法院對賣方提起告訴，故英國上訴法院給予禁訴令禁止當事人於瑞士之程序。而且這種外國判決於英國是不會被執行的[5]。英國上訴法院又於Continental Bank NA v Aeakos Compania Naviera SA[6]中，決定給予被告禁訴令禁止其於希臘之程序。這是因為被告之行為違反契約之約定，而英國法院依布魯塞爾公約17條有著專屬管轄權之故。

於The Angelic Grace中上訴法院對於當事人違反準據法為英國法之仲裁條款而於外國提起訴訟程序之行為給予禁訴令，法院認為只要申請人儘早提出申請並且於外國程序進行太深入前，法院應有信心可以給予禁訴令[7]。Cheshire and North在其較早論述中說[8]：「於The Angelic Grace中，在義大利被禁止的程序裡看來是有關民商之事情，但由於被告之住所是歐洲共同市場外。因此，看起來禁訴令的許可依本案之事實是不會與（布魯塞爾）公約不一致。」這些對司法正義有著令人敬佩造詣的英國資深同僚在信心滿滿的作完這個符合法律邏輯的論述後，相信他們很快就發現他們對人性的缺點（至少歐洲的缺點）似乎非常的陌生[9]。「消滅英國法」已

3 Aggeliki Charis Compania Maritima SA v Pagnan SpA, The Angelic Grace [1995] 1 Lloyd's Rep 87, CA, at 96.

4 [1981] 1 WLR 1026 at 1031.

5 Civil Jurisdiction and Judgments Act 1982, s. 32. Tracomin SA v. Sudan Oil Seeds Ltd (No. 1) [1983] 1 WLR 1026.

6 [1994] 1 WLR 588, CA.

7 Aggeliki Charis Compania Maritima SA v Pagnan SpA, The Angelic Grace [1995] 1 Lloyd's Rep 87, CA, at 96.

8 P M North, JJ Fawcett, Cheshire and North's Private International Law, 13th ed., p. 272, "In The Angelic Grace, the proceedings in Italy which were restrained appear to have involved a civil and commercial matter but one where the defendant was domiciled outside the EC. Accordingly, it seems that on the facts of the case there was no inconsistency with the Convention in granting the injunction."

9 見Case C-116/02, Erich Gasser GmbH v MISAT Srl, [2003] ECR I-14693; Case C-159/02, Turner v. Grovit, 2004 E.C.R. I-3565; Allianz SpA, Generali Assicurazioni Generali SpA, v West Tankers Inc. [2009] EUECJ C-185/07.

經是歐洲法學界最頂尖的時尚。

於The Angelic Grace中，Lord Justice Leggatt[10]認為違反仲裁條款構成「迅速作成禁止令之模範案例」（the paradigm case for the prompt issue of an injunction.）。其認為[11]如果義大利法院拒絕管轄，那麼那些程序會構成時間與金錢的浪費；反之，如果義大利法院接受管轄，那麼作成禁止令會造成與義大利法院有意的接受管轄之直接衝突。但是如果將其認定為當事人接受義大利之管轄，那麼就會產生兩組平行訴訟，而這正是仲裁條款以契約來設定確保就只有一組程序之目的，其又認為義大利法院於這種情形下不會認為英國禁訴令是違反國際禮誼[12]：「依我的觀點，我不認為如果在英國法決定英國仲裁條款之範圍後，然後以禁止令去限制傭船人再次於義大利法院重複提出程序以試其運氣之方式去執行這個決定，會使得義大利法院認為這是干擾國際禮誼。我認為如果英國法院採取下列的態度那就極度的自以為是，亦即如果義大利法院拒絕管轄，那就認同英國法院之態度，反之若義大利法院接受管轄，那時英國法院就會考慮是否在那個階段應以禁止令來介入。這非但是不好的而且是逆向的國際禮誼。」

但是更有趣的觀點來自Lord Justice Millett，其主張[13]禁訴令應於極度謹慎下才可被使用及甚少被使用的「儀式性經咒」（ritual incanta-

---

10 The Angelic Grace, [1995] 1 Lloyd's Rep. at 94.

11 同上，at 94-95, "Proceedings in a foreign Court are in breach of contract, so an injunction can issue to restrain them. If no injunction issues, a foreign Court will either decline or accept jurisdiction. If, as we are entitled to assume it would, the Italian Court were to decline jurisdiction, those proceedings would have constituted a waste of time and money. If, on the other hand, the Italian Court were to accept jurisdiction, any injunction then issued would directly conflict with the deliberate assumption of jurisdiction by the foreign Court … But if there were held to have been a submission, there would follow two parallel sets of proceedings where the arbitration clause had been contractually designed to ensure that there was only one."

12 同上，at 95, "For my part, I do not contemplate that an Italian Judge would regard it as an interference with comity of the English Courts, having rules on the scope of the English arbitration clause, then seek to enforce it by restraining the charterers by injunction from trying their luck in duplicated proceedings in the Italian Court. I can think of nothing more patronising than for the English Court to adopt the attitude that if the Italian Court declines jurisdiction, that would meet with the approval of the English Court, whereas if the Italian Court assumed jurisdiction, the English Court would then consider whether at that stage to intervene by injunction. That would be not only invidious but the reverse of comity."

13 同上，at 96.

tion）應是被放棄的時候。其觀點似乎與個人有所出入[14]：「已經有著許多權威性的論述在警告著對於外國法院程序的不當干擾的顯現。當……於沒有違反契約之情形時這種對外國法院感覺之敏銳性是非常值得稱許的。於前一種情形時，應該非常需要去注意去避免對外國法院程序的適當性或公平性加以懷疑。於後一種情形，該程序是否構成困擾性或壓迫性之問題是主要由訴訟所繫屬之法院所決定。但是在我的判斷下，被告已經承諾不去提起這些程序的明白而簡單的理由，已經不構成沒有信心去給予一個禁訴令以限制外國程序的好理由。……於兩種情形下給予禁訴令的理由皆是，如若沒有禁訴令在損害賠償是明顯的不構成適當的救濟時，原告契約上之權利會被剝奪。這種管轄權的行使自然是屬於裁量性質，而且不能理所當然的被行使，但是於任何案件中若其未被行使則應被給予好理由。」如前述個人是認為「困擾性」或「壓迫性」、「濫用程序」、「不公正之行為」、或「違反誠信之行為」於全球化法學中是大致上有一共同核心政策，反而是仲裁或管轄條款的效力、形成、或平衡性應嚴格的受到契約法原則之制約。對於契約法基本原則的要求，可能通常不是「簡單而明白」，沒有經過契約法原則的檢驗是不能「不構成沒有信心」的好理由。

Lord Justice Millett又說[15]：「像義大利這種國家是布魯塞爾及魯加

---

14 同上，"There have been many statements of great authority warning of the danger of giving an appearance of undue interference with the proceedings of a foreign Court. Such sensitivity to the feelings of a foreign Court has much to commend it where …no breach of contract is involved. In the former case, great care may be needed to avoid casting doubt on the fairness or adequacy of the procedures of the foreign Court. In the latter case, the question whether proceedings are vexatious or oppressive is primarily a matter for the Court before which they are pending. But in my judgment there is no good reason for diffidence in granting an injunction to restrain foreign proceedings on the clear and simple ground that the defendant has promised not to bring them ..... . The jurisdiction for the grant of the injunction in either case is that without it the plaintiff will be deprived of its contractual rights in a situation in which damages are manifestly an inadequate remedy. The jurisdiction is, of course, discretionary and is not exercised as a matter of course, but good reason needs to be shown why it should not be exercised in any given case."

15 同上，"The courts in countries like Italy, which is a party to the Brussels and Lugano Conventions as well as the New York Convention, are accustomed to the concept that they may be under a duty to decline jurisdiction in a particular case because of the existence of an exclusive jurisdiction or arbitration clause. I cannot accept the proposition that any Court would be offended by the grant of an injunction to restrain a party from invoking a jurisdiction which he had promised not to invoke and which it was its own duty to decline."

諾公約及紐約公約之會員，其法院是習慣於因為專屬管轄或仲裁條款的存在而可能有著責任去拒絕某個特定案件之管轄之概念。當一個當事人承諾不去起訴時，法院許可一個禁訴令禁止其去起訴而這亦是該其他法院自己之責任去拒絕管轄時，我不能接受有建議主張任何其他法院會被冒犯。」Lord Justice Millett這段於英國著名的論述沒有被英國同僚所批評，個人是覺得有些訝異。

首先歐盟布魯塞爾及魯加諾公約採的是死硬的先繫屬優先原則，而這個原則是優先於當事人之管轄條款，於Erich Gasser GmbH v. MISAT Srl[16]中歐盟法院之表態是斬釘截鐵的沒有迴旋之餘地，而這亦是歐盟與2005海牙選擇法院公約不同之處。遊樂場中有一種遊戲機是用槌子打冒出頭之地鼠，整個歐洲司法遊樂場正流行用歐盟法院當搥子打冒出頭的英國判例法。Lord Justice Millett不可能不知道司法遊樂場中最流行的打英國判例法老鼠的遊戲，或者至少時間證明其為錯誤的。

至於紐約公約，個人近年一再聲嘶力竭的提醒其他同僚公約2(3)條中規定，如果該「條約是無效、不適用、或不能被履行」則繫屬法院可以不遵守。而這個論述亦為美國聯邦仲裁法[17]（the Federal Arbitration Act (FAA)）所採納，及英國自己1996年的仲裁法（Arbitration Act 1996）第9(4)條所採納[18]。更有趣的是在Lord Justice Millett這個論述15年後，歐盟法院於Allianz SPA, Generali Assicurazioni Generali SPA, v West

---

16 Case C-116/02, Erich Gasser GmbH v. MISAT Srl, [2003] ECR I-14693.
Article 21 – Where proceedings involving the same cause of action and between the same parties are brought in the courts of different Contracting states, any court other than the court first seised shall of its own motion stay its proceedings until such time as the jurisdiction of the court first seised is established. Where the jurisdiction of the court first seised is established, any court other than the court first seised shall decline jurisdiction in favour of that court.
Article 21 of the Brussels Convention must be interpreted as meaning that a court second seised whose jurisdiction has been claimed under an agreement conferring jurisdiction must nevertheless stay proceedings until the court first seised has declared that it has no jurisdiction.

17 9 U.S.C. § 2, "shall be valid, irrevocable, and enforceable, save upon such grounds as exist at law or in equity for the revocation of any contract."

18 (4) On an application under this section the court shall grant a stay unless satisfied that the arbitration agreement is null and void, inoperative, or incapable of being performed.

Tankers Inc.[19]中不偏不倚的引用紐約公約2(3)條來駁回英國法院禁訴令之要求。事實上除了紐約公約2(3)條外，類似的規定亦規定於5(1)(a)條[20]有關承認及執行條款上。另外1985年的模範公約（UNCITRAL Model Law on International Commercial Arbitration）的8(1)條[21]、34(2)(a)(i)條[22]、及36(1)(a)(i)條[23]中有更詳細而相對應紐約公約條款之規定。故而Lord Justice Millett所說[24]：「如果它（禁訴令）是快速的被申請及在外國程序進

---

19 [2009] EUECJ C-185/07.

20 Article V
1.Recognition and enforcement of the award may be refused, at the request of the party against whom it is invoked, only if that party furnishes to the competent authority where the recognition and enforcement is sought, proof that:
(a)The parties to the agreement referred to in article II were, under the law applicable to them, under some incapacity, or the said agreement is not valid under the law to which the parties have subjected it or, failing any indication thereon, under the law of the country where the award was made.

21 Article 8. Arbitration agreement and substantive claim before court
(1)A court before which an action is brought in a matter which is the subject of an arbitration agreement shall, if a party so requests not later than when submitting his first statement on the substance of the dispute, refer the parties to arbitration unless it finds that the agreement is null and void, inoperative or incapable of being performed.

22 Article 34. Application for setting aside as exclusive recourse against arbitral award
(1)Recourse to a court against an arbitral award may be made only by an application for setting aside in accordance with paragraphs (2) and (3) of this article.
(2)An arbitral award may be set aside by the court specified in article 6 only if:
(a)the party making the application furnishes proof that:
(i) a party to the arbitration agreement referred to in article 7 was under some incapacity; or the said agreement is not valid under the law to which the parties have subjected it or, failing any indication thereon, under the law of this State; or

23 Article 36. Grounds for refusing recognition or enforcement
(1)Recognition or enforcement of an arbitral award, irrespective of the country in which it was made, may be refused only:
(a) at the request of the party against whom it is invoked, if that party furnishes to the competent court where recognition or enforcement is sought proof that:
(i) a party to the arbitration agreement referred to in article 7 was under incapacity; or the said agreement is not valid under the law to which the parties have subjected it or, failing any indication thereon, under the law of the country where the award was made.

24 Aggeliki Charis Compania Maritima SA v Pagnan S.p.A (The Angelic Grace), [1995] 1 Lloyd's Rep 87, 96 (Eng. C.A.), "Moreover, if there should be any reluctance to grant an injunction out of sensitivity to the feelings of a foreign Court, far less offence is likely to be caused if an injunction is granted before that Court has assumed jurisdiction than afterwards, while to refrain from granting it at any stage would deprive the plaintiff of its contractual rights altogether.
In my judgment, where an injunction is sought to restrain a party from proceeding in a foreign Court in breach of an arbitration agreement governed by English law, the English Court need feel no diffidence in granting the injunction, provided that it is sought promptly and before the foreign proceedings are too far advanced."

展太過深入前被申請，則我的判斷是，當禁止令是被申請來禁止一個當事人於違反準據法為英國法之仲裁條款下去外國法院提起訴訟，英國法院不需要對許可禁止令感到沒有信心。」或許英國法院不需要對許可禁訴令感到沒有信心——但顯然前提是不能違反上述的國際公約、契約法的平衡性、及訴訟法要求當事人立足點平等的超越性考量。

(二)德、英司法戰爭與國家主權

有趣的是在Lord Justice Millett作出「英國法院不需要對許可禁訴令感到沒有信心」，及「這亦是該其他法院自己之責任去拒絕管轄時，我不能接受有建議主張任何其他法院會被冒犯」之充滿自信之論述後，德國法院隨即以行動表示德國法界完全不認同其看法。在一個包含於倫敦仲裁之條款之消費者契約之案件中[25]，面對英國禁訴令德國法院並不認為在這種情形下自己有義務去停止自己之程序，因為這會侵犯到自己之主權（sovereignty），並且拒絕允許禁訴令的被送達。

因此於Philip Alexander Securities and Futures Ltd v. Bamberger[26]中，申請人PASF是一家債券公司，於過去在德國與德國客戶有著相當的商業行為。被告客戶們是在德國透過德國經銷商與PASF交易。他們的交易契約中有包含在倫敦依倫敦國際仲裁協會（‘LCIA’）之規則去仲裁之條款。這些客戶於不同的德國法院對原告PASF提起訴訟，而PASF則主張應將爭執交付倫敦仲裁。但是德國法院對於其他客戶之訴訟並未停止訴訟以交付仲裁，反而作成對PASF不利之實體上判決；而對相同客戶PASF卻取得對其有利之仲裁。因此PASF認為德國法院可能會不承認仲裁條款之效力，故於英國商業法庭申請禁訴令及要求確認依英國法該仲裁條款為有效並應被加以執行。一審的高院及二審的上訴法院皆拒絕給予禁訴令之許可。

---

25 Re the Enforcement of an English Anti-Suit Injunction [1997] IL Pr 320.
26 [1997] 1 ILPr. 73.

於商業法庭中一審的Waller J.[27]說：「有關中間禁訴令，因為基於這會造成對德國主權的干擾德國法院是拒絕加以送達。.....大致上說，德國法院所說的是1.依德國程序法德國法院是需仰賴當事人之合作，故因此對當事人所下的禁訴令會直接影響到法院的程序；2.每個個別的公民應有權利自由的利用德國法院；及3.對於每個案件之管轄權是應由德國法院自己去決定，而外國法院之嘗試去保障自己之管轄權是不能超越（德國法院）這個責任的。」

更有趣的是如個人所一再強調的仲裁及管轄條款不能超越強行法之觀點，亦為Waller J.所一開始即引為基礎論述[28]：「在一開始我就想陳述一或二個基本觀點。首先，並沒有任何抗辯呈現在我之前足以說明德國客戶並非消費者。這在我的看法裡是與本案中不只一部分有關連而已。布魯塞爾公約承認消費者應有著一個特殊的地位（見第4章第13-15條）。在羅馬公約有關消費者亦有著特殊的條款（見第5條）。在許多案件中德國

27 "I should add that problems have also arisen in relation to service of the interim injunctions, the German Courts refusing to serve on the basis that there would be an interference with German Sovereignty. At the most recent hearing before me I have had produced to me a Judgment of The Dusseldorf Higher Regional Court which explains in clear terms in relation to the injunction obtained against Gilhaus why the Court takes that there is an interference with the Jurisdiction of the Federal Republic, and why the documents will thus not be served. Putting the matter broadly, what the German Court is saying is that 1. under German procedure the Courts are dependent on the collaboration of the parties, and thus an antisuit injunction directed against a party does have a direct influence on the activities of the court; 2. free access to the German courts is a right of each individual citizen; and 3. it is for the German court to decide its competence in particular cases, and a foreign court's attempt to safeguard its own competence will not override that responsibility."

28 "At the outset I would like to make one or two general points. First, there has not been any argument placed before me to the effect that the German customers are not consumers. This in my view has a relevance in more than one area of the case. There is a recognition in the Brussels' convention that consumers have a special position (see s 4 arts 13 to 15).
In the Rome Convention there are special provisions relating to consumers (see art 5). It is by reference to local consumer legislation in many of the cases that the German Courts have refused to recognize the Arbitration provisions, and have felt not free to order a stay of the proceedings under the New York Convention.
One is already thus, as it seems to me, in a different area from that in which the Court was operating in 'The Angelic Grace', [1995] 1 Lloyds Rep 96 and Continental Bank NA v Aeakos Compania Naviera SA [CA] [1994] 2 All ER 540, [1994] 1 Lloyd's Rep 505 cases. I also believe the situation to be different to that confronting Longmore J in RCS Editori SPA v Bankers Trust International Plc transcript 23 January 1996 (unreported)."

法院會拒絕承認仲裁條款就是引用當地的消費者立法，並且依據這些法律得以自由的不依紐約公約之規定而去停止訴訟。」因此法院認為本案是與The Angelic Grace及Continental Bank NA v Aeakos Compania Naviera SA不一樣的。而法院亦指出英國在某些消費者契約上，亦有立法使得仲裁條款不生效，這是與德國立法相平行的，特別是The consumer Arbitration Agreements Act 1988（the CAAA）中的有些條文是與本案相關的[29]。故而個人不厭其煩的在此再次重申——在本案中德國及英國判例法又一次的證明仲裁條款的超越性是個虛擬的神話。

---

[29] 1 Arbitration agreements
(1) Where a person (referred to in s 4 below as "the consumer") enters into a contract as a consumer, an agreement that future differences arising between parties to the contract are to be referred to arbitration cannot be enforced against him in respect of any cause of action so arising to which this section applies except –
(a) with his written consent signified after the differences in question have arisen; or
(b) where he has submitted to arbitration in pursuance of the agreement, whether in respect of those or any other differences; or
(c) where the court makes an order under s 4 below in respect of that cause of action.
(2) This section applies to a cause of action –
(a) if proceedings in respect of it would be within the jurisdiction of a country court; or
(b) if it satisfies such other conditions as may be prescribed for the purposes of this paragraph in an order under s 5 below.
(3) Neither s 4(1) of the Arbitration Act 1950 nor s 4 of the Arbitration Act (Northern Ireland) 1937 (which provide for the staying of court proceedings where an arbitration agreement is in force) shall apply to an arbitration agreement to the extent that it cannot be enforced by virtue of this section.
4 Power of court to disapply s 1 where no detriment to consumer
(1)The High Court or a country court may, on an application made after the differences in question have arisen, order that a cause of action to which this section applies shall be treated as one to which s 1 above does not apply.
(2)Before making an order under this section the court must be satisfied that it is not deterimental to the interests of the consumer for the differences in question to be referred to arbitration to in pursuance of the arbitration agreement instead of being determined by proceedings before a court.
(3)In determining for the purposes of subsection (2) above whether a reference to arbitration is or is not deterimental to the interests of the consumer, the court shall have regard to all factors appearing to be relevant, including, in particular, the availability of legal aid and the relative amount of any expense which may result to him –
(a)if the differences in question are referred to arbitration in pursuance of the arbitration agreement; and
(b)if they are determined by proceedings before a court.
(4) This section applies to a cause of action –
(a) if proceedings in respect of it would be within the jurisdiction of a country court and would not fall within the small claims limit; or
(b)if it satisfies the condition referred to in s 1(2)(b) above and the order under s 5 below prescribing the conditions in question provides for this section to apply to causes of action which satisfy them.

更有趣的是個人請兩岸「所有」的同僚特別注意，Waller J.引用個人近幾年來一再引用的紐約公約第2(3)條來說明會員國是有權利，亦有可能，認定該仲裁條款「不適用」[30]：「因此看起來紐約公約的會員國是可能可以使得約定（仲裁條款）『不適用』，並且在消費者契約上是已經這麼作。這正是德國立法所已經完成的情形。」

或許因太重要故Waller J.對這個論述又重複了兩次[31]：「在本案中，認定Riedel（被告客戶）於德國提起訴訟之行為是困擾性行為是很困難的，特別是很明顯的德國法院的觀點是，基於德國法仲裁條款是無效的，做為消費者他們的公民有權利到他們的法院。…….於本案中很明顯的德國法院是覺得受到禁訴令許可之侵犯，並且視其為一種干擾性之行為。並且，德國法院明顯的認為基於在德國因為消費者法律之適用，德國之程序沒有義務依紐約公約而去被加以停止。」Waller J.雖然宣示[32]通常違反英

---

30 "In my view it is difficult to justify objectively the discrimination on the basis of nationality. The one area which has obviously given me cause for concern on this aspect relates to the United Kingdom's Treaty obligations under the New York Convention. Article 2(3) of that Convention provides: -
'The court of a Contracting State, when seized of an action in a matter in respect of which the parties have made an agreement within the meaning of this article, shall, at the request of one of the parties, refer the parties to arbitration, unless it finds that the said agreement is null and void, inoperative or incapable of being performed.'
It would thus appear possible for a Contracting State under the New York Convention to render an agreement 'inoperative' and to do so in consumer context. This indeed may well be what the German legislation has done."

31 "In the instant case, it would be difficult to suggest that Riedel's commencement of proceedings in the German Courts was vexatious, particularly since the German Courts were apparently taking the view that their citizens had the right, as consumers, to come to their Courts on the basis that under German law arbitration agreements were invalid.
Furthermore, neither Leggatt LJ nor Millett LJ (see pp95/96) in The Angelic Grace contemplated that the Italian Judge in that case would be offended by the grant of an injunction or would regard it as an interference. Indeed Leggatt LJ considered that the Italian Court would in fact decline jurisdiction. In the instant case it is clear that the German Court is offended by the grant of an injunction and does regard it as an interference. Furthermore, the German Court clearly takes the view that there is no obligation to stay the German proceedings pursuant to the New York Convention on the basis of the consumer laws being applied in Germany."

32 "It would seem to me prima facie that if someone proceeds in breach of, and with notice of, an injunction granted by the English court to obtain judgments abroad, those judgments should not, as a matter of public policy, be recognized in the United Kingdom."這個見解為上訴法院所再次引用，並認同如下："Unless, therefore, the apparent breaches of those respondents could be excused, their German judgments would not be enforceable."

國禁訴令而所取得的外國判決，基於公共政策，是不會於英國被承認的。但其又認為[33]在該階段並非對有關是否執行德國判決之確認之好時機，合適之時間應是德國客戶要求於英國執行德國判決之時，故確認之申請亦被駁回。

德國法院與英國法院在確認英國禁訴令之效力上，意外的在Philip Alexander Securities and Futures Ltd v Bamburger and others中證明了仲裁條款的超越性是個神話。更有趣的是兩國法院於爭執中，更意外的顯示出紐約公約第2(3)條維護契約誠信原則及保護弱勢的最重要功能。除了禁訴令支持者經常主張仲裁條款之超越性外，兩國之法院可能沒有預測到近十年後2005年海牙選擇法院公約亦主張管轄條款之超越性，並企圖成為紐約公約的「司法版本」[34]。但是2005年海牙選擇法院公約及禁訴令之支持者必須嚴肅的面對在本案之「法律戰爭」中，英德兩國法院以司法戰火赤裸裸的揭開紐約公約尊重契約法誠信原則的第2(3)條之真正功能[35]。如前述紐約公約第2(3)條給予「人民司法保護的形式」，歐盟最

33 "What difference should the above make to the granting of declarations? I do not think it right to grant declarations at this stage in relation to the enforceability of judgments. One does not know if the German customers will actually seek to enforce their judgments or what steps German customers may now take before seeking to enforce them. I am not absolutely clear whether there could be any contest as to whether notification of the injunctions was given. The appropriate time to consider the question is when, and if, the German customers seek to enforce their judgments in this country.
Conclusion
These applications for injunctions and declarations are thus dismissed."這個駁回確認之要求亦為上訴法所認同："In our judgment the judge's discretion not to grant declarations was exercised on correct principles. He was entitled to refrain from rendering the issue res judicata, and so to leave it open to the respondents to attempt enforcement, even though they have not so far resisted the appellants' proceedings here."

34 Masato Dogauchi and Trevor C. Hartley, para 1, Introduction, Prel. Doc. No 26, Preliminary Draft Convention on Exclusive Choice of Court Agreements: "The objective of the Convention is to make exclusive choice of court agreements as effective as possible in the context of international business. The hope is that the Convention will do for choice of court agreements what the New York Convention of 1958 has done for arbitration agreements."

35 "147. Paragraphs a) and b) of Article 6 correspond to the 'null and void' provision in Article II(3) of the 1958 New York Convention on the Recognition and Enforcement of Foreign Arbitral Awards, while paragraphs d) and e) cover the same ground as 'inoperative or incapable of being performed' in the same provision of the New York Convention …. These exceptions may seem more complex than those in the New York Convention, but on closer examination it will be seen that they are similar to, and no wider than, those in the New York Convention. This was also the clear intent of the Diplomatic Session.

高法院在2009年時為了消滅英國禁訴令在West Tankers案中已公開闡述並支持第2(3)條這個功能。而且事實上在West Tankers案之前，個人早已引述紐約公約第2(3)條以作為2005年海牙選擇法院公約霸凌第三世界弱勢人民之證據[36]，於此不再贅述細節。事實上如前述紐約公約第2(3)條亦為1985聯合國模範公約、美國聯邦仲裁法（the FAA）、及英國仲裁法（Arbitration Act 1996）所採納。如今在本案中，經由德國法院與英國法院在禁訴令的司法戰爭中，雙方猛烈砲火的交織照明下，紐約公約第2(3)條誠信原則及保護弱勢的真相終能大白——請問2005年海牙選擇法院公約及禁訴令之支持者如何面對這個德英司法戰爭所蹂躪出來的真相？仲裁條款及管轄條款超越性神話的超大氣泡難道沒有被這兩個號稱大陸法及英美法先進國家間之司法戰爭所刺破？

如Waller J.之判決主文所述，其一開始就定調「消費者應有著一個特殊的地位」。而「消費者特殊位」之承認，不只於程序上布魯塞爾公約（及規則）於管轄上之規定，在實體法上羅馬公約（及規則I）亦有著規定。另外在不涉及本案之情形，布魯塞爾公約及規則在程序上，羅馬公約及規則在實體法上尚有一些對弱勢的特別保障條款，例如勞工與保險契約等。另外毫無疑問各國尚有著有關自己法院地內保護弱勢、環保、金融、及安全之公共政策及強行法，這些皆不是當事人以契約條款就可迴避。

管轄、仲裁、及選擇準據法條款超越性的神話，在大陸法規避法律及誠信原則，與英美法合理性要求的基本政策前根本無所遁形，實在不需要德英司法戰爭的戰火來照明其不真實性。就只有信仰資本主義追逐市場利益的貪婪人性，才會利欲薰心的將一個本可與紐約公約平行的曠世司法版本的公約建築在一個神話泡沫上。任何罔顧司法正義企圖將海牙公約建築

The apparent complexity of the provisions is due to the fact that the Diplomatic Session was aiming for greater clarity and precision than that found in the rather skeletal provisions of Article II(3) of the New York Convention." Para. 147, Explanatory Report by Trevor Hartley and Masato Dogauchi.（但是最大的問題是弱勢一方仍經常須去強勢一方所指定之法院去應訴）

36 陳隆修，《2005年海牙法院選擇公約評析》，台北，五南圖書公司，2009年1月，初版1刷，3-18頁。

在第三世界人民的血肉、淚水、及生命上之公約，在人類歷史上不會留下神話的記錄，只會留下黑暗醜陋的記錄——例如美式的不方便法院法學。

如Cardozo J.所說「法學的概念應受到常識的限制」，最尊敬的恩師Prof. Graveson所說「邏輯一致性的目的應受到判例法實現正義的目的之限制」，ALI/UNIDROIT Principles of Transnational Civil Procedure第3條的comment認為「合理性的概念是排除過分技術性的法律論述」，而這就是我們二千五百年來所謂的「道法自然」。個人於一開始試圖研究中國式法學時，即主張應以「王道」為基礎，而避免以「利益」為法學之目的[37]。中國式法學的以「王道」為基礎論述，亦為黃進教授的共同主張。聯合國高峰會於Rio Declaration on Environment and Development（1992）第5、6條及於Johannesburg Declaration on Sustainable Development（2002）第13、14、及15條中所作之宣言，是與我們二千多年來「不患寡患不均」之「禮運大同」精神一致，故而個人認為二十一世紀全球化法學之共同核心基礎應為上述聯合國宣言及中國「王道」文化。

面對德國司法對英國法院禁訴令之全面反彈，於Philip Alexander Securities and Futures Ltd v Bamburger and others[38]中英國上訴法院除了維持一審之原判外，又再次重申德國法院認為依德國法該仲裁條款為無效或不適用[39]。其結論並認為在本案之事實下，可能英國有關禁訴令之相關作法需要再加以考慮[40]：「基於這個案件之事實英國法院於許可禁訴令以限

37 見陳隆修，《歐盟經驗論中國式國際私法之建立》，高雄大學法學論叢6卷2期，2011年，第37-39頁，註94。

38 [1997] IL Pr 73, CA.

39 "In each of the judgments the German Court rejected the appellants' submission that the Court had no jurisdiction because of the binding arbitration agreement, and ruled, as a distinct ground of its decision, that the arbitration agreements were under German law either invalid or inapplicable."

40 "The practice of the courts in England to grant injunctions to restrain a defendant from prosecuting proceedings in another country may require reconsideration in the light of the facts of this case. The conventional view is that such an injunction only operates in personam with the consequence that the English courts do not and never have regarded themselves as interfering with the exercise by the foreign court of its jurisdiction. In cases where the defendant lives or has assets of substance in England that view may have some reality for there is reason to think that the injunction may be enforced so as to

制被告在其他國家提起訴訟程序之作法可能需要再加以考慮。傳統的觀點是這種禁訴令只是產生對人之效力，以致於英國法院並不，並且從未，認為他們自己干擾到外國法院管轄權之行使。當在被告於英國居住或有著重大之財產之情形下，這個看法或者有些真實性，因為有理由去相信禁訴令得被執行以致可以防止違反該命令而於外國法院提出程序。但是於被告並未居住於英國並且未於這裡有財產之情形下，除非經由外國法院的承認及執行該禁訴令，或在其拒絕如此作時，經由本院去拒絕承認不承認該禁訴令之外國命令，該禁訴令是不可能被執行的。於本案中德國法院視禁訴令為侵犯到他們的主權並且拒絕允許他們於德國的被送達。除此之外他們更對案件的實體加以判決。」因此上訴法院駁回上訴。

在The Angelic Grace中Millett LJ自信滿滿的論述[41]：「當一個當事人承諾不去起訴時，法院許可一個禁訴令禁止其去起訴而這亦是該其他法院自己之責任去拒絕管轄時，我不能接受有建議主張任何其他法院會被冒犯。」事實上這種論述過去，甚或現在，是許多英國同僚一廂情願的想法——既然當事人已承諾不去起訴，外國法院自己有責任去拒絕管轄，故外國法院之管轄權自然不可能被冒犯。但是2005年海牙選擇法院公約及禁訴令的支持者必須摸著良心回答一個問題——外國法院有責任去接受當事人契約條款之約束嗎？若是有其他非契約當事人之相關第三人之權利呢？

prevent proceedings taken in breach of it from reaching the foreign court. But in cases in which the defendant does not live in England and does not have assets here the injunction is unlikely to be enforceable except by the foreign court recognizing and giving effect to the injunction or, where it refuses to do so, by this court refusing to recognize the order of the foreign court made without such recognition. In the present case the German courts regarded the injunctions as an infringement of their sovereignty and refused to permit them to be served in Germany. In addition they proceeded to give judgments on the merits. It was for that reason that the amici curiae were appointed in this case. In practice that point has not been developed in these proceedings. But in future cases it may assume greater importance. In cases concerning the European Union what would best meet the predicament is a Directive defining the extent of the recognition which the orders of the courts of each Member State are entitled to receive from the courts of other Member States."

41 Aggeliki Charis Compania Maritima SA v Pagnan S.p.A, (The Angelic Grace), [1995] 1 Lloyd's Rep 87, 96 (Eng. C.A.). "I cannot accept the proposition that any Court would be offended by the grant of an injunction to restrain a party from invoking a jurisdiction which he had promised not to invoke and which it was its own duty to decline."

實體契約法平衡性原則之考量呢？訴訟程序上當事人立足點平等及財富不均之考量呢？個人於此公開的對2005年海牙選擇法院及禁訴令的支持者再次重申——當事人選法條款、仲裁條款、及管轄條款的超越性自一百多年前他們誕生之日起就是個神話。

對於The Angelic Grace的這種論述德國法院在Philip Alexander Securities and Futures Ltd v Bamburger中著實的當著英國法院的面給他們上了一課：依德國法該仲裁條款是無效的；德國法院認為他們的主權被侵犯；而且「每個案件之管轄權是應由德國法院自己去決定，而外國法院之嘗試去保障自己之管轄權是不能超越（德國法院）這個責任的。[42]」依國際法德國法院的論述是站得住的。紐約公約第2(3)條及1985年模範公約8(1)條皆有規定法院得認定仲裁條款無效、不適用、或無法被履行之情形，而這個規定亦為美國聯邦仲裁法[43]（FAA）及英國1996年仲裁法第9(4)條[44]所採納。

在管轄條款上同樣的法理亦是被成文法化。英國的Civil Jurisdiction and Judgments Act 1982第32條2及3項[45]分別規定於承認外國判決時英國法院得不受外國法院對該事項之認定之拘束，而認定該管轄條款為非

---

42 "I should add that problems have also arisen in relation to service of the interim injunctions, the German Courts refusing to serve on the basis that there would be an interference with German Sovereignty. ...... it is for the German court to decide its competence in particular cases, and a foreign court's attempt to safeguard its own competence will not override that responsibility."

43 9 U.S.C. § 2, "shall be valid, irrevocable, and enforceable, save upon such grounds as exist at law or in equity for the revocation of any contract."

44 (4) On an application under this section the court shall grant a stay unless satisfied that the arbitration agreement is null and void, inoperative, or incapable of being performed.

45 32.-(1) Subject to the following provisions of this section, a judgment given by a court of an overseas country in any proceedings shall not be recognised or enforced in the United Kingdom if-
(a) the bringing of those proceedings in that court was contrary to an agreement under which the dispute in question was to be settled otherwise than by proceedings in the courts of that country; and
......
(2) Subsection (1) does not apply where the agreement referred to in paragraph (a) of that subsection was illegal, void or unenforceable or was incapable of being performed for reasons not attributable to the fault of the party bringing the proceedings in which the judgment was given.
(3) In determining whether a judgment given by a court of an overseas country should be recognised or enforced in the United Kingdom, a court in the United Kingdom shall not be bound by any decision of the overseas court relating to any of the matters mentioned in subsection (1) or (2).

法、無效或不能被執行、或不能被履行。個人於此鄭重要求主張管轄及仲裁條款之超越性及2005年海牙選擇法院公約之必要性之支持者必須對這個成文法加以回應。另外除了禁訴令之支持者外，主張管轄及仲裁條款獨立性之同僚亦必須回應這個條文，因為這個條文給予繫屬法院（非被指定法院）不受外國法院認定之影響而認定管轄條款為無效之自主性權力。

(三)超越性強行基本政策

至於在選法條款上所受的限制更多，羅馬I規則充斥著強行法之概念，而且經常是與布魯塞爾規則有著相當程度的配合。最明顯的例子為羅馬I規則第9條的強行法規定，第1項[46]規定：「超越性強行法就是一個國家為了保障其公共利益，例如其政治、社會或經濟組織而認定很重要的條款，這些條款重要到無論依本規則契約本應適用的法律為何，只要是符合其範圍內，皆應被適用。」第2項[47]規定本規則不得限制法院地強行法之適用。第3項[48]則規定履行地強行法應被加以考慮適用。這個第3項的規定於著名的英國判例法Ralli v. Compania Navivera Sota y Aznar[49]中，Scrutton LJ即表示契約已默認契約之條款必須符合履行地之法律。而這個法理亦為美國第2新編202條2項[50]所引用，只是很奇怪的美國判例法對這個法理似乎不甚重視，而且經常忽略。個人早期基於實務經驗亦一再強調[51]契

46 Article 9 Overriding mandatory provisions
1. Overriding mandatory provisions are provisions the respect for which is regarded as crucial by a country for safeguarding its public interests, such as its political social or economic organisation, to such an extent that they are applicable to any situation falling within their scope, irrespective of the law otherwise applicable to the contract under this Regulation.

47 2. Nothing in this Regulation shall restrict the application of the overriding mandatory provisions of the law of the forum.

48 3. Effect may be given to the overriding mandatory provisions of the law of the country where the obligations arising out of the contract have to be or have been performed, in so far as those overriding mandatory provisions render the performance of the contract unlawful. In considering whether to give effect to those provisions, regard shall be had to their nature and purpose and to the consequences of their application or non-application.

49 [1920] 2K. B. 287, at p. 394.

50 Second Restatement, s. 202(2): "When performance is illegal in the place of performance, the contract will usually be denied enforcement."

51 見陳隆修，《國際私法契約評論》，台北，五南圖書公司，民國75年2月，初版，80、81頁。

約履行地法學應受尊重，除非當地之法律是違反文明的公理。更有趣的是Unidroit Principles of International Commercial Contract 2004的7.2.2條(a)款[52]將這個法理採納為實體契約法之內容。這個發展個人以為是明顯的印證了國際案件之解決方法應以相關實體法之內容為「傳統上公平與實質正義之概念」之依據。

另外羅馬I規則中尚有第3(3)條（選法自由）、第5條（運送契約）、第6條（消費者契約）、第7條（保險契約）及第8條（個別僱傭契約）等強行法之規定。而這些有關選法條款的強行法規通常於布魯塞爾規則I亦有相對應的管轄規則強行法規，例如第3章的保險規則、第4章的消費者規則、及第5章的個別僱傭契約規則等。另外對這些強行法規羅馬I（Rome I）的序言（Recitals）中亦有著相對應的強行政策之宣示。例如序言23即規定[53]：「有關於被視為較弱勢之當事人所以訂之契約，這些當事人在有關他們的利益上應受到較一般規則更有利的國際私法規則之保護。」序言32即規定於運送契約及保險契約上，旅客及保單持有人應受到特別法規適當之保護[54]。序言35規定於個別僱傭契約中保護受僱人之強行法只能對其有利下才能被違反[55]。最有趣的是序言37規定公共利益使得各會員國法院於例外之情形下得適用自己的公共政策及超越性強行法[56]。

---

52 Article 7.2.2 (Performance of non-monetary obligation)
Where a party who owes an obligation other than one to pay money does not perform, the other party may require performance, unless
(a) performance is impossible in law or in fact;
(b) performance or, where relevant, enforcement is unreasonably burdensome or expensive;
(c) the party entitled to performance may reasonably obtain performance from another source;
(d) performance is of an exclusively personal character; or
(e) the party entitled to performance does not require performance within a reasonable time after it has, or ought to have, become aware of the non-performance.

53 (23) As regards contracts concluded with parties regarded as being weaker, those parties should be protected by conflict-of-law rules that are more favourable to their interests than the general rules.

54 (32) Owing to the particular nature of contracts of carriage and insurance contracts, specific provisions should ensure an adequate level of protection of passengers and policy holders. Therefore, Article 6 should not apply in the context of those particular contracts.

55 (35) Employees should not be deprived of the protection afforded to them by provisions which cannot be derogated from by agreement or which can only be derogated from to their benefit.

56 (37) Considerations of public interest justify giving the courts of the Member States the possibility, in exceptional circumstances, of applying exceptions based on public policy and overriding mandatory

甚至在有關非契約責任的羅馬II（Rome II）亦是充斥著強行法，例如第14(2)條[57]與第16條[58]。其序言31規定[59]：「於確認約定之存在時，法院應尊重當事人之意思。應以對當事人之選擇加以某些條件之方式來對弱勢當事人給予保護。」故而選法條款、管轄條款、及仲裁條款受到法院地及履行地強行法的制約是一個國際法上的常態，亦是一個合理的習慣法。

即使是現代社會中一般被視為是奉行資本主義的美國，較近在修訂統一商法時亦不得不順應全球化法學的潮流，而對消費者加以適度保護。於2004年的U.C.C. § 2A-106[60]中，新版之統一商法對消費者租賃契約之準據法條款及指定法院管轄條款，皆有嚴格之限制，以期保護弱勢之承租人。這個條文對消費者嚴格之保護，使得選法條款及管轄條款的當事人自主原則變得是神話。其立法理由解釋[61]：「有一個真實性的危險就是，出

---

provisions. The concept of 'overriding mandatory provisions' should be distinguished from the expression 'provision which cannot be derogated from by agreement' and should be construed more restrictively.

57 2. Where all the elements relevant to the situation at the time when the event giving rise to the damage occurs are located in a country other than the country whose law has been chosen, the choice of the parties shall not prejudice the application of provisions of the law of that other country which cannot be derogated from by agreement.

58 Article 16 Overriding mandatory provisions
Nothing in this Regulation shall restrict the application of the provisions of the law of the forum in a situation where they are mandatory irrespective of the law otherwise applicable to the non-contractual obligation.

59 (31) To respect the principle of party autonomy and to enhance legal certainty, the parties should be allowed to make a choice as to the law applicable to a non-contractual obligation. This choice should be expressed or demonstrated with reasonable certainty by the circumstances of the case. Where establishing the existence of the agreement, the court has to respect the intentions of the parties. Protection should be given to weaker parties by imposing certain conditions on the choice.

60 U.C.C. § 2A-106
LIMITATION ON POWER OF PARTIES TO CONSUMER LEASE TO CHOOSE APPLICABLE LAW AND JUDICIAL FORUM
(1)If the law chosen by the parties to a consumer lease is that of a jurisdiction other than a jurisdiction in which the lessee resides at the time the lease agreement becomes enforceable or within 30 days thereafter or in which the goods are to be used, the choice is not enforceable.
(2)If the judicial forum chosen by the parties to a consumer lease is a forum that would not otherwise have jurisdiction over the lessee, the choice is not enforceable.

61 "There is a real danger that a lessor may induce a consumer lessee to agree that the applicable law will be a jurisdiction that has little effective consumer protection, or to agree that the applicable forum will be a forum that is inconvenient for the lessee in the event of litigation. As a result, this section invalidates these choice of law or forum clauses, except where the law chosen is that of the state of the consumer's residence or where the goods will be kept, or the forum chosen is one that otherwise would

租人可能誘導承租之消費者去同意對消費者幾乎沒有有效之保護之管轄區之法律為準據法，或去同意應適用的管轄法院會於訴訟時對承租人是個不方便之法院。因此，除非所選定的準據法是消費者居所之州法或貨品所被放置之州法，或所被選擇之法院是本就應對承租人有著管轄權之法院，本條文會使得這些選法或管轄條款無效。」因此正如英國法院在Philip Alexander Securities and Futures Ltd v. Bamberger[62]中由德國法院所狠狠的學到的一課，美國統一商法這個條文亦認為消費者會面對「一個真實性的危險」，因此消費契約的效力應受到很大的限制。

但是弱勢者所面對的「一個真實性危險」自然不只是侷限於消費契約中，尚有於羅馬I號規則及布魯塞爾規則中所特別規定的保險契約、個別僱傭契約、及運送契約等，弱勢者皆需要司法及立法之特別保護。另外法院地及契約履行地自然還有其他「公共利益上之考量」，在特別之情形下得基於公共政策及強行法，而超越當事人契約條款之效力。這些「公共利益上之考量」可能適用於安全、衛生、經濟、環保、或甚至於是有關道德上之考量，如果這些大範圍包山包海的考量可以明文列舉，歐盟就不需要訂立羅馬公約7條規則9條的爭議性條款。這數十年來歐盟於這種強行法條款上之爭議，充分顯示人類社會對這些「公共利益的考量」不確定性之無奈，但更顯現出近代人類社會維護個案正義的決心。

如個人所一再指出管轄與仲裁條款的效力絕對不是如2005海牙選擇法院公約及禁訴令支持者所吹噓的具有超越性的效力，於主要近代文明國國家之判例法上是受到節制的。美國最高法院於The Bremen v. Zapata Off-Shore Co.[63]中認為，管轄條款必須「沒有牽涉詐欺、不當誘導或一方過分強大議價能力下」才能生效，若當事人能證明「該執行是不合理並且不公平，或者基於詐欺或過分操弄」則會使得該條無效[64]。而歐盟最高

have jurisdiction over the lessee."

62 [1997] 1 ILPr. 73 CA.

63 407 U.S. 1 (1972).

64 Ibid. at 11-15, "There are compelling reasons why a freely negotiated private international agreement, unaffected by fraud, undue influence, or overweening bargaining power, such as that involved here,

法院為了「消滅」英國之禁訴令，在Allianz SpA, Generali Assicurazioni Generali SpA, v West Tankers Inc.[65]中引用紐約公約第2(3)條來否認仲裁條款的超越性：「當事人之一方只要依賴該條款就可避免訴訟程序，而申請人，他認為該條款是無效、不適用、或不能被履行，則將會被禁止依44/2001規則第5(3)條去法院提出訴訟，並因此而會被剝奪他所應享有的司法保護的形式。[66]」「這個結論是受到紐約公約第2(3)條所支持的，根據該規定，有關當事人所訂定之仲裁條款範圍內之訴訟所繫屬的會員國法院，在當事人一方之請求下，應命令當事人去仲裁，除非法院認定該條款是無效、不適用、或無法被履行。[67]」

直至1958年美國聯邦法院仍然拒絕執行管轄條款，其理由為[68]：「在糾紛尚未產生前之約定，其目的乃是在排除法院之管轄權，是違反公共政策並不能被執行的。」在其時英國法院早已承認被指定之法院通常即為合適之法院，但又認為在「正義且合適」（just and proper）下管轄條款

should be given full effect." "…… could clearly show that enforcement would be unreasonable and unjust, or that the clause was invalid for such reasons as fraud or overreaching."

65 [2009] EUECJ C-185/07.

66 Para. 31, "Lastly, if, by means of an anti-suit injunction, the Tribunable di Siracusa were prevented from examining itself the preliminary issue of the validity or the applicability of the arbitration agreement, a party could avoid the proceedings merely by relying on that agreement and the applicant, which considers that the agreement is void, inoperative or incapable of being performed, would thus be barred from access to the court before which it brought proceedings under Article 5(3) of Regulation No 44/2001 and would therefore be deprived of a form of judicial protection to which it is entitled."

67 Para, 33, "This finding is supported by Article II(3) of the New York Convention, according to which it is the court of a Contracting State, when seised of an action in a matter in respect of which the parties have made an arbitration agreement, that will, at the request of one of the parties, refer the parties to arbitration, unless it finds that the said agreement is null and void, inoperative or incapable of being performed."

68 Carbon Black Export, Inc. v. The Monrosa, 254 F. 2d 197, at 300-01 (en banc), cert. dismissed, 359 U.S. 180 (1959), "agreements in advance of a controversy whose object is to oust the jurisdiction of the courts are contrary to public policy and will not be enforced."於Scherk v. Alberto-Culver Co., Inc. 417 U.S. 506 (1974)中，最高法院承認國際仲裁條款之效力："A contractual provision specifying in advance the forum in which disputes shall be litigated and the law to be applied is, therefore, an almost indispensable precondition to achievement of the orderliness and predictability essential to any international business transaction. Furthermore, such a provision obviates the danger that a dispute under the agreement might be submitted to a forum hostile to the interests of one of the parties or unfamiliar with the problem area involved." at 515.

之效力應被超越[69]。Brandon J.在The Eleftheria[70]中之意見後來又於The El Amrid[71]中再次被重申：(1)當原告違反契約應將爭執交付外國法院之約定而於英國法院起訴，假定英國法院有管轄權，而被告要求停止訴訟時，英國法院有裁量權去決定是否停止訴訟。(2)除非有相當強的理由，否則應停止訴訟。(3)原告應負起證明此相當強的理由的責任。(4)於行使裁量權時法院應考慮到個案中之所有情況。(5)於第(4)款之規定下應特別考慮下面情況：(a)案件事實的爭點的證據在那個國家或那個國家較容易取得，比較英國與外國法院的便利性與訴訟之費用。(b)是否該外國法院之法律會被適用，如果被適用，是否會與英國法有重大不同。(c)當事人是否與這些國家有密切關連。(d)被告是否真正的希望於外國審判，或只是希望取得程序上的優勢。(e)原告若於外國起訴是否會遭受到下列的不利：(i)他們的請求會沒有擔保；（ii）沒有辦法強制執行取得之判決；（iii）遭受到英國所沒有的時效的限制；（iv）因為政治、種族、宗教及其他的理由而無法公平的受到審判。這個論述於1985年時在The Sennar（No. 2）[72]為英國最高法院所確認。

---

69 The Fehmarn [1958] 1 All ER 333.見陳隆修、許兆慶、林恩瑋、李瑞生四人合著，《國際私法-管轄與選法理論之交錯》，台北，五南圖書公司，2009年3月，初版1刷，198-200頁。

70 [1970] p 94.

71 Aratra Potato Co Ltd v. Egyptian Navigation Co., The El Amria [1981] 2 Lloyd's Rep 119, CA.

72 The Sennar (No.2) [1985] 1 WLR 490 at 500, "The principles established by the authorities can, I think, be summarized as follows: (1) Where the plaintiffs sue in England in breach of an agreement to refer disputes to a foreign court, and the defendants apply for a stay, the English court, assuming the claim to be otherwise within its jurisdiction, is not bound to grant a stay but has a discretion whether to do so or not. (2) The discretion should be exercised by granting a stay unless strong cause for not doing so is shown. (3) The burden of proving such strong cause is on the plaintiffs. (4) In exercising its discretion the court should take into account all the circumstances of the particular case. (5) In particular, but without prejudice to (4), the following matters, where they arise, may properly be regarded: (a) In what country the evidence on the issues of fact is situated, or more readily available, and the effect of that on the relative convenience and expense of trial as between the English and foreign courts. (b) Whether the law of the foreign court applies and, if so, whether it differ from English law in any material respects. (c) With what country either party is connected, and how closely. (d) Whether the defendants genuinely desire trial in the foreign country, or are only seeking procedural advantages. (e) Whether the plaintiffs would be prejudiced by having to sue in the foreign court because they would: (i) be deprived of security for their claim; (ii) be unable to enforce any judgment obtained; (iii) be faced with a time bar not applicable in England; or (iv) for political, racial, religious or other reasons be unlikely to get fair trial."

個人一再重申[73]聲名卓越的法院所累積出來的實務判例法，歷經時空的淬鍊，不但是我們祖先智慧及生活經驗的結晶，亦是大自然進化的一環。如果沒有明確的理由就率性不遵守判例法的規則，就是近乎逆天而行違抗「自然道法」之行為。在Sun Oil Co[74]中美國最高法院說：「如果一件事於大眾同意下已被實行二百年，那麼需要很強的證據才能以十四修正案去影響它。」**很明顯的在選法、管轄、及仲裁條款上，如果美國、歐盟、及英國的最高法院長久以來對其效力皆給予相當的限制，那麼不可否認的是在這個議題上全球化法學的共同核心是存在的，而這個共同核心是與中國的「王道」「禮運大同」政策是一致的。2005年海牙選擇法院公約及禁訴令支持者「需要很強的證據」才能同時推翻美國、歐盟、及英國最高法院的判例法。他們的證據在哪裡？在資本主義攫取第三世界自由市場的掠奪性新殖民地主義法學裡**[75]。

做為一個法律學生個人無法相信任何同僚可以直視The Bremen、West Tankers、及The Sennar（No.2）所代表的全球化法學，而仍然對管轄及仲裁條款的超越性說得出口。最基本的界線是選法、管轄、及仲裁條款皆為契約條款，因此皆應受到契約法基本政策的制約。即使主張2005年海牙選擇法院公約最力的資本主義大本營美國，自己應記住其2004年新版的U.C.C. 1-302條[76]中亦如大陸法一般的規定，誠信原則、合理性、

73 陳隆修，《2005年海牙法院選擇公約評析》，台北，五南圖書公司，2009年1月，初版1刷，108頁。

74 Sun Oil Co. v. Wortman, 486 U.S. 717, 730, "If a thing has been practiced for two hundred years by common consent, it will need a strong case for the Fourteenth Amendment to affect it."

75 新約馬太福音第七章：「你們要防備假先知。他們來到你們這裡來、外面披著羊皮、裡面卻是殘暴的狼。憑著他們的果子、就可以認出他們來。荊棘上豈能摘葡萄呢。蒺藜裡豈能摘無花果呢。這樣、凡好樹都結好果子、惟獨壞樹結壞果子。好樹不能結壞果子、壞樹不能結好果子。凡不結好果子的樹、就砍下來、丟在火裡。所以憑著他們的果子、就可以認出他們來。凡稱呼我主阿、主阿的人、不能都進天國。惟獨遵行我天父旨意的人、纔能進去。」

76 1-302. VARIATION BY AGREEMENT

(a) Except as otherwise provided in subsection (b) or elsewhere in [the Uniform Commercial Code], the effect of provisions of [the Uniform Commercial Code] may be varied agreement.

(b) The obligations of good faith, diligence, reasonableness, and care prescribed by [the Uniform Commercial Code] may not be disclaimed by agreement. The parties, by agreement, may determine the standards by which the performance of those obligations is to be measured if those standards are not manifestly unreasonable. Whenever [the Uniform Commercial Code] requires an action to be taken within a

勤奮性、及適當注意性皆為當事人所不可於契約中違反之強行法。至於習慣於強行法的歐盟契約法原則[77]第1:201條[78]亦規定：「(1)每個當事人之行為必須符合誠信及公平交易。(2)當事人不得排除或限制這個責任。」其註釋A[79]說明：「這個條文規定了貫穿整個（歐盟契約法）原則中之基本原則。誠信及公平交易於當事人依契約之責任於成立、履行、及執行時皆被要求，及在當事人依契約而行使權利時亦同樣的被要求。」註釋B更說明誠信原則之超越性[80]：「它補充本（歐盟契約法）原則條款不足之處，並且在如果嚴格的遵守本原則的其他條文會造成明顯的不公正的後果時，它得超越該些其他條文而被適用。」而這個概念事實上就是一般認為Judge Cardozo所闡釋的公共政策[81]：「會侵犯到一些正義的基本原則，一

---

reasonable time, a time that is not manifestly unreasonable may be fixed by agreement.

77 見the Commission of European Contract Law, Principles of European Contract Law, edited by Ole Lando and Hugh Beale (2000),

78 Article 1:201: Good Faith and Fair Dealing
(1) Each party must act in accordance with good faith and fair dealing.
(2) The parties may not exclude or limit this duty.

79 A. *Good Faith and Fair Dealing*
This Article sets forth a basic principle running through the Principles. Good faith and fair dealing are required in the formation, performance and enforcement of the parties' duties under a contract, and equally in the exercise of a party's rights under the contract. Particular applications of this rule appear in specific provisions of the present Principles such as the duty of a party not to negotiate a contract with no real intention of reaching an agreement with the other party (Article 2:301), not to disclose confidential information given by the other party in the course of negotiations (Article 2:302), and not to take unfair advantage of the other party's dependence, economic distress or other weakness (Article 4:109). Good faith and fair dealing are an important factor when implied terms of a contract are to be determined (Article 6:102); and they give an debtor a right to cure a defective performance before the time for performance (Article 8:104) and to refuse to make specific performance of a contractual obligation if this would cause the debtor unreasonable effort and expense (Article 9:102).

80 B. *Not Confined to Specific Rules*
The concept is, however, broader than any of these specific applications. It applies generally as a companion to Article 1:104 on Usages. Its purpose is to enforce community standards of decency, fairness and reasonableness in commercial transactions, see Article 1:108 on Reasonableness. It supplements the provisions of the Principles, and it may take precedence over other provisions of these Principles when a strict adherence to them would lead to a manifestly unjust result. Thus, even if the non-performance of an obligation is fundamental because strict compliance with the obligation is of the essence of the contract under Article 8:103, a party would not be permitted to terminate because of a trivial breach of the obligation.

81 "would violate some fundamental principle of justice, some prevalent conception of morals, some deep-seated tradition of the commonweal." Loucks v. Standard Oil Co. of New York, 224 N.Y. 99, 111, 120 N.E. 198, 202 (1918).另外Restatement of the Law, Second, Conflict of Laws的第90條規定外國訴因若違反法院地之強烈公共政策，則可以拒絕接受該訴訟。

些盛行的道德觀念，一些公益上根深蒂固的傳統。」故而如歐盟契約法委員會在1:201條中對會員國誠信原則信守的程度所作的調查顯示[82]，各會員國皆承認誠信原則，只是以基本原則或判例個案達成目的之方法不同。

另外與羅馬公約7條規則9條所規定之強行法直接有關的為，歐盟契約法委員會後來增加的15:101條[83]：「契約違反歐盟會員國之法律所認為基本原則之部分為無效。」其註釋B[84]認為這是有關「整個歐盟普遍承認的法律基本原則的必須性寬廣概念」。其指標性基本原則為歐盟公約、歐洲人權公約、及歐盟基本權利憲章中的許多條文。由這個最強行的法規我們可以見到引起德英禁訴令司法戰爭的保護消費者政策只是這個法規範圍的一小部分，禁訴令與管轄、仲裁、選法條款被排除適用的範圍是「必須

---

§ 90 Action Contrary to Public Policy
No action will be entertained on a foreign cause of action the enforcement of which is contrary to the strong public policy of the forum.

82 Notes
1. *Survey of the Laws*
The principle of good faith and fair dealing is recognized, or at least appears to be acted on as a guideline for contractual behaviour, in all Member States. There is, however, a considerable difference between the legal systems as to how extensive and how powerful the penetration of the principle has been. At the one end of the spectrum figures a system where the principle has revolutionized the contract law (and other parts of the law as well) and added a special feature to the style of that system (GERMANY). At the other end we find systems which do not recognise a general obligation of the parties to conform to good faith, but which in many cases by specific rules reach the results which the other systems have reached by the principle of good faith (ENGLAND and IRELAND).

83 Article 15:101: Contracts Contrary to Fundamental Principles
A contract is of no effect to the extent that it is contrary to principles recognised as fundamental in the laws of the Member States of the European Union.

84 B. *Contrary to Principles Recognised as Fundamental in the Laws of the Member States*
The formulation of Article 15:101 is intended to avoid the varying national concepts of immorality, illegality at common law, public policy, *ordre public* and *bonos mores*, by invoking a necessarily broad idea of fundamental principles of law found across the European Union, including European Community law. Guidance as to these fundamental principles may be obtained from such documents as the EC Treaty (e.g. in favour of free movement of goods, services and persons, protection of market competition), the European Convention on human Rights (e.g. prohibition of slavery and forced labour (art. 3), and rights to liberty (art. 5), respect for private and family life (art. 8), freedom of thought (art. 9), freedom of expression (art. 10), freedom of association (art. 11), right to marry (art.12) and peaceful enjoyment of possessions (First Protocol, art. 1)) and the European Union Charter on Fundamental Rights (which includes many of the rights already mentioned and adds such matters as respect for personal data (art. 8), freedom to choose an occupation and right to engage in work (art. 15), freedom to conduct a business (art. 16), right to property (art. 17), equality between men and women (art. 23), children's rights (art. 24), rights of collective bargaining and action (art. 28), protection in the event of unjustified dismissal (art. 30), and a high level of consumer protection (art. 38).

性的寬廣」[85]。很明顯的英德司法戰爭中的英國法院、2005年海牙選擇法院公約、禁訴令的愛好者、及資本主義者，在鋪天蓋地席捲而來的全球化法學中是處於時代浪潮逆流的一端。而且違反歐盟這些「基本原則」的契約條款，無論當事人之動機為何，一定會被法院認定無效[86]。

類似的概念亦規定於Unidroit Principles of International Commercial Contracts 2004中，其中自然有著甚多強行法之概念，例如誠信原則之不可排除即規定於第1.7條[87]中。但是個人覺得最有趣的是其將第3章整個契約效力之問題，幾乎全部列為強行法[88]。很明顯的，2005年海牙選擇法院公約及禁訴令支持者所主張之的管轄條款及仲裁條款的超越性及獨立性，是一個建築在泡沫上的神話。或許他們在二十一世紀的全球化法學中——是一個十八世紀所遺留的資本主義法學的黑色神話。

(四)管轄及仲裁條款之獨立性

有關管轄條款及仲裁條款之存在或效力應獨立於包含該條款之主契約之其他條款而被單獨認定之論述，亦為英國法界所認為天經地義之事。有關這方面之代表性公約，或許2005年海牙選擇法院第3(d)條[89]可為管轄條款獨立性之代表，而UNCITRAL Model law on International Commercial

---

85 "Thus Article 15:101 extends to contracts placing undue restraints upon individual liberty (for example, being constraints of excessive duration or convenants not to compete), upon the right to work, or upon being otherwise in restraint of trade, contracts which are in conflict with the generally accepted norms of family life and sexual morality, and contracts which interfere with the due administration of justice (e.g. champertous agreements in England, pacta de quota *litis* elsewhere)."

86 D. *No Discretion*
Unlike the position in Article 15:102, the judge or arbitrator is given no discretion to determine the effects of a contract which is contrary to European fundamental principles of law: such a contract is to be given no effect at all. The intentions and knowledge of the parties are irrelevant.

87 Article 1.7 (Good faith and fair dealing)
(1) Each party must act in accordance with good faith and fair dealing in international trade.
(2) The parties may not exclude or limit this duty.

88 Article 3.19 (Mandatory character of the provisions)
The provisions of this Chapter are mandatory, except insofar as they relate to the binding force of mere agreement, initial impossibility or mistake.

89 d) an exclusive choice of court agreement that forms part of a contract shall be treated as an agreement independent of the other terms of the contract. The validity of the exclusive choice of court agreement cannot be contested solely on the ground that the contract is not valid.

Arbitration 1985第16(1)條[90]可為仲裁條款獨立性之代表。而1985年模範公約16(1)條又為許多國家之仲裁法引為模範[91]。個人一向務實的認為管轄與仲裁條款的獨立性與超越性是違反契約法基本原則的資本主義市場利益的神話[92]，是個將強勢者要求法律可預測之利益置於弱勢者要求正義之利益之上之黑色法學。

美國聯邦第8巡迴上訴法院之論述可為仲裁與管轄條款獨立性不符合一般人之生活經驗與常識之代表。於Farmland Indus. Inc. v. Frazier-Parrot Commodities, Inc.[93]中，原告農業公司與被告期貨公司訂立一個契約，契約中有約定任何與契約相關之糾紛，皆應至伊利諾州起訴，後原告宣稱其一職員與被告之職員們收取回扣，並且成立一個假公司。故於密蘇里州起訴，主張詐欺、違反信賴義務，違反證券及期貨交易之相關法規，及觸犯詐欺與貪污組織條例，告期貨公司、仲介公司、及相關職員。聯邦上訴法院同意聯邦地院之看法如下：「這個問題不只牽涉到原告與期貨公司及期貨公司之相關人員間之糾紛而已。原告宣稱有一個複雜的詐欺計畫，不只牽涉到期貨公司及其相關人，並且牽涉不受到原告與期貨公司約定所拘束之其他問題及與證券仲介公司及假公司以外之人[94]。」故而聯邦法院認為本訴訟之範圍大於管轄條款。上訴法院亦同意地院之看法，認為

---

90 (1) The arbitral tribunal may rule on its own jurisdiction, including any objections with respect to the existence or validity of the arbitration agreement. For that purpose, an arbitration clause which forms part of a contract shall be treated as an agreement independent of the other terms of the contract. A decision by the arbitral tribunal that the contract is null and void shall not entail ipso jure the invalidity of the arbitration clause.

91 例如英國的Arbitration Act 1996就稱其第7條為「仲裁調款的分離性」（Separability of arbitration agreement）：
7. Unless otherwise agreed by the parties, an arbitration agreement which forms or was intended to form part of another agreement (whether or not in writing) shall not be regarded as invalid, non-existent or ineffective because that other agreement is invalid, or did not come into existence or has become ineffective, and it shall for that purpose be treated as a distinct agreement.

92 見陳隆修，《2005年海牙法院選擇公約評析》，台北，五南圖書公司，2009年1月，初版1刷，51頁。

93 806 F.2d 848 (8th Cir. 1986); 1986 U.S. App. Lexis 34626.

94 同上，"this matter involves more than a dispute between plaintiff, Heinold, and those associated with Heinold. Plaintiff has alleged an elaborate scheme of fraud involving not only Heinold and individuals associated with Heinold, but also involving other individuals outside the securities brokerages, sham corporations, and other matters not subject to the agreement between plaintiff and Heinold."

原告之訴因並非直接的或間接的由契約而來，並且原告無法預測於伊利諾州提起這些請求之訴訟，故而原告之數個請求並非故意規避管轄條款。地院決定於這種情形下去執行管轄條款，會造成不合理（non reasonable）之情形，上訴法院同意地院之決定，並且認為其並未濫用裁量權（abuse of discretion）。美國聯邦法院的認為訴訟之「範圍」（scope）大於管轄條款，就是英國判例法Donohue[95]所謂的有非訂定管轄條款的第三當事人之利益牽連在案中，故拒絕作成禁訴令。無論是以訴訟範圍大於管轄條款或有第三人之利益被牽連之名義，為了避免判決不一致以達到集中審理案件之目的，英美之判例於此處皆不約而同的超越管轄條款之拘束力。但更有趣的是於Farmland Industries中，上訴法院不但將管轄條款視為實體事項而尊重密蘇里州之公共政策[96]，更語出驚人的挑戰管轄條款獨立性的潮流。上訴法院平實樸素的訴諸人類生活經驗所累積的直覺似乎更強而有力[97]：「原告宣稱被告有詐欺行為，該行為如果能被證實，應足夠能使得包含管轄條款在內之契約無效。被告們引用數個判決，這些判決認為詐欺使得管轄條款無效的情形，只有於管轄條款的被納入契約中是詐欺的後果時方適用。但是，我們相信一個因契約而產生的信賴關係（例如期貨仲介公司與其客戶之關係）如果有涉及詐欺之情形，被詐欺之人不能被要求遵守契約上管轄條款之義務。做任何相反之解釋皆會對Farmland極大不公

95　Donohue v Armco Inc [2001] UKHL 64, [2002] 1 All ER 749.

96　806 F.2d 848; 1986 U.S. App. Lexis 34626, "Whether a contractual forum selection clause is substantive or procedural is a difficult question. On the one hand the clause determines venue and can be considered procedural, but on the other, choice of forum is an important contractual right of the parties. Because of the close relationship between substance and procedure in this case we believe that consideration should have been given to the public policy of Missouri."

97　806 F.2d 848 ,851; 1986 U.S. App. Lexis 34626, "Farmland alleges fraudulent acts on the part of the defendants which, if proved, would be sufficient to vitiate the contract and along with it the forum selection clause. Defendants cite several cases holding that fraud will vitiate a forum selection clause only if the inclusion of that clause in the contract was the product of fraud. However, we believe that in a situation where a fiduciary relationship (such as between a commodities broker and its customer) is created by a contract tainted by fraud, the person defrauded can not be held to the contractual forum selection clause. To hold otherwise would be grossly unfair to Farmland because it would force Farmland to comply with an agreement which never would have been made had the existence of the fraud been known."

平，因為它會迫使Farmland去遵守一個如果詐欺被發現的話永遠不會被簽訂的契約。」

基本上人類的生活經驗是如同上訴法院所說「如果當事人發現的話永遠不會被簽訂的契約」，要求當事人去遵守這種管轄條款是「極度不公平」的。故而如個人前述the UNIDROIT Pronciples中之第3章幾乎將有關契約之效力皆列為強行法，其第3.8條[98]即規定當事人得主張詐欺而使得契約無效，第3.9條為有關脅迫[99]，第3.1條[100]即為當事人間之不平衡亦可使得契約無效。事實上聯邦上訴法院的論述不但是全球化契約法的共同核心政策，亦是人類生活經驗中之常識。

ALI/UNODROIT Principles of Transnational Civil Procedure第3條當事人程序平等條款之comment P-3A[101]說：「合理性的概念並且排除過

---

98 Article 3.8 (Fraud)
A party may avoid the contract when it has been led to conclude the contract by the other party's fraudulent representation, including language or practices, or fraudulent non-disclosure of circumstances which, according to reasonable commercial standards of fair dealing, the latter party should have disclosed.

99 Article 3.9 (Threat)
A party may avoid the contract when it has been led to conclude the contract by the other party's unjustified threat which, having regard to the circumstances, is so imminent and serious as to leave the first party no reasonable alternative. In particular, a threat is unjustified if the act or omission with which a party has been threatened is wrongful in itself, or it is wrongful to use it as a means to obtain the conclusion of the contract.

100 Article 3.10 (Gross disparity)
(1) A party may avoid the contract or an individual term of it if, at the time of the conclusion of the contract, the contract or term unjustifiably gave the other party an excessive advantage. Regard is to be had, among other factors, to
(a) the fact that the other party has taken unfair advantage of the first party's dependence, economic distress or urgent needs, or of its improvidence, ignorance, inexperience or lack of bargaining skill, and
(b) the nature and purpose of the contract.
(2) Upon the request of the party entitled to avoidance, a court may adapt the contract or term in order to make it accord with reasonable commercial standards of fair dealing.
(3) A court may also adapt the contract or term upon the request of the party receiving notice of avoidance, provided that that party informs the other party of its request promptly after receiving such notice and before the other party has reasonably acted in reliance on it. The provisions of Article 3.13(2) apply accordingly.

101 P-3A The term "reasonable" is used throughout the Principles and signifies "proportional," "significant," "not excessive," or "fair," according to the context. It can also mean the opposite of arbitrary. The concept of reasonableness also precludes hyper-technical legal argument and leaves a range of discretion to the court to avoid severe, excessive, or unreasonable application of procedural norms.

分技術性的法律論述並且避免……..不合理的程序上之形式規則。」Cardozo J.說[102]：「但實際上，因為法學上的概念很少，如果曾經存在的話，被執行至邏輯的極限，它的意義並不是絕對的，而是受制於自我設限的常識及公平原則的限制，正如同我們於內戰後之訴訟所學到的一般。」最尊敬的恩師Prof. Graveson於闡釋英國附隨問題之判例法時如此睿智的論述[103]：「這個解決方法的可接受性乃基於邏輯並非判例法的最高價值。英國國際私法實現正義的概括性目的給予邏輯一致性的政策必要的限制。因此於附隨問題上一個英國法院可能判定一個小孩為婚生子女，而於主要問題上卻認定其父母之婚姻為無效[104]，為了達成這個目的可能會使用不同制度的國際私法，判例法的法官將規則視為工具，而非束縛，去提昇，而非防止，他們功能的實現。」「人法地，地法天，天法道，道法自然。」契約中之仲裁及管轄條款之效力不但超越其他法規，並且應獨立於該主契約之其他條款之效力，這種論述不但匪夷所思，違反全球化契約共同核心的基本原則，亦違反了英、美、歐盟各自最高法院歷經時空所淬鍊之自然判例法。這種「橫柴入灶」理論完全是站在資本主義一方面要求攫取自由市場的利益，一方面又要規避法律以剝奪弱勢者「司法保護的形式」之「掠奪性新殖民地主義法學」之立場。這種「過分技術性的法律論述」不但因為「不合理」而應受排除，這種極端的法律邏輯亦應受到人類生活經驗所累積的「常識」所限制，「法學邏輯一致性」的要求更應受到「實現正義

[102] Boris N. Sokoloff v. The National City Bank of New York
[2]39 N.Y. 158, 165, "Juridically, a government that is unrecognized may be viewed as no government at all, if the power withholding recognition chooses thus to view it. In practice, however, since juridical conceptions are seldom, if ever, carried to the limit of their logic, the equivalence is not absolute, but is subject to self-imposed limitations of common sense and fairness, as we learned in litigations following our Civil War."

[103] R.H. Graveson, Conflict of Laws, p.79 (7th ed. 1974), "The acceptability of this solution rests in the fact that logic is not the highest value in the common law. The necessary limits on the policy of logical consistency are imposed by the general purpose of positive justice of English private international law. An English court may thus uphold the legitimacy of children as the subsidiary question and declare null and void the marriage of their parents as the principal question, using different systems of conflict of laws for the purpose. Common law judges regard rules as tools, not as fetters, to promote, not prevent, the fulfillment of their function."

[104] In Hashmi v. Hashmi [1972] Fam. 36.

的基本目的」的限制，「天道無親，恆與善人」如此才是二十一世紀全球化法學之「自然道法」。

(五)禁止濫用程序

在Phillip Alexander Securities & Futures Ltd v Bamberger & Ors中，英國上訴法院承認「英國於許可禁訴令之作法上基於這個案件之事實需要再考慮」，這個論述得到許多教科書之認同[105]，但除了「即使於牽連到違反契約仍可能應加以小心」[106]外，「再考慮」之認同似乎並無具體之結果。個人是極度認同Lord Scarman的論述[107]：「衡平法的寬度及靈活性是不可以被類別化所破壞。」例如當係爭的糾紛的範圍大於契約條款，或有非訂約第三人之利益被牽連於訴訟中時，仲裁或管轄條款的效力就可能會屈服於整個糾紛判決一致的目的下。

但是如果就法院較通常會允許當事人所申請之禁訴令之情形而分類，可能較常發生的為他方當事人於外國所提之訴訟屬於是，他方當事人違反契約約定或其行為是不公正（unconscionable）的。對於前者，個人

---

105 J. G. Collier, Conflict of Laws, 3rd ed., p.108, "It has been suggested that the courts may be becoming more careful in asserting their jurisdiction under an exclusive jurisdiction clause; indeed, in the case just mentioned the Court of Appeal suggested that the courts' existing approach might need reconsideration."

106 PM North, JJ Fawcett, Cheshire and North's Private International law, 13th ed., p. 372, "WALLER J in Philip Alexander Securities and Futures Ltd v Bambeger, aware of the fact that the German courts were offended by the grant of an anti-suit injunction by the English courts, distinguished The Angelic Grace, inter alia, on this ground, and held that it was not a case where it was appropriate to grant an injunction. The Court of Appeal in the same case, recognizing the comity problem where effect needs to be given to the injunction by a foreign court, thought that the English practice in relation to the grant of anti-suit injunctions may need reconsideration in the light of the facts of this case. It may be that a degree of caution is necessary even in cases involving breach of an agreement."
但是因為無法面對契約法平衡性及訴訟法立足點平等之法學共同核心之基本需求，英國後續判例法顯得不知所措，教科書亦不知所云為何。見14th ed.,p. 473: "However, many subsequent cases have followed the principles in *The Angelic Grace*, ignoring the reaction of foreign courts to the grant of an inhunction. Nonetheless, it is submitted that where there is clear evidence that a foreign court would be offended a degree of caution is desirable even in cases involving breach of an agreement. When it comes to whether a foreign court will be offended by the grant of an injunction it may be necessary to distinguish common law jurisdictions which are used to granting such an injunction themselves and are therefore not likely to be offended and civil law jurisdictions which are not and are therefore likely to be offended."

107 Castanho v. Brown & Root (U.K.) Ltd., [1981] A.C. 557, 573 (H.L.) (appeal taken from Eng.), "the width and flexibility of equity are not to be undermined by categorization."

並不反對一般商業上之仲裁或管轄條款之效力，但是其效力必須受到一般契約法上強行法之制約，例如誠信原則、合理性、平衡性要求、及其他基本原則之規定。另外如前述歐盟契約法原則15:101條所特別要求的「寬廣」人權法規自然亦不能被違反，而這些人權法規並不侷限於契約履行地或法院地之強行政策。

而所謂「不公正」的行為，就是對被告造成「困擾性或壓迫性」（vexatious or oppressive）之行為，或是「濫用程序」（abuse of the process）之行為。於Johnson v Gore Wood & Co中Lord Bingham解釋這種法院權力之使用情形[108]：「於RSC Ord. 18, r. 19中可發現這種權力之一種表現，這使得法院在任何階段之程序中，去駁回任何顯示不合理的訴因或防禦之主張，或其為不名譽、輕率、或困擾性，或是其可能濫用法院之程序。現在於CPR r. 3.4亦有相同之權力。」而在Hunter v Chief Constable of the West Midlands Police中Lord Diplock[109]說：「雖然與其程序規則之實際適用並沒有不一致，但仍然會對訴訟當事人造成明顯的不公平，或者於思考正確的人間造成正義的實施會有不名譽之情形下，任何法院皆一定要有此種既存的主動權去防止這種不當的運用其程序之行為。濫用程序可能發生於非常不同的情形；會上訴到本院（最高法院）一定是非常特別的。我認為如果本院若藉此機會去陳述任何會被認為去限制或訂定這種情形之種類之事情是很不智的，而這些情形是法院有義務（我拒絕裁量權之名詞）去行使這個有益的權力的。」故而英國最高法院是認為禁

[108] [2002] 2 AC 1, “One manifestation of this power was to be found in RSC Ord 18, r 19 which empowered the court, at any stage of the proceedings, to strike out any pleading which disclosed no reasonable cause of action or defence, or which was scandalous, frivolous or vexatious, or which was otherwise an abuse of the process of the court. A similar power is now to be found in CPR r 3.4.”

[109] “inherent power which any court of justice must possess to prevent misuse of its procedure in a way which, although not inconsistent with the literal application of its procedural rules, would nevertheless be manifestly unfair to a party to litigation before it, or would otherwise bring the administration of justice into disrepute among right-thinking people. The circumstances in which abuse of process can arise are very varied; those which give rise to the instant appeal must surely be unique. It would, in my view, be most unwise if this House were to use this occasion to say anything that might be taken as limiting to fixed categories the kinds of circumstances in which the court has a duty (I disavow the word discretion) to exercise this salutary power.” [1982] AC 529, 536.

止濫用程序是不應被類別化，而且這種權力的行使並非是法院之裁量權，而是法院之責任。另外於Johnson v Gore Wood & Co中Lord Bingham又說[110]：「於濫訴被認定前，我不同意有必要去確認例如不誠實或對前決定之附隨攻擊等任何附帶因素，但當這些因素是存在時，後面的程序則較明顯的是濫訴，並且除非後面的程序是被法院認定為不公正的騷擾他方，否則甚少被認定為濫訴。但是僅因為一個問題得於前程序被提起，就認為其應被提起，以致於在後面的程序它被提起就必定會被認為是濫訴。如此則是一種過分教條化之方式，而我認為應採的方式是，一種寬廣、以實體為基礎之判斷，應考慮到所牽連之公的及私的利益，並且應考慮到所有案件之事實，注意力應集中在一個重要的問題上，亦即於考慮所有的情形下，一個當事人對以前可以提起的爭點現在試圖於法院前將其提起，是否為錯用或濫用法院的程序。由於我們無法將所有可能濫用的形式皆廣泛的加以表列，故而我們亦無法組成任何死硬的規則，以便於一些特定的事實上可以決定其是否構成濫訴。因此當我會接受缺乏資金通常是不會造成沒有於前訴訟中去提起一個在其時應被提起之爭點之藉口時，我亦不會認定它是一定沒有關連的，特別是這種缺乏資金之情形是由於被請求之人所造成之

[110] “I would not accept that it is necessary, before abuse may be found to identify any additional element such as a collateral attack on a previous decision or some dishonesty, but where those elements are present the later proceedings will be much more obviously abusive, and there will rarely be a finding of abuse unless the later proceeding involves what the court regards as unjust harassment of a party. It is, however, wrong to hold that because a matter could have been raised in earlier proceedings it should have been, so as to render the raising of it in later proceedings necessarily abusive. That is to adopt too dogmatic an approach to what should in my opinion be a broad, merits-based judgment which takes account of the public and private interests involved and also takes account of all the facts of the case, focusing attention on the crucial question whether, in all the circumstances, a party is misusing or abusing the process of the court by seeking to raise before it the issue which could have been raised before. As one cannot comprehensively list all possible forms of abuse, so one cannot formulate any hard and fast rule to determine whether, on given facts, abuse is to be found or not. Thus while I would accept that lack of funds would not ordinarily excuse a failure to raise in earlier proceedings an issue which could and should have been raised then, I would not regard it as necessarily irrelevant, particularly if it appears that the lack of funds has caused by the party against whom it is sought to claim. While the result may often be the same, it is in my view preferable to ask whether in all the circumstances a party’s conduct is an abuse than to ask whether the conduct is an abuse and then, if it is, to ask whether the abuse is excused or justified by special circumstances. Properly applied, and whatever the legitimacy of its descent, the rule has in my view a valuable part to play in protecting the interests of justice.” [2002] 2 AC 1.

情形時。雖然適用之結果是通常一樣的，我認為去詢問是否於所有之情形下當事人之行為是否為濫訴，是比起去詢問該行為是否為濫訴，然後如果是濫訴的話，就去詢問是否將濫訴於特殊情形下應為有理由的或應被原諒的較好。如果適當的使用下，並且在其後續判例的法規下，在我看來這個規則是於保證正義的利益之目的下一個很重要的部分。」因此濫用程序是不應被教條化，亦「無法組成任何死硬的規則」，但卻是「於保證正義的利益之目的下一個很重要的部分」。

雖然說禁止濫訴是不能被「組成任何死硬的規則」，但英國的CPR rule 3.4(2)仍然規定[111]：「法律得排除案件之陳述，如果對法院而言它顯示出：(a)該案件之陳述並未表達抗辯對方之請求，或提出請求，之任何合理的理由；(b)該案件之陳述是濫用法院之程序，或是可能造成公平正義的處理該訴訟程序的障礙……」而於美國禁止濫訴亦同樣的有著成文法之規定，其被規定於美國聯邦民事訴訟法規則（FRCP）的Rule 11(b)[112]中，並且於(c)[113]項中規定為著不當之目的而進行程序者得被加以處罰。另

[111] Civil Procedures
3.4 Power to strike out a statement of case
"(1) In this rule and rule 3.5, reference to a statement of case includes reference to part of a statement of case.
(2) The court may strike out a statement of case if it appears to the court –
(a) that the statement of case discloses no reasonable grounds for bringing or defending the claim;
(b) that the statement of case is an abuse of the court's process or is otherwise likely to obstruct the just disposal of the proceedings......"

[112] (b) Representations to the Court.
By presenting to the court a pleading, written motion, or other paper – whether by signing, filling, submitting, or later advocating it – an attorney or unrepresented party certifies that to the best of the person' s knowledge, information, and belief, formed after an inquiry reasonable under the circumstances:
(1) It is not being presented for any improper purpose, such as to harass, cause unnecessary delay, or needlessly increase the cost of litigation;
(2) the claims, defenses, and other legal contentions are warranted by existing law or a nonfrivolous argument for extending, modifying, or reversing existing law or for establishing new law;
(3) the factual contentions have evidentiary support or, if specifically so identified, will likely have evidentiary support after a reasonable opportunity for further investigation or discovery; and
(4) the denials of factual contentions are warranted on the evidence or, if specifically so identified, are reasonably based on belief or a lack of information.

[113] (c) Sanctions.
(1) In General.
If, after notice and a reasonable opportunity to respond, the court determines that Rule 11(b) has been

外有趣的是ALI/UNIDROIT Principles of Transnational Civil Procedure於相關禁止濫訴的11條[114]又例行的將大陸法的誠信原則與英美訴訟法上的要求連結[115]。其第1項規定當事人必須依誠信原則而行事；第2項規定當事人不得濫用程序；第3項規定當事人必須呈現詳細之事實陳述；第4項規定若當事人不能反駁對方重大之爭辯則視為其接受爭辯。其comment P-11A[116]闡釋當事人於法律上或事實上之主張或抗辯不可以不合理，否則

---

violated, the court may impose an appropriate sanction on any attorney, law firm, or party that violated the rule or is responsible for the violation. Absent exceptional circumstances, a law firm must be held jointly responsible for a violation committed by its partner, associate, or employee.

....

(4) Nature of a Sanction.

A sanction imposed under this rule must be limited to what suffices to deter repetition of the conduct or comparable conduct by others similarly situated. The sanction may include nonmonetary directives; an order to pay a penalty into court; or, if imposed on motion and warranted for effective deterrence, an order directing payment to the movant of part or all of the reasonable attorney's fees and other expenses directly resulting from the violation.

[114] 11. Obligations of the Parties and Lawyers

11.1 The parties and their lawyers must conduct themselves in good faith in dealing with the court and other parties.

11.2 The parties share with the court the responsibility to promote a fair, efficient, and reasonably speedy resolution of the proceeding. The parties must refrain from procedural abuse, such as interference with witnesses or destruction of evidence.

11.3 In the pleading phase, the parties must present in reasonable detail the relevant facts, their contentions of law, and the relief requested, and describe with sufficient specification the available evidence to be offered in support of their allegations. When a party shows good cause for inability to provide reasonable details of relevant facts or sufficient specification of evidence, the court should give due regard to the possibility that necessary facts and evidence will develop later in the course of the proceeding.

11.4 A party's unjustified failure to make a timely response to an opposing party's contention may be taken by the court, after warning the party, as a sufficient basis for considering that contention to be admitted or accepted.

11.5 Lawyers for parties have a professional obligation to assist the parties in observing their procedural obligations.

[115] 其28.3條之註釋亦將英美法的衡平禁反言與誠信原則相連接"A broader scope of issue preclusion is recognized in many common-law systems, but the more limited concept in Principle 28.3 is derived from the principle of good faith, as it is referred to in civil-law systems, or estoppel in pais, as the principle is referred to in common-law systems.「誠信原則」於實體法上是經常與英美法的「合理性」連接並論的。這到底是「大陸法系」半套拳走天下，還是「誠信原則」是法學中之最基礎的基本原則？可能兩者皆是。

[116] P-11A A party should not make a claim, defense, motion, or other initiative or response that is not reasonably arguable in law and fact. In appropriate circumstances, failure to conform to this requirement may be declared an abuse of the court's process and subject the party responsible to cost sanctions and fines. The obligation of good faith, however, does not preclude a party from making a reasonable effort to extend an existing concept based on difference of circumstances. In appropriate circumstances, frivolous or vexatious claims or defenses may be considered an imposition on the court and may be

可能被宣布為濫用程序。若被法院認為輕率或困擾性時，可能遭受敗訴及罰金之處罰。

因此無論是禁止「不公正」行為、「困擾性」或「壓迫性」行為、「濫用程序」行為、或「不誠信」行為，全球化法學於此方面是有一個共同核心的基本政策（而這個政策可能表現在實體法或程序法上）之存在。如若在這個全球化法學基本政策下，有任何外國法院作成禁訴令以禁止當事人「不公正」或「不誠信」之行為，這是不會妨礙到其他大陸法或英美法法院之管轄權的。如在British Airways Board v Laker Airways Ltd中Lord Scarman所說的[117]：「如果於外國法院所提起的訴訟之情形是如此的不公正，以致依照我們『寬廣及靈活』的衡平法原則是可以被認為侵犯了申請者之衡平權利，那麼英國法院許可禁止令之權力是存在的。」

因此對於外國禁訴令是否應加以承認，或甚至大陸法法院是否應自己本身許可禁訴令之作成，如果由二十一世紀全球化法學共同核心政策之觀點而言答案是很清楚的。如果當事人於外國所提的程序是「困擾性」或「壓迫性」之行為、濫用程序、或違反誠信[118]原則，則禁訴令之許可是符

---

subjected to default or dismissal of the case, as well as cost sanctions and fines.

[117] British Airways Board v Laker Airways Ltd 「1985」AC 58 at 95, "The power of the English court to grant the injunction exists, if the bringing of the suit in the foreign court is in the circumstances so unconscionable that in accordance with our principles of a 'wide and flexible' equity it can be seen to be an infringement of an equitable right of the applicant."

[118] ALI/UNIDROIT Principles of Transnational Civil Procedure 的第11條可為全球化法學於禁止濫訴上之代表，該條文規定當事人及其律師對法院及其他當事人之行為，必須符合誠信及道德上之標準，並應避免程序上之濫用。

11. Obligations of the Parties and Lawyers

11.1 The parties and their lawyers must conduct themselves in good faith in dealing with the court and other parties.

11.2 The parties share with the court the responsibility to promote a fair, efficient, and reasonably speedy resolution of the proceeding. The parties must refrain from procedural abuse, such as interference with witnesses or destruction of evidence.

11.3 In the pleading phase, the parties must present in reasonable detail the relevant facts, their contentions of law, and the relief requested, and describe with sufficient specification the available evidence to be offered in support of their allegations. When a party shows good cause for inability to provide reasonable details of relevant facts or sufficient specification of evidence, the court should give due regard to the possibility that necessary facts and evidence will develop later in the course of the proceeding.

11.4 A party's unjustified failure to make a timely response to an opposing party's contention may be taken by the court, after warning the party, as a sufficient basis for considering that contention to be ad-

合正義的利益，其他法院亦應接受這個禁訴令之效力。但若當事人於外國所提之程序是違反仲裁或管轄條款，則如英國同僚於Philip Alexander Securities and Futures Ltd v Bamberger & others中所學到之寶貴一課：「即使於牽連到違反契約仍可能應加以小心」。亦即該契約之成立、存在、效力皆應受到傳統上全球化契約法共同核心強行法之制約，特別是有關契約法強行法中之當事人平衡條款之規定及各種人權公約之強行規定之制約。就只有在符合契約法之基本原則及人權法上，該違反契約之行為才能被給予禁訴令，而其他國家之法院亦才能承認該禁訴令之效力。

(六)國際禮誼與習慣不要求承認禁訴令

雖然於濫用程序及契約法基本原則上全球化法學是有著大致上之共同核心政策，但於各國法院若對這些共同核心政策有著不同立場時，禁訴令之效力應為何？很簡單，各國沒有義務去接受他國基於不同立場而作成之禁訴令。英國之判例法上並不見得永遠接受美國法院之禁訴令。在General Star International Indemnity Ltd v. Stirling Cooke Brown Reinsurance[119]中Judge Langley即認為管轄權之問題應由係屬法院自己決定，而非由當事人間接的在其他法院加以訴訟，因此對於紐約法院之禁訴令再對當事人給予一個反禁訴令。

---

mitted or accepted.

11.5 Lawyers for parties have a professional obligation to assist the parties in observing their procedural obligations.

Comment:

P-11D It is a universal rule that the lawyer has professional and ethical responsibilities for fair dealing with all parties, their lawyers, witnesses, and the court.

[119] [2003] EWHC 3, para. 16 (Eng. Q.B.).又見後續之Tonicstar Ltd. v. Am. Home Assurance Co., [2004] EWHC 1234, para. 13 (Eng. Q.B.), "It seems to me that AHA have tried to hijack the decision which is presently before this court, namely whether the arbitration clause is apt to embrace the disputes between the parties, and, if so, where its seat should be ... The effect of their conduct is to seek to pre-empt this court from reaching its own decision on the arbitration questions. AHA no doubt hoped that their tactic would lead to an earlier determination by the New York Court which would then be invited to restrain the English Court from considering the issue; or at the least, arguing that the decision of the New York court was final and binding as between the parties. The essential facts in this case are sufficiently close to the facts in the case of General Star ... to make what Langley J held in that case worth citing as appropriate in this case too."

美國Restatement of the Law, Second, Conflict of Laws之第102條[120]雖然規定非金錢給付之外州法院之判決，包括禁止命令在內，得被加以執行。但是其第103條[121]卻明文規定若一個州判決之承認或執行會不適當的干擾到姊妹州之重要利益，則充分互信條款之國家政策並不要求其之承認或執行[122]。但最權威的來自美國最高法院於Baker v. General Motors Corp.中之明確意見[123]：「當一個州之判決是欲達成其他姊妹州所專屬範圍之公務上之行為，或是干擾到該作成判決命令之州沒有權力的訴訟時，這種命令作某行為或禁止某行為之判決已經在其他姊妹州被拒絕執行過。」又說[124]：「即使是作為限制受命令當事人之行為之指示，其之作成是符合適

---

[120] § 102 Enforcement of Judgment Ordering or Enjoining Act
A valid judgment that orders the doing of an act other than the payment of money, or that enjoins the doing of an act, may be enforced, or be the subject of remedies, in other states.

[121] § 103 Limitations on Full Faith and Credit
A judgment rendered in one State of the United States need not be recognized or enforced in a sister State if such recognition or enforcement is not required by the national policy of full faith and credit because it would involve an improper interference with important interests of the sister State.

[122] 又見其comment (b)所述充分互信政策之例外，"On these extremely rare occasions, the policy embodied in full faith and credit will give way before the national policy that requires protection of the dignity and of the fundamental interests of each individual State. So, full faith and credit does not require a State to recognize a sister State injunction against suit in its courts on the ground that it is an inconvenient forum. This is because a State, subject to jurisdictional limitations, should be permitted to decide for itself, and without dictation from another State, what cases its courts will hear. Similarly, a State may apply its local statute of limitations to refuse enforcement to a sister State judgment (see § 118, Comment c). The Supreme Court has also held that, in the case of sister State ex parte divorce decrees, the court of the State where recognition is sought is not foreclosed from reexamining the question of domicil in the State of rendition by the fact that 'warrant' could be found in the record of the rendering court for its conclusion that the plaintiff spouse had been domiciled within its territory at the time of the decree, and that it thus had jurisdiction to render the divorce. Williams v. North Carolina, 325 U.S. 226 (1945)."

[123] 522 U.S. 222, 235 (1998), "Orders commanding action or inaction have been denied enforcement in a sister State when they purported to accomplish an official act within the exclusive province of that other State or interfered with litigation over which the ordering State had no authority. Thus, a sister State's decree concerning land ownership in another State has been held ineffective *to transfer title*, see *Fall v. Eastin*, 215 U.S. 1 (1909), although such a decree may indeed preclusively adjudicate the rights and obligations running between the parties to the foreign litigation, see, e.g., Robertson v. Howard, 229 U.S. 254, 261 (1913).

[124] 522 U.S. 222, 236 (1998), And antisuit injunctions regarding litigation elsewhere, even if compatible with due process as a direction constraining parties to the decree, see *Cole v. Cunningham,* 133 U.S. 107 (1890), in fact have not controlled the second court's actions regarding litigation in that court. See, *e.g. James v. Grand Trunk Western R. Co.*, 14 I11. 2d 356, 372, 152 N.E. 2d 858, 867 (1958); see also E. Scoles & P. Hay, Conflict of Laws s. 24.21, P.981 (2d ed. 1992) (observing that antisuit injunction "does

當程序的……有關其他地方訴訟的禁訴令，於實際上對於有關於在該法院之訴訟之第2個法院之訴訟是無法控制的。」

至於歐盟對英國法之特點近年來所持「消滅英國判例法」之態度已是個公開之事實[125]，於Allianz SpA, Generali Assicurazioni Generali SpA, v West Tankers Inc.[126]中歐盟法院更是奇怪的引用紐約公約2(3)條來否認英國禁訴令的正當性（但該2(3)條卻是與2005年海牙選擇法院公約不相容的）。故而若是於不認同外國作成禁訴令法院之立場時，任何法院的不承認外國禁訴令之作法並未違反美、歐、及英國判例法之國際慣例，從而很難指責該不承認行為是違反國際禮誼。

但是無論禁訴令之是否作成，或是否承認外國禁訴令，皆必須僅記英國Civil Procedure Rules 1998, Rule 1.1公正處理案件之「超越性目的」，特別是其第2款所考量之首要因素為「當事人立足點之平等」及亦應衡量當事人之經濟地位[127]。對於第三世界的人民而言，這些考量超乎一切的其他法律基本原則。

二十一世紀全球化法學的心與靈魂在於個案正義是否能被達成，故

---

not address, and thus has no preclusive effect on, the merits of the litigation [in the second forum]").

125 Trevor C. Hartley, The European Union and the Systematic Dismantling of the Common Law of Conflict of Laws, 54 I.C.L.Q. 813, 828 (2005). "The crass insistence that common law rules must be abolished even where no Community interest is at stake is the feature of this judgment that will cause most difficulty for lawyers in England. It seems that the continental judges on the European Court want to dismantle the common law as an objective in its own right. The brushing aside of all practical considerations is also disturbing."

126 [2009] EUECJ C-185/07.

127 (1) These Rules are a new procedural code with the overriding objective of enabling the court to deal with cases justly.
(2) Dealing with cases justly includes, so far as practicable –
(a) ensuring that the parties are on an equal footing;
(b) saving expense;
(c) dealing with the case in ways which are proportionate –
(i) to the amount of money involved;
(ii) to the importance of the case;
(iii) to the complexity of the issues; and
(iv) to the financial position of each party;
(d) ensuring that it is dealt with expeditiously and fairly; and
(e) allotting to it an appropriate share of the court's resources, while taking into account the need to allot resources.

而在這個法學的基本核心政策下，二十一世紀全球化法學於管轄規則的心與靈魂是在於個案正義的真正利益在那裡最能被達成。「道法自然」，個人以為這種論述是符合英國判例法長久以來的傳統。於Lopez v Chavarri中，英國法院認為於數個國家皆有管轄權之情況下，英國法院決定管轄的標準應為[128]：「到底將問題交給外國法院，或於此地解決，才是最能符合正義結果的真正利益。」但是在跨國訴訟中，尤其牽連到第三世界弱勢之人民及中小企業，欲決定「個案正義的真正利益在那裡最能被達成」時，「當事人間立足點平等」及「當事人間之經濟地位」之超越性考量是超越了資本主義者要求法律預測性及穩定性之考量。這亦是個人強烈的認為聯合國人權公約之普世價值及各國之強行法規超越2005年海牙選擇法院之理由。

二、全球化共同核心管轄基礎

最後有個法學方法論上的問題值得再次提出來加以探討。於Airbus Industrie GIE v. Patel中Lord Goff說[129]：「國際禮誼要求英國法院與爭執中的事情必須有著一個充足的利益或關連，以便禁訴令所產生對外國法院的間接干擾是合理的」。這個要求「充足的利益或關連」難道不是英國版的「最低限度關連點」標準嗎？於Allstate Insurance Co., v. Hague, Personal Representative of Hague's Estate[130]中，美國聯邦最高法院立下法院

[128] [1901] W.N. 115, 116, "whether the true interests of justice would be best served by trying the question here, or leaving it to the foreign tribunal."

[129] Airbus Industrie GIE v. Patel [1999] 1 AC 119 at 138, "As a general rule, before an anti-suit injunction can properly be granted by an English court to restrain a person from pursuing proceedings in a foreign jurisdiction in cases of the kind under consideration in the present case, comity requires that the English forum should have a sufficient interest in, or connection with, the matter in question to justify the indirect interference with the foreign court which an anti-suit injunction entails."

[130] 449 U.S. 302; 101 S. Ct. 633; 66 L. Ed. 2d 521; 1981 U.S. LEXIS 52; 49 U.S.L.W. 4071; 1981 Auto. Cas. (CCH) P 10,911。本案為各州選法之基準，故各州皆須遵循本案，例如見James A. Meschewski, Choice of Law in Alaska: A Survival Guide for Using the Second Restatement 16 Alaska L. Rev. 1, 32, 33 (1999); Lsura B. Bartell, the Peripatetic Debtor: Choice of Law and Choice of Exemptions 22 Bank, Dev. J. 401, 408 (2006).

選法規則的基本規範[131]：「一州之實體法如果要在符合憲法之規範下被選為準據法，該州必須要有一個重要的關連點，或一群重要的關連點，而產生州利益，以使得其法律之被適用而不會造成武斷或基本上不公平之後果」。這個規則已成為美國適用法院地法之最基本的少量要求。無論是英國最高法院在禁訴令，或是美國最高法院在選法規則的最低標準上，都有著濃厚的「最重要關連說」及「利益說」的影子，而且符合一般的直覺都將兩者一起使用。這種將兩種不同的理論合併使用的做法，自兩個理論的創世紀判例法Babcock v. Jackson[132]開始後便為許多美國法院所沿用。而個人亦一再的認為這兩個理論，無論單獨使用或合併使用，皆是障眼法。個人一向主張必須依相關的實體政策才能確認系爭中糾紛的公平正義的解決方法，而符合「傳統上公平與實質正義的概念」。禁訴令的作成，事實上與國家的利益及關連是沒有直接關係的，而是與當事人是否濫用程序及其契約是否符合契約法上之基本原則較有直接關連。故而個人自年輕時主張「主流價值」，後來又主張「立法實體化」，到後來配合美國聲音較大的同僚改為「實體法論」，現今全世界最時髦的「全球化法學」亦為個人本文中所一再使用。「全球化法學」的創世紀在那裡？或許在數十年後的今日時間還給個人的信仰一個公道？

(一)司法帝國主義

Professor Adrian Briggs於評論大陸法與英美法同僚在禁訴令上之對話是如同[133]：「雞同鴨講；並且如果是如此的話，去論述一種方式是對的而他種方式是錯，那就沒有意義。」對於歐盟法院對英國判例法的趕盡殺絕Prof. Briggs更是直言是個「可恥」的行為[134]：「歐盟法院對英國法院

---

[131] 449 U.S. 302, 312, 313, "For a State's substantive law to be selected in a constitutionally permissible manner, that State must have a significant contact or significant aggregation of contacts, creating state interests, such that choice of its law is neither arbitrary nor fundamentally unfair."

[132] 12 N.Y. 2d 473, 191 N.E. 2d 279 (1963).

[133] Adrian Briggs, The Impact of Recent Judgments of the European Court on English Procedural Law and Practice, Zeitschrift Fur Schweizerisches Recht 124 (2005) II 231, 234, 144. "chickens talking to a duck; and if it is, it is pointless to say that one approach is right and the other is wrong."

[134] Arian Briggs, *The Impact of Recent Judgments of the European Court on English Procedural Law and*

於法律及實務上之影響，可以說是非常不友善的，而且可以充分的被認為是對商業訴訟的道德性構成威脅。我們很難避免去認為歐盟法院應該為自己感覺可恥。」而最尊敬的恩師Prof. Trevor C. Hartley更是令人震驚的揭穿歐盟大陸法「消滅英國判例法」的真相[135]：「這個判決的特點在於，即使與歐盟的利益無關，卻仍然粗魯的堅持英國判例法必須被消滅，這對英國的法界人士會造成最大的困難。看起來似乎歐盟法院中大陸法系的法官，認為他們是有著確定的權利，去將拆毀英國判例法當成是一個目標。另外（歐盟法院）將事實上的考慮完全忽略也是令人不安的。」

於英國法界哀鴻遍野之際，美國同僚卻經常對大陸法投以豔羨之眼光，Prof. Patrick J. Borchers鄰居的草比較綠的說[136]：「很明顯的，歐盟在布魯塞爾公約，其是規定歐洲共同市場會員國間之對人管轄，的經驗是很正面的。因為如同布魯塞爾公約所顯示，從立法上去努力是一定會較成功的，特別是相較於企圖由憲法不確定之基礎上去建立一個以個案為基本的理論，在可預測性及清晰性上一定是較好的。」為什麼他會將英國同僚的惡夢憧憬為美國夢呢？因為他認為[137]：「美國於對人管轄的歷史是非常

Practice, 124 Zeitschrift Fur Schweizerisches Recht 231 et seq. (2005). "The European Court has had an impact on the law and practice of English courts which is far from benign and which fully deserves the description of a menace to the morality of commercial litigation. It is difficult to avoid the sense that it should ashamed of itself."

135 Trevor C. Hartley, *The European Union and the Systematic Dismantling of the Common Law of Conflict of Laws*, 54 I.C.L.Q. 813, 828 (2005). "The crass insistence that common law rules must be abolished even where no Community interest is at stake is the feature of this judgment that will cause most difficulty for lawyers in England. It seems that the continental judges on the European Court want to dismantle the common law as an objective in its own right. The brushing aside of all practical considerations is also disturbing."又見Trevor C. Hartley, Unnecessary Europeanization under the Brussels Jurisdiction and Judgments Convention: The Case of the Dissatisfied Sub-Purchaser, 18 E.L. Rev. 506 (1993).

136 Patrick J. Borchers, The Death of the Constitutional Law of Personal Jurisdiction: From Pennoyer to Burnham and Back Again, 24 U.C. Davis L. Rev. 19, 104 (1990-1991), "Certainly the European experience with the Brussels Convention, which regulates personal jurisdiction among member nations of the European Common Market, has been very positive. As the Brussels Convention demonstrates, legislative efforts are bound to be more successful, particularly from the standpoint of clarity and predictability, than attempting to create doctrine on a case-by-case basis from uncertain constitutional underpinnings."

137 "The history of American personal jurisdiction is a rocky one. The Court set off in the wrong direction in *Pennoyer* and compounded its navigational error in *Menefee*. Since then, personal jurisdiction doc-

不平順。於Pennoyer中最高法院一開始就走錯了，而且又加上了於Menefee中方向之錯誤。自從那時起，對人管轄的法理就無目的的漂流著，產生出一套令人無法接受的混亂而不合理的管轄『規則』。最高法院最近於Burnham中之決定提供了一些希望。雖然由Justice Scalia所代表的多數意見之憲法方法論與Justice Brennan所代表的贊同意見之立場是極度對立的，但是在兩種意見中最高法院看起來比以前更了解，做為一個一般性之建議，對人管轄並不是一個憲法上之問題。如果最高法院真正願意去擱置其管轄權上之拼圖遊戲，或許由這個混亂中可以建立起一些規則。無論是經由國會或州，立法的行為提供了一些希望以減少奇怪的結果對目前所產生的傷害之方式，及對於問題之最基本所產生的不必要訴訟：我可以在那裡起訴？」另外他又稱美國管轄規則為「叢林法則」[138]；亦有其他美國同僚稱為「一團混亂」[139]或「浩劫」[140]。因此個人戲稱「最低限度關點」在美國於管轄規則上可能已造成最大程度之混亂（minimum contacts cause

---

trine has drifted aimlessly, producing an unacceptably confused and irrational set of jurisdictional 'rules.' The Court's most recent decision in *Burnham* offered some hope. Although the constitutional methodology of the plurality opinion written by Justice Sclaia and the concurrence written by Justice Brennan stood at polar opposites, in both opinions the Court appeared closer than ever to realizing that personal juriadiction is not, as a general proposition, an issue of constitutional law. If the Court is truly willing to shelve its jurisdiction jigsaw puzzle, perhaps some order can be created out of the chaos. Legislative action, either by the states or Congress, offers some promise in reducing the toll currently taken in the form of bizarre results and unnecessary litigation over the most elementary of questions: Where can I sue?" 24 U.C. Davis L. Rev. 105 (1990-1991).

[138] "the Brussels convention is a far more successful effort at rationally regulating jurisdiction than the 'minimum contacts' test and the 'patchwork of legal and factual fictions' that dominate American jurisdeiction." "The fallback to signing the Lugano Convention would be to negotiate as many bilateral agreements as possible. Although this would be cumbersome, a few successful bilaterall agreements might pave the way for a multilateral agreement. Even if a multilateral agreement does not eventually result, some bilateral agreements would be an improvement over the current 'law of the jungle.'" Patrick J. Borchers, Comparing Personal Jurisdiction in the United States and the European Community: Lessons for American Reform, 40 Am J. Comp. L. 121, 153, 156 (1992).

[139] "The United States' law of territorial jurisdiction in civil cases is a mess. Many commentators, here and abroad, have said so for a long time." Kevin M. Clermont, Jurisdictional Salvation and The Hague Treaty, 85 Cornell L. Rev. 89 (1999).

[140] "But, as matters stand, such hopes seem vain. Beyond the internal havoc they have caused, International Shoe and its progeny present formidable obstacles to international harmonization. Because our own house is in disarray, we are unable to render a contribution to the world at large." Friedrich K. Juenger, A shoe Unfit for Globetrotting, 28 U.C. Davis L. Rev. 1027, 1044 (1994-1995).

maximum chaos）。

無論是美國同僚的稱呼美國對人管轄規則是「叢林法則」，或英國同僚的認為歐盟法院於管轄規則上之判例法是「可恥的」，國際私法在管轄規則上似乎是「一團混亂」。更驚悚的是大陸法與英美法似乎在管轄權上極端的對立。除了前述英國與德國在禁訴令上之司法主權的爭端外，德國同僚對於美國司法在懲罰性賠償、反托辣斯法、或集體訴訟法之運作上，指責美國制度為「霸權法律制度」[141]（hegemonic legal system）或「司法帝國主義」[142]（judicial imperialism）。即使是英國同僚亦對Protection of Trading Interests Act 1980之立法，稱之為對美國之「法律戰爭」[143]（legal warfare）。而Professor Ralf Michaels則如此陳述歐洲同僚之不滿[144]：「歐洲人經常指控美國法院的司法霸權主義，這是因為美國法院會去主張管轄權而不顧慮到其他的國家。」

在近代國際私法上通常我們會見到在國際間如若牽連到利益上之衝突時，沒有煙硝的「法律戰爭」是四處蔓延，國與國間捉對厮殺，甚至第一世界與第三世界會在國際公約上展開掠奪性的新殖民地法學的無聲戰爭。然而國際私法在管轄規則之運用上真的是「一團混亂」、「浩劫」、「叢林法則」、「應感到可恥」嗎？個人自年輕時即主張「主流價值」，而現今則承認「全球化法學之共同核心政策」，於管轄規則上個人亦認為全球化管轄規則之共同核心早已存在多時。

---

141 "The *Campabell* decision has been hailed as a welcome contribution given European apprehension of a perceived excessive and hegemonic legal system in the United States at the hands of American plaintiff." Oliver Furtak, Application of Foreign Law to Determine Puntive Damages, in Conflict of Laws in a Globalized World, edited by Eckart Gottschalk, p. 272.

142 Jens Adolphsen, *The Conflict of Laws in Cartel Matters in a Globalised World: Alternatives to the Effects Doctrine*, 1 J. PRIVATE INT'L L. 151, 157 (2005), "has clearly reduced the tendency towards judicial imperialism in U.S. cartel law."

143 P M North, JJ Fawcett, Cheshire and North's Private International Law, 13th ed, p.488,於較近所出版之14th ed.,又於p.561中再次重申。

144 "Europeans frequently accuse U.S. courts of judicial hegemonialism, because U.S courts assert jurisdiction without regard to other countries." Ralf Michaels, Two Paradigms of Jurisdiction, 27 Mich. J. Int'l L. 1003, 1058 (2006).

(二)所在權力與裁量權之行使

因為大陸法的「一般管轄」及「特別管轄」之概念已為有些德裔美國同僚所引進美國[145]，縱使其並未為英國所接受，而且於美國只是發光而未放熱，但個人仍願由此開始分析。美國法律協會（American Law Institute）第三新編外交關係法第421條之報告人註解中[146]，對一般管轄解釋為「不限制於請求權是由於在法院地之行為或活動而引起之管轄權」；而特別管轄是「法院地之法院只有管轄權去審判相關與法院地有關連所引起之請求。」一般而言大陸法之一般管轄基礎為被告之住所地，英美法則為被告之所在於法院地。大陸法之代表規則應為布魯塞爾公約第2條[147]，而美國則為Pennoyer v. Neff[148]所代表的美式用語「所在權力」（presence power）。

或許一般同僚在論及大陸法在一般管轄上是以住所為基礎，故與英美法的以所在為基礎是不一致的——但是跌破眼鏡的個人於此認為英美法於事實上（非名義上）住所亦為一般之管轄基礎。英國於法院之許可下送達境外的Civil Procedure Rules 1998之第1款[149]即規定對住所於法院地內之人之請求之救濟得送達至境外。而美國法律學會的Restatement (Second) of Conflict of Laws § 29 （1988 Revision）[150]亦規定，除非在當事人與

---

145 von Mehren and Trautman, "Jurisdiction to Adjudicate: A Suggested Analysis," 79 Harv. L.Rev 1121 (1996)

146 Restatement (Third) of Foreign Relations Law § 421 (1987)，Reporters' Notes, 3. General and specific jurisdiction. Jurisdiction under Subsections (2)(a)-(e) and (h) is general jurisdiction to adjudicate, i.e., the jurisdiction is not limited to claims arising out of conduct or activity in the forum state. Jurisdiction under Subsection (2)(f), (i), (j), and (k) is sometimes called specific jurisdiction, i.e., the courts of the forum state have jurisdiction to adjudicate only with respect to claims arising out of a the contact with the forum state. Whether jurisdiction under Subsection (2)(g) is general or specific depends on the scope of the consent.

147 Article 2
1. Subject to this Regulation, persons domiciled in a Member State shall, whatever their nationality, be sued in the courts of that Member State.
2. Persons who are not nationals of the Member State in which they are domiciled shall be governed by rules of jurisdiction applicable to nationals of that State.

148 95 U.S. 714 (1877).

149 (1) a claim is made for a remedy against a person domiciled within the jurisdiction.

150 1988 Revision:
A state has power to exercise judicial jurisdiction over an individual who is domiciled in the state,

州之關係極為薄弱，以致管轄之行使為不合理，否則該州對住所於州內之人得行使司法管轄權。其註釋(a)[151]認為最高法院早在1940年就承認這個基礎，並與英國法學一般，認為在這個世界上至少應確保有一個地方一個人是應該接受法院之管轄的。相同的規定亦規定於Restatement (Second) of Conflict of Laws § 30 (1971)[152]有關居所上面。至於有關住所之定義各國仍然南轅北轍，布魯塞爾規則I 59條[153]是交由各會員國依其國內法而定。但是於全球化法學之潮流中，不爭的事實是在一般管轄中——以住所為一般管轄基礎之全球化管轄規則共同核心是存在的。雞跟鴨講不講都沒有關係，反正都是鳥類，都受到禽流感之威脅。

有關所在權力美國法律協會Restatement (Second0 of Conflict of Laws § 28 (1988 Revision)[154]規定，除非州與個人之關係如此薄弱以致管轄權之行使為不合理，否則一個州對境內之人得行使管轄權。但是或許二十世紀末期國際法界對於過度管轄的撻伐，法律協會在其Restatemen (Third) of Foreign Relations Law § 421（1987）之2(a)款[155]中，將單純

---

except in the highly unusual case where the individual's relationship to the state is so attenuated as to make the exercise of such jurisdiction unreasonable.

151 a. Rationale. Except in a highly unusual situation, a person will in the nature of things have a sufficiently close relationship to the state of his domicil to make that state a fair and reasonable forum for the maintenance there of an action against him. So much was recognized by the Supreme Court in Milliken v. Meyer, 311 U.S. 457 (1940). This basis of jurisdiction assures the existence of a place in which a person is continuously amenable to suit.

152 § 30. Residence
A state has power to exercise judicial jurisdiction over an individual who is a resident of the state unless the individual's relationship to the state is so attenuated as to make the exercise of such jurisdiction unreasonable.

153 Article 59
1.In order to determine whether a party is domiciled in the Member State whose courts are seised of a matter, the court shall apply its internal law.
2.If a party is not domiciled in the Member State whose courts are seised of the matter, then, in order to determine whether the party is domiciled in another Member State, the court shall apply the law of that Member State.

154 1988 Revision:
A state has power to exercise judicial jurisdiction over an individual who is present within its territory unless the individual's relationship to the state is so attenuated as to make the exercise of such jurisdiction unreasonable.

155 (a) the person or thing is present in the territory of the state, other than transitorily.

過境管轄排除於所在權力外[156]。但是針對這個問題，法律協會在Restatement (Second) of Conflict of Laws § 28 (1988 Revision) comment (c)中給予一個完美的答案，而且這個答案是與英國判例法及學界之意見完全一致的[157]：「由一個實際的角度而言，是否一個人短暫的停留於一個州會給予該州司法管轄的基礎，這個問題可能只是學術性的。這是因為一個訴訟只是基於這種短暫停留於一個州而沒有其他相關連之情形，可能會基於不方便法院之理由而被駁回或被移轉。」

或許是二十世紀後期大陸法對「所在權力」之撻伐，英國的Dicey and Morris對「所在權力」作出與美國法律協會上述評論一樣的答辯[158]：「任何所在於英國之個人是有責任於對人訴訟之程序中受到送達，無論其於英國所在之期間是如何的短暫皆是如此。因此一個美國人其由紐約飛至

---

[156] 其comment (e) 認為「刺殺管轄」依國際法通常是不能被接受的，故而單純「過境」是不能夠成「所在」。於機場換機、由郵輪下船遊樂、或與訴的請求無關的逗留數日是不能構成(2)(a)款的「所在」，但比「居所」之構成較為短暫的停留是可以的。

e. Transitory presence. "Tag" jurisdiction, i.e., jurisdiction based on service of process on a person only transitorily in the territory of the state, is not generally acceptable under international law. "Presence" in Subsection (2)(a) is satisfied by a less extended stay than is required to constitute residence, but it does not include merely transitory presence, such as while changing planes at an airport, coming on shore from a cruise ship, or a few days' sojourn unconnected with the activity giving rise to the claim.

[157] See Restatement Third, Foreign Relations Law of the United States § 421, which states that service of process on a person only transitorily in the territory of the state is not generally acceptable under international law.

c. Forum non conveniens. From a pragmatic standpoint, the question may be academic whether an individual's momentary presence in a state provides that state with a basis of judicial jurisdiction. This is because a suit based on such presence in the state without other affiliating circumstances would probably be dismissed or transferred on forum non conveniens grounds. See Comments a and c of § 84.

[158] "Any individual who is present in England is liable to be served with process in proceedings in personam, however short may be the period for which he is present in England. Thus an American who has flown from New York to London and intends to leave on the same day is liable to be served with process in proceedings brought to recover a debt due to the claimant incurred by the American and payable in New York. No doubt in some cases the exercise of such a jurisdiction may be exorbitant, and it has been contended that process cannot rightly be served on a foreigner who is not strictly speaking resident in England. But temporary presence as a basis of jurisdiction was emphatically affirmed by the Court of Appeal and has the support of weighty dicta by Lord Russell of Killowen. The history of English procedure bears out this view; the right of an English court to entertain an action depended originally upon a defendant being served in England with the King's writ, and this again was only part of the general doctrine that any person whilst in England owed at least temporary allegiance to the King. But the court has a discretion to refuse to entertain proceedings if to do so might work injustice, where, for example, the claim is contested and the case has no connection with England." Dicey and Morris, the Conflict of Laws, 14th ed, p. 346.

倫敦並且意圖同一天離開，是有責任接收訴訟程序之通知，而該訴訟是由於請求人要求該美國人給付其應於紐約支付之債務而被提起。無疑的於某些情形下這種管轄之行使是可能會構成過度管轄，並且亦有主張認為這種程序不能被合適的送達給嚴格而言並非居住於英國之外國人。但以短暫性的所在（停留）做為管轄基礎是為上訴法院所強力的認同[159]，並且是為Lord Russell of Killowen於其有份量的判決中之附帶意見所支持[160]。英國程序法的歷史證明了這個觀點；英國法院審理案件之權力之依據，是源自依據被告於英國受到國王命令之送達而來，而同樣的這只是基本理論之一部分而已，該理論是任何人當於英國時至少對國王負有短暫忠誠的義務。但是法院在如果可能會造成不正義之情形下，是有著裁量權去拒絕接受訴訟程序的，例如當該請求是被加以抗辯並且該案件與英國沒有關連時。」而所謂依「所在權力」而來的管轄，這顯然包括美國所謂的「過境管轄」（transient jurisdiction）在內，「法院在如果可能會造成不正義之情形下，是有著裁量權去拒絕接受訴訟程序的」，Dicey and Morris於註解中即指明此即為規則31之不方便法院之裁量權。英美法寬廣的管轄基礎本就與其靈活的法院裁量權之行使（方便與不方便法院）是同一制度下不可分割之兩面，如同人行進時之雙腿一般。做為一個判例法的學生，個人實在無法諒解大陸法對英美管轄權行使之粗暴裂解閹割。

雖然以今日之觀點以「所在」作為管轄基礎，可能會產生「法院為不方便法院」之情形[161]，但是這是由於判例法基於歷史所產生的緣故。故而

---

[159] *Colt Industries Inc v Sarlie* [1966] 1 W.L.R. 440 (CA); *Maharance of Baroda v Wildenstein* [1972] 2 Q.B. 283 (CA), *Adams v Cape Industries Plc* [1990] Ch. 433, 518 (CA).

[160] *Carrick v Hancock* (1895) 12 T.L.R. 59m 60.

[161] Dicey and Morris, the Conflict of Laws, 14th ed., p. 591, 592, ""“But some of the older cases also suggest that presence, rather than residence, is a sufficient basis, and presence as a basis of jurisdiction is strengthened by those authorities which suggested that ‘temporary allegiance’ to the local sovereign was one of the reasons why a defendant might be under an obligation to comply with the judgment of its courts. For this reasoning is no less applicable where a defendant is merely present within the foreign country concerned. It is also supported by the authorities on the jurisdiction of the English court over persons present in England: the temporary presence of an individual defendant in England gives the English court jurisdiction at common law and the test for the presence of corporations in that context is the same as that for corporations in the context of the jurisdiction of foreign courts, although in

Cheshire and North[162]說：「英國判例法有關對人訴訟管轄權之規則上最顯著的特點就是他們純粹是程序上之性質。只要如果被告已被請求文件送達，任何人皆可主張或受到管轄。」判例法母法這種對人訴訟之核心管轄基礎自然亦為美國所承襲，於McDonald v Mabee[163]中Holmes J.說：「所在權力就是管轄之基礎」。

事實上「所在權力」不但是英國法院行使管轄之基礎，亦是其承認外國判決之基礎[164]。於Sirdar Gurdyal Singh v Rajah of Faridkote中Lord Selborne[165]說：「所有的管轄權應皆是地域性的」，「並且是extra territorium jus dicenti, impune non paretur……於一個對人屬性之訴訟中，被告無論於何種情形下皆未承認法院之管轄，而該外國法院卻作成缺席判決，於國際法上是個絕對無效的判決。被告是沒有任何義務去遵守該判決；並且除了在作成判決法院之國家外〈當該國有特別的當地法規允許時〉，該判決應是被每一個國家之法院視為無效。」於Pemberton v Hughes中Lord Lindley[166]說：「如果一個外國法院所宣佈的判決是對在

---

the latter context it is described as residence rather than presence. It may be doubted, however, whether casual presence, as distinct from residence, is a desirable basis of jurisdiction if the parties are strangers and the cause of action arose outside the country concerned. For the court is not likely to be the forum conveniens, in the sense of the appropriate court most adequately equipped to deal with the facts or the law."

[162] P M North, JJ Fawcett, Cheshire and North's Private International Law, 13th ed, p. 285, "The most striking feature of the English common law rules relating to competence in actions in personam is their purely procedural character. Anyone may invoke or become amenable to the jurisdiction, provided only that the defendant has been served with a claim form."14th ed., p.353.

[163] 243 US 90 at 91 (1971), "the foundation of jurisdiction is physical power".

[164] 於領頭案例*Buchanan v Rucker* (1808) 9 East 192, 194中，Tobago島的法院於被告從未到過該島，亦未接受其管轄，卻依該島法將訴訟通知釘於法院門口作為替代送達，Lord Ellenborough戲謔的問說："Can the Island of Tobago pass a law to bind the rights of the whole world? Would the world submit to such an assumed jurisdiction?"

[165] [1894] A.C. 670, 683-684 (PC), "All jurisdiction is properly territorial," "and extra territorium jus dicenti, impune non paretur ... In a personal action, ⋯ a decree pronounced in absentem by a foreign court, to the jurisdiction of which the defendant has not in any way submitted himself, is by international law an absolute nullity. He is under no obligation of any kind to obey it; and it must be regarded as a mere nullity by the courts of every nation, except (when authorised by special local legislation) in the country of the forum by which it was pronounced."

[166] [1899] 1 Ch. 781, 790 (CA), "If a judgment is pronounced by a foreign court over persons within its jurisdiction and in a matter with which it is competent to deal, English courts never investigate the propriety of the proceedings in the foreign court, unless they offend against English views of substantial

其管轄區域內之人，並且是其有管轄權去處理之事項，除非他們違反了英國實質正義的概念，英國法院是永遠不會去探究外國法院程序的合適性。」Dicey and Morris認為[167]：「這段話是指程序上之不規則」，但很明顯的當事人必須於外國管轄區內是先決要件。於對人管轄上判例法在John Russell & Ltd v Cayzer, Irvine & Co Ltd中早已宣佈[168]：「任何接到國王的命令（於現今英國稱為請求文件），並且於後來能被強迫去服從所作成之命令的人，就是法院能對其有管轄權之人。」於Adams v Cape Industries Plc中上訴法院認定被告未承認外國法院之管轄權時，外國法院之管轄權得依據被告所在於外國法院地而來[169]：「只要其繼續身體所在於該國，其就享有該國法律上之利益，並應以接受該國法院程序徵召之方式，來顯示其接受該國法律之順與不順之全部。在沒有判例法顯示出相反之結論下，無論是永久性或暫時性及無論是否伴隨著居所而來，我們會認定一個人自願的出現於外國而短暫的所在於該地，根據我們國際私法的規則已經是足以給予該國法院地域管轄權。」

若單以所在權力之本身做為管轄基礎而沒有加上法院裁量權之節制時，的確可能產生過度管轄之不正義情形。但於「不方便法院」標準之節制下，通常自然原告（主張權利受損者）會對自然被告（被主張造成損害

justice."

167 Dicey and Morris, the Conflict of Laws, 14th ed., pp. 633, 634, "This passage refers to irregularity in the proceedings, for it is clear that a foreign judgment, which is manifestly wrong on the merits or has misapplied English law or foreign law, is not impeachable on that ground. Nor is it impeachable because the court admitted evidence which is inadmissible in England or did not admit evidence which is admissible in England or otherwise followed a practice different from English law." See Jacobson v Frachon (1927) 138 L.T. 386, 390, 393 (CA); Adams v Cape Industries Plc [1990] Ch. 433, 569 (CA); *De Cosse Brissac v Rathbone* (1861) 6 H. & N. 301 (the sixth plea); *Scarpetta v Lowenfeld* (1911) 27 T.L.R. 509; *Robinson v Fenner* [1913] 3 K.B. 835; *Boissière v Brockner* (1899) 6 T.L.R. 85.

168 [1916] 2 AC 298 at 302, HL, "whoever is served with the King's writ [now called a claim form] and can be compelled consequently to submit to the decree made is a person over whom the courts have jurisdiction"

169 [1990] Ch. 433 at p. 519, "So long as he remains physically present in that country, he has the benefit of its laws, and must take the rough with the smooth, by accepting his amenability to the process of its courts. In the absence of authority compelling a contrary conclusion, we would conclude that the voluntary presence of an individual in a foreign country, whether permanent or temporary and whether or not accompanied by residence, is sufficient to give the courts of that country territorial jurisdiction over him under our rules of private international law."

者）於自然法院（the most real and substantial connection；「最真實與重大關連」）提起自然訴訟便是順其自然而符合「自然道法」之發展。個人不但主張「不方便法院」應為管轄權行使之限制，亦更主張應仿效美國立法[170]於外國法院之判決違反自然或實質正義時，得據以為不承認外國判決之理由。早在1837年時在Price v Dewhurst中Shadwell V-C就說[171]：「無論何時只要正義很明顯的被忽視，法院就必須將判決視為沒有價值與沒有重要性。」

(三)司法的自大被司法的禮誼取代

早期英國於停止法院地之訴訟上是採較為嚴謹的「困擾性或壓迫性」（oppressive or vexatious）法學，因為被告必須同時對正面及負面的兩個要件負起舉證責任[172]，故是較為傾向保護原告的私人及司法上之利益。個人認為這種較為嚴格的標準較能符合憲法於程序上之要求，於國際上亦可能較符合國際禮誼之要求。但是近年來由於全球化之變遷，使得世界的結構變為更具流動性，如Dicey and Morris所說[173]：「由於許多因素

---

170 美國的UNIFORM FOREIGN MOMEY JUDGMENT RECOGNITION ACT, s.4(6), "in the case of jurisdiction based only on personal service, the foreign court was a seriously inconvenient forum for the trial of the action."故不方便法院亦可為不承認外國判決之理由，個人認為這是相當先進之思想，足以為全世界效法。但是這個規定是限制於管轄基礎是本於送達而來，亦即或許可能是只是針對「短暫過境管轄」而已。個人以為過度管轄之種類繁多，應不只侷限於「短暫過境」而已。不但所有的過度管轄皆應受到「方便與不方便法院」法學之節制，即使在「一般或特別管轄」之情形，於「正義之需求」下亦可在特殊情形下去拒絕承認外國判決。

171 (1837) 8 Sim 279 at 302 "whenever it is manifest that justice has been disregarded, the court is bound to treat the decision as a matter of no value and no substance"

172 (1) A mere balance of convenience is not a sufficient ground for depriving a plaintiff of the advantages of prosecuting his action in an English court if it is otherwise properly brought. The right of access to the King's court must not be lightly refused.
(2) In order to justify a stay two conditions must be satisfied, one positive and the other negative:
(a) the defendant must satisfy the court that the continuance of the action would work an injustice because it would be oppressive or vexatious to him or would be an abuse of the process of the court in some other way; and
(b) the stay must not cause an injustice to the plaintiff. On both, the burden of proof is on the defendant. 見Lord Justice Scott, St. Pierre v. S. Am. Stores (Gath & Chalves) Ltd., [1936] 1 K.B. 382, 398(Eng. C.A. 1935).

173 Dicey and Morris, the Conflict of Laws, 14th ed., p. 465, "This topic has become of the highest importance as a result of a variety of factors including the greater ease of communication and travel; the tendency of courts in many countries to extend their jurisdiction over events and persons outside their territory; and a greater awareness of foreign laws and procedures, which in turn may lead to 'forum-

的結果，包括旅行與通訊的較為容易；許多國家的法院傾向對於在他們管轄區域外之事情或人擴張其管轄權；及對於外國法與程序上的較為知悉，而這可能造成『選購法院』的現象，這個議題已經成為最重要的議題。」而這個鏗鏘有力之論述亦為其他英美法院所認同及引述[174]。於國際複數訴訟中，無論是以什麼名義，承審法院於個案中為了主持正義而行使的裁量權（discretionary power），無論是停止法院地之訴訟、允許送達訴訟之通知至境外之被告、或對有著對人管轄權的當事人作成禁訴令，於市場全球化的今日世界裡已變為「最重要的議題」。

故而為了配合全球化下的寫實，英國最高法院亦不得不採納Lord Kinnear於Sim v. Robinow中所論述的蘇格蘭「不方便法院」法學：「這種主張（基於不方便法院之理由而要求停止訴訟程序）是永遠不能被許可的，除非法院能確定還有著其他有充分管轄權的法院，且於該法院中該案件可以為了所有當事人之利益及正義之目的下而被更合適的加以審判。[175]」Lord Diplock於The Abidin Daver中語出驚人的如此說[176]：「至少於一個程度上司法的自大已經被司法的禮誼取代，亦即我認為現在應是坦白的承認的時候，在有關這個上訴的法律之部門是與蘇格蘭的不方便法院法律原則無法區分的。」最後於Spiliada Maritime Corp v Cansulex Ltd[177]中，英國最高法院（the House of Lords）決定Lord Diplock對於英國停止訴訟重新論述之兩個基本原則太過注重原告之「合法個人或司法利益[178]」（legitimate personal or juridical advantage），而公開的採用不

shopping'."

174 Amchem Products Inc v Worker's Compensation Board [1993] 1 S.C.R. 897, 904 (Sup Ct Can).

175 1892 Sess. Cas. 665, 668 (Scot. 1st Div.), "The plea [for staying proceedings on the ground of forum non conveniens] can never be sustained unless the court is satisfied that there is some other tribunal, having competent jurisdiction, in which the case may be tried more suitably for the interests of all the parties and for the ends of justice."

176 [1984] A.C. 398, 411, "judicial Chauvinism has been replaced by judicial comity to an extent which I think the time is now right to acknowledge frankly is, in the field of law with which this appeal is concerned, indistinguishable from the Scottish legal doctrine of *forum non conveniens*."

177 [1987] A.C. 460.

178 有關原告之「合法私人或司法利益」，見陳隆修、許兆慶、林恩瑋、李瑞生四人合著，《國際私法-管轄與選法理論之交錯》，台北，五南圖書公司，2009年3月，初版1刷，211-215頁。

「方便法院法則」，認為訴訟只能基於「不方便法院」之理由而被加以停止。

英國最高法院（the House of Lords）於領導案例Spiliada Maritime Corp v Cansulex Ltd[179]中，由Lord Goff說明以不方便法院法則為基礎而停止法院之訴訟程序之適用規則如下[180]：「基本原則是法院之訴訟只能基於不方便法院而被停止，而其要件是法院能確認有其他有管轄權之法院存在，並且該法院是合適處理該訴訟之法院，亦即該訴訟可以為了正義的目的及所有當事人的利益，可以在該法院更合適的被加以審判。」而對於以方便法院法則為基礎而行使裁量權，允許將訴訟的文件送達境外之適用規則，Lord Goff說明所謂方便法院即為：「去辨別出案件可以在所有當事人的利益及達到正義的目的下而被合適的審判法院」[181]。故自Spiliada Matitime Corp v Cansulex Ltd後，英國法院於允許送達境外裁量權之行使是以方便法院法則為基礎，而於特定情形下停止英國法院訴訟進行之裁量權之行使則是以不方便法院法則為基礎。

基於方便法院之原則而將通知送達至境外，與基於不方便法院之原則於通知送達至境內後方停止訴訟，兩個裁量權行使的裁量因素、內容、甚至判例基本上皆相似，故而個人稱之為一體之兩面，但仍有相異之處。首先送達至境外基本上就被認定為過度管轄[182]，而於不方便法院之情況基本上法院是已有管轄權之後才去裁量是否停止管轄。另外於方便法院之情況下，舉證責任在於原告，並且於請求之階段因不須通知他方，故必須完全而且公平的陳述[183]；而於不方便法院的情況，至少於第一階段舉證責任在

179 [1987] A.C. 460.

180 Spiliada Maritime Corpn v. Cansulex Ltd [1987] AC 460 at 476, “The basic principle is that a stay will only be granted on the ground of forum non conveniens where the court is satisfied that there is some available forum having jurisdiction, which is the appropriate forum for trial of the action, i.e. in which the case may be tried more suitably for the interests of all the parties and the ends of justice.”

181 同上，at 480, “to identify the forum in which the case can be suitably tried for the interests of all the parties and for the ends of justice”.

182 Spiliada Maritime Corpn v. Cansulex Ltd [1987] AC 460 at 481.

183 Kuwait Oil Co. (KSC) v. Idemitsu tankers KK, The Hida Maru [1981] 2 Lloyd’s Rep 510.另外在對法律解釋有疑問時，應以對被告有利之方式解決。

於不方便法院的被告[184]。

但為了避免與美式不方便法院無法區別，所應注意的是如Lord Justice Scott於St. Pierre v. S. Am. Stores (Gath & Chalves) Ltd.[185]中所說的：「只是便利因素的平衡是不足的」。為了避免對「不方便法院」或「方便法院」中「conveniens」一詞產生混淆，Dicey and Morris還特別說明[186]：「conveniens並不是指『方便』」。故而於此「conveniens」所指的通常或許應是「appropriate」（合適）之意，這雖然包含證人、證據、及準據法的便利及當事人的利益，但最主要的還是指「更合適達成正義目的」（more suitable for the ends of justice）之法院。事實上於一百多年前面對國際訴訟上可能形成之複數訴訟之問題，在Lapez v Chavari中英國判例法甚早就對此問題之核心加以論述如下[187]：「是否於本地審理該問題，或將其交付外國法院，最能達成正義的目的。」

(四)送達境外為過度或例外之管轄

雖然自the Spiliada後英國法院正式於停止法院地之程序是採用不方便法院法學，而於允許將訴訟之通知送達境外被告是採用方便法院法學之標準，但事實上於境外送達上英國判例法長久以來就認為是過度（exorbitant）或例外（extraordinary）之管轄[188]，並且有著一系列之判例法來規範裁量權之行使[189]。而成文法亦明確的規定法院允許送達境外時應謹慎的考慮一些因素。Civil Procedure Rules 1998, s. 6.20(3)(a)[190]要求

---

[184] The Spiliada, [1987] AC 460, at 474.

[185] "(1) A mere balance of convenience is not a sufficient ground for depriving a plaintiff of the advantages of prosecuting his action in an English court if it is otherwise properly brought. The right of access to the King's court must not be lightly refused." St. Pierre v. S. Am. Stores (Gath & Chalves) Ltd., [1936] 1 K.B. 382, 398 (Eng. C.A. 1935).

[186] Dicey and Morris, the Conflict of Laws, 14th ed., p. 465, note 25, "*Conveniens does not mean 'convenient': see The Atlantic Star* [1974] A.C. 436, 475; *GAF Corp v Amchem Products Inc* [1975] 1 Lloyd's Rep. 601, 607; *Spiliada Maritime Corp v Cansulex Ltd* [1987] A.C. 460, 474-475."

[187] [1901] W.N. 115, 116, "whether the true interests of justice would be best served by trying the question here, or leaving it to the foreign tribunal".

[188] Spiliada Maritime Corpn v. Cansulex Ltd [1987] AC 460 at 481.

[189] 陳隆修，《國際私法管轄權評論》，台北，五南圖書公司，民國75年11月，初版，45-47頁。

[190] (3) a claim is made against someone on whom the claim form has been or will be served and –

請求人與被告間「必須有一個真正的爭點合理的需要法院去審判」；s. 6.21(1)(b)[191]規定原告必須以書面證明「其請求有著合理勝訴的機會」；而s. 6.21（2A）[192]則明示「除非法院能同意法院地是個合適去提起請求之地，否則法院不會去允許送達境外」。故而在方便法院法則之相關判例法與成文法之交叉規範下，英國法是謹慎的避免對境外被告之人權與被告國家之主權加以侵犯。大陸法國內法及歐盟布魯塞爾規則第5條雖然於管轄權上皆要求法院地與訴因有著關連，但對於境外與境內被告之送達並未加以區分，這是與一般常識上之認知及訴訟於實務上之困難不合的。對於境外被告加以送達、起訴，不但應注意到應訴被告之人權及其母國之尊嚴、主權之問題，更應務實的謹記法院判決於被告母國之執行性之問題。

英國判例法傳統上認為送達訴訟之通知至境外基本上是一種「過度」或「例外」之管轄基礎，經常冒著不被外國法院承認之風險，因而必須於非常謹慎之情形下方得行使此裁量權送達通知至境外之認知[193]，亦為ALI/UNIDOROT Principles of Transnational Civil Procedure有關當事人於程序上平等之第3條[194]所採。其第3.1條除了規定法院必須確保當事人間之平等外，第3.2條又特別規定應避免基於國籍與居所而來的歧視，而後

(a) there is between the claimant and that person a real issue which it is reasonable for the court to try.

191 6.21 Application for permission to serve claim form out of jurisdiction
(1) An application for permission under rule 6.20 must be supported by written evidence stating –
(a) the grounds on which the application is made and the paragraph or paragraphs of rule 6.20 relied on;
(b) that the claimant believes that his claim has a reasonable prospect of success; and
(c) the defendant's address or, if not know, in what place or country the defendant is, or is likely, to be found.
(2) Where the application is made in respect of a claim referred to in rule 6.20(3), the written evidence must also state the grounds on which the witness believes that there is between the claimant and the person on whom the claim form has been, or will be served, a real issue which it is reasonable for the court to try.

192 (2A) The court will not give permission unless satisfied that England and Wales is the proper place in which to bring the claim.

193 Cardova land Co. Ltd., v. Victor Bro Inc [1966] 1 WLR 793 at 796.

194 3. Procedural Equality of the Parties
3.1 The court should ensure equal treatment and reasonable opportunity for litigants to assert or defend their rights.
3.2 The right to equal treatment includes avoidance of any kind of illegitimate discrimination, particularly on the basis of nationality of residence. The court should take into account difficulties that might be encountered by a foreign party in participating in litigation.

半段則規定「法院應考慮到一外國當事人於參加訴訟時所可能遭遇之困難」。其註釋P-3A[195]又補充解釋整個ALI/UNIDROIT Principles是充斥著「合理性」的要求。除了跨國公司間之訴訟外，要將被告拖曳（hale）至「一個遙遠的外國法院」[196]，使其面對費用、語言、文化、制度、法律、及習慣上之困難，除了要有正當性及迫切之理由外，另外必須顧及英國Civil Procedure Rules 1998, Rule 1中所要求的「立足點平等」及「貧富差距」之問題。

如果於跨國訴訟中法院地的決定不是那麼的重要，第一世界為什麼要花數十年的時間去形成2005年海牙選擇法院公約共識成立之假象？於跨國訴訟中任何人都知道法院地的決定就幾乎是勝負的決定，以原告就被告的訴訟法原則的歷史之建立可能遠遠久過國際管轄規則之建立。於跨國訴訟上忽視外國被告參加本國訴訟的困難，這不僅是不符合Cardozo J.所說的「常識」，亦違反了Prof. Graveson所說的「正義的目的」，更違反了人類生活經驗所累積的「自然道法」。

個人於此再次引用先前著作之論述[197]：**「或許是無論於英國方便法院原則之公開確認，或美國於Burnham198對短暫過境管轄之確認，至今皆不滿二十年，個人甚為訝異的發現國際私法界有一個驚天動地的新潮流又鋪天蓋地的席捲而來，而全世界仍然白目的視而不見—英國與美國皆不約而同的對送達至境外加以重新規範，英國以『方便法院』原則而美國以『最低限度關連點』原則為裁量權行使之規範。雖然學理與名稱不同，但**

---

[195] P-3A The term "reasonable" is used throughout the Principles and signifies "proportional," "significant," "not excessive," or "fair," according to the context.

[196] Carnival Cruise Lines Inc v. Shute, 499 U.S. 585 (1991), para, 26, "Furthermore, the Court of Appeals did not place in proper context this Court's statement in The Bremen that 'the serious inconvenience of the contractual forum to one or both of the parties might carry greater weight in determining the reasonableness of the forum clause.' 407 U.S., at 17, 92 S. Ct., at 1917. The Court made this statement in evaluating a hypothetical 'agreement between two Americans to resolve their essentially local dispute in a remote alien forum.' *Ibid*. In the present case, Florida is not a 'remote alien forum'."

[197] 陳隆修、許兆慶、林恩瑋、李瑞生四人合著，《國際私法-管轄與選法理論之交錯》，台北，五南圖書公司，2009年3月，初版1刷，204、205頁。

[198] Burnham v. Superior Court, 495 U.S. 604 (1990).

基本精神乃是將送達至境外的過度管轄權加以適度合理的規範，如前述歐盟與海牙會議數十年來忙著對過度管轄消極的加以撻伐及限制，然而最近不到二十年來英國及美國卻不約而同的以不同的手段積極的對送達至境外加以制度化及合理化。或許歐陸國家應擺脫消極禁止的態度，而積極的去制度化境外送達。個人不知是否有其他衝突法的同僚注意到英、美此處異曲同工之創見，如若是沒有，那麼如同個人近三十年前於實體法方法論一般，於此處管轄權理論驚濤駭浪般澎湃洶湧的新趨勢中，本文很榮幸的於此為衝突法管轄權歷史作一個大時代潮流的新見證。國際私法的江山如此的多嬌，難怪60、70年代的前輩美國選法革命論者直以生死相許。」

個人真誠的認為任何國際管轄的規則如果不能嚴肅的面對外國當事人於本國參加訴訟的困難，那就是藐視訴訟法要求「當事人間立足點平等」的最基本原則。尤其對於第三世界的人民而言這已是構成違反人權法及憲法的基本人權之問題。個人於此再次語出驚人的宣佈：我們人類不但在一般管轄上有著共同核心，在特別管轄上亦早已存在著共同核心，但是在心態上我們對跨國管轄的最基礎認知上卻沒有共同核心。英國判例法[199]一百多年來對境外被告人權之考量，為美國「最低限度關連點」所跌跌撞撞的實施者，而歐盟大陸法卻無知、野蠻、落後到完全不區分當事人是否有著「外國當事人之困難」。

(五)一般管轄與特別管轄的共同核心

如前述一般管轄的以住所為全球化法學在管轄規則的共同核心是已存在之事實，而以「身體所在」的英美管轄基礎既已受到不方便法院法學的限制，故是否會構成「過度管轄」已是個「學術上之問題」而已。

---

[199] 英國有關法院行使裁量權的標準，於The Hagen中有規定如下：
1.使居住於國外之被告到法院地來為其權利辯護不是不正當。
2.當法院對於是否應適用法規而將訴訟之通知送達於國外，若有疑問時，對於外國被告之利益應給予優先之考慮（benefit of doubt）。
3.由於被告居於國外，並且通常無代理人，故原告有義務將案件之事實完全告訴法院，並且說明法院將訴訟之通知送達於國外是符合法律上之規定。
[1908] p. 189.

至於有關特別管轄在契約履行地（或訂定地）、侵權行為地[200]（通常包含行為發生地及損害發生地）、不當得利地、因分行之活動而產生之訴因以分行所在地等，一般各國之過內及國際管轄上是皆有規定。代表大陸法於此方面之規定者應為Council Regulation (EC) No 44/2001 December 2000 on jurisdiction and the recognition and enforcement of judgments in civil and commercial matters（布魯塞爾規則I）第5條[201]。至於英美法因為所在於境內之人皆必須接受管轄，故特別管轄只能適用於送達給境外被告之「過度」或」例外」之管轄權之行使。英國Civil Procedure

---

[200] 除了英國送達境外包含侵權行為地與損害賠償發生地（CPR 1998, s. 6.20(8)）為基礎外，歐盟最高法院（ECJ）於Case 21/76 Bier BV v. Mines de Potasse D'Alsace SA [1976] E.C.R. 1735中，認定Brussels Convention的第5(3)條是給予請求者選擇行為發生地或損害發生地去起訴之機會。

[201] Article 5

A person domiciled in a Member State may, in another Member State, be sued:

1.(a) in matters relating to a contract, in the courts for the place of performance of the obligation in question;

(b) for the purpose of this provision and unless otherwise agreed, the place of performance of the obligation in question shall be:

—in the case of the sale of goods, the place in a Member State where, under the contract, the goods were delivered or should have been delivered,

—in the case of the provision of services, the place in a Member State where, under the contract, the service were provided or should have been provided,

(c) if subparagraph (b) does not apply then subparagraph (a) applies;

2. in matters relating to maintenance, in the courts for the place where the maintenance creditor is domiciled or habitually resident or, if the matter is ancillary to proceedings concerning the status of a person, in the court which, according to its own law, has jurisdiction to entertain those proceedings, unless that jurisdiction is based solely on the nationality of one of the parties;

3. in matters relating to tort, delict or quasi-delict, in the courts for the place where the harmful event occurred or may occur;

4. as regards a civil claim for damages or restitution which is based on an act giving rise to criminal proceedings, in the court seised of those proceedings, to the extent that that court has jurisdiction under its own law to entertain civil proceedings;

5. as regards a dispute arising out of the operations of a branch, agency or other establishment, in the courts for the place in which the branch, agency or other establishment is situated;

6. as settlor, trustee or beneficiary of a trust created by the operation of a statute, or by a written instrument, or created orally and evidenced in writing, in the courts of the Member State in which the trust is domiciled;

7. as regards a dispute concerning the payment of remuneration claimed in respect of the salvage of a cargo or freight, in the court under the authority of which the cargo or freight in question:

(a) has been arrested to secure such payment, or

(b) could have been so arrested, but bail or other security has been given;

provided that this provision shall apply only if it is claimed that the defendant has an interest in the cargo or freight or had such an interest at the time of salvage.

Rules 1998之s. 6.19是有關不需法院之許可即可送達境外之被告之情形，這是通常是有關歐盟會員國之公約或有其他立法之情形。但Civil Procedure Rules 1998之s. 6.20[202]即可相對於大陸法所謂的特別管轄與一般管轄

[202] 6.20 Service out of the jurisdiction where the permission of the court is required
In any proceedings to which rule 6.19 does not apply, a claim form any be served out of the jurisdiction with the permission of the court if-
(1) a claim is made for a remedy against a person domiciled within the jurisdiction.
(2)a claim is made for an injunction ordering the defendant to do or refrain from doing an act within the jurisdiction.
(3) a claim is made against someone on whom the claim form has been or will be served and –
(a) there is between the claimant and that person a real issue which it is reasonable for the court to try; and
(b) the claimant wishes to serve the claim form on another person who is a necessary or proper party to that claim.
(3A) a claim is a Part 20 claim and the person to be served is a necessary or proper party to the claim against the Part 20 claimant.
(4) a claim is made for an interim remedy under section 25(1) of the 1982 Act.
(5) a claim is made in respect of a contract where the contract –
(a) was made within the jurisdiction;
(b) was made by or through an agent trading or residing within the jurisdiction;
(c) is governed by English law; or
(d) contains a term to the effect that the court shall jurisdiction to determine any claim in respect of the contract.
(6) a claim is made in respect of a breach of contract committed within the jurisdiction.
(7) a claim is made for a declaration that no contract exists where, if the contract was found to exist, it would comply with the conditions set out in paragraph (5).
(8) a claim is made in tort where –
(a) damage was sustained within the jurisdiction; or
(b) the damage sustained resulted from an act committed within the jurisdiction.
(9) a claim is made to enforce any judgment or arbitral award.
(10) the whole subject matter of a claim relates to property located within the jurisdiction.
(11) a claim is made for any remedy which might be obtained in proceedings to execute the trusts of a written instrument where –
(a) the trusts ought to be executed according to English law; and
(b) the person on whom the claim form is to be served is a trustee of the trusts.
(12) a claim is made for any remedy which might be obtained in proceedings for the administration of the estate of a person who died domiciled within the jurisdiction.
(13) a claim is made in probate proceedings which includes a claim for the rectification of a will.
(14) a claim is made for a remedy against the defendant as constructive trustee where the defendant's alleged liability arises out of acts committed within the jurisdiction.
(15) a claim is made for restitution where the defendant's alleged liability arises out of acts committed within the jurisdiction.
(16) a claim is made by the Commissioners of the Inland Revenue relating to duties or taxes against a defendant not domiciled in Scotland or Northern Ireland.
(17) a claim is made by a party to proceedings for an order that the court exercise its power under section 51 of the Supreme Court Act 1981 to make a costs order in favour of or against a person who is not a party to those proceedings.

（住所；s.6.20(1)），如果忘掉其只適用於境外送達之方面，s. 6.20之規定以個人而言是非常類似大陸法的國內管轄規定，甚或更為詳細。至於s.6.20(3)(b)及3A是有關對該請求為必須或合適之第三人；或對抗請求人之主張為必須或合適之第三人。這種類似第三人訴訟或共同訴訟於布魯塞爾規則亦有類似之規定[203]，但表達方式並不一致。

至於美國因為亦採所在理論[204]，故對境內之人皆有著一般管轄，特別管轄亦只能適用於域外之被告，而域外管轄是受到「最低限度關連點」之限制。個人早期如此寫著[205]：「依上述『最低限度關連點』理論，只要訴訟是基於被告與法院地有重大關係之行為，並且法院審理該訴訟並不違反傳統上公平及正義之原則時，則法院對非居民被告有管轄權。但以上乃為美國憲法有關適當程序條款之要求，各州仍須將此理論制成法規，以便州法院對非居民被告有管轄權，這些法規於美國稱為『長手法規』（long arm statutes）。沒有這些『長手法規』，無論非居民被告於法院地之活動為何，及與法院地之關連點（contacts）為何，州法院對其無管轄權。一般美國各州最常採用之長手法規，為伊利諾州所採用的長手法規。此類長手法規明文列舉各種特定之行為，如果行為人於法院地做成這些行為，則法院對於任何基於這些行為所引起之訴訟，對行為人有管轄權。另外加州於1970年所通過之長手法規，並未列舉出各種特定之行為，其允許法

(17A) a claim is –
(a) in the nature of salvage and any part of the services took place within the jurisdiction; or
(b) to enforce a claim under section 153, 154 or 175 of the Merchant Shipping Act 1995(a).
(18) a claim is made under an enactment specified in the relevant practice direction.

[203] Article 6
A person domiciled in a Member State may also be sued:
1.Where he is one of a number of defendants, in the courts for the place where any one of them is domiciled, provided the claims are so closely connected that it is expedient to hear and determine them together to avoid the risk of irreconcilable judgments resulting from separate proceedings;
2.as a third party in an action on a warranty or guarantee or in any other third party proceedings, in the court seised of the original proceedings, unless these were instituted solely with the object of removing him from the jurisdiction of the court which would be competent in his case;

[204] Burnham v. Superior Court, 495 U.S. 604 (1990).

[205] 陳隆修，《國際私法管轄權評論》，台北，五南圖書公司，民國75年11月，初版，136頁。又見136-147頁。

院於憲法適當程序條款之範圍內，接受案件之管轄權，亦即美國憲法適當程序條款為其管轄權唯一之限制。」但其長手法規所規定之內容亦大致上與大陸法特別管轄之內容相去不遠，如商業行為地、侵權行為地、財產所在地、婚姻住所地、及契約履行地等。

因為涉及五十州之長手法規較難比較，但或許美國法律協會（the American Law Institute）有關司法管轄的規定較具有代表性。其有關州對個人之司法管轄規定於Restatement (Second) of Conflict of Laws § 27（1971）[206]中；另外於Restatement (Third) of Foreign Relations Law § 421（1987）[207]中，其又規定各州之對人或對物之管轄。故而美國法通常

[206] § 27. Bases Of Judicial Jurisdiction Over Individuals
(1)A state has power to exercise judicial jurisdiction over an individual on one or more of the following bases:
(a) presence
(b) domicil
(c)residence
(d) nationality or citizenship
(e) consent
(f) appearance in an action
(g) doing business in the state
(h) an act done in the state
(i) causing an effect in the state by an act done elsewhere
(j) ownership, use or possession of a thing in the state
(k) other relationships to the state which make the exercise of judicial jurisdiction reasonable
(2) The circumstances in which, and the extent to which, these bases are sufficient to support an exercise of judicial jurisdiction over an individual are stated in § § 28-39.

[207] § 421 Jurisdiction To Adjudicate
(1) A state may exercise jurisdiction through its courts to adjudicate with respect to a person or thing if the relationship of the state to the person or thing is such as to make the exercise of jurisdiction reasonable.
(2) In general, a state's exercise of jurisdiction to adjudicate with respect to a person or thing reasonable if, at the time jurisdiction is asserted:
(a) the person or thing is present in the territory of the state, other than transitorily;
(b) the person, if a natural person, is domiciled in the state;
(c) the person, if a natural person, is resident in the state;
(d) the person, if a natural person, is a national of the state;
(e) the person, if a corporation or comparable juridical person, is organized pursuant to the law of the state;
(f) a ship, aircraft or other vehicle to which the adjudication relates is registered under the laws of the state;
(g) the person, whether natural or juridical, has consented to the exercise of jurisdiction;
(h) the person, whether natural or juridical, regularly carries on business in the state;

是以住所或居所做為一般管轄基礎（甚至包含「所在」），這是與歐盟（布魯塞爾規則I第2條）及英國相似，並以於法院地內之行為做為有關該行為之特別管轄。至於以當事人之承認做為管轄基礎，這是各文明國家於國內法及國際法之共通規定。略有爭議的是美國式的以經營商業做為一般管轄基礎，這不但為其他國家所沒有，大部分美國同僚亦認為這是個不存在的管轄基礎，但若做為特別管轄基礎則為舉世皆有的。至於物之所在地之訴訟必須與該物有關連方能以物之所在為管轄基礎，這是舉世皆然[208]。

故而無論是一般管轄或特別管轄，全球化管轄規則的共同核心是存在的，但是這種分法的阿奇里斯腳踝是其不符合人道的忽視了「外國當事人參加訴訟的困難」。

(六)方便法院與不方便法院

另外Restatement (Second) of Conflict of Laws § 24 (1988 Revision)[209]規定只要州與個人之關連是合理的即可行使管轄。而Restatement (Second) of Judgments § 4 (1982)[210]則規定聯邦與州法院必須於法院地與

(i) the person, whether natural or juridical, had carried on activity in the state, but only in respect of such activity;

(j) the person, whether nature or juridical, had carried on outside the state an activity having a substantial, direct, and foreseeable effect within the state, but only in respect of such activity; or

(k) the thing that is the subject of adjudication is owned, possessed, or used in the state, but only in respect of a claim reasonably connected with that thing

(3) A defense of lack of jurisdiction is generally waived by any appearance by or on behalf of a person or thing (whether as plaintiff, defendant, or third party), if the appearance is for a purpose that does not include a challenge to the exercise of jurisdiction.

208 陳隆修、許兆慶、林恩瑋、李瑞生四人合著，《國際私法-管轄與選法理論之交錯》，台北，五南圖書公司，2009年3月，初版1刷，176-180頁。

209 1988 Revision:

(1) A state has power to exercise judicial jurisdiction over a person if the person's relationship to the state is such as to make the exercise of such jurisdiction unreasonable.

(2) The relationships which are sufficient to support an exercise of judicial jurisdiction over a person are stated in §§27-52.

210 § 4. Constitutional And Legislative Determinants Of Territorial Jurisdiction

(1) A state court may exercise territorial jurisdiction over persons in an action if:

(a) The state has a relationship to the action or the parties thereto stated in §§ 5 to 8; and

(b) The exercise of jurisdiction is not impermissible under federal law, the law of the state itself, or other applicable restriction.

(2) A federal court may exercise jurisdiction over persons in an action if:

(a) The court has a territorial jurisdiction relationship to the action prescribed by statute or rule of court;

個人間有關連才能行使地域管轄。這種說法為ALI/UNIDROIT Principles of Transnational Civil Procedure第2條[211]對人管轄之規定所論述的更為清楚。第2.1.1規定當事人之同意得構成管轄基礎。第2.1.2條規定法院與當事人、行為、或事件有重大關連即有對人管轄；而行為或事件的顯著部分發生於法院地，慣居地、公司成立地或主要營業地、或與爭執有關之物之於法院地，皆構成重大關連之存在。故而很聰明的避開了一般及特別管轄之區分。其註釋P-2B[212]認為「重大關連」之標準是於國際紛爭中所一般會接受的，並且拒絕「所在權力」及「經營商業」之一般管轄。另外其2.5條[213]又接受「不方便法院」法學，而3.2條[214]又規定「應考慮外國當事人於參加訴訟所可能遭遇之困難」。於Airbus Indus. G.I.E. v. Patel中Lord Goff高調的宣示在Spiliada[215]、Connelly[216]、Lubbe[217]等領導案例之適

---

and

(b) The exercise of jurisdiction is not impermissible under federal law or other applicable restriction.

211 2. Jurisdiction Over Parties

2.1 Jurisdiction over a party may be exercised:

2.1.1 By consent of the parties to submit the dispute to the tribunal;

2.1.2 When there is a substantial connection between the forum state and the party or the transaction or occurrence in dispute. A substantial connection exists when a significant part of the transaction or occurrence occurred in the forum state, when an individual defendant is a habitual resident if the forum state or a jural entity has received its charter of organization or has its principal place of business therein, or when property to which the dispute relates is located in the forum state.

212 P-2B The standard of "substantial connection" has been generally accepted for international legal disputes. Administration of this standard necessarily involves elements of practical judgment and self-restraint. That standard excludes mere physical presence, which within the United States is colloquially called "tag jurisdiction." Mere physical presence as a basis of jurisdiction within the America federation has historical justification that is inapposite in modern international disputes. The concept of "substantial connection" may be specified and elaborated in international conventions and in national laws. The scope of this expression might not be the same in all systems. However, the concept does not support general jurisdiction on the basis of "doing business" not related to the transaction or occurrence in dispute.

213 2.5 Jurisdiction may be declined or the proceeding suspended when the court is manifestly inappropriate relative to another more appropriate court that could exercise jurisdiction.

214 3.2 The right to equal treatment includes avoidance of any kind of illegitimate discrimination, particularly on the basis of nationality or residence. The court should take into account difficulties that might be encountered by a foreign party in participating in litigation.

215 Spiliada Mar. Corp. v. Cansulex Ltd., [1987] 1 A.C. 460, 460 (H.L. 1986) (appeal taken from Eng.).

216 Connelly v. RTZ Corp. PLC, 1998 A.C. 854, 872 (H.L. 1997) (appeal taken from Eng.).

217 Lubbe v. Cape PLC, [2000] 1 W.L.R. 1545 (H.L.) (appeal taken from Eng.).

用下，「不方便法院」法學[218]：「可被視為最文明之法學原則之一」：又因為ALI/UNIDROIT Principles of Transnational Civil Procedure公開宣示：「『重大關連』的標準已於國際紛爭中普遍的被接受。」故而於全球化管轄規則中管轄規則的共同核心之存在已是不爭之事實。更加上ALI/UNIDROIT Principles of Transnational Civil Procedure不但採納不方便法院法學，其又如傳統的英國判例法及成文法一般的公開宣示：「應考慮外國當事人於參加訴訟所可能遭遇之困難」（亦即「方便法院」法學所代表的境外送達政策）。因此為了確保訴訟法上例如英國的（Civil Procedure Rules 1998, Rule 1）當事人立足點之平等之要求（ensuring that the parties are on an equal footing），及降低貧富差距所可能帶來之不公平現象（the financial position of each party），個人曾屢次建議[219]：「**於民商管轄規則上，歐盟Council Regulation No.44/2001之第2及5條、1999海牙草約、美國各州送達境外被告之長手法規及英國法院允許送達境外被告之R.S.C. Order 11, rule 1 (1)（即現今之1998 C.P.R. s. 6. 20），與大陸法各國之國內管轄規則相去並不遠，故個人建議於行使民商管轄權時220：各國仍得以既有的國內或國際管轄規則為基礎（英美則仍為所在權力理論及送達境外之規則）。但訴訟之通知若於境內已適當的送達給被告，或被告承認法院之管轄權時，法院得以『不方便法院』法則為拒絕或停止訴訟裁量之依據（例如訴因與法院地沒有合理之牽連時）；而若法院欲允許送達至境外時，首先必須認知此為一種例外之過度管轄，其判決有可能不為外國法院所承認，應以『方便法院』法則來確認法院是否為合適、自然之管轄法院以作為允許送達境外之適用基礎（例如為了公平正義之目的或訴因與法院地有強烈之牽連時）。」但是有鑑於美國法院的利用**

---

[218] Airbus Indus. G.I.E. v. Patel, [1999] 1 A.C. 119, 141 (H.L. 1998), "can be regarded as one of the most civilised of legal principles".

[219] 陳隆修、許兆慶、林恩瑋、李瑞生四人合著，《國際私法-管轄與選法理論之交錯》，台北，五南圖書公司，2009年3月，初版1刷，見「序言」及248頁。

[220] 有關婚姻案件管轄基礎之建議，見陳隆修、許兆慶、林恩瑋、李瑞生四人合著，《國際私法-管轄與選法理論之交錯》，台北，五南圖書公司，2009年3月，初版1刷，251、252頁。

「不方便法院」法則去剝奪第三世界弱勢人民人權法上保障的訴訟權及財產法，個人於此必須不厭其煩的再次重申英國判例法中之核心超越性考量—「conveniens」並不是指「方便」之意[221]，而是合適去達成正義之目的之意。

事實上這個大膽的建議完全不是一個建議——它只是英國判例法歷經近兩百年時空淬鍊順天應人所形成判例法的寫實。如Cheshire and North所說[222]：「現在所已經被見證的是允許將訴訟的文件送達至境外的裁量權是依據方便法院的基礎而被加以行使。另外亦有著裁量權於有些特定之情形下依不方便法院之基礎（亦即特別是當英國不是審理案件之合適法院時而外國法院卻明顯的合適）去停止訴訟之進行。」在全球化之潮流下，個人之「建議」只不過將英國判例法一百多年來演進之經驗推上全球化法學之舞台而已。

同樣的論述亦為Dicey and Morris所敘述，但有別於大陸法於國際複數訴訟時只倚賴先繫屬優先原則[223]，英國法除了「方便與不方便法院」外，尚使用容易引起爭端的禁訴令[224]：「英國法院是事實上已有著固有的

---

[221] Dicey and Morris, the Conflict of Laws, 14th ed., p. 465, "conveniens does not mean 'convenient': *see The Atlantic Star* [1974] A.C. 436, 475; *GAF Corp v Amchem Products Inc* [1975] 1 Lloyd's Rep. 601, 607; *Spiliada Maritime Corp v Cansulex Ltd* [1987] A.C. 460, 474-475."

[222] PM North, JJ Fawcett, Cheshire and North's Private International Law, 13th ed, 313.這個論述又於14th ed., pp. 426, 427,被再次確認如下："It has already been seen that the discretionary power to allow service of a claim form out of the jurisdiction exercised on the basis of forum conveniens. There is also a general discretionary power to stay actions on the basis of forum non conveniens (ie where the clearly appropriate forum for trial is abroad). Whilst there has been such a power in Scotland and the USA for a considerable length of time, it is only relatively recently that a general doctrine of forum non conveniens has been accepted in England. The English discretion to stay is now indistinguishable from the Scottish doctrine of forum non conveniens. That this is the case has been endorsed by the House of Lords in the leading authority on stays of action, Spiliada Maritime Corpn v Cansulex Ltd. It is clear from this case that the same basic criterion applies in cases involving stays of action as in cases involving the exercise of the discretion to serve a claim form out of the jurisdiction."

[223] ALI/UNIDROIT Principles of Transnational Civil Procedure之先繫屬優先則較有彈性。見
2.6 The court should decline jurisdiction or suspend the proceeding, when the dispute is previously pending in another court competent to exercise jurisdiction, unless it appears that the dispute will not be fairly, effectively, and expeditiously resolved in that forum.

[224] Dicey and Morris, the Conflict of Laws, 14th ed., pp. 464,465, "English courts have an inherent jurisdiction, reinforced by statute, to stay or strike out proceedings, whenever it is necessary to prevent injustice. The court also has an inherent power to order a stay to await the outcome of proceedings in

管轄權，而這種權力是被成文法所再加強的，於無論何時有必要之情形下為防止不正義之發生，而去停止或駁回訴訟程序。於行使處理案件之程序權上，法院亦有著固有的權力去命令訴訟之停止，以等待外國法院或仲裁程序之結果。這種管轄權之行使可能適用在與衝突法無關之案件上，或是訴因或抗辯的理由是基於在外國發生的事實之案件上。但是訴訟當事人依此管轄權而請求停止程序之案件是經常，至少於某些方面上，與在外國發生的交易或於外國進行之訴訟有關。根據英國衝突法的概念，於此種案件英國法院及某些外國法院可能被承認皆會有著管轄權去處理訴訟程序，及英國法院經由使用其允許或拒絕請求者要求停止英國訴訟程序之權力，或經由行使或拒絕行使其權力去允許請求者將訴訟之文件送達境外，或經由行使其權力去禁止一個受到其管轄之當事人，但該當事人於外國法院卻已成為或威脅著要去成為原告，去於該外國法院提起或繼續訴訟程序，而使得其（英國法院）具有裁量權去決定該紛爭應於那一個法院而被決定。」故而面對日益複雜詭譎多變的複數國際訴訟，英國法院（及同樣的美國法院，但卻無方便法院之名稱）有著固有的裁量權（an inherent discretion）去依方便法院法則而允許送達境外，或依不方便法院法則而停止英國訴訟，或在對當事人有對人管轄權下作成禁止當事人於外國法院提起或繼續訴訟之禁訴令。相對於大陸法於複數訴訟時所引以為傲的「先繫屬優先原則」，英美法院固有裁量權之行使顯得較具彈性而較能維持個案正義。「先繫屬優先原則」不但過於機械式的硬性以致可能有時無法顧及個

---

a foreign court or arbitration in the exercise of case management. The jurisdiction may be exercised in cases which have nothing to do with the conflict of laws, or with the fact that a cause of action or ground of defence arises in a foreign country. But the cases in which a party to proceedings applies to have them stayed under this jurisdiction are very often, in some way or another, connected with transactions taking place in a foreign country or with litigation being conducted abroad. In such cases, according to English notions of the conflict of laws, an English court and a court in some foreign country may both be recognized as having jurisdiction to entertain proceedings, and the English court has a discretion to determine in which forum the dispute will be resolved, by using its power to grant or refuse a stay of the proceedings by the claimant in the English court, or by exercising or refusing to exercise its power to authorise the claimant to serve process out of the jurisdiction, or by using its power to enjoin a party subject to its jurisdiction, but who is or is threatening to become a plaintiff in the foreign court, from commencing or continuing proceedings in that court.

案正義，並且造成鼓勵當事人於和解前先下手為強選擇對自己有利之法院先行起訴之可能會發生現象。這種違反自然原告至自然法院提起自然訴訟以起訴自然被告之法律原則，是明顯的違反人類文明的常識，踐踏司法追求正義的基本目的，亦是違反國際訴訟法的倫理道德。對中國人而言這是違反易經「訟，終凶」[225]二千多年來之傳統文化。

歐盟大陸法的同僚經常認為大陸法的管轄規則甚為嚴格，故不需要如英美法院採用不方便法院原則。個人並不認同這種論述，因為國際上公認的過度管轄中，大陸法至少有著「物之所在」及「國籍」之過度管轄基礎。另外如ALI/UNIDROIT Principles of Transnational Civil Procedure之comment P-2B所述「『重大關連』之標準是於國際法律糾紛上所普遍接受的」，除非迫於正義的需求，否則各國法院通常是不會接受與法院地沒有關連之案件。例如Restatement (Second) of Judgments § 4 (1982)[226]就規定州及聯邦法院於行使地域管轄權時必須與當事人或案件有關連。而Restatement (Second) of Conflict of Laws § 24 (1988 Revision)[227]則規定如果州與當事人有合理的關連則得行使司法管轄。如個人所述，無論是於一般管轄或特別管轄全球化管轄規則在此方面是有著共同核心，但是對於「外國當事人參加訴訟之困難」卻沒有共同的心態。

---

225 坎下乾上
訟
有孚，窒惕，中吉，終凶。利見大人，不利大川。

226 § 4. Constitutional And Legislative Determinants Of Territorial Jurisdiction
(1) A state court may exercise territorial jurisdiction over persons in an action if:
(a) The state has a relationship to the action or the parties thereto stated in § § 5 to 8; and
(b) The exercise of jurisdiction is not impermissible under federal law, the law of the state itself, or other applicable restriction.
(2) A federal court may exercise jurisdiction over persons in an action if:
(a) The court has a territorial jurisdictional relationship to the action prescribed by statute or rule of court; and
(b) The exercise of jurisdiction is not impermissible under federal law or other applicable restriction.

227 § 24. Principle Underlying Judicial Jurisdiction Over Persons
(1) A state has power to exercise judicial jurisdiction over a person if the person's relationship to the state is such as to make the exercise of such jurisdiction reasonable.
(2) The relationships which are sufficient to support an exercise of judicial jurisdiction over a person are stated in § § 27-52.

這種英美法與大陸法在國際管轄之隔閡，即使於英國加入歐盟後仍發生。於1984年Lord Diplock在*Amin Rasheed Shipping Crop v Kuwait Insurance Co*中仍舊認為英國送達境外之管轄為「過度管轄」（exorbitant jurisdiction），因為[228]：「依據一般之英國國際私法，除非有著條約規定應加以承認，它並非英國法院承認外國法院所擁有（之管轄權）。」但於加入歐盟甚久之後英國資深同僚終於先後駭然發現他們所如履薄冰的境外過度管轄是為許多（或所有）大陸法所視為理所當然的。Prof. Collins不平等的反擊如下[229]：「但是非常遺憾的是過境管轄規則是否可以應用（如同現在於美國所稱呼的）是為布魯塞爾公約所冠以過度之名而未考慮到不方便法院之效力，以及更加令人遺憾的是，在Lord Diplock的影響下，英國法院將依Order 11而行使之管轄（境外送達）是過度管轄視為一個已經確立之概念。於The Siskina……中，其所表達之觀點為對外國人行使管轄權之Order 11中之數個項目（管轄基礎），是較英國法院所承認外國法院所擁有之管轄權為廣；這些是違反了『文明國家間所有的禮誼之正常規則』的過度管轄。」對於境外送達是違反了「文明國家間所有的禮誼之正常規則」之看法，不但Prof. Collins提出抗議，Dicey and Morris亦於英國加入歐盟數年後恍然大悟[230]：「但是亦有論述認為依C.P.R., r. 6. 20而

---

[228] [1984] A.C. 50. 65, “it is one which under general English conflict rules, an English court would not recognize as possessed by any foreign court in the absence of some treaty providing for such recognition.”

[229] Lawrence Collins, Temporary Presence, Exorbitant Jurisdiction and the U.S. Supreme Court, Vol. 107, L.Q.R. 1991, pp. 10, 13, 14, “If there is a genuine dispute which has no connection with the forum, then the exercise of jurisdiction may be excessive if the defendant has no opportunity to contest its exercise under a forum non conveniens doctrine; this is perhaps why it is so regarded under the Brussels Convention régime, where forum non conveniens plays no part. But it is regrettable that the transient jurisdiction rule (as it is called in the United States) was branded as exorbitant by the Brussels Convention without regard to the effect of forum non conveniens, and even more regrettable that, under the influence of Lord Diplock, the English courts have come to regard it as established that the jurisdiction exercised under Order 11 is exorbitant. In The Siskina [1979] A.C. 210 at p. 254 he expressed the view that in several of the heads of Order 11 the jurisdiction exercised over foreigners was wider than that which was recognized in English law as being possessed by courts of foreign countries; these were exorbitant jurisdictions which ran counter to ‘to normal rules of comity among civilized nations’.”

[230] Dicey and Morris, the Conflict of Laws, 14th ed., pp. 364, 605, “But it is suggested that the jurisdiction exercised under CPR, r.6.20 is not exorbitant, since it is similar to the jurisdiction exercised by many countries, and is also in many respects similar to the rules in the Judgments Regulation and the 1968

行使的管轄權並非是過度的，因為他與許多國家所行使的管轄權是相似的，而且於許多方面亦是和布魯塞爾規則與公約以及Lugano公約的條文於許多方面是相似的」。**故而個人一再主張正如於實體法之其他部門，於國際訴訟上「許多國家所行使的管轄權是相似的」，事實上在二十一世紀我們是已有一個管轄權之全球化共同核心存在—而且更驚人的是這個全球化的共同核心可能自有國際管轄之概念即早已存在。**

故最後於加入歐盟數十年後，英國資深同僚才驚駭莫名的發現全球化管轄規則共同核心之存在：「亦有論述認為依C.P.R., r. 6.20而行使的管轄權並非是過度的，因為他與許多國家所行使的管轄權是相似的，而且於許多方面亦是和布魯塞爾規則與公約以及Lugano公約的條文於許多方面是相似的」。但是在這些共同核心管轄基礎上英美法是有裁量權去決定是否行使，而大陸法是沒有裁量權的。更重要的是英國同僚忽略了一個「可視為最文明的法學原則之一」——境外送達基本上是「過度」或「例外」之管轄。雖然全世界主要文明國家的管轄規則是「相似的」，但是「心態」卻是南轅北轍的。將一個人「拖拽」」至「一個遙遠的外國法院」，「外國當事人參加訴訟所可能遭遇之困難」是可以預期的，因此為確保當事人間於國際訴訟上「真正立足點之平等」及彌平跨國企業與平民間「貧富之差距」，英國Civil Procedure Rules 1998所規定的法院允許將訴訟之通知送達境外之要求，必須成為全球化法學：**(a)當事人間「必須有一個真正的爭點（事實或法律上）合理的需要法院去審判」；(b)原告必須以書面去證明「其請求有著合理勝訴的機會」；及最重要的(c)「法院地是個合適去提起請求之地」，必須成為全世界各法系於送達境外被告之考慮要件—亦即為對境外被告管轄權基礎之全球化法學。**

---

and Lugano Conventions." "Although Lord Diplock was wrong to describe what is now CPR, r.6.20 as an exorbitant jurisdiction, he was certainly expressing the orthodox view on recognition of foreign judgments in cases where the debtor was neither within the foreign jurisdiction nor had submitted to it."

三、最低限度關連製造最大程度之混亂

最低限度關連點之標準被美國同僚形容為「浩劫」、「一團混亂」、及「叢林法則」，因此個人認為「最低限度關連已造成最大程度之混亂」，有些人認為它是「無法對世界有貢獻的」。個人認為或許美國國際私法基本上是通常為適應美國各州之衝突而產生，於同文同種、同一國家、同一制度及社會上，美國同僚較易忽視對境外被告「所產生之困難」，因而忽視了英國母法「境外送達基本上是過度或例外管轄」之判例法。最低限度關連點已造成最大限度之混亂，或許美國同僚應返璞歸真的直視英國母法之區分境內與境外管轄，而對境外管轄基本上視為例外或過度管轄。對於「最低限度關連點」的回歸「不方便法院」法學的趨勢，Prof. Weintraub於評論Asahi Metal Industry v. Superior Court[231]時，便訝異的發現「最低限度關連點」與「不方便法院」的相似性[232]：「如此一來，通常與裁量權行使的不方便法院理論相關的一些概念便被提升至憲法的位階。」如果時光能倒流，或許美國同僚能將精力集中於英格蘭的困擾性或壓迫性法學、蘇格蘭的不方便法院、及送達境外的方便法院，則最低限度關連點不但不會「於國內造成浩劫，於國際和諧上亦造成無可跨越的障礙」，更進一步會「有辦法對世界各地產生貢獻」。

(一)Pennoyer v. Neff

Pennoyer v. Neff[233]通常是美國以「所在權力」（presence power）做為最基本管轄基礎的代表案例。Justice Field代表大多數法官發表意見[234]：「每一個法院之權力是必須受限於其之所在地之州之地域範圍內。

---

[231] 480 U.S. 102(1987)

[232] "Thus, concepts usually associated with the discretionary doctrine of forum non conveniens were elevated to consitutuinal status." Russell J. Weintraub, A Map Out of the Personal Jurisdiciton Labyrinth, 28 U.C. Davis L. Rev. 531, 539 (1994-1995).

[233] 95 U.S. 714 (1877).

[234] 95 U.S. 714, 720, "The authority of every tribunal is necessarily restricted by the territorial limits of the State in which it is established. Any attempt to exercise authority beyond those limits would be deemed in every other forum, as has been said by this court, in illegitimate assumption of power, and be resisted as mere abuse. D'Arcy v. Ketchum et al., 11 How. 165. In the case against the plaintiff, the property

正如同本院已說過，任何權力的行使企圖超過這些界限是會被每一個其他法院視為非法僭越權力，並被以濫權而加以抗拒。……於對原告起訴之案件中（奧州判決），依判決而被拍賣之係爭財產並未被扣押，亦未被置於法院之管轄。它與案件的第一個關連是因執行而被徵收。因此它並非是根據任何判決而被處份，而是只為了執行與財產無關的對人判決，而該判決是針對一位於訴訟中未受到送達之非居民，並且其亦未出席訴訟。」有趣的是Justice Field對於非居民於州內之財產得被本州公民以對該非居民求償而加以管轄，特別引用Justice Story之判決而加以論述[235]。美國這種所謂「準對物」之管轄或許於交通不便之早期有必要，但現今國際上一般認為「物之所在地」之管轄只能限於與物有關之訴訟。最多只能如UNIDROIT Principles[236]一般，如與該物無關，則「物之所在地」只能

---

here in controversy sold under the judgment rendered was not attached, nor in any way brought under the jurisdiction of the court. Its first connection with the case was caused by a levy of the execution. It was not, therefore, disposed of pursuant to any adjudication, but only in enforcement of a personal judgment, having no relation to the property, rendered against a non-resident without service of process upon him in the action, or his appearance therein."

235 95 U.S. 714, 723, 724, "So the State, through its tribunals, may subject property situated within its limits owned by non-residents to the payment of the demand of its own citizens against them; and the exercise of this jurisdiction in no respect infringes upon the sovereignty of the State where the owners are domiciled. Every State owes protection to its own citizens; and, when non-residents deal with them, it is a legitimate and just exercise of authority to hold and appropriate any property owned by such non-residents to satisfy the claims of its citizens. It is in virtue of the State's jurisdiction over the property of the non-resident situated within its limits that its tribunals can inquire into that non-resident's obligations to its own citizens, and the inquiry can then be carried only to the extent necessary to control the disposition of the property. If the non-resident have no property in the State, there is nothing upon which the tribunals can adjudicate." Picquet v. Swan, 5 Mas. 35, Mr. Justice Story, "Where a party is within a territory, he may justly be subjected to its process, and bound personally by the judgment pronounced on such process against him. Where he is not within such territory, and is not personally subject to its laws, if, on account of his supposed or actual property being within the territory, process by the local laws may, by attachment, go to compel his appearance, and for his default to appear judgment may be pronounced against him, such a judgment must, upon general principles, be deemed only to bind him to the extent of such property, and cannot have the effect of a conclusive judgment in personam, for the plain reason, that, except so far as the property is concerned, it is a judgment coram non judice." Boswell's Lessee v. Otis, 9 How. 336, Mr. Justice McLean, "Jurisdiction is acquired in one of two modes: first, as against the person of the defendant by the service of process; or, secondly, by a procedure against the property of the defendant within the jurisdiction of the court. In the latter case, the defendant is not personally bound by the judgment beyond the property in question. And it is immaterial whether the proceeding against the property be by an attachment or bill in chancery. It must be substantially a proceeding in rem."

236 ALI/UNIDROIT Principles of Transnational Civil Procedure

作為預備之第二線「必要管轄」。故而在一百三十多年前之領頭案例Pennoyer中，美國最高法院是如英國判例法般的遵循「所在權力」，並且對域外管轄是視為侵犯他州之主權而通常應加以禁止——亦即區分境內與境外管轄，而境外管轄是被視為「不正常」管轄。若以二十一世紀的術語，很可能域外管轄通常是被視為「過度」或「例外」管轄，只能於案件或當事人與法院地有「重大關連」時才能「間接」行使。

(二)International Shoe Co. v. Washington

如前述Dicey and Morris所說，隨著交通與通訊之進展各國不得不擴大管轄基礎並給予法院更大之裁量權。最明顯的近代例子就是ALI/UNIDROIT Principles of Transnational Civil Procedure第2.2條將傳統上被認為是過度管轄的「所在」、「國籍」、及「物之所在」管轄基礎，列為預備的第二線「必要法院」管轄基礎。繼英國司法於19世紀中期後就發現必須以近似「方便法院」之裁量權而將訴訟之通知送達境外之被告[237]，美國則晚至1945年才正式建立這方面之法學。International Shoe Co. v. Washington是一般認為建立「最低限度關連點」（minimum contacts）之經典領頭案例[238]。

Stone C.J.代表最高法院提出震驚美國法界的「最低限度關連點」理論[239]：「歷史上法院作成對人訴訟判決的管轄權是本於他們對於被告人身

2.2 Jurisdiction may also be exercised, when no other forum is reasonably available, on the basis of:
2.2.1 Presence or nationality of the defendant in the forum state; or
2.2.2 Presence in the forum state of the defendant's property, whether or not the dispute relates to the property, but the court's authority should be limited to the property or its value.

[237] 陳隆修，《國際私法管轄權評論》，台北，五南圖書公司，民國75年11月，初版，45-48頁。

[238] 326 U.S. 310 (1945).

[239] 326 U.S. 310, 316, "Historically the jurisdiction of courts to render judgment in personam is grounded on their de facto power over the defendant's person. Hence his presence within the territorial jurisdiction of court was prerequisite to its rendition of a judgment personally binding him. Pennoyer v. Neff, 95 U.S. 714, 733. But now that the capias ad respondendum has given way to personal service of summons or other form of notice, due process requires only that in order to subject a defendant to a judgment in personam, if he be not present within the territory of the forum, he have certain minimum contacts with it such that the maintenance of the suit does not offend 'traditional notions of fair play and substantial justice.'"

的實際上權力而來。因此其於法院地域管轄區內之所在是法院於作成對其個人有拘束力之判決之必要條件。……但是現今capias ad respondendum[240]已經被訴訟的命令或其他形式的通知之親自送達所取代，適當程序只是要求，如果被告之所在不在法院地域內，為了使其受到對人判決之管轄，其必須與法院地有著某些最低限度關連點以至於訴訟的被提起不會違反『傳統上公平與實質正義的概念』。」

Stone C.J.又說[241]：「因為公司人格是個假設……因而所謂『所在』或『身體所在』通常只是指公司代理人於州內之行為，而法院認為足夠滿足適當程序條款之規定。這些規定得經由公司於法院地之州內之關連點而使得其合理……一個遠離其『家鄉』或主要營業地之訴訟對公司所造成的『不方便的評估』於此方面是相關的。」接著又說[242]：「即使是未曾同意被訴或未曾授權給代理人去接受程序之送達，當公司之行為不但是持續的且是有制度性的，並且造成被起訴之責任時，於此方面會構成『所在』於該州是從未被懷疑的。」事實上美國所有的同僚，七十年前與現今的同僚皆包含在內，皆應冷靜的思考一個簡單的事實——英國母法[243]對於在法院

[240] 依照Black's Law Dictionary, 7th ed., p. 200,為命令警長拘捕被告以確保其出庭之意："A writ commanding the sheriff to take the defendant into custody to ensure that the defendant will appear in court."

[241] 326 U.S. 310, 316, 317, "Since the corporate personality is a fiction, although a fiction intended to be acted upon as though it were a fact, Klein v. Board of Tax Supervisors, 282 U.S. 19, 24, 51 S.Ct. 15, 16, 73 A.L.R. 679, it is clear that unlike an individual its 'presence' without, as well as within, the state of its origin can be manifested only by activties carried on in its behalf by those who are autorized to act for it. To say that the corporation is so far 'present' there as to satisfy due process requirements, for purposes of taxation or the maintenance of suits against it in the courts of the state, is to beg the question to be decided. For the terms 'present' or 'presence' are used merely to symbolize those activities of the corporation's agent within the state which courts will deem to be suffucuent to satisfy the demands of due process. L. Hand, J., in Hutchinson v. Chase & Gilbert, 2 Cir., 45 F.2d 139, 141. Those demands may be met by such contacts of the corporation with the state of the forum as make it reasonable, in the context of our federal system of government, to require the corporation to defend the particular suit which is brought there. An 'estimate of the inconveniences' which would result to the corporation from a trial away from its 'home' or principal place of business is relevant in this connection."

[242] 326 U.S. 310, 317, "'presence' in the state in this sense has never been doubted when the activeties of the corporation there have not only been continuous and systematic, but also give rise to the liabilities sued on, even though no consent to be sued or authorization to an agent to accept service of process has been given."

[243] Civil Procedure Rules 1998, s. 6.20,
(5) a claim is made in respect of a contract where the contract –

地營業之外國公司如前所述是允許送達至境內之營業地的（限於與當地業務有關），而若契約訂定地、履行地或準據法為英國法亦可送達至境外，另外若契約透過境內之代理而訂定亦可送達境外。於母法有詳盡且確實的規定時，美國同僚為什麼要「燒盡午夜的油」去幻想出一個日後引起不斷爭議的學術理論，不遵守母國判例法就是不遵守「自然道法」。美國同僚這種詭異的行徑不僅是脫乎判例法母法的常軌，亦與大陸法長久以來習以為常的認知脫離。例如現今的布魯塞爾規則的第5條第1項[244]即規定契約履行地或買賣交貨地法院有管轄權；而第5項[245]又規定有關分行、代理、或其他機構之行為，該分行、代理、或其他機構之行為地法院有管轄權。而又如個人所一再強調大陸法之管轄基礎是不分境內或境外，故而皆可送達至境外之外國法人。美國最高法院在沒有迫切而明顯的理由下，竟然違背了聲名卓越的母法，又與歐洲大陸的其他文明國家的慣例脫離，於這麼大的動作下卻造成了半個世紀美國管轄法規的「浩劫」，美國同僚是否可以對目瞪口呆的其他同僚做一個說明？於美國同僚「燒盡午夜的油」去建立「最低限度關連點」後，個人只想知道所為何來？

個人真誠的認為如果最低限度關連點欲「取代」英國母法對外送達

(a) was made within the jurisdiction;
(b) was made by or through an agent trading or residing within the jurisdiction;
(c) is governed by English law; or
(d) contains a term to the effect that the court shall have jurisdiciton to determine any claim in respect of the contract.
(6) a claim is made in respect of a breach of contract committed within the jurisdiction.
(7) a claim is made for a declaration that no contract exists where, if the contract was found to exist, it would comply with the conditions set out in paragraph (5).

244 1. (a) in matters relating to a contract, in the courts for the place of performance of the obligation in question;
(b) for the purpose of this provision and unless otherwise agreed, the place of performance of the obligation in question shall be:
— in the case of the sale of goods, the place in a Member State where, under the contract the goods were delivered or should have been delivered,
— in the case of the provision of services, the place in a Member State where, under the contract, the services were provided or should have been provided,
(c) if subparagraph (b) does not apply then subparagraph (a) applies.

245 5. as regards a dispute arising out of the operations of a branch, agency or other establishment, in the courts for the place in which the branch, agency or other establishment is situated.

或大陸法特別管轄之管轄基礎，那麼其自一出生便已失敗，並且其於美國管轄基礎上造成長久以來之「一團混亂」、「叢林法則」、及「浩劫」。但是如果最低限度關連點被加以適用的心態是，做為英國法境外送達或大陸法特別管轄行使之「輔助基礎與行使之限制」，那或許是較為可被接受之一種方式。Stone C.J.於創立「最低限度關連點」時便將其與「不方便法院」法學相提並論，或許可以這麼的說—「最低限度關連點」一出生便與「不方便法院」相連結。或許個人可以更務實的這麼的主張—「最低限度關連點」只能做為「方便或不方便法院」裁量權行使的補助考量因素之一。而鑑於ALI/UNIDROIT Principles of Transnational Civil Procedure的以「重大關連」為管轄基礎，英國境外送達與大陸法特別管轄都亦有著「明確或特別」的關連點做為管轄基礎，美國式的「最低限度關連點」之要求皆已明顯的被滿足，故而除非有著更進一步的發展，否則其功能並不會明顯。

本案之所以日後會產生「叢林法則」的「一團混亂」，可能即為其於實際上是遵守判例法母法對境外送達加以謹慎之態度，但其卻未對這個判例法之傳統法律邏輯加以確認。反之，其庸人自擾的對域外之被告以其於域內之行為而假設其「所在」於域內，更糟糕的是其「鬼打牆」式的在沒有明顯迫切需要之情形下，脫離英國送達境外之母法而自創一個新的法學概念「最低限度關連點」。於英國母法送達境外之既有的傳統規則下，以一個比較法學生之地位個人看不出最低限度關連點之功能性在那裡。而美國同僚之意見則有些已如前述。

另外有趣的是Black J.於贊同意見中則對「自然主義」概念之適用加以節制如下[246]：「目前所能辨認出之已被適用之標準應如下：適當程序的

[246] 326 U.S. 310, 323, 324, "The criteria adopted insofar as they can be identified read as follows: Due process does permit State courts to 'enforce the obligations which appellant has incurred' if it be found 'reasonable and just according to our traditional conception of fair play and substantial justice.' And this in turn means that we will 'permit' the State to act if upon 'an 'estimate of the inconveniences' which would result to the corporation from a trial away from its 'home' or principal place of business', we conclude that it is 'reasonable' to subject it to suit in a State where it is doing business."

確允許州法院去『執行上訴人所引起之義務』如果其是在『我們公平及實質正義的傳統概念下是合理及公正的』。而這個又接著意味著在『一個不方便的評估』下我們會『允許』一個州之行為，這會造成公司去面對一個不在其『家園』或主要營業地之訴訟之結果，我們認為要求其於其所營業之州接受訴訟之管轄是『合理的』。」又說[247]：「將自然正義[248]之概念加於憲法之明確禁令上，會對他們所包含的民主制度上之保障，例如言論、出版及宗教、與詢問律師之自由，產生重大之刪減。而這已發生。……因為這個自然法概念之適用，無論是以『合理』、『正義』、『公平原則』之名詞，使得法官成為這個國家之法律與執行上之最高仲裁者。……這個結果，我相信，會改變我們憲法所規定之政府的形式。我不能同意。」最

[247] 326 U.S. 310, 325, 326, "There is a strong emotional appeal in the words 'fair play', 'justice', and 'reasonableness.' But they were not chosen by those who wrote the original Constitution or the Fourteenth Amendment as a measuring rod for this Court to use in invalidating State or Federal laws passed by elected legislative representatives. No one, not even those who most feared a democratic government, ever formally proposed that courts should be given power to invalidate legislation under any such elastic standards. Express prohibitions against certain types of legislation are found in the Constitution, and under the long settled practice, courts invalidate laws found to conflict with them. This requires interpretation, and interpretation, it is true, may result in extension of the Constitution's purpose. But that is no reason for reading the due process clause so as to restrict a State's power to tax and sue those whose activities affect persons and businesses within the State, provided proper service can be had. Superimposing the natural justice concept on the Constitution's specific prohibitions could operate as a drastic abridgment of democratic safeguards they embody, such as freedom of speech, press and religion, and the right to counsel. This has already happened. Betts v. Brady, 316 U.S. 455, 62 S.Ct. 1252. Compare Feldman v. United States, 322 U.S. 487, 494-503, 64 S.Ct. 1082, 1085-1089, 154 A.L.R. 982. For application of this natural law concept, whether under the terms 'reasonableness', 'justice', or 'fair play', makes judges the supreme arbiters of the country's laws and practices. Polk Co. v. Glover, 305 U.S. 5, 17-18, 59 S.Ct. 15, 20, 21; Federal Power Commission v. Natural Gas Pipeline Co., 315 U.S. 575, 600, 62 S.Ct. 736, 750, note 4. This result, I believe, alters the form of government our Constitution provides. I cannot agree."

[248] 又如前述，因為基於對「正義」概念之可能產生之歧異，英國傳統判例將「自然正義」侷限於程序正義。但較近亦有判例法認為程序上重大的被違背之效果，亦可能產生「實質正義」被侵犯。但亦有英國同儕認為「自然正義」仍應只是指程序上之問題，有關「實質正義」之問題仍應在相關政策上去解決。而美國同儕對「實質正義」與「自然正義」之區分，似乎並不如此絕對涇渭分明。個人以比較法學生的角度去觀察，或許法律基本功夫的馬步仍應紮實，否則長久以後可能於正義之目的上會陷入走火入魔的歧途，例如不方便法院及最低限度關連點之適用上。

後其引用[249]Mr. Justice Holmes於1930年之論述[250]作為結論：「對於第14修正案在刪減我所認為應是各州於憲法上之權利之被授與範圍之一直增加，我尚未恰當的表示我所感覺到超過焦慮的想法。如同現今的判例所代表的，如果這些州之權利恰巧觸及本最高法院的大多數法官認為具備任何不受歡迎的任何理由，除了天空以外我幾乎見不到任何去限制使得這些州權利無效之權力。」

於Price v Dewhurst[251]中Shadwell V-C說：「無論何時只要正義很明顯的被忽視，法院就必須將判決視為沒有價值與沒有重要性。」美國衝突法選法規則的強調政策分析，羅馬I規則的強調強行法，歐盟契約法的以「誠信」為基本原則，美國UCC的以「合理性」為基本原則，美國法律協會（ALI）的以「合理性」為管轄基礎，而ALI/UNIDROIT Principles of Transnational Civil Procedure亦一再強調「合理性」的貫穿整個原則。近幾十年來全球化法學所顯示的是偏向以實體政策分析為方法論，以「合理性」及「誠信原則」為基本法理之共同趨勢，而這些都指向一個二十一世紀文明進化的特徵——亦即人類文明已進化到二十一世紀全球化法學是注重在個案公平正義的達成。在二十一世紀全球化法學中，人類文明對正義的要求更為嚴格，程序自然正義與實質正義被加以結合以期能達成個案正義的確保，已是一個二十一世紀法學的自然寫實[252]。

---

249 326 U.S. 310, 326, “True, the State’s power is here upheld. But the rule announced means that tomorrow’s judgment may strike down a State or Federal enactment on the ground that it does not conform to this Court’s idea of natural justice.”

250 “I have not yet adequately expressed the more than anxiety that I feel at the ever increasing scope given to the Fourteenth Amendment in cutting down what I believe to be the constitutional rights of the States. As the decisions now stand, I see hardly any limit but the sky to the invalidating of those rights if they happen to strike a majority of this Court as for any reason undesirable.” Baldwin v. Missouri, 281 U.S. 586, 595, 50 S.Ct. 436, 439, 72 A.L.R. 1303.

251 (1837) 8 Sim 279 at 302 “whenever it is manifest that justice has been disregarded, the court is bound to treat the decision as a matter of no value and no substance”.

252 Kekewich J.認為公共政策無法被給予定義，亦不能輕易的被解釋。Davies v. Davies (1887) 36 Ch D 359 at p. 364, “Public policy does not admit of definition and is not easily explained”.而更早期著名的論述即為Burrough J.所說的公共政策：「是一匹極度脫繮的野馬，當你其上牠之後你永遠不會知道牠會載你到那裡。」但是後來Lord Denning MR卻如此的回答：「但是如果一個好人騎在馬鞍上，這匹野馬是可被加以控制的。」Richardson v. Mellish (1824) 2 Bing 229 at p. 252, “is a very unruly horse, and when once you get astride it you never know where it will carry you.” *Enderby*

(三)Shaffer v. Heitner

這個「最低限度關連點」標準，後來又於Shaffer v. Heitner[253]中再次被確認除了對人訴訟外亦應適用於準對物及對物訴訟中。亦即憲法適當程序條款（the Due Process Clause）要求被告、法院地、及訴訟間必須有著最低限度關連點，以使得法院於行使管轄權時，不會違反「傳統上公平原則及實質正義的概念」（traditional notions of fair play and substantial justice）。Marshall J.代表法院發言如下[254]：「汽車的來到，伴隨著依據Pennoyer並非受到對人訴訟管轄之人於一些州所造成傷害之增加，司法管轄權力於地域上之限制必須被加以修改。正如為了配合跨州際上公司之行為之必須修改之現實，這個修改是以使用法律上之假設而使得Pennoyer所建立起之概念上之架構於理論上沒有被改變之方式而完成。」Marshall J.又做了下面著名的論述[255]：「因此，訴訟、法院地、及當事人間之關係成為對人管轄問題的主要考量，而非Pennoyer規則所依據的各州間主權互相的獨立性。這種與Pennoyer整個概念的脫離之直接效果是，使得州法院對非居民被告取得對人訴訟管轄能力之增加。」在美國同僚受到這個有力的論述所感動，並且一再重覆引用這個論述時，作為

Town Football Club v. Football Association [1971] Ch. 591 at p. 606H, “With a good man in the saddle, the unruly horse can be kept in control”.

253 443 U.S. 186 (1977)，但海商案件因有特殊商業需求，例如船及船員可能離港甚久，故因而不適用

254 433 U.S. 186, 202, “The advent of automobiles, with the concomitant increase in the incidence of individuals causing injury in States where they were not subject to in personam actions under Pennoyer, required further moderation of the territorial limits on jurisdictional power. This modification, like the accommodation to the realities of interstate corporate activities, was accomplished by use of a legal fiction that left the conceptual structure established in Pennoyer theoretically unaltered. Cf. Olberding v. Illinois Central R. Co., 346 U.S. 338, 340-341 (1953). The fiction used was that the out-of-state motorist, who it was assumed could be excluded altogether from the State’s highways, had by using those highways appointed a designated state official as his agent to accept process. See Hess v. Pawloski, (1927). Since the motorist’s “agent” could be personally served within the State, the state courts could obtain in personam jurisdiction over the nonresident driver.”

255 433 U.S. 186, 204, “Thus, the relationship among the defendant, the forum, and the litigation, rather than the mutually exclusive sovereignty of the States on which the rules of Pennoyer rest, became the central concern of the inquiry into personal jurisdiction. The immediate effect of this departure from Pennoyer’s conceptual apparatus was to increase the ability of the state courts to obtain personal jurisdiction over nonresident defendants.”

同樣是英美法的學生，個人不得不煞風景得請美國同僚冷靜下來並且想一想——英國母法至今仍固守所在理論，但其對境外被告送達之作法與理論至今仍大致上未多加改變。美國同僚的熱血是否太容易沸騰？

Marshall J.代表法院下結論如下[256]：「『傳統上公平與實質正義之概念』可以輕易的因執行不符合時代的古老程式而被侵犯，正如同引用與我們憲法傳統上之基本價值不一致之新程序一般的被侵犯……對物管轄之主張並非是對該物所有人管轄之主張的虛構，是支持一個沒有得到現代社會實質合理的認可之古老程式。它的繼續被接受只會允許州法院去擁有對被告基本上不公平之管轄權。我們因此認定所有的州法院管轄權之主張應依照International Shoe及其後面所延續判例之所設下的標準去衡量。」非常有趣的是在Shaffer v. Heitner中美國最高法院引為論述主軸的「對物訴訟於事實上皆為對人的」之概念，亦為歐盟最高法院[257]及母法英國最高法院[258]所採納——而很明顯的歐盟最高法院與英國最高法院之認定是與「最

---

[256] 433 U.S. 186, 211, 212, "This history must be considered as supporting the proposition that jurisdiction based solely on the presence of property satisfies the demands of due process, cf. Ownbey v. Morgan, 256 U.S. 94, 111 (1921), but it is not decisive. 'Traditional notions of fair play and substantial justice' can be as readily offended by the perpetuation of ancient forms that are no longer justified as by the adoption of new procedures that are inconsistent with the basic values of our constitutional heritage. Cf. Sniadach v. Family Finance Corp., 395 U.S., at 340; Wolf v. Colorado, 338 U.S. 25, 27 (1949). The fiction that an assertion of jurisdiction over property is anything but an assertion of jurisdiction over the owner of the property supports an ancient form without substantial modern justification. Its continued acceptance would serve only to allow state-court jurisdiction that is fundamentally unfair to the defendant. We therefore conclude that all assertions of state-court jurisdiction must be evaluated according to the standards set forth in International Shoe and its progeny."

[257] The Tatry, Case C- 406/92 [1994] E.C.R. I-5439, para. 47, "In Article 21 of the Convention, the terms 'same cause of action' and 'between the same parties' have an independent meaning (see Gubisch Maschinenfabrik v Palumbo, cited above, paragraph 11). They must therefore be interpreted independently of the specific features of the law in force in each Contracting State. It follows that the distinction drawn by the law of a Contracting State between an action in personam and an action in rem is not material for the interpretation of Article 21."

[258] 於Republic of India v India Steamship Co (No 2)中，英國最高法院認為對物訴訟於實際上是對船東之訴訟，依s.34 Civil Jurisdiction and Judgment Act 1982之規定，相同當事人對外國勝訴判決不得於英國對相同訴因再提起訴訟，故而外國判決中已決定之事情應有禁反言（estoppel）之適用。
[1998] AC 878.
Section 34: "No proceedings may be brought by a person in England and Wales or Northern Ireland on a cause of action in respect of which a judgment has been given in his favour in proceedings between the same parties, or their privies, in a court in another part of the United Kingdom or in a court of an

低限度關連點」無關的。與其將精力與注意力無謂的放在一個可有可無的創見上，不如直接的面對全球化的事實所必然引發的法學全球化之共同核心基本政策，而加以更腳踏實地的詳細探討。

對於扣押管轄的以物之所在做為對人訴訟之過度管轄基礎，於國際上早已由學術上之撻伐，進入公約上之禁止階段。海牙會議1999年之草約18(2)(a)條[259]即將這個過度管轄列為禁止之第1項目：「(2)特別是，訂約國法院管轄權之行使不能只是依據下列之一個或數個管轄基礎——(a)被告於該國財產之所在或被扣押，但若該紛爭是直接與該財產有直接關連則為例外」。而歐盟早期的布魯賽爾公約及現今的布魯塞爾規則[260]皆於第3條之附件一中禁止這個過度管轄。不但是國際公約或歐盟大陸法內部規則禁止這種過度管轄，事實上判例法的母法亦是沒有這種以物之所在做為對人管轄基礎。英國有關境外送達管轄基礎之Civil Procedure Rules 1998, s.6.20(10)[261]規定必須「請求之整個主體（實體）是有關位於境內之

---

overseas country, unless that judgment is not enforceable or entitled to recognition in England and Wales or, as the case may be, in Northern Ireland."

259 Article 18 Prohibited grounds of jurisdiction

1. Where the defendant is habitually resident in a Contracting State, the application of a rule of jurisdiction provided for under the national law of Contracting State is prohibited if there is no substantial connection between that State and the dispute.

2. In particular, jurisdiction shall not be exercised by the courts of a Contracting State on the basis solely of one or more of the following –

a) the presence or the seizure in that State of property belonging to the defendant, except where the dispute is directly related to that property.

260 Article 3

1.Persons domiciled in a Member State may be sued in the courts of another Member State only by virtue of the rules set out in Sections 2 to 7 of this Chapter.

2.In particular the rules of national jurisdiction set out in Annex I shall not be applicable as against them.

261 又見早期R.S.C., Ord 11, r 1(1)(i), "the claim is made for a debt secured in immovable property or is made to assert, declare or determine proprietary or possessory rights, or rights of security, in or over movable property, or to obtan authority to dispose of movable property, situate within the jurisdiction." Detusche National Bank v Paul [1898] 1 Ch 283.另外對於蘇格蘭及大陸法式之扣押管轄及美國之準對物訴訟，Cheshire and North直言：「英國法與這個理論保持距離，除非被告於英國時受到請求之通知或經由成文法規定所授予之權力被告於外國受到請求之通知，它堅持不可以對被告提起對人訴訟。」「但是實際上，被告於此地有財產及請求是有關該財產時，請求人通常是可能依11條去送達請求之通知至境外，或於境內找到一個合適的英國被告去加以送達。」P M North, JJ Fawcett, Cheshire and North's Private International Law, 13th ed., pp.323, 324, "English law stands aloof from this doctrine. It insists that no action in personam will lie against a defendant unless

物」，法院才得允許通知被送達境外。故而以物之所在做為對人訴訟之管轄基礎，必須訴因與該物有關連（或應有直接關連）才不會於國際上被視為過度管轄。這種國際法上之共識早已為前輩同僚所提倡，更進而為歐盟布魯塞爾公約及規則所立法，為1999年海牙草約所明示，更重要的這亦是判例法母法於送達境外時所實施以久之法則。對於這個全球化的共同核心管轄規則的自然形成，個人請教美國同僚與美國最高法院——這個全球化共同核心管轄的形成與「最低限度關連點」有何關係？

所謂「最低限度關連點」之憲法最低限度要求，因其只為「最低要求」故可輕易的為傳統的管轄基礎所輕易滿足，例如契約履行地、侵權行為地、不當得利地、代理人行為地等長久以來即為全世界國際法所共同接受、認可之管轄基礎。這個論點由上述個人仔細的逐一翻譯歐盟布魯塞爾規則I第5條、英國送達境外的CPR 1998, s. 6.20，及UNIDROIT Principles 2.1.2條的「重大關連」管轄基礎可以印證。契約履行地、侵權行為地、不當得利地、代理人行為地等各國國內法特別管轄基礎不但為歐盟及其他國際公約所接受，亦為英國對外送達之CPR 1998, s. 6.20及美國各州對外送達之長手法規所共同接受與執行之共同管轄基礎，而這些人類文明社會長久以來之共同傳統上之管轄基礎，亦應滿足較近2004年之UNIDROIT Principles於2.1.2條中所規定的「重大（或實質）關連」之要求。這些傳統上全世界文明國家所共同接受之「重大（或實質）關連」之管轄基礎，自然是輕易的能滿足美國最高法院管轄規則上「最低」限度關連點之要求。 因此或許最低限度關連點只能與聯邦間州際憲政權力之劃分有關，對美國州際間國際私法上個案正義之追求無所助益。個人於此再次不客氣的直接請教美國最高法院——對於國際間傳統上盛行已久之

---

he has been served with a claim form while present in England or unless by virtue of some statutory power a claim form has been served on him abroad……. If the claimant asserts some interest in or right to movables the position is very different. Although there is no separate basis of jurisdiction founded on the presence of movables in England, in practice, in cases where the defendant has assets here and the claim relates to those assets, it is often possible for the claimant either to serve a claim form out of the jurisdiction under Order 11 or to find a suitable English defendant upon whom a claim form can be served within the jurisdiction."又見14th ed., pp. 413,414,對現今s.6.20(10)之論述更為保守。

「重大（實質）關連」管轄基礎之國際管轄規則上之全球化共同核心之存在，「最低限度關連點」與這個可能已存在數百年之共同核心有何關連？

(四)Burnham v. Superior Court

於Shaffer後許多美國同僚懷疑，並或贊同，所在權力之基礎是否應被推翻。但1990年之Burnham v. Superior Court[262]則於驚濤駭浪中終於確定「最低限度關連點」只有適用於被告不在法院地而主張之管轄權基礎，而與於法院地受到送達之被告之管轄權無關。Scalia J.代表其他三位大法官敘述法院之意見[263]：「這裡的問題是對於一個短暫停留於一個州之非居民加以親自送達，而訴訟是與其於該州之行為無關之訴訟中，14修正案之適當程序條款是否拒絕給予該州管轄權。」法院認為[264]：「於美國傳統上有關對人訴訟上所已最為堅定的被建立之原則即為一個州的法院對於身體所在於該州的非居民有著管轄權。早期所發展的見解是對於任何於州境內之個人每個州法院有著權力去將其強拖至法院，並且在經由合適的送達而對其取得管轄權後，無論其之造訪是如何的短暫，該州能保留對其不利判決之管轄權……」因此對於上訴人依據International Shoe的標準，主張在缺乏與法院地有著「持續而制度性」的關連時，非居民被告只能在與其於法院地之關連點有關之事情上受到判決，法院認為[265]：「這個抗辯是根據對我們判例的完全誤解而來。」因此法院明確的再次維護傳統的「所在

---

262 495 U.S. 604 (1990).

263 "The question presented is whether the Due Process Clause of the Fourteenth Amendment denies California courts jurisdiction over a nonresident, who was personally served with process while temporarily in that State, in a suit unrelated to his activities in the State."

264 Among the most firmly established principles of personal jurisdiction in American tradition is that the courts of a State have jurisdiction over nonresidents who are physically present in the State. The view developed early that each State had the power to hale before its courts any individual who could be found within its borders, and that once having acquired jurisdiction over such a person by properly serving him with process, the State could retain jurisdiction to enter judgment against him, no matte how fleeting his visit ... .

265 "Despite this formidable body of precedent, petitioner contends, in reliance on our decisions applying the International Shoe standard, that in the absence of 'continuous and systematic' contacts with the forum, a nonresident defendant can be subjected to judgment only as to matters that arise out of or relate to his contacts with the forum. This argument rests on a thorough misunderstanding of our cases."

權力」規則如下[266]：「簡言之只是根據身體所在而來之管轄權就能符合適當程序，這是依據我們在法律制度上之繼續性的傳統之一，對於『傳統上公平與實質正義的概念』在適當程序上之標準的定義。這個標準之發展是與『身體所在』相比擬，並且如果說其現在可以被反過來對抗這個管轄權的試金石是會造成詭異的情形的。」

Brennan J.雖然認同判決，但其代表另外三位大法官對Scalia J.的論述並未完全認同，加以評述如下[267]：「我同意Scalia J.的意見，亦即十四修正案的適當程序條款在被告志願的所在於法院地州而被加以送達時，通常會允許該州法院對其行使管轄權。但是我並不認為有需要去決定，就只因為其『起源』於一個『非常長久以來就是這個土地於事實上之法律』之管轄規則，就自動符合適當程序法。雖然我同意於建立一個管轄規則是否符合適當程序之要件時歷史是個重要的因素，我不能承認它是唯一的因素，以至造成所有的傳統管轄規則皆永遠符合憲法的事情。不同於Scalia J.，我會行使一個『獨立的調查……去查明現在盛行的境內送達規則之公平性』。因此我只能同意於判決之部分。」Brennan J.又說[268]：「我相信

266 "The short of the matter is that jurisdiction based on physical presence alone constitutes due process because it is one of the continuing traditions of our legal system that define the due process standard of 'traditional notions of fair play and substantial justice.' That standard was developed by analogy to 'physical presence,' and it would be perverse to say it could now be turned against that touchstone of jurisdiction."

267 "I agree with JUSTICE SCALIA that the Due Process Clause of the Fourteenth Amendment generally permits a state court to exercise jurisdiction over a defendant if he is served with process while voluntarily present in the forum State. I do not perceive the need, however, to decide that a jurisdictional rule that 'has been immemorially the actual law of the land,' automatically comports with due process simply by virtue of its 'pedigree.' Although I agree that history is an important factor in establishing whether a jurisdictional rule satisfies due process requirements, I cannot agree that it is the only factor such that all traditional rules of jurisdiction are, ipso facto, forever constitutional. Unlike JUSTICE SCALIA, I would undertake an 'independent inquiry into the ··· fairness of the prevailing in-state service rule.' I therefore concur only in the judgment."其使用「過境管轄」名詞，並加以定義如下：" I use the term 'transient jurisdiction' to refer to jurisdiction premised solely on the fact that a person is served with process while physically present in the forum State."

268 "I believe that the approach adopted by JUSTICE SCALIA's opinion today -- reliance solely on historical pedigree -- is foreclosed by our decisions in International Shoe Co. v. Washington. In International Shoe, we held that a state court's assertion of personal jurisdiction does not violate the Due Process Clause if it is consistent with 'traditional notions of fair play and substantial justice.' In Shaffer, we stated that 'all assertions of state-court jurisdiction must be evaluated according to the standards set

今日Scalia J.之論述所採用之方式——完全依賴歷史之起源——是被我們於International Shoe之決定所終結。於International Shoe我們認定一個州法院在對人訴訟之主張如果符合『傳統上公平與實質正義之概念』則不會違反適當程序條款。於Shaffer，我們說『所有州法院管轄之主張必須依International Shoe及其後續判例所規定之標準而被衡量。』Shaffer批評性之見解即為所有之管轄規則，即使是古老的規則，必須符合適當程序於現代之觀念。對於『所在權力就是管轄權之基礎』及『對於其境內之人及物每一州皆擁有專屬管轄及主權』之宣示，我們在管轄權上之分析再也不會只是受限於這些宣示而已。……我同意這個方式並且繼續相信『於International Shoe中所發展之最低限度關連點分析……比起Pennoyer判決中所產生之法律及事實上假設之碎片式理論，代表著一個對州法院管轄權行使之遠較為合理之解釋』。」但是令人訝異的是在Brennan J.根據International Shoe及Shaffer而對Pennoyer所代表的「所在權力」大肆加以強烈反對後，亦並且堅決的重申「所有州法院管轄之主張必須依International Shoe 及其後續判例所規定之標準而被衡量」，他的態度卻大為逆轉。於引用Story J.認為過境管轄之「創世紀是個神話」，並且認為其規則之歷史「起源」是受到懷疑的之後，他又大迴轉的認為[269]：「過境管

forth in International Shoe and its progeny. 'The critical insight of Shaffer is that all rules of jurisdiction, even ancient ones, must satisfy contemporary notions of due process. No longer were we content to limit our jurisdictional analysis to pronouncements that '[t]he foundation of jurisdiction is physical power,' and that 'every State possesses exclusive jurisdiction and sovereignty over persons and property within its territory.' While acknowledging that 'history must be considered as supporting the proposition that jurisdiction based solely on the presence of property satisfie[d] the demands of due process', we found that this factor could not be 'decisive.' We recognized that '[t]raditional notions of fair play and substantial justice' can be as readily offended by the perpetuation of ancient forms that are no longer justified as by the adoption of new procedures that are inconsistent with the basic values of our constitutional heritage.' I agree with this approach and continue to believe that 'the minimum-contacts analysis developed in International Shoe··· represents a far more sensible construct for the exercise of state-court jurisdiction than the patchwork of legal and factual fictions that has been generated from the decision in Pennoyer v. Neff.'..."

269 "Regardless of whether Justice Story's account of the rule's genesis is mythical, our common understanding now, fortified by a century of judicial practice, is that jurisdiction is often a function of geography. The transient rule is consistent with reasonable expectations and is entitled to a strong presumption that it comports with due process. 'If I visit another State, ··· I knowingly assume some risk that the State will exercise its power over my property or my person while there. My contact with the State,

轄是與正當期待一致的，並且應該受到其是符合適當程序之強烈假設。」

Brennan J.要求非居民被告「自願性的出現在法院地」，而Scalia J.則遵守傳統的並未加以限制。但是Brennan J.真的有對「所在權力」加以修正嗎？Brennan J.派與Scalia J.派兩派大法官真的對「所在權力」管轄基礎之行使有歧異嗎？美國法律協會（American Law Institute）早在本案之前已陳述一個為美國及全世界所有文明國家所共同承認之一個全球化法學之共同核心。其Restatement (Second) of Conflict of Laws § 82（1971）規定[270]：「如果對一個被告或其財產之司法管轄權之取得，是經由詐欺或非法之暴力，則該州不能行使管轄權。」其comment (a)說[271]：「一個人不能被允許經由詐欺或非法暴力而取得利益。當原告可能是透過這種方法而對被告或其物取得這種司法管轄權時，一個州得拒絕行使這種司法管轄。」依英國母法雖然管轄基礎亦本於「所在」而來，但詐欺並不能構成取得管轄權之方式[272]。

(五)鬼打牆法學

任何有著「不乾淨的手」之人不能據此而取得利益之衡平法，無論於程序法或實體法皆為全世界文明國家之共識及常識。Brennan J.對於「所在權力」之「革命」居然是以在傳統規則上加個「自願性的出現在法院地」之條件為其革命性論述之基礎。請問Brennan J.——Pennoyer中所建

---

though minimal, gives rise to predictable risks."

270 "A state will not exercise judicial jurisdiction, which has been obtained by fraud or unlawful force, over a defendant or his property."

271 a. Rationale. A person is not permitted to profit from his use of fraud or unlawful force. A state will refuse to exercise such judicial jurisdiction as the plaintiff may obtain by such means over the defendant or his property.

272 Carrick v Hancock (1895) 12 T.L.R. 59m 60, *See also Forbes v Simmons* (1914) 20 D.L.R. 100 (Alta); Laurie v Carroll (1958) 98 C.L.R. 310, 323.但是當一個人依法被帶至加拿大的另一省，或澳洲的另一州時，該第二省或州是被認定為有權力對其加以送達。*Doyle v Doyle* (1974) 52 D.L.R. (3d)143 (Newf.); *John Sanderson Ltd v Giddings* [1976] V.R. 421; *Baldry v Jackson* [1976] 1 N.S.W.L.R. 10, affirmed on different grounds [1976] 2 N.S.W.L.R. 415.但是若一個外國人被以詐欺之方式而誘引至法院地，該送達得被撤銷。*Stein v Valkenhuysen* (1858) E.B.E. 65; *Watkins v North American Lands*, etc. Co. (1904) 20 T.L.R. 534 (HL); *Perrett v Robinson* [1985] 1 Qd.R. 83.見Dicey and Morris, 14th ed., p. 346, note 70; p.595, note 36.

立的「所在權力」管轄基礎可以允許對被告加以詐欺或脅迫而取得嗎？「所在權力」基礎之母法為英國判例法，請問美國最高法院你們的「常識」會允許你們去假設英國「所在權力」管轄基礎是准許對被告加以詐欺或脅迫而取得嗎？請問美國同僚，如果美國管轄基礎或契約權利——無論國內法或國際法——允許當事人以詐欺或脅迫取得利益，美國的法律秩序可以維持嗎？請問Scalia J.及Brennan J.你們對「所在權力」的解釋有任何差異嗎？請問美國最高法院可敬的同僚及全美國「所有」法律界之同僚冷靜的捫心自問——無論在國際法或國內法，亦無論在實體法或程序法，包括美國在內的全世界文明國家會有那一個國家會不顧法律與秩序的允許任何當事人經由詐欺或脅迫去取得利益？

自International Shoe以後「最低限度關連點」顯然在傳統的「所在權力」管轄基礎上掀起一片腥風血雨，故美國同僚有人形容其為「浩劫」或「叢林法則」。而Burnham則至少號稱在被告「有意」的進入法院地時兩派法官皆一致同意「所在權力」之管轄基礎是符合適當程序的[273]。個人戲稱「最低限度關連點」在International Shoe的崛起是個「鬼打牆法學」，如果因為有四位法官要求必須「自願性」的出現，故因此在Burnham因為於「所在權力」上達成一致的見解而消弭紛爭，那麼其紛爭的終止亦是個「鬼打牆法學」。「鬼打牆法學」的威力真是有趣的可怕。

對於傳統的「所在權力」之「公平性或妥適性」有必要交給「國會去作判斷」或加以一個莫須有的「自願性」條件嗎？如前所述自「最低限度關連點」之一出世其就與「不方便法院」連結，對於傳統的「所在權力」之「公平性妥適性」事實上依「不方便法院」法則加以衡量是較為可接受之作法。以「不方便法院」法則來對「所在權力」之過度管轄加以節制，如前述已為英國法界、美國法律協會自己（認為過境管轄是個「學術性」問題[274]）、及UNIDROIT Principles 2.2及2.5條所公開的認可之作法。如

---

[273] Patrick J. Borchers, The Death of the Constitutional Law of Personal Jurisdiction: From *Pennoyer to Burnham* and Back again, 24 U.C. Davis L. Rev. 19, 78 (1990-1991).

[274] Restatement (Second) of Conflict of Laws § 28, comment (c),

果「所在權力」之母法英國判例法對「所在權力」之可能過度管轄之情形，可以依「不方便法院」而加以節制，同為判例法之美國最高法院並未加以解釋為何英國母法不能適用於美國。這又是一個不遵循享有崇高聲譽之判例法之不良示範，這不是「道法自然」之作風。這亦是個人一再認為Burnham中之辯論及其「自願性」之折衷法則是個「鬼打牆法學」之故。

坦白說個人覺得Burnham之辯論及結論皆是嚴重失焦，其重點不應放在非居民被告是否「自願性」的所在於法院地，或非居民被告於該州之行為是否與訴訟有關。兩派法官皆承認非居民被告所在，或自願性的所在，於法院地是可以滿足14修正案的適當程序的，亦即居民或非居民被告皆能於法院地內被親自給予送達而受到法院之管轄——那麼「最低限度關連點」或「傳統上公平與實質正義的概念」基本上只成為適用於對境外被告加以送達之標準。因此做為一個英國法的學生個人不得不善意的提醒美國最高法院的同僚及其他所有的美國同僚，不好意思，近七十年來你們的重點可能有點失焦了——應如英國母法一般，重點是在公開的承認送達境外被告通常是一種「例外」或「過度」之管轄。

四、逆向不方便法學

(一)Gulf Oil Corporation v. Gilbert

美國所行使的「不方便法院」法學是被1999年海牙草約22(3)條[275]及UNIDROIT Principles 3.2條[276]所公開禁止其基於國籍或居所而對外國當

c. *Forum non conveniens*. From a pragmatic standpoint, the question may be academic whether an individual's momentary presence in a state provides that state with a basis of judicial jurisdiction. This is because a suit based on such presence in the state without other affiliating circumstances would probably be dismissed or transferred on forum non conveniens grounds.

[275] 3. In deciding whether to suspend the proceedings, a court shall not discriminate on the basis of the nationality or habitual residence of the parties.

[276] ALI/UNIDROIT Principles of Transnational Civil Procedure

3.2 The right to equal treatment includes avoidance of any kind of illegitimate discrimination, particularly on the basis of nationality or residence.

又見其註釋：

P-3B Illegitimate discrimination includes discrimination on the basis of nationality, residence, gender,

事人加以歧視之行為。而個人於較近著作之結論亦如此的論述「這種邪派理論」[277]：「美國法院於『不方便法院』之發展上，造成人類國際私法歷史上最黑暗的紀錄。」這個二十世紀的霸主為什麼會在其霸業即將結束的二十一世紀留下這樣野蠻不光彩的紀錄？即將再度成為二十一世紀霸主的中華民族必須認真的探其究竟。或許1947年的Gulf Oil Corporation v. Gilbert[278]是「不方便法院」法學在蘇格蘭式以「正義為目的」及美國式對第三世界採「掠奪式新殖民地法學」之死亡交叉點。

Jackson J.代表法院作成判決[279]：「不方便法院原則很簡單的就是一個法院得抗拒加於其身上之管轄權，即使是管轄權是依一般管轄條款之規定而來時亦是一樣。這些條款必須以一般性的方式而被規定，並且通常會給予原告去選擇法院的機會，以便其被確保至少有地方去提起救濟之請求。但是這種開放的方式可能會去允許那些不只要求正義，而或許是正義混雜一些騷擾的行動。有時原告可能受到誘惑去訴之在對手最不方便之地方強行訴訟之策略，即使是對他自己會有些不方便亦會如此。」Jackson J.又說[280]：「許多州是以給予法院裁量權去基於許多理由而去改變審判地

---

race, language, religion, political or other opinion, national or social origin, birth or other status, sexual orientation, association with a national minority. Any form of illegitimate discrimination is prohibited, but discrimination on the basis of nationality or residence is a particularly sensitive issue in transnational commercial litigation.

277 陳隆修，《2005年海牙法院選擇公約評析》，台北，五南圖書公司，2009年1月，初版1刷，306頁。

278 330 U.S. 501 (1947); 91 L.Ed. 1055; 67 S. Ct. 839.

279 同上，para. 11,
The principle of forum non conveniens is simply that a court may resist imposition upon its jurisdiction even when jurisdiction is authorized by the letter of a general venue statute. These statutes are drawn with a necessary generality and usually give a plaintiff a choice of courts, so that he may be quite sure of some place in which to pursue his remedy. But the open door may admit those who seek not simply justice but perhaps justice blended with some harassment. A plaintiff sometimes is under temptation to resort to a strategy of forcing the trial at a most inconvenient place for an adversary, even at some inconvenience to himself.

280 同上，para. 12,
Many of the states have met misuse of venue by investing courts with a discretion to change the place of trial on various grounds, such as the convenience of witnesses and the ends of justice. The federal law contains no such express criteria to guide the district court in exercising its power. But the problem is a very old one affecting the administration of the courts as well as the rights of litigants, and both in England and in this country the common law worked out techniques and criteria for dealing with it.

點之方式以應付審判地之濫用，例如證人的便利性及正義的目的。聯邦法並無明示之標準以便指引地院去行使其權力。但這是一個非常古老的問題，它影響到法院的行政程序及當事人之權利，並且英國及這個國家的判例法皆同時創造出應付它之技術及標準。」

於1947年Jackson J.即提出對「不方便法院」法學所應加以考量之因素的經典論述[281]：「如果對於造成既定結果所必須的因素的份量及結合去加以敘述或預測是有困難的，但是那些應該被加以考慮的去將其陳列出來並無困難。一個應考量的利益，並且這個利益可能會是最應優先的，就是訴訟者之私人利益。其他重要的考量為證據來源接近的相對容易性；不情願出庭證人強迫程序的可供利用性，及取得願意出庭證人之費用；如果地點的視察對於訴訟是有必要的，視察的可能性；及使得案件之審判能夠簡單、快速、及便宜之所有其他之實際問題。另外可能有關之問題為取得判決後之強制執行問題。為了能達成公平的審判法院會衡量相關的益處及障礙。通常是認為原告不得經由選擇一個不方便的法院去加諸被告費用或依

有趣的是Jackson J.在2005年海牙選擇法院公約約60年前即斬釘截鐵的宣示，當事人之同意只是給予法院對人之管轄，而法院仍有裁量權去決定是否接受該訴訟。見para. 10, But the general venue statute plus the Neirbo interpretation do not add up to a declaration that the court must respect the choice of the plaintiff, no matter what the type of suit or issues involved. The two taken together mean only that the defendant may consent to be sued, and it is proper for the federal court to take jurisdiction, not that the plaintiff's choice cannot be questioned. The defendant's consent to be sued extends only to give the court jurisdiction of the person; it assumes that the court, having the parties before it, will apply all the applicable law, including, in those cases where it is appropriate, its discretionary judgment as to whether the suit should be entertained. In all cases in which the doctrine of forum non conveniens comes into play, it presupposes at least two forums in which the defendant is amenable to process; the doctrine furnishes criteria for choice between them.

281 同上，para. 14,
If the combination and weight of factors requisite to given results are difficult to forecast or state, those to be considered are not difficult to name. An interest to be considered, and the one likely to be most pressed, is the private interest of the litigant. Important considerations are the relative ease of access to sources of proof; availability of compulsory process for attendance of unwilling, and the cost of obtaining attendance of willing, witnesses; possibility of view of premises, if view would be appropriate to the action; and all other practical problems that make trial of a case easy, expeditious and inexpensive. There may also be questions as to the enforcibility of a judgment if one is obtained. The court will weigh relative advantages and obstacles to fair trial. It is often said that the plaintiff may not, by choice of an inconvenient forum, 'vex,' 'harass,' or 'oppress' the defendant by inflicting upon him expense or trouble not necessary to his own right to pursue his remedy. But unless the balance is strongly in favor of the defendant, the plaintiff's choice of forum should rarely be disturbed.

其權利去要求救濟之不必要之麻煩，以『困擾』、『騷擾』、或『壓迫』被告。但是除非是考量的平衡是強烈的對被告有利，原告所選擇的法院是應極少被干擾的。」這個論述很明顯的與英國母法先前的「困擾性或壓迫性」主義一般，禁止原告對被告造成「困擾或壓迫」之行為。另外本案中美國最高法院認為「原告所選擇的法院是應極少被干擾的」，這與早期英國法院極度尊重當事人原告之利益事一致的[282]。即使現在採用「不方便法院」法學，個人較近亦如此論述[283]：「故而第一階段是被告必須證明除了英國法院外，還有其他有管轄權的法院很明顯的（clearly or distinctly）較英國法院合適。除了要有其他有管轄權之法院外，該法院必須很明顯的較英國法院合適，只是證明英國法院不是合適或不是自然的法院並不符合要件。所謂『明顯的合適』之要件，事實上於英國採納不方便法院之前，英國已有自然法院（natural forum）之概念。」

個人認為或許Jackson J.於下面之論述是美國判例法於裁量權上與母法英國判例法上於裁量權在行使上之分水嶺[284]：「公共利益之因素在適用

---

[282] 見陳隆修，《國際私法管轄權評論》，台北，五南圖書公司，民國75年11月，初版，84頁。「因為英國法院於訴訟會造成困擾（vexation）或壓迫（oppression）之情形下，為避免造成不正當（unjust）的後果，可以命令停止（stay）或駁回（dismiss）當事人於英國之訴訟，甚至可以禁止（injunction）當事人於國外起訴或繼續進行國外之訴訟，或強制執行國外之判決。此種管轄上之權力為英法院之自由裁量權（discretionary power），法院必須很謹慎地使用此種權力。法院必須於當事人之一方，若繼續進行其於法院地或法院外之訴訟，會很明顯地對他方當事人造成困擾或壓迫，或著濫用法院之訴訟程序時才可使用此種權力。另一要件為法院欲停止訴訟之進行時，必須不能對原告造成不公平（injustice）之現象。而上述兩要件之舉證責任在於被告。」

[283] 陳隆修、許兆慶、林恩瑋、李瑞生四人合著，《國際私法-管轄與選法理論之交錯》，台北，五南圖書公司，2009年3月，初版1刷，208頁。另外於209頁中如此敘述：「總之所謂『明顯的合適』的概念，事實上與前述方便法院一般，法院不但會注意當事人居住或經商之地，證人的便利性及花費，還有交易之準據法等。至於當事人若有指定管轄法院及提起否認債權之訴時，學理上亦與前述方便法院一致。」「當事人若提出否認之訴時，英國法院因怕會與其他國家之法院發生管轄之衝突，故通常會允許停止訴訟之請求，但於Smyth v. Behbehani (1999) Times, 9 April, CA中，為了使得類似的訴訟可同時一起被處理，在正義的需求下，否認之訴被允許提起。」另外210頁：「但是除了於第一階段被告須證明有明顯的更合適的有管轄權的外國法院外，於第二階段法院必須考慮到是否為了正義的需求，停止訴訟之請求應被駁回，此時原告須證明其於英國提起訴訟之正當性。故而第二階段的舉證責任在於原告」。

[284] 330 U.S. 501, para. 15,

Factors of public interest also have place in applying the doctrine. Administrative difficulties follow for courts when litigation is piled up in congested centers instead of being handled at its origin. Jury duty is a burden that ought not to be imposed upon the people of a community which has no relation to the

這個法理上亦占有著地位。當訴訟是被堆積在一個擁塞的中心而不是在其起源處被解決，則對法院會造成行政上之困難。陪審團的義務是一種負擔，而若訴訟是與社區無關這種負擔不應加諸在該社區的人民身上。若是於牽涉及許多人之事情之訴訟，審判應以他們的觀點及可接觸的範圍內進行是合乎道理的，而不應是於一個遙遠角落的國家進行，而他們只能經由報告而知道該訴訟。當地是有個利益去使得當地的紛爭於家園之地解決。另外並且有一種合適性是存在著，亦即在審判不同州籍之案件時，應於對案件準據法之州法較為熟悉之法院中審理，而不是使得其他地方之法院去解決衝突法及對其陌生之法律之問題。」如前述準據法是否為法院地法為英、美兩國不方便法院法學所應考慮之重點，而於英國的CPR 1998, s.6.20(5)(c)中契約準據法為英國法甚至是訴訟通知送達境外之一種基礎（方便法院）。但是使美國「不方便法院」法學與英國於此方面之裁量權不同的是在美國法院於「公共利益」上之考量，這是英國母法所沒有的。

(二)公共利益與法律恐怖主義

基於「公共利益」之考量，後續的美國案例經常以「法院案件擁塞」、「人民沒有義務當陪審員」、或「訴訟程序耗費人民稅金」為理由，而拒絕第三世界人民於當地受到美國跨國公司傷害之請求。這種以「公共利益」去拒絕外國請求者基於外國訴因而對美國被告所提起的請求是有道理嗎[285]對於美國法院基於「公共利益」所行使的拒絕管轄之裁量

---

litigation. In cases which touch the affairs of many persons, there is reason for holding the trial in their view and reach rather than in remote parts of the country where they can learn of it by report only. There is a local interest in having localized controversies decided at home. There is an appropriateness, too, in having the trial of a diversity case in a forum that is at home with the state law that must govern the case, rather than having a court in some other forum untangle problems in conflict of laws, and in law foreign to itself.

[285] 類似之案情亦發生於英國之Lubbe v. Cape PLC, [2000] 1 W.L.R. 1545 (H.L.)。於該案中被告英國母公司之南非子公司於南非開採石棉礦，其被主張其子公司於南非未遵守安全規則故造成死傷，三千多請求者中只有一人為英國公民及居民，其餘皆為南非公民與居民。被告不方便法院之主張為一審所接受，二審亦認為南非為明顯的合適法院。最高法院採納Spiliada及Connelly之原則，認為請求人若沒有法律扶助或律師抽成制，則無法起訴，拒絕美式公共利益之考量，允許訴訟之進行。Lord Bingham (Lubbe v. Cape PLC, [2000] 1 W.L.R. 1545, 1561 (H.L.))認為公共利益是與當事人的利益及正義的目的無關："public interest considerations not related to the private

權，個人基於第三世界法律學生之身分，於此謹代表十三億中國人質問美國法院——請問美國跨國公司在第三世界所榨取的大量「利益」及資源是否為美國投資者及美國政府所受益？所謂的「公共利益」就只有避免「法院程序的擁塞」與「人民加入陪審團的負擔」而已嗎？美國跨國公司在第三世界造成環境汙染，侵害當地人民身體、健康、生命，及甚至造成種族滅絕之暴行[286]，因而所獲得的巨額利益及所產生之稅收難道不屬於美國社會的「真實性公共利益」？美國於「不方便法院」上所賴以行使裁量權之「公共利益」理論，一方面幫助美國以WTO及自由貿易之名於第三世界憑藉著資金、技術、行銷之絕對優勢大肆掠奪自然資源及獲取高額商業利潤，一方面卻又拒絕給予第三世界之被害者到美國法院要求正義，因此個人習慣性的稱美國「不方便法院」法學對第三世界人民所實施的是「法律恐怖主義」（legal terrorism）或「掠奪性新殖民主義」（predatory neo-colonialism）。

於Shaffer中Marshall J.即公開表示為了簡化管轄權問題而去犧牲自然法上公平正義之概念，「代價太高了」[287]：「並且，當一個特定法院依

interests of the parties and the ends of justice have no bearing on the decision which the court has to make. Where a catastrophe has occurred in a particular place, the fact that numerous victims live in that place, that the relevant evidence is to be found there and that site inspections are most conveniently and inexpensively carried out there will provide factors connecting any ensuing litigation with the Court exercising jurisdiction in that place. These are matters of which the Spiliada test takes full account."又認為（at 1559）如果在「更合適的」南非法院進行訴訟會等同於「正義的拒絕」："if these proceedings were stayed in favour of the more appropriate forum in South Africa the probability is that the plaintiffs would have no means of obtaining the professional representation and expert evidence which would be essential if these claims were to be justly decided. This would amount to a denial of justice. In the special and unusual circumstances of these proceedings, lack of the means, in South Africa, to prosecute these claims to a conclusion, provides a compelling ground, at the second stage of the Spiliada test, for refusing to stay the proceedings here."而Lord Hope (Lubbe v. Cape PLC, [2000] 1 W.L.R. 1545, 1561)則採用「司法自尊與政治上之責任或利益不能被適用」之原則 ("questions of judicial amour proper and political interest or responsibility have no part to play.")其認為蘇格蘭判例已於此方面一再證明這個原則，La Societe du Gaz de Paris v. La Societe Anonyme de Navigation "Les Armateurs Francaise", 1926 Sess. Cas. 13, 21 (H.L. 1925) (appeal taken form Scot.) "Obviously the Court cannot allege its own convenience, or the amount of its own business, or its distaste for trying actions which involve taking evidence in French, as a ground for refusal⋯." (Lord Summer)

286 陳隆修，《2005年海牙法院選擇公約評析》，台北，五南圖書公司，2009年1月，初版1刷，294、295、304-306頁。

287 433 U.S. 186, 211, "It might also be suggested that allowing in rem jurisdiction avoids the uncertainty

International Shoe其管轄權之存在是不清楚時，以迴避管轄問題來簡化訴訟的代價可能是犧牲了『公平與實質正義』。這個代價是太高。」事實上在國際訴訟上，於複數訴訟（平行訴訟）時英國判例法Lopez v Chavarri於一百多年前即對法院之選定下個萬世不移之基礎論調[288]：「是否正義的真正利益是將問題於此審判或將其交付外國法院最能被達成。」因此在「正義的真正利益」之核心基礎下，於國際訴訴上當面對複數訴訟時，不但歐盟助長選購法院鼓勵濫訴之先繫屬優先死硬原則不能被加以合理化，美國法院對第三世界弱勢被害者加以歧視之「公共利益」之不當運作更應被視為非法。

如同前述所謂「不方便法院」的「conveniens」指的並不是「便利」之意思，而所謂自然原告對自然被告於「自然法院」提起自然訴訟，所謂「自然法院」當然不是「資本主義之利益被達成之法院」，亦不完全是「具有重大關連管轄基礎之法院」，而應是「正義的真正利益最能被達成之法院」。二十一世紀全球化法學於國際管轄——這自然包含裁量權之行使——之心與靈魂（heart and soul）是在於「是否正義的真正利益最能被達成」。個人經常舉Connelly v. RTZ Corpn. plc[289]為例，最密切關連地之法院不見得永遠是「最能達成正義之真正利益」的法院。如Lord Goff於Spiliada Maritime Corpn v. Cansulex Ltd中所說的[290]：「如果有著其他可供起訴之法院而該法院對於該訴訟之審判是表面上明顯的為更合適時，除非由於正義要求停止訴訟之請求是不可以被允許之情形下，否則通常

inherent in the International Shoe standard and assures a plaintiff of a forum. We believe, however, that the fairness standard of International Shoe can be easily applied in the vast majority of cases. Moreover, when the existence of jurisdiction in a particular forum under International Shoe is unclear, the cost of simplifying the litigation by avoiding the jurisdictional question may be the sacrifice of 'fair play and substantial justice.' That cost is too high."

288 Lopez v Chavarri [1901] W.N. 115, 116, "whether the true interests of justice would be best served by trying the question here, or leaving it to the foreign tribunal".

289 [1998] AC 854, HL.見陳隆修、許兆慶、林恩瑋、李瑞生四人合著，《國際私法-管轄與選法理論之交錯》，台北，五南圖書公司，2009年3月，初版1刷，210頁。

290 The Spiliada [1987] AC 460 at 476. Lord Goff: "... if there is some other available forum which prima facie is clearly more appropriate for the trial of the action, it will ordinarily grant a stay unless there are circumstances by reason of which justice requires that a stay should nevertheless not be granted."

停止之請求會被允許。」故而由Connelly或Spiliada所顯示與案件最具有密切關連之地之法院或明顯的更為合適之法院雖然通常是自然原告對自然被告順理成章應該提起自然訴訟之法院（亦即通常表面上可能直覺的會認定為自然法院），於例外之可能情形下，他們的所謂表面上之自然管轄權應在個案正義之要求下退讓[291]。亦即真正的自然法院（不同於表面上合適之自然法院）是在自然正義程序及實質正義的要求下，於國際複數訴訟中「正義的真正利益最能被達成」之法院。這亦是中國式法學「道法自然」的詮釋之一種。

如果相較於英國判例法於裁量權上近兩百年來之經驗，在國際複數訴訟上，美國「公共利益」之運作，及歐盟本於「重大關連管轄」而來之

---

[291] 於Connelly v. RTZ Corp. PLC, [1998] A.C. 854, 872 (H.L. 1997)中英國最高法院雖然認為："if a clearly more appropriate forum overseas has been identified, generally speaking the plaintiff will have to take that forum as he finds it, even if it is in certain respects less advantageous to him than the English forum."但是請求者若於外國法院會受到不公正之對待，英國法院不會允許訴訟停止之請求。例如外國司法之不獨立，訴訟可能會拖延10年才會受到審判，或過低之賠償等，皆構成正義之拒絕。The Abidin Daver, 1 A.C. 398, 411 (H.L. 1984); The Vishva Ajay, 2 Lloyd's Rep. 558, 560 (Q.B. 1989); BMG Trading Ltd. v. A.S. McKay, 1998 I.L. Pr. 691 (Eng. C.A.).而後來在Lubbe v. Cape PLC, [2000]1 W.L.R. 1545, 1554 (H.L.)中，正如以前所發生於Connelly, [1998] A.C. at 874中，請求者於原來外國「合適法院」，由於缺乏外國法律貧民扶助或律師抽成制度，故無法起訴。英國最高法院將這個「私人利益」放置於整個分析的重點。嚴格而論，由於涉及英國法律扶助，故「公共利益」的分析對英國是不利的。於經過Connelly案後，英國政府對於外國人申請法律扶助去對英國公司起訴之情形，於2000年修改法律扶助辦法，但仍保留交換律師抽成制度。Access to Justice Act 1999, c. 22, 4-10 (Eng.); Conditional Fee Agreements Regulations, (2000) SI 2000/692. 見C.G.J. Morse, Not in the Public Interest? Lubbe v. Cape PLC, 37 Tex. Int'l L.J. 541, 549, 550 (2002). 事實上在Lubbe, [2000]1 W.L.R. at 1558, 1559, 1560中，南非法院雖為Lord Bingham所認為是「更為合適之法院」("the more appropriate forum")，但是由於南非當時尚未有完整的集體訴訟法規，故其認為於南非進行訴訟，會構成「正義的拒絕」(This would amount to a denial of justice)。有趣的是由於法制的不完備，許多第三世界的政府皆認為訴訟若於當地進行是與當地的公共利益無關。在Lubbe v. Cape PLC中，南非政府於第三審時介入，認為被告與南非沒有關連，更於南非沒有財產，故公共利益指向應於英國進行訴訟。Peter Muchlinski, Corporations in Internatinoal Litigation: Problems of Jurisdiction and the United Kingdom Asbestos Cases, 50 Int'l & Comp. L.Q.1, 21 (2001); C. G. J. Morse, Not in the Public Interest? Lubbe v. Cape PLC, 37 Tex. Int'l L.J. 541, 552 (2002).**相同的在舉世震驚且傷害更達數十倍以上的**In re Union Carbide Corp. Gas Plant Disaster at Bhopal, India in Dec. 1984, 634 F. Supp. 842 (S.D.N.Y. 1986), affd, 809 F.2d 195 (2nd Cir. 1987), cert. denied, 484 U.S. 871 (1987).**案件中，印度政府亦表明其司法無法承受數十萬請求之能力，但美國法院仍堅守「逆向帝國主義」法學。個人基於比較法學之立場，請教WTO及諾貝爾和平獎——美國沒有進行「保護貿易主義」嗎？美國法院沒有侵犯第三世界人權公約中所保障的訴訟權、財產權、生命權嗎？更重要的1966年人權公約第1(2)條中第三世界的生存權沒有被踐踏嗎？相較之下在Lubbe中約7500個請求者取得兩千一百萬英鎊的和解金。**37Tex. Int'l L.J. 541, 557.

先繫屬優先法則，或許有時無法於個案上達成「實質正義」之要求，因此即使是具有「重大關連管轄」或「最密切關連管轄」之法院，亦不應該被認為是永遠符合「自然法院」之要件。二十一世紀全球化法學在國際管轄上，無論是英國式的「方便與不方便法院」，美國式的「最低限度關連點」與「不方便法院」，及大陸法的「禁止濫用訴訟程序」，這些裁量權法學行使的心與靈魂都應是在於「是否正義的真正利益最能被達成」[292]。而對這個二十一世紀全球化國際管轄法規於裁量權之心與靈魂，我們中國文化早在近二千多年前即領先宣示「天道無親恆與善人」。「不患寡患不均」之「禮運大同」「王道」法律哲學與二十一世紀全球化法學於國際管轄法規裁量權行使之心與靈魂是相配合的。

(三)Piper Aircraft Co. v. Reyno

如果Gulf Oil Corporation v. Gilbert[293]案可說是正式的定立下美國不方便法學之定義與基礎，則Piper Aircraft Co. v. Reyno[294]可謂是美國法院光明正大理直氣壯的以不方便法院之名，而拒絕給予外國原告基於外國訴因而來之請求之濫觴[295]。於案中一小型商用包機於蘇格蘭墜毀，駕駛與5名乘客立即死亡，他們皆為蘇格蘭公民及居民。原告被上訴人代表5名乘客之遺產而對被告上訴人於加州法院提起不當死亡之訴訟。被告為一於賓夕法尼亞製造飛機之公司及一於俄亥俄製造螺旋槳之公司。飛機於英國登記並為英國公司所擁有及經營。死亡乘客之繼承人及最近家屬皆為蘇格蘭人，而事故之調查是由英國官方所進行。基於無過失責任或過失責任

---

[292] 調查顯示於英美若案件以不方便法院而被停止，則訴訟甚少在其他法院再被提起。David W. Robertson, Forum Non Conveniens in America and England: A Rather Fantastic Fiction, 103 Law Q. Rev. 398 (1987).

[293] 330 U.S. 501 (1947).

[294] 454 U.S. 235 (1981).

[295] 對這種現象加以批評之評論見Jacqueline Duval-Major, Note, One-Way Ticket Home: The Federal Doctrine of Forum Non Conveniens and the International Plaintiff, 77 Cornell L. Rev. 650 (1992); John R. Wilson, Note, Coming to America to File Suit: Foreign Plaintiffs and the Forum Non Conveniens Barrier in Transnational Litigation, 65 Ohio St. L.J. 659 (2004). 又見Ronald A. Brand & Scott R. Jablonski, Forum Non Conveniens: History, Global Practice, and Future Under the Hague Convention on Choice of Court Agreements 58 (2007).

原告要求被告損害賠償，蘇格蘭法並不承認無過失責任。原告承認其於美國提告是因美國法於責任、訴訟資格、及損害賠償上是較蘇格蘭法對原告有利。後被告要求將訴訟移至加州聯邦法院，再後又根據28 U.S.C. § 1404(a)[296]而被移至賓州聯邦法院。賓州地院准許被告之請求，以不方便法院而駁回訴訟。法院依據Gilbert之標準[297]，而「分析影響到當事人便利之『私人利益因素』及影響到法院便利之『公共利益因素』，正如同Gilbert所定下之標準，地院認定蘇格蘭是合適之法院。」但是上訴法院更改其判決，認定地院於進行Gilbert之分析時已經濫用裁量權，並且當另一個法院之法律是較原告所選之法院之法律不利時，訴訟之駁回是會被自動禁止的。美國最高法院認同地院之決定而更改高院之判決。

Justice Marshall代表法院作成判決。首先其注意到地院認為另一有管轄權之法院存在於蘇格蘭，兩個被告皆同意接受蘇格蘭法院之管轄，並且若時效屆至他們同意拋棄時效之抗辯[298]。死者之家屬另外於蘇格蘭對駕駛、飛機經營商、及所有人另外提起訴訟。地院唯恐美國被告無法加入蘇格蘭第三當事人被告，因此認為「如果相關的所有的證人之可供利用之證據整個案件式呈現在一個陪審團前，對於所有的當事人是會更公平及花費較少」[299]。地院亦擔心由於美國採無過失責任，而蘇格蘭採過失責任，因

296 Section 1404(a) provides:
"For the convenience of parties and witnesses, in the interest of justice, a district court may transfer any civil action to any other district or division where it might have been brought."

297 454 U.S. 235, 236, Syllabus, "The District Court granted petitioners' motion to dismiss the action on the ground of *forum non conveniens*. Relying on the test set forth in Gulf Oil Corp. v. Gilbert, 330 U.S. 501, and analyzing the 'private interest factors' affecting the litigants' conenience and the 'public interest factors' affecting the forum's convenience, as set forth in Gilbert, the District Court concluded that Scotland was the appropriate forum. However, the Court of Appeals reversed, holding that the District Court had abused its discretion in conducting the *Gilbert* analysis and that, in any event, dismissal is automatically barred where the law of the alternative forum is less favorable to the plaintiff than the law of the forum chosen by the plaintiff."

298 454 U.S. 242, "It began by observing that an alternative forum existed in Scotland; Piper and Hartzell had agreed to submit to the jurisdiction of the Scottish courts and to waive any statute of limitations defense that might be available."

299 454 U.S. 243, "[I]t would be fairer to all parties and less costly if the entire case was presented to one jury with available testimony from all relevant witnesses."

而會造成不一致之判決[300]。布魯賽爾規則I的第6(1)條[301]有著共同訴訟之規定，而第28條[302]亦有著避免相關訴訟造成不一致判決之規定。故而聯邦地院之作法並未與其他文明國家之慣例在表面上會有脫節之處。但真正的問題似乎不在這裡。依個人所主張的實體法方法論，真正的問題在於產品的無過失責任在任何文明國家都是一種公共政策之問題，而如前述英國法院在有關英國公共政策時是經常不會將案件交付無法執行該政策之外國法院的。例如歐盟的羅馬II（Rome II）的第16條即規定無論非契約責任之準據法為何，法院地強行法之適用是不會被禁止的[303]。做為一個死忠的實體法論者，個人認為這個案件的重點不在法院於管轄權上裁量權之行使，而在於其公共政策（產品之無過失責任政策）被執行之強度（是否適用於外國消費者之保護上）。

但美國最高法院認為[304]：「只是經由證明於另一個替代法院所適用之

---

[300] Footnote 7,
"The District Court explained that inconsistent verdicts might result if petitioners were held liable on the basis of strict liability here, and then required to prove negligence in an indemnity action in Scotland. Moreoner, even if the same standard of liability applied, there was a danger that different juries would find different facts and produce inconsistent results."

[301] Article 6
A person domiciled in a Member State may also be sued:
1. Where he is one of a number of defendants, in the courts for the place where any one of them is domiciled, provided the claims are so closely connected that it is expedient to hear and determine them together to avoid the risk of irreconcilable judgments resulting from separate proceedings.

[302] Article 28
1.Where related actions are pending in the courts of different Member States, any court other than the court first seised may stay its proceedings.
... .
3.For the purposes of this Article, actions are deemed to be related where they are so closely connected that it is expedient to hear and determine them together to avoid the risk of irreconcilable judgments resulting from separate proceedings.

[303] REGULATION (EC) No 864/2007 OF THE EUROPEAN PARLIAMENT AND OF THE COUNCIL of 11 July 2007 on the law applicable to non-contractual obligations
Article 16
Overriding mandatory provisions
Nothing in this Regulation shall restrict the application of the provisions of the law of the forum in a situation where they are mandatory irrespective of the law otherwise applicable to the non-contractual obligation.

[304] 454 U.S. 247, "The Court of Appeals erred in holding that plaintiffs may defeat a motion to dismiss on the ground of *forum non conveniens* merely by showing that the substantive law that would be applied in the alternative forum is less favorable to the plaintiffs than that of the present forum. The possibility

實體法是比起現在法院所適用之法是對原告為較不利，原告即可挫敗基於不方便法院而要求駁回訴訟之請求，上訴法院這種認定是不對的。於探詢不方便法院之適用時，實體法可能之改變通常不應被給予決定性或甚至重大的份量。」但是更有趣的是最高法院說[305]：「的確，藉由認定不方便法院的諮詢之中心重點是便利性，Gilbert默示的承認不能僅因一個法律上不利之改變之可能即可禁止駁回之請求。依據Gilbert，當訴訟是於原告所選定之法院舉行時會對被告及法院產生重大負擔，並且原告是無法給予任何有關便利之明確理由以支持其選擇時，駁回訴訟是通常會是合適的。但是，如果對於法律不利的改變之可能性是給予重大的份量時，即使是所選定法院之審判地是明顯的不便利時駁回訴訟之要求仍可能被禁止。」另外又說[306]：「當家園地之法院被選定時，去假設這個選擇是便利的是為合理的。但是當原告是外國人時，這個假設就是非常的沒有那麼合理。因為任何不方便法院的諮詢之中心目的就是去確保審判是便利的，一個外國原告的選擇是較不值得順服的。」

但是「不方便法院的諮詢之中心重點是便利性」這個論述是正確的嗎？請允許個人再次引用Dicey and Morris 的教科書如下[307]：「不方便法院法學，亦即所謂其他法院是更『合適』指的就是為了正義的目的是更適

---

of a change in substantive law should ordinarily not be given conclusive or even substantial weight in the *forum non conveniens* inquiry."

305 454 U.S. 249, "Indeed, by holding that the central focus of the forum non conveniens inquiry is convenience, Gilbert implicitly recognized that dismissal may not be barred solely because of the possibility of an unfavorable change in law. Under Gilbert, dismissal will ordinarily be appropriate where trial in the plaintiff's chosen forum imposes a heavy burden on the defendant or the court, and where the plaintiff is unable to offer any specific reasons of convenience supporting his choice. If substantial weight were given to the possibility of an unfavorable change in law, however, dismissal might be barred even where trial in the chosen forum was plainly inconvenient."

306 454 U.S. 255, 256, "When the home forum has been chosen, it is reasonable to assume that this choice is convenient. When the plaintiff is foreign, however, this assumption is much less reasonable. Because the central purpose of any f*orum non conveniens* inquiry is to ensure that the trial is convenient, a foreign plaintiff's choice deserves less deference."

307 Dicey and Morris, the Conflict of Laws, 14th ed., p.465, "The doctrine of forum non conveniens, i.e. that some other forum is more 'appropriate' in the sense of more suitable for the ends of justice, was developed by the Scottish courts in the nineteenth century, and was adopted (with some modifications) in the United States."

合」。故而所謂「合適」的自然法院指的就是為了正義的目的更適合之意思。彷彿這樣還不夠明確，其又於註解中引用判例法而更白紙黑字的明確宣示[308]：「conveniens不是指『便利』」。於確立「方便與不方便法院」法學之領導案例Spiliada中，Lord Goff宣示[309]所謂「合適法院」就是能更妥善的處理所有當事人之利益及正義之目的之法院。因此個人於此請求美國同僚注意，你們判例法的母法鏗鏘有力的宣布「conveniens不是『便利』」，因此「不方便法院的諮詢中心的重點是便利性」是與母法之判例法不合的。

個人認為任何「方便與不方便法院」法學之重點若不是以正義為目的，就不是「道法自然」之行為。「外國原告之選擇較不值得順服」之論述就是這種謬誤理論之產物，它不但違反UNIDROIT Principles第3條禁止歧視之規定，亦違反1999海牙草約第22(3)條禁止歧視之規定，更是違反所有人權公約中的生存權、財產權、及訴訟權。因此個人於此再唸一次經咒——方便與不方便法院的心與靈魂在於「正義的真正利益是否最能被達成」。

有關產品責任的過失或無過失責任，於大部分之文明國家皆是屬於重大的政策。歐盟的羅馬II規則（Rome II）第5條準據法順序依序為被害

308 同上，"*Conveniens* does not mean 'convenient': see The Atlantic Star [1974] A.C. 436, 475; *GAF Corp v Amchem Products Inc* [1975] 1 Lloyd's Rep. 601, 607; *Spiliada Maritime Crop v Cansulex Ltd* [1987] A.C. 460, 474-475."

309 Spiliada Maritime Crop v. Cansulex Ltd [1987] 1 AC460, at 480, "to identify the forum in which the case can be suitably tried for the interests of all the parties and for the ends of justice"
Spiliada Maritime Crop v. Cansulex Ltd [1987] 1 AC460, at 476, "The basic principle is that a stay will only be granted on the ground of forum non conveniens where the court is satisfied that there is some available forum having jurisdiction, which is the appropriate forum for trial of the action, i.e. in which the case may be tried more suitably for the interests of all the parites and the ends of justice."但是在Spiliada Mar. Corp v. Cansulex Ltd.的「不方便及方便法院」原則確立之前，英國法院已累積了一些前置判例。例如於The Atlantic Star, [1974] 1 A.C. at 478 (H.L.)中對「困擾性或壓迫性」給予更開放之解釋。及Lord Justice Scott於MacShannon v. Rockware Glass Ltd., [1978] A.C. 795, 812 (H.L.)中對停止訴訟所立下之要件："In order to justify a stay two conditions must be satisfied, one positive and one negative: (a) the defendant must satisfy the court that there is another forum to whose jurisdiction he is amenable in which justice can be done between the parties at substantially less inconvenience or expense, and (b) the stay must not deprive the plaintiff of a legitimate personal or juridical advantage which would be available to him if he invoked the jurisdiction of the English court."

人慣居地、取得產品地（銷售地）、或損害發生地（銷售地），其政策就是本於在今日高科技的社會中，應將產品責任的風險加以分散，並藉此保護消費者、刺激創造力[310]。如果美國法院認為其對美國所生產之物品沒有利益那就是不合常理。對於地院認為與蘇格蘭之關係為是「壓倒性」的，最高法院認為[311]：「這種定性是有些誇張。特別是有關證據來源取得的比較容易性的問題上，私人利益指向雙方。如被上訴人所強調，有關發動機及飛機的測試、製造、及設計的記錄皆位於美國。如果審判是在這裡舉行，對於其無過失及過失責任理論之相關證據來源她會較能取得。」基本上美國最高法院是已存在著不受理外國人本著外國訴因對美國被告所提起之訴訟之心態。事實證明自本案後，於美國跨國企業在第三世界所造成的災害中，有許多「外國法院所提供的救濟是如此明顯的不合適或令人不滿意，以致形成根本上沒有救濟」，美國法院仍舊駁回訴訟。就如同本案一般，現今美國的跨國企業已經得到美國法院之強力背書，經常以「不方便法院」請求駁回訴訟之策略，而對第三世界之受害者進行「逆向選購法院」[312]（reverse forum-shopping）。當一個文明國家的法院有意的在產

---

310 見其Recital 20, “The conflict-of-law rule in matters of product liability should meet the objectives of fairly spreading the risks inherent in a modern high-technology society, protecting consumers’ health, stimulating innovation, securing undistorted competition and facilitating trade. Creation of a cascade system of connecting factors, together with a foreseeability clause, is a balanced solution in regard to these objectives. The first element to be taken into account is the law of the country in which the person sustaining the damage had his or her habitual residence when the damage occurred, if the product was marketed in that country. The other elements of the cascade are triggered if the product was not marketed in that country, without prejudice to Article 4(2) and to the possibility of a manifestly closer connection to another country.”

311 454 U.S. 257, “In analyzing the private interest factors, thc District Court stated that the connections with Scotland are overwhelming. 479 F.Supp. at 732. This characterization may be somewhat exaggerated. Particularly with respect to the question of relative ease of access to sources of proof, the private interests point in both directions. As respondent emphasizes, records concerning the design, manufacture, and testing of the propeller and plane are located in the United States. She would have greater access to sources of proof relevant to her strict liability and negligence theories if trial were held here.”

312 Professor Juenger認為「選購法院」是有著「一個壞名聲」(“has a bad name.”) Fredrich K. Juenger, Forum Shopping, Domestic and International, 63 Tul. L. Rev. 553(1989).但是於p.570中其又認為有些是可以被允許的，因為這些行為於法律上或道德上並非可受譴責的：”Not all forum shopping merits condemnation. Some clearly does, such as the ‘pennoyering’ of casual travelers and, worse yet, the kidnapping of hapless children. But can anyone blame the solicitors who retained American attorneys, instead of the barristers with whom they normally deal, to litigate the Paris air-crash cases? Far

品責任上淡化風險的分散及保護消費者的全球化共同核心基本政策，並且公開的為跨國企業為了規避責任所採取的「逆向選購法院」之行為加以背書時，做為一個終生的國際法學生，個人理解到這已超出國際法學之範圍——這是一個二十世紀的唯一霸主赤裸裸的展現出其逆天而行不可一世之暴力法學，中國文化自古稱之為「霸道」法學。

最高法院又說[313]：「地院承認通常對原告所選定之法院是存在著一個有利之強烈假設，這個假設只能於公與私的利益因素清楚的指向於另一個法院審理時才能被超越。但現在已是被認定，當原告或有利益的真正當事人是外國人時，這個假設被適用時是較無力道的。地院的區分居民或公民原告及外國原告是充分的有道理的。在Koster中，法院表示當原告選擇家園之法院時，原告之選擇法院應受到較大之尊重。……當家園之法院被選擇時，去假定該選擇是便利的是為合理的。但是當原告是外國人時，這個假設就非常的沒有合理性。因為任何不方便法院的諮詢之中心目的就是去確保該審判是便利的，一個外國原告的選擇是較不值得尊重。」對於「因為任何不方便法院諮詢之中心目的就是去確保該審判是便利的」之錯誤論述，個人再次引用聲名卓越法院之判例法來證明其走火入魔-「conveniens並非便利之意」。另外對於最高法院所說的：「地院的區分居民或公民原告及外國原告是充分的有道理的。」個人卻認為可能是沒有道理的。

---

from doing anything legally or morally reprehensible, the solicitors simply served their clients well." 又見Friedrich K. Juenger, Jurisdiction, Choice of Law and the Elusive Goal of Decisional Harmony, in Law And Reality, Essays on National and International Procedural Law in Honour of Cornelis Carel Albert Voskuil 137 (M. Sumampouw et al. eds., 1992); Friderich K. Juenger, What's Wrong with Forum Shopping?, 16 Sydney L. Rev. 5, 10 (1994).

313 454 U.S. 255, 256, "The District Court acknowledged that there is ordinarily a strong presumption in favor of the plaintiff's choice of forum, which may be overcome only when the private and public interest factors clearly point towards trial in the alternative forum. It held, however, that the presumption applies with less force when the plaintiff or real parties in interest are foreign. The District Court's distinction between resident or citizen plaintiff and foreign plaintiffs is fully justified. In Koster, the Court indicated that a plaintiff's choice of forum is entitled to greater deference when the plaintiff has chosen the home forum. 330 U.S. at 330 U.S. 524. When the home forum has been chosen, it is reasonable to assume that this choice is convenient. When the plaintiff is foreign, however, this assumption is much less reasonable. Because the central purpose of any forum non conveniens inquiry is to ensure that the trial is convenient, a foreign plaintiff's choice deserves less deference." Koster v. Lumbermens Mut. Cas. Co., 330 U.S. 518 (1947).

請問美國最高法院如何去面對「actor sequitur forum rei」這個國內及國際訴訟法上最基本之法理？原告至被告處之法院起訴是個自然的萬國公法[314]。於一般管轄上，英美法經常是以被告之所在為基礎（所在權力），大陸法的布魯塞爾公約及規則第2條是以被告之住所為基礎，而海牙草約第3條是以被告之慣居地為基礎[315]。又即使在送達境外之管轄上，英國C.P.R. 1998, s. 6.20(1)[316]及美國的相關判例[317]，被告的住所皆構成一個可

314 美國the American Law Institute的Restatement (Second) of Conflict of Laws之29及30條亦承認對於住所或居所（非不合理之情形下）於州內之人，州法院有著司法管轄權。
§29. Domicil (1988 Revision)
A state has power to exercise judicial jurisdiction over an individual who is domiciled in the state, except in the highly unusual case where the individual's relationship to the state is so attenuated as to make the exercise of such jurisdiction unreasonable.
§30. Residence
A state has power to exercise judicial jurisdiction over an individual who is a resident of the state unless the individual's relationship to the state is so attenuated as to make the exercise of such jurisdiction unreasonable.
又見29條之註解(a)及(d)。
a. Rationale. Except in a highly unusual situation, a person will in the nature of things have a sufficiently close relationship to the state of his domicil to make that state a fair and reasonable forum for the maintenance there of an action against him. So much was recognized by the Supreme Court in Milliken v. Meyer, 311 U.S. 457 (1940). This basis of jurisdiction assures the existence of a place in which a person is continuously amenable to suit.
d. Necessity for statute. Domicil was not generally recognized as a basis of judicial jurisdiction at common law. When the question has arisen, the courts have usually held themselves without authority under their local law to exercise jurisdiction on bases not recognized at common law unless authorized to do so by statute. Due process does not prevent retroactive application of such a statute to claims that arose prior to its enactment. See McGee v. International Life Insurance Co., 355 U.S. 220 (1957).

315 Article 3 Defendant's forum
1. Subject to the provisions of the Convention, a defendant may be sued in the courts of the State where that defendant is habitually resident.

316 (1) a claim is made for a remedy against a person domiciled within the jurisdiction.

317 陳隆修，《國際私法管轄權評論》，台北，五南圖書公司，民國75年11月，初版，111頁。「即使被告不在於其住所之州內，住所地之法院對其亦有充分之對人訴訟管轄權。從憲法上之觀點而言，住所係一充分之關連點（sufficient contact）。因為當事人既於住所地享有許多權利，自然其亦應於住所地被起訴。而且即使訴之原因發生於他處，被告仍可能預期其會於住所地被起訴。何況於複雜之國際情形下，被告至少應有一處之法院對其有管轄權。」Milliken v. Meyer, 311 U.S. 457(1940). 又見Restatement, Second, Conflict of Laws §27
(1) A state has power to exercise judicial jurisdiction over an individual on one or more of the following bases:
(a) presence
(b) domicil
(c) residence
(d) nationality or citizenship

能的過度管轄基礎。這種以原就被之國際法及訴訟法之萬國公法亦是為美國所遵守的，如果以較近時髦的說法，這即可能是自然原告對自然被告於自然法院提起自然訴訟。如果美國最高法院承認美國被告是經常「逆向選購法院」，那麼美國法院的操作不方便法院就是一種「逆向不方便法院」法學。

最高法院認為[318]「蘇格蘭在這個訴訟中有著一個非常強烈的利益」，「如同於Gilbert中所說的當地存在著一個利益，以使得當地的紛爭於家園中被決定」。「被上訴人之抗辯中主張美國公民有著一個利益去確保美國製造商會被嚇阻去生產有瑕疵之產品，並且如果Piper及Hartzell是在美國被審判的話會有額外的嚇阻效果被產生，亦即於美國他們可以同時被以過失及無過失責任之基礎而被起訴。但是如果這個審判是在一個美國法院進行所可能得到的增加的嚇阻是應該會是不重要的。如果這個案件是於此進行審判，那麼不可避免的須要投入龐大的司法資源與時間，很簡單的在這個事故中美國的利益不足以合理化這種投入。」在註解19中美國最高法院說[319]：「當然的我們承認Piper and Hartzell（被告）可能在操作逆向選購法院（reverse forum-shopping）。但是這個可能性通常不應於地

[318] 454 U.S. 260, 261, "Scotland has a very strong interest in this litigation. The accident occurred in its airspace. All of the decedents were Scottish. Apart from Piper and Hartzell, all potential plaintiffs and defendants are either Scottish or English. As we stated in Gilbert, there is 'a local interest in having localized controversies decided at home.' 330 U.S at 330 U.S. 509. Respondent argues that American citizens have an interest in ensuring that American manufacturers are deterred from producing defective products, and that additional deterrence might be obtained if Piper and Hartzell were tried in the United States, where they could be sued on the basis of both negligence and strict liability. However, the incremental deterrence that would be gained if this trial were held in an American court is likely to be insignificant. The American interest in this accident is simply not sufficient to justify the enormous commitment of judicial time and resources that would inevitably be required if the case were to be tried here."

[319] Footnote 19, "We recognize, of course, that Piper and Hartzell may be engaged in reverse forum-shopping. However, this possibility ordinarily should not enter into a trial court's analysis of the private interests. If the defendant is able to overcome the presumption in favor of plaintiff by showing that trial in the chosen forum would be unnecessarily burdensome, dismissal is appropriate – regardless of the fact that defendant may also be motivated by a desire to obtain a more favorable forum. Cf. Kloechner Reederei und Kohlenhandel v. A/S Hakedal, 210 F.2d 754, 757 (CA2) (defendant not entitled to dismissal on grounds of *forum non conveniens* solely because the law of the original forum is less favorable to him than the law of the alternative forum), *cert. dism'd by stipulation,* 348 U.S. 801 (1954)."

院[320]在分析私人利益時被加以考慮。如果被告可以經由證明審判於被選定的法院舉行會造成有著不必要的負擔，則就可以超越對原告有利的假設，那麼駁回訴訟就是合適的——無論於事實上被告之動機可能亦是在於企圖取得一個更有利的法院。」

在英國於不方便法院之考量上，一般是認為法院所考慮的主要因素為當事人（私的）利益與正義的（公的）利益。現今由於困擾性或壓迫性法學轉向不方便法院法學，英國法院對原告利益之解釋較為嚴格[321]。但是如個人所一再重述，如Connelly v. RTZ Corpn. plc[322]所顯示，於特殊情形下實質正義（substantial justice）的考量應超越其他表面上更為合適之考量。美國為世界第一大國，其農工商之產品由飛機、麥當勞、至可口可樂行銷至世界每一角落，其金融及服務業亦經常操控世界市場。「很簡單的在這個事故中美國的利益不足以合理化這種（司法）投入」——很簡單的是個神話[323]。在全球化的市場下，無論是第一世界還是第三世界都必須

---

320 454 U.S. 257, "The forum non conveniens determination is committed to the sound discretion of the trial court. It may be reversed only when there has been a clear abuse of discretion; where the court has considered all relevant public and private interest factors, and where its balancing of these factors is reasonable, its decision deserves substantial deference."「不方便法院」通常主要是由地院來行使裁量權，這亦為英國判例法所認同。於Spiliada Mar. Corp. v. Cansulex Ltd., [1987] A.C. 460, 465中，Lord Templeman說這個問題「最主要是第一審法官的問題」（"pre-eminently a matter for the trial judge"），只能依法官的經驗，而沒有引用判例法，於「數小時內而非數日內」（"in hours and not days"）解決。這是因為第一審法官較上訴審法官接近事實，因此有較好的地位去決定問題。

321 Cheshire and North, Private International Law, 13th ed. p. 345, 14th ed., p.437, "At one time great weight was attached to this factor, and if the claimant obtained a substantial advantage from trial in England the courts were unlikely to grant a stay of the English proceedings. The House of Lords in the Spiliada case sought to reduce the weight given to the advantage to the claimant when exercising the discretion to stay. Hence the principle that the mere fact that the claimant has a legitimate personal or juridical advantage in proceedings in England cannot be decisive."見陳隆修、許兆慶、林恩瑋、李瑞生四人合著，《國際私法-管轄與選法理論之交錯》，台北，五南圖書公司，2009年3月，初版1刷。213、214頁。Spiliada Maritime Corpn v. Cansulex Ltd [1987] AC 460 at 482.

322 [1998] AC 854, HL.

323 見Peter Muchlinski, Corporations in International Litigation: Problems of Jurisdiction and the United Kingdom Asbestors Cases, 50 Int'l & Comp. L.Q. 1, 16 (2001). "Surely, if a firm is undertaking hazardous industrial activities it must be prepared to take on at least part of the risk, given that if it does not it will have a greater incentive to act in a negligent way. Furthermore, if it is willing to take all the profit on the venture the enterprise must carry some of the associated risk."另外有趣的是又見OECD Guidelines for Multinational Enterprises 27 June 2000 "Concepts and Principles" p.3,跨國企業對關係企業之行為所產生之責任標準，或許已由對關係企業之控制權而擴展至「活動之配合」。"[U]sually

在全球化的「商業潮流」（stream of commerce）中「一起游泳或下沉」（swim or sink together）。沒有任何有關產品責任的契約可以規避瑕疵擔保責任或無過失責任，亦沒有任何有關產品所造成的傷害可以規避其侵權行為責任。這些基本常識是不必等待法學的全球化即早已存在。利益與責任是如影隨形的，美國的跨國企業在全球化的「商業潮流」中所取的巨大利益，自然使得他們必須與其產品的受害人「一起游泳或下沉」。中國人吃芝麻一定掉屑，這是什麼法學又要吃芝麻又不掉屑？

(四)逆向不方便法院神話法學

保障跨國企業「逆向選購法院」[324]及「取得更有利之法院」，藉以減

comprise companies or other entities established in more than one country and so linked that they may co-ordinate their operaions in various ways. While one or more of these entities may be able to exercise a significant influence over the activities of others, their degree of autonomy within the enterprise may vary from one multinational enterprise to another. Ownership may be private, state or mixed."如若依這種標準則第一世界無法再指責中國之「血汗工廠」，因為該些跨國企業皆應對中國「血汗工廠」之「配合性活動」而負起責任。WTO一直強調自由市場之比較經濟利益，在WTO得庇護下第一世界的跨國公司攫取了第三世界市場及資源上的絕大利益，在「配合性活動」之責任標準下，他們自應負起「比較利益」上所帶來之「比較則責任」——而這亦符合中國式「王道」之「禮運大同」「不患寡患不均」之傳統文化。諾貝爾和平獎的無視於第一世界及其跨國公司於掠奪第三世界市場及資源時在第三世界所造成人權及環境上之傷害，故與WTO皆是第一世界及跨國企業附屬的岳不群機構，其目的是在忠誠的執行第一世界的「掠奪性新殖民地主義」。

324 在Lubbe v. Cape PLC, [2000] 1 Lloyd's Rep. 139,161中，上訴法院之認定雖為最高法院所不採納，但Lord Justice Pill於上訴審中卻企圖引用惡名昭彰的In re Union Carbide Corp. Gas Plant Disaster at Bhopal, India in Dec. 1984, 634 F. Supp. 842 (S.D.N.Y. 1986), aff'd, 809 F.2d 195 (2nd Cir. 1987), cert. denied, 484 U.S. 871 (1987)中Judge Keenan之論述："In the court's view, to retain this litigation in this forum, as plaintiffs request, would be yet another example of imperialism, another situation in which an established sovereign inflicted its rules, its standards and values on a developing nation. This Court declines to play such a role. The Union of India is a world power in 1986, and its courts have the proven capacity to mete out fair and equal justice. To deprive the Indian judiciary of the opportunity to stand tall before the world and to pass judgment on behalf of its own people would be to revive a history of subservience and subjugation from which India has emerged."這種駭人聽聞的岳不羣論述，被具有純正謙謙英國君子血統的恩師Prof. Morse諷刺性的稱呼為一個「特別的紫色言詞」（a particularly purple passage;過分高尚的言詞；台灣話叫「蓋高尚」），甚至挑明其為「逆向帝國主義」："While disagreeing with the use of the expression 'imperialism,' Lord Justice Pill thought that this 'general approach' appeared 'apt in the context of personal injury litigation such as the present. These personal injury actions concern operations conducted in South Africa and are concerned with their effect on persons employed and resident there.' In other words, perhaps , South Africa was the 'origin' or 'home' of this litigation as it was the country with which the litigation has the 'most real and substantial connection.' Whether Lord Justice Pill's derivation actually reflects what Judge Keenan (in more grandiose terms) actually meant must be open to question. For Judge Keenan, India had an obligation to throw off the colonial yolk, to stand tall, and to hear the Bhopal litigation because of its strong interest in so doing; this conclusion is slightly peculiar given that the Union of India was, in fact,

輕個別企業之損害賠償責任，並不是二十一世紀全球化法學於產品責任之共同核心主流政策。對於過失及無過失責任的「額外嚇阻效果」，「如果這個審判是在一個美國法院進行所可能得到的增加的嚇阻是應該會是不重要的」，這種論述是與產品責任在全球化法學的共同核心政策——包括美國自己的國內政策在內——相違背。美國在農工商產品、高科技產品、及金融服務業，經常是藉著行銷的獨占而幾乎壟斷市場，進而攫取龐大的利益。但是在被害人依「以原就被」的傳統訴訟法規則到被告家園的法院要求跨國企業負起全球化法學共同核心的產品責任時，美國法院卻說出這樣的神話——「很簡單的在這個事故中美國的利益不足以合理化這種（司法）投入」。美國憲法所膨風出來的「商業潮流」、「一起游泳或下沉」的泡泡，都被這個以「資本主義」及「自由貿易」為基礎的「神話法學」所徹底刺破。本著Piper Aircraft Co. v. Reyno的「神話法學」，我們可以正確的去解讀WTO的「自由貿易」及「比較經濟利益」就是——經濟力量比較強勢地區的資本家可以自由的在經濟弱勢地區攫取比較高的利益，而經濟弱勢地區的受害者無法在經濟強勢地區要求資本家負起責任。

事實上受到這個資本主義及自由貿易主義所創造的「神話法學」所荼毒的亦不限於極低度開發國家。1998年美國跨國企業本著「金融自由流通」的概念於東南亞攫取暴利而造成亞洲金融風暴，而2009年更變本加厲的造成全世界金融海嘯。所有全世界的受害者皆無能力到美國求償，所有的美國跨國企業皆受到這個「神話法學」的保護[325]。美國法院的「神

---

seeking to have the trial before an American court. From another perspective, Judge Keenan might be thought to be patronizing, or as engaging in what one might call 'reverse imperialism.'" C, G. J. Morse, Not in the Public Interest? Lubbe v. Cape PLC, 37 Tex. Int'l L.J. 541, 551, 552 (2002).

[325] 事實上歐盟早於金融風暴之前，便明確的要求投資公司必須誠實、公正、及專業的促進市場的完整。見DIRECTIVE 2004/39/EC OF THE EUROPEAN PARLIAMENT AND OF THE COUNCIL of 21 april 2004 on markets in financeial instruments,

Article 25

Obligation to uphold integrity of markets, report transactions and maintain records.

1. Without prejudice to the allocation of responsibilities for enforcing the provisions of Directive 2003/6/EC of the European Parliament and of the Council of 28 January 2003 on insider dealing and market manipulation (market abuse) (1), Member States shall ensure that appropriate measures are in place to enable the competent authority to monitor the activeities of investment firms to ensure that they

話法學」不但違反「以原就被」及一般管轄的訴訟法共同核心，亦違反產品責任於實體法上之共同核心。這個「神話法學」不但違反實體法及程序法上之全球化共同核心，亦違反了幾乎所有文明國家憲法及人權公約中所保障的訴訟權、財產權、生命權、平等權、及適當程序權，更應特別指出的是它違反了聯合國1966年兩個人權公約第1條2項中之生存權。第2項[326]規定：「在他們自己的目的下，所有的人得自由的處分他們的自然財富及資源，但不得違反基於國際法與互利原則而來的國際經濟合作所產生的任何義務。無論於何種情形下，沒有任何人得被剝奪其賴以生存之依據。」很明顯的，在1998年及2009年美國跨國企業以金融自由之名所引起的金融風暴，已違反了「自然財富之處分不得違反互利原則下國際經濟

act honestly, fairly and professionally and in a manner which promotes the integrity of the Market.
並且亦規定資訊必須以合理的術語而對大眾達成透明化。
Article 44
Pre-trade transparency requirements for regulated markets
1. Member States shall, at least, require regulated markets to make public current bid and offer prices and the depth of trading interests at those prices which are advertised through their systems for shares admitted to trading. Member States shall require this information to be made available to the public on reasonable commercial terms and on a continuous basis during normal trading hours.
而第9條及37條更要求投資公司管理人必須有著好聲譽及經驗以確保健全及謹慎之管理。
Article 9
Persons who effuseively direct the business
1. Member States shall require the person who effectively direct the business of an investment firm to be of sufficiently good repute and sufficiently experienced as to ensure the sound and prudent management of the investment firm.
Article 37
Requirements for the management of the regulated market
1. Member States shall require the person who effectively direct the business and the operations of the regulated market to be of sufficiently good repute and suddiciently experienced as to ensure the sound and prudent management and operation of the regulated market. Member States shall also require the operator of the regulated market to inform the competent authority of the identity and any other subsequent changes of the persons who effectively direct the business and the operations of the regulated market.
有關金融、消費投資於各國皆屬於強行法規，但由於霸權母國的支持，美國跨國企業通常都是超乎各國強行法規之上，而不必負起符合比例之責任。故而個人一再指責美國、WTO、及諾貝爾和平獎的聯手唱和，霸凌第三世界人民聯合國1966年兩個人權公約第1(2)條中所保障的基本生存權。

326 2. All peoples may, for their own ends, freely dispose of their natural wealth and resources without prejudice to any obligations arising out of international economic co-operation, based upon the principle of mutual benefit, and international law. In no case may a people be deprived of its own means of subsistence.

合作所產生之義務」，對第三世界人民而言這更是「剝奪其賴以生存之依據」。美國法院違反實體法與程序法在全球化法學的共同核心，允許跨國企業「逆向選購法院」以躲避其產品責任，這是一種「逆向不方便法院」（reverse forum non conveniens）之行使。對這違反「傳統上公平與實質正義」的「逆向不方便法院」神話法學，個人再次重申——這是一個二十世紀的唯一霸主赤裸裸的展現出逆天而行不可一世之暴力法學，中國文化自古稱之為霸道法學。

跨國企業的藉著「霸權法律制度」或「法律帝國主義」以攫取自由市場上的暴力之行為，除了表現在「逆向不方便法院」之行使外，另外又表現在其母國於反托辣斯法過分的擴張適用，及商標專利法的專制執行上。這種優勢經濟力量與優勢法律科學之結合，不但扭曲了自由市場自由貿易的真正公平性，對第三世界而言，第一世界已違反1966年人權公約第1(2)條的「互利原則下國際經濟合作之義務」，並剝奪第三世界「賴以生存之依據」。WTO對這種妨礙真正公平貿易之行為從未加以禁止，而諾貝爾和平獎亦對第一世界違反1966年人權公約第1(2)條之義務並剝奪第三世界生存權之邪惡暴行視而未見。故而WTO與諾貝爾和平獎是第一世界黑暗勢力終極掠奪性新殖民地主義法學之執行組織，是岳不群法學巔峰的表現。

當美國跨國企業在全世界造成金融海嘯，或在第三世界為了掠奪自然資源而造成環境污染或種族滅絕，或其產品在第三世界造成傷亡時，外國被害人本著外國訴因依訴訟法的基本原則到跨國企業的家園（住所、居所）法院起訴時，美國最高法院脫離英國母法的宣示：「美國的利益不足以合理化這種司法投入」。但是當肇事的美國企業「事實上之動機可能亦是在於取得一個更有利的法院」時，美國最高法院又說：「這個可能性通常不應於地院在分析私人利益時被加以考慮。」最尊敬的恩師Prof. Graveson說「法律邏輯一致性的政策必須受限於實現正義的概括性目的」，很明顯的在替美國跨國企業的「逆向選購法院」加以背書時，美國最高法院所行使的「逆向不方便法院」神話法學所信仰的是資本主義的

「法律邏輯一致性的政策必須受限於跨國企業實現利益的概括性目的」。中國人沒有那麼高雅精緻的法學傳統，我們或許可以很粗俗的稱這種現象為人嘴兩片皮——兩片皮法學。

第10章 李雙元、黃進的王道法學

當Lord Denning豪情萬丈氣吞河嶽的宣示[1]：「沒有人到這些法院來要求正義會徒勞無功……這個到這裡來的權力並不只侷限於英國人。它拓展至任何友好的外國人。如果他願意如此做，他可以要求我們法院的幫助。如果你願意你可以稱這是『選購法院』，但如果法院是在英國，同時在貨的品質及服務的速度上，它是一個選購的好地方。」而Lord Goff 亦高調的宣佈英國的「不方便法院」法學[2]：「可被視為最文明的法學原則之一」。請問「所有」的美國同僚——你們可以直視第三世界人民的眼睛而重覆這些話嗎？請問WTO與諾貝爾和平獎——你們可以直視第三世界人民的眼睛而重覆這些話嗎？

美國藉著高技術的「逆向不方便法院」血淚斑斑的迫害第三世界受害者於憲法、人權公約上之平等權、訴訟權[3]、財產權、生命權。事實上第

1 "No one who comes to these courts asking for justice should come in vain ... . This right to come here is not confined to Englishmen. It extends to any friendly foreigner. He can seek the aid of our courts if he desires to do so. You may call this 'forum shopping' if you please, but if the forum is England, it is a good place to shop in, both for the quality of the goods and the speed of service." The Atlantic Star, [1973] 1 Q.B. 364, 381-82 (C.A.).但是於House of Lords中Lord Reid卻對Lord Denning這個磅礡雄偉的論述，認為過分屬於「舊時代的好日子」："the good old days, the passing of which many may regret, when inhabitants of this island felt an innate superiority over those unfortunate enough to belong to other races." The Atlantic Star, [1974] 1 A.C. 436, 478 (H.L. 1973) (appeal taken from Eng.)

2 Airbus Indus. G.I.E. v. Patel, [1999] 1 A.C. 119, 141 (H.L. 1998), "can be regarded as one of the most civilised of legal principles."

3 歐盟1950年人權公約第6(1)條規定："In the determination of his civil rights and obligations or of any criminal charge against him, everyone is entitled to a fair and public hearing within a reasonable time by an independent and impartial tribunal established by law." 但是Lord Bingham認為第6條不會視Spiliada為違反這個人權條款（Spiliada, 1987 A.C. 460），故於實際上他亦是據此而認定Lubbe之結果（Lubbe, [2000] 1 W.L.R. 1545）是符合公約的，反而停止訴訟會造成對原告構成「正義之拒絕」，故會違反公約。（Lubbe, [2000] 1 W.L.R. 1545, 1561）如於Connelly v. RTZ Corp. PLC, [1998] A.C. 854 (H.L. 1997)中所顯示的，如果因為經濟或其他原因以致請求者不能於其他另一個法院請求，則構成正義的拒絕，Lubbe案亦顯示同樣的結果。個人近年來之所以聲嘶力竭的指控

一世界、WTO、及諾貝爾和平獎憑藉著第一世界於科技、經濟、行銷、資金、及法律科學的優勢，迫害第三世界人民的惡行罄竹難書。例如台灣社會在反托辣斯法及智慧財產權[4]上所受到的壓迫，就是歐盟及美國藐視

美國「逆向不方便法院」法則違反人權公約，乃是其肆無忌憚的違反ALI/UNIDROIT Principles of Transnational Civil Procedure第3條的公平保護條款，對外國居民構成「正義之拒絕」之非法情形。如恩師所說：「於是否訴訟當事人間有著平等的立足點之問題上，特別是由於跨國公司於外國之行為所引起的人身傷害請求權上，人權問題可能會發生。這個因素反映了當事人相較上之私人利益，並且再加強了於英國不方便法院之諮詢上，私人利益超越其它因素之看法。」"Human rights issues might also arise in relation to the question of whether parties to litigation are on an equal footing, particularly in the context of personal injury claims against multinational companies that arise out of the activities of those companies in foreign countries. This factor reflects the comparative private interests of the parties and reinforces the view that in the English forum non conveniens inquiry, private interests dominate." C.G.J. Morse, Not in the Public Interest? Lubbe v. Cape PLC, 37 Tex. Int'l L.J. 541, 555 (2002).

4 事實上2002年聯合國高峰會即宣布「應以現代科技來促進發展，及確保科技的移轉」。見Johannesburg Declaration on Sustainable Development
18. We welcome the focus of the Johannesburg Summit on the indivisibility of human dignity and are resolved, through decisions on targets, timetables and partnerships, to speedily increase access to such basic requirements as clean water, sanitation, adequate shelter, energy, health care, food security and the protection of biodiversity, At the same time, we will work together to help one another gain access to financial resources, benefit from the opening of markets, ensure capacity-building, use modern technology to bring about development and make sure that there is technology transfer, human reasource development, education and training to banish underdevelopment forever.
故而除非2002年聯合國宣言的第18條被推翻，否則「應以現代科技來促進發展及確保科技的移轉」仍應是現代全球化法學於智慧財產權方面的共同核心政策。因此歐盟及美國對大中華經濟區產業於此方面過度擴張的追殺，不但妨礙中國人1966年聯合國人權宣言第1(2)條之生存權，亦踐踏了全球化智慧財產權法學的共同核心強行超越性基本政策。
事實上專利權的過分擴張，亦反過來傷到跨國企業自己。並且如美國聯邦上訴法院的法官所說，這個已經不合時宜的舊專利法，已經在真實世界造成「混亂」。見Charles Duhigg and Steve Lohr, An Arms Race of Patents- Legal Warfare Threatens to Stymie Innovation, The New York Times International Weekly, Tuesday. October 16, 2012: "Technology giants have also waged wars among themselves. In the smartphone industry, according to a Stanford University analysis, as much as $20 billion was spent on patent litigation and purchases in the last two years – an amount equal to eight Mars rover missions. Last year, spending by Apple and Google on patent lawsuits and unusually big-dollar patent purchases exceeded spending on research and development of new products." "many people argue that America's patent rules, intended for a mechanical world, are inadequate in today's digital marketplace. Patents on software often effectively grant ownership of concepts, rather than tangible creations. Some patents are so broad they allow patent holders to claim ownership of seemingly unrelated products built by others. Often, companies are sued for violating patents they never knew existed. 'There's a real chaos.' said Richard A. Posner, afederal appellate judge who has helped shape patent law. 'The standards for granting patents are too loose.'"
不合時宜的舊專利法之適用，不但妨礙到「創新」，更是違反了公平交易法自由競爭的基本強行政策，而扼殺了小企業的生存空間。"'Apple could get a chokehold on the smartphone industry,' said Tim O'Reilly, a publisher of computer guides and a software patent critic. 'A patent is a government-sanctioned monopoly, and we should be very cautious about handing those out.'" "The shift, inventors say, markes life harder for small entrepreneurs. Large companies with battalions of lawyers can file thousands of pre-emptive patent applications in emerging industries. Start-ups, lacking similar

他們於國際經濟上所應合作之義務及中國人民基本生存權之殘酷事實，而這是1966年聯合國兩個人權公約所於開宗明義的第1(2)條所列為應優先禁止之惡行。

如果一幅畫勝過千句言語，那麼一顆正義的心勝過一千個人權公約。無論「方便與不方便法院」法學之邏輯一致性為何，必要時應如Connelly v. RTZ Corpn. PLC[5]案所顯示，於特殊情形下實質正義（substantial justice）的達成應超越其他考量[6]，亦即「方便與不方便法院」法學的心與靈魂在於「是否正義的真正利益最能被達成[7]」——而個人認為

resources, will find themselves easy prey once their products show promise."
對於專利法形成「國家所許可的獨占行為」，美國聖路易的聯邦儲備銀行更要求廢除專利；而Posner法官則明言經過5年後這些專利已構成陷害對手的陷阱。"But the Federal Reserve Bank of St. Louis recently published a working paper calling for the abolition of patents, saying they do more harm than good. This year, Judge Posner tossed out patent arguments made by Apple and Motorolar Mobility. Cleaning up the patent mess, Judge Posner said in an interview, might also require reducing the duration of patents on digital technologies, which can be as long as 20 years. 'After five years,' he said, 'these patents are mainly traps for the unwary.'"

5 [1998] AC 854, HL.

6 或許如Peter Muchlinski, 50 Int'l & Comp. L. Q. 1, 20, 21 (2001)，所說的英國最高法院於Lubbe v. Cape PLC, [2000] 1 W.L.R. 1545 (H.L.)中，將「武器平等」原則加入「不方便法院」法學中。"This has serious implications in relation to litigation between MNEs and individual claimants in personal injury cases. First, the right to present the evidence by a party may have implications for the exercise of discretion over jurisdiction. It may curtail the freedom of the court to characterise an issue involving MNE group liability for the acts of a subsidiary as one involving the latter entity alone, where this results in a finding of no jurisdiction. By such reasoning important issues of evidence showing group liability will be excluded from the court, especially where there is no effective alternatve forum that is willing to take on the litigation. Secondly, as already noted, in personal injury cases, especially those where there is no insurer involved, the claimants are very unlikely to have the same reasources as the MNE in relation to the conduct of litigation. In a democratic society based on the rule of law, this places a duty on the courts to ensure that such differences between the parties do not impact adversely on the ability of the individual claimants to have a fair hearing of their case. Therefore, factors of the kind identified by the claimants in relation to the South African legal system, which materially impact on the economic ability of the claimants to pursue their claims, must be given significant weight under the substantial justice aspect of *Spiliada*. The effect on the claimants was much the same as the absence of legal aid was on the claimant in *Connelly*. Thus the House of Lords appears to be adding an 'equality of arms' requirement to the *Spiliada* doctrine as part of a wider due process element."

7 如最尊敬的恩師Prof. Morse對於Lubbe v. Cape PLC, [2000] 1 W.L.R. 1545 (H.L.)案之結果所加以之評論：「很難相信這個結果是對任何合法之公共利益是有害的。」"it was reported in The Times of London on January 15, 2002, that some 7500 claimants had settled their claims against Cape PLC for ￡21 million. It is hard to believe that this outcome is inimical to any legitimate public interest." 37 Tex. Int'l L.J. 541, 557.
又如英國Civil Procedure Rules 1998, Rule 1,
第1項規定程序法則的「超越性目的」（"Overriding Objective"）就在於幫助法院去「公正」的

這亦是中國思想下二十一世紀全球化法學的心與靈魂。

如前述德國同僚認為禁訴令的行使構成法律戰爭，而英國同僚則認為美國反托拉斯法的行使導致法律戰爭。個人則認為美國法院「逆向不方便法院」法學之行使並非是一個戰爭，而是以第三世界為殺戮戰場的對第三世界人民展開一連串違反人權公約的大屠殺（holocaust）。WTO則提供這些違反人權的酷行充分之平台與工具，諾貝爾和平獎則在旁邊大聲吆喝，故意將違反人權的施暴者渲染成既有秩序的慈悲和平維護者。因此個人認為對抗這種「逆向不方便法院」法學最名正言順之作法是仿效大英國協——亦即在遵守過去三十年來先進國家之國際慣例下——去採用保護貿易利益法[8]：「這個法案的背景為中國對美國逆向不方便法院法學適用之不滿。對於構成政治以及經濟、法律問題於外交上嘗試之解決作法之失敗，導致法律上之戰爭。根據這個法律，對於影響到在中國之人之貿易利益的外國規範國際貿易的措施，國務院是被給予寬廣的權利去應付[9]。」

處理案件：
(1) These Rules are a new procedural code with the overriding objective of enabling the court to deal with cases justly.
(2) Dealing with cases justly includes, so far as practicable –
(a) ensuring that the parties are on an equal footing.
而(2)(a)中「確保當事人間公平的立足點」（ensuring that the parties are on an equal footing）就是大陸法所謂「武器平等」之近義，亦是ALI/UNIDROIT Principles of Transnational Civil Procedure第3條所謂的「公平保護」條款之內涵，這些都是明顯的站在美國「逆向不方便法院」法學之對立面。

8 P M North, JJ Fawcett, Cheshire and North's Private International Law, 13th ed., p.488, "The background to this Act is the United kingdom resentment at the extra-territorial application of anti-trust laws by the United States. Diplomatic attempts at solving what is a political as well as an economic and legal problem failed and led to legal warfare. Under the Act, the Secretary of State is given wide powers to counter foreign measures for regulating international trade which affect the trading interests of persons in the United Kingdom."
這個論述又在其較近之14th ed. P.561中再次被確認。
British Nylon Spinners Ltd v ICI Ltd [1953] Ch 19; Re Westinghouse Electric Corpn Uranium Contract Litigation NDL Docket No 235 [1978] AC 547.

9 The Protection of Trading Interests Act 1980
1.-(1) If it appears to the Secretary of State-
(a) that measures have been or are proposed to be taken by or under the law of any overseas country for regulating or controlling international trade; and
(b) that those measures, in so far as they apply or would apply to things done or to be done outside the territorial jurisdiction of that country by persons carrying on business in the United Kingdom, are damaging or threaten to damage the trading interests of the United Kingdom,

正如美國法院在適用「逆向不方便法院」法則以維護跨國企業之利益，所有的第一世界國家皆經常在WTO及諾貝爾和平獎的交叉掩護下，挾著優勢科技、經濟、行銷，藉著複雜的法律科學技術[10]，而對第三世界加以霸凌獲取利益。以目前看來，保護貿易利益法的成立，是二十一世紀中十三億中國人帶領全世界第三世界的人民，要求第一世界遵守1966年人權公約第1(2)條「互利原則下國際經濟合作之義務」，及爭取第三世界最基本的「生存之依據」，之順乎國際慣例法之天賦人權。

聯合國1948年的Universal Declaration of Human Rights的序言[11]要求各會員國維持友好關係及尊重人類的價值、尊嚴、平等與促進生活水準、社會進步，美國的「逆向不方便法院」法學顯然是違反聯合國之人權宣言。另外其25條1項[12]又規定：「每個人對於自己及其家人皆有權去要求符合健康及有益之適當的生活標準」。

對於第一世界之跨國企業在第三世界中大肆開採石油、礦產、設立

The Secretary of State may by order direct that this section shall apply to those measures either generally or in their application to such cases as may be specified in the order.雖然英國的重點是在於反托辣斯法，但以中國處境之艱辛，或許應擴大適用於一般民生上。

10 2004年ALI/ UNIDROIT Principles of Transnational Civil Procedure的第3條是有關當事人之平等保護條款，其註解中說明「合理性」是於整個2004年之規則中皆被貫穿使用。而所謂「合理性的概念是並且排除過分高度技術性的法律論述」，以及「避免嚴重、過分、或不合理的適用程序上之方式」。2004年的規則亦採不方便法院法學，這個規則的3.2條本就在禁止美式不方便法院之適用。這個註解又在禁止「逆向不方便法院」之「過分高度技術性的法律論述」，及避免程序上「過分、不合理」之適用。P-3A The term "reasonable" is used throughout the Principles and signifies "proportional," "significant," "not excessive," or "fair," according to the context. It can also mean the opposite of arbitrary. The concept of reasonableness also precludes hyper-technical legal argument and leaves a range of discretion to the court to avoid severe, excessive, or unreasonable application of procedural norms.

11 Preamble
Whereas it is essential to promote the development of friendly relations between nations. Whereas the peoples of the United Nations have in the Charter reaffirmed their faith in fundamental human rights, in the dignity and worth of the human person and in the equal rights of men and women and have determined to promote social progress and better standards of life in larger freedom.

12 Article 25
1.Everyone has the right to a standard of living adequate for the health and well-being of himself and of his family, including food, clothing, housing and medical care and necessary social services, and the right to security in the event of unemployment, sickness, disability, widowhood, old age or other lack of livelihood in circumstances beyond his control.
個人真誠的認為這個第25條之宣言，不折不扣的就是21世紀現代版的禮運大同宣言。

污染性工業，導致環境破壞河川污染，以至傷害到當地居民，甚至沿岸部落遭受到種族滅絕之威脅，1992年聯合國的Rio Declaration on Environment and Development第13條[13]規定：「有關污染被害人之損害賠償及責任與其他環境上之損害賠償，各國應發展其相關法律。對於因為在他們管轄區或控制區域內之行為導致在他們域外所發生之負面環境效果之損害賠償及責任，各國應以快速及更果決之態度以便合作發展此方面之國際法。」第5條[14]規定各國應將消除貧窮、減少生活水平差距視為「主要任務」；第6條[15]規定發展中國家，特別是最落後國家，之需求與情況「應被給予特別優先」。第7條[16]後半段又規定：「在考慮已開發國家的社會對全球環境所造成之壓力及他們所掌握的技術及經濟資源，已開發國家承認於追逐國際永續發展上他們所承擔之責任。」對於弱勢之原住民第22條[17]規定如下：「原住民及其社會與其他當地社會於環境控制及發展上是有重要的地位，這是由於他們的知識及傳統的作法。各國應承認及適度的

---

[13] Principle 13
States shall develop national law regarding liability and compensation for the victims of pollution and other environmental damage. States shall also cooperate in an expeditious and more determined manner to develop further international law regarding liability and compensation for adverse effects of environmental damage caused by activities within their jurisdiction or control to areas beyond their jurisdiction.

[14] Principle 5
All States and all people shall cooperate in the essential task of eradication poverty as an indispensable requirement for sustainable development, in order to decrease the disparities in standards of living and better meet the needs of the majority of the people of the world.

[15] Principle 6
The special situation and needs of developing countries, particularly the least developed and those most environmentally vulnerable, shall be given special priority. International actions in the field of environment and development should also address the interests and needs of all countries.

[16] Principle 7
States shall cooperate in a spirit of global partnership to conserve, protect and restore the health and integrity of the Earth's ecosystem. In view of the different contributions to global environmental degradation, States have common but differentiated responsibilities. The developed countries acknowledge the responsibility that they bear in the international pursuit of sustainable development in view of the pressures their societies place on the global environment and of the technologies and financial resources they command.

[17] Principle 22
Indigenous people and their communities and other local communities have a vital role in environmental management and development because of their knowledge and traditional practices. States should recognize and duly support their identity, culture and interests and enable their effective participation in the achievement of sustainable development.

幫助他們的認同、文化、及利益，並且於達成永續發展上幫助他們能有效的參加。」

聯合國高峰會又後續於2002年之Johannesburg Declaration on Sustainable Development之14條[18]公開宣示：「全球化的利益及代價並未平均分配，面對這個挑戰開發中國家遭遇著特別的困難」。而第15條[19]則承認：「我們有著加深全球化不平均之危險，除非我們行動的方式能由基本上改變他的生活，貧窮世界可能失去對我們仍舊深信的民主制度及他們的代表之信心，而視他們的代表只不過是會發聲的管樂器及發亮的鐃鈸。」於聯合國高峰會連續對全球化所產生貧富不均的負面效果加以作成正式宣言後，作為法律學生我們對全球化法學於二十一世紀之發展，自然應以這些宣言為全球化法學之基礎原則及警察原則。全球化法學無論是於實體法或程序法自然皆應以這些宣言為核心共同政策。

無論是於契約法上之要求平衡性原則，於訴訟法上要求立足點平等[20]及避免當事人貧富不均所產生之不公正，及最重要的聯合國數次高峰會針對「全球化的利益及代價並未平均分配」，因而要求「降低生活水平之差距」，以上這些實體法、訴訟法、及聯合國高峰會宣言不但是二十一世紀全球化法學的共同核心基本政策，更是中華民族二千五百年來我們祖先的「不患寡患不均」「禮運大同」的「王道」思想[21]。

---

[18] 14. Globalization has added a new dimension to these challenges. The rapid integration of markets, mobility of capital and significant increases in investment flows around the world have opened new challenges and opportunities for the pursuit of sustainable development. But the benefits and costs of globalization are unevenly distributed, with developing countries facing special difficulties in meeting this challenge.

[19] 15. We risk the entrenchment of these global disparities and unless we act in a manner that fundamentally changes their lives the poor of the world may lose confidence in their representatives and the democratic systems to which we remain committed, seeing their representatives as nothing more than sounding brass or tinkling cymbals.

[20] 大陸法系或許較習慣於「武器平等」之名詞，歐洲人權法院認為這個原則是指當事人必須與其對手有著同樣合理的抗辯機會（包括於提供證據上）。Dombo beheer v. Netherlands ECtHR Ser. A. 274 at para. 33 (1993), “equality of arms implies that each party must be afforded a reasonable opportunity to present his case — including his evidence — under conditions which do not place him at sunstantial disadvantage *vis-à-vis* his opponent”.

[21] 較近於著名的Microsoft Corp. v Commission of the European Communities, 2007 ECR II-03601中，歐盟第一審法院以微軟違反歐洲公約82條而處罰其5億歐元。法院認為有獨占地位的企業只有於

符合下列情形下之拒絕授權才能構成濫用專利，paras. 331, 332, 333:
331. It follows from the case-law cited above that the refusal by an undertaking holding a dominant position to license a third party to use a product covered by an intellectual property right cannot in itself constitute an abuse of a dominant position within the meaning of Article 82 EC. It is only in exceptional circumstances that the exercise of the exclusive right by the owner of the intellectual property right may give rise to such an abuse.
332. It also follows from that case-law that the following circumstances, in particular, must be considered to be exceptional:
- in the first place, the refusal relates to a product or service indispensable to the exercise of a particular activeity on a neighbouring market;
- in the second place, the refusal is of such a kind as to exclude any effective competition on that neighbouring market;
- in the third place, the refusal prevents the appearance of a new product for which there is potential consumer demand.
333. Once it is established that such circumstances are present, the refusal by the holder of a dominant position to grant a licence may infringe Artucle 82 EC unless the refusal is objectively justified.
微軟一如往常的抗辯授與專利權會妨礙其創新之能力，但這個資本主義的美國神話為法院所拒絕，para. 697:
697. The court finds that, as the Commission correctly submits, Microsoft, which bore the initial burden of proof (see paragraph 688 above), did not sufficiently establish that if it were required to disclose the interoperability information that would have a significant negative impact on its incentives to innovate.
於同一事件中，微軟於美國則較為雲淡風清的逃過重責，這或許是因為美國對於獨占採取較為寬鬆之態度。Rita Coco, *Antitrust Liability for Refusal to License Intellectual Property: A Comparative Analysis and the Internation Setting*, 12 Marq. Intell. Prop. L. Rev. 1, 47 (2008).美國最高法院於Verizon Commc'ns Inc. v. Law Offices of Curtis V. Trinko, LLP, 540 U.S. 398, 407 (2004)中，認為由於產品的優良、生意上的精明、或歷史的因故，而導致獨占的地位是合法的。並且認為在自由市場的制度中，獨占是刺激經濟成長及創新的重要因素：It is settled law that offense requires, in addition to the possession of monopoly power in the relevant market, "the willful acquisition or maintenance of that power as distinguished from growth or development as a consequence of a superior product, business acumen, or historic accident." *United States v. Grinnell Corp*., 384 U.S. 563, 570-571, 16 L.Ed. 2d 778, 86 S. Ct. 1698 (1966). The mere possession of monopoly power, and the concomitant charging of monopoly prices, is not only not unlawful; it is an important element of the free-market system. The opportunity to charge monopoly prices--at least for a short period-- is what attracts "business acumen" in the first place; it induces risk taking that produces innovation and economic growth. To safeguard the incentive to innovate, the possession of monopoly power will not be found unlawful unless it is accompanied by an element of anticompetitive conduct.
於這個舉世矚目的案件中，我們目睹了兩個當今最有權勢的經濟體為了利益而反目。但於中國法學革命崛起之際，我們見證了中國「禮運大同」、「不患寡患不均」法學的再次驗證。宣稱其「創新」能力會嚴重受損的微軟，事實上全世界見證了其於歐盟法院受到挫敗後，仍然繼續努力——或許更加努力——於全世界的自由市場中攻城掠地。於二十一世紀的開始中國式法學即見證了資本主義美國式黑色神話法學的虛偽、貪婪。或許中國式法學的共同基礎核心思想應是：「君子喻於義（正義），小人喻於利（利益）」。
當第一世界於WTO極力鼓吹自由競爭的經濟法學時，OECD的報告卻顯示禁止不公平貿易的法規妨礙內部市場的競爭：
"While competition policy is designed to preserve competitive domestic market structures and the efficient allocation of resources, laws dealing with unfair trade practices aim to protect domestic industry from unfair import pressures causing injury to domestic competitors......some actions brought under the unfair trade laws can reduce competition in domestic markets, particularly where high levels of concen-

於2009年黃進、趙相林教授在兩岸國私會議時提倡「中國式法學」，2010年黃進教授與個人皆認為「中國式法學應以『王道』傳統思想為基礎」，於2012年李雙元教授亦認同這個方法論。而很明顯的中國的「王道」哲學是與聯合國數次宣言之理想是一致的，故而二十一世紀的全球化法學自然應以中國「王道」思想及聯合國上述宣言為基礎及共同核心。「天道無親，恆與善人」，二十一世紀文明的進展使得全球化法學提昇至以個人之人權為中心[22]，故個人認為二十一世紀全球化法學之心與靈

tration already exist, through the foreclosure of foreign firms." (C(86)65(Final), Competition Policy and International Trade: OECD Instruments of Co-operation, OECD 1986, p.19.)
接著更令人吃驚的是OECD內部的學術研究顯示依WTO及有些國家的反傾銷法規，「大部分情形並無反公平競爭的效果，外國公司之行為是看起來完全合理，並且不容易發現有不公平之因素。」
"In most of those situations no anti-competitive effects arise, the behavior of the foreign firms appears completely rational and it is difficult to detect an element of unfairness."
而在有關「掠奪性傾銷」以便摧毀國內競爭力上，於主要之OECD國家內是甚難發現的。
"The second category where dumping can raise competition concerns would be situations where an exporting firm in a position of market power charges below cost prices with the intent of destroying domestic competition ('predatory dumping'). The analysis of anti-dumping cases in major OECD countries showed that such instances were hard to detect." (Competition Policy and Antidumping, Chapter 1: The Economic Effects of Anti-Dumping Policy, OECD 1994, DAFFE/CLP/WP1 (94) 11 (unpublished))
因此OECD報告之結論為：「於超過絕大部分的反傾銷程序之案件中，對於內部市場之競爭性而言並不存在威脅的可能。」「但是反傾銷程序的適用，卻造成各種減少競爭的結果」。
"That in the overwhelming majority of cases where anti-dumping procedures were applied, there was no plausible threat to competition in the domestic market. The application of anti-dumping procedures, however, has led to a variety of competition-reducing outcomes, including the application of duties, undertakings to rise prices or reduce quantities, voluntary export restraint agreements and the perhaps unintended facilitation of collusion." (Competition Policy and Antidumping, Chapter 9, Summary and Conclusions, OECD 1995, DAFFE/CLP/WP1 (95) 3 (unpublished)).
而令人遺憾的是根據OECD歐洲區資深顧問的報告，由於「一個有影響力的會員國基於政治性動機的抗拒」，上述報告「很不幸的不能被發表」。
"This statement contained in the 1984 report of the Competition Committee was further underpinned by a subsequent study which could unfortunately not be published over the politically motivated resistance of one influential Member state." (見Rainer Geiger, The Development of the World Economy and Competition Law, in The Development of Competition Law Global Perspectives, Edited by Roger Zach, Andreas Heinemann, Andreas Kellerhals, pp. 243,244)
當WTO及美國一再的以自由市場之名於第三世界執行「掠奪式新殖民地主義」("predatory neo-colonialism")法學及經濟學之實，全第三世界六十億人民皆於水深火熱中啞巴吃黃蓮。而WTO及諾貝爾和平獎對於跨國企業及歐美所實施的岳不?法學，在舉世第三世界人民的哀號聲中卻無恥的假裝這等「法律恐怖主義」("legal terrorism")自始至終不存在。OECD內部的報告白紙黑字的刺穿了資本主義所供奉的自由市場、自由經濟、比較利益的黑色神話法學的國王外衣。WTO及諾貝爾和平獎所真正擎舉的大纛或許不是自由市場及人權，而是不聽、不見、不說三隻猴子哲學，而更或許他們應該再增添一隻猴子——沒天良("unconscionability")。

22 歐盟Charter of Fundamental Rights of the European Union (2003/C 364/01)的序文開宗明義的宣

魂在於個案之正義是否能被達成[23]，而二十一世紀全球化管轄規則之心與靈魂在於個案正義的真正利益在那裡最能被達成[24]。

示：「經由建立聯盟的公民權，及創造自由、安全及正義的空間，歐盟將個人置於其活動之中心。」歐盟於此昭告全世界，其立國之宗旨及社會之基石為——創造正義的空間及以個人為國家制度之中心"It places the individual at the heart of its activities, by establishing the citizenship of the Union and by creating an area of freedom, security and justice."

23 Price v Dewhurst (1837) 8 Sim 279 at 302 "whenever it is manifest that justice has been disregarded, the court is bound to treat the decision as a matter of no value and no substance". (Shadwell V-C). Pro Swing Inc. v. Elta Golf Inc., 2006 Can. Sup. Ct. LEXIS 52; 2006 SCC 52; [2006] S.C.J. No. 52 para. 1: "Modern-day commercial transactions require prompt reactions and effective remedies. The advent of the Internet has heightened the need for appropriate tools. On the one hand, frontiers remain relevant to national identity and jurisdiction, but on the other hand, the globalization of commerce and mobility of both people and assets make them less so. The law and the justice system are servants of society, not the reverse." (Deschamps J.) Trevor C. Hartley, Internation Commercial Litigation, Preface, "Law is made for man, not man for the law." 新約哥林多後書第3章：「你們明顯是基督的信、藉著我們修成的。不是用墨寫的、乃是用永生上帝的靈寫的。不是寫在石版上，乃是寫在心版上。我們因基督所以在上地面前纔有這樣的信心。並不是我們憑自己能承擔什麼事、我們所能承擔的、乃是出於上帝。他叫我們能承擔這新約的執事。不是憑著字句、乃是憑著精意。因為那字句是叫人死、精意是叫人活。精意或作聖靈」

24 Lopez v Chavarri [1901] W.N. 115, 116, "whether the true interests of justice would be best served by trying the question here, or leaving it to the foreign tribunal".

國家圖書館出版品預行編目資料

中國思想下的全球化管轄規則／陳隆修著.
－－初版.－－臺北市：五南，2013.04
面；　公分
ISBN 978-957-11-7056-5（平裝）
1.國際私法　2.論述分析
579.9　　102004860

1T81

中國思想下的全球化管轄規則

作　　者— 陳隆修
發 行 人— 楊榮川
總 編 輯— 王翠華
主　　編— 劉靜芬
責任編輯— 游雅淳
封面設計— P.Design視覺企劃
出 版 者— 五南圖書出版股份有限公司
地　　址：106台北市大安區和平東路二段339號4樓
電　　話：(02)2705-5066　　傳　　真：(02)2706-6100
網　　址：http://www.wunan.com.tw
電子郵件：wunan@wunan.com.tw
劃撥帳號：01068953
戶　　名：五南圖書出版股份有限公司

台中市駐區辦公室/台中市中區中山路6號
電　　話：(04)2223-0891　　傳　　真：(04)2223-3549
高雄市駐區辦公室/高雄市新興區中山一路290號
電　　話：(07)2358-702　　傳　　真：(07)2350-236

法律顧問　元貞聯合法律事務所　張澤平律師

出版日期　2013年4月初版一刷
定　　價　新臺幣600元